The Secret Life of
MATH

Discover how (and why) numbers have survived from the cave dwellers to us!

Ann McCallum

Illustrated by Carolyn McIntyre Norton

Williamson Books • Nashville, TN

Library of Congress Cataloging-in-Publication Data
McCallum, Ann.
    The secret life of math: discover how (and why) numbers have survived from the cave dwellers to us / Ann McCallum ; illustrated by Carolyn McIntyre Norton.
        p. cm.—
    (A Williamson's kids can! book)
    Includes bibliographical references and index.
ISBN 0-8249-6779-8 (casebound: alk. paper) — 0-8249-6755-0 (softcover : alk. paper)
    1. Numeration—History—Juvenile literature. 2. Mathematics—History—Juvenile literature. I. Norton, Carolyn McIntyre, ill. II. Title.
    QA141.3.M355 2005
    510' .9—dc22
                                    2005002763

Printed in Italy
10 9 8 7 6 5 4 3 2 1

Kids Can!® series editor: **Susan Williamson**
Interior design: **Carolyn McIntyre Norton**
Illustrations: **Carolyn McIntyre Norton**
Craft styling and photography: **Carolyn McIntyre Norton**
Research: **Carolyn McIntyre Norton, Emily Stetson**
Cover design and cover illustration: **Michael Kline**

Published by Williamson Books
An imprint of Ideals Publications
A division of Guideposts
535 Metroplex Drive, Suite 250
Nashville, Tennessee 37211
800-586-2572

Kids Can!®, *Little Hands*®, *Quick Starts for Kids!*®, *Kaleidoscope Kids*®, and *Tales Alive!*® are registered trademarks of Ideals Publications, a division of Guideposts.

Good Times Books™, *Little Hands Story Corners*™, and *Quick Starts Tips*™ are trademarks of Ideals Publications, a division of Guideposts.

Permissions

Permission to use the following is granted by these people and institutions:

Page 17: Museum of Natural Science, Brussels, Belgium; Ishango bone website: <http://www.naturalsciences.be/expo/ishango/en/ishango/introduction.html>

Page 24: Science Museum/Science and Society Picture Library, London, Great Britain

Page 25: Photo used with permission of the New York State Stock Exchange, Inc.

Page 26: Science Museum/Science and Society Picture Library, London, Great Britain

Page 40: Bildarchiv Preussischer Kulturbesitz / Art Resource, NY

Page 65: Réunion des Musées Nationaux /Art Resource, NY

Page 72: Erich Lessing /Art Resource, NY

Page 84: British Museum, London, Great Britain/HIP/Art Resource, NY

Pages 6-9, 12-15, 29, 37-39, 47, 48, 55, 58-62, 65, 70, 71, 77-79, 89-91, 100-102, 109, 110, 119-123: Susan Williamson

DEDICATION

To Chloe, Chris, and Brent.

ACKNOWLEDGMENTS

I would like to acknowledge
Susan Williamson and Emily Stetson for their untiring efforts
and true talent in the making of this book.
Also, my sincere appreciation goes to Carolyn McIntyre Norton
for her amazing ability to make things beautiful.
Last, a debt of gratitude goes to Ruth and Helmut Klughammer,
who supported me throughout this process and always.

Ann McCallum

DEDICATION

For Daniel, Brian, Caitlin, and Grant.

Carolyn McIntyre Norton

What's Inside

What's the Big Secret, Anyway?

(Yeah, like I really care…)

Okay, that's fair enough. How can you be interested in something that you never really thought about before? For that matter, why would you—or anyone else—care about anything that has to do with math's secret life? Well, maybe, like us, you think that looking back to the beginning of something is a pretty cool thing to do. Or, you just might be a curious kid. If so, then you are one of the lucky people who is about to go on an adventure to discover just how and why math has led such a mysterious and secretive life—and a very, very, very long life at that!

Make that about 35,000 years long! Whoa! So, math has survived longer than languages, longer than ancient civilizations, longer than just about anything that we humans invented

Yes, definitely, this is more of a detective book than a math book or history book. No question about it.

and discovered. Yes, you can place math and the discovery of fire right at about the same time, historically speaking. And that is even before that most famous invention, the wheel. So, there must be something mighty important about math—or else its long life is just an amazing fluke of history.

If you think about that, you'll come up with some questions that may begin to tickle your curiosity. Maybe you're wondering …

• "Thirty-five thousand years is a long time. How could anything 'survive' that long? And how do you know math has been around that long, anyway?"

• "Who invented math—and why? I didn't even know there were people who could speak that long ago, so how did they begin math? And with all of the things that hadn't been invented, why would math be one of the first?"

• "Did dinosaurs or some other prehistoric animal invent math or stumble across it in some way? Is this some kind of a joke or trick question?"

• "Who kept math alive and who taught it to new generations? And hey—were there schools back then? I thought everyone lived in caves and in huts, trapping animals and looking for shelter."

• "Is this whole book a way to get us to doing math or is it some kind of way to get us to do math and history homework at the same time? If it is, we're already on to you."

"Reserve your right to think, for even to think wrongly is better than not to think at all."

—Theon,
father of Hypatia
(hy-PAY-sha)

Hypatia lived in the area now called Egypt from A.D. 370 to A.D. 415 and is believed to be the world's first female mathematician.

Now, wait a minute. We didn't say that you should be *suspicious* of everything. We said that you might become *curious*, and that is a completely different thing. But to clarify: This book is sort of about math—more as an invention that survived an amazing length of time than about math facts and problems. Because math seems to have "survived" for so long and "traveled" to so many places, it is a lot like history, too.

You were on the right track when you asked about the people, because they play a big role in our detective work, even though they lived so very long ago. Our sleuthing adventure is mostly about discovering and searching for answers. Yes, definitely, this is more of a detective book than a math book or history book. No question about it.

What is a "sleuth" and how do you get to be one?

You have everything you need to be a sleuth with you right now. But to be a Super Sleuth, well, that is something that only you can control. First off, *sleuth* is another word for "detective." And if you are going to be a detective, there is only one kind to be: an excellent one. Otherwise, quite bluntly, why bother?

Here is exactly what you need to be a Super Sleuth:

1. An open mind. That means that you are willing to think about some things that at first glance may seem downright ridiculous to you or at best impossible.

2. Excellent observation skills. In fact, they need to be sharp—even when you are tired. Your five senses will be working overtime. (We didn't say this would be easy.)

3. Curiosity and an adventurous spirit. Without those, you won't get anywhere. But if you keep that mind of yours open to new ideas, curiosity will follow naturally. Trust us on that one.

4. Respect. Respect for what? Why, respect for all of the ideas, beliefs, people, traditions, and ways of doing things that are different from what you know and are accustomed to. Without respect for differences, that open mind of yours will simply slam shut.

That's it. You will want to bring along a small notebook and pencil, just as all good detectives do, but don't stick your head in your notebook when you could be observing and absorbing these experiences firsthand. And for fun, if you have a small camera, bring that along. Ready to move forward—uh, make that move *backward*—in time and place? Great! We're off!

Part I

Keeping Track:

How Humans Invented Methods

Sticks, Stones, Fingers & Bones

So, you're playing the game of Pick-Up Sticks. How do you keep score? *Count the sticks you picked up!* Say you have 2½ weeks until your cousin comes to visit. How do you keep track of the days? *Mark them off on a calendar.* What if your mouth is full of marshmallows, and a friend asks you how many s'mores you've eaten? *You hold up three fingers.*

You get the point. Counting and keeping track—these are things you do every day, many times over. And if you think about it, people from every corner of the globe do these things, too. Actually, as it turns out, people have been using these methods, along with others, for thousands upon thousands of years to answer their

own questions about how many sheep and cows they had, when to plant and when to harvest, and how close by or far away water supplies were. How did they keep track before there was any real concept of numbers? Well, how might *you* have kept track if numbers hadn't been invented yet?

People of long ago, like you, were resourceful. Using what they had available to them—sticks, bones, shells, or clay—all ancient peoples developed systems for keeping track. You'll get a good sense of just how resourceful people were—and how creative they were in their thinking—as we see how different civilizations at different times and in distant lands all came up with systems for keeping track. Whether it was the ancient Greeks and Romans in what is now Europe, using pebbles, balls, and tokens; the people in what is now the continent of Africa using finger counting, or the Inca in South America and the Chinese and Japanese in Asia using knots, ingenuity was alive and well. Other peoples used different objects —pebbles, beans, coconuts, and even dried animal manure—for keeping track.

"It is not once nor twice but times without number that the same ideas make their appearance in the world."

—Aristotle, who lived in ancient Greece, 384 B.C. to 322 B.C.

Any missing?

Is that a clue?

In a way. That people used natural materials to help them keep track is a clue to something quite amazing—the resourcefulness of people—but it is not a direct clue to the secret of math's *longevity*, or long life. In detective work, you need to look beyond the obvious to get to the heart of the clues, just as in a good mystery book or on TV detective shows, the puzzle isn't solved until all the clues are put together. Then, the detectives ask questions such as "*Why* did that happen?" or "*How* could they have managed to do that?" Those questions take detectives to the next level of thinking and closer to uncovering the answer.

How will we know what is important?

That is a good question.

Before we get deep into our detective work uncovering the secret to the life of numbers, we should establish the scope of what we are looking at. We all need to begin our adventure with an understanding that we are not looking at the past few decades (10 years), nor at the past few centuries (100 years), nor at even the past few millennia (1,000 years). We are looking back as far as 35,000 years ago ... and as recent as yesterday.

Yes, this is a major sleuthing operation that may well cause you to question assumptions that you believe are absolutely true.

And, as each of us knows, that is a very difficult thing to do. For often, it is easier to think more highly of what we know than to do the work of exploring what we don't know. But you're up to the task, aren't you?

Here's a BIG clue to get you started

What is so interesting and so amazing is that *people who lived on different continents and thousands of years apart all developed similar number and counting systems.* How could that be? Those people didn't even know that other humans existed, so they certainly weren't communicating with one another.

What would lead people to develop such similar systems? How could information have been passed along? Or, were these things invented over and over, each time anew? Did numbers have some kind of secret life of their own or were they just a part of the human way of doing things, sort of like walking on two feet?

As we begin, please remember that to be a really good Super Sleuth, you need to keep your mind open to new thoughts, new ideas, and new understanding. Weigh your earlier assumptions against what you read about and think about here. It is only then that you can discover the secrets that are hidden from those who won't entertain new ideas nor seek out answers; it is only then that you may be able to discover the secret to the long life of numbers.

Hatch Marks

How a counting system spanned 35,000 years and several continents

For our first around-the-world (and back-in-time) sleuthing adventure, let's start by looking at an aspect of numbers and keeping track in which we can verify its early use and its use today. This way, we can come to terms with how long ago some of these systems were in place.

To do that, we need to go way back to about 35,000 years ago. Sometime after the discovery of fire but before the invention of the wheel, people began to use bones to make tools and hunting weapons; to make skins into clothes and shelters; to create art on cave walls; and to fashion jewelry out of stones, bones, ivory, shells, and teeth.

And they began to keep track, or count.

They didn't really have numbers, at least not the kinds of numbers that we think of today, but they did have a very simple

40,000 B.C.
Modern humans make tools, art, shelters.

35,000 B.C.
Western Europe: Oldest known notched bones.

30,000 B.C. or earlier
Europe: Earliest known cave paintings.

20,000 B.C.
Africa: Ishango bone with quartz was created.

Quartz

This bone was found in the ancient fishing village of Ishango in what is now the Democratic Republic of the Congo, Africa. It is more than 20,000 years old! The notches are thought to represent a six-month calendar. The quartz was used for making marks.

system that served them well.

These early cave dwellers didn't call it counting or tallying, of course, but the idea was there. People began to *tally* (keep track of) the number of animals hunted or the passage of time by marking notches on bones, or sticks. The oldest examples of these ancient markings have been found on bones in western Europe and Africa.

We call these notched bones *tally sticks*. They are one of the oldest human inventions, along with fire, still in use today.

Today? Yes, we still use tally marks. Have you ever kept track by writing like this? 卌

Tally marks are great for keeping track of items of equal value, such as quarters or dollars you've stashed away or for keeping score in a game. All over the globe, from early humans to today, people have been tallying up!

10,000 B.C.   0   A.D. 10,000

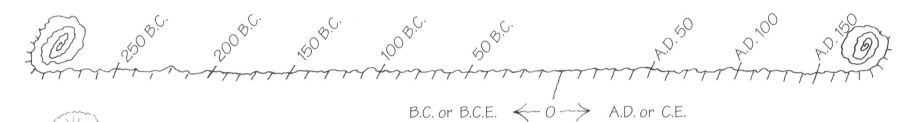

250 B.C. 200 B.C. 150 B.C. 100 B.C. 50 B.C. A.D. 50 A.D. 100 A.D. 150

B.C. or B.C.E. ←—O—→ A.D. or C.E.

THINK QUICK!

Figure out this baffling birthday to see if you've got these ABCDE's straight:

How old would someone born in 1990 B.C. be in 2004 B.C.?

Answer to the question is at bottom of page.

TIME TRAVELS

What's all this about B.C.? These letters after the number are a way of marking the modern Western calendar. The people who established our present-day calendar, based on the Christian calendar, divided history into two time periods—the years *before* Christ was born, written as B.C. ("before Christ") and the years *after* his birth, written as A.D. (an abbreviation for the Latin *anno Domini* that means "in the year of our Lord").

Here's the trick: The years in B.C. time start large, way back at the beginning of "modern" human time (40,000 B.C., for instance) and work their way down to more recent time (50 B.C.). The years from Christ's birth forward start with A.D. 1 and increase to the present year.

Many scholars prefer to leave religion out of timekeeping altogether. So you may also see the terms B.C.E., meaning "before the common era," and C.E., for "common era."

Think Quick! answer:
Not old at all! The person wouldn't even be born yet!

Make an Ancient-Styled Tally Stick

Since it's not likely many of you need to keep track of animals herded or hunted, you can make a fairly authentic-looking tally stick to keep track of other things. Perhaps you want to mark off every time you manage to save a dollar. Keep track for a few months, or better yet, for a whole year. How much have you managed to save?

You will need:
❖ Cleaned cooked chicken leg bone (remove all meat and wash) or a short stick (with the bark still on)
❖ Penknife (with adult supervision only), or dull butter knife, or fine-pointed marker

What you do:
1 Once the chicken bone has been cleaned, let it air-dry. For those who have permission to use a penknife with the supervision of an adult, use a small branch or twig from a tree or shrub that is about $\frac{1}{4}$" (.5 cm) to $\frac{1}{2}$" (1 cm) in diameter. Shorten it to about 7" (17.5 cm) long. (Leaving the bark on actually helps reveal the markings.)

2 Use the knife or marker to put notches on the bone or stick, similar to the tally sticks found from many thousands of years ago in Europe and Africa.

3 Use it to keep track of your savings or something else like the number of books you've read, or items added to a collection of favorite things!

Tallying in North America

The native peoples in North America also kept track of what was important to them by making tally marks, using feather pens and homemade dyes to make marks on animal hides and tree bark. Do you suppose that they began this practice after learning of it from elsewhere, or do you think that they, too, devised a system that suited their needs?

The three symbols (above) from a Dakota Indian buffalo hide recorded that 30 Dakota Indians were killed in the year A.D. 1800, that food was plentiful in 1845, and that cattle arrived in 1868.

Use Tallies to Take an

TRY THIS! Try keeping count like the American Indians did. Use tally marks to keep track of the wildlife that share your backyard or a nearby park. If you like, take part in the Audubon Society's Christmas Bird Count, too, or other bird counts. Anyone can participate. Just contact the Audubon Society at <www.audubon.org>.

You will need:
❖ Piece of fake suede fabric, or a brown paper grocery bag
❖ Scissors
❖ Markers for the fabric or oil pastels for the paper bag
❖ Piece of string, dried cornhusk, or yarn

American Indian-Styled Nature Count

What you do:

1 Cut a piece of fake suede fabric to look like an animal hide, or cut the bag apart at the sides and smooth it flat. Tear off the edges, giving it a rough shape, like an animal skin.

2 Note the dates you begin and end your count.

3 Design symbols for each kind of wildlife you find and draw them on your paper animal hide. You may want to have a symbol for small birds, one for large ground birds such as wild turkeys and pheasant, another for small critters such as squirrels and chipmunks, and one for larger animals such as deer or fox.

4 Each time you spot a critter, tracks, or other evidence that an animal was nearby, mark a single tally mark line next to its symbol.

5 Store your count by rolling it up and tying it with a piece of string, dried cornhusk, or yarn. Each year, do a new nature count on a new piece of fabric or bag, and compare results year to year. Do you spot any trends? Are you concerned because there are fewer varieties of critters to observe? Are you encouraged by healthy numbers for all types of animals?

KEEP IT SIMPLE: TALLY PROS & CONS

BE A SECRET SUPER SLEUTH

As you track birds and animals, notice how easy it is to use tally marks. You can easily see how many of each type of animal you have observed without using any real numbers. Plus, you can look at the whole "skin" and note what you have seen most frequently and what you've spotted least often. Tally marks are quite an impressive, yet very simple, number system that is as handy today as it was about 35,000 years ago!

On the other hand, when you were saving your spare change (see page 19), you may have noticed one of the problems with tally sticks: Each slash needs to be of equal value. So, if the slash equaled $1.00, did you hold out your spare change until you had a whole dollar or did you jot down the amount with modern numerals until you could make a slash? Either way, without real numbers (which was how tallying was used when it started), it wouldn't have worked for partial amounts. It really was meant for equal whole amounts, as was used on early tally markings. That is not a problem with tallying, of course, but more a limitation as to how it could be used most effectively. Does that tell you anything about the kind of counting skills that were needed when tallies first developed?

Fair with Double Tally Sticks

ver borrowed
om a family
omised to do
nge for a spe-
u keep track of
ep from being
xt time you
r chores, make
sticks. Give
who lent you
stockholder),
r your own

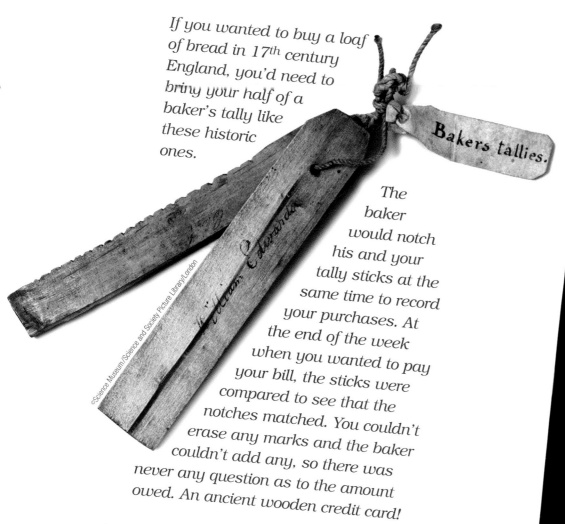

©Science Museum/Science and Society Picture Library/London

If you wanted to buy a loaf of bread in 17th century England, you'd need to bring your half of a baker's tally like these historic ones.

Bakers tallies.

The baker would notch his and your tally sticks at the same time to record your purchases. At the end of the week when you wanted to pay your bill, the sticks were compared to see that the notches matched. You couldn't erase any marks and the baker couldn't add any, so there was never any question as to the amount owed. An ancient wooden credit card!

Double Tally Sticks

A s tallies were used over thousands and thousands of years, new needs actually *did* improve on the original idea. Take a single tally stick. Notch it and then split it in two to keep track of transactions. What do you get? The invention of the *double tally stick!*

The lender kept one half of the stick and the borrower kept the other. Later, when the debt was being repaid, the sticks were compared to check the amount. There was virtually no way to cheat, because the two sides of the tally stick had to fit together and match exactly. So no one could change the amount owed by substituting another stick, as the notches wouldn't match up. Imagine that— tally sticks keeping people honest!

This drawing of an early double tally stick from the Middle Ages in England illustrates how the double tally was made and used.

TRY THIS! Break off a few green twigs from a shrub. Split one in half (horizontally or vertically), and notice the break marks. Set both pieces aside. Now repeat with a second twig, but this time try to match a piece of the first twig with a piece of the second. Do they fit perfectly, or are there indications that this is not a real match?

Keep It Fair with Double Tally Sticks

Have you ever borrowed money from a family member or promised to do some chores in exchange for a special favor? How did you keep track of what was owed? To keep from being foiled ("fooled") the next time you owe someone money or chores, make your own double tally sticks. Give the stock to the person who lent you the money or favor (the stockholder), and you keep the foil for your own records.

If you wanted to buy a loaf of bread in 17th century England, you'd need to bring your half of a baker's tally like these historic ones.

Bakers tallies.

©Science Museum /Science and Society Picture Library/London

The baker would notch his and your tally sticks at the same time to record your purchases. At the end of the week when you wanted to pay your bill, the sticks were compared to see that the notches matched. You couldn't erase any marks and the baker couldn't add any, so there was never any question as to the amount owed. An ancient wooden credit card!

foil, and the piece kept by the lender was called the *stock*. (One meaning of the word stock is "stick" or "log of wood.") The person with the stock was the *stockholder* and owned a little piece of the bank until he was paid back. Aha! Do you see where this is headed now? If you are thinking of the *stock market*, where people buy and sell ownership in parts of companies (i.e., buy and sell *stock*), then you are right! And to think it all began with hatch marks, about 35,000 years ago.

Finally, in 1826, bank authorities decided to turn to a newer method of record keeping. In 1834, the massive collection of tally sticks stored in the House of Parliament was burned. Unfortunately, the fire got out of control and ended up burning down the entire House of Parliament. Those tally sticks really went out with a roar!

I'M A STOCKHOLDER!

FAST-FORWARD

Today, many countries have a financial center where stocks are traded. There, investors can lend money to different companies by buying stocks, or shares, from the company. Investors then own a little piece of that company until they sell their stocks. The main stock market of the United States is the New York Stock Exchange, located on Wall Street in New York City.

On the trading floor of the exchange, brokers buy and sell securities (stocks). The computer age has completely taken over the exchange now, but the transactions are still all about numbers!

MAKE IT REAL! If you ever visit New York City in the United States, be sure to include a fun visit to Wall Street in your plans. That is where the impressive New York Stock Exchange building is located. While you're down on Wall Street, go to the South Street seaport for a great lunch and to see the sights!

Photo used with permission of the New York Stock Exchange, Inc.

Double Tally Sticks

As tallies were used over thousands and thousands of years, new needs actually *did* improve on the original idea. Take a single tally stick. Notch it and then split it in two to keep track of transactions. What do you get? The invention of the *double tally stick!*

The lender kept one half of the stick and the borrower kept the other. Later, when the debt was being repaid, the sticks were compared to check the amount. There was virtually no way to cheat, because the two sides of the tally stick had to fit together and match exactly. So no one could change the amount owed by substituting another stick, as the notches wouldn't match up. Imagine that—tally sticks keeping people honest!

This drawing of an early double tally stick from the Middle Ages in England illustrates how the double tally was made and used.

TRY THIS! Break off a few green twigs from a shrub. Split one in half (horizontally or vertically), and notice the break marks. Set both pieces aside. Now repeat with a second twig, but this time try to match a piece of the first twig with a piece of the second. Do they fit perfectly, or are there indications that this is not a real match?

Tallies & Taxes in Old England

©Science Museum/Science and Society Picture Library/London

In about A.D. 1100, people living in England used double tally sticks to keep track of taxes, fines, rents, and other money owed.

The founders of the Bank of England also used double tally sticks at this time. When money was put into the bank, the amount

The double tally stick is a perfect example of the secret life of numbers.

As you track numbers' routes from 35,000 years ago, remember the development of the double tally stick. It's an important clue.

These carved tally stocks belonged to an English exchequer in A.D. 1440.

was carved with tally marks onto the double tally stick. The stick was then split in two; the piece retained by the bank was called the

Head, Knuckles, Knees & Toes:
"Digit" counting in ancient times

What's your earliest memory of numbers and counting? What are your family members' and friends' first memories of numbers? Are there lots of similarities in the answers you get? Yes, we all did it and most of us still do! Most of us began keeping track of the important things in life—like our ages and how many cookies we ate—by holding up our fingers! After all, our fingers are always with us, and anyone can understand what we mean—no language barriers with finger counting, right?

But if you think counting on your fingers is something new, well, by now you realize that numbers and keeping track go way, way back. Finger counting was probably used by those same

40,000 B.C.   30,000 B.C.   20,000 B.C.

From then to now and there to here!

So, in the space of a few pages, we have revisited a system of number-like markings and ways to keep track that began about 35,000 years ago and that we still use today. And it was a system that probably began in the areas where the Middle East and Africa are and then eventually traveled to England and North America. Plus, it all began long before different peoples even knew of one another's existence, let alone traveled and spoke to each other.

Turn the page to see how the secret life of numbers managed to keep going in other ways over thousands of years and thousands of miles, too.

cave dwellers who drew hatch marks on cave walls.

When people began counting larger and larger amounts, patterns for counting numbers on fingers began to appear. By adding the use of knuckles, joints, and bones of the hand, people could count much higher. (The Chinese even figured out how to count to 100,000 with one hand and to one million if they used both hands.) In New Guinea, people counted using their whole bodies!

Based on a language thousands of years old, the Kewa people of Papua New Guinea use their word for "hand" to mean "five." In North America, the Takelma people, who lived for thousands of years in what is now southwestern Oregon, used the word *ixdil,* meaning "hands," to mean "ten." In South Africa, the Zulu people have used a system of finger counting since the development of their need for accurate number communication. Fingers and toes: These handy *digits* are the original counting machines—and they are not about to go out of style!

10,000 B.C.

2500 B.C.   0
(North Africa) Egypt:
Earliest concrete evidence
of finger counting.

A.D. 10,000

"BUT, EVERYONE COUNTS WITH THEIR FINGERS!"

BE A SECRET SUPER SLEUTH

Well, here we are—and there we were—people the world over using fingers and toes to count. And even with the ability of the Chinese and others to do some very fancy finger figuring, this practical system of counting was used mostly when there was no need for extremely large numbers. So, Super Sleuth, do you suppose that using fingers or toes—in groups of ten—had anything to do with how our modern-day counting system was developed?

Could the idea of grouping by tens have been "planted" as long as 35,000 or more years ago? Hmmm …

Egyptians finger counting, as depicted here from a monument made about 2500 B.C.

Eenie, Meenie, Minie, Morra!

TRY THIS!

Play Morra, the simple and very popular finger-counting game that's been enjoyed by people the world over throughout time. Even though it is an ancient game, it is still played in Italy, France, Spain, Portugal, Morocco, Greece, Egypt, Syria, Iraq, and China. It's also a good way to choose someone to be "It" for other games!

To play: Two players stand face to face, each holding out a closed fist. On the count of three ("one, two, three!"), each player shows as many fingers as he chooses and at the same time calls out a number from 1 to 10. (If you use both hands, you call a number from 1 to 20.) If the number called by a player is the same as the number of *all* the fingers shown by *both* players, then that player wins a point. Play a certain number of rounds, or play to a certain point score.

P.S. If no one is winning, then either narrow the choices by using only one hand each, or play that the person wins who comes the closest without going higher than the real number.

One, Two, Three . . . Nye, Bili, Thathu?

TRY THIS!

Learn how the Zulu count by placing your palms face up with all fingers, including the thumbs, bent inward, then follow the pictures below. A Zulu usually says the word for the number as she shows the sign. Notice anything interesting about the meanings for the Zulu words?

①
nye
(NAY)
"state of being alone"

②
bili
(BEE-lee)
"raise a separate finger"

③
thathu
(TAH-too)
"to take"

④
ne
(neh)
"to join"

⑤
hlanu
(THAH-new)
(all the fingers) "united"

⑥
isithupa
(ee-see-TOO-pa)
"take the
(right) thumb"

⑦
isikhombisa
(ee-see-com-BEE-sa)
"point with the forefinger
of (right) hand"

⑧
isishagalombili
(ee-see-shi-a-ga-lom-BEE-lee)
"leave out
two fingers"

⑨
isishiyagalunye
(ee-see-sha-ga-lo-LOO-nay)
"leave out
one finger"

⑩
ishumi
(ee-shu-MEE)
"cause to stand"

Finger Counting, Zulu-Style

Within the country of South Africa today lies an area known as Zululand. This beautiful homeland of the Zulu people is also home to many exotic animals, such as elephants, lions, and zebras, as well as fantastic birds and butterflies. Each hut in a traditional Zulu village typically has a woven roof placed on top of a round base structure made from branches and sticks. Inside the hut, the floor is a lovely polished green produced by a mixture of tightly compacted anthill sand (without the ants!) and cow manure (imagine that!). Of course, the Zulu people have been influenced by modern things, but this is how they traditionally live.

In the Zulu marketplace, many people today still use a sophisticated system of finger counting, based on the original Zulu method of counting. A specific finger gesture equals a particular number, and even when the people are gesturing very, very quickly, they manage to understand one another quite well.

> In the Zulu marketplace, many people today still use a sophisticated system of finger counting, based on the original Zulu method of counting.

TRY THIS!

Play Zulu Says

Once you've practiced your Zulu number gestures, see how quickly you can form each one! Gather some friends together to play a game of Zulu Says. Using the same rules as Simon Says but with the gestures for the Zulu numbers, have the leader call out "Zulu says" followed by a number. (You can begin by saying the number in English, but then once you get better at it, use the Zulu word.) The rest of the group forms the number. If the leader doesn't begin by saying "Zulu says," the participants shouldn't respond. If you do, you are out of the game.

Learn American Sign Language! For another version of Zulu Says, use these American Sign Language number gestures!

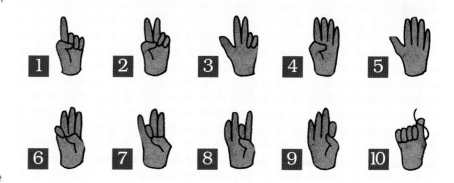

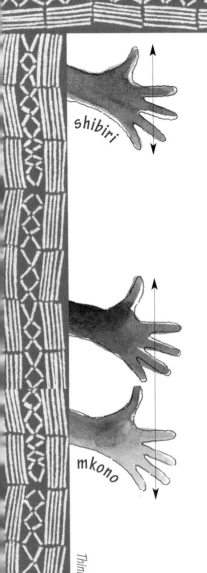

shibiri

mkono

A Swahili Way to Measure— Body-Style

Farther up the African coast, the African Swahili people also used to rely on body-part math, but in this case it was to measure length, rather than to count.

Having an approximate measure worked fine when someone was making one thing at a time, but this system could cause problems in the marketplace. For example, the customer with the longest hand span would get the best deal when buying some cloth. Or, looking at it another way, the seller with the shortest hand span would make the largest profit. Knowing your hand span now, imagine when you would have wished you had bigger hands and when small hands would have suited you just fine, thank you!

A shibiri *was the distance from the tip of the pinkie finger to the tip of the thumb in a spread hand.*

The mkono *was two of these hand spans.*

The pima *was four mkono, or eight hand spans.*

THINK QUICK!

How many shibiri was a pima?

Answer to the question is up the side of this page.

pima

We're off to meet the *quipucamayoc!*

You know, the *quipucamayoc,* or "quipu-maker." Realizing that finger counting in Zulu is a skill far beyond anything most of us have ever managed, we thought you would thoroughly enjoy another skill you may believe you have mastered already—tying knots. Of course, these aren't just any knots tied any which way or in any place. With math and its many secrets, placement, or shall we say, *place value,* are very important. So if you are feeling adventurous and if you are trying to put all of this together to figure out the secret to math's longevity, join us as we head to Peru! (Or, would you prefer China, where knots were used at a much earlier time?)

Would You Like a Receipt? Knot!

How knots & numbers go together

Knots and math?
Uh—this is getting really weird!

Are you one of those people who is good at tying knots? You know—able to tie a bowline, a double fisherman's knot, or a taut-line hitch without a second thought (and without looking it up!). Or, are you more like some of us who have always found tying knots to be somewhat of a mystery? Tying shoelaces is one thing, but knowing the knots that will hold a kayak onto the roof of a car, well, that is something else entirely. And surely, none of us ever really considered our knot-tying skills as having much to

2000 B.C.　　　　1500 B.C.　　　　1000 B.C.　　　　500 B.C.
(Asia) China:
Recording numbers on knotted strings mentioned in I Ching.

In the Inca empire
knots were
the preferred method
of keeping track.

THINK QUICK!

Knotty record keeping

There are earlier mentions of knots and numbers, too. In 500 B.C. in China, knots used in record keeping were mentioned in the *I Ching*, an ancient Chinese book about the basic ideas of everyday life. It is also called the *Book of Changes*. The idea of tying a knot to represent a number has also been found in the Middle East, Nigeria, Hawaii, Japan, and many American Indian cultures, from ancient to recent times.

What is a common memory aid used by many people today that is somewhat similar to the knotted string custom?

Answer to the question is up the side of this page.

do with our number skills, right?

Uh-uh. Sorry to disappoint you, but knots and numbers go together, or at least they went together long ago, especially if you lived in the Inca empire in western South America (about where Peru is today) along about A.D. 1200 to A.D. 1500. There, knots were the preferred method of keeping track.

| 0 | A.D. 500 | A.D. 1000 | A.D. 1200 | A.D. 1500 | A.D. 2000 |

(South America) Peru:
Quipus used
for record keeping.

Why Knots?

A story of what might have happened

Picture this: You are a very wealthy emperor whose land stretches far and wide into the mountains of western South America. It's A.D. 1475 and it is time to collect taxes from those who live on and work the lands. But how do you keep track of who owes what?

(That part is true. The emperor at that time, who lived in the capital city of Cuzco, ruled an enormous expanse of rugged land. And, this family of royals was very wealthy, thanks to the taxes they collected from all the citizens of their empire, called Tahuantinsuyu [TA-wan-tin-suyu], or "The Land of the Four Quarters." There was an incredible system of roads linking all parts of this prosperous empire, and there were even engineered bridges to cross the deep ravines.)

Tracking taxes is the same issue that was solved in earlier times by using tally sticks and by finger counting. We'll learn that the ancient civilization in Mesopotamia, in an area of the Middle East today, at first used pebbles for keeping track (page 60). Pebbles may have proved difficult for the tax collectors of the Inca empire to carry, especially across rugged terrain. The Mesopotamian ancients later used clay tablets with notations on them, but those, we imagine, would have been breakable ... and heavy. So, what could they do instead?

The Inca people raised many llamas, and they certainly knew how to weave the wool into yarn. Hmmm ... use what is naturally plentiful, right?

So, how did the Inca keep track of everyone's taxes so efficiently? They didn't have a system of notation or symbols for numbers yet. The Inca people invented their own method of record keeping—something permanent, and more important, something easy to carry along the long roads leading to and from the capital. The Inca invented a system of knotted strings!

This amazing quipu was made by an Inca in A.D. 1400- A.D.1532. It is attached to a carved wooden stick.

©Bildarchiv Preussischer Kulturbesitz/Art Resource, NY
Ethnologisches Museum, Staatliche Museen zu Berlin, Berlin, Germany

A system
of runners
in relay
was brilliant.
Are you
impressed by
how inventive
humans are?

Instant Messaging—Knot!

Even if there were a system of knots, how to get the message from here to there was the next obstacle. We're talking about a huge empire. And keep in mind the lack of transportation, or anything technological such as phones, e-mails, and the like. How did the Inca overcome that hurdle?

Not to worry, as it wasn't a problem for the Incas! They developed a system of trained runners, called *chasquis* (CHA-skis), to carry information from one place to another. These speedy runners ran as fast as they could between station houses, passing their message on to the next runner, much like a baton is passed on in a relay race. In this

giant relay race, a series of runners could cover about 300 miles (480 km) in 24 hours!

How did the runners remember the messages they had to deliver after such a long run? Each runner carried a *quipu* (KEE-pooh), a special record-keeping device that was made out of knotted string. When rolled up, each quipu looked sort of like a mop full of knots, but it was actually a sophisticated way to record amounts such as taxes owed or collected, or how much metal had been taken from one of the Inca mines. Each Inca town, village, and district had a *quipucamayoc*, or "quipu maker," who was in charge of creating and then interpreting the meaning of the knotted strings. String is light and runners are swift. A system of runners in relay was brilliant. Are you impressed by how inventive humans are?

THINK QUICK!

Word clues

What do you suppose is the Inca word for "knot"?

Answer to the question is up the side of this page.

"I THOUGHT OF IT FIRST!"

The Japanese people had a similar system using knotted string called the *ketsujo* (ke-TWO-joe). And Darius, King of Persia (522 B.C. to 468 B.C.), used knotted string, not in the sophisticated way that the quipu was used, but nonetheless it was related to keeping track and using string. Darius is said to have tied 60 knots in a leather strap. He ordered the soldiers, whom he left behind to defend an important bridge, to untie one knot each day. If he didn't return by the time the last knot was untied, all of the soldiers were instructed to return to their homes.

Now, how clever was that!

These diverse examples illustrate that similar devices used for keeping track of amounts appeared in areas far away in time and space. How could these ideas have spread from one civilization to another? Or, maybe they didn't spread at all. Maybe each civilization developed its own system without knowledge of the others. That begs the question: Do you think that humankind is so alike that different people developed similar methods without ever knowing about one another? We think this is very curious and exciting to think about.

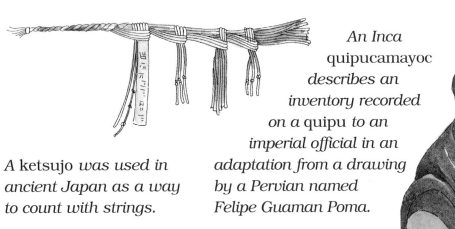

A ketsujo was used in ancient Japan as a way to count with strings.

An Inca quipucamayoc describes an inventory recorded on a quipu to an imperial official in an adaptation from a drawing by a Pervian named Felipe Guaman Poma.

A Closer Look at Quipus

A quipu was a means of recording information. It provided a system for keeping track. These knotted strings were a sophisticated way to document such things as the population, taxes, or amount of livestock or crops. A quipu could be very simple with just a few cords. Or, it could have up to 2,000 cords tied together!

Here's how a quipu worked:

The main, or top, cord had the summation cord and pendant cords tied onto it. The cords could be different colors to represent different items.

Numbers were recorded by using knots in various positions on the quipu. Their placement on the string referred to a power of ten, like 10, 100, or 1,000. The number of knots represented the digits from 1 to 9.

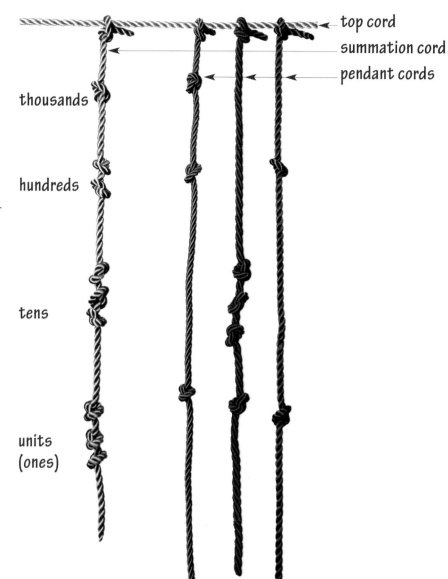

top cord

summation cord

pendant cords

thousands

hundreds

tens

units (ones)

Make an Inca Quipu

TRY THIS!

Here's a "knotty" bit of fun. Let's say it's your birthday and three relatives have given you money: $35 from your aunt and uncle, $20 from your grandma, and $46 from your parents (they included $16 allowance they owed you for the past month). Wow! That's more than you can earn mowing lawns for your neighbors.

So, how can you keep track of how much everyone gave you so that you can write thank-you cards? And, how can you keep track of how much you have altogether so that you can figure out if you have enough for a new computer game or a CD player? Keep track like the people of the Inca empire and make a usable Inca quipu!

thousands

hundreds

tens

units
(ones)

You will need:

❖ Three different colors of cord or yarn:

    ❖ One piece 12" (30 cm) long for the *top cord* (ours is gold)

    ❖ 3 pieces of another color string (we used red) about 36" (90 cm) long for the *pendant cords*

    ❖ One piece 36" (90 cm) long of another color string (ours is green) for the *summation cord*

What you do:

1 First, make the blank quipu. Lay the *top cord* horizontally on a flat surface. Then tie the *summation cord* on the left and the three *pendant cords* to the right.

2 Use the pendant cords to record the amounts you want to remember, each on a separate cord. Tie knots onto the correct positions on the cord. Two knots in the tens place, for example, mean 20; six knots in the ones (or units) place represents 6, and so on.

3 Record the total amount of all three numbers ($101, in this example) on the summation string of your quipu.

P.S. If you want to keep your quipu as a piece of art, see the box on this page for a way to frame it.

A Zero?

We write a zero in modern numbers when we want to show that there are none of that number—to show the difference between 3 free tickets (really 03, or no tens and 3 ones) to the movies and 30 tickets (3 tens, or 3 x 10, and no ones), for example. The Inca left a blank space on a quipu when they wanted to show "nothing" in a certain space. Do you think they were starting to see the need for a zero? (See page 90 for more on the zero question.)

How to "frame" your quipu

Even though a quipu was used like a slip of paper to put notations on, yours probably looks more like a piece of interesting art today. To frame it, simply use a piece of thick corrugated cardboard or a corkboard. Spread your quipu out. Then, using sewing pins or pushpins, pin your quipu in place. You can make a frame or just hang your matted quipu on a wall. How many people can figure out what it means?

Quipucamayoc Quest

Feel as if you have mastered the art of quipu-making? Test your quipucamayoc skill by taking on a more challenging project, such as recording the number of kids in your school or the number of relatives you have. You should end up with an amazing-looking quipu, but if you want to go for a new record you'll have to tie a lot of knots. The largest number so far discovered on a real quipu is 97,357! Oh, my aching fingers!

You will need:
❖ Many different colored pieces of yarn

What you do:

1 Collect all the numbers you want to record.

2 Make a blank quipu. To organize your numbers, make groups of cords separated by a little space, and use different colors of cord. (Use one color for each class in one grade, for example, then add another color for each class in the next grade.) Choose a separate color for the summation cord of each category and a summation cord for the whole quipu.

3 Record the numbers on the appropriate cords.

4 Explain your magnificent quipu to someone. Congratulations! You're now an honorary quipucamayoc!

COLORFUL MATH!

FAST-FORWARD

On the quipu, the Inca used different colors and different strings to distinguish between various number data, such as comparing the populations of different villages. Although using color in mathematics may seem unusual, it was (and still is) quite common around the world. The Chinese used red and black rods for counting—the red ones for positive numbers (pluses) and the black ones for negative numbers (minuses). The idea of red and black numbers has even survived into today's business world. Just ask any businessperson if she is "in the red" or "in the black." Today, "red" means losing money or spending more than you are bringing in, so businesspeople tend to feel blue when they are "in the red!"

A Major Turning Point Ahead

Let's journey on to see what happened when people moved from simply keeping track to writing numerals and counting! Hmmm. Are you curious to know if people went in completely different directions, or if they came up with similar ways of using numbers? Guess we'll have to do some more sleuthing to find out. One thing is for sure: You can count on us to continue the search for the secret life of numbers!

Counting the Roman Way

Where do Roman numerals belong in math's secret life?

Where, oh where?

Where should we put Roman numerals in this book? It seems to us that most people would date Roman numerals back in the time of the Roman Republic, say anywhere from 500 B.C. to 44 B.C., when Julius Caesar was assassinated. In that way of thinking, it belongs right about where the discussion of zero (page 90) is now. But, then again, maybe it belongs here at the end of Part I, as a transition from earlier forms of keeping track. Let's take a closer look.

2000 B.C.

1500 B.C.

1000 B.C.

500 B.C.
(Europe) Italy:
Roman numerals
begin to be used.

IT'S NOT AS EASY AS KNOWING WHEN!

BE A SECRET SUPER SLEUTH

One of the problems as to where to put Roman numerals is that this book isn't about the date that things happened. This is because there wasn't communication between peoples in the earliest times covered in this book. Thus, we can't organize this book *chronologically*, or in the order of years, because, as you know, math moved across the boundaries of time and place in order to survive. And that is part of the mystery of the secret life of math. We are more interested in where Roman numerals belong as far as how numbers developed from using them, first as a means of keeping track, then as a way to record information, and finally, to using them for computation. So, let's start looking at Roman numerals right here!

0   A.D. 500   A.D. 1000   A.D. 1500   A.D. 2000

Europe, Great Britain, Asia, Africa:
Roman numerals
in widespread use.

What's so confusing?

Why is it so difficult to place Roman numerals in the life of math? After all, most historians agree that Rome was built on seven hills in 753 B.C. by Romulus, who named the city after himself. If you remember, Romulus was the surviving twin in "the fight to the finish" with his twin brother, Remus. Talk about sibling rivalry! So, if we know about all of these details, why is it that we don't just place the invention of Roman numerals somewhere in the time of the Romans?

That does make sense, but we have one little thing that bothers us about placing Roman numerals that way. Bear with us, okay? See what you think. Take a look at the Roman numeral for three, for example:

III

Now, think back a bit to some of the earliest ways of keeping track. Remember those hatch marks (pages 16–29)? They spanned time from about 35,000 B.C. all the way to today! Now, how do you show a count of three using hatch marks?

Notice anything? Take a good look at the two things—the Roman numeral for three and the hatch marks for a count of three.

So, what do you observe? And, what do you think? Are Roman numerals an outgrowth of hatch marks from about 34,000 years before the founding of Rome? If people didn't yet know of one another, how did these hatch marks travel in both time and place to where Italy is today over so many years? Could it be possible that Roman numerals existed before Rome? Or, is it a natural progression (since we know

that somehow hatch marks stayed around) to believe that the Romans, who were exceedingly smart, took the hatch marks and then invented a numeral system using them?

And keep in mind that most people would agree that lines for V's and X's are the easiest shapes to carve into bone or wood. So no matter where or when people decided to record numbers on tally sticks, they all used the same kinds of symbols. Some would say that we still use them today and call them Roman numerals.

That type of thinking has led some to believe that the I, V, and X are the oldest kind of writing ever! Yes, even older than any other kind of alphabet or numerals. If that were true, then they would likely be direct followers of the hatch marks used on sticks and found in caves and on cave walls. Now that is very, very old, and that would make you think this discussion of Roman numerals really belongs right after our exploration of hatch marks. Should we move it there?

NO PARROTS NEEDED!

THINK QUICK!

What does the Roman numeral for five remind you of?

Hint: If I ask you to communicate the number for two without speaking or writing, what might you do? What's the possible math link here?

Answer to the question is at the bottom of this page.

Think Quick! answer: Holding up two fingers—especially your two middle fingers—just might remind you of finger counting. Those two fingers sure do look like two Roman numerals for one, as well as the Roman numeral for five. Hmmm!

BE A SECRET SUPER SLEUTH

What's that? What do parrots have to do with sleuthing? Nothing really, except that parrots simply repeat back to you whatever you say to them. And sleuths, or detectives, can't do that if they are to be successful. Historians (and just about anyone else who wants to learn) can't do that, either. The only way to discover the truth is to think and to question. And that's what we

need here. Where Roman numerals belong in this book is going to take some careful thought and consideration on your part to come to the best conclusion. And even then, we may not know the real answer, because there is still so much that we don't know from way back then. But what we *can* do is examine what we are aware of at this particular time in the history of humankind, and then we can evaluate it to come to our own best guess.

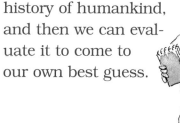

Polly want a cracker?

Aha! And the answer is...

Write Like a Roman!

Use Roman numerals to write the following information on some index cards, and then write the same numbers in Arabic numbers on separate index cards. Shuffle all of the cards together and spread them out face down. Now, play Memory and see if you can match up the same numbers in Roman and Arabic numerals.

❖ your house or apartment number
❖ the grade you are in school
❖ the number of people in your immediate family
❖ your height in inches or centimeters
❖ the year you were born
❖ your phone number
❖ your zip code

To refresh our memories, here's what the Roman numerals look like and what their values are.

I	= 1	**C**	= 100
V	= 5	**D**	= 500
X	= 10	**M**	= 1,000
L	= 50		

To read Roman numerals, follow these rules:

When a numeral of equal or lesser value follows a numeral, add them together.
VI = 5 + 1 = 6
XX = 10 + 10 = 20

When a numeral is immediately followed by one of greater value, subtract the first from the second.
IV = 1 from 5 = 4
XL = 10 from 50 = 40
CD = 100 from 500 = 400
CM = 100 from 1,000 = 900

Have any problems? If you have a zero in any of those numbers, you are out of luck! The Roman system, like many other number systems of long ago, did not include a symbol for zero. (See page 90 for more about that.)

CLXXVII

The Secret Life of Math

Break it down

If you are having any trouble decoding Roman numerals, here is a way to do it: Break the numeral down into its parts. Let's say you want to write the year 2968, Roman-style. Break it down; then decode each number and you will have the Roman numeral.

2968 =
2000 + 900 + 60 + 8 =
MM (1000 + 1000) + **CM** (1000 - 100)
+ **LX** (50 + 10) + **VIII** (5 + 1 + 1 + 1) =
MMCMLXVIII =
2968

COUNTING THE ROMAN WAY

FAST-FORWARD Some historians say that from about 500 B.C. to A.D. 1500, the ancient Romans used I's, V's, and X's—as well as C's, D's, L's, and M's—to write their numbers. Even today, you can often see Roman numerals on many clocks and watch faces, or in the credits at the very end of a movie. Look on the sides of buildings, too, where the year the building was built is often engraved in Roman numerals.

TRY THIS! Go on a Roman numeral treasure hunt. If you can, have all of the players take a disposable camera with them (you can buy them at most grocery stores). Snap a photo when you see a Roman numeral being used. You can click each time or you can click only different kinds of uses. Who found the most Roman numerals?

P.S. If you take your photos carefully, you can make a really nice Roman numeral collage!

(Note: Be sure that an adult accompanies you on your treasure hunt and knows where you are at all times. Thank you.)

Another perspective on computing with Roman numerals

Welcome to ancient Rome! The city of Rome was founded in 753 B.C. and became the center of a powerful empire throughout what are now Europe, Great Britain, and parts of Asia and Africa. In ancient Rome many people lived comfortably in well-planned cities. The ancient Romans engineered and built amazing theaters and buildings, chariot racetracks, huge public baths, and special plumbing called *aqueducts* to bring fresh water to Rome. Have you heard of the saying "All roads lead to Rome"? The Romans also built an incredible road system, including bridges. Clearly, the Romans used Roman numerals to do all of this!

So, you might ask, who are we to say that Roman numerals weren't particularly easy to use and were probably used for keeping track rather than for computations? After all, the brilliant Romans engineered, designed, and built all of these amazing systems. You would be correct to make all of those points. You decide if Roman numerals were too awkward to use.

Keeping track or doing math?

One way to think about all of this is to decide what you think Roman numerals were used for: keeping track of things, as hatch marks were used, or for calculating things, like we use numerals today. Here is a little scheme to help you discover your answer.

Add CLXII + MCCCV. What is your answer—in Roman numerals, of course?

Now, add 2,365 + 3,488. Write your answer in regular Arabic numerals, our Western numbering system. (Answers up the side of this page.)

Which took you the longest? Did you have to rewrite the Roman numerals into Arabic numerals and then put the answer back in Roman numerals again?

Actually, *adding* in Roman numerals is the easiest computation to do with them. You should try multiplying and dividing Roman numerals! So what do you think they were meant to be used for, computations or keeping track?

Given your answer, where do *you* think this section on Roman numerals belongs? At the beginning or end of Part I (KEEPING TRACK), Part II (WRITING IT DOWN), or Part III (FASTER FIGURING)?

Did we choose correctly?

Actually, we went though a similar thought process ourselves. In the end, we decided to put this topic where it would serve to demonstrate our confusion. Many historians believe that Roman numerals were symbols derived from the notched stick markings of ancient peoples and that standardized Roman numerals were modified from these ancient tally markings. Thus, the modern system of Roman numerals was not used until well into Roman times (509 B.C. to A.D. 475). To back this up, historians point out that the earliest known use of the numeral L for 50 is in 44 B.C.

These are very sound arguments, indeed. Yet, we believe Roman numerals don't belong in Part II where numbers were being used for computation, because they were too difficult to work with. And we don't really think they belong right after the discussion of hatch marks, although some historians might make that argument. So, we decided to compromise and place Roman numerals at the end of Part I, but you could very likely make an argument for placing them later in the book.

If you are confused, well, that is a good thing, because it lets you know that being a Super Sleuth is not a matter of right or wrong, but rather a matter of thoughtful consideration. Good job!

Part II

Writing It Down:

Toward a Universal Language

A Major Leap Forward for Humankind

Well, perhaps Einstein was correct that not everything is worth counting, but we humans sure have invented a lot of ways to do just that—and in a lot of different languages, too!

There is not a language in the world today that does not include numerals and words for numbers. Around the world, people seem to have invented similar systems for counting, keeping track, and using numerals, yet the languages we speak are so different.

Why is that? Why would math develop in similar ways across thousands of miles and years, but language went every which way? More precisely, what is it about math that made it almost universal? And how did it happen?

A Clue to the Clues

These questions set the stage for your sleuthing. As we discover the ins and outs of written symbols and try

our hand at using counting balls, writing in cuneiform, and then using some hieroglyphs (just for the pure fun of it!), look for the "how" and "why" clues. Try to get a handle on why math developed in similar ways around the globe, but when it came to language, it was every civilization for itself!

Who decided to write things down?

Who actually wrote a number symbol on a piece of clay for the very first time in the history of humankind? Well, that is quite a difficult question. You see, once again we need to think more broadly. So instead of looking for the exact person, we'll ask: Who moved away from the rather broad and clumsy ways of keeping track, such as hatch marks and quipus, to actually putting notations down, much like we write today? And, once again, how and why did people make that change, each in a similar way, although still using whatever natural materials they had around them? After all, this was a giant leap forward. And even more amazing, writing down numbers crossed thousands of years and miles, as if it were a simple thing to have happened. Meanwhile, the life of math remains on a singular track, unlike the multiple tracks of language. What was it that made math and writing down notations such a universal thing even though each pocket of civilization developed independently?

Match these countries to the children counting to three in their native languages.

- Japan
- Germany
- Mexico
- France
- South Africa
- Russia

Un, Deux, Trois

Odin, Dva, Tri

Uno, Dos, Tres

From Pebbles to Symbols

Moving from tokens to written notations

If you live in a city with a subway or metro system, you are likely to be very familiar with tokens. Tokens are basically substitute money. You pay for a token, put it in the subway turnstile, and you are able to enter to ride the subway. It's a very clever system.

Well, guess what? Today's tokens are designed after relics of the very distant past. The huge span of time during which pebbles and stones were used—from about 40,000 B.C. (we are assuming that they were just beginning to be used back then) to the period of 8000 B.C. to 3000 B.C.

40,000 B.C.
Europe, Africa, Middle East:
Pebbles used to track amounts.

30,000 B.C.

20,000 B.C.

Today's tokens are designed after relics of the very distant past.

MESOPOTAMIA IS HERE

(there are many examples of tokens from that period)—sure does make us wonder about the secret to the long life of numbers! For now, let's focus on those tokens found in the area of southwest Asia once called Mesopotamia, the region of the early civilizations of Babylonia, Sumer, Akkad, and Assyria (now all part of the Middle East).

How do you think today's subway tokens got started so long ago and survived to now? Finding the answer—or at least making an "educated guess" (that means you have good background information but you can't prove it yet with "hard"—the kind you can hold in your hand and say "See!"—evidence) is our job as sleuths. How did an idea get all the way from then to now?

Middle East:
Specific clay tokens represent amounts.
3500 B.C.

8000 B.C.
Middle East:
Earliest clay tokens symbolize items.

3300 B.C.
Middle East:
Earliest form of written numerals.

0

A.D. 10,000

CALCULATING CLUE

BE A SECRET SUPER SLEUTH

There are going to be clues flying right and left in this section of our search for math's mysterious secret life, but let me just say one word: *Calculate*. No, let's make that two words: *Calculate* and *calculus*. More precisely, get this: The Latin word for "pebble" is *calculus*. Aha!

P.S. Latin was the language of the ancient Romans whom you just visited on pages 48 to 55.

OOPS!

FAST-FORWARD

Have you ever made something of clay, and then had it fired (baked) in a kiln until it was hard? If you have, we're guessing that at least once after finishing a baked clay hand-made object, your clay masterpiece got knocked off a shelf or dropped on the floor, and . . . crash! Your clay object had broken into more pieces than Humpty Dumpty. Sound familiar? Here's our quandary: How do you suppose these clay tokens made anywhere from 10,000 to 5,000 years ago are still being found today?

1032 x 347!

1032 x 347?

And we're off!

In 8000 B.C. there were still no written numbers, but people had gotten pretty good at keeping track using pebbles, shells, bones, or other small things available to them, in addition to using tallies or fingers. But as cities formed and flourished, and as trade between them began to expand—well, can you imagine hauling around thousands of pebbles to keep track of what people bought or owed?

You see, Mesopotamia was the site of some of the oldest civilizations, starting out as a cluster of villages and then turning into larger urban areas. The people traded and used metal tools such as saws to build innovations including—ta-da!—the wheel. (Yes, it's finally here! Although we are not sure what group of people invented the wheel, the oldest wheel found as of now is believed to be 5,500 years old and was found in Mesopotamia.)

In this region, clay was easily found, shaped, and dried. Archaeologists have found thousands and thousands of clay tokens used from about 8000 B.C. to 3000 B.C., when trading became quite brisk in this region. Some tokens were very simply shaped objects; many were in geometrical shapes. Some were used in a similar way to early hatch marks: One token equals one item. Others stood for varying amounts depending on their shapes. And some, from about 3500 B.C. to 3300 B.C., were even found grouped inside *clay counting balls.*

PEBBLE POCKETS

MAKE IT REAL

Well, maybe you *can't* really imagine what it would be like doing transactions with a couple of hundred pebbles hauled around in your pockets, after all! It would be a lot heavier than the same number of pennies (and you probably know how annoying a pocketful of pennies can be). Just for the fun of it, gather together about a hundred pebbles (or as many as you can find). Wearing a pair of old pants or shorts, stuff the pebbles in as many pockets as possible. Then, just leave them there for the day. What do you think, eh? In this case, they probably are not "worth their weight in gold," as the saying goes!

NOT JUST CIRCLES!

MAKE IT REAL

A lot of people living in the U.S. might think that all tokens are round, because all of the coins used as money in the U.S. are round. But that is not the case the world over. Countries such as China, Aruba, and the United Arab Emirates have coins in varied shapes. We wonder where that idea came from?

In ancient China you could have used the square hole in the middle of these ancient coins to thread them together and keep them safely around your neck. Today you could easily get one of these small hexagonal five fils coins as change in the United Arab Emirates or fifty pence coins in England.

Good-bye to pockets full of pebbles!

When you have a group of similar items, what do you usually do? If you said that you find a way to store them together, such as by using a rubber band, a shoe box, or an envelope, then you and these ancient peoples think alike. Some very clever accountants in the Mesopotamia region thought to store their tokens according to the type of transaction. Tokens representing, for example, the number of sheep sent to graze for the summer were placed in a *counting ball*—a hollow ball made out of clay that could be sealed shut and kept safe over periods of time. When the herd came back at summer's end, the ball was broken open, revealing the tokens, and the record-keeper could make sure all the sheep had returned. It was an ingenious counting and record-keeping system!

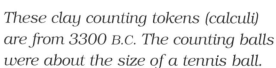

These clay counting tokens (calculi) are from 3300 B.C. The counting balls were about the size of a tennis ball.

Record It in a Counting Ball!

TRY THIS!

No paper and pencil? Make a counting ball and counting tokens to keep your records organized. Then, imagine what you would think of this new invention if the alternative were to carry around heaps of pebbles!

You will need:

❖ Salt Clay (see recipe) or modeling clay, for tokens
❖ Balloon
❖ Newspaper, torn into 1" x 4" (2.5 x 10 cm) strips
❖ Papier-Mâché Paste (see recipe)
❖ Brown paint
❖ Paintbrush
❖ Masking tape

Salt Clay:

❖ 2 cups (500 ml) flour
❖ 1 cup (250 ml) salt
❖ ¾ to 1 cup (175 to 250 ml) water
❖ 2 tablespoons (25 ml) vegetable oil

In a bowl, mix together the flour and salt. Slowly add the water and the oil to the flour mix. Stir until dough forms.

Papiér-Mâché Paste:

❖ ½ cup (125 ml) flour
❖ ½ cup (125 ml) water

Stir the flour and water together in a bowl. The paste should look thick and creamy. Add more water or flour, if necessary. Store in a container in the refrigerator until ready to use.

What you do to make the tokens:

Make a different token shape out of the Salt Clay or modeling clay for each kind of item for which you want to keep a record. (For example, one token shape for the books you read this month and another token shape for the times you mowed the lawn.)

What you do to make the counting ball:

1 Slip the different tokens inside the balloon; then, blow it up.

2 Cover the inflated balloon with strips of newspaper dipped in the Papiér-Mâché Paste, overlapping the strips. Build up several layers, leaving a small hole where the balloon is tied. Let them dry.

3 Paint your counting ball to look like it is made of clay. Let dry. Pop the balloon and remove the balloon bits, throwing every bit away.* Tape over the small opening to seal the ball shut. Later, when you want to remember how many books you've read, open the counting ball and take out the tokens.

*Warning: Balloons and pieces of balloons are very dangerous for young children. It takes just a small piece for a child to choke. Please check very carefully that every piece of balloon or any extra balloons are thrown away immediately. Thank you.

3-D Tokens Morph to 2-D Symbols!

Still, there was a problem with those clay "envelopes": You couldn't see what was inside once they were sealed! At some point, someone decided to press the token symbols into the outside of the clay ball before the clay dried to remember what was inside ... and—in about 3300 B.C.—the idea of using symbols to show numbers was born! Although not like the numbers we use today, the idea of writing symbols to show amounts had begun.

For a while—from 3300 B.C. to 3200 B.C.—people used solid counting balls with notations on the outside. Then, around 3200 B.C. to 3100 B.C., the Sumerians made the giant leap to using number symbols on slabs of clay, and it was soon good-bye to counting balls. Imagine! Something could become obsolete in 3100 B.C.!

FOCUS ON "OBSOLETE"

BE A SECRET SUPER SLEUTH

We think that the idea of counting balls becoming obsolete way back in 3100 B.C. must be a major clue. After all, keeping track of things was coming along just fine. So, here are our clues for you:

Clue #1: Why do things become obsolete?

Clue #2: What could that have to do with the secret life of numbers?

Are any bells going off in your head? Do you think you are getting close to what controls the mysterious secret life of numbers? Don't tell if you do. Just keep your thoughts to yourself and test them out against what happens next.

Imagine! Something could become obsolete in 3100 B.C.!

TRY THIS! Ask someone about your grandparents' ages how many things they can think of that have become obsolete, or out of date. Do they have anything in the attic or basement that they can show you?

Are we there yet?

Well, Super Sleuths, we've made some progress here. We've moved from the simplest methods of keeping track to a very early method of notation, using symbols, wet clay, and a stylus. It feels downright modern—and it is only about 3200 B.C.!

Using Cuneiform

A step backward—or not?

The life of math seems to be progressing nicely. But let's not get lulled into thinking that everything moved along in a *linear* fashion—that is, everything moved from one year to the next, making progress as the years went by. That was *not* the case in the secret life of math. No way! The years would move along, but remember that these were still separate civilizations that encompassed pockets of people who had minimal, if any, contact with other cultures. What one group invented was not passed along to

40,000 B.C.　　　　　30,000 B.C.　　　　　20,000 B.C.

How is it that very similar number systems developed, invented by different peoples, in different times, often separated by thousands of miles and thousands of years? What is the—to use a math term—common denominator that kept numbers and math moving ahead?

another group. It wasn't as if they could teach one another what they discovered or invented. *Au contraire, mon ami!** (Just checking to see if you are still there!)

People of each group had to invent their number systems

*Translated from French: *To the contrary, my friend!*

themselves. And that is where the secret comes in. How is it that very similar number systems developed, invented by different peoples, in different times, often separated by thousands of miles

and thousands of years? What is the—to use a math term—*common denominator* that kept numbers and math moving ahead? That common denominator, or common element, will solve the mystery of how numbers have survived from the cave dwellers to today!

Middle East:
Archaic numbers on clay
slabs develop in Sumer.
3200 B.C.

10,000 B.C.   2700 B.C.   0   A.D. 10,000

Middle East:
Cuneiform numbers
introduced.

Please pass in your homework!

Here's a case in point. It is now the year 2700 B.C., 500 years after the first use of clay tablets by the Sumerians. It's an ordinary day, with the children—boys only, still!—in school.

The Babylonians also recorded numbers in a rather "bulky" way. They adopted the special kind of writing from the Sumerians called *cuneiform* (coon-EE-a-form) that they engraved on slabs of wet clay, using the shaped end of a reed as a writing tool, or stylus. (The word *cuneiform* means "wedge-shaped" and refers to both the letters and numbers used.)

Boys in wealthy families went to schools called *edubbas*, meaning "tablet houses." They did their work on these clay tablets. Whenever written work needed to be saved, the clay tablet was dried in the sun or baked in an oven fueled by animal manure. (Oh my! No wonder kids might have forgotten to "save" their homework!) Can you imagine how hard it must have been to carry your homework home on those days when the teacher

(Math) all seemed to happen in spurts of growth and spurts of repetition. That it happened at all is what we are curious about, because that kept math alive.

"piled on the work"?

Does all this sound somewhat familiar to what was done when the people who lived in Sumer moved from counting balls to tablets in about 3200 B.C.? Well, you are right. That was in a different time but there you have it! How could this have happened? The idea of the tablet and the writing stylus sure do sound alike.

This is an actual clay tablet that was used in 2100 B.C. to calculate an area of land.

COUNTING IN CUNEIFORM

The Babylonian number system, which developed from the earlier form of writing numbers, was a *sexagesimal* system, which means it was based on the number 60 that, when written in cuneiform, looks sort of like a Y or wedge shape. The number 10 had its own symbol in cuneiform. It looked sort of like a hook.

Cuneiform numbers 1 through 10:

1	Y	6	
2	YY	7	
3	YYY	8	
4		9	
5		10	

Can you guess what the numbers 11 and 12 looked like? Think "hooks," "wedges," or Y's.

11

12

And 20? Two hooks. (Hey, this is easy!)

20

You get the idea. Numbers 1 to 59 followed the same system. After that, it got a little trickier: The wedge symbol could represent 1 or 60, depending on where it was placed in relation to the other number symbols. (This is where the *sexagesimal*, or "based on the number 60," idea comes in.)

60

The number 61 would be written like this, with a wedge for the sixties place and a wedge in the ones place.

61

Can you tell what this number is?

Let's see ... the symbols for 60 and 10 and 2. Add them together and you get the number 72! (For more on cuneiform numbers, see page 92.)

THINK QUICK!

How about decoding this cuneiform number?

Answer to the question is up the side of this page.

Think Quick! answer: YY *means 2 x 60,* ◄ *is 10 and* YYY *is 7. Thus, 120 + 10 + 7 = 137!*

Create a

The longer we wait, the more we learn!
Isn't it interesting that the further away from the time something took place—even thousands of years later—the more we seem to eventually learn? Of course, that is not always true, but thanks to serious researchers and Super Sleuths like you, and now with advanced technology such as carbon dating, we are learning more about the ancients as the years go by. For instance, there is some evidence being found of ancient trade routes and therefore some minimal contact between ancient cultures. The "incense road" (where incense was traded) that connected Egypt with Arabia and the Indies is now thought to have been in existence since at least 1800 B.C.

THINK QUICK!

Can you figure out the birth date on the cuneiform birthday tablet we've made?

Answer to the question is up the side of this page.

TRY THIS! Take the Babylonian challenge and make your own cuneiform birthday tablet!

You will need:
❖ Newspaper, to protect work surface
❖ Salt Clay (see recipe)
❖ Waxed paper
❖ Red and green food coloring
❖ Rolling pin or glass jar
❖ Pencil
❖ Paper

Salt Clay:
❖ 2 cups (500 ml) flour
❖ 1 cup (250 ml) salt
❖ ¾ to 1 cup (175 to 250 ml) water
❖ 2 tablespoons (25 ml) vegetable oil

In a bowl, mix together the flour and salt. Slowly add the water and the oil to the flour mix. Stir until dough forms.

Cuneiform Birthday Tablet

What you do:

1 Spread the newspaper over your work surface. Soften the clay by kneading it with your hands for a minute or so. Working on waxed paper, add a few drops of the food coloring to get the brown tablet color.

2 Roll out the clay so that it is roughly oval shaped and about 1/2" (1 cm) thick.

3 Write the month and day you were born on paper in cuneiform numbers. Once you are certain you have the correct numbers, use the pencil as a *stylus* (the original writing tool) to make cuneiform shapes by pressing into the clay.

4 Allow the clay to dry for at least two days in a sunny place, or ask permission to bake it in the oven at 300°F (150°C) until hardened. Then, say happy birthday with your cuneiform tablet!

THINK QUICK!

Something's missing

Do you notice anything missing in the cuneiform numeral system?

Here's a hint: Some might say
what is missing is very, very important;
others might say
it is a whole lot of nothing.

Answer to the question is up the side of this page.

Let's call it "Vacationatus"

The Babylonians depended on planting crops to give them most of their food. To do this, they needed to know when to plant seeds and when to harvest the crops to make the most of the growing season. So the Babylonians invented a calendar that alternated between a 29- and 30-day-month schedule. The year was 12 months long, or 354 days. Because a real year is actually just over 365 days (as we know now, but they didn't know then), over time the calendar would become less and less accurate. The ancient Babylonian king would, therefore, order a new month every so often when the calendar got too far off track. When would you order the new month? During summer vacation, we bet!

Using Cuneiform: A Step Backward–or Not?

We've just taken a glimpse on our back-in-time sleuthing adventure at one example of how math didn't just keep moving forward one year after another. It all seemed to happen in spurts of growth and spurts of repetition. That it happened at all is what we are curious about, because that kept math alive.

Was math taking a step backward or a step forward with cuneiform numbers? To our way of thinking, based on what we know, it doesn't really seem to be either. (In fact, it seems we are asking the wrong question, which we have found can be a real stumbling block to solving a dilemma.)

• Math was neither going forward nor stepping backward.

• Using cuneiform was neither good nor bad.

• Math was neither making progress nor marking time.

It just was.

The use of cuneiform written on tablets 500 years after the first tablets with symbols were used just shows us that the life of math continued. Why or how? Well, we each need to look beneath the surface of the facts to find the secret to its survival.

Hieroglyphics

Using pictures to write and keep track

Since we've been leaping around the world in time and place, allow us please to further confuse you. It is still around the year 2000 B.C. We are in northern Africa, in what is called Egypt today, along the Nile River. But when we take a look at the secret life of math here, we discover that it is going through a major growth spurt! What's up with that?

3500 B.C.

3000 B.C.
(North Africa)
Egypt: Hieroglyphic
numbers in use.

2500 B.C.

(North Africa)
Egypt: Rhind
papyrus copied
by Ahmose.
1650 B.C.

About 1850 B.C.
(North Africa)
Egypt: Original
Rhind papyrus
written.

1500 B.C.
(North Africa)
Egypt: Hieroglyphic
numbers found on
stone carving.

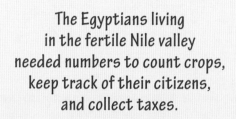

The Egyptians living
in the fertile Nile valley
needed numbers to count crops,
keep track of their citizens,
and collect taxes.

It's all about decoding!

"I can't read that. It looks like it was written in hieroglyphics!" Have you ever said that? Usually we mean that we have no way of understanding what is being written because we don't know what the written symbols mean.

But we are about to change that, as we discover the secret life of *hieroglyphics*. By 3000 B.C., the Egyptians living in the fertile Nile valley needed numbers to count crops, keep track of their citizens, and collect taxes for the *pharaoh*, or leader. So they invented *hieroglyphics*, a system of writing that uses pictorial symbols, called *hieroglyphs* (HI-row-glifs), or just *glyphs*.

500 B.C.   0   A.D. 500   A.D. 1000   A.D. 1500   A.D. 1858
                                                                          (Europe) Scotland:
                                                                          A. Henry Rhind
                                                                          purchases
                                                                          Rhind papyrus.

Ancient School Days

What was school like in ancient Egypt? Well, going to school cost money, so most Egyptians never learned to read, to write, or to use numbers and understand math. Usually, only the sons of powerful people had the opportunity to go to school. (Sorry to say, no girls were allowed.) The students used very different writing materials for their math problems back then. To record lessons, they used a wooden tablet covered with plaster. To write, they used a special paintbrush with red and black ink. The tablet could be wiped clean after each use, ready to be used again.

Usually, only the sons of powerful people had the opportunity to go to school. (Sorry to say, no girls were allowed.)

EGYPTIAN NUMBERS

BE A SECRET SUPER SLEUTH

Egyptians had been using finger counting since 2500 B.C., or earlier. The first Egyptian number system, however, used *hieroglyphs* (HI-row-glifs), numbers based on picture symbols. Another system that came along later (and was much more convenient) was called *hieratic*, meaning "sacred," because Egyptian priests invented it. This is the system that was used to write on papyrus (see page 82).

| 1 | 10 | 100 |
| (stroke) | (cattle hobble) | (coil of rope) |

Hieroglyphic Handiwork

The ancient Egyptians used hieroglyphs to write their numbers, just as they used drawings to make up the written Egyptian language. There were distinct characters to represent 1, 10, 100, 1,000, and so on up to 10,000,000! (Don't worry, they didn't have to memorize ten million different glyphs. The characters were simply repeated.) Below are the main symbols used for numbers up to a million.

"Pretty easy, right? To read these numbers simply find the value of each of the symbols and add them up. For example, two coils of rope equal 200. Five tadpoles equal 500,000. To make things easier, first find the value of the symbols having the greatest value. Then, keep adding all the symbols to decipher the Egyptian number."

1,000
(lotus plant)

10,000
(finger)

100,000
(tadpole)

1,000,000
(a god with arms
supporting the sky)

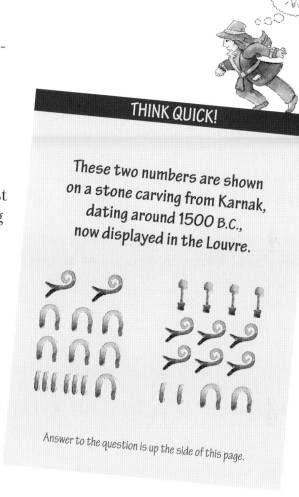

THINK QUICK!

These two numbers are shown on a stone carving from Karnak, dating around 1500 B.C., now displayed in the Louvre.

Answer to the question is up the side of this page.

Think Quick! answer: The numbers are 276 and 4622. How did you do?

Papyrus—a kind of paper product

For very important documents where the information needed to be saved, *papyrus* was used, but usually the practice draft was composed on the wooden tablet first. (The word *paper* comes from the word *papyrus*, even though paper isn't really made from papyrus.) Papyrus paper was made by weaving stalks of the papyrus marsh weed that grew on the banks of the Nile River. Layers of the woven strips were soaked in water, pounded with a mallet, and left to dry in the sun. Once dry, the surface was scraped smooth and the papyrus "paper" was ready to write on. (Papyrus feels more like rough cardboard than writing paper to us, though.) To give proper credit, the very first paper was not made in the land now called Egypt, but was invented in China, where one of the oldest pieces can be seen today in a museum in Xian. Of course, that shouldn't surprise us! It is just one more example of math having many lives that seemed to repeat themselves in faraway places and times.

ANOTHER IMPORTANT CLUE

BE A SECRET SUPER SLEUTH

What do you suppose the Egyptian students used to "take notes" or to write things they wanted to remember? (After all, if they wiped the tablet clean each time, they would have to wipe away their notes.) The answer to this—in a way—is a clue to how and why humans the world over invented things—including numbers and math!

Maya Glyphs in Central America!

While the Egyptian use of glyphs was certainly much earlier, the Maya (MY-uh), who lived in what is now southern Mexico and parts of Central America, also used glyphs, beginning in about A.D. 250. That was the height of the *El Mundo Maya*, the ancient Maya empire that helped this amazing civilization of long ago to prosper.

In most villages, the Maya rulers, who were mathematical astronomer priests, governed the people. These rulers came up with incredible number systems that were mostly organized in groups of 20. (Could this number have been chosen because it is related to our 20 digits—our fingers, thumbs, and toes?)

Maya-Style Numbers

System One
One number system the Maya used was a series of symbols

combined with pictures of heads (glyphs) of gods like the ones shown on the side of this stela carved in A.D. 731. There were 19 head glyphs in all, representing the 13 gods of the Superior World, with six variations. A separate head glyph represented zero. This special system of head glyphs was used only for special occasions, and you can understand why: Writing out numbers was literally like drawing portraits, a real form of "art"—a lot different than writing out our numbers today!

System Two

Although the glyph numbers are fun to look at, we think you will agree that the second number system of the Maya was much more practical. This second system was based on a pattern of dots and bars, with a shell symbol used to represent the Maya idea of "nothing," or zero. (Some historians think that

the shell that represents the Maya zero symbolized an empty oyster shell. Oysters were served on shell halves at important feasts. Empty shells meant no oysters, or "nothing!" How clever is that?)

a shell = 0
a dot = 1
a bar = 5

In different positions, these symbols could represent numbers up to infinity, not unlike our own system! Sound a little tricky? It's actually easy, once you get the hang of it.

TRY THIS!

Here are the Maya numbers from zero to 11:

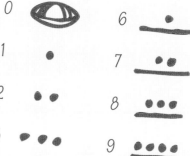

0
1
2
3
4
5
6
7
8
9
10
11

Can you guess what number this is?

Let's see . . . two bars and four dots—that's 5 + 5 + 1 + 1 + 1 + 1. You've got it; it's 14! Great! Why don't we try another one?

Three bars, meaning 5 + 5 + 5. Wow! Now you are counting like the Maya!

For numbers above 19, the counting got a little trickier. (For more about Maya numbers, see pages 90 to 96.)

WILL THE REAL INVENTOR PLEASE RECEIVE CREDIT?

FAST-FORWARD

The *Rhind papyrus* is an important record of 87 ancient Egyptian math problems. It was written by a scribe named Ahmose, who copied it in 1650 B.C. from an older document, written about 200 years earlier. The Rhind papyrus is named after the Scotsman, A. Henry Rhind, who purchased it in 1858 and realized its importance. Now it is also referred to as the *Ahmes papyrus,* after the scribe Ahmose who copied it from an unknown author. Some people feel that the name Ahmes papyrus gives credit to the person who most deserves it. Who do you think—Ahmes, or Rhind, or the unnamed earlier scribe—should have his name associated with this famous and valuable math document?

You are looking at the mathematical "Rhind" (or "Ahmes") papyrus that was created about 1650 B.C. in Thebes, Egypt!

THINK QUICK!

In the paragraph "Will the real inventor please receive credit?" why isn't the date 1858 marked either B.C. or A.D.?

Answer to the question is up the side of this page.

Think Quick! answer: The date couldn't be B.C. because the Rhind papyrus couldn't have been purchased, as it wouldn't have been written yet! So it goes without saying that we're talking about A.D. time here.

SEVEN CATS ... AND MORE!

MAKE IT REAL

Try to solve problem 79 on the Rhind/Ahmes papyrus. Figure it out in hieroglyphics for a greater challenge, using numerals on a piece of scrap paper for a little less challenge, or use a calculator for the easiest method by far. No matter which method you use, read the problem carefully and don't peek at the answer at the bottom of this page.

Seven houses each have seven cats. The seven cats each kill seven mice. If not for the cats, each of the mice would have eaten seven ears of wheat. Each ear of wheat would have produced seven measures of flour. How many measures of flour did the cats save?

Many years later, a traveler took the "seven cats" idea from the Rhind/Ahmes papyrus and introduced a similar problem in Europe, in the form of a poem that you may have heard:

As I was going to St. Ives,
I met a man with seven wives.
Every wife had seven sacks.
Every sack had seven cats.
Every cat had seven kits.
Kits, cats, sacks and wives,
How many were going to St. Ives?

Seven Cats answer: 7 houses x 7 cats x 7 mice x 7 ears of wheat x 7 measures of flour = 16,807 measures of flour total!

St. Ives Answer: Ah-ha! A trick question! Remember to read the questions carefully. The answer is 1! The narrator of the poem is the only one going to St. Ives. The others—the 1 man, his 7 wives, 49 sacks, 343 cats, 2,401 kittens—were all going the other way!

Fractions... Already?

By the year 1800 B.C., Egyptians were using unit fractions! Why do you think the very clever Egyptians invented these? (Another clue to the secret to math's life.) The Egyptians were considered very advanced for using the fractions ½, ¼, ⅛, ¹/₁₆, ¹/₃₂, ¹/₆₄ in a diagram called the *Eye of Horus.*

Who's Horus and what did he have to do with fractions? This picture shows the eye of Horus, son of Osiris, one of Egypt's principal gods. (The name Horus was associated with kings, who were thought to be godlike. When a king died, he became Osiris, and the new ruler became Horus.) The eye represents 1 hekat (unit) of grain and is considered a good-luck symbol. By today's standards, 1 hekat of grain is the equivalent to about 4.8 liters, or approximately 5 quarts. That's a little over a gallon, or just over the amount that fits in a gallon milk jug.

Make an Eye

TRY THIS! Each of the parts of the Eye of Horus is a hieroglyphic symbol for one of the fractions in the series ½, ¼, ⅛, ¹/₁₆, ¹/₃₂, and ¹/₆₄. Cleverly arranged, these symbols make the Eye of Horus.

# of Horus Amulet

You will need:

- ❖ Newspaper, to protect the work surface
- ❖ Scrap paper and pencil
- ❖ Cardboard
- ❖ White craft glue
- ❖ Small bowl or clean container for mixing glue
- ❖ Water
- ❖ Tissue paper
- ❖ Gold spray paint (or yellow if gold is not available), or gold or yellow tempera paint and a paintbrush
- ❖ Scissors, to cut finished amulet
- ❖ Nail, to make a hole
- ❖ Ribbon, yarn, or piece of leather, to make a necklace

What you do:

1 Practice drawing the fraction hieroglyphs on a piece of scrap paper. When you are comfortable, draw the Eye of Horus on your piece of cardboard.

2 Prepare the glue in the container by mixing it in thirds: 2 parts glue plus 1 part water. Tear off pieces of the tissue paper and moisten them in the glue mixture.

3 Form the tissue into "snakes" and place these strips over the lines you've drawn on the cardboard. You will have a raised Eye of Horus design. Use plenty of the glue mixture to attach the tissue.

4 Allow the design to dry for a day or two. When dry, take it outdoors to spray-paint it gold (or yellow). If indoors, just paint it with paint and a brush.

5 Cut out the amulet, punch a hole through the top using a nail. String it on a piece of yarn, ribbon, or leather, and wear the necklace for good luck!

½   ¼   ⅛   1/16   1/32   1/64

THINK QUICK!

Do you notice anything strange about the series of fractions in the Eye of Horus?

Here's a clue: Add them up. (Remember to use a common denominator of 64, so 1/32, for example, would equal 2/64.) Discover anything now?

Answer to the question is up the side of this page.

A Civilization Ahead of Its Time

Whoa! How'd we advance so quickly? Well, not everyone *did* advance so quickly. While people of ancient Europe were living in Stone Age (primitive) conditions, the people of ancient Egypt were wearing fine linens, devising calendars and an intricate writing system based on pictures, and growing grains like barley and corn that could be stored for hard times.

Ancient Egypt was so advanced for its time! Egyptian doctors performed brain surgery (successfully!), Egyptians built the pyramids, and people prospered and worked hard in the fields. It all serves to remind us, however, that communication between various cultures was not very efficient. Information about what one community of peoples did was mostly *not* shared with other cultural groups, even though there is evidence that there was some trading at this time.

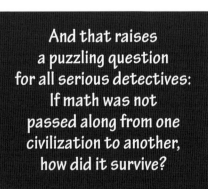

And that raises a puzzling question for all serious detectives: If math was not passed along from one civilization to another, how did it survive?

Forward or Back?

Now that we've seen how quickly one civilization moved ahead, it is important to remind ourselves that most civilizations at this time were, well, far from civilized. And since these civilizations did not interact with one another, they had a lot of catching up to do if the secret life of math were to continue moving ahead.

And that raises a puzzling question for all serious detectives: If math was not passed along from one civilization to another, how did it survive?

Zip, Zephirum, Zero

Why bother with nothing?

It isn't really all that curious that ancient peoples, for the most part, weren't interested in zero. Why bother with nothing? After all, would you want zero ice cream, zero popcorn at the movies, zero recess, or even worse, zero vacation? You'd be hard-pressed to find someone who would say, "Oh, please, please, give me a zero on the test!" The same held true for most civilizations: Zero was a no-show when it came to numbering systems.

While including zero as a number might seem to make perfect sense to us today, remember that it had to be invented in order for it to be used. And it had to be used a lot to survive. It seems that many ancient civilizations thought "zero" about zero.

2000 B.C.   1500 B.C.   1000 B.C.   700 B.C.   400 B.C.

700 B.C.
Middle East:
Babylonians use
3 hook marks to
indicate empty
space in number.

400 B.C.
(Asia) China:
Use of
empty space
to differentiate
numbers.

400 B.C.
Middle East:
Babylonians use 2
wedge-shaped marks to
mean empty space to
differentiate numbers.

BANISHING ZERO?

MAKE IT REAL

Imagine life without zero. How would you record the difference between receiving a $1 or $10 allowance? How would you indicate that you aced a quiz and got a 90—not a 9! And when someone hands you $1.00 in change when it was supposed to be $10.00—well, exactly how would you explain that?

TRY THIS! For a whole day, try not to use a zero in numerals or numbers, nor the word zero in conversation, nor any other word that means zero in your language. (So if someone asks you if you would like extras on peas and broccoli, no fair saying, "Actually, I don't want any," or "None, please," because that is the same as saying zero.)

(Asia) India:
Aryabhata develops place-value number system.
A.D. 500

(Asia) India:
First concrete evidence that Indian mathematicians recognize zero as a real value.
A.D. 876

0

A.D. 665
Central America:
Maya use zero in place-value number system.

A.D. 1000

A.D. 1200
(Europe) Italy:
Leonardo Fibonacci spreads use of zero in Europe.

A.D. 1600
Europe:
Zero used by most peoples of Europe.

A.D. 2000

Uh-oh! Something's wrong here!

Remember the clever people who lived in what is now part of the Middle East who developed a whole system of numerals called *cuneiform*? (See page 72.) It seemed like everything made sense when writing in cuneiform, right? Well, not exactly. If you remember, they had numbers for 1 through 59; then they began all over again for 60. Big problem! You see, there was no way to tell the difference between 1 and 60, unless you knew what the numbers referred to or the spacing of the other written numbers.

If you left a note for your Mom back then (written on a tablet, of course), telling her that you ate one (1) fig, what would she think? Did you eat all 60 figs that were set aside for guests? Or, did you just help yourself to 1 fig? The cuneiform wedge symbol could mean both of these numbers.

The rule of position

A number's value depended on its *situation*, or place, in the number. Mathematicians refer to that as the *rule of position*.

The rule of position was discovered at different times in the history of the world. For example, the Babylonians, the Chinese, the Maya peoples, and the people of India all developed positional number systems. Then, with the rule of position as the basis for a method of recording numbers, it was soon realized that a zero was needed. Different cultures developed the idea of zero, though often in a different form (more of a placeholder) than the zero we know today.

At first, zero was not thought of as an actual value. Instead, it was either ignored completely, or a space or symbol was used to show an empty position in a number. For example, by 700 B.C. in Babylonia, zero was used only to show how the two and six were related. Zero as a number didn't exist. By 400 B.C., the Chinese were using an empty space to show the difference between a number like 2 or 20. In India, a heavy dot was used to mark an empty number position. (It wasn't until A.D. 876 that we have concrete evidence that Indian mathematicians recognized zero as a real value!)

The Inca left a blank space on a quipu (see page 45) when they wanted to show "nothing." The Maya in what is now southern Mexico and Central America were on top of things in A.D. 665 when they included a real zero in their number system despite their earlier knowledge about zero. Believe it or not, zero didn't appear in Europe

> It isn't really all that curious that ancient peoples, for the most part, weren't interested in zero. Why bother with nothing?

until about A.D. 1200! Even then, the City Council in Florence, Italy, did not welcome zero with open arms. They said that it would be too easy to make a zero into a 6 or 9, and so they made using zero against the law! It wasn't for another 400 years that using *zephirum* became common in Europe.

Numbers, Take Your Places!

Let's compare the Maya system and our present-day system. Both are *place value* number systems. That means the number symbols, or *digits* (the 1, 2, or 3, or the dots and bars), have different values depending on what position they occupy in a number. For instance, what would you rather have, 4 free rides at an amusement park, or 40? How about 400! (See? It's the same digit 4, but in a different *place*.)

   The Maya used the same idea with their dot and bar digits, except that the place-value positions were listed up and down, not sideways! Reading from top to bottom, here's the number for 447, Maya-style (remember, the Maya number system was based on 20):

1 dot in the
four hundreds place,
or 1 x 400 = 400

2 dots in the
twenties place,
or 2 x 20 = 40

a bar and 2 dots
in the *units* (ones) place,
or 5 + 2 = 7

Put it all together, and you get
400 + 40 + 7, or 447!

THINK QUICK!

Ready for a challenge? Try this one:

Answer to the question is up the side of this page.

Think Quick! answer: From the bottom, 4 dots in the units place = 4; the shell symbol in the twenties place means no 20, that is it means zero; and 2 dots and 1 bar in the four hundreds place means 7 x 400, or 2,800. So 4 + 2,800 = 2,804!

Munchin' Maya Number Cookies

Let's make a batch of Maya Number Cookies, based on the place values we've just seen in use. And since Maya number systems were based on a base of 20, let's make a batch of 20 cookies!

You will need:
❖ One 1.55-ounce (43 g) chocolate bar
❖ Zip-locking bag
❖ Bowl
❖ 1 package ready-made sugar cookie dough
❖ Mixing spoon
❖ Waxed paper
❖ Rolling pin or glass jar

❖ Cookie sheet or large baking pan
❖ Icing (homemade or store-bought) to "glue" decorations onto each cookie
❖ Malt balls or other small round candies for the dots
❖ Black or red licorice pieces for the bars

What you do:
1 Preheat oven to 350°F (180°C). Place the unwrapped chocolate bar in the zip-locking bag and crush it until it resembles coarse crumbs.

2 Put the prepared cookie dough and chocolate crumbs into the bowl. Mix lightly.

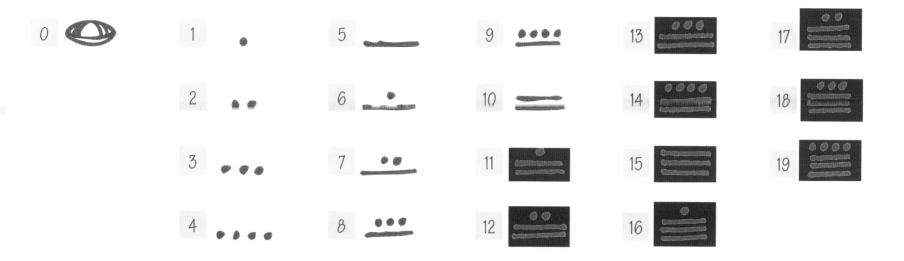

3 Place a portion of the dough between two pieces of waxed paper. Roll out the dough so that it's about 1/2" (1 cm) thick.

4 Cut the dough into rectangular-shaped cookies and place each on the cookie sheet. Leave about 2" (5 cm) of space between each cookie.

5 Bake the cookies according to the package directions.

6 Remove the cookie sheet from the oven. Cool the cookies on a rack for at least 30 minutes. Use icing to "glue" the candy decorations onto the cookies to construct Mayan numerals. Each cookie should have one Maya number on it, and each cookie eater has to try to figure out what that number is!

THE DECI-DECA DUO

MAKE IT REAL

If the Maya-style number system is based on 20, what is the Western style based on? Yes, 10 is correct. In English, we use the prefix *deci* to mean "one-tenth" and *deca* to mean "ten." What words can you think of that use these prefixes? Decimeter ($\frac{1}{10}$ of a meter)? Decade (a period of 10 years)? Decathlon (a sports contest of 10 different events)?

What else comes in ten or tenths? Use the *deci-* or *deca-* prefix to make up names that will come in handy for what you find. After you cut a large pizza into 10 pieces, you might call out, "Come and get it! The deci-pizza is ready." If you need your brother to buy you 10 pencils in a package, you might say, "Yo! Bro! Would you mind stopping at the store to buy me a deca-pack of pencils?" And, if a scoop of ice cream costs 10 cents, you might order (dare we write it?) … a double-deca!

FIBONACCI'S NEW NUMBERS

FAST-FORWARD

In about A.D. 1200, Leonardo Fibonacci introduced the digits we use today (1, 2, 3, 4, 5, 6, 7, 8, 9, and 0) to the people of Europe. Although they were new to Europe, these symbols for numbers were nothing new to the Indian and Arab peoples of that time. This "new" system was called the *Hindu-Arabic system,* named after the people who used it first. Fibonacci had learned about it during his childhood when he lived in northern Africa with his father, who was a customs official there. Fibonacci explained this new system in a book: "There are nine figures of the Indians, 1 2 3 4 5 6 7 8 9. With these nine figures and the symbol 0, which in Arabic is called *zephirum,* any number can be written."

Unfortunately, many people didn't want to try this new method of counting. They preferred using their old system of Roman numerals, even though it was harder and more complicated to use. Finally, though, by about A.D. 1600, nearly everyone was using the Hindu-Arabic numerals.

Zero: From Zilch to Value

Although zero didn't catch on quickly even after people had been introduced to it, it did eventually gain use, first as a placeholder, and then as a number with its own value. If you can figure out why zero didn't catch on more quickly in math, you might be very close to solving the secret about math's long life.

Part III

Faster Figuring:

Knowing More—Sooner!

The Keys to the Mystery of Math

You need to tease clues out of hiding, uncovering them from thousands of years of dirt and dust.

You have to be clever enough to know a clue when you are staring it in the face, so to speak!

"What's the rush? Slow down and smell the flowers. Why is everyone in such a hurry to finish one thing so they can rush off and do another?"

Sooner or later, we can practically guarantee that you will feel that way, if you haven't already. It seems we humans are always in a hurry to accomplish more, faster.

It's a chicken-and-egg thing

Interestingly, we can learn a lot about ourselves just from what we have observed about math's long life. And if we are correct in linking the development of math with the life of individuals, it is clear that finding answers fast, then faster, then fastest is a key not only in the life of math, but in our lives, too. On closer inspection, we are faced with a *conundrum*, or puzzle: Did math drive people's lives, or did humans drive math's long life? After all, math has been here through it all, while people and their civilizations have come and gone.

According to Plato, many would say that it is necessity that drives people to invent things. And we humans sure are resourceful. But there are those who believe that often an idea catches on and before we realize it, we have changed how we do things. In no time at all, we have forgotten why we made the changes in the first place or whether they improved on anything.

As long ago as 1000 B.C., counting boards were used in China. To do what? Why, to speed up math processes! If we people were already in such a hurry more than 3,000 years ago, maybe it *is* fair to say that math was invented to help people move ahead faster and faster. After all, we haven't slowed up yet!

You need to look at some things one way and then turn them around and look at the same things another way.

You'll need to give the "handy five"—your five senses—a tough workout, because clues don't just sit around waiting to be found.

Keep that sleuthing cap on

Remember when you asked how you would know what was important? (See page 14.) Well, now that you have so many thoughts and impressions rolling around in your head, it's time for a last reminder of what it takes to be a good sleuth (see the keys on these pages).

As we near the end of our adventure, those clues will be flying by fast. Even so, take the time to have a lot of fun on this last leg of your journey, because algorithms and the high-tech abacus are definitely a good time. So, smell those flowers, while keeping your eye on the prize!

You need to question, put forth new ideas, and listen to what others are saying.

Be an Algorithm Detective

Using numbers to solve problems

How would you teach someone to tie her shoes? What is the recipe for preparing cinnamon toast? And, more to the point, what does math have to do with either of these processes? Good question. Many of us tend to think of math as times tables, figuring out problems for homework, and generally as something that is taught in school but is not particularly useful anyplace else. But, if that were all there is to math, why would it still be around after 35,000 years?

Despite the fact that on some days numbers might seem as if they were designed to keep you up

2000 B.C.   1500 B.C.   1000 B.C.   500 B.C.

Lots of things that we aren't familiar with are easier to do when we have a series of smaller steps to follow. That's math at work inside and outside ot schools and businesses!

too late doing your homework, this is not their real purpose! Believe it or not, the process of using step-by-step instructions to complete a task, such as tying a special knot, is math at work. The instructions are called an *algorithm* (AL-geh-ri-thim). The recipe for cinnamon toast—take a piece of bread, pop it in the toaster, and when ready, spread it with butter, sugar, and cinnamon—is an algorithm, too. Lots of things that we aren't familiar with are easier to do when we have a series of smaller steps to follow. That's math at work inside and outside of schools and businesses!

TRY THIS!

An Algorithm a Day Keeps Confusion Away

It really is true that algorithms keep our levels of confusion and frustration much lower. Chances are you use a lot more than one algorithm each day, which means—surprise!—you use math many times a day. Just out of curiosity, jot down all of the math, including algorithms, that you use in one whole day. If you learn a new game, for instance, the rules of the game that tell you how to play are an algorithm. What other step-by-step algorithms can you think of? In how many ways have numbers sneaked into your life?

0	A.D. 500	A.D. 800	A.D. 1000	A.D. 1500	A.D. 1945
		Middle East: Al-Khwarizmi writes books on algorithms.		(North America) United States: George Polya publishes book on problem-solving.	

SWISH! IT'S GONE!

FAST-FORWARD

In about A.D. 800 in the Middle East, individuals were using tables covered in dust or sand to work out math problems. Similar to a chalkboard, a problem would be worked out step-by-step with the beginning parts erased as more space was needed. (Uh-oh. What do you think happened when somebody sneezed! *Gezundheit!*)

AN ALGORITHM MISTAKE!

Because *algorithm* is a rather difficult-sounding word, many people think it involves some type of complex mathematical process. Not so, most of the time! The word is actually the result of a mistake. A brilliant man by the name of Muhammad Bin Musa Al-Khwarizmi spent most of his life working things out on a "dust table" at his home in the Middle East. But Al-Khwarizmi's name, after it was translated from Arabic into Latin, was misread and mispronounced as "algorithm." So not only is the name misleading as to how difficult algorithms tend to be, but the word itself is just plain incorrect, too!

Lots of things that we aren't familiar with are easier to do when we have a series of smaller steps to follow.

THINK QUICK!

Lattice and algorithms

Why is the lattice multiplication method an algorithm?

Answer to the question is up the side of this page.

Make a Lattice Multiplication Puzzle

TRY THIS!

One useful algorithm that was developed in the Middle East and then later introduced to Europe by Leonardo Fibonacci is called the *lattice method of multiplication.* The grid you'll make looks like a lattice pattern. For fun, try making your own lattice puzzle.

3

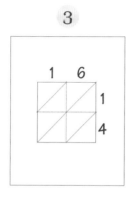

4

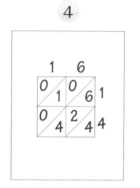

5

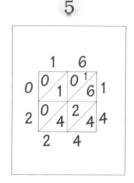

6

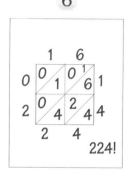

224!

You will need:
- Square sticky note
- Paper, 1 sheet
- Pencil
- Scissors

What you do:

1 Fold the square diagonally. Then flatten the paper. Refold it twice into quarters. Unfold the paper.

2 Make two more folds by turning in the top left and bottom right couners so that each quarter of the paper is divided into two triangles. Trace over the diagonal folds.

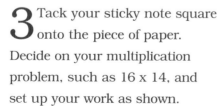

3 Tack your sticky note square onto the piece of paper. Decide on your multiplication problem, such as 16 x 14, and set up your work as shown.

4 Work with each of the four main squares separately. Multiply the aligning numbers and record the answer placing the tens in the top triangle (put 0 if there are none) and the ones in the bottom triangle. (See the example of 1 x 1 in red.)

5 Add the *diagonals*, carrying when needed. (In the example 6 + 2 + 4 = 12, you carry the 1 to the next diagonal.)

6 The answer is revealed! Read it counter-clockwise on the larger paper.

JUST FOR FUN! Draw a picture on the back of the lattice paper. It is helpful if it is of big things, like a cat, a tree, or the sun.

Cut each section apart. Challenge a friend to figure out the original number sentence. (Need help? Have her put the picture together.)

PROBLEM-SOLVING MADE OH-SO-EASY (FINALLY!)

FAST-FORWARD

"The first rule of discovery is to have brains and good luck. The second rule of discovery is to sit tight and wait until you get a bright idea."

George Polya, the mathematician who said that, moved to the United States from Europe in 1940. One of his bright ideas was to come up with a neat four-step algorithm for solving problems:

1. Understand the problem:
What is it that you want to find out?

2. Devise an algorithm:
Make a plan and use a strategy to figure out the answer. For example, you can use a strategy such as starting with what you know, looking for a pattern, making a list, drawing a picture, working backward, or making a guess and then checking it. You can also invent your own strategy.

3. Carry out your plan:
Carefully follow the steps in the plan.

4. Examine the solution:
Does the result make sense? Did the algorithm work?

TRY THIS!
Conduct an Algorithm Investigation
Think up your own problem-solving investigation. Use Polya's four-step plan to figure out the solution. Write down the algorithm, or the steps you will take to find the solution. Here are some ideas to get you started.

- What is the average number of pets owned by members of your class?

- Which person in your family reads the most?

- Where did I leave my overdue library book (or my baseball cap, favorite sweater, etc.)?

Or, make up your own algorithm on a topic that interests you!

Do Some Math in the Egyptian Style!

TRY THIS!

In ancient Egypt, many students learned math inside temple schools where boys (boys only, again!) worked out problems from papyrus study scrolls. These were called the *Kempt*. What algorithm would you use to solve this problem: 17 x 6? Is there another way to solve this? You bet there is! If you lived in ancient Egypt, you would multiply like an Egyptian, of course. Use the following algorithm to set up the number sentence 17 x 6 and solve it the Egyptian way!

```
   17
 x  6
   42
   60
  102
```

1	6
2	12
4	24
8	48
16	96

✓1	6	
2	12	
4	24	
8	48	
✓16	96	

✓1	✓6	
2	12	
4	24	
8	48	
✓16	✓96	

```
    6
 + 96
  102
```

What you do:

1 You will need to make two columns of numbers on your paper. In the right-hand column, start with the 6 from your math problem. Complete the column by doubling the previous number.

2 Always start with a 1 in the left-hand column, placing it beside the first right-hand entry. Then continue to double the numbers in this column as well.

3 Stop doubling in the left when you have enough numbers to make the 17. Put a check beside the numbers that add to 17. This would be 16 and 1 for this math problem.

4 To find the product of 6 x 17, add the numbers in the right column that correspond to the checked numbers in the left. So, add 6 + 96 to get 102. The product of 17 x 6 is 102!

Want to impress your teacher? Try doing your math homework like an ancient Egyptian. Not so tricky once you get the hang of it, is it?

SOLVING OUR QUEST TO MATH'S SECRET LIFE!

BE A SECRET SUPER SLEUTH

Now that you have written an algorithm about something you know quite well, see if you can come up with a way to use an algorithm to find the answer to our quest: Why has math survived for more than 35,000 years?

1. Understand the problem. (What it is you want to find out?): What is the secret to math's long life?

2. Devise an algorithm. Make a plan to solve the problem. You could use the strategies of making and then checking a guess by looking back in the book for clues. Or you could make the problem simpler by relating it to how *you* need math in everyday life. Is your life, like the lives of others before you, riddled with math situations and needs?

3. Carry out your plan. Think about the answers to your questions. Find the clues throughout the book and write them down. Then, make a list of how you use math every day. Imagine what it would be like if you couldn't calculate, measure, estimate, or count all day. What would happen?

4. Examine your solution. Does your solution to why numbers survived make sense? What do people think when you share your answer to the mystery?

What's this have to do with math's secret life?

That's a very good question. Do you know why? If you ask *why* something is included, then the answer should be an important clue. It should either contribute to your ideas thus far, or it should convince you that it is just included to confuse you. Which is it? Would we spend all of these pages just to confuse you? Here's a clue to what's going on here: Read the headlines above each section in this chapter—the big ones *and* the small ones. Together they give you some strong hints, but one headline in particular practically tells you the key to math's secret life. Another tells you how to set up your sleuthing algorithms, so you turn out a winner either way! Then, give this algorithm a try. You just might have the answer to our quest!

Hi-tech Math, the Low-tech Way

From bamboo rods to the abacus

Ask anyone who grew up in math classes without calculators, and they are sure to tell you that they did a lot of math in their heads and that long division and the like took them "forever" on paper. While most kids still use pencil and paper to do homework in elementary school, people in China have been using early calculators since about 1000 B.C. So, from then to within the time that your grandparents or great-grandparents may have been in school, math was still moving around secretively. What one group of peoples invented sometimes took thousands of years to cross borders.

Meet the Chinese!

Did you know that the ancient Chinese invented gunpowder, umbrellas, leather money, and handy calculating tools? If you were visiting ancient China and you were trying to figure out how much to pay for your steamed dumpling lunch, you could

2000 B.C.

1500 B.C.

1000 B.C.
(Asia) China:
Counting boards
used for calculation.

540 B.C.
(Asia) China:
Counting rods in use.

CHINA

use your *counting rod* type of calculator or, a little later in history, an *abacus* calculator made from beads and sticks. (The modern-type abacus that you may be familiar with didn't come into use until around A.D. 1200.) Then, when you *did* figure out how much to pay, you might store your cash on a string! (Yes, the Chinese invented some of the first metal coins, too. They made them with holes in the middle so they could carry around a "string of money.")

How could people in one country have invented so many things, far ahead of the rest of the world? Let's look at a map for clues.

See how huge the continent of Asia is? China takes up the better part of Asia, and it has a huge population. So it's no surprise that the Chinese invented many things. Ancient China had a population that probably equaled the rest of the world combined! Clearly, the Chinese were looking for ways to do math to keep track, record numbers, and then to calculate.

| 0 | A.D. 500 | A.D. 1200 | A.D. 1500 | A.D. 2000 |

(Asia) China:
Modern-type abacus
commonly used.

A Bamboo Calculator

More than 2,500 years ago, the Chinese had a convenient carry-around calculating system. It was a set of bamboo rods, or sticks. Some people who came from wealthy families might have had a set of rods made from ivory or jade. Whatever they were made of, these rods were a huge help in adding, subtracting, multiplying, and dividing. Sound a little like a calculator? You decide for yourself. After a little practice, see if you can do your math calculations more accurately and more quickly than with a pencil and paper.

Make Your Own Chinese

TRY THIS! You can make your own set of Chinese counting rods to see for yourself how helpful these were. Who knows? You may decide that these are more fun to use than a "plain old calculator!"

You will need:
❖ About 30 clean Popsicle, craft, or other sticks (see MAKE IT REAL, page 114)
❖ A piece of string, ribbon, or yarn
❖ Four sheets of paper taped together lengthwise (end to end) to make a place-value grid

What you do:

1 Practice making the Chinese rod numerals 1 to 9. Then practice some of the larger numbers. The rods that are placed vertically are called *tsungs* (ZONG) and the ones that are placed horizontally are called the *hengs* (HENG).

Counting Rods

2 Now that you've got the hang of the tsungs and hengs, practice making some larger numbers using the place-value grid. Place sticks in the place-value grid like this:

thousands	hundreds	tens	units
☰	Π	☰	T

What number have you made? (Answer is on page 112.)

Why do you think the vertical rod numeral alternates with the horizontal rod numeral? That's right, the units and hundreds are set up vertically and the tens and thousands are set up horizontally.

What a clear and easy way to keep track of the units, tens, hundreds, and thousands digits!

Chinese rod numbers

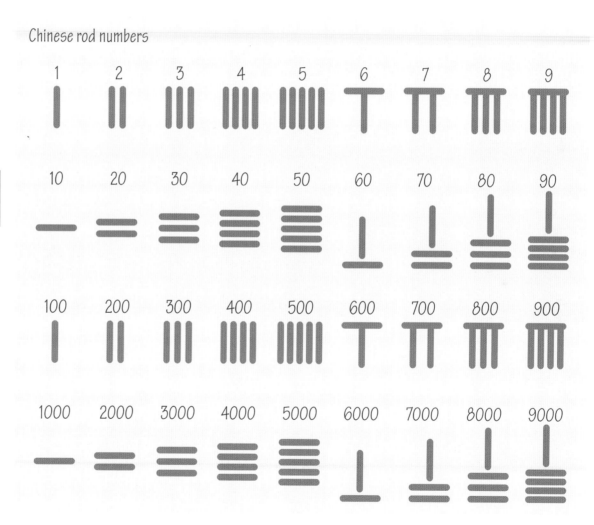

TRY THIS!

READY, SET, ADD!

Now that you are getting the "hang of the hengs," why not try adding using the rod set? It's fun! Start by setting up your rod number sentence as shown for 8 + 6:

Then, simply gather together the sticks, regrouping as necessary.

HINT: You will need to exchange two 5s in the *units* place for one 10 in the *tens* place. (Don't forget that numerals in the tens place are hengs—that is, they are placed horizontally.)

In this case, gather the four vertical rods and place them together in the units place. Next, add the two horizontal rods. They each

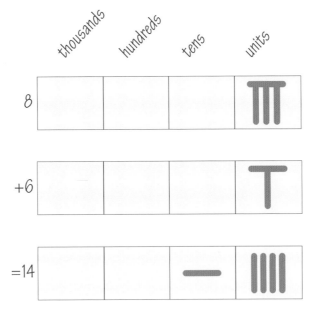

equal 5, so exchange them for one horizontal rod in the tens place.

You've done it! You have used Chinese ingenuity to work out 8 + 6! How about trying a more difficult number sentence?

For more of a challenge try something harder: How about 26 + 47?

Now, tie a ribbon or piece of yarn around your set of counting rods to keep them together until the next time you need to do some fast figuring.

WHAT'S LIGHT AND HANDY?

MAKE IT REAL

One characteristic throughout math's long life is that people did math using what was handy. At first it may have been pebbles, shells, or bones. Then people made clay counting balls with the clay that was plentiful. The quipus of long ago were made with string fashioned from the sheep's wool. It was light so that runners could traverse the empire easily and it could be carried without losing it.

The Chinese, too, wanted something that they could carry with them. Bamboo was very plentiful in ancient times and it is very light. It was the perfect choice to make rods.

When you make your calculating rods (see page 112), you can buy Popsicle or craft sticks or you can use something readily available, free, and—as with the other cultures—preferably something that is lightweight. What would you use for your calculating rod invention if you were living where you do right now, only in ancient times?

Almost Magical: The Abacus!

Did you ever have a toy abacus when you were a little kid? Lots of people had them when they were toddlers, yet traditionally they were used as calculating devices by adults. You see, around A.D. 1200, another kind of math tool was popular, also in China. The *suan pan,* the Chinese *abacus,* is still popular nowadays. (There we go again—math inventions traveling over distant miles and distant times all the way to today.) In fact, some people still prefer to use the abacus instead of using a modern electronic calculator. Those may be the same people who say that technology doesn't always help us. Can you think of a time when it was easier to do something by hand, rather than by using a machine? Hmmm.

One of many?

If you were to hold an international abacus convention, who should come? The participants from Greece, Rome, China, Japan, Russia, and other places would definitely be your honored guests. That's because China wasn't the only place to develop and use an abacus as a math tool!

Here are examples of the Chinese *suan pan,* the Japanese *soroban* (sore-oh-ban), and the Russian *schoty* (SHAW-tee).

Can you see the differences between the Chinese abacus and the others? Which of these do you think would be the easiest to use?

If you were to hold an international abacus convention, who should come?

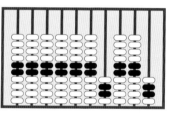

Russian schoty (SHAW-tee)

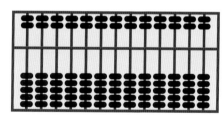

Chinese suan pan

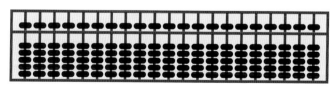

Japanese soroban (*sore-oh-ban*)

Make Your Own Chinese Abacus

TRY THIS!

Whether you decide this is the ultimate early invention or you are doing just fine with that handy little inexpensive calculator in your backpack, you'll want to make one of these and give it a try. It is amazing to think that this was invented so long ago. It's hard to believe. Just think, you are using a piece of early history!

You will need:
❖ Ruler
❖ Pen and pencil
❖ A shoe-box lid
❖ Wire (We like the plastic-coated kind from the hardware store.)
❖ 8 "heaven" beads of one color
❖ 20 "earth" beads of another color
❖ 1 dowel slightly wider than the box for a dividing rod

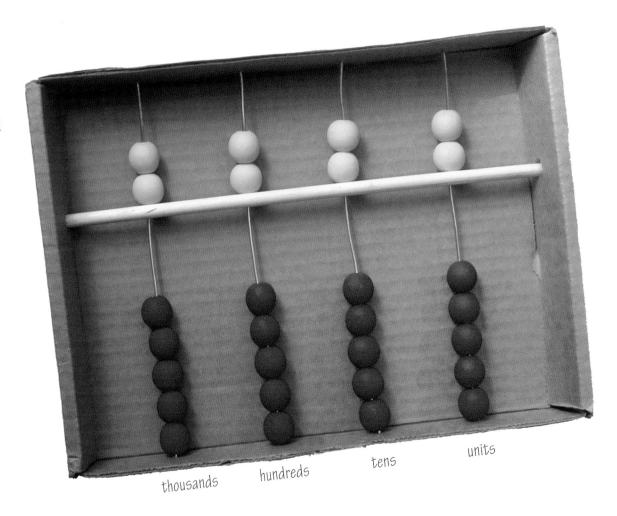

thousands   hundreds   tens   units

What you do:

1 Make marks across the lower side of the box where the holes for the wire rods will go. Use a ruler and a pencil to make four evenly spaced marks far enough away from the back so that the beads can move. Mark the upper side in the same way.

2 Have an adult help you use a pen point to poke a hole through each of the marks you made.

3 Cut four wires about 2" (5 cm) longer than the box. Push the wire through the holes and bend each end so that the wire doesn't fall out.

4 Place five earth beads of one color and two heaven beads of another color onto the wire as shown.

5 Put three more wires into place and add the heaven and earth beads.

6 Make a mark on the left and right sides of the box for the dividing rod. Place the marks about one-third of the way from the top, make sure they are even. Pake a hole through each of the marks. Push the heaven beads up and the earth beads down. Then push the dowel through to make a dividing rod.

7 Starting from the right, label the wires: units, tens, hundreds, and thousands. Now you can learn to form numbers. (See page 118.)

thousands   hundreds   tens   units

Because we know how you like added challenges (right?), you can use the abacus to practice decimal numbers if you label the right-hand wire hundredths, the second wire tenths, the third wire units, and the left-hand wire tens.

TRY THIS! Moving Heaven and Earth on the Abacus!

It's fun to practice forming numbers on the abacus! You'll need to move heaven and earth (beads, that is) to form these numbers, though! Just like in our modern number system, each beaded string is a place value, starting at the right with the units place. On each string, the (top) heaven beads are each worth five units and the (bottom) earth beads

Just think, you are using a piece of early history!

are each worth one unit. (Psst! Heaven = above or top; earth = below or bottom. But you were already using that mnemonic device, weren't you?)

After you learn to make these, try a few others until you feel comfortable.

How about making the number for the year you were born? Aha, right, got it?

(If not, not to worry; just go back to some double-digit numbers until you feel more comfortable with it.)

1. Get ready by pushing all the beads away from the center.

thousands   hundreds   tens   units

2. Make the number 7 like this:

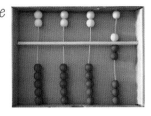

3. Now, try making 37. Your abacus should look like this:

TAKE THE ABACUS CHALLENGE

MAKE IT REAL

In 1945, a calculating race was held using a Japanese soroban that cost about 25 cents against a United States Army adding machine that cost $700. The outcome surprised many people! Kiyoshi Matsuzaki, nicknamed "The Hands," used a soroban to win the contest against Thomas Ian Deering on an electric adding machine. With fewer mistakes and time to spare, the soroban won hands down!

Are you ready to take the abacus challenge—you on the abacus versus someone else on a calculator?

1. Ask someone to be a referee. For a warm-up, the referee has a stopwatch and two dice to generate the numbers.

2. At the count of three, the referee starts the stopwatch and then rolls the dice. Race against your calculator opponent to be the first one to show the sum of the two dice on your Chinese abacus.

3. Now, try something more challenging, like a number sentence.

The referee randomly calls out two larger numbers to add. Race your opponent again. Who was able to show the answer first?

The Abacus Appeal

So, what do you think? Is an abacus more fun and more efficient than the math tools you use today? Do you feel as if you are really involved in the process because you are moving the beads and thinking fast? Those are interesting issues, because a lot of inventive thinking comes about when you are "into," or involved in, something. Is the calculator too separate from you and your thought process?

What is really of interest with regard to our search for the secret to the long life of math and numbers is that while a quick and accurate calculaing device (the abacus) was invented in one part of the world, Roman numerals that were very awkward to calculate with were in use in another part of the world. Assuming all peoples are equally capable of invention, what is the difference? Answer that and you will have solved the mystery!

Solve the Mystery of Math's Longevity

Find the "common denominator" across the ages (& pages)

Well, we're at a good stopping place for now. Of course, there is so much more to math's mysterious ability to sustain itself (or to be sustained by us). Times were definitely changing at this point in math's life, and independent civilizations were becoming aware of one another's existence. Ideas were being carried across the oceans, first in the simplest of ways as ships began to bring food and spices as well as observations about others from one continent to another, and then in more immediate ways. Today, it seems as if ideas travel almost as fast as we can think of them!

Understanding the secret to math's role in global culture and its longevity is no longer a matter of searching through ancient cultures to unearth artifacts as we try to reconstruct how math has shaped us or how we have shaped it.

Yet, the "common denominator" remains very much the same today as it was back then. (We use the math term "common denominator" in the sense that these are shared attributes, or themes, that kept numbers and math alive.) The most important of those common denominators embodies the mysterious secret to math's long, long life.

The Secret Super Sleuth reveals the secret to math's life

You don't really need us anymore. Truthfully, you already know the answer to math's secret life, even if you don't feel as if you do—yet. You can give your detective summation now if you like, or you can use these last clues. We're proud of you for all you've accomplished and for being such an amazing detective. We hope you've had fun, too, and that what you've learned about math, about human nature and people the world over, and about yourself will stay with you a long time.

So here we go—the last clues!

The last clues!

Clue #1
Blurt it out—right off the top of your head!

That's right. Spontaneity is a great thing. Don't think about it too much, just say it! Or, brainstorm with some others.

• Jot down the ideas or answers that interest or amuse you—and especially the ones that take you totally by surprise.

Clue #2
Why, oh why, did math grow here?

Have you noticed how much we have learned about human nature (that is how human beings seem to react, behave, and live their lives) by looking at how math has "lived" its life? In a way, you might say that math reveals characteristics about people that repeat themselves from one civilization to another.

• Look at the different cultures we visited and ask yourself "why" math and numbers took root there.

Clue #3
One-word impressions

Flip through the pages and jot down *single words* about the different kinds of keeping track and how and why they were used. Why tally sticks? Why counting balls? Why quipus?

• Look over your words and see if a theme develops. That will be a big clue as to how math survived and why.

Clue #4
People! People! People!

You've met people who lived in the far corners of the earth, thinking they were the only humans. You've met people who developed complex civilizations from scratch. You've met people who made hatch marks 35,000 years ago and people who used double tallies in England as recently as 200 years ago.

• What conclusions have you drawn about people the world over throughout all time? What does this have to do with the secret to math's longevity?

Clue #5
Across great distances?

Ask yourself (and then answer yourself): Could math have traveled "on its own" from here to there?

• Explain how math traveled great distances without a lot of human communication.

Clue #6
Throughout thousands upon thousands of years?

Think about the enormous time spans separating similar math concepts. How is it that some "math inventions" were so similar?

• Explain how math traveled back and forth in time without human communication or even human contact with artifacts. How is it that so many similar ideas came about even when separated by time and distance?

Clue #7
Try 'em on!

You know how it is when you are trying on a new pair of jeans in the store. Maybe a friend keeps telling you that each pair looks fine, but you keep trying different ones. And then, you put on a pair and you don't even ask how it looks on you. You just know this is the pair because it feels right. Well, that is what we all need to do right now. That is, we need to try on different ideas to find the key to math's long and secret life.

• You'll know when you find the answer, just as you know when you find the perfect pair of jeans. It will feel just right!

Index

Index

Resources

RESOURCES FOR READERS

The Adventures of Penrose the Mathematical Cat by Theoni Pappas (Wide World Publishing, 1997)

Ask Dr. Math (website) <http://mathforum.org/dr.math/>

From Zero to Ten: The Story of Numbers by Vivian French and Ross Collins (Oxford University Press, 2000)

The History of Counting by Denise Schmandt-Besserat (Morrow Junior Books, 1999)

How to Count Like a Martian by Glory St. John (Random House Children's Books, 1975)

The MacTutor History of Mathematics Archive (website) <http://www-history.mcs.st-andrews.ac.uk/history/index.html>

Moja Means One: Swahili Counting Book by Muriel L. Feelings (Dial Books for Young Readers, 1971)

REFERENCES

Ascher, Marcia. *Ethnomathematics: A Multicultural View of Mathematical Ideas.* Belmont, CA: Wadsworth, Inc., 1991.

Ascher, Marcia. *Mathematics Elsewhere: An Exploration of Ideas Across Cultures.* Princeton, NJ: Princeton University Press, 2002.

Ascher, Marcia. *Mathematics of the Incas: Code of the Quipu.* New York: Dover Publications, 1997.

Closs, Michael P., ed. *Native American Mathematics.* Austin, TX: University of Texas Press, 1986.

Gerdes, Paulus, ed. *Geometry from Africa: Mathematical and Educational Explorations.* The Mathematical Association of America, 1999.

Gillings, Richard J. *Mathematics in the Time of the Pharoahs.* Cambridge, MA: MIT Press, 1972.

Ifrah, Georges. *The Universal History of Numbers: From Prehistory to the Invention of the Computer.* New York: John Wiley & Sons, Inc., 2000.

Joseph, George Gheverghese. *The Crest of the Peacock: Non-European Roots of Mathematics.* Princeton, NJ: Princeton University Press, 2000.

Katz, Victor J. *A History of Mathematics: An Introduction.* New York: HarperCollins, 1993.

Zaslavsky, Claudia. *Africa Counts: Number and Pattern in African Culture.* Chicago: Lawrence Hill Books (an imprint of Chicago Review Press), 1999.

Zaslavsky, Claudia. *Math Games and Activities from Around the World.* Chicago: Chicago Review Press, 1998.

More Good Books from Williamson

The following Williamson Kids Can! ® Books are for ages 7 to 14 are each 128 to 160 pages, fully illustrated, trade paper, 11 x 8 1/2, $12.95 U.S. (Prices may be higher in Canada.) To order, please see below.

Real-World Math for Hands-On Fun!
by Cindy A. Littlefield

Parents' Choice Recommended

The Kids' Book of Weather Forecasting
Build a Weather Station, "Read" the Sky & Make Predictions!
with meteorologist Mark Breen & Kathleen Friestad

Parents' Choice Silver Honor Award

Awesome OCEAN SCIENCE!
Investigating the Secrets of the Underwater World
by Cindy A. Littlefield

Benjamin Franklin Best Juvenile Nonfiction Award
Learning® Magazine Teachers' Choice Award

Super Science Concoctions
50 Mysterious Mixtures for Fabulous Fun
by Jill Frankel Hauser

Parents' Choice Silver Honor Award

Fizz, Bubble & Flash!
Element Explorations & Atom Adventures for Hands-On Science Fun!
by Anita Brandolini, Ph.D.

Parents' Choice Recommended
Children's Digest Health Education Award

The Kids' Guide to FIRST AID
All about Bruises, Burns, Stings, Sprains & Other Ouches
by Karen Buhler Gale, R.N.

Parents' Choice Gold Award
Dr. Toy Best Vacation Product

The Kids' Nature Book
365 Indoor/Outdoor Activities & Experiences
by Susan Milord

Using Color in Your Art!
Choosing Colors for Impact & Pizzazz
by Sandi Henry, full-color

Parents' Choice Gold Award
Oppenheim Toy Portfolio Best Book Award

The Kids' Multicultural Art Book
Art & Craft Experiences from Around the World
by Alexandra M. Terzian

Selection of Book-of-the-Month; Scholastic Book Clubs

Kids Cook!
Fabulous Food for the Whole Family
by Sarah Williamson and Zachary Williamson

Parents' Choice Approved

Great Games!
Old & New, Indoor/Outdoor, Travel, Board, Ball & Word
by Sam Taggar

Kids Write!
Fantasy & Sci Fi, Mystery, Autobiography, Adventure & More!
Rebecca Olien

Parents' Choice Gold Award
Benjamin Franklin Best Juvenile Nonfiction Award

Kids Make Music!
Clapping and Tapping from Bach to Rock
by Avery Hart and Paul Mantell

WordPlay Café
Cool Codes, Priceless Punzles® & Phantastic Phonetic Phun
by Michael Kline

Parents' Choice Recommended

Kids' Easy-to-Create Wildlife Habitats
for small spaces in the city, suburbs & countryside
by Emily Stetson

Oppenheim Toy Portfolio Best Book Award
Parents' Choice Approved

Summer Fun!
60 Activities for a Kid-Perfect Summer
by Susan Williamson

American Institute of Physics Science Writing Award
Parents' Choice Honor Award

Gizmos & Gadgets
Creating Science Contraptions that Work (& Knowing Why)
by Jill Frankel Hauser

In the Days of Dinosaurs
A Rhyming Romp through Dino History
by Howard Temperley
64 pages, 8 1/2 x 11, full-color, $9.95

Visit Our Website!
www.williamsonbooks.com
or www.1dealsbooks.com

What Parents Are Saying about
The Super Baby Food Book

Ruth,
Your book is awesome! I didn't know a thing about feeding my baby and don't know how I could have gotten along without your book! It tells me all I need to know! I used many of your suggestions and now my baby is one of the original Super Babies! Thanks for giving us Moms a Super Guideline to follow!

Terri, mother of Nicky (Manheim, PA)

Ruth-
I love your book! Thank you! My four and half month old son, Connor, is eating sweet potatoes, bananas, and avocados. I am amazed at how simple it is to prepare safe and healthy foods for him. I especially enjoyed the section on nutrition and I have my husband eating healthier also. Your book is invaluable.

Sarah

Ruth-
...I have a full time job,... Kayla is a very happy, active, content baby and has NEVER had a real cold/flu. ... Even my doctor says she's been exceptionally healthy. Many people I meet say she looks so healthy, and she does due to nursing and organic food. I know good nutrition plays a good part in this. ... The day care is very supportive of my nursing and homemade baby food ... My husband is also supportive, especially after I showed him the food savings! Thank you for making it so easy!

Robin ... America On Line

Ruth,
...What I really appreciate about your book is how thorough it is - it's great to see an eating schedule for William's age, and when you recommend certain foods, you always mention where you can see how to prepare them. And such a lovingly written book too - I think your kids are pretty lucky to have you for a mom. As I am working full time outside the home, it makes me feel great to think that even when I can't be with him, William will be enjoying his super food cubes at the day care. Thanks for all the inspiration.

Lisa (The Netherlands)

Ruth,
I have an almost 6 month old and we couldn't make it without your book. My husband is in chiropractic school, so we love saving money by making our own food, but best of all, we love the totally natural diet that our little one is consuming! We have shared this book with all of our friends, family, and our pediatric chiropractor, who has in

turn shared with all of her patients! I was so excited when the doctor said that your book confirmed everything that she had already recommended to her patients! Thank you again.

Hunter's mom, Staci

Ruth,
I recently purchased the Super Baby Food book and have found it GREAT! It has helped me a great deal in determining what foods my 5 month old boy can have and how much he should be getting each day - (I had been feeding him homemade carrots for a couple of days, before getting the book - aah!). I enjoy making his meals for him, knowing that they are nutritious, and the book has helped me a lot in putting together a good combination of foods. ... Again, thanks for writing a great, informative book.

Theresa (& Scott)

Ruth--
I received your book a couple of weeks ago and I have sent one to a friend in St. Louis. I can't believe the time it takes to prepare a month's worth of food for my 6-month old. Virtually none!! I can't believe how much money I've saved as well by not buying commercial baby food, plus I know this has to be better for my daughter. I encourage all mothers to try this. I feel confident that Kelsey is getting the best I can give her, too, as she has been breast-fed since her birth and I plan to continue until she weans herself.

Carrie (Central Nebraska)

Ruth,
Just a note to thank you for your book. My daughter, Schuyler, is just turning one next week, and has never had a single jar of baby food. She loves everything I make for her. The super porridge cereal is her favorite. Now she eats much of the same food as my husband and I do right from our table. As a full time working mom, I found your book very easy and informative. While I was pregnant I began to question all that commercial baby food lining the shelves of the food store. It made my head spin! I couldn't understand if I was buying fresh fruits and veggies for myself, why not for my baby too?? ...Both my husband and our baby sitter find it easy to use the cube method also. I just bring over enough cubes for the week along with her super porridge cereal for a 2 day supply for the sitter and that's it! Our baby sitter is always commenting on how much healthier Schuyler is and what a better eater she is compared to the other children in her care. Once again, thanks for making my baby a healthy and happy eater.

Denise

(PS. With all that good food in the house, I have begun to eat healthier too!)

Super Baby Food

Absolutely everything you should know about feeding your baby and toddler from starting solid foods to age three years.

Ruth Yaron

Second Edition, Revised

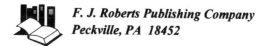
F. J. Roberts Publishing Company
Peckville, PA 18452

Super Baby Food

Absolutely everything you should know about feeding your baby and toddler from starting solid foods to age three years.

by Ruth Yaron

Library of Congress Catalog Card Number: 98-65653

ISBN 0-9652603-1-3

Published by:

 F. J. Roberts, LLC
20 Blythe Drive
Peckville, PA 18452 U.S.A.
570-487-2846 Voice 570-487-2845 Fax
866-BABYBOOK (866-222-9266) For orders only
http://www.SuperBabyFood.com
http://www.SuperBabyStore.com

First Printing, May 1996, ...Eighteenth Printing, February 2005
Nineteenth Printing, September 2005, Twentieth Printing, March 2006
Twenty First Printing, October 2006,
Twenty Second Printing, May 2007
Twenty Third Printing, August 2007

Cover by Maryrose Snopkowski
Images copyright, New Vision Technologies, Inc.
Printed by Bang Printing, Brainerd, Minnesota

Updates and corrections to this book can be found at:
www . SuperBabyFood . com

How to Use this Book to Get the Most Information in the Least Amount of Time

A new parent like yourself does not have time to do an in-depth study of this book before you begin feeding your baby solid foods! I designed this book so that, after some initial introductory reading, you should read only a small part of this book every month as your baby grows. I recommend that you read the parts below in the order given.

Introductory Reading

1. Review the Table of Contents on the next two pages and read all pages up to and including the *Introduction*.
2. Read Part I up to the chapter entitled *Feeding Your Super Baby at 6 Months*. If your baby is older than 6 months, continue to read Part I up to the chapter associated with your baby's current age.
3. Read the *Super Baby Food Diet* chapter (pages 119-148), which is the heart of this book. It will give you an overview of the healthy diet that your baby and future toddler eventually should be eating.
4. Take no more than 10 minutes and skim Part II and Part V to get an idea of the information included. When you introduce each new age-appropriate food to your baby, read and follow the preparation and storage instructions for that particular food.

Future Reading

5. A month from now, read the chapter in Part I associated with your baby's age. Every month thereafter, read the age-appropriate chapter.
6. In your leisure time (ha ha), you can peruse the other parts: the recipes (Part III) and the fun part (Part IV).

You Don't Need A Good Memory to Read this Book

Any parent knows that a frequent side effect of caring for a baby (or maybe it's from the premature aging caused by caring for a baby ☺) is memory loss. After you do the introductory reading recommended above, I assume that you may be picking up this book as infrequently as once a month. During the time lapse, you will forget some of what you read and where you read it. To remind you, I have filled this book with many cross references: "see page x," "for more information, turn to page y," and "go to page z, read it, then come back here and continue reading." Some readers think these references are great, others don't like the flipping back and forth. Either way, the cross references should help you to remember every single solitary thing!

Table of Contents

Part III Toddler (and Grown-Up) Recipes

Part IV Fun Stuff!

Part V Reference and Appendices

Bibliography

vii

From the Author

Dear Fellow Parent,

*Thank you for buying this book! Thirteen years ago,
when my twin sons were born 9½ weeks premature
and very sick, I knew that the most important thing I
could do for them (besides giving them my love) was to
feed them the healthiest diet possible. It was the mid
80's and America was into "health foods." But as
much as I read about health and nutrition, I found that
there was no single complete book about how to feed a
baby healthy food.*

*I fed the twins a diet of homemade, mostly-organic, whole grain cereals, fruits, and
home-cooked vegetables. At the mother-of-twins club meetings, I would listen to all
the other moms—including those with full-term twins with good birth weights—talk
about projectile vomit, diarrhea, high fevers, and often hospitalization for
pneumonia. I listened in silence, thinking about how blessed I was to have healthy
babies. As my pediatrician is my witness, my sons never got sick, NEVER! She told
me that my twins were THE healthiest babies she had ever seen in all her years of
practice, including those babies who were full-term singletons. The average baby
gets sick 6-12 times per year just as the twins' father and I (according to our
mothers) did when we were babies, so I don't think my sons have inherited a super
immune system. I have not done a statistically accurate medical study to prove it,
but I claim that it was the Super Baby Food Diet that made my sons so very
healthy. Let some scientist prove me wrong!*

*My sons' diet became my mission and I could not read enough about nutrition and
health food. Back then I was an inexperienced cook and used dozens of natural
foods cookbooks to learn my way around the kitchen. I was a fanatic, and my
friends and family got tired of hearing me talk about healthy diets. Some refused to
eat my tofu-carob wheat germ holiday pie; others laughed about it! Since then, to
their relief (and mine), I have lightened up.*

*Three years ago, my third son was born and I again pulled out the mini-blend
containers and ice cube trays. This time I was fortunate enough to be able to quit
my job at the local university and stay home with my baby. As I made my son's
Super Porridge while watching Sesame Street, I thought about other moms feeding
their babies over-priced, nutritionally-inferior, commercially-processed boxed rice
cereal, and the idea for the Super Baby Food book was born. I had written books
previously on un-important subjects like computers and statistics. Nothing ground-
breaking like healthy baby food! I was so excited to be able to work at home on
something that I love so much and that interests me so much.*

About the Second Edition

I received a lot of feedback from readers of the first edition, and I want to thank the hundreds of moms from all over the world who took some of their precious time to email me, phone me, and write me letters! Of course I loved the compliments, but I especially appreciated the criticisms and comments on how to improve and add to the first edition. I listened carefully to each idea and used many of them for this second edition. I became aware of some common concerns of new parents and discuss them more thoroughly in this edition.

The main changes to this second edition are the new sections on baby-safe, environmentally-friendly baby products and household cleaning products, and the fun stuff in Part IV. I've added hundreds of new tips and included new nutrition and diet facts which have come out since the last printing, including the warning about peanut allergies (page 32). Remember that the information in this book is recent only up to the copyright date; I can't predict future findings. For example, some baby food cookbooks still on library shelves today contain recipes with raw eggs and honey. The authors simply had no way of knowing about the dangers at the time. New facts come out continuously, which is why it is imperative that you collaborate the information in this book with the advice of your pediatrician, who has the latest information on feeding your baby. Start by showing her the schedule on pages 86-87. Check in with me periodically on the world wide web at http://www.superbabyfood.com for updates and corrections to this book. If you don't have Internet access from home, go to your local library. A librarian or any web surfer can get you to my website in a matter of seconds. Also at my site are frequently-updated links to other websites with the latest information about child care, nutrition, and safety. Drop me an email while you're there!

A metric equivalents appendix is now included for international readers; some have told me that they find it strange that we still haven't converted to the metric system. With regard to publishing technicalities, the text layout has been changed for better readability, and I've expanded the index by more than double. This book is quite large, but believe it or not, some information has been deleted since the first edition. Most of my readers who gave me feedback felt that I went a little overboard in the first edition about food drying and homemade bread baking, so I removed about half of that information. Hope you won't miss it! If so, you can read the other books I've listed as references on those subjects.

Part I Feeding Your Super Baby

discusses for each month of your baby's first year from before six months to twelve months:

- *which foods to introduce to your baby at that age*
- *the amount of food you can expect your baby to eat daily*
- *the amount of daily liquid that you baby should be drinking or the number of times she should be breastfeeding per day*
- *the average size of a food serving for a baby at that age*
- *a sample daily feeding schedule for a baby at that age*
- *information on baby's digestive system at that age*

Part I's Mealtimes and Your Baby's Development *chapter covers fascinating facts about your baby's development and includes when to start offering finger foods, snacks, teething foods, and table foods. Included is the age when your baby should start self-feeding with a spoon and fork, and when and how to introduce the cup. The details of the Super Baby Food Diet are in this part, with food groups and worksheets to help you feed your baby a balanced and nutritious diet. Part I also includes safety precautions and lists food hazards, such as those foods likely to cause choking or allergies or digestive problems in a young baby.*

Part II Preparation and Storage of Super Baby Foods

assumes you know practically nothing about cooking, and includes complete, easy-to-read, detailed instructions on how to buy, clean, prepare, store, freeze, re-heat, and feed the Super Baby Foods to your Super Baby. Food safety and an explanation of how bacteria grows will give you knowledge and confidence to handle, prepare, and store baby's food (and your family's food) safely.

Part III Recipes for Your Toddler (and for Grown-ups, too)

contains hundreds of recipes that your toddler will love. They are super healthy for baby and family, but are designed to be quick and easy for busy parents. Dozens of cooking tips are interspersed within the recipes to save you time, money, and energy.

Part IV Fun Stuff!

includes food decorating and other ideas for entertaining your toddler and making meals fun! Toddler party-throwing tips are included, as well as economical recipes for arts and crafts projects, homemade toys, and homemade gifts.

Part V Reference and Appendices

includes detailed instructions on how to choose, prepare, and store specific vegetables and fruits for your baby. General instructions are given in Part II. There are two appendices on nutrition: one is a brief overview of nutrition and the other contains nutrient tables with baby-sized portions. The nutrition appendices will help you to be sure that your baby is getting all the nutrients needed for healthy development. Another appendix contains recipes for homemade baby products and household cleaning products—you don't need toxic, expensive commercial cleaning products! The appendix Your Kitchen Window is a Green Mine *includes directions for growing edible houseplants. Plant growing is fun and educational and it teaches your child that food comes from the Earth and not from boxes and cans at the supermarket.*

Hope you enjoy reading the book as much as I enjoyed writing it! Please feel free to write or email me with questions or to give me feedback on the second edition. I would love to hear from you!!

Email me at ruth@superbabyfood.com

or write me:

Ruth Yaron
% F. J. Roberts Publishing
900 Henry Street
Archbald, PA 18403

*I have previously answered **all** of my mail and plan on continuing to do so. I usually return email within a day or two, but it sometimes takes me weeks to get around to responding to a paper letter. Hope to hear from you soon!*

Thanks and enjoy the ride!

This book is lovingly dedicated to my Super Mother, Regina

♡

Acknowledgments

I'd like to thank my wonderful husband, who is always there whenever I need him. Sweety, thanks for your support throughout the years of work on this project, and for knowing just the right things to say when I was tired and unsure. My appreciation to the best boys in the world: Freddy and Johnny, my grown-up twin Super Babies; and Super Baby Bobby, for all of their patience and understanding throughout this project. I love you guys, you are great! And to Mom, thanks for watching Bobby for all of those hours and for letting me use your Cray. My appreciation to my dear friend and sister-in-law, Terri McCloskey, who suffered with a half-written draft of this manuscript throughout her baby's first year. And thanks to my parents-in-law, Helen ("Meme") and Charlie, for their constant encouragement, and especially to Meme, who kept me fed when I was working on this book. Love to my siblings, Linda, John, and David, who are too much like their big sister ☺.

My gratitude to Sue Gilbert, nutritionist at ParentsPlace.com on the web, for her very helpful comments and for answering my many questions. My thanks go to the people at the libraries of the University of Scranton and Marywood University, and to the Lackawanna County Library System in Northeastern Pennsylvania. My sincere thanks to the folks at the Interboro Library, who let me take out hundreds of books and dozens of interlibrary loans without complaint. (At least, they didn't complain to me!) Thanks so much for your help: Mary Barna, Director; Karen Slachta, Children's Services; Patty Fitch, Interlibrary Loan (who so kindly did not cringe outwardly when she saw me coming with those yellow slips!); Clarita Piccotti, Circulation; Kim Stritchfield, Terri Zadzura, Barbara Melodia, Henry Heflin, Milly Brzostowski, and volunteer Ed Testa. My gratitude to Taylor Fitterer at Bang Printing for his infinite patience.

I'd especially like to thank all of the Moms, Dads, and friends of young babies who have written to me with very kind compliments and helpful criticisms—you've really helped improve this second edition!

WARNING — DISCLAIMER

This book is designed to provide information on the child care and feeding of babies and toddlers. It is sold with the understanding that neither F. J. Roberts Publishing Company nor Ruth Yaron are engaged in rendering professional opinions or advice. If professional assistance is needed, the services of a competent pediatrician or registered dietician should be sought. F. J. Roberts Publishing Company and/or Ruth Yaron shall have neither liability nor responsibility to any parent, person, or entity with respect to any illness, disability, injury, loss, or damage to be caused, or alleged to be caused, directly or indirectly by the information contained in this book.

The book should be used only as a supplement to your pediatrician's advice, not as a substitute for it. It is not the purpose of this book to replace the regular care of, or contradict the advice from, the American Academy of Pediatrics, or any pediatrician, nutritionist, registered dietician, or other professional person or organization. This text should be used only as a general guide and should not be considered an ultimate source of child care, child feeding, food preparation, food storing, or as the ultimate source of any other information. You are urged to read other available information and learn as much as possible about child care, safe methods of food preparation and storage, and the nutrition and feeding of young children. For more information, see the many references in the bibliography at the back of this book.

Every reasonable effort has been made to make this book as complete and as accurate as possible. However, **there may be mistakes both typographical and in content**. Therefore, this text should be used as only a general guide. You should discuss with your pediatrician the information contained in this book before applying it. This book contains information only up to the copyright date. New information, or information contradicting that which is found in this book, should be actively sought from your child's competent professionals.

If you do not wish to be bound by the above, you may return this book to F. J. Roberts Publishing for a prompt and full refund.

Introduction

Congratulations on the birth of your new little one! Only those of us who have experienced parenthood understand the joy that comes from watching a child grow. You feel that you want to give the world to your baby. But the most important thing you can give your baby is not toys or a college fund, but YOU—your time and your love. You've heard it a million times, but I'll say it again: Enjoy them while they're young. They do grow so very fast.

You want the best of everything for your new baby, including the most nutritious food possible. The best food for your baby comes out of your kitchen, not from an industrial food plant. Making your own baby food gives you the power to insure that only healthy, whole foods are used as ingredients. Homemade food is more natural, more tasteful, and much more economical.

The easiest way to feed your baby homemade food is to feed her along with the rest of the family. Take some of their unseasoned plain food, purée it, and feed it to her. However, if your house is like mine, the family sometimes doesn't eat together. Most of the time I end up feeding my baby with no one else around. I don't think I'd ever go through the trouble of cooking and puréeing a few ounces of fresh vegetables each time I gave my baby a meal—I'd be much too tempted to pop open a jar instead. Using the Super Baby Food System, baby-sized portions of vegetables, fruits, and cereals are at the ready. In literally **two minutes**, you can whip up an entire home-cooked baby meal, complete with cereal, two vegetables, and a fruit or juice. This amazing feat is done by grabbing pre-measured, pre-cooked foods out of the freezer and refrigerator and thawing them in the microwave or on the stove top.

The Commercial Baby Food Industry

Advertising works. It worked a few decades ago, when mothers didn't even consider breastfeeding because advertisers convinced them that commercial infant formula was somehow better than mother's milk and more convenient. It's working now. How else would generations of parents be influenced to pay exorbitant prices for nutritionally inferior baby foods? The medical profession seems to go along with the advertising. In March, when my baby was 4 months old, his pediatrician gave me a copy of the daily diet I should be feeding him. It consisted of a *jar* of baby fruit, two *jars* of baby vegetables, and a few tablespoons of iron-fortified commercially-processed baby rice cereal. When I asked her if I could make homemade baby food, she looked at me like I was from another planet. This reminds me of the comment my mother's doctor made when she asked about breast-feeding her newborn back in the 50's. He said that her breasts were too small to have enough milk to feed her baby.

Modern society has come so far from nature that we sometimes forget where real food comes from. Last week, as I was feeding my baby orange juice, my husband asked me where I had gotten it (because we had finished our last carton the day before). When I said that I squeezed it out of an orange from our refrigerator, he joked that he thought orange juice came from cartons.

Orange juice comes from fresh, whole oranges. Baby rice cereal should come from whole brown rice and other whole grains, with all their nutrients intact and not processed out during refinement. All baby food should come from fresh, whole, minimally-processed food—and you can make it easily and cheaply in your own kitchen.

Myth: Commercial baby food is superior to homemade baby food.
The food that you make at home from fresh whole vegetables and fruits is nutritionally superior to any jarred commercial variety on your grocer's shelf. The cereals you can quickly and easily make at home from brown rice (and other whole grains) cannot be compared to the processed, refined white rice commercial baby cereals.

Myth: It takes too much time to make homemade baby food.
Making homemade baby food is much easier than you think. Yes, I agree that popping open a jar is less work than preparing a fresh fruit for your baby, but not by much. Would you feed yourself and your family TV dinners every night because they are so convenient?

Myth: **Homemade baby food may cause my baby to get sick or get food poisoning.**

Some parents think that there's something magical that goes into the preparation of commercial baby food that cannot be done at home, which somehow makes it the only food suitable and safe for their baby. I hope this book will dispel this notion.

Myth: **The convenience of commercial baby food is worth the price.**

On page 5, I do a cost comparison of commercial baby food and homemade baby food. I think most parents, once they realize how much the convenience of commercial baby food really costs, will choose to make at least some of their own baby food at home.

You Don't Have to Go "All the Way"

There's no rule that says that you cannot have some jars of commercial baby food in your cabinet and still be a good parent. Yes, even I confess to keeping a few jars on hand for emergencies, like when I run out of homemade, or for long-distance travel. I use the Earth's Best brand, because it's organic and the cereal is whole grain.

The Super Baby Food System

The Super Baby Food System is a method of preparing and storing extremely nutritious homemade baby food. The method saves time, energy, and money. Once you get the system down, it becomes part of your routine. The system is so easy that, if you spend any time whatever in the kitchen, you will be able to prepare baby food simultaneously while doing your other kitchen tasks. Preparing homemade baby food will take only a few extra minutes in the kitchen each day.

You do not need to be a good cook to use the Super Baby Food System. I hate to cook—that's why I came up with such a quick and easy system. When I told my friends I was writing a baby food cookbook, they rolled on the floor laughing. If you are concerned that you need advanced (or even average!) kitchen knowledge to use the system, fear not, because I assume you know practically nothing about cooking. Did you worry that you wouldn't know how to take care of your baby after you brought her home? We all did. Within days, we knew how to give better care to our new little one than anyone else in the world. Give the Super Baby Food System the same time, and you'll be a pro after only a couple of batches of cooked vegetables!

Super Baby Food is Better

The Super Baby Food Diet is based on the fact that anything the commercial baby food manufacturers can do, you can do in your own kitchen better. When you prepare your own baby foods, you can be sure that only wholesome ingredients, with no additives or fillers, are used.

Instead of these commercial baby foods:	Feed your baby these homemade Super Baby Foods:
baby fruits in jars	fresh ripe fruits
baby vegetables in jars	fresh cooked and puréed vegetables
refined, processed baby rice and other cereals in boxes	Super Porridge, a super healthy homemade cereal made from whole grains, and when your baby is 9 months old, from whole grains and legumes for complete protein
commercial dinners, either the mixed junior dinners in jars with additives, or the high-sodium frozen dinners marketed for children, or the pasta dinners in cans	homemade and frozen toddler TV dinners made from whole, healthy foods with no added salt or preservatives

How Much Time Is This Going To Take?

The answer is: as much time as you want. You don't have to feed your baby the entire diet. For instance, you could choose to use just the idea of adding a teaspoon of wheat germ to commercial baby cereal for a nutritional boost. Time: 30 seconds. Or you can choose to peel and fork-mash a fresh ripe peach instead of buying the commercial jarred baby peaches. Time: 2 minutes. Or you can go all the way and do the whole diet. Time: **average of less than a few minutes per meal—guaranteed!** The keyword here is "average." You may put in an hour making a month's supply of broccoli, or you may put in 12 minutes making 6 servings of cooked brown rice cereal, but it all averages out to only a few minutes per meal.

The Super Baby Food System works this way: You spend some time preparing and refrigerating/freezing batches of baby food. The secret is batch cooking—cooking large batches of food at once. Just as you would not prepare a single bottle of formula at a time, you should not prepare one baby-sized food portion or meal at a time. When mealtime comes, you pull out already-prepared baby-sized portions of food, thaw or re-heat them for a minute or two in the microwave, and—voila!—fast food for baby. If you're willing to spend an hour or two a month to prepare cooked veggies and a few minutes every two or three days preparing cereal, you can prepare a whole diet of extremely nutritious, natural Super Baby Food.

How Do I Do This Preparation?

Each type of food is prepared and stored using a different method. For example, vegetables are cooked, puréed, and frozen in ice cube trays—the perfect size for baby portions. Brown rice and other grains or cereals are ground to a coarse powder in the blender, cooked, and refrigerated. Or, just as easy, brown rice or other grains can be cooked first, then puréed, and refrigerated or frozen. The table on page 7 gives a summary of how each type of Super Baby Food is prepared and stored, and the time necessary for preparation.

Detailed step-by-step instructions for each category of food in the table are given in Part II of this book.

It's Like Making Money At Home

Let's figure out how much more you pay for commercial baby food by analyzing a very common jarred commercial baby food—carrots. At the time

this book was published, my local supermarket was selling a four-ounce jar of brand name puréed baby carrots for 35¢. That works out to $1.40 a pound (35¢ for four ounces or ¼ pound, times 4). However, there are less than 4 ounces of carrots in each jar, because water is added during processing, and your actual cost is more than $1.40 per pound.

How much water is added to commercial jarred baby vegetables and fruits? I called two major baby food manufacturers to try to find out. They would not tell me exactly. In both cases, after I told them the information was for my book, the supervisor was called to the phone. One hinted that it was about 15%. Assuming this is true, the price of commercial baby carrots is more like $1.64 a pound ($1.40 divided by 85%).

Fresh carrots at my local supermarket cost about 50¢ a pound. Therefore, commercial baby carrots at $1.64 a pound are more than *three times* the cost of fresh carrots! Maybe you think that it's worth the extra cost for the convenience of commercial baby food. After all, you just pop open a jar. But it is not difficult or very time consuming to make your own baby food using the Super Baby Food System. Following the method described in this book, you can make a month's supply of vegetables for your baby in about an hour. If your baby eats 3 jars of veggies a day, and you're paying 35¢ per jar, that's $1.05 a day or about $30 a month. If you make your own baby food, it will cost you only ⅓ of that or $10 a month. **In approximately 1 hour, you're saving $20**—and that's tax free! In fact, if you get fresh veggies on sale at the supermarket, it is possible to make healthy homemade Super Baby Food for as little as 3 cents a serving! (See page 194.)

If that's not enough to motivate you to make homemade baby food, remember that you're making food that is *nutritionally superior* for your precious baby. I always feel great after feeding my baby homemade food—it's another way I have to give him my love.

I have done the same analysis with rice and barley cereals and oatmeal, and the difference in price is even greater than three times. The difference in nutritional quality between commercial baby cereals and the whole grain cereals you can easily prepare at home is, in my opinion, *shocking*. The typical baby rice cereal on the market today is made from processed white rice, which has most of its natural nutrients and fiber removed during refinement. Then, one nutrient, iron, is put back into the cereal, and it may be in a form that is not as well assimilated by your baby as the iron found in whole, natural food. Brown rice is much healthier for your growing baby, and you can make two or three days' worth in minutes.

Add up the savings from feeding your baby homemade vegetables, fruits, and cereals, instead of the overpriced, nutritionally inferior commercial variety, and you'll find that making homemade baby food is well worth your time. You save literally **hundreds of dollars!**

MONEY SAVER: We busy parents need the convenience of commercial baby foods sometimes. You can save money by buying food products which are essentially equivalent to commercial baby foods. Buy unsweetened regular applesauce instead of commercial baby food applesauce— they are essentially equivalent and the regular applesauce is much cheaper. Buy regular canned fruits packed in juice (not syrups) and no-salt-added canned vegetables instead of toddler diced fruits and vegetables and dice them yourself. Instead of baby fruit juices, buy regular, pasteurized, vitamin C-fortified, no-sugar-added 100% juice and dilute (see how to dilute juice in the section *Juice* on page 64). Be sure to follow instructions for safe handling of baby food and leftovers on page 26 and pages 163-165.

Preparation and Storage of Super Baby Foods

Food	Preparation Method	Time Needed for Preparation	Frequency of Preparation
vegetables	cook in large batches, purée, and freeze	one or two hours	once every month or two
fruits	fork-mash or purée, then feed immediately or freeze	a few minutes	once or twice a day
grains and cereals	grind large batches, cook two days' supply (about 4 to 6 servings), and refrigerate	several minutes to grind a large batch, 10 minutes wait while cooking	grind a large batch once a month, cook every two or three days, and refrigerate
	Brown rice cereal and other whole grain cereals can also be cooked and puréed in batches and refrigerated or frozen. Waiting time to cook any-sized batch is about 45 minutes. Puréeing takes several extra minutes.		
lentils, split peas, soybeans, and other legumes	Add dried beans and other legumes to the grains and cereals above and prepare them together to make high-protein whole grain baby cereals. Requires no additional time.		
egg yolks	hard cook and refrigerate	15 minutes to cook	once a week
nuts and seeds	grind and feed immediately	2 minutes	once a day
miscellaneous foods: yogurt, tofu, wheat germ, and many more	none	a few seconds to add to foods as nutritional enhancers	as often as once a meal

Why Doesn't Every Parent Make Homemade?

I imagine that it's for a lot of reasons, perhaps the most common one being that they just never thought of it, so ingrained in us are those little glass jars of baby food. Or maybe they think they don't have a choice and just assume that you must feed a baby commercial baby food. They may think it takes too much work to make homemade, or maybe they even think it's dangerous. Our society still tends to trust manufactured products more than homemade natural products.

Pressure from Parents and In-Laws

If your family is pressuring you to feed your baby jarred foods, believe me, I know what you're going through. Twelve years ago, when I was making my own baby food for my twins, I was practically accused of abusing them. One day, I was so upset that I was ready to quit and buy commercial baby food. Luckily, on that very day, I just so happened to have a pediatrician appointment. She told me that she had never seen such healthy babies, which was amazing because they were 10 weeks premature and very sick when they were born. That did it!

Since then, I had forgotten about all this pressure until I received a letter from a young mother saying that her mother was insisting that she use Gerber. I'm in my forties now and no one dares tell me what to do with my new baby, but somehow people feel they have the right to give unwanted advice when you're in your twenties. Just politely listen to them. Don't get angry because their motives are good—they care about you and your baby and they want to help.

You're Not Alone

One young mother wrote to me and said, "I feel like I'm the only one doing this!" Well, she is certainly not! I have received many letters from parents all over the country, and even from the other side of the world, who feel very strongly about feeding their babies only homemade foods. Just as breastfeeding was not accepted a few generations ago (in fact, I got flack about it just 12 years ago!), homemade baby food is not fully accepted now. But, in the future, you will be proud to tell your children that you cared enough to make them homemade Super Baby Food. And they will be proud of you too!

Part I

Feeding Your Super Baby

1. BEGINNING SOLID FOODS

The term "solid foods" refers to food (baby cereals, fruits, vegetables, meats, and mixed foods) especially prepared for a baby, usually by cooking and puréeing or straining. "Baby food" includes solid foods and baby juices. Breast milk and commercial infant formula, although the major part of a baby's diet, do not come under either the category baby food or solid foods.

When Should I Start Feeding My Baby Solid Foods?

The answer is: when your pediatrician tells you that it's OK to start solid foods. She will probably agree with the American Academy of Pediatrics, whose guidelines state that the best time to begin feeding your baby solid foods is between 4 and 6 months of age. And the closer to 6 months the better, especially if you are breastfeeding. Your baby's body in its first few months was designed to digest breast milk, or something similar to it. And, calorie for calorie, no solid food has the nutritional quality of breast milk or formula for your young baby. If you feed your baby solid foods too early, her milk intake may decrease. You'd be replacing milk, the best food for your baby, with foods that are nutritionally inferior and not as digestible. Solid foods should not *replace* breast milk, they should *supplement* it.

Why You Should Wait Until At Least 4 Months

Your baby is not physically ready to eat solid foods until he is around 4 months old. Although your mother or grandmother will strongly disagree, saying that she gave her babies solids when they were only 2 weeks old, there are several reasons to wait at least 4 months before starting your baby on solid foods.

Reason 1. Your baby's digestive system is too immature for solid foods before 4 months. Although he can suck very well, he does not have a lot of saliva to help digest food. Until he is at least 3-4 months old, his system lacks certain digestive enzymes, such as an enzyme called *amylase*, needed for digesting cereals (starches or complex carbohydrates). His body has trouble digesting some fats before he is 6 months old. Some foods will pass through him undigested and end up in his diaper;

10

in fact, stool analyses of babies under three months of age who have eaten solid foods show undigested food particles. And some high protein foods, like eggs, meat, and even cow's milk, given too early may cause problems with your baby's immature kidneys.

Reason 2. Your baby is not developmentally ready to eat solid foods. His throat muscles are not developed enough to swallow solid foods until he is at least 4 months old. And, it is not until about 4 months that he is able to use his tongue to transfer food from the front to the back of his mouth. In fact, when you touch his tongue, he reacts by pushing his tongue outward or forward. This response, called the *extrusion reflex* or the *tongue-thrust reflex,* is an inborn mechanism designed to protect your baby from choking on foreign substances that he cannot yet properly swallow. This reflex will not disappear until he is around 16-18 weeks old. The first time you feed him with a spoon, it may seem that he is spitting out the food and closing his mouth at the wrong time. But his tongue movement is simply the result of the not-yet-unlearned extrusion reflex and not because he doesn't want the food. It is not until he is about 5 months old that he will see the spoon coming and open his mouth in anticipation.

Reason 3. Your baby must have a way of telling you that he is satiated. He lets you know that he is finished breast or bottle feeding by stopping his sucking or by falling asleep. But until he becomes able to turn his head to refuse food, which occurs at around 4 or 5 months, he has no way of letting you know he has had enough solid food. Because of this inability, when you feed solid foods to a too-young baby, you may be unintentionally force feeding him. This practice can interfere with his body's self-regulating eating mechanism and lead to overweight later in life. As with adults, your baby should eat only when he is hungry.

Reason 4. Beginning solid foods too early has been associated with other problems later in life, such as obesity, respiratory problems like bronchial asthma, and food allergies. For more information on how food allergies are caused by too-early introduction of solid foods, see page 30.

Reason 5. Solid foods will not make your baby sleep through the night. Studies show that ¾ of all babies sleep through the night at 3 months of age, whether or not they are eating solid foods. Even if solid foods will help your baby sleep longer, that is still not a good reason to begin solid foods early. I know sleep deprivation is torture—most of us have been there. Hang in there. One night he'll sleep right through, and then you can start feeling normal again.

Reason 6. If you are breastfeeding and give your baby solid foods too early, your milk production may be decreased.

Don't Wait Longer than 8 Months

After six months, your baby begins to need solid foods for some nutrients, such as iron, vitamin C, protein, carbohydrates, zinc, water, and calories, and delaying food may cause delayed growth. Besides playing a nutritional role, solid foods help your baby developmentally, as discussed under the section *Do Not Use an Infant Feeder* on page 21. It is important that your baby start developing eating and chewing skills between the ages of 7 to 9 months. And if you delay the introduction of solid foods past 8 or 9 months, your baby may refuse textured foods when you finally do offer them to her.

NOTE: Some exclusively breastfed babies have successfully begun solid foods after their first birthday. There are parents who feel very strongly that solid foods should not be started until after their babies' first birthdays. If you want to wait to introduce solid foods, discuss it with your pediatrician, and do whatever you and your pediatrician agree is best for your baby. Your pediatrician probably will be concerned that your baby gets enough iron in her diet.

Signs of Readiness for Solid Foods

Your pediatrician looks for certain signs of readiness in your baby before advising you to begin solid foods. Here are some of them:

- She is at least 4 months old.
- She weighs twice as much as her birth weight.
- She weighs at least 13-15 pounds.
- She can sit with support, allowing her to lean forward when she wants another spoonful and backward to refuse.
- She has control over her head and neck muscles and can turn her head to refuse food.
- She has stopped exhibiting the extrusion reflex when you put a spoon in her mouth. If, after several tries, food comes right back out of her mouth when you spoon feed her, she is not yet ready for solid foods.
- She is drinking at least 32-40 ounces of formula per 24 hours and still wants more.
- She is breast feeding at least 8-10 times per 24 hours (after the first few weeks), empties both breasts at each feeding, and still wants more.
- The time between feedings becomes shorter and shorter over a period of several days.
- She can bring an object in her hand directly to her mouth.
- She shows interest in others eating around her.
- She becomes fussy in the middle of the night, whereas before she slept through with no problem. Or her sleep periods are becoming shorter instead of longer.

Baby Food Mathematics

The signs of readiness for solid foods tend to occur around the same time in your baby's life because of a few simple mathematical facts about calories and your baby's body weight. (Math phoebes may skip the next paragraph.)

The average baby needs about 50 calories per day per pound of body weight. Breast milk and formula provide about 20 calories per ounce. Therefore, for every pound of body weight, your baby requires about 2½ ounces of milk. At 13 pounds, your baby needs about 650 calories or about 32 ounces of milk. These two signs of readiness—a minimum weight of 13 pounds and a daily intake of at least 32 ounces of formula per day—are related. So you see, it's no happenstance that some of the signs of readiness coincide.

Which Food Should Be First?

The first foods you should feed your baby are those that are easily digested and least likely to trigger an allergic reaction. Opinions vary, but the most often recommended first food is commercial iron-enriched baby rice cereal. Other popular first foods are avocado, sweet potato, ripe banana, and if your baby is older, millet cereal and yogurt. You and your pediatrician should decide which food should be given to your baby at her very first meal.

Commercial Rice Cereal

Commercial iron-fortified baby rice cereal is the first choice of the American Academy of Pediatrics. Rice is very easily digested, is rarely an allergen, and thins readily when added to liquid. Most commercial cereals are refined and processed. Earth's Best is not—it is made from whole brown rice and is organic. If you wish to use commercial baby cereal, I highly recommend Earth's Best. Find it at some supermarkets, all natural foods stores, or order from some baby product catalogs or from mail order natural foods companies (page 142). Store opened boxes of cereal in a cool, dry place for up to one month. After one month, the cereal's nutrient content begins to decrease.

Homemade Whole Grain Cereals

If your baby is at least 6 months old, I recommend homemade whole grain brown rice or millet cereal as baby's first food. These cereals are easily digested, but your baby must be at least 6 months old before he has the necessary digestive enzymes to handle the complex carbohydrates in these cereals. Instructions on how to prepare and store homemade whole grain cereals (Super Porridge) begin on page 207 in Part II. Although homemade cereals do contain iron, most experts agree that the iron amounts are not enough for a growing baby. It is important that you read about iron beginning on page 69.

Banana

Mashed ripe banana is an excellent first food for baby. As discussed on page 427, bananas are nutritious and very easy for your baby to digest. Many other cultures use banana exclusively as their first baby food. However, some experts caution that the sweet taste of bananas may give your baby a "sweet tooth" and cause him to refuse less sweet tasting foods later. I personally wouldn't be concerned about that. My baby started on bananas and he now happily eats brewer's yeast! If you've ever tasted brewer's yeast you know what I mean.

> **WARNING:** Some experts recommend against feeding a young baby bananas because of the fungicides with which they (and all other imported fruits) are sprayed. Banana skins are porous, allowing the fungicides to be absorbed into the flesh. Try to buy only certified organically-grown bananas.

Avocado

Mashed ripe avocado is also an excellent first food for baby. They are so nutritious that some claim humans can live on them exclusively. Avocados are also an excellent source of the unsaturated fatty acids that your baby needs for brain development. See page 426 for more information on avocados.

Cooked Sweet Potato

Cooked mashed sweet potato is another favorite first food. It is highly nutritious and rich in beta-carotene (vitamin A). This is a great first food for your 4-month old baby, if you don't wish to start her out on sweet bananas or a processed baby cereal. Sweet potatoes are discussed in detail on page 461.

Yogurt

Yogurt is a good first food for babies who are at least 6 months old. Yogurt is a Super Baby Food which contains beneficial bacteria that promote intestinal health. It is similar-tasting to milk, which is a benefit to a beginning eater who is familiar only with breast milk or formula. Whole milk yogurt, instead of low-fat yogurt, is recommended because your baby needs fats. Baby yogurt should be of the plain variety. Don't buy the yogurt with sugary fruit added or, worse yet, the yogurt that contains artificial sweetener (Nutrasweet®, saccharin®). There is more information on yogurt, including how to save lots of money by making your own (it's easy!), beginning on page 252.

Although yogurt made from cow's milk may be given to a baby younger than one year old, cow's milk should not be fed to babies *in place of* breast milk or formula before age one year (page 60).

> NOTE: If allergies to milk run in your family, you shouldn't feed your baby yogurt made from cow's milk. Babies with milk allergy can have yogurt made from other milks—see page 129. Talk to your pediatrician. Milk allergy and lactose intolerance are discussed in more detail on page 33.

2. The Feeding Area and Equipment

The Feeding Area

Set up a feeding area in your home where you will feed your baby most of the time. Babies like stability and predictability. She'll know just what's coming if you feed her in the same high chair in the same corner of the kitchen each day.

Make the feeding area as comfortable for you as it is for your baby. Place your chair in front of your baby's feeding chair so that you can be face-to-face with him, to chat and smile at him as he eats. Feeding time will become another pleasant bonding time for the two of you. It's very nurturing to give food to your baby, as it is to breast or bottle feed him.

Have a table top or counter surface within your reach and out of your baby's reach. Place on it wipe-up towels, vitamin supplements, bibs, and anything else you use during baby's mealtime.

If the floor in the feeding area is carpeted or covered with some other material that will be ruined when baby starts dropping food to the floor, protect it by covering it with something waterproof. Baby stores and catalogs sell machine-washable plastic sheets and mats specifically for baby feeding areas. A piece of plastic tarp, an old waterproof table cloth, or an old shower curtain (by the way, shower curtains are machine washable) will work; but use only if it's not slippery. Or you can get a leftover piece of non-slip linoleum remnant from the nearest floor covering store (ask them if it will ruin carpeting if placed over it). If you're at Grandma's or a friend's house, rip a big plastic garbage bag at the seam so that it lays flat in one layer. Be very careful not to slip on it, because plastic garbage bags are as slick as ice. Layers of newspaper, brown paper bags from the grocery store, or even a flattened large cardboard box also can be used to temporarily protect floors.

The walls near the feeding chair should not be covered with fine velvet wallpaper; if so, protect them also. The nicest babies have been known to throw food. Walls are also threatened by the ominous full-mouthed sneeze, which has been known to project wet food as far as several feet in all directions. Practice a quick draw with a wipe-up towel to cover baby's mouth when you suspect one is about to occur.

> **WARNING:** Make sure that wall mountings, electrical outlets, and objects on counter tops are out of baby's reach from the feeding chair. Also, your baby should not be able to grab something and use it for leverage to tip the chair over.

The High Chair

Safety First

Thousands of children are injured each year because of careless practices with high chairs, so please read the warnings in this section carefully.

> **WARNING:** Never leave your baby alone in a high chair. High chairs are safe only when an adult is present to make sure that our energetic babies don't try any acrobatics while seated in them.

Stability

There now exists a vast array of high chairs on the market. Safety should be your first criterion in choosing a high chair. Pick one with a wide base for stability. Before buying a chair, shake it and push it sideways to see just how much it takes to tip it over.

Always place the chair on a level floor surface to prevent instability. And if your chair has wheels, always make sure the wheel locks are in good working condition and fully engaged before seating your baby. A wiggly baby can maneuver a mobile chair to the nearest staircase in the twinkling of an eye.

> **WARNING:** Never allow your older children to play in baby's high chair or hang onto it. Their weight may tip the chair over, causing injury. Keep older children and pets away from your baby when he's in his high chair.

JPMA Certification

Make sure that the chair you buy is certified safe by the Juvenile Products Manufacturers Association (JPMA). The JPMA is a national trade organization representing most of the companies that manufacture or import infant products. Call them at 609-231-8500.

> **WARNING:** Do not assume that because one chair model from a specific manufacturer is certified by the JPMA, that all models from that manufacturer are. Some manufacturers have only a few of their chair models certified. Make sure that the specific model that you have chosen is certified by looking for the JPMA seal on the box or on the high chair itself.

The Consumer Product Safety Commission (CPSC)

The CPSC is an independent Federal regulatory agency that helps keep American families safe by reducing the risk of injury or death from consumer products. If you have any question about the safety of a high chair or another type of feeding chair or just about any product—from mini-blinds to portable cribs—call the CPSC Hotline at 800-638-CPSC (800-638-2772) or write CPSC, 5401 Westbard Avenue, Bethesda,

MD 20816. You can also call or write the CPSC to report an unsafe product. CPSC TTY for the Hearing Impaired is 800-638-8270.

Safety Strap

The high chair should have a waist strap to prevent your baby from standing up in the chair and/or climbing out the top, possibly causing it to teeter over. A crotch strap also should be part of the restraint system to prevent your baby from sliding out the bottom. Some babies love to slither down slowly until they are under the tray, while others prefer a rapid chute.

> **WARNING:** All kidding aside—always use the full restraint system including the waist and crotch straps when seating your baby in the high chair—never use just the tray alone. The tray is not intended to be a restraint. Numerous deaths have occurred from babies slipping down in the seat and catching their heads on the tray (called "submarining entrapment"). Submarining entrapment can also occur in strollers and other baby seats—always use the full restraint system as described in the manufacturer's instructions.

> **REMEMBER:** For your child's safety, remember to clean the chair and its restraint system on a regular basis. Clumps of food and dried liquids can prevent the restraint system and tray from working properly.

> **WARNING:** A high chair safety strap is wonderful for preventing babies from sliding out, but it can be life-threatening if your baby is choking and you can't quickly release her from the chair. Practice opening that buckle until you're as quick as lightning and you can do it blindfolded. There is a chance that she could be moving so much that you can't get to the buckle. Study the chair and see where you can cut the strap with a knife or scissors to release her, in the rare case where this would be necessary. Find a place on the back or side of the chair where you can safely and easily cut the strap and not your baby.

The Tray

Choose a high chair with large tray that is removable, so that you can take it to the kitchen sink and give it a good washing and so that you can use the sink hose to rinse off every last trace of soap. Your baby will be eating finger foods directly off the tray, so you want to keep it as clean as possible.

If you can remove the tray with only one hand, all the better. Plan on spending some time in the store when you shop for a high chair. Remove each high chair's tray and see which feels easiest and best to you. You shouldn't have to peer under the tray to find the catch to remove it—it should be easily found by touch.

The tray should have a raised lip around the edge to stop inevitable spills from getting to the floor or baby's lap. The lip may also help prevent baby from pushing food pieces and dishes off the tray and onto the floor, although I wouldn't count on it. The tray should be angled so that liquids spill to the front.

Another reason for a removable tray is the ability to move the chair to the family table when your baby gets older. Make sure the instructions say that the chair is safe at a full-sized adult table without its tray.

WARNING: After your baby is seated, always make sure that the full restraint system is in place and that the tray is securely locked into position. An unlocked tray is a danger to your baby. Give the tray a good forward yank to verify that it's locked in place.

REMEMBER: Get into the habit of knowing where tiny fingers are *before* you slide the tray onto the high chair so that you don't accidentally pinch them. Always give a quick look before you close or collapse anything: high chair trays, folding strollers, car doors, house doors, cabinets, reclining living room chairs, lawn chairs, etc. To do a quick check of several children at one glance before slamming a car door, play "Simon says 'Hands on Your Head.'" Odds are that this quick check habit, which takes only a second, will eventually save your child pain and injury.

TIP: If the high chair tray is no longer sliding on and off smoothly, try rubbing the metal runners with a sheet of waxed paper, or rub them with a bar of mild soap, or put a little petroleum jelly on the runners, or use vegetable oil spray (Pam® or homemade, page 275) to lubricate them. Use the same to make metal crib runners move smoothly and noiselessly, for sticking dresser drawers, squeaky doors, etc.

Adjustable Height

The ability to raise and lower the height of the high chair is a nice feature. This will allow you to adjust the seat height when you are feeding your baby so that you and your baby can be face-to-face. The adjustable height feature is also nice for when your baby moves to the family table.

Comfort

Padded seats are usually more comfortable for babies than wooden seats. The covering should be thick so it will not puncture easily. Feel the seams to make sure they are smooth and won't scratch your baby's legs. Check over the entire chair for any protrusions or sharp edges that can injure your baby. If you have your baby with you, and she is willing, test her in your favorite chair before you buy it. She'll let you know if she doesn't like it!

If your baby looks uncomfortable in a high chair, as is common with babies younger than 6 or 7 months, place her in your lap in an upright position to feed her her first meals. Move her to the high chair when she gets a little older and is sitting well without support.

MONEY SAVER: Some high chairs recline to an infant seat-type angle, an expensive option that is useful for a very short time. If he's uncomfortable in a high chair and your lap, why not just use your infant seat until he's older? Remember to always strap him in securely and never place the seat on a chair or table because it can fall off and cause your baby serious injury. Place the infant seat on the floor and sit on the floor next to him to feed him. He can't fall off the floor!

WARNING: Your baby should be seated in an upright position, whether it be in the high chair, an infant seat, or your lap, in order to prevent choking during eating. Also, don't let your baby crawl around with a cracker or other food, as he may lie facing upward and choke.

TIP: If your baby sits up well but tends to wobble sideways in the high chair, use a few rolled-up terry towels to support her on each side.

Cleanability

Avoid high chairs with intricate carvings, which serve only to gather hardened glop. Some feeding chair trays have built in toys which not only make the chair more expensive, but make cleaning more difficult. Your baby's high chair will eventually become a modern art piece of crusty layers of dried food. To clean a non-wooden high chair, take it in the bathtub (place rags under the legs to prevent scratches in the tub) and give it a shower massage with an old vegetable brush or toothbrush. Or use the hose outside on a nice warm sunny day, or take it to the carwash and blast it with the pressure hose (make sure to rinse very well to get all the harsh detergent off). First cover any cracks in the cushioned seat with duct tape, so that the inside foam doesn't become a water-logged sponge.

> **TIP:** For those really dried on food splatters, lay a wet towel or sponge on them for an hour or so, and they'll wipe right off. If food is dried around the arms of the chair or in corner crevices, take a dripping wet rag and drape it or tie it around the hard-to-reach dried food. Let it sit for a few hours and then use an old toothbrush or vegetable brush to scrub out the softened food. If you're in a hurry, try using a baker's bench knife to get stuck-on food off a high chair or counter top. They are available in kitchen stores.

"Previously Owned" or Older High Chairs

If you have inherited an older-model high chair or purchased a used chair, make sure that it is safe. It should be sturdy with a working complete restraint system and tray. Older chairs with only a crotch bar do not prevent a child from climbing out the top. If parts are missing, call or write the manufacturer to see if you can get replacements.

> **MONEY SAVER:** If you've inherited a chair without a crotch strap and you cannot get a replacement from the manufacturer, place a flat piece of foam under your baby or glue non-stick bathtub appliques onto the seat to prevent him from slipping under the tray. (See the warning about "submarining entrapment" on page 17.) Call the JPMA to make sure that using foam/appliques will not cause a safety problem with your particular chair model.

> **TIP:** If the chrome on your high chair (stroller, playpen, etc.) has gotten dingy looking, try rubbing it with a wadded up ball of aluminum foil.

Call the JPMA to verify that a used or older chair has been certified, that there have been no recalls or safety problems, and to obtain any other warnings or information on that particular model chair from that manufacturer.

> **NOTE:** No matter which feeding chair you are using, take the time to read and follow all instructions carefully. Periodically check all assembly screws to make sure that they are fully tightened. Check that all clamps and locking mechanisms are working properly. The instructions will include details on how to clean and maintain the chair.

> **REMEMBER:** Remember to stop using the seat when your child has reached the recommended maximum height OR weight; it may help you to remember this if you write yourself a note with the height and weight where you will see it often. Busy parents of young children have a tendency to forget things!

Other Feeding Chairs

There are other types of chairs for the purpose of feeding babies—feeding tables, legless hook-on-table chairs, and booster seats. Let's get **booster seats** out of the running immediately. I don't recommend them for toddlers (and they are not made for babies) because most of these seats don't attach to the chair onto which they are placed. Children can easily fall off the chair, with or without the booster seat. Some suggest saving money by building a homemade booster seat by stacking and taping several telephone books together. The same danger of falling and serious head injury exists with these homemade booster seats.

If you want to purchase only one feeding chair, a high chair is probably your most economical choice because of its long lifetime. A high chair can be used for years if you move it to the family table when your child gets older, which cannot be done with a feeding table. However, one advantage of **feeding tables** is the fact that they are safer than high chairs because they will probably never tip over. But it is more difficult to maneuver your child in and out of them.

Hook-on-table seats are also second in maneuverability to high chairs. More importantly, you cannot sit directly in front of your baby for face-to-face interaction during mealtime. These seats must be clipped onto a firm, strong table with a thick strong top; for example, don't hook them onto a card table, a glass-topped table, a table with a loose top, or a table with a single pedestal. Never attach the seat to a table's extension leaf. Don't clip the chair onto anything that might interfere with its gripping the table, such as a tablecloth or placemat. The table should be dry and clean where the chair's arms will grip it, and the arms and clamps should be kept very clean and dry. If the chair's grip depends on suction cups, make sure that they are all there and that they, too, are clean and dry. Be sure your child's feet cannot reach a table leg, a wall, a counter, or anything he may use to kick-off from and loosen the seat from the table. Keep pets and other children away from under baby's chair as they may dislodge it from the table. Before seating your baby, the chair should be fully opened and the locking device should be fully engaged. After mealtimes, always remove your baby from the seat first, and then remove the chair from the table—never remove the chair from the table with your baby still in the seat and never carry your child in it.

> **WARNING:** Many parents using a hook-on-table seat place an adult chair under it to "give it a safety net." This practice actually causes accidents! Your baby may push on the adult chair, which decreases her weight on the hook-on seat. Your baby's weight is part of the cantilever system of the hook-on seat and is necessary to keep the seat firmly clipped to the table.

> **NOTE:** Now that you know all of these dangers lurking in baby feeding chairs, dining out with your baby sitting in a restaurant's feeding chair will be a nightmare for you. Just be careful to inspect the restaurant's chair, or take your own chair from home. Try to relax and enjoy, which should be easy in a restaurant with a baby! ☺

The Spoon

Baby's gums are sensitive. Instead of using a hard metal spoon that might irritate her gums, feed her with a plastic coated baby spoon. The spoon should be small and shallow so that it fits easily into baby's tiny mouth, and should have no sharp edges. If you don't want to buy a special baby spoon, you can use a demitasse spoon or a small plastic disposable spoon, like the one you get with ice cream cups, or even a plastic toy spoon from your older child's toy tea set. (Do not give your baby anything small enough to be a choking hazard, pages 40-42.) A small wooden tongue depressor or even a popsicle stick, with any loose slivers of wood removed, will work in a pinch. For non-self-feeding babies, the longer the spoon handle, the easier on mom's or dad's back muscles and the easier for reaching baby food in the bottom of tall jars. When your baby begins to feed himself, give him a plastic spoon made specifically for this purpose with a curved handle to decrease the danger of an eye poke. A spoon with a pointed end is not safe for a young child. Plastic coated spoons are often sold with plastic coated forks. Although your baby will not be old enough for a fork until the latter half of her second year (page 81), you may save money by buying the set and stashing the fork away until later.

NOTE: The latest fad in baby feeding accessories is flashy-handled spoons and forks, or those with sparkly toys built into the handles, or those with handles shaped like airplanes, etc. These utensils may only serve to distract your baby from what he is supposed to be doing—concentrating on learning how to eat. Your baby doesn't need them.

Do Not Use an Infant Feeder

Although first foods are very liquidy, they should not be fed to your baby through a bottle with an enlarged nipple hole, or with one of those bottle-type infant feeders, which I am surprised are still sold in baby stores. These feeders actually delay learning how to swallow, do not help in desensitizing the gag reflex, and delay the development of other eating skills. They may cause your baby to choke. Solid foods should be given to your baby at a time when they are needed both nutritionally *and developmentally*. Nutritionally, they add calories and nutrients to your baby's milk diet. Developmentally, eating solid foods helps in the maturation of a new set of muscles in the tongue that allow swallowing, which were not used in breast or bottle feeding. Proper development of these muscles help to promote clear speech patterns later in life. If your baby is not developmentally ready to eat from a spoon, then she is not yet ready for solid foods.

When baby eats from a spoon, she starts becoming aware of the process of eating: taking a bite, chewing and swallowing the bite, waiting a moment before taking another bite, and stopping when satiated. Infant feeders do not allow this process and drastically increase the amount of food your baby eats, which may cause problems with overweight and bad eating habits. The chapter *Mealtimes and Your Baby's Development* beginning on page 71 discusses more about the learning that takes place when your baby eats.

Bibs

Babies are messy eaters. Make sure your baby dons a bib for her first meals. Actually, you'll need bibs for your baby's first few years. Cloth bibs or even wipe-up towels tucked into baby's shirt will help keep his clothes clean. Try to buy cloth bibs without tie strings, which can be strangulation hazards—look for bibs with snaps or Velcro®. Bibs with pockets will help stop food from dropping on the chair's seat and to the floor. If you are going to invest in a plastic bib, buy a larger size so that your baby won't grow out of it in a few months. They now sell very heavy stiff plastic armor-like bibs that wipe clean. Keep the receipt in case your baby doesn't like the heaviness. There's more about bibs on page 465.

> **TIP:** If your baby cries when he sees the bib coming, try this: Give him an interesting toy to distract him. While he's playing, move in back of his high chair and sneakily and deftly slip the bib on from behind. Start using a bib at his first meal to get him used to it and possibly avoid this problem.

There's nothing wrong with letting your baby eat topless on warm days—skin cleans off so easily! Or you can feed your baby non-staining foods while she is bib-less and fully clothed, if you know you're going to bathe her and change her clothes/pajamas immediately after she finishes eating (and soon afterwards pooping).

> **TIP:** To prevent food from smearing on baby's face when you pull her dirty shirt over her head, pull her arms out of her sleeves and roll the shirt up tightly before removing.

Wipe-Up Towels

I always keep a few dozen "wipe-up towels" on hand in my kitchen. They are life savers! Please read the section on wipe-up towels on page 159 in the chapter on *Kitchen and Baby Food Hygiene*. Always keep a few wipe-up towels within arm's reach. I find it convenient to dampen a corner of the towel to clean the crusty leftovers from my baby's face. Then I use the dry part of the towel to dry him up.

> **TIP:** Wipe the cleanest thing first and the dirtiest thing last, and then you will need only one wipe-up towel. For example, at the end of the meal, wipe your baby's face first, her hands next, then the high chair tray and seat, and last the floor. If you've used the towel to wipe the floor first, then you'll need another clean towel to wipe her face.

> **TIP:** If your baby acts insulted when you try to wipe his face with a towel, use your wet fingers to clean him up, and wipe your fingers instead of his face with the towel.

> **TIP:** You as a new parent should get used to wearing sturdy, stain-resistant, machine washable clothing. It's K-mart clothes for the next few years—so put away those designer clothes ☺ !

3. Baby's Very First Meal

It's Time to Start Solid Foods!

One day you just know it's time to start. Your pediatrician has given you the OK and together you have decided on the food that will be the first, and there's some ready and waiting in your kitchen. The suggestions below will help make your baby's very first meal a pleasant experience.

The Best Time of Day for the Very First Meal

The best time to give your baby her very first meal is in the morning or early afternoon. Sometimes babies have allergic reactions to foods. If you feed her in the evening, and she does have a reaction, it will probably occur in the middle of the night. It is better for you, the parent, if you don't have to comfort a gassy baby at 2 am, while you're tired and half asleep.

> **REMEMBER:** Here is a sleep saving tip. Always introduce *any new food* to your baby at breakfast or lunch, never supper. If he has an allergic reaction, it is less likely to occur in the middle of the night.

There is another reason why you should feed your baby during the earlier part of the day. It is usually a time when your baby (and you!) is not tired or colicky, as he may be toward evening. We want everybody happy and energetic when your baby has his first special meal. Choose a time when your baby is not tired, fussy, or cranky, such as after his morning nap.

Give Your Baby His Very First Meal When He is Not Too Hungry

Yes, when he is not too hungry. He should be hungry enough to want to eat, but not ravenous. A too-hungry baby urgently wanting to eat may become frustrated during this new unfamiliar eating method, with this strange contraption called a spoon. Feed him his very first meal after he has had a *partial* breast or bottle feeding. Give him half a feeding, then introduce his first solid food, and then finish the feeding. Giving him a partial feeding will also help to maintain his milk intake. Or you can give him his first solid food halfway through the time between two breast or bottle feedings, when he's just a little hungry.

The Food's Temperature

Remember that your baby's mouth is much more sensitive to heat than yours, so please do not go by how warm you like your food when heating up your baby's food. The temperature of your baby's food should be *moderately warm*. Breast-fed babies are accustomed to the temperature of breast milk—body temperature, 98.6°F—and will be comfortable with their first solid food if it is also at body temperature. However, your baby does not mind cool food and heating is not really necessary, although warmed food does have more flavor. If you do wish to warm your baby's food, you can do so on the stove top or in the microwave for just a few seconds.

> **WARNING:** Please be sure to carefully read the section *How to Safely Thaw Frozen Baby Foods* beginning on page 175, especially if you are using the microwave.

The Amount of Food for Your Baby's Very First Meal

You may be surprised at how little food you should give your baby at her first meal—no more than a teaspoon or two (before it's mixed with liquid). Remember that she will not be very hungry because you will first give her half of a breast or bottle feeding. Or, if you're giving her first meal halfway between breast or bottle feedings, it will be at a time that is at least an hour before she expects her next feeding.

The Consistency of the First Solid Food is Not!

"Solid" is a misnomer—to eat foods that are actually solid, your baby would need a good set of teeth, which she won't have for quite some time! Your baby's first food, after breast milk or formula, should be more liquid than solid. In fact, it should be so liquid that it pours off the spoon. Thick food may make him gag or choke. If you're feeding him commercial rice cereal, use only a teaspoon and mix it with about 2 tablespoons of liquid. For liquid, you can use water, but using breast milk or formula is more nutritious and will make the food taste more familiar to him. If you're using cooked sweet potato, ripe banana, or ripe avocado, mash or purée it until it is very smooth and has absolutely no lumps. Then take only a teaspoonful and mix with liquid until it pours off the spoon. To yogurt, add just a little liquid. Or scoop yogurt out from the top, where that yellow-tinged watery liquid (called whey) gathers. Mix the whey into the yogurt to liquify it so that it pours off the spoon.

> **TIP:** If you tend to hold the bowl of baby food while you feed your baby, you may find it easier to use a coffee cup with a handle.

One More Thing Before You Start Feeding Your Baby

We all know that mealtimes are important to a baby's health and physical growth and development. But before you go wielding that baby spoon, you might want to become more aware of how important mealtimes are to your baby's intellectual, psychological, and emotional development, and to her development of self-confidence and feelings of trust and security. In other words, mealtimes can mess her up in more ways than one! ☺ Because mealtime is much more important than you may have previously thought, you may want to read *Chapter 9. Mealtimes and Your Baby's Development* beginning on page 71 before you feed your baby her very first meal.

Get Ready,

Now that everything is physically ready for baby's first meal, prepare yourself mentally. Decide that you will not be disappointed or upset if she doesn't do well with the food. Be ready to keep your facial expression pleasant, no matter what happens.

I didn't realize how important my facial expression was as a guide to my babies until one afternoon when I was sitting outside with my twin sons. Unexpectedly, a very loud crack of thunder sounded, and this was a new noise to my sons. They both immediately looked questioningly at my face to see if they should be afraid. When I looked at them and smiled, they were quite relieved and returned the smile. Since then, we love thunderstorms. The point to remember is to keep your face pleasant at baby's meal times. If your face looks anxious, your baby will be anxious, and mealtimes will turn out to be anxiety producing.

Even a baby can see through feigned calmness. I smiled at my sons through an entire commuter flight in a plane the size of a phone booth. My sons didn't fall for it, and they watched me worriedly the whole time. Don't fake it. Be determined beforehand that you will not get frustrated if baby refuses to eat or spits food at you, and then you won't have to pretend.

> **REMEMBER:** The more relaxed, confident, and tolerant you are at mealtime, the smoother the feeding will go.

Get Set, Go!

Your baby and you are both seated comfortably and you have a relaxed expression on your face. You have just finished giving him half a breast or bottle feeding and he is still hungry. It's time to go! Put a pea-sized amount of the liquidy food on the spoon, no more than ¼ teaspoon. Place the spoon lightly on your baby's lower lip and slip it gently into his mouth, so that it's on top of his tongue. Let him suck the food off the spoon. If he doesn't, then tip the spoon slightly so that the food pours slowly into his mouth. You may also want to try placing the food a little farther back on his tongue, because of his tendency to thrust his tongue forward. Be careful not to gag him.

Whatever Happens, Smile and Say "Mmmmm!!!!"

Remember that this is a first time for your baby. Don't show disappointment if she thrusts her tongue forward and seems to spit out the food—remember the extrusion reflex (page 11). The younger she is, the longer it will take her to learn to swallow. The closer she is to 6 months, the better she will do. If she is spitting out the food, gently scrape it off her chin with the spoon and re-feed it to her. A baby who is truly ready for solid foods will, after a few tries, begin to get the hang of it and retain more of the food in her mouth than she spits out.

If she doesn't handle the spoon well or if she seems at all uncomfortable, put the food away and wait a few days before trying to feed her again. Remember that your baby's health will not suffer if she doesn't start eating solid foods today. *Take it slowly and never push her to eat.* You want your baby to look forward to her meals as relaxing and enjoyable times with you. After a few days, try feeding her again, keeping things relaxed and pleasant. If she still has problems, discuss your concerns with your pediatrician.

> **REMEMBER:** Your baby will look adorable when he is eating, but try not to laugh when he spits out his food. It may encourage him to continue to do this after it's no longer cute.

Watch Carefully for Signs that You Should End the Meal

Continue to feed her as long as she wants to cooperate. Keep feeding her until the food is gone, or until she turns her head away or closes her little mouth when she sees the spoon coming. Fussiness is also a sign that your baby is finished eating. Never force your baby to continue eating if she does not want to. Please read the section *You Can Put Your Baby in a High Chair, but You Can't Make Him Eat* beginning on page 53 for more information on the importance of never forcing your baby to eat. When she is finished eating, offer her a little water (see next paragraph) and the rest of her breast or bottle feeding.

Water

When your baby begins eating solid foods, it increases the load on the kidneys and necessitates the addition of a small amount of water to your baby's diet. Please read about water on page 61.

What to Do with the Leftovers

Whether you are using commercial jars of baby food or making homemade baby food, it is important for your baby's and family's health and safety that the food preparer in the home understand the basics of hygiene and bacterial contamination. Please be sure to read *Chapter 21 Kitchen and Baby Food Hygiene,* especially the Baby Food Precautions on page 165.

> **WARNING:** Do not keep baby food—either opened commercial jars or homemade—in the refrigerator for more than 1-2 days. Baby food can be spoiled without necessarily smelling bad. If commercial infant cereal has been mixed with liquid, serve it immediately; discard any leftovers and do not use them for another meal.

> **WARNING:** If leftover food has come in contact with your baby's saliva, because the spoon from your baby's mouth has been dipped into it, throw the food away. The bacteria and enzymes in your baby's saliva will continue digesting the food in the bowl, breaking down the vital nutrients and causing it to begin to spoil.

If you are using avocado or banana as baby's first food, you will have plenty of leftovers. You can always eat the rest of the banana yourself, but even an adult has trouble finishing a whole avocado minus one teaspoon!

One method that will help prevent leftovers and food waste is the Frozen Food Cube Method. The method is explained in detail in Part II of this book (page 166), but very briefly you would: purée or fork-mash a very ripe avocado, spoon portions into the cubes of an ice cube tray, cover with aluminum foil to prevent freezer burn and nutrient loss, freeze until solid, and transfer the frozen food cubes into a plastic freezer bag. When mealtime comes, thaw a food cube or two (following the directions and precautions in Part II) and feed it to your baby. The Food Cube Method can be used for cooked puréed sweet potatoes and almost all other Super Baby Foods.

MONEY SAVER: Don't cook large amounts of a new food until you know that your baby likes it and will eat it.

Poop Panic!

Beware that your baby's bowel movements (now a major part of your life ☺) will change considerably when he starts eating solid foods. They will have a stronger odor, and they may also take on the color of the food eaten several hours before. My baby's first post-beet poop looked so much like blood I almost went into a panic. Beets and beet greens cause the most severe color change, followed by kale and the other greens. You may also notice orange veggies, like carrots, at the other end too. Beets may also cause red urine, although this is not as common. Asparagus sometimes lends a strong "fragrance" to a baby's urine.

Your baby's stool may also contain undigested foods. For example, you may see in your baby's diaper the little black seeds from kiwi fruit, which will pass unscathed through your young baby's digestive tract. Sometimes undigested foods are accompanied by small quantities of mucus, especially when your baby starts feeding himself more textured foods. You probably have no cause to be concerned, but it's a good idea to discuss it with your pediatrician.

WARNING: If your baby's stool becomes loose and watery and contains mucus, inform your pediatrician. You may want to retain a stool sample for your doctor to analyze. Your baby's digestive tract might be irritated from a food that he has been eating and you may have to temporarily reduce his solid food intake, especially the suspect food.

WARNING: Too much fruit juice or even too much fresh fruit can cause your baby's stool to be acidic. This irritates baby's tender skin and may cause a painful, bright-red diaper rash that hurts when you wipe. Inform your pediatrician.

REMEMBER: Remember to keep your facial expression pleasant when you are changing your baby's diaper. (With some poops, this may be a real challenge!) He will notice any look of disgust on your face, which may teach him that his private parts are repulsive and lead him to believe that sex is "dirty" when he gets older.

Baby's Second Meal and Beyond

Tomorrow, when it's time for your baby's second meal of solid foods, please follow the directions in *Chapter 11. Feeding Your Super Baby During the First Few Weeks* beginning on page 88. Please read the next few chapters before feeding your baby his second meal, as they contain important information on keeping your baby safe. If it is impossible for you to read them in their entirety before your baby's second meal, then please take a few minutes now to skim through them and read just the subheadings.

4. Food Allergies and The Four-day Wait Rule

Food Allergies

An allergy is an abnormal reaction by the body's immune system to some substance. An allergic reaction to food occurs when the body perceives an ingested food as a threat and overproduces antibodies to counteract it.

A 4 to 7 Day Waiting Period after the Introduction of Each New Food

It is possible that your baby has one or more food allergies, especially if food allergies run in your family. When your baby eats a food that he is allergic to, a reaction (like hives) can occur immediately, or a reaction can be delayed and occur SEVERAL DAYS LATER. Because of this, it is important that you wait several days after the introduction of any new food in order to see if that new food will trigger an allergic reaction. In other words, follow the Four-day Wait Rule.

The Four-day Wait Rule

Introduce only one new food at a time. After you introduce your baby to a new food, do not introduce another new food for at least four days. During the 4-day waiting period, watch carefully for signs of allergies.

Note: Some experts recommend a 3-day waiting period, some recommend waiting 5 days, and still others recommend a full week of waiting between new foods. Consult with your pediatrician and follow his recommendation.

It is important that you understand that a 4-day wait does NOT mean that you feed your baby lots of that one new food, or that you feed him only that new food during the waiting period. In fact, only one small feeding of the new food can be enough to cause an allergic reaction. During the waiting period, feed him a variety of foods to which he has been previously introduced as well as some of the new food.

Wait No Longer than One Week

Some authors recommend waiting a full week after each new food. A one-week trial period is fine, but please don't wait any longer than a week before giving your baby other foods. Feeding him one food for too long a time may produce a sensitivity in him to that food (see *Overfeeding of a Particular Food* on page 31). A 4- to 7-day wait is a long enough time to determine if your baby has an allergy to a food.

Introduce Single Foods Only

Be careful that each new food is a single food. For example, don't feed your baby yogurt for the first time that is mixed with peaches, if peaches haven't been introduced before either. If there is an allergic reaction, you won't know whether it was the peaches or the yogurt. The same goes for commercial "mixed dinners;" do not feed them to your baby until each ingredient in the dinner has been previously introduced individually using the Four-day Wait Rule. Same goes for multi-ingredient stews and soups.

Watch for Signs of Allergies

After each new food is introduced, watch your baby carefully during the 4-day period for any of the signs of allergies listed in the box on the next page. Most allergic reactions manifest themselves in vague symptoms, which you may not notice if you're not watching carefully. Although a lot of these symptoms are commonly caused by a cold or other illness, there is a possibility that they are instead indications of an allergy to the last-introduced new food. Consult your pediatrician to be sure.

Allergy symptoms can occur in almost any part of the body, but most commonly they manifest in the digestive tract (nausea, diarrhea, etc.), the respiratory system (runny nose, wheezing, etc.), and the skin (rashes, hives, etc.). And as you can see in the list of Signs of Allergies in the box on the next page, they range from mild to severe, and even death can result. I certainly don't mean to unduly alarm you. Incidence of serious food allergy is extremely rare in healthy babies, especially when solid foods are delayed until at least 4 months of age. And parents are usually aware of food allergies that run in the family. So please don't worry excessively over possible serious allergic reactions.

Signs of Allergies			
nausea	cough	lip swelling	headache
vomiting	wheezing	face swelling	irritability
gas	breathing	rashes	fatigue
diarrhea	difficulties	diaper rash	behavior
frequent bowel	asthma	hives	problems
movements	runny nose with	itching	convulsions
abdominal pain	clear secretions	eczema	shock
bed wetting	eye swelling	mouth ulcers	death

TIP: If your baby has problems with gas, you may want to consider giving her simethicone drops. These drops act as an antiflatulent to help relieve your baby's gas pains and are claimed to be safe. They are not absorbed by your baby's intestinal system and pass right through it. Sold over the counter under the name Mylicon® Drops, they also come in generic brands which probably work just as well but are much cheaper. They really helped whenever my third son was screaming with gas pain. As always, get an OK from your pediatrician before you administer any medications to your baby, even those you can buy without a prescription.

TIP: Some experts swear that the carminative oil in fennel is an excellent remedy for colic. Make fennel tea for your baby by pouring 4-5 cups of boiling water over 1 teaspoon fennel seeds. Steep for 10 minutes, strain well, and cool. Administer 1-2 ounces at a time. As always, consult your pediatrician to get his advice first before administering fennel, other medicinal herbs, or any medication to your baby.

Causes of Food Allergies

Introducing Solid Foods Too Early

A young baby's digestive system is immature. Their intestines are more permeable to large food molecules and they have relatively low quantities of something called sIgA, making them more prone to allergic reactions. This is why it is so important to introduce the proper foods at age-appropriate times, when your baby's system is mature enough to handle them.

Heredity

Allergies run in families. If one parent has an allergy, her child has a one out of four chance (25%) that he will also have that allergy. If both parents have an allergy, there is a 40% chance that their child will have it. Inform your pediatrician of any food allergies in your family.

Overfeeding of a Particular Food

Feeding your baby too much of a new food over a long period of time may introduce a sensitivity to that food, which may not have occurred during a one week or less waiting period (see *Wait No Longer than One Week*, page 29).

An Existing Allergy to a Similar Food

Be aware that if your baby is allergic to a food, he may also be allergic to similar foods. For example, if your baby is allergic to cabbage, then he may also be allergic to other vegetables in the cabbage family, such as broccoli, Brussels sprouts, and collards. A baby allergic to oranges may also be allergic to grapefruit, limes, lemons, tangerines, and kumquats.

People with allergies to milk must also avoid: canned milk, dried powdered milk, milkshakes, ice cream, yogurt made from cow's milk, butter, margarine, cheese, cream, sour cream, buttermilk, custards made with milk, some hot dogs, some canned tuna, and any products containing whey, casein, milk solids, and other foods containing milk products.

People with allergies to eggs must also, if they are very sensitive, avoid any products with eggs as an ingredient: breads and bread products; cookies, cakes, doughnuts, pies and other desserts; pretzels; salad dressings and mayonnaise; some pasta noodles; and many other products made with eggs.

People with strong allergies to gluten must avoid many products containing it: wheat, rye, and other grains containing gluten, breads and bread products; wheat flour, wheat germ, wheat bran; doughnuts, cakes, cookies, pies, and many other desserts made with flour; some gravy and sauces; malt, as in malted milk; MSG (monosodium glutamate); Ovaltine®; tamari; some processed cheeses and meats; some coffee substitutes; and many other products containing wheat.

> **TIP:** Your natural foods store has a variety of wheat-free and dairy-free food items. Bio-Designs by Allergy Resources has food products, home, cleaning and personal care products, and many more items for the allergic and health conscious. Ask for a catalog by calling 303-438-0600. Another company specializing in allergy products is The Allergy Relief Shop, Inc.®. A catalog from can be obtained by calling 800-626-2810.

The Foods Most Likely and Least Likely to Trigger Allergies

Please be aware that any child can be allergic to any food, even if there is no family history of food allergy. But the foods listed in this section are frequently found to be allergens.

Cow's Milk

The food most notorious for causing allergies in young babies is cow's milk. Typically, it's the protein casein in cow's milk that is the culprit. It is estimated that more than one in ten babies have sensitivities to milk, which explains the big market for soy-based baby formulas. Fortunately, the majority of these children outgrow milk allergy during their second year of life. Most experts recommend postponing the introduction of cow's milk until age one year (page 60). The difference between milk allergy and milk intolerance is discussed on page 33.

Soy, Egg White, Wheat, and Others

The next most common food allergy is that of soy, followed by egg whites and wheat. Other common allergens are citrus, berries, tomatoes, fish (especially shellfish), corn, pork, nuts, and those listed in the next table. Most of these allergies subside as children get older, with the exception of wheat, eggs, cow's milk, nuts, and fish, which often remain throughout life. Some ice cream contains egg white, so don't feed your baby ice cream until he is at least one year old. In fact, avoid feeding your baby ice cream for as long as possible—it contains too much sugar and other additives to be considered a Super Baby Food.

Artificial Additives

Foods containing artificial additives, chemicals, and artificial sweeteners often cause allergies. Never feed your baby (or any living being) carbonated or artificially sweetened beverages. They have no nutritional value and are nothing but water, sugar, and chemicals. It is typical for 12 ounces of soft drink to contain 7 or more teaspoons of sugar! (See page 499). Some carbonated beverages also contain caffeine, even the light colored sodas.

Peanut Allergies

Some experts recommend waiting until age three before introducing a baby to peanuts, peanut butter, peanut oil, or anything containing these foods. A peanut allergy is a dangerous one and is similar to bee-sting allergies in that the reaction can be quick and deadly. Peanut-allergic children may suffer serious reactions and even death from eating peanut-containing foods. A serious reaction may result when a child leans on a counter smeared with peanut butter or peanut oil, even if it has been wiped off!

Ask your pediatrician when you should begin the introduction of peanut foods into your baby's diet. Be sure to make her aware if you have a peanut allergy in your family.

High Risk Allergy Foods		Low Risk Allergy Foods
beans and other	mustard	apples
legumes	nuts	applesauce
berries	onions	apricots
buckwheat	papaya	asparagus
cabbage	peanuts	bananas
chocolate	peas	barley
cinnamon	pork	beets
citrus fruits	rye	carrots
citrus juices	semolina	lettuce
coconut	shellfish	millet
corn	strawberries	oats
cow's milk	soybeans	peaches
cheese	tofu	pears
dairy products	tomatoes	plums
egg whites	wheat	rice
mango	yeast	squash
melons	artificial food	sweet potatoes
milk products	additives	tapioca

NOTE: Some experts recommend that all high allergy foods be withheld until your baby's first birthday, especially if food allergies run in the family. Please ask your pediatrician for advice on the age to begin introducing your baby to the high allergy foods listed above.

WARNING: It is possible that your child may have no noticeable reaction when he eats a small quantity of food to which he is allergic, whereas a larger quantity of the food will cause a reaction.

Lactose or Milk Intolerance

Lactose intolerance (or milk intolerance) is different from milk allergy. Children with lactose intolerance lack the enzyme *lactase* in their intestines. Lactase's job is to break down the milk sugar, lactose, which is present in milk and milk products. If a child's intestines lack lactase, lactose is not digested and remains in the intestines where it absorbs water and becomes food for bacteria, which cause gas, abdominal cramps, and diarrhea. These symptoms usually occur one to two hours after ingestion, but can start as soon as 30 minutes after eating.

Children with lactose intolerance can sometimes eat yogurt with no problem, because it contains much less lactose than does milk. Some children do well with goat's milk. Some natural, aged cheeses, such as Swiss, cheddar, and Colby, may also be well accepted by lactose-intolerant children, because some of the lactose is drained off with the whey. Fresh, unripened cheeses (mozzarella, cream cheese, cottage cheese, ricotta) are not aged and will probably have to be avoided by the lactose intolerant. LactAID®, a brand of milk containing lactase, is available at most supermarkets. You can also buy lactase products (LactAID® and Dairy Ease®) in the antacid section of most supermarkets. Be sure to check with your pediatrician before using.

Although yogurt is often recommended as a first food, check with your pediatrician, especially if there is milk intolerance in your family. Children with milk *allergy* should not eat yogurt or any of the milk products listed on page 31. Read more about yogurt and lactose intolerance on page 253.

What to Do If Your Baby Has an Allergic Reaction

First and foremost, inform your pediatrician. If your baby has a small reaction to a particular food, such as a runny nose, your doctor will probably suggest that you try feeding your baby that food again a month later. If he still shows sensitivity, wait to try again until he is at least one year old. Of course, if your baby has a serious reaction, you should not feed your baby that food culprit again.

For More Information about Food Allergies

The bibliography in the back of this book contains the names of some books, including cookbooks, on the subject of food allergies.

The American Academy of Allergy, Asthma and Immunology (AAAAI) is a non-profit medical specialty organization representing allergists, clinical immunologists, allied health professionals, and other physicians with a special interest in allergy. Call its toll-free Physician Referral Hotline, 800-822-ASMA (822-2762), to request information brochures or to find a doctor in your community who specializes in allergies.

The Food Allergy Network is a nonprofit organization established to help families living with food allergies, and to increase public awareness about food allergies. Contact them at: The Food Allergy Network, 10400 Eaton Place, Suite 107, Fairfax, VA 22030 800-929-4040.

5. Important Safety Warnings

Safety First

The importance of safety in the kitchen and in the home cannot be overemphasized. Thousands of accidents and deaths occur in homes each year because people are either careless or just not aware of the hazards. In this chapter, I discuss the dangers associated with preparing food in the kitchen and feeding your baby. I certainly don't intend to make you a basket case about your baby's safety. My intention is to make you aware of some precautions that you can take to minimize the chance of food problems and kitchen accidents.

Other rooms in your home besides the kitchen can be dangerous, of course, but this book's focus is on baby food and the kitchen. The section *Toxic Substances Found in the Human Body* (page 556) discusses some other safety precautions. For a more thorough coverage of household safety, read one of the many good books available on the subject, such as Vicky Lansky's *Baby Proofing Basics*. Although Debra Lynn Dadd's book, *Home Safe Home*, is not specifically a baby safety book, I highly recommend it as an overall home safety book. These and other books on safety are listed in the bibliography in the back of this book. If you don't want to buy a safety book, your local library is a good source of free information.

For baby-safe and environment-friendly household cleaning solutions, see page 474.

Possibly Poisonous Foods

Food borne Illness

Probably the best way to allay your fears about food poisoning is to learn about bacteria, how it grows, and how you can prevent its growth. Reading the chapter *Kitchen and Baby Food Hygiene* beginning on page 155 is a good place to start.

Honey, Corn Syrup, and Infant Botulism

Do not feed uncooked honey or corn syrup to your baby before she is one year old. Honey and corn syrup may contain spores of bacteria that cause clostridium botulism, a disease that can be fatal. Because infants have not yet developed intestinal flora (their bowel is alkaline, not acidic) or defense mechanisms that fight this bacteria, it can multiply in the intestines. By one year, a baby's stomach acidity is close to that of an adult's. Symptoms of botulism include constipation, poor appetite, and weakness.

What about *cooked* honey/corn syrup? If baked into food, such as breads, it is *probably* safe for a baby to eat, but not definitely. Although bacteria is killed during baking, the bacterial spores are very hardy and need to be in high temperatures for extended periods of time in order to die. The spores can survive through baking and possibly cause botulism, especially if your baby is younger than 6 months. Why take the chance? Don't feed your baby honey or corn syrup, even if it has been cooked or baked into foods. I suggest that you be safe and wait to give your baby those delicious whole grain honey graham crackers from the natural foods store until after her first birthday! (Please know that the corn syrup used as an ingredient in infant baby formulas is safe.)

Raw Eggs and Salmonella

Eggs are a regular part of the Super Baby Food Diet for babies older than seven or eight months. But eggs must be cooked thoroughly to be safe for baby and adults. Raw eggs, especially if they contain cracks in the shell, are a hospitable breeding ground for salmonella bacteria. Even perfect and un-cracked fresh eggs can contain bacteria inside their shells, because chickens (and other animals) actually have harmful bacteria in their intestines, which get deposited into the egg before it comes out of the chicken! So washing it on the outside does not make a raw egg safe. Eggs must be hard-cooked or scrambled and cooked solid to be safe for your baby. For more information on eggs and how to cook them, see page 266.

REMEMBER: Never eat raw eggs or any foods that contain raw eggs, such as eggnog, Caesar salad, whipped raw egg whites, easy-over eggs with partially raw parts. And this one's a killer for me because I love raw cake batter, especially chocolate: Don't let your children "lick the bowl" or beaters or eat from the mixing bowl from cake batter/cookies if you've used raw eggs as an ingredient.

WARNING: While we're on the subject of salmonella, you may be surprised at the fact that 90% of reptile-like pets, such as iguanas, turtles, and others, have been found to contain salmonella. Some babies have died from salmonella poisoning after touching or being near these animals. (As if we parents didn't have enough to worry about.) For more animal worries, see warning about puppies on page 156.

Meat

Meat is not part of the Super Baby Food Diet. Some parents who have used the first edition of this book requested that I include instructions on how to safely prepare meat as baby food. In my effort to make this second edition complete for those parents who choose to feed their babies meat, I have included these instructions. (See chapter on meat beginning on page 278.)

WARNING: Do not eat rhubarb leaves; they are toxic and can be fatal. See *Rhubarb*, page 457.

Canned Foods

In general, canned foods are nutritionally inferior to fresh or frozen foods, and canned vegetables and other foods are frequently high in sodium, as discussed on page 545. There should no longer be a problem with lead in canned foods manufactured in the United States. For more information, see *Lead* on page 557.

WARNING: When you buy a can of foods, check it out carefully. Don't buy cans or jars that are sticky or those with stains. Make sure there are no bulges, dents, broken seams, rust, or small holes in the can. These indicate spoiled or contaminated food.

WARNING: Carefully examine the color and clarity of any liquids, syrups, or juices from cans. If liquid is supposed to be clear but looks cloudy, do not use it—throw it out.

After opening cans of food, do not store leftovers in the original can. Transfer them to a sterile air-tight glass or plastic container and place them in the refrigerator. Metal elements from the can may cause the food acquire a "tinny" taste, and some may even leach into the food.

TIP: Opening canned foods, such as red beets and sticky fruits, can cause a mess. Use a manual triangular-tipped can opener to gently poke a hole in the can. Pour out some liquid and splatters will be avoided when you finish opening the can.

Wash Cans and Jars Before Opening

You never know what's on the outside of cans/jars of food from the supermarket—dust, dirt, germs, and who knows what else. Some supermarkets even spray insecticides directly on the shelves. So make sure to wash the outside of food containers thoroughly and rinse, rinse, rinse before you open them to prevent contamination of the food inside while opening, and to keep your clean hands from getting dirty. And remember to keep your can opener clean—use detergent and a sterile toothbrush after every opening to scrub off dried food and rinse well with hot water.

"Pop!" Goes the Jar or Throw it Out

Most baby foods are packaged in vacuum-sealed jars. Listen carefully while you twist open a jar of baby food. If the button on the jar's lid doesn't pop up when you open it, discard the entire jar because it may be contaminated. Or, better yet, return it to the store and get your money back.

WARNING: Never bang on a glass jar to loosen a top that won't open, which can cause little pieces of glass to get into the food. Use one of those rubber grasper gadgets sold explicitly for the purpose of opening tight-lidded vacuum-packed jars, or use rubber gloves, a large rubber band like those that comes with broccoli bunches, a damp wipe-up towel, or sandpaper. Or let hot tap water run over the top to loosen it. A gritty or grating sound when opening a glass jar may be caused by small pieces of broken glass—so listen carefully and discard the whole jar if you hear anything suspicious.

TIP: It is best to avoid breakable dishes when there's a baby in the house. I recommend Corelle® bowls and dishes because they don't break easily and they do better in the dishwasher then plastic, which tends to flip and gather pockets of water. They also stack compactly in the cabinet and in the dishwasher. (Please know that I have no affiliation with the Corning® company, financial or otherwise.) I called the company and they said that their dishes do not contain any lead now.

TIP: If glass gets broken, pick up every sliver before your baby does. Pick up the largest pieces by hand. Vacuum thoroughly or sweep with a broom, using a damp newspaper as a dustpan. Use damp paper towels to wipe up the entire area. Glass can fly far from the break site so do the entire floor area, table tops, and any other surfaces that may have caught some glass. Turn the lights off and use a flashlight to search carefully from every angle for small . Hopefully, any glass you missed will twinkle. I do one final step (being the self-sacrificing parent that I am): I walk around in my bare feet over the entire area—better for me to get glass in my foot than my baby.

Food and Drug Administration (FDA)

The Federal Government's Food and Drug Administration (FDA) is an agency which ensures that all the food (except meat and eggs) we eat is safe and wholesome, that the cosmetics we use won't harm us, and that medicines, medical devices, and radiation-emitting consumer products, such as microwave ovens, are safe and effective. For general questions on food safety, you can call the FDA's Consumer Hotline at 800-532-4440. If the situation is critical, phone the agency's emergency number, 301-443-1240, which is staffed 24 hours a day. The FDA's Center for Food Safety and Applied Nutrition and Seafood Hotline toll-free number is 800-FDA-4010 (800-332-4010). In the Washington, DC metropolitan area, call 202-205-4314. For questions about prescription or non-prescription medicines or to report a problem with an adverse reaction to medicines, call the FDA MedWatch Hotline, 800-FDA-1088; but first, of course, you should call your doctor immediately. For the USDA's meat safety hot-line, see page 280.

Pesticides

Pesticides kill living things. Let me repeat that. Pesticides **kill** living things. Who knows what long-term effects these supposedly safe levels of pesticides used on our nation's crops will have on your baby (or you for that matter), especially since "safe" pesticide levels on our nation's crops are set according to tolerances by adults and not babies! Another problem with pesticides and your baby is this: Your baby eats much more food per pound of body weight than we do (page 495), so pesticides get more concentrated in her little body. Babies are especially vulnerable to pesticides because their immune system, their organs, and their developing brains are so immature.

WARNING: The American Academy of Pediatrics recommends that you wait until your baby is between 7-9 months old before you introduce homemade carrots, beets, turnips, spinach, or collard greens. In some parts of the country, these crops contain nitrates, and may cause a type of anemia (methemoglobinemia) in young infants. Nitrates also form cancer-causing nitrosamines. Commercial baby food manufacturers can test for nitrates, but we parents can't. Some health professionals believe that any health risk from high-nitrate vegetables in babies under 7 months is so small that restriction is not really necessary. I recommend that no matter how small the risk, do not take the chance. Wait until your baby is at least 7 months old before feeding her these homemade foods.

Certified Organic Foods are Best for Baby

Only certified organic foods should be used to make food for your precious baby. "Certified" organic means that the food has been grown and handled according to strict uniform guidelines and that the farm fields and processing facilities have been inspected to assure that organic standards are being met, according the Organic Foods Production Act of 1990. For more information about organic food, contact the Organic Trade Association, PO Box 1078, Greenfield MA 01301 413-774-7511. Supermarkets, natural foods stores, and mail order organic food companies are discussed beginning on page 140.

NOTE: If your child is eating a lot of one single food, she may be getting much more of a particular pesticide than a child who is eating a variety of foods.

The EPA

The United States Environmental Protection Agency (EPA) is responsible for protecting human health, safeguarding the environment, and establishing safe levels of pesticides for humans. If you have questions on pesticides, call the EPA's National Pesticide Telecommunication Network (NPTN) at Oregon State University: 800-858-PEST (858-7378). For questions about drinking water, call the EPA's Safe Drinking Water Hotline at 800-426-4791.

For More Information on Pesticides

Contact the National Coalition Against Misuse of Pesticides (NCAMP), 701 East Street, SE, Washington, DC 20003 202-543-5450; fax: 202-543-4791.

See Anne Witte Garland's book (listed in the bibliography) entitled *For Our Kids' Sake: How to Protect Your Child Against Pesticides in Food*.

Choking Hazards

There is a risk that young babies will choke on any foods, but hard, whole foods are especially dangerous. The foods in the table below are all considered choking hazards and should not be fed to a baby before he is at least three years old. Choking is not uncommon in children, even children older than three to five years old.

Foods That Are Choking Hazards to Avoid Before Age Three Years and Older	
popcorn marshmallows grapes ice cubes celery sticks cherries blueberries all berries olives peas raisins any dried fruit pretzel pieces meat chunks pieces of bacon gristle from meat hard candy chewy candy gum jelly beans all candy	sliced hot dog "coins" and any other windpipe-sized foods hard, underripe fruit pieces peels of vegetables and fruits strings from vegetables, such as celery, sweet potatoes, and winter squash watermelon seeds and other seeds from vegetables and fruits leafy vegetables whole corn kernels (cooked or uncooked) raw carrot, celery, mushroom, and other hard vegetable pieces apple pieces and other hard fruit pieces too-thin carrot sticks (pieces can break off) peanut butter (unthinned or chunky style) any nut butter (unthinned or chunky style) caramel candy and other thick, sticky foods whole or partially chopped nuts and seeds nuts hidden in candy bars potato chips, corn chips, and other chips lollipops that may come off the stick wrappers from candy

WARNING: A child who has choked should be examined by a doctor in order to determine if any food pieces remain lodged in his upper respiratory tract. Food pieces may cause swelling and strangulation to occur within a few days.

Prevent Your Baby from Choking

❧ Always watch your baby carefully while he is eating, and never turn your back or leave the room. Forget about your housework until after he is finished eating. Use his mealtimes as quality times to bond with your beautiful baby.

❧ Food pieces should be small enough so that, even if baby doesn't chew them at all and swallows them whole, they won't become lodged in the throat or food pipe.

❧ Before feeding your baby tofu dogs, toddler meat sticks (or hot dogs, which are the complete opposite of Super Baby Food), do NOT slice them crosswise into round coin-shaped pieces. These pieces are dangerous choking hazards and the perfect size and shape to block a child's windpipe. First slice the whole dogs lengthwise and then into small pieces less than an inch long.

❧ Never let baby eat unless he is seated and in an upright position. For example, don't let him lie on the floor and eat a cracker. Eating while he is walking or running may also cause choking.

❧ Be especially careful to watch a baby who has had teething medicine rubbed in his mouth. His ability to swallow may be impaired.

❧ Give your baby only a few bits of finger food at a time so that he doesn't cram too much in his mouth at once and possibly choke.

❧ Foods like cookies, crackers, muffins, breads, and biscuits should be either too hard for baby to bite off a piece or so soft that they dissolve almost immediately when put into baby's mouth.

❧ Be careful with slippery foods, such as wet fruits, which your baby can easily inhale into his windpipe. See tip and warning about slippery foods on page 80.

❧ Do not prop your baby's bottle, as your baby may choke.

❧ Baby's mealtimes should be pleasant and fun. However, a baby laughing too much may choke on his food, and that's not fun. Use your own judgement as to how much is too much.

❧ Stress to your children to take small bites and chew carefully and thoroughly before swallowing.

❧ Balloons and broken balloon pieces are not food, of course, but they are known choking hazards for young children, especially when deflated.

❧ Choking hazard measures are available at major toy stores for a few dollars. Any toy, toy part, or item that is smaller than 1¾ inch should be considered a choking hazard to children, especially children under three years old. Supposedly, a toilet paper core is the same size as a baby's windpipe—any item that can fit in it is a choking hazard. I wouldn't trust the toilet paper core though; I'd much rather use an official measuring device.

NOTE: Some of the foods listed as choking hazards above are very nutritious and it would be a shame to miss their nutrients. When baby is older and chewing and swallowing very well, you may want to feed her some of the foods above if you watch her very carefully. Ask your pediatrician for advice.

Warn Older Children about Choking

Older children should be made aware of the dangers of choking and your baby. Tell them never to leave food where baby can reach it and never to feed your baby anything that has not been OK'd by you. Warn even the babysitter about feeding unapproved snacks/foods to your baby. I heard of a case where the babysitter fed a candy bar to a baby who choked on a nut inside the candy bar. Nuts are especially dangerous because nut oils may cause lung infections if inhaled.

Know What to Do If Your Baby Is Choking

Reading about the Heimlich maneuver and CPR (cardio-pulmonary resuscitation) in a book cannot prepare you like real-life practice under an expert's instruction. Call your local chapter of the American Red Cross or contact your hospital or pediatrician for information on classes given in your area.

I can't say enough good things about the American Red Cross. Their volunteers are extremely understanding and helpful. My twins had premature apnea and were on monitors for 6 months after they came home from the hospital. A trained Red Cross volunteer actually came right into my house to give instruction on infant CPR and the Heimlich maneuver to a group of my twins' significant others, including grandmas, grandpas, aunts, uncles, neighbors, and babysitters. Any donation you give to the American Red Cross goes to a very worthy cause.

I warn you that this paragraph is upsetting and scary: I once took an American Red Cross First Aid course where the instructor related a very sad true story. It was about a panicking mother who, in an effort to help her choking baby, hurriedly pushed her hand into the baby's mouth without looking, and accidentally drove the food further down the baby's throat, causing him to suffocate. Never reach into baby's mouth unless you can see the food piece. Swipe it sideways and out, do not push it back. It's a good idea to keep a working flashlight handy to look into baby's mouth for food pieces.

It is probably best not to interfere with choking if the person can breath, cough, or speak. If he cannot breathe, call for help immediately

You are less likely to panic in an emergency situation if you know what to do. Emergency training will take only a few hours of your time. Your baby is well worth it.

If, for some reason, you cannot attend a first-aid class, probably the next best thing is to watch an instructional video, such as the 60-minute VHS videotape entitled *Baby Alive*. Phylicia Rashad of *The Cosby Show* and top medical experts present a step-by-step guide for prevention and treatment of life threatening situations facing children from birth to 5 years old, including choking, drowning, poisoning, head injuries, and cuts. The cost of *Baby Alive* is $19.95 plus shipping and handling of $4.95. It is available from the American Academy of Pediatrics. To order with MasterCard or Visa, call 800-433-9016 (Canada and outside USA call 847-228-5005) or send check, money order, or credit card authorization to: American Academy of Pediatrics Publications, PO Box 927, Elk Grove Village, IL 60009-0927.

Foods That May Cause Digestive Problems
Which Should be Avoided Before 18 Months

Your baby may still have some trouble digesting some foods after his first birthday. Listed below are some of the common offenders, which should be avoided until your baby is at least 18 months old.

chocolate	corn
cucumbers	raw onion
cabbage	vanilla flavoring with alcohol added

Preventing Burns in the Kitchen

I'm sure you've heard a lot of warnings lately to be careful with hot food in the kitchen. We sometimes don't think that accidents will happen to us and that they happen only to other people. It's only those that have been through pain and misfortune that understand how important it is to be cautious. I still remember, when I was a 12-year-old candy striper, the sight of a 2-year-old child who was hospitalized for months. She had been burned over most of her body from scalding liquid that her mother accidentally spilled on her. She cried out in pain whenever touched, making it impossible for her mother to pick her up and hold her. The baby couldn't even be covered with a bed sheet because it hurt too much. I'm telling you this horror story, which I know is making you cringe or cry (I get bleary-eyed every time I think about it), so that you will have a healthy fear of burns from kitchen accidents. Perhaps it will prompt you to be extra cautious in the kitchen. These memories have made me so phobic of burn accidents that I note the whereabouts of all of my children and even my dog to make sure that they are completely out of the kitchen before I move a hot pot.

Preventing Burns in the Kitchen

Please use these safety precautions:

- Use the back burners on your stove, so if your baby reaches up and touches the front burners, she won't burn her fingers. Buy a stove shield and switch covers for your stove—ask for them at your local toy/department store or look for them in baby catalogs.

- Turn the handles of the pots toward the back of the stove, so they are not extending out in front of the stove. Your baby can reach up and pull an extended handle and cause a pot of boiling food to pour on her. ALWAYS turn pot handles backward, even when you are home alone, so that it becomes a habit. Get other family members into the habit too.

🐾 Pack your table cloths away until baby is older. He can pull the table cloth down on himself along with heavy items and hot food.

🐾 When you are moving pots of hot food, verify that baby is not in your path, and that you cannot possibly spill hot food on him. Never hold your baby by a hot stove. If possible, keep your baby out of the kitchen while you are cooking. If no one is around to watch your little one while you cook, place him in the high chair in the kitchen. He'll love to sit and watch you, especially if you talk and sing to him or even dance around to entertain him (as a drastic measure). Strap him in so that he won't surprise you underfoot and get burned. Also, don't set him in your path or in the path of any hot pot you're moving from stove to counter. Make it impossible to fall on him with hot food or to spill hot food on him.

🐾 Don't drink hot coffee, hot liquids, or eat hot soup or other food while holding your baby. You may accidentally spill some on him.

🐾 Keep a fire extinguisher and a fire blanket in your kitchen. Put them in a convenient and visible place, where they will be away from possible fires. For example, don't place them on back of the stove where you won't be able to reach them when the stove is on fire!

🐾 Don't smoke around your baby or allow anyone else to. Besides the danger of cigarette burns, second-hand smoke is very unhealthy. Don't worry about hurting their feelings; simply tell them kindly to put it out. People who would smoke around a baby are probably just unaware, and you're doing many others a favor by bringing it to their attention.

🐾 Do not lean with your back on the range top or reach over or across the stove top, especially if you have long hair or are wearing loose-fitting clothing or an untucked shirt. Of course, never allow your child to climb on the stove top.

🐾 While dining out, keep baby out of the paths of waiters/ waitresses. Be especially careful to keep servers carrying hot coffee pots to refill customers' cups away from your baby. Some have no experience around babies and they just don't think.

🐾 Always put dangerous objects, such as hot pots, sharp knives, etc. on the back of the counter towards the wall out of baby's reach and not near the edge of the counter. Divide kitchen counters with an imaginary line or with red strips of tape to remind the family to keep dangerous objects *behind the line* where baby's hands cannot reach.

🐾 Don't forget to keep wax paper and other wraps with a sharp cutting edge built into the box away from baby so she doesn't get cut. And keep plastic wrap, garbage bags, freezer bags—all suffocation hazards—away from baby too.

🐾 Mark the hot water faucets in the kitchen and the bathroom with red tape, stickers, or nail polish, and warn your toddler not to touch them. Set your hot water heater's thermostat to a safe temperature to prevent scalding. The American Academy of Pediatrics recommends a setting of 120°F. There now exist anti-scald devices for spigots—inquire at your local hardware store or ask a plumber.

🐾 Be careful not to burn your baby's mouth. As discussed in the chapter *Baby's Very First Meal* (page 24), your baby's mouth is more sensitive to heat than yours and baby's food should be only moderately warm. Please be sure to read the section *How to Safely Thaw Frozen Baby Foods* beginning on page 175, especially if you are using a microwave.

🐾 Before turning on your oven, always first check inside for teddy bears, plastic toys, used diapers, and the cat.

Be Ready for an Unexpected Phone Call to the Poison Control Center

Please put this book down and do this *right now*. Look up the number of the Poison Control Center in your phone book. Call it and make sure that the number has not changed. Write the phone number on the handset of every phone in the house. Many poisonings can be managed over the phone if you call the Poison Control Center right away. If you even think there is a possibility of a poisoning, do not hesitate and call the center immediately. When you call, the Poison Control Center will want to know:

- The age and weight of the child.
- The substance that the child swallowed—take the open pill bottle or other container to the phone. Or take the container of the substance that was splashed on the child's skin or in the child's eyes.
- An estimate of the amount of the substance swallowed by the child.
- An estimate of how long ago the child swallowed the substance.
- Symptoms: vomiting, irregular breathing, rapid sweating, weak pulse, a change in skin color or unusual skin color, drowsiness, sluggishness, diarrhea, burns around the mouth, odor on breath, poison still in mouth or on child's teeth, etc. If the child is old enough, ask her how she feels and if it hurts: head, stomach, can she see clearly, etc.
- Keep anything you find for analysis by medical personnel. The pill bottle, the cleaning container, parts of the houseplant or outdoor plant. Keep some of the vomit; this is not time to be squeamish—a life could be at stake.
- Follow the Poison Control Center's instructions. The center will call you back with a follow-up call later to make sure the child is OK.
- If the child is unconscious, call 911 first, then administer CPR.

Syrup of Ipecac

Buy some syrup of ipecac, which is a liquid used to induce vomiting (an "emetic"). Buy the bottle with the latest expiration date. Place the syrup of ipecac bottle in an easily seen, easy to reach, centrally located place in your home, but out of baby's reach. Point out to everyone that it is there and what its purpose is. You may want to stick it right onto the wall in a center hallway. Store another bottle of syrup of ipecac with the first aid/medical supplies, a bottle in the glove compartment of each car, and one in the diaper bag.

WARNING: Do not use syrup of ipecac to induce vomiting unless the Poison Control Center specifically instructs you to. Bringing some poisons back up through the esophagus and throat through vomiting can cause more damage than if it remained in the stomach.

Vitamin/Mineral Supplements

The most common cause of poisoning deaths for children under age six in the United States is the swallowing of iron-containing products. So be as careful about keeping vitamin bottles out of baby's reach as you are with your other medicines. Children can die by consuming as few as five iron-containing pills.

Don't Let Children Mimic You

Do not let your children see you using cough syrups, pills, throat sprays, or any other medications. Babies love to imitate you. Even something as seemingly innocuous as eye drops can cause a child to go into a coma if he drinks enough of them. ALL prescription and over-the-counter medications should be locked up and out of sight.

Child-Resistant Caps Are Not To Be Trusted

Don't be mislead into thinking that a poisonous substance in a child-resistant bottle is child-proof. Manufacturers claim that the purpose of child-resistant caps is to give you *some extra time* to remove your baby from the danger. They are meant only to give you a few extra seconds to prevent your baby from eating or drinking the toxic product inside.

Baby-Safe Cleaning Products

Do NOT keep poisonous household cleaning products in your home, grandma's home, the babysitter's house, or any other place your child may be. You just do NOT need them—see the recipes for non-toxic, environmentally-friendly, and economical cleaning products in the chapter *Children Are More Important than the Carpet* beginning on page 474.

NOTE: If you cannot find a poison control center in your phonebook, write: The American Association of Poison Control Centers, 3201 New Mexico Avenue, NW, Suite 310, Washington, DC 20016

Emergency Phone Numbers

Create several copies of the emergency sheet in the box on the next page and hang them in strategic places and near every phone in your home. Update the emergency information sheet every few months or whenever the information changes. Keep a copy in your purse, the diaper bag, the glove compartment, your office, at the babysitter's or day care, etc. along with the syrup of ipecac bottles.

Review the emergency sheet with babysitters, grandparents, neighbors, and anyone else who will be staying with your baby. Tell them to take a copy to the hospital with them. Tape a copy next to the door so it can be seen and grabbed quickly on the rush to the hospital.

NOTE: It has been my experience that people hesitate to make emergency calls because they are nervous or afraid, and the younger the person is, the more s/he hesitates. Stress to them that they should not hesitate to call the Poison Control Center or 911 IMMEDIATELY. Make it clear that it is much better to have an ambulance when it is not needed than to need an ambulance to save your child's life and not have one.

TIP: For the babysitter, leave a Post-A-Note® by each phone with the phone number and name of the place you can be reached. (Save the notes for re-use.)

TIP: If you are a parent on the go, consider getting a beeper. They now cost as little as $2 per week. Give the number to the day care, the babysitter, your mother, and anyone who may need to get you in an emergency.

REMEMBER: Know exactly where your children are before you begin driving your car.

Emergency Information and Phone Number Sheet

Write up a sheet of paper with important facts and phone numbers. Make several copies and hang them all over the house and near every phone. Include this information:

- Poison Control Center's phone number.
- Fire department, ambulance, and police department phone numbers
- Electric company's and gas company's emergency phone numbers.
- The precise address and phone number of your home.
- Directions to your home from the main street or well-known landmark in your town and the time it will take to get there.
- The full name of the baby, the hospital where she was born, blood group, immunizations, and medical problems. State any unusual fears your child may have.
- Pencil in your baby's current age and weight—keep it updated.
- Information on allergies to foods or medications. If your baby has no allergies, state that she has "no known allergies."
- Mom's and Dad's work numbers, full names, and work addresses. (I highlight these phone numbers with a yellow highlighter pen.)
- Any other phone numbers where Mom and Dad might be, such as cellular phone numbers, beeper numbers, the golf course, frequently visited restaurants, etc.
- Phone numbers of other people to call in case Mom and Dad cannot be reached, such as Grandpa, Aunt Jane, Uncle Leroy, the neighbor you trust, another babysitter. These should be listed in the order of the ones to call first.
- Names, addresses, and emergency phone numbers of your baby's pediatrician, pediatric dentist, ophthalmologist, and the nearest all-night pharmacy that delivers. Leave an emergency cash envelope with your babysitter. If you have a preferred hospital in your community, list its name.
- A copy of your medical insurance cards. (Copy them and cut and paste them directly onto this emergency sheet.)
- A notarized note signed by you saying that any hospital or emergency facility can administer emergency treatment to your baby. Hospitals will not give emergency treatment to your baby unless her life is in danger or unless they have permission from a parent. Call the emergency room of every hospital in your community and ask for the necessary procedures to have your written permission on file.
- The location of keys to doors in the house, in case your child locks himself in the bathroom or some other room in the house. Or drape a thick towel over the tops of doors to prevent them from fully closing.
- The date that this sheet was last updated.

Preventing Dental Problems

Take good care of your baby's teeth, even though they will eventually fall out and be replaced by permanent teeth. Baby teeth are important for holding permanent teeth in their proper positions.

> **TIP:** For an approximation of the number of teeth your baby should have at a given age, subtract 6 from your baby's age in months. For example, a baby 10 months old should have about 4 teeth. Use this rule for babies under 2 years old.

Fluoride

Your baby may also need a fluoride supplement if her drinking water is not fluoridated or be at risk of fluorosis (discolored teeth) from getting too much fluoride, as discussed on page 70 and page 553.

Nutrition and Sweets

Good nutritious food and a minimum of sweet junk foods help promote dental health. Acids produced by sugars in foods actually remove calcium from the enamel of teeth.

> **WARNING:** After your child eats a sweet food, make sure that you clean his teeth, or at least make him rinse with water, immediately afterward to prevent tooth decay. Blackstrap molasses and dried fruits, such as raisins and apricots, are especially bad to leave on the teeth because of their concentrated sugars and stickiness, which prolongs contact with tooth enamel. Chewy candy, hard candy, and lollipops are definite no-no's. Besides being choking hazards, they bathe the teeth in sugars for extended periods—tooth decay's heaven. Good snack foods that have a cavity-fighting effect include cheese, yogurt, milk, peanut butter, and apples. See how to clean baby's teeth below.

Drink Water or Rinse after Meals

Get your child into the habit of drinking a little water after every meal, which he should be doing anyway as soon as he starts on solid foods (see page 61). Teach an older child to brush or at least rinse with water after every meal.

> **WARNING:** Do not allow your child to suck or chew on ice cubes. Besides being a choking hazard (page 40), biting and chewing on ice cubes may cause the teeth to crack or may cause parts of the teeth to break off.

Clean Your Baby's Teeth Often

When your baby's teeth start coming in, "brush" them at least once a day with a piece of gauze, a handkerchief, a washcloth, or a Q-tip® cotton swab. Some experts recommend cleaning the gums before the first tooth appears. After there are a few more teeth, you can switch to a soft toothbrush. The brush should be very soft to prevent wearing down of baby's enamel and irritation to baby's sensitive gums.

> **NOTE:** There are all kinds of baby toothbrushes now on the market. Toothbrushes that fit on your fingertip, brushes with cartoon characters on them, glow-in-the-dark toothbrushes,

disposable cloth finger slips, and who knows what else they'll think of. Use a toothbrush that has been approved by the American Dental Association.

Clean your baby's teeth within 5-10 minutes after each meal. Ideally, you should clean your baby's teeth after every meal, but do so especially at bedtime after the last feeding. Don't forget to floss between his teeth, as soon as he has two next to each other.

Do not use toothpaste until your baby is at least two years old, and then use only a pea-sized bit or a drop the size of a match head. Be careful about letting your baby swallow fluoridated toothpaste, because too much fluoride can actually cause dental and other problems (pages 70 and 554).

> **TIP:** If you can't prevent your child from eating toothpaste, use a toothpaste without fluoride or a "milk tooth" paste with low fluoride levels. Many natural toothpastes without fluoride and artificial sweeteners are available at your natural foods store.

Your child will not be able to proficiently brush his own teeth until he is at least 7 years old. Teach him how by standing behind him in front of a mirror and holding his hand over the toothbrush while you show him how to move it. Use a *gentle* up and down motion and be careful not to gag him. Place an hour glass minute egg timer on the bathroom sink and instruct your child to use it for timing his tooth brushing.

> **WARNING:** Bacteria accumulate in toothbrushes. Experts recommend discarding toothbrushes after six weeks of use. Regularly soak toothbrushes in Listerine or similar mouthwash and rinse very well before placing in baby's mouth. Or run toothbrushes through the dishwasher in the silverware basket, which will also remove those annoying accumulations of gel toothpaste.

No Sleeping with Bedtime Bottles or While Breastfeeding

Don't let your baby fall asleep with a bottle of milk or juice—make sure that he finished his bedtime bottle before he falls asleep. First, the liquid can pool in his mouth and cause tooth decay, even if his teeth have not yet come through the gums. Second, when your baby falls asleep, his saliva flow significantly diminishes. Saliva helps bathe the teeth and washes away food particles, helping to prevent cavities. So teeth get a double whammy when the baby falls asleep with milk or juice, and dental cavities may form. Referred to as *nursing bottle caries* or *bottle-mouth caries*, this tooth decay is most common in children between eighteen months and three years old. It is more likely to occur in the top teeth, because the tongue tends to cover and protect the bottom teeth. Nursing bottle caries are not limited to bottle-fed babies. Breastfeeding baby for long periods during the night while Mom falls asleep also can cause this decay. Perhaps Dad can let Mom sleep and take baby away. Incidentally, sleeping with bedtime bottles or while breastfeeding may also cause ear infections, because liquids may flow through the Eustachian tube and into the inner ear.

Some experts recommend that you give your baby a bottle of plain water at bedtime, if he insists on keeping and sleeping with a bottle. Although this will not cause dental problems, there is still a chance that the baby can choke on it. Always hold your baby close when giving him a bottle in order to bond with him, as well as for safety reasons.

Another cause of dental caries is the feeding of sweet food before bedtime, because the sugar may remain in his mouth. Always brush your child's teeth after sugary, sticky treats, like those listed in the warning on page 48.

Please read page 66 for a warning about juice bottles.

No Honey-Coated Pacifiers

It used to be a common practice to place honey on a baby's pacifier. Raw honey will not only promote cavities, but also may cause botulism poisoning in babies younger than one year old, as discussed on page 36.

Bland is Best for Baby

Hold the Salt and Sugar

When you are preparing homemade baby food, never add salt or sugar. Sugar causes cavities in the teeth and adds empty calories to your baby's diet. Not only does sugar contain no nutrients, it actually uses up your baby's existing nutrients from other foods for its digestion. If your baby fills up on sugar, there won't be room for the Super Baby Foods with their important nutrients. Sugar is discussed on page 496 of the nutrition part of this book.

Although salt or sodium is needed by your baby's body, he gets plenty of it from natural unsalted foods. Salt is an acquired taste, and you should not promote a love of salt in your baby's taste buds. Too much salt is a problem in the typical American diet. See sodium on page 546 in the nutrition part.

Additives in Commercial Baby Food

If you are going to buy commercial baby food, read the labels carefully for added sugar and salt. Some commercial baby food manufacturers still add sugar and salt to their jars of baby food, especially to the "dessert" types of baby food. Avoid buying baby food that has added preservatives, such as BHA, BHT, and EDTA. Also, if you buy baby food, go for the single ingredient jars, which are less likely than the "dinners" to have added salt and the bad type of fat (page 504).

6. How Much Should My Baby Eat?

A Healthy Baby Will Eat The Proper Amount of Food

The question "How much should my baby be eating?" is so often asked of pediatricians, that it is clear that food amount is a great concern to new parents. They are worried that their babies are either eating too much or too little. Don't worry. Your baby will tell you how much he should eat. Your concern should be to include as much nutrition as possible into every calorie that goes into your baby's mouth. Feed your baby a balanced variety of healthy foods and you can be confident that he's eating right. If you would like more reassurance, read the appendix *Nutrition 101: A Crash Course in Nutrition* (page 495). The *Nutrient Tables with Baby-sized Portions* (page 520) make it easy to do a nutritional analysis of your baby's diet.

The Amount Your Baby Eats Will Vary from Day to Day

The quantity of food your baby will eat will vary from day to day, sometimes by great amounts. Don't be surprised if she acts like you starve her one day and eats like a little bird the next. An extended period in which she eats very little is usually followed by a period where she eats a lot. Remember that it is atypical for a baby to be consistent in the amount of food she eats and with her food likes and dislikes from one day to the next.

You know your baby. You can tell if she's not eating because she is sick. If you have any doubt, it's always best to call and ask your pediatrician. Don't be afraid to "bother" your doctor when you have a concern. If he makes you feel like you are a nuisance, find another doctor.

Growth Spurts

The "average" baby doubles her birth weight by 5 months and triples it by 1 year. That means if your baby weighed 7 pounds at birth, she should weight about 14 pounds at 5 months and about 21 pounds at 1 year. Imagine tripling your weight in one year! Your baby's entire first year is a growth spurt, with temporarily bigger growth spurts occurring at certain times. The first several growth spurts are signaled by increased milk consumption. The first growth spurt occurs about a week after birth, the next at 3 weeks, then 6 weeks, and then at about 3 months. After about 5 or 6 months, you may notice that your baby is eating less, which may be because he is growing at a slower rate at this time or because of teething pain. Another growth spurt begins between 8-10 months of age, when you will see a significant increase in the food your baby eats. You may notice an increase in your baby's appetite when he begins crawling and walking, an effect of his using more energy. When he begins his second year of life, his growth rate again decreases and he will consequently eat less. It is at this time, sometime after the first birthday, that many parents become concerned in the drop in their baby's appetite (see *A Decrease in Appetite at One Year*, page 116). Your pediatrician will be watching your baby's growth and development. Discuss with her any changes in appetite you notice in your baby, not only to make sure that your baby is OK, but also to reassure you.

NOTE: Steady weight gain is not necessarily an indicator of a healthy baby. Rely on your pediatrician's expertise to monitor your baby's growth and development.

I'm Worried That
My Baby is Eating Too Much

A Healthy Baby Will Stop Eating When Full

Your baby's appetite is self-regulating. If your baby is eating a lot, he needs to. As long as he's not eating junk foods and stays with Super Baby Food, there's probably no need to worry.

REMEMBER: When your baby cries, first try to comfort him by holding and talking to him. Use food to stop him from crying as a last resort, when you are sure that he is crying because he is hungry.

My Baby is Too Fat

Many babies, even breast-fed babies, are fat before they start crawling and walking. But when they start to move, they quickly slim down. Never put your baby on a reducing diet. And never feed your baby under one year old skim (nonfat) milk, because it contains too much protein and salt and because babies need fat in their diet. Estimates on the percentage of fat from calories that should be in a baby's diet range from 30% to 55%, which is higher than the percentage recommended for us adults. (The nutrition part discusses how to compute percentage of calories from fat on page 525.) If you are concerned about your baby's weight, consult your pediatrician before making any changes in your baby's diet.

Height and Weight Charts

Weight and height charts for children up to three years old are included on the next pages for your convenience. If you are concerned about your baby being too heavy (or too thin), have a talk with your pediatrician. Metric equivalents for the growth charts can be found on page 560.

I'm Worried That My Baby Is Not Eating Enough

A Healthy Baby Will Not Starve Himself

You know your baby. You can tell when he is sick or if something is wrong. If your baby is not losing weight, seems healthy and happy, and your pediatrician says that he is developing well, you probably have no cause to worry.

I've heard on more than one occasion a mother say, "My baby won't eat for me." That statement indicates that a power struggle has developed between Mom and baby. Baby does Mom a favor by eating, and punishes her by not eating. How to prevent this? Don't over-react when your baby refuses to eat. And always keep mealtimes relaxed and pleasant.

You Can Put Your Baby in a High Chair, But You Can't Make Him Eat

Never force your baby to eat. When that little head turns or those little lips close tight, it's time to put the food away. *Never, never, never force a baby to eat.* Never make him finish the last spoonful in the bowl—throw it away. Never make him finish the last half-ounce in the bottom of the bottle—throw it away. Finishing that last bite will start your baby in the bad habit of eating when he is not hungry and throws off his body's self-regulating mechanism, which may lead to overweight later in life.

Some parents are so concerned about their baby's lack of appetite that they may resort to shoving a spoonful of food into baby's open mouth when he is not paying attention, or forcing or manipulating food into their baby by some other means. This kind of feeding is doing more harm than good. If you find that you are resorting to such methods, give yourself an A for effort and for the fact that you care so much about your baby. But please stop it, and instead, ask your pediatrician for advice on what to do about your baby "not eating enough."

WARNING: If your baby begins to hold food in her mouth for extended periods, or spit, gag, or vomit food, this may be an indicator that your baby views mealtimes as stressful. Re-evaluate your feeding methods and make sure that you are not force feeding your baby—either purposely or unintentionally.

Source of data for graphs: National Health Survey, US Dept of Health, Education, and Welfare, 1977.

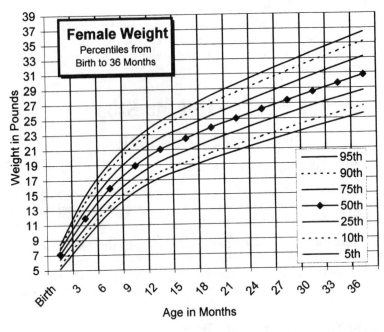

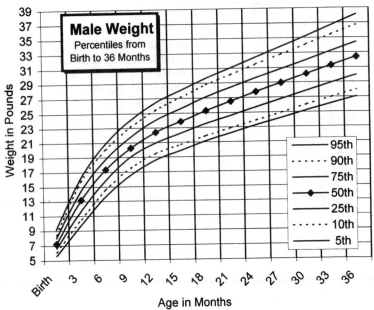

Source of data for graphs: National Health Survey, US Dept of Health, Education, and Welfare, 1977.

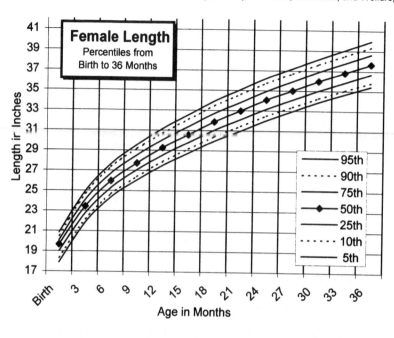

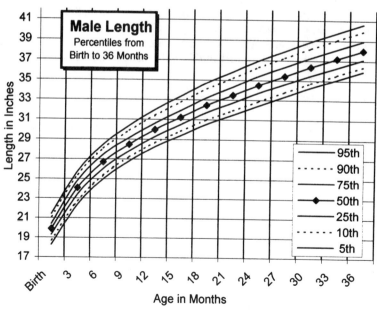

What to Do When Your Baby Won't Eat a Certain Food

Don't push it. Put it away and try again in a few weeks. There are certain things in the Super Baby Food Diet that even I won't eat alone, such as brewer's yeast. It tastes awful. It must be mixed in small amounts with other food to hide its bitterness. Sometimes your baby will not eat something that is sweet and tastes good to you. With my baby, it was applesauce. I was surprised (but not upset!) that he simply would not eat it. A few months later, he began eating it with gusto and has loved it ever since. It must have been something about the acidy flavor...

If you are afraid a toddler will not like a particularly healthy new food, such as kale, use a little reverse psychology to get her interested. Don't give her any and eat it in front of her; have the whole family eat it in front of her. She will want some. Be hesitant, but agree to give her some. If you're lucky, she will love to eat it because it makes her feel like a big girl who fits in with the rest of the adults in the family.

REMEMBER: Babies will almost always make a face when offered a new food, especially if it has a strong flavor. Do not go by her facial expression. Offer her another spoonful and if her little mouth opens to accept a refill, continue feeding.

TIP: You may wish to have this rule in your home: You have to try one bite of a new food. If you don't like it, you don't have to eat it, but you have to try it. Remind your child of Dr. Suess's *Green Eggs and Ham.* You may like them, Sam I am. ☺

Small Amounts of Food Frequently Throughout the Day

It's not unusual for a baby to eat only one major meal a day, with the rest of his food coming from snacking. Snacks are necessary in a baby's diet and should consist of smaller portions of the same healthy foods that are part of larger meals. A baby may not begin eating three baby-sized meals until he is 10 months old, although he may start as early as 4 months.

Snacks should be offered at scheduled, predictable times every day and not at random. Snacks should be eaten in the feeding area, as main meals are, because they ARE meals. See more about the Super Snacks of the Super Baby Food Diet on page 131.

The "Average" Food Amounts Given in this Book

In the chapters for each month of your baby's first year, I have included a section about the daily amounts of foods that you can expect your baby to eat at that age. For example, see the section entitled *Daily Amount of Food for Babies 7 Months Old* on page 99. These amounts are based on the hypothetical "average" baby. Babies differ enormously in height, weight, activity level, and appetite. However, sometimes a great deviation from the average may be a sign that something is wrong. If your baby eats a VASTLY different amount of food than the one stated for her age, you may have a reason to be concerned. The section *How Many Calories Does My Baby Need?* on page 511 and *Your Baby's Caloric Needs* on page 522 in the nutrition part of this book may be of help. Also, see the table for the *Average Daily Recommended Calories and Fat* for your baby on page 523.

Table of Baby Food Portions

The table on the next page is a brief summary of the complete information given in Chapters 13-17. The table is meant to give you only a rough sketch of the number of meals and the size of food servings that your baby *might* eat at those ages. Please be very flexible when you feed your baby and go by her cues that she is still hungry or satisfied.

Baby Food Diary

If you are concerned that your baby is eating too much or too little, begin keeping a baby food diary. Include a description and amount of each food and drink your baby has consumed with the day and time of each meal or snack. After you have gathered several days of "data," consult with your pediatrician.

REMEMBER: Your pediatrician should be a person you feel comfortable with. You should not hesitate to ask him or her a question. Many Moms have come to me with questions and when I asked them what their pediatricians advised, they tell me that it never even crossed their minds to ask their doctors!! Do not hesitate to pick up the phone and call your pediatrician's office with a question. There are no "dumb" questions. If your doctor makes you feel like there are, or in any other way makes you feel uncomfortable about the concerns you have for your baby, find another doctor.

Super Baby Food Daily Servings and Portion Sizes
See details in Chapters 13 - 17.

Age / Food	7 Months	8 Months	9 Months	10 and 11 Months
Vegetables and Fruits	3-4 servings Each serving is 1-2 tablespoons	4-5 servings Each serving is 2-3 tablespoons	4-5 servings Each serving is 2-4 tablespoons	4-5 servings Each serving is 3-4 tablespoons
Super Porridge Cereals	1-2 servings Each serving is 1-2 tablespoons dry cereal or ¼-½ cup cooked cereal.	2-3 servings Each serving is 1-2 tablespoons dry cereal or ¼-½ cup cooked cereal.	3-4 servings Each serving is 1-2 tablespoons dry cereal or ¼-½ cup cooked cereal.	4 servings Each serving is 1-2 tablespoons dry cereal or ¼-½ cup cooked cereal.
Legumes Nuts and Seeds	1-2 tablespoons of tofu purée every day or every second day	1-2 servings For serving sizes, see protein foods on page 103.	2-3 servings For serving sizes, see protein foods on page 108.	2-3 servings For serving sizes, see protein foods on page 112.
Dairy	1 serving per day or every other day ⅓-½ cup yogurt ¼ cup cottage cheese	1 serving per day or every other day ½ cup yogurt, ¼-⅓ cup cottage cheese, or ½-1 ounce of natural grated cheese	1 serving per day or every other day ½ cup yogurt, ⅓ cup cottage cheese, or 1 ounce of natural grated cheese	1 serving per day ½ cup yogurt, ⅓ cup cottage cheese, or 1 ounce of natural grated cheese
Egg Yolks	One egg yolk every second day or 3-4 egg yolks per week.			
Nutritional Enhancers	none	Add ½-1 teaspoon of brewer's yeast and a pinch of kelp into Super Porridge at least once a day, and maybe ½-1 teaspoon of desiccated liver too.		
Solid Food Meals per Day	2-3 meals per day with 2-3 food servings each	3 meals per day with 3 food servings each and a snack or two	3 meals per day with 3 food servings each and a snack or two	3 meals per day with 3 food servings each and 2 or more snacks

Be very flexible with meals and food serving sizes. This table is meant to give you only a rough idea of what your baby might eat at these ages.

7. How Much Should My Baby Drink?

Breast Milk/Formula Amounts Before The Introduction of Solid Foods

As a general rule of thumb, a baby drinking breast milk or formula exclusively—that is, one who has not yet been started on solid foods—should be drinking about 2½ ounces of milk per day for each pound of body weight. Age plays an important factor; for example, a baby younger than 6 weeks may drink over 3 ounces of formula per pound of body weight because of a fast growth rate, whereas a baby 15 weeks old may drink only 2⅓ ounces per pound. Of course, a 20-week old baby who has begun eating solid foods may be drinking only 2 ounces per pound of body weight, due to the increased calories from the solid food. Examples of the number of average daily ounces according to pounds of body weight are given below.

Average Amounts of Daily Breast Milk/Formula by Body Weight for Babies Not Yet Eating Solid Foods

6 pounds	15 ounces per 24 hours
7 pounds	17½ ounces per 24 hours
8 pounds	20 ounces per 24 hours
9 pounds	22½ ounces per 24 hours
10 pounds	25 ounces per 24 hours
11 pounds	27½ ounces per 24 hours
12 pounds	30 ounces per 24 hours
13 pounds	32 ounces per 24 hours

Make Sure Your Baby is Drinking Enough Breast Milk or Formula

Breast milk or formula is the most important food for your baby during her first year, and especially in her first 8 months. **It is very important that the introduction of solid foods not decrease her breast milk or formula intake during the first eight months.** Calorie for calorie, there is no solid food that is as nutritious for your baby as breast milk or formula. Initially, solid foods should supplement milk, not replace it. Chapters 11-17 each contain a section entitled *Daily Amounts of Liquids*; for example, turn to page 90 to see the amount of liquids recommended for a beginning eater. If your baby is not drinking the recommended amount of breast milk/formula for her age, cut back on her solid food intake so that she will be hungrier for breast milk or formula. For smaller babies, this may not work; please consult your pediatrician.

> **WARNING:** When mixing formula, always use the recommended ratio of water to formula. Parents who are concerned that their babies are not drinking enough formula may think that less water is the answer. Do NOT make formula more concentrated than it should be by adding less water than instructed. Sodium, protein, and other ingredients in the formula must be mixed with the proper amount of water so as not to strain your baby's kidneys and for other health reasons.

Formula-fed Babies and the 32-ounce Rule

If your baby is older than 6 months, most experts agree that your baby should not be drinking more than 32-40 ounces of formula per day. If your baby wants more than this limit, offer her a bottle of water instead. If she won't drink water, offer her pasteurized and diluted juice as described in the *Juice* section beginning on page 64.

Please note that the "no more than 32 ounces per day" rule holds only for babies older than 6 months. Before the age of 4-6 months, experts say that too much formula is not a problem and that a hungry baby should be given a bottle instead of solid food. Your pediatrician may not agree; follow her advice on this issue.

No Cow's Milk Until One Year

Breast milk or formula is the only milk you should give to your baby throughout her first year. Cow's milk is different in composition than human milk—it's "designed" for baby cows, not baby humans. Cow's milk contains more salt than breast milk/formula and its protein content is different from human milk, which may strain your baby's kidneys. Introducing your baby to cow's milk too early can cause milk allergy to those who are susceptible.

> **NOTE:** Cow's milk should not be used as a replacement for breast milk or formula during the first year, but it is OK to introduce it as an ingredient of solid foods in the rest of the diet, such as yogurt.

Parents may wish to begin cow's milk as early as possible because it is less expensive than formula. Some experts are more lenient about this one-year rule and advise that once your baby is getting half of his calories from solid foods, it's OK to start him on cow's milk. Others say it's OK when your baby is eating at least six ounces of solid foods a day. Go by your pediatrician's advice.

Cow's milk leaves an infant at risk for anemia because it is low in iron, a very important nutrient for your baby in her first years of life. Cow's milk is also low in vitamin C, another important nutrient. Vitamin C also helps in the absorption of iron, so the lack of it in cow's milk increases the risk of anemia. And to even further risk Iron-deficiency anemia, cow's milk can irritate the digestive tracts of very young infants (younger than 6 months) and cause tiny amounts of bleeding, with a consequent loss of blood and its iron.

> **TIP:** When it comes time to make the transition from formula to cow's milk, it may be easier for your baby if you start by mixing a small amount of cow's milk into your baby's cup of formula or breast milk. Gradually decrease the amount of formula and increase the amount of cow's milk until the mixture is all cow's milk with no formula.

Once your baby starts on cow's milk, it should be whole milk and not skim or low-fat, which is too high in salt and protein. Your baby needs the fat from whole milk for calories and nutrition. You can find organic milk at the natural foods store and at some large supermarkets. Don't confuse organic milk with raw milk, which may contain dangerous bacteria. Organic milk is milk from cows that haven't been administered drugs or fed hormones. It is usually pasteurized, but don't buy it unless it states that it is pasteurized on the label.

Most experts recommend that you keep your baby on whole milk until he is at least 1 year old, and some recommend 2 years. Again, ask your pediatrician.

Baby's Bottle Should Contain Only Formula or Breast Milk

Some experts recommend that your baby's bottle contain only formula or breast milk. In other words, although it is fine to let your baby drink milk or water or juice from the cup, some authorities advise that it is best to offer only milk, and never water or juice, in the bottle.

Water

Water Is Important to Kidney Functioning

When you introduce solid foods, begin giving your baby a little water after and between meals. It will help her kidneys dilute the more concentrated waste products of solid foods.

The amount of water needed varies with the baby. You may start by giving your baby a tablespoon of water after his meal and before the rest of the breast or bottle feeding. Gradually increase the amount of water until he's drinking a maximum of 4-6 ounces of water per day. Maintain this maximum until your baby is about one year old, so as to insure that his milk intake is not being decreased by his drinking other liquids.

Besides helping the kidneys, water is needed by your baby's body to replace that which is lost through the urine, feces, sweating, evaporation, and breathing (as can be seen in cold weather). This he gets from milk, water, juice, and food, which is part water. You must make sure your baby gets enough liquids to prevent dehydration, especially on hot days. Ask your pediatrician how much water your baby should drink.

Getting enough liquid is as important for a baby as for an adult, maybe even more so, because a baby's body is made up of a higher proportion of water than an adult's. While adults require a daily an amount of water equal to 2-3% of their body weight, a baby requires about 15%! (That's about 2½ ounces or almost ⅓ cup of liquid per pound of body weight.) If you're not interested in the math, go on to the next paragraph. For example, a 20-pound baby requires approximately .15*20=3 pounds (48 ounces) of water every day. Let's say he drinks 32 ounces of formula, 2 ounces of juice, and 2 ounces of water, for a total of about 36 ounces. That leaves about 12 ounces to be obtained from food. If he eats 2 half-cup servings of cereal, 4 quarter-cup servings of vegetables, and 2 quarter cup servings of fruits, that's 2½ cups or 20 ounces of food. It's safe to say that more than half of these foods is water (see *Drying Foods*, page 200), and so there you have it—12 ounces of water.

Babies do not dehydrate easily because the main part of their diet is fluid. But your baby may dehydrate if she is vomiting or has diarrhea, so be sure to consult with your pediatrician.

Tap Water

Tap water may be safe for your baby to drink. Ask your pediatrician, who should be familiar with the local water supplies. If your pediatrician isn't sure and you are concerned about lead and other tap water dangers, call the EPA's Safe Drinking Water Hotline at 800-426-4791 (see EPA, page 39) for a list of certified water testers in your area. National Testing Laboratories, Ltd. in Cleveland, Ohio at 800-458-3330 does testing of drinking water. Beware of free water testing offers. If you are going to use a home lead test kit, first call the EPA to make sure that they approve of the manufacturer. If a test determines that a problem exists with your water, get it re-tested by another certified water tester.

> **WARNING:** Never use tap water that has been sitting in your pipes for an extended period of time, because it may contain heavy metals (cadmium, mercury, lead) that leached in from the plumbing. For example, you wouldn't want to drink the first glass of water out of the kitchen tap in the morning, because that water has been sitting in the pipes all night. Flush out stagnant water from the pipes by letting the water run for a few minutes, until it gets as cold as it will get. Don't waste this water: rinse dirty dishes with it or save it to water plants.

WARNING: Never use hot tap water for drinking or cooking purposes. The warmth helps lead and other heavy metals from your pipes leach into the water. If you need warm/hot water, draw cold water and heat it on the stove or in the microwave.

No Standards for Bottled Waters

When you buy bottled water, you may be wasting money. Most bottled waters are not natural mineral water at all, and are actually nothing more than processed local tap or well water. This is true if the label says "spring fresh", "spring type" or "spring pure." Some bottled waters have added sodium and may have more bacteria than your tap water, and even more lead! There are no FDA (page 38) limits on bottled water when it comes to levels of pesticides and organic chemicals. And there are no federal standards on any bottled waters if they are bottled and sold in the same state!

One type of bottled water, distilled water, has nothing in it but H_2O. Distilled water has no minerals and may even absorb minerals from your body. Drinking water should be a dietary source of many healthful minerals, so distilled water is not good to drink. (Note: Some people disagree with this, and claim that drinking distilled water is healthful.)

Hard Water vs Soft Water

Hard water refers to water that has high levels of minerals, specifically calcium and magnesium. Hard water is known for making white clothes gray after washing, leaving a bathtub ring, and depositing crystals in your tea kettle and hot water heater. Water softeners were invented to undo the hardness of water. But soft water contains high levels of sodium. It makes more bubbles in the bathtub and causes soap to lather more readily, so that you can use less soap. Soft water more easily dissolves metals from your plumbing. Hard water is the more healthy drinking water, so if you plan on buying a water softener, hook it up to your hot water pipes only and drink only from the cold.

Hard Water is Healthier than Soft Water		
Water hardness (ppm)	Minerals-grains per gallon	Parts per million
soft	0-3.5	0-60
moderately hard	3.6-7	61-120
hard	7.1-10.5	121-180
very hard	10.6 and above	181 and above

Call your local water company to determine your water hardness.

MONEY SAVER: If you have soft water, although it's not good for drinking, it sure is good for saving money on detergents. We have very soft water in our community and I get away with using less than half the recommended amount of laundry detergent and dishwasher liquid! I use the money I save on detergent to have heathy drinking water delivered to our doorstep.

The Best Drinking Water

The best water you can drink is probably a water bottled directly from a local spring. The spring should be in an area with little or no industry, so pollutants can't get into the water. The bottle will say something like, "Natural spring water bottled directly from the source." Call the company and ask them about their water's hardness and if and how often they test their water for pollutants, lead and other heavy metals, and other toxic substances.

Baby's Water must Be Boiled and Cooled

The water you give to your very young baby must be boiled to kill all bacteria. Boil it for 5-10 minutes and store it in a sterile container in the refrigerator. Make sure that it is thoroughly cool before giving it to baby, of course. Do not keep it at room temperature for more than a few minutes. Store in the refrigerator for no more than 1-2 days and then discard it. It will not be long before you can feed your baby water without boiling it first. Ask your pediatrician when it is no longer necessary to boil your baby's water.

Juice

At about 7 months, you can begin giving your baby diluted, mild fruit juice. Your pediatrician may advise the introduction of juice several months earlier.

It's Important that Juice Not Replace Baby Milk

To keep your baby's breast milk/formula intake up, limit your baby's juice intake to 3-4 ounces of juice per day. Babies who drink too much juice may not be drinking enough breast milk or formula to obtain the fat, calories, and protein they need for proper development. Too much juice and not enough breast milk/formula may adversely affect your baby's growth and may lead to decreased weight and height.

Start with Mild Fruit Juices

Start with mild juices, such as apple, apricot, white grape, papaya, pear, peach, and prune, remembering to use the Four-day Wait Rule (page 28). Although some experts recommend orange juice and other citrus juices at 6 months, others recommend waiting until 12 months, especially if allergy to citrus runs in the family. Citrus is one of the foods that is a common allergen (page 33) and the acidity may be a problem. Ask your pediatrician when you should start giving your baby orange juice.

Apple juice seems to be very popular because it has a low chance of allergy, although a friend of mine uses it because it doesn't stain the carpet. It certainly is no more nutritious than other non-citrus juices, unless it is vitamin C-fortified. If you're going to give your baby apple juice, infant juice is probably your best bet because adult apple juice may still contain the pesticide alar. Although alar is no longer used on apple crops, there may be some still remaining in stored apples or juice concentrates somewhere. Why take the chance? Use apple juice that is purposely for babies and more carefully screened for alar.

Juices for Baby Must Be Pasteurized

You may be aware of the recent problem with E. coli bacteria in commercial unpasteurized apple juice and apple cider. Make sure that any juice fed to your baby is pasteurized—it should be indicated on the label. Beverages in bottles, cans, and juice boxes stored on the supermarket shelf at room temperature are supposedly pasteurized. I recommend that you not trust them, though, unless it specifically says that they are pasteurized on the label.

> **WARNING:** Do not feed your baby apple cider, juices, or any beverages bought from roadside stands. And do not feed your baby "fresh" juices, as they are not pasteurized.

Refrigerate and Discard Opened Bottles of Juice Within Two Days

If you are feeding your baby commercial baby juices, make sure to refrigerate any opened bottles with unused portions immediately. Do not leave opened jars of baby juice at room temperature for more than a few minutes. Store opened jars of baby juice tightly covered in the refrigerator. Keep for no more than two days before discarding.

How to Pasteurize Juice

If you are not sure that juice for baby has been pasteurized, bring it to a full boil and boil it for it for 3-5 minutes to kill any bacteria. Store in a sterile container in the refrigerator immediately. Never leave it for more than a few minutes at room temperature and keep refrigerated. Discard after 2 days.

Juice Should Be Diluted When First Introduced

Juice contains large amounts of sugar, and natural or not, too much sugar is not good for your baby. For example, it takes an entire apple to make one ounce of apple juice, therefore four ounces of juice contain the natural sugar in four apples—that's a lot of sugar! Excessive sugar from fruit juices may cause susceptibility to yeast overgrowth (specifically *candida albicans*), which manifests in throat and ear infections, eczema, and chronic nasal congestion. Too much sugar causes a temporary decrease in your baby's white blood cell count, and consequently a decrease in the strength of her immune system—yet another reason why too much sugar causes illness. Sorbitol (a sugar alcohol found in pear and apple juices) has been shown to cause gastrointestinal disorders, such as gas and bloating, abdominal pain, and diarrhea. Please read more about the ills of excessive sugar in the nutrition appendix under *Simple Carbohydrates or Sugars* on page 496.

Bottled baby juice is 100% juice with no water added, therefore it should be diluted. If your pediatrician OKs it, you can save money and use regular adult juices and dilute them yourself. Buy those juices that are only 100% juice and make sure they are pasteurized. Do not feed your baby "pretend" juices—those juice *drinks*, which have added sugar. These nutritionally-void drinks are nothing but sugar, water, and food coloring. Read the label and watch out for the OSE's (pages 498-499). Although natural juice does contain a lot of sugar, it does contain some other nutrients. It is best to buy baby juice fortified with vitamin C, a necessary nutrient that will also help with iron absorption.

At first, dilute 1 ounce of juice to 3 ounces of water, giving a 4-ounce serving. Over a month's time, gradually increase to half juice and half water. In subsequent months as your baby grows older, you can, if you wish, gradually increase to 100% juice with no added water, as directed under the *Daily Amount of Liquids* section in Chapters 11-17.

> **REMEMBER:** There is really no need to build up to 100% juice, which contains so much concentrated sugar. If you wish, you can continue feeding your baby diluted juice throughout his childhood and even into adulthood. It's a good idea to start diluting your family's and your juice, too. We're better off without all that concentrated sugar!

Some Juices Must Be Strained to Prevent Choking

Most natural foods stores have a nice selection of organic fruit juices, but they sometimes have solid particles that should be strained out to prevent baby from choking. Home-squeezed juices also need straining. See how to strain juices on page 152. As discussed above, remember to check that all juice has been pasteurized.

Home-squeezed Juice

If you squeeze juices at home manually or with a juice extractor, feed them to your baby immediately after squeezing so that bacteria do not have a chance to multiply. Drinking home-squeezed juices is similar to eating fresh fruit. However, do not store home-squeezed juices (even in the refrigerator or freezer) for baby unless you first pasteurize them as directed in the previous paragraph. After pasteurizing, strain the juice. Refrigerate in a sterile bottle. As with all juice, discard after two days.

Before juicing, remember to wash the fruit/vegetable well to remove as much of the pesticides as possible. Although pasteurization kills bacteria, it does not remove the pesticides. I recommend using only certified organically-grown produce for making home-squeezed juices.

Protect Your Baby's Teeth from the Sugar in Juice and Other Beverages

Use a baby cup instead of the bottle to feed your baby juice in order to minimize the time the juice remains in his mouth. (Introducing the cup is discussed on page 76.) Don't let your baby sip from a bottle or cup of juice, milk, formula, or any other carbohydrate-containing liquid throughout the day. The natural sugars and acids in the liquid will remain for extended periods on his teeth and may cause dental caries. If your baby insists on sipping from a bottle, make it water. For more information on protecting your baby's teeth, see page 48.

> **WARNING:** Too much fruit juice or even too much fresh fruit can cause your baby's stool to be acidic. This irritates baby's tender skin and may cause a painful, bright-red diaper rash that hurts when you wipe. Inform your pediatrician.

Cola and Other Carbonated Beverages

NEVER give your baby cola drinks or other sweet carbonated beverages, even when she's 21 years old. Besides gobs of unhealthy sugar (see page 499), some of these drinks also contain caffeine, which has a much greater affect on a 20-pound baby than it does on a 150-pound adult.

Nut/Seed Milks

Other Super Baby (and Super Adult) beverages are nut milks and seed milks. As discussed in the chapter beginning on page 240, nuts and seeds are one of nature's most nutritious foods. Nut/seed milk is not actually what we tend to think of as "milk;" it is actually water with added liquified nuts or seeds, which makes the water look like a thin and watery milk. Nut/seed milks are very easy to make if you have a blender—see the Super Milk recipes beginning on page 359. Beginning at about 8 months, you can introduce your baby to these Super Milks (page 104). But just as with juice and water, nut/seed milks should supplement and not replace breast milk or formula.

Some experts advise using nut/seed milks for non-breastfeeding babies who cannot tolerate any brand of formula. If your baby has this intolerance, discuss with your pediatrician the use of nut/seed milks.

REMEMBER: For your baby to develop properly, he needs a recommended amount of breast milk/formula every day. Water and juice should not replace breast milk/formula. Limit your baby's juice intake to 3-4 ounces of undiluted juice per day until he is one year old. Limit your baby's total daily intake of juice, water, and other beverages to 6-8 ounces per day so that he will drink his recommended amount of breast milk/formula. On hot days, your baby may need a little more water to replace perspiration.

8. Vitamin and Mineral Supplements

Prescription Vitamins

Your pediatrician has probably prescribed "ACD" vitamin drops, so called because they contain vitamins A, C, and D. When your baby gets a little older, a more complete vitamin supplement may be prescribed.

Your baby should get vitamins from whole foods, which also contain cofactors and other substances needed to work with vitamins. Do not count on vitamin supplements to make up for a bad diet. Vitamin supplements are called "supplements" because they are meant to do just that—supplement a baby's good diet, not replace it. I recommend vitamin supplements, because even a good diet can be lacking in nutrients due to improper storage of foods, too-early harvesting, and the lack of nutrients in our country's depleted soils from poor farming methods.

Exclusively breast-fed babies are often prescribed a supplement containing vitamin D. The American Academy of Pediatrics recommends this because breast milk may not have enough of this nutrient, which is produced by sunlight on skin. (See vitamin D in nutrition part, page 530.)

> **WARNING:** Never give your child vitamin or mineral supplements without your pediatrician's OK, especially for those supplements sold without a prescription.

I make sure my baby gets his prescription multi-vitamin drops every day. In fact, I divide the dose and give him half a dropper with breakfast and half a dropper with supper. Some vitamins, such as vitamin C, are better utilized if you administer them in two smaller doses than in one large daily dose (page 539). I was concerned that I would not be accurate enough in the dosage by dividing it this way, because there is no mark on the dropper at the halfway point. My pediatrician said that you do not have to be that accurate, and that it was OK to divide up the dose by eye-balling it. If you wish to do the same, please OK it with your pediatrician first.

Give vitamin supplements to your baby with her meals, and not on an empty stomach. Vitamins work *with* food to help with chemical reactions in the body. Fat-soluble vitamins (A, D, E, and K) are best utilized when taken with food containing some fat, such as whole milk or yogurt, egg yolks, soybeans, peanut butter, tahini, and ground nuts and seeds. They should not be fed with an all-fruit snack, because there is virtually no fat in fruit.

Iron

Enough Iron in Your Baby's Diet Is Extremely Important

A full-term baby is born with enough iron stores from Mom to last him about 4-6 months, or until his birth weight doubles. Premature and underweight babies may have only enough iron stores for 2 months. At these ages, babies must be fed foods high in iron, such as iron-fortified formula or iron-fortified cereal. Although breast milk has low levels of iron, its iron is used much more efficiently by the baby's body than iron from formula or food. But most experts still recommend that a breast-fed baby get some form of iron supplementation, whether it be from iron-fortified cereal or iron drops.

If you plan on feeding your baby homemade whole grain cereal instead of commercial iron-fortified cereal, and your baby is not drinking an iron-fortified formula, your baby may not get enough iron. Brown rice and millet contain iron, as do egg yolks and other foods in the Super Baby Food Diet. However, most experts consider their iron levels too low for a baby. *Iron from plant sources like rice and millet is not as well assimilated as iron from meat and other animal products.*

WARNING: Iron deficiency during the first eighteen months of your baby's life may cause serious health and behavior problems and may delay your baby's development.

Ask your pediatrician about giving your baby a daily iron supplement, which you can buy over-the-counter (no prescription needed). Similar to prescription vitamins, iron drops are in liquid form and dispensed through a dropper into your baby's mouth.

WARNING: Some brands of iron drops have been known to stain the teeth. Your pediatrician will advise you on which brand to buy.

Your pediatrician may advise that iron drops are not needed if you are feeding your baby iron-fortified cereal or iron-fortified formula. Too much iron is not healthy, and may lead to constipation. Go by your pediatrician's advice, which may depend on the results of the blood test for anemia given routinely to babies.

The nutrition part has more information on iron beginning on page 547.

Babies may continue to need iron supplementation until they are at least 18 months old, as discussed in the chapter *Feeding Your Super Toddler* on page 116.

Combine Iron with Vitamin C

Iron from meat is better assimilated by the body than iron from grains. To help increase the absorption of iron, feed your baby a vitamin C food or vitamin drops containing vitamin C at the same time your feed your baby egg yolk or cereals. This combination of foods is built into the Super Baby Food Diet (pages 124-125).

Iron-fortified Adult Cereals

Don't feed your baby iron-fortified adult cereals and feel safe about your baby getting enough iron. As is discussed in the nutrition part of this book (page 547), there are different forms of iron, some of which are very poorly absorbed. Adult cereals may contain the poorly-absorbed type. Top brand baby cereals are fortified with the correct form of iron, the form that is well-assimilated by your baby.

Fluoride

Discuss a fluoride supplement with your pediatrician, especially if you have un-fluoridated drinking water. The daily dose of fluoride depends on the level of fluoride in your baby's drinking water and her age. If there is no fluoride in her drinking water, supplements are usually started before or during baby's sixth month. See more about fluoride in the nutrition part, page 553.

WARNING: Excessive intake of fluoride by your child from supplements, fluoridated water, concentrated baby formula mixed with fluoridated water, and the swallowing of fluoridated toothpaste and mouthwashes, can also cause dental problems. Remember to keep toothpaste, mouthwash, and fluoride supplements out of baby's reach. High fluoride levels have been found in some commercial baby foods, specifically chicken, which may put baby at risk for developing fluorosis if he regularly eats more than a few ounces. See more about fluorine toxicity on page 554.

REMEMBER: If you are using fluoridated water to mix your baby's formula, remember to discuss this fact with your pediatrician. Keep in mind that boiling fluoridated water does NOT remove the fluoride. As the water evaporates, the fluoride actually becomes more concentrated.

9. Mealtimes and Your Baby's Development

Feeding with Love

Your baby's feeding area should be a happy place to be! You will be spending a lot of time feeding your baby in the next few years. Try not to look at baby's mealtime as a chore. Rather, use it as a quality time for bonding with your beautiful baby. Spoon feeding your baby will then make you feel very loving and nurturing towards him, and he will become closer to you as he does when you breast or bottle feed him. Mealtimes are important to your baby's social development. During your baby's first year, he should develop a sense of trust, and relaxed mealtimes are a large part of the process. If his first experiences with food are within an atmosphere of tension and frustration, eating problems may develop that can last a lifetime. Your baby will actually grow and develop better if he is fed in a loving environment rather than one that is emotionally negative. **Feeding your baby involves much more than food.**

Entertainment with Dinner

Make silly faces at your baby, smile, and talk to her during mealtime. Do the classic "airplane into the hangar" routine. Sing her songs. My baby's favorite is "How Much Is That Doggie in the Window?" because I say "WOOF! WOOF!" between phrases. (My older boys have asked me to refrain from doing this when they have friends over.) However, you should not drag out baby's mealtimes beyond a 20-30 minute limit. The high chair's main purpose should be meal eating, and not entertainment.

If your baby gets antsy while you're getting her food ready, give her some finger food to keep her busy. Or place an interesting toy on her high chair, one that she doesn't get to play with at other times and that will endure crashing to the floor after hundreds of throws off the high chair tray. The invention of the suction toy has saved parents many backaches. During the actual meal, remove all toys so that your baby can concentrate on eating. Keep distractions to a minimum.

> **TIP:** Save her absolute favorite small toy for when you're dining out and she's ready to let out a howl. Please remove her from the restaurant if she's noisy. There are a lot of people around you paying for dinner and a babysitter so that they can enjoy a quiet, romantic meal

on a rare night out without the baby. By the way, if you are going to take a baby or toddler out to dinner, it's a good idea to take some Super Baby Food with you. You can slowly feed her to keep her busy during the wait for the meal (and it's a long wait if you have a toddler with you ☺).

Eating Is an Important Learning Process

Baby mealtimes are the foundation for a lifetime of the healthy attitudes and the eating habits so necessary for the prevention of adult eating disorders. Allow your baby to participate as much as possible in the feeding process. Eating, like walking or any other skill, must be learned. Self-feeding is important to your baby's physical development, eye-hand coordination, and manual dexterity. It is also important to her intellectual development. *Allowing your baby to freely self-feed shows her that you have confidence in her abilities, which increases her self-confidence, independence, and self-esteem.* Your tolerance, patience, and acceptance teaches her that the world is not a restrictive, formidable place and that she is free to be creative.

REMEMBER: Remember how important it is to have a positive, cheerful attitude each time you place your baby in his high chair or when you find yourself getting frustrated about the mess.

Pay close attention and you will see that meals are a special education in themselves. Learning begins with your baby's very first meal, as discussed under the section *Do Not Use an Infant Feeder* on page 21. Your baby also learns about cause and effect while eating: Raise my hand this way and the cracker reaches my mouth, tip the cup to this angle and liquid will flow out and into my mouth or onto the tray, drop the spoon and it falls to the floor and goes "ting" and mom/dad picks it up. The concept of object permanence is reinforced: The spoon still exists, even when it's on the floor and I cannot see it.

WARNING: Restricting a baby from self-feeding during his first year may cause feeding problems later on.

Praise the Good, Ignore the Bad

Most babies spit out food, throw food and dishes on the floor, and do other seemingly mischievous acts in the high chair. Your reaction will determine whether the behavior will continue, or worse, become a power ploy. Giving "normal baby behavior" attention, even negative attention, may reinforce the behavior. Keep a poker face when your baby does something in the high chair that annoys you—he will notice if you look upset and may begin to practice tormenting you.

TIP: Try making a game of eating to prevent food on the floor. Draw circles on the high chair tray with washable, non-toxic markers. The cup goes in one circle, the bowl stays in another, etc. You'll want to keep finger foods away from marker ink, though, even though it's non-toxic. Marker ink is not a Super Baby Food!

WARNING: If your baby looks adorable when she experiments and spits food over her chin for the first time, don't smile or laugh. She may enjoy your response and repeat the spitting after it's no longer cute.

DO Play with Your Food

Babies are messy eaters, so make sure that you have the feeding area set up properly (page 15). It is perfectly normal for a baby to dip his fingers into bowls of food, suck his fingers and fist, squeeze and smear food onto his face and the tray with his palm and fingers, mash it into his hair, spit it out or let it drool down his chin, blow it at you or on the wall, throw it on the floor along with cups and bowls, and spill his drinks. Be assured that to everything, there is a learning purpose. Your baby is not doing these things to provoke you—he is experimenting and learning about his environment and the texture and feel of his food. (See *House Rules*, page 118.) She explores her food just as she explores her toys. Restrain your impulse to be neat and encourage self-feeding. Your baby doesn't need Miss Manners's approval.

> **TIP:** Before self-feeding mealtimes, roll up baby's sleeves to keep them clean. Bibs and other "how to keep baby clean" tips are discussed on page 22.

> **TIP:** Although a wet wipe-up towel works fairly well to clean a baby's fingers, a finger bowl (like in fancy restaurants) works even better. Dip your little one's hands into the water and dry them with a wipe-up towel.

> **TIP:** When some babies begin self-feeding, their Moms get them used to wearing a hat or shower cap to keep their hair clean. Make it fun and your baby just might go for it.

Self-Feeding Babies Eat Slowly

It seems to take forever for a baby to feed himself, but once again, be patient. Grin and bear it when he endlessly explores his food before putting it in his mouth. As long as *some* eating is taking place, let him be. When it becomes all play, it's time to end the meal.

Self-Feeding Babies DO Eat Enough

Your baby will feed herself inefficiently, and you may wonder if more food is going into her mouth or onto the floor. She will consume much less food than when you spoon feed her, but be assured that she will eat enough for her growing needs. Remember the discussion on pages 51 and 53—a healthy baby will eat the proper amount of food and will not starve herself. Coincidentally, by the time your baby is skilled enough to self-feed, she will also be growing at a much slower rate and need fewer calories.

Eating and Your Baby's Physical Development

Babies develop at different rates. My premature twins did not start walking until they were 16 months old (!), but my youngest son walked at 11 months. The ages that babies walk and develop other skills quoted in baby books are based on studies of many babies, of course. For example, let's say 100 babies were observed and 75 of them walked by 13.5 months. The baby that walked the earliest did so at 10 months and the baby that took the longest walked at 15 months. This sample gives an age range when you can expect the normal baby to walk, but it certainly does not predict the exact age a particular baby will walk. Because of this averaging, you may find that one baby book author says your baby will walk by 12 months and another author says 13 months.

In this section, certain ages are quoted based on averages. If you are concerned that your baby is developing late according to these averages, please discuss the matter with your pediatrician. Do not be concerned and start losing sleep over it unless your pediatrician says that you should!

Although babies develop at different rates, they learn certain skills in predictable sequences. For example, all babies sit up before they walk. It's fascinating the way a baby develops! Did you know that your baby develops from the head down (called cephalocaudal)? She lifts her head before she gets up on elbows and hands, sits before she stands, and crawls before she walks. She develops from the center line of her body outward (proximodistal). Her shoulders move causing whole-arm movements before she makes fine movements with her fingers. She also develops from front to back (ventrodorsal). She uses her abdominal muscles to sit up before she uses her back muscles to sit unsupported. If you are interested in learning more, visit your local public library or a local university library and pick up some books on child development and/or pediatric nursing. You'll find much more detail in these college text-type books than you will in the paperbacks from bookstores.

Gross Motor Development vs Fine Motor Development

Gross motor development refers to maturation in large motor skills: posture, head balance, sitting, creeping, standing, and walking. Fine motor development refers to fine motor behavior, specifically the use of the hands and fingers in the reaching for, grasping, and manipulating an object (prehension). Gross and fine motor skills are functionally integrated together with other skills, such as visual acuity. Again, check out those textbooks. For an excellent graphic overview of the ages where gross and fine motor skills develop, look up *Denver Developmental Screening Test* in the index.

Here are some skills shown in the Denver Test and the ages (or range of ages) when you can expect your baby to develop them. The age when most babies will exhibit each skill is shown at the end of each line.

Sits without support : between 5-9 months : most by 6½ months.
Feeds self cracker : between 5-8 months : most by 6 months
Rakes raisin and attains : between 5-8 months : most by 6½ months
Thumb finger grasp : between 7-10½ months : most by 9½ months
Neat pincer grasp of raisin : between 9-14 months : most by 12½ months
Drinks from cup : between 10-16 months : most by 14 months
Walks well : between 11-15 months : most by 13½ months
Uses spoon, spilling little · between 13½-23½ months : most by 18 months

Oral Motor Development and Swallowing Development

As you surely have noticed, your newborn is a veritable sucking machine! A newborn's tongue is large in the mouth and is flat with sides thinned and cupped up to provide a channel for moving liquid backward for swallowing. Sucking pads in the cheeks help provide stability for sucking. Sucking automatically triggers swallowing. A newborn does not yet recognize the nipple by sight, because cognitive development is too immature. Your newborn will keep crying even though you are directly in front of him obviously getting ready the breast or bottle. But if you touch his lip or cheek, his mouth begins searching for the nipple (the rooting reflex). His mouth opens wide in order to accept the nipple and his lips move forward in order to surround the nipple. If you place your finger in his mouth, strong sucking is triggered almost immediately. His tongue will wrap around your finger and try to pump liquid from it. If you place your finger in the side of the mouth on top of the gum, his mouth will move up and down in a biting motion. This "phasic bite" is practice for the true chewing he will master in the future.

Between 4 and 6 months, your baby begins to move her mouth more voluntarily, overriding the primitive reflexes with which she was born. She now visually recognizes the nipple and moves forward deliberately. While you feed her, she is learning to handle solid foods within her mouth. Her tongue juts in and out to move the food back into her mouth for swallowing. But her jaw, tongue, and lips move together as one unit and she cannot control them independently. Between 6-7½ months, she will begin to chew foods, or because she has no molars at this age, to "gum" foods.

At around 7 to 9 months, your baby learns to move his jaw independently of his tongue and lips. He now opens his jaw to accept the spoon, and his lower lip and upper lip work to remove food from the spoon. He's beginning to coordinate the taking in of food with swallowing and breathing. He can transfer food from the center of his tongue to the sides of his mouth and from the side of his mouth to the center of his tongue, but not yet all the way across the inside his mouth from one side to the other. Although he can get a cracker into his mouth, close his mouth and break off a piece, he will not use precise jaw movements until he is about 9 months old. By then he will be able to make a controlled and more mature bite. By 9½ months, drooling will be significantly reduced because he can better control his lips, tongue, and jaw.

When your baby is 10 to 12 months of age, you will notice that her eating is becoming much more mature. Her bite is more controlled. Her upper lip works better to clean food off the spoon than it did when she was younger. Her cheeks and mouth work to move food around in her mouth, and her mouth is more often closed while she is eating. Her swallowing skills are much improved.

Eating skills continue to mature as your child goes through the toddler years. By the time he is 18 months he will lose very little food from his mouth while eating. His jaw, lips, tongue, and cheek movements will become more finely graded. From 18-24 months, he will begin to practice transferring food from one side of his mouth to the other—a motion that will be perfected by his second birthday.

At two years old, he probably will use his tongue to lick his lips clean and will use his upper teeth to clean his lower lip. He will be able to chew with his mouth closed and has learned to move food around well in his mouth. His jaw openings become better sized for the incoming food.

By his third birthday, he will be able to keep his mouth fully closed while chewing, and even while transferring food across the mouth. He will be able to "feel" food on his lips, and use his tongue to clean it off, and he will use his tongue to clean between his gums and cheeks. The first semblance of adult table manners may appear by your baby's second birthday, but many babies prefer to remain very messy until they are well into their third year. Be patient—civility is bound to come before your child's third birthday. ☺

The Cup

At First, Hold the Cup While Your Baby Drinks

It may take many months (perhaps until age 16-18 months) for your baby to learn to drink *neatly* from a cup, but until then keep plenty of those wipe-up towels around. Beginning at about 5 or 6 months, let your baby take small sips from a cup while you hold it. There may be a few chokes rather than swallows at first. Your baby should be drinking water as soon as he begins eating solid foods (page 61), and it's a good idea to give him this water in a cup after he finishes eating and between meals. Start with about a tablespoon of water and gradually increase the amount. He'll soon become comfortable enough with the cup to grab it and try to drink himself. Let him. He may play with it for a while first, which is a step in learning. It's OK if he spills because there is only a little water in it.

Training Cups—Baby Cups with Spouts

You can buy baby cups that have spouts with holes to minimize spilling. If there is an air hole on the opposite side of the spout, it means that liquid will come out faster—you may want to start with a cup without the extra air hole (or cover the hole with tape until baby is older). Some baby cups have different spout attachments that allow for varying liquid flow speeds. The newest invention is the spill-less cup, which doesn't spill even when it tips over.

Young babies have an easier time handling a cup with handles on both sides. I found that the light plastic cups with handles don't do well in the dishwasher—their handles get caught on everything and they are so light that they flip upside down. Handle-less baby cups made from a heavy plastic stay in place on the top rack. Put the tops from the cups in one of those dishwasher baskets.

TIP: To help baby's wet hands get a grip around a handle-less cup, wrap one or two thick rubber bands (like those around broccoli bunches) around the middle of the cup. Or use adhesive tape or pieces of self-sticking bathtub appliques instead of rubber bands, although it gets cruddy after a while. Or cut off the cuff from a small clean sock and stretch it around the cup.

MONEY SAVER: If you don't want to invest in a dishwasher basket, use those green plastic containers in which strawberries are sold. Connect two together with twist ties to form a box for holding silicon nipples, baby bottle caps, cookie cutters, and other small items. Mesh onion bags also work well as dishwasher baskets. Or place small items in a partition in the silverware basket and stuff a net scrubber in the top to hold them in.

By 7-8 months, let him feed himself his single daily serving of diluted fruit juice from the spouted cup. Remember that he may want to just play with it for the first several weeks. Until about 9 months, your baby will drink from it using the same sucking pattern as he would from a bottle.

When he becomes fairly skilled, go all the way and give him an uncovered plastic cup, but fill with only small amounts of liquid to make clean-up easier. Don't make him feel bad when he spills—everyone has to start somewhere. Remember that learning to handle the cup is helping to develop his hand-to-mouth coordination.

TIP: Drink from a cup while your baby is watching. Babies love to imitate and it's a fun, natural way for them to learn.

From 10-15 months, he will still hold the cup with both hands and may drop it on the floor when finished. Gradually, he will stop using those up and down jaw movements as he is drinking. He will become more skilled at taking several continuous swallows without stopping to take a breath. Observe how his hands, wrist, and elbows consciously work in unison to adjust the angle of the cup in order to successfully move it to his mouth. During these months he will eventually perfect the motion and get the liquid into his mouth without spilling most of the time. By 18 months, he will use the rim of the cup for stability.

TIP: If you can't stand the spills, let your baby practice drinking from a cup in the bathtub, but make sure he doesn't try to drink the bath water when you turn your head.

TIP: Tuck a wipe-up towel between his neck and his bib to prevent drips from going down his shirt. Fold the towel in half to give an extra layer of protection.

TIP: Protect your furniture by teaching baby to place her cup on a coaster. A large plastic lid from a margarine tub makes a large coaster—a bigger target on which baby can place her cup.

By 18-24 months, she no longer needs both hands to hold a cup. Your one-fisted drinker has perfected the tilt of the cup at just the right moment to tip liquid into her mouth. There will continue to be some loss of liquid and spillage until her second birthday, but at least now she is putting the cup back on the table and not throwing it to the floor. Sometime after her second birthday, she will be able to get herself a drink and will even be able to pour from a pitcher and will most likely insist, in the stubborn toddler fashion, on doing it herself.

Gradual Weaning to the Cup

At about 8-10 months, experts recommend that you start weaning your baby off the bottle or breast by giving her formula or expressed breast milk in a cup with meals. Many pediatricians recommend discontinuing the bottle entirely by the age of 18 months.

> **REMEMBER:** The need to suck will continue well into your baby's second year. In my opinion, there's no need to hurry your baby off the breast/bottle. Weaning should be done slowly and gradually and with love. Force should never be used, neither should subtle coaxing or manipulation.

Wean your baby slowly by eliminating one bottle at a time. Begin by substituting the bottle with a cup of formula at the midday meal. Wait several days or weeks before omitting another bottle. The next bottle to be replaced with the cup should be the bottle with supper, then the morning bottle, and last the bedtime bottle. It may take more than 6 months before your baby gets all of his liquids from the cup and completely gives up the bottle. Formula should continue to be given in the cup until your baby becomes one year old, when you can start giving cow's milk.

> **TIP:** To help your baby adjust to drinking from a cup, let him drink directly from his open-topped bottle. Or stick a straw into the bottle.

> **TIP:** When your baby begins drinking from a straw, cut it down to baby-size. Cut the straw so that it extends no more than an inch or two above the rim of the cup. And how much fun it is when she discovers how to blow bubbles in her cup! (By the way, bubble blowing is great for your baby's oral muscle development.)

Some Babies Abruptly Stop Breastfeeding

Be aware that some babies wean themselves from the breast at about 10 months, an age where physical progress advances quickly. A friend of mine felt abandoned and rejected when her baby decided one day to quit breastfeeding cold turkey. It is very disconcerting to suddenly have to give up that special intimacy with your baby. If you ever need someone to talk to about breastfeeding, there is a compassionate ear available at your local La Leche League. To find your local La Leche representative, call 800-LALECHE or call the maternity department of your local hospital. I found my rep very knowledgeable and helpful whenever I had a problem with breastfeeding.

Finger Foods

Finger foods are food pieces that your baby can pick up and eat by himself. Place them in front of your baby directly on his clean high chair tray, on his feeding table, or on an unbreakable plate. Ideas for finger foods are listed in the box on page 291.

First for Practice, Then for Nutrition

At first, finger foods are mostly tools for practice in self-feeding, which will help your baby to develop manual dexterity and give him more control of his jaw muscles. Practice at finger feeding also promotes the skills necessary for later self-feeding with a spoon. It may take up to his 9th or 10th month until he aims accurately enough to get good amounts of finger foods into his mouth. When these skills develop, finger foods will become an important nutritional part of your baby's diet. Until then, your baby will get the majority of his food from your spoon-feeding.

The Rake

Before the age of 6 months, your baby scoops up small objects by using the outer palm (pinky finger side) of his hand in a rake-like motion. Because he's not yet skilled at picking up small bits of food, first finger foods should consist of larger food pieces, such as teething biscuits or crackers, strips of bread, French toast, soft fruit wedges or veggies cooked until they're soft, whole bagels, pancakes, etc.

The Palmar Grasp

At around 5 months, the palmar grasp develops. Finger foods are pulled against the palm with the fingers—the thumb is not used and sticks out like a sore thumb. By about 7 months, thumb opposition begins to develop and finger foods will be held against the palm by both the fingers and the thumb (radial-palmar grasp). At around 8-9 months, the fingertips, instead of the palm and fingers, begin to hold the food against the tip of the thumb (radial-digital grasp).

> **REMEMBER:** Along with learning the skill of grasping food comes the repeated practice of opening the hand to release the food—much of the time to the floor! Your baby must practice releasing objects voluntarily, so please be patient with your little one.

The Pincer Grasp

Beginning sometime between 8 and 10 months, your baby will begin to use her index, ring, and pinky fingers against the lower thumb to grasp an object. This *crude pincer grasp* eventually develops into a *neat pincer grasp*, where index finger and thumb delicately meet to pick up a small object. This neat pincer grasp (also called the *fine pincer grasp*), which usually develops around 12 months, allows baby to become skilled at finger feeding small bits of food.

Small and Soft Food Bits

The food bits should be small enough to prevent choking, about the size of a Cheerio®. And they should be soft so that baby can easily chew them or "gum" them with her sensitive gums. On page 291 in the recipes part, you will find a list of finger food ideas. Next time you go to the supermarket, look in the baby food section for jarred finger foods. Name brands include ½-inch pieces of diced apples, peaches, carrots, and green beans. Some of these have added salt and all of them, in my opinion, are overpriced. You can easily make your own finger foods by cooking, dicing, and freezing foods yourself— see page 292.

WARNING: Give your baby only 2 or 3 bits of finger foods at a time, otherwise he will probably stuff his cheeks until he looks like a chipmunk. An overfull mouth may lead to choking.

TIP: Sometimes a baby will have trouble picking up pieces of wet fruits or other foods because they are slippery. Help your baby to get a grip by rolling the food pieces in rolled oats/oatmeal ground to a fine powder in the blender. Of, if your baby is old enough for wheat products, use whole wheat flour or wheat germ. If the wheat germ is too chunky, grind it to a fine powder in the blender.

WARNING: Be careful with slippery pieces of food. They are more likely to slide into the throat or be inhaled into the windpipe. Coat them to make them less slippery as described in the previous tip.

From 12-18 months, you should continue giving your baby plenty of finger foods. At this age, finger feeding will cause more food to reach his mouth than when he spoon feeds. A sandwich is likely to get ripped apart for its filling alone, with the bread discarded. My little guy liked to eat only the peanut butter and leave the crumbled bread in tatters on his tray. When his appetite waned, the food flinging or finger painting began.

Your toddler will become a real pro at finger feeding between 18-24 months.

Teething Foods

Your baby will be getting teeth from 4 months to 24 months, maybe even sooner. You can start giving her teething foods when she is able to bring them to her mouth with her hand—sometime after 5-6 months. Chewing on hard or cool foods will help relieve the teething pain in her gums. Offer her hard toast, hard crackers, cool juices, or a cool baby-safe spoon. Freeze a fat hard carrot and let her suck on it, but make sure that no pieces will break off and that it is thick enough so that it will not split and cause choking.

WARNING: With all frozen foods, make sure they are not so cold that they will burn your baby's mouth (example is a child's tongue stuck on a metal pipe at the playground). Rinse frozen food under cool water for a few seconds to prevent ice burns.

TIP: An inexpensive teether is a sterilized sturdy nipple filled with sterile water and frozen. Screw nipple on top of a bottle and baby will hold it easily.

WARNING: Never give your baby paregoric to relieve teething pain, as your mother or grandmother tells you was common several decades ago. Paregoric contains barbiturates and may be habit forming.

Self-Feeding with a Spoon and Fork

Sometime between 8 and 12 months of age, your baby may grab the spoon and attempt to feed herself. Let her. Encourage her. Before she attempts to grab the spoon herself, give her a spoon to play with during mealtimes. Accept the banging and clanging—again, it's part of the learning process. When she begins to use the spoon for its real purpose, she will have trouble and will most likely turn the spoon upside down immediately before it gets to her mouth. To help her along, give her foods that will tend to stay stuck to the spoon when it turns over, such as mashed banana, cereal, or yogurt thickened with a little ground cooked grain or wheat germ.

TIP: When your baby first starts to use the spoon and has not yet developed enough skills, use two spoons. Let her practice feeding herself with one spoon, while you get a few spoonfuls in with another. Or use two spoons and swap with your baby—an empty spoon for a full spoon.

Proficiency at self-feeding with the spoon takes many months. She will master moving the spoon from bowl to mouth at around 11-12 months of age, before she is able to successfully scoop food from the bowl into the spoon. You can help by filling the spoon with food for her, but let her move it to her mouth and eat. This will help develop her eye-hand coordination. At 12 months, she may still be turning her spoon upside down right before it reaches her mouth, but within the next few months she will master the spoon and get most of the food into her mouth. Eat with a spoon while your baby is watching. Your baby loves to imitate and it's a fun, natural way for her to learn.

MONEY SAVER: If she keeps spilling the bowl, you can buy a baby bowl with suction cups on the bottom to anchor it to the tray. I find that a double-sided suction soap holder under a Corelle® bowl is cheaper and better. Corelle dishes are unbreakable and better than plastic in the dishwasher. The suction soap holder can be washed with the wipe-up towels.

At 15 months, your baby will probably use the spoon to feed himself, although much of the food gets spilled accidentally or deliberately. By 18-21 months, he becomes more skilled with the spoon, but still looks baby-ish as he uses it because he holds his elbow, arm, and spoon horizontally and raises all three to move spoon to mouth. (This is the proximodistal development mentioned on page 74.) His other hand comes in handy to help with food on his lips that hasn't quite made it into his mouth. The helping hand may also place dropped food or food from the bowl into the spoon.

From 18-24 months, whole grain cereals (Super Porridge) should remain part of his daily diet. The oatmeal-like consistency of Super Porridge makes it easy for him to self-feed with a spoon. His other meals should become more coarse in texture and have many soft lumps of food in them. It's time to start letting him use a safe plastic baby **fork** for learning to spear lumps of food.

By her second birthday, even though her spoon feeding skills are mature, she may still resort to fingers and feeling the food's texture. She may even smell the food. Let her be.

> **WARNING:** Watch your toddler carefully as he eats: Toddlers sometimes get tired of chewing in the middle of a meal and tend to swallow food whole.

Between 24-36 months, your toddler knows whether to use his fingers or a spoon to eat the food before him. He has his black belt in spoon use, although he occasionally spills because his eye-hand coordination is still developing . His skills with the fork are improving and by the end of his third year he will hold it fisted. At three years, he will be able to cut food with his fork. He will be able to spoon his individual portion of food from a serving dish. His mature chewing pattern now mimics that of an adult, with a circular action of the jaw. He may choose moist food over drier foods because he knows from experience that they are easier to chew. Although he may still enjoy playing with his food, don't end the meal as long as there is *some* eating occurring. Your little one is probably still a messy eater, but he is improving and spilling less and less food from his spoon and his cup.

Table Foods

As early as 7 months, your baby might start eating at the same time as the rest of the family, although she will be eating her own baby foods. Pull her high chair up to the table and let her join the clan. Most table foods are not appropriate for your baby until she is at least one year old. At 9 or 10 months, she can start eating some unseasoned foods from the family table to which she has been previously introduced, such as mashed potato. Mash the potatoes and take out a baby-sized portion BEFORE you add the salt, pepper, and butter. Or fork-mash some soft unseasoned vegetables, pasta, cheese, etc. By her first birthday, she should be ready to become a full-fledged member at the family table.

> **TIP:** If your family uses placemats, use a paper towel or two for your baby's placemat. Replace when spills occur. At meal's end, wipe up with the paper towel.

Babies imitate the things they see grown-ups do, so try not to let your baby see you using the salt shaker. The salt habit is something our babies (and we adults) can do without.

> **TIP:** Feeding your baby at the table can take your attention away from the other members of your family. You may want to compromise and feed your baby most of his meal before family mealtime, and let baby finger feed himself at the table while you enjoy the rest of your family.

Traveling Foods

Unfortunately, homemade frozen baby food cubes don't travel well and neither does homemade Super Porridge because it keeps in the refrigerator for only 2-3 days. Traveling is the time to use Earth's Best organic jars of baby food and boxed whole grain baby cereals.

For baby emergencies, it's a good idea to keep a baby travel bag in the trunk of your car. This is in addition to the usual diaper bag that you carry everywhere. The travel bag is for when you have forgotten to pack something in the diaper bag, for when your baby gets wet or dirty and needs a change of clothes, or for other emergencies. I keep my baby emergency supplies in the trunk in an old duffle bag.

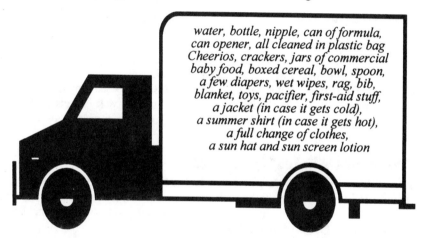

water, bottle, nipple, can of formula,
can opener, all cleaned in plastic bag
Cheerios, crackers, jars of commercial
baby food, boxed cereal, bowl, spoon,
a few diapers, wet wipes, rag, bib,
blanket, toys, pacifier, first-aid stuff,
a jacket (in case it gets cold),
a summer shirt (in case it gets hot),
a full change of clothes,
a sun hat and sun screen lotion

TIP: If you're short on clothes, keep a change of clothes in the trunk that is slightly too big or too small. Who cares if they don't fit perfectly in a baby emergency!

MONEY SAVER: Don't buy expensive travel sizes of wipes and lotions. When your regular size wipes or lotions have only a few more uses, open new ones and put the "almost empties" in the trunk. Squeeze every last bit out of a diaper cream (or toothpaste) tube by rolling up a pencil from the end, or use a small rolling pin to push the contents up from the end of the tube, or just step on the tube with your foot. In a pinch, use wax paper or a plastic freezer bag as a waterproof changing mat.

TIP: Keep a large paintbrush in the trunk of your car to dust sand and dirt from kids' shoes. Or keep empty freezer bags for kids' muddy shoes to save your car's carpet.

TIP: Let your kids use a homemade lap table (page 286) for doing artwork in the car. Use it to store art materials when not in use.

10. A Month-By-Month Summary Schedule for the Introduction of Foods in Baby's First Year

Pages 86-87 show a summary table with the ages to introduce your baby to most of the Super Baby Foods. There seems to be no consensus among the experts on which new foods to introduce at which ages. And the more books you read, the more confused you become. The one fact that experts agree on is: Wait until your baby is at least one year old before introducing egg whites, honey, or corn syrup. Most experts say to wait until one year (some say 6-9 months old) before introducing citrus fruits/juices and wheat.

Always Consult with Your Pediatrician

Be sure to discuss your baby's diet with your pediatrician. And remember that if her advice and mine conflict, follow her advice. New knowledge about diet and nutrition is constantly being discovered. Your pediatrician will have the latest information on what is best for your baby.

Take this book with you to your pediatrician's office. Hand it to her opened to the time schedule on the next two pages. Give her a red pen and ask her to modify the schedule as she sees fit.

Remember to ask your pediatrician about:

❧ The **amount of water and juice** your baby should be drinking and whether she would recommend the local **tap water**, bottled water, or filtered water. If she recommends a drinking water that is not fluoridated, ask her if she recommends prescription vitamins containing **fluoride**.

❧ If you're going to feed your baby homemade cereals and your baby is breast feeding and not drinking an iron-fortified formula, remember to ask her if you should give your baby supplemental **iron drops**.

TIME SAVER: You probably will be constantly referencing the summary schedule on the next two pages. Save time and frustration when looking for it by folding a piece of clear tape over the edge of the page like a tab. You can even place a small piece of paper within the tape with a description of the page. Do this for all pages that you use frequently. See Quick Reference Pages Index on page 593.

TIP: Keep notes on what you want to ask your pediatrician and remember to take the notes with you when you go for those well-baby visits. I've had the experience of forgetting to ask questions I was SURE I was going to remember to ask. There's something about being in charge of a baby, especially when you are out in public, that makes you incapable of thinking clearly. At least I hope that's how it is with everyone—it's certainly that way with me. ☺

Questions I must remember to ask my pediatrician:

Summary Schedule for Introduction of Foods During Baby's First Year

Best First Foods for Baby	Best Foods for the Beginning Eater	Foods for Baby 6 Months or Older	Foods for Baby 7 Months or Older
ripe avocado ripe banana iron-fortified infant rice cereal cooked, puréed sweet potatoes	single grain iron-fortified commercial infant cereals: barley millet oatmeal whole-milk yogurt (for babies older than 6 months) cooked, strained fruits: apricots nectarines peaches pears plums prunes	homemade whole grain cereals: brown rice millet oat raw mild fruits: mango papaya pears winter squash	homemade mixed cereals tofu cottage cheese hard-cooked egg yolk (not egg white) peaches cooked, puréed: asparagus carrots green beans peas summer squash white potatoes diluted, strained, mild fruit juices: apple apricot grape papaya pear peach prune maybe orange juice
Mix finely puréed food with enough liquid until it pours off the spoon into baby's mouth. Food should be only slightly thicker than breast milk/formula.		Food should still be puréed or mashed until it is a smooth and lumpless consistency. Food can be slightly thicker than for beginners— the consistency of thick cream.	

Please remember to verify this schedule with your pediatrician.

Summary Schedule for Introduction of Foods During Baby's First Year

Foods for Baby 8 Months or Older	Foods for Baby 9 Months or Older	Foods for Baby 10 Months or Older	Foods for Baby One Year or Older
tahini ground nuts ground seeds brewer's yeast powdered kelp natural cheeses apricot apple cantaloupe honeydew kiwi fruit plums watermelon broccoli okra cooked parsley maybe wheat germ peeled and quartered grapes (not whole grapes)	dried beans, lentils, split peas, ground and cooked pineapple Brussels sprouts cauliflower spinach beets kale eggplant rhubarb rutabaga turnips finely chopped raw parsley cooked greens cooked onion	thinned creamy (not chunky) peanut butter other thinned nut butters homemade bulgur cereal cooked whole grain cornmeal with the germ whole grain pasta ground sprouts finely grated, raw: summer squash carrots greens sweet peppers	cow's milk citrus fruits citrus fruit juices tomatoes tomato juice hard-cooked egg white honey strawberries, blueberries, and other berries (not whole, cut into small pieces)
Gradually increase thickness, then chunkiness of food. Offer bite-sized pieces of soft finger foods. Watch very carefully for choking or gagging.		Foods should still be fork-mashed or puréed. Never leave your baby alone while eating.	

Please remember to verify this schedule with your pediatrician.

11. Feeding Your Super Baby During the First Few Weeks

> **INTRODUCE THESE FOODS TO BEGINNING EATERS:**
>
> *ripe avocado*
>
> *ripe banana*
>
> *sweet potatoes*
>
> *yogurt, whole-milk (6 months or older)*
>
> *commercial iron-fortified single-grain infant cereals:*
> *rice*
> *barley*
> *millet*
> *oatmeal*
>
> *mild fruits, cooked and strained:*
> *apricots*
> *nectarines*
> *peaches*
> *pears*
> *plums*
> *prunes*

Baby's Second Meal of Solid Foods

Your beginning eater has had his very first meal. It's now day two of solid foods and he's ready for another meal. The amount he is eating depends on his age and weight and his unique appetite. If he is 6 months or older, you may want to look at the additional foods that you can give him listed on page 94 at the beginning of the next chapter, *Feeding Your Super Baby at 6 Months*.

The First Week of Solid Foods

For the first week (or at least 4 days), give her one meal each day consisting of one single food—the same food you fed to her in her very first meal. As with her first meal, give her some breast milk or formula before the solid food so that she is not too hungry when you spoon-feed her. After she finishes the food, you can give her a little boiled and cooled water (pages 61-64) and the rest of the breast or formula feeding. For the first few days, each meal should be no more than a tablespoon before mixing with liquid.

The Second Week of Solid Foods

At the beginning of the second week of solid foods, introduce your baby to one new food from the list above. Wait 4-7 days (the Four-day Wait Rule, page 28) and watch for allergy symptoms before introducing another new food.

Until Your Baby is 6 Months Old

Continue introducing foods from the list above using the Four-day Wait Rule (page 28). Your baby will gradually (or quickly if he is older) eat larger food servings and be ready for two meals per day, as discussed later in this chapter.

As your baby nears 6 months, he will become more interested and cooperative in the feeding process. Your beginning eater will develop more mouth and lip control as he gains practice in eating. You may notice him using his lower lip to "hold" the spoon as you feed him. He may draw his lips together as the spoon is exiting his mouth in order to keep the food inside. As his trunk control improves and he sits with more stability, his hands and arms will become active during feeding and he will eventually reach for food or the spoon. At first he may insert a finger or two into his mouth to help him to swallow food. The fingers help him to suck—the only method he employed for swallowing before the advent of solid foods. At about 5½ months he may be able to use his hands to feed himself a teething biscuit. If you have not already done so, please read the chapter *Mealtimes and Your Baby's Development* beginning on page 71.

Preparation of Foods for Beginners

Avocado, banana, cooked sweet potatoes, and yogurt were discussed in *Baby's Very First Meal*, pages 13-14, 574. The single grain cereals listed in the box on the previous page are referring to store-bought, brand-name, iron-fortified cereals. Simply mix the cereal with breast milk, formula, or water, or follow the directions on the box. I suggest using Earth's Best brand, because it is organic and whole grain (page 13). If your baby is 6 months or older, you may want to skip to the next section, *Feeding Your Super Baby at 6 Months*. Six-month olds have digestive systems mature enough to handle homemade whole grain cereals, which are much healthier for your baby and pocketbook than commercial brands.

Most Fruits Should Be Cooked for Babies Younger than 6 Months Before 6 months of age, it is best not to feed raw fruits to your baby (except for bananas and avocado). Cook fruits to make them soft and more digestible for your baby's immature system. Directions on how to cook fruits are in Part II, page 200. If the fruit contains little bits of peel, it is important to strain them out so that your baby doesn't choke on them. I strongly suggest straining all cooked fruits, even though you think there are no peel pieces, just to be on the safe side. See how to strain foods on page 152.

Food Consistency for Beginners

As in your baby's very first meal, food should be puréed to the smoothest consistency. Mash foods very well with a fork or purée in a blender until all lumps are completely gone. Mix the finely puréed food with enough liquid (breast milk, formula, or water) until the food is very thin and will pour off the spoon into your baby's mouth. *Food should be only slightly thicker than breast milk or formula.*

Daily Amount of Foods for Beginners

Your baby's first meal consisted of only one teaspoon of solid food. Over the next few weeks, very gradually increase this serving size to 3-4 tablespoons of solid food (before mixing with liquid).

Sample Daily Feeding Schedule for Beginners
One Meal Per Day

Upon Awakening	breast/bottle
Morning	breast/bottle
Noon	give partial feeding from breast/bottle, then solid food, then water, then finish with the breast/bottle
Afternoon	breast/bottle
Evening	breast/bottle
Bedtime	breast/bottle or bottle of cooled boiled water

Daily Amount of Liquids for Beginners

Breast milk or formula is the top priority food. Your baby should be breastfeeding at least 5 times a day or drinking 32 ounces of formula a day. If your baby is not drinking this amount, decrease the amount of solid foods. Your baby should drink a little bit of water after each meal, as discussed on pages 61-64. Limit your baby's water intake to at most 4-6 ounces (maybe more on hot days) per day in order to assure she is drinking enough breast milk or formula.

Two Meals a Day

When you think your baby is hungry enough for two meals a day, offer her a second meal in the late afternoon/early evening, as shown in the schedule on the next page. Each meal should consist of only one food serving. For the first few days, make the evening meal the same food as the morning meal. Then the evening meal can be a different food from the morning. Remember that a new food introduced in the evening can cause an allergic reaction in the middle of the night. To prevent loss of sleep, introduce new foods early in the day.

Sample Daily Feeding Schedule for Beginners
Two Meals Per Day

Upon Awakening	breast/bottle
Morning	partial feeding from breast/bottle and a new food
Noon	breast/bottle
Afternoon	partial feeding from breast/bottle and one food serving (same food as in morning or a previously introduced food)
Evening	breast/bottle
Bedtime	breast/bottle or bottle of cooled boiled water
Plus water after and between meals.	

Two Different Foods in the Same Meal

Several days after your baby is eating two different foods a day, you may feed her two different foods in the same meal, such as cereal with bananas. Refer to the feeding schedule on page 95, which is the feeding schedule for babies 6 months old. Remember not to introduce two new foods at the same time, because if your baby has an allergic reaction, you won't know which food caused it.

Which One First, the Food or the Breast Milk/Bottle?

After your baby has been eating solid foods for about a month, you can start the meal by feeding her the solid food first and then end with the breast/bottle. The first time you try this, see how she reacts to it. If she'll take the solid food first before any milk from the breast/bottle, fine; otherwise, give her the breast/bottle first and try again a week later.

How Large is a Food Serving?

In the previous table, you see the words "food serving." The amount of food in a serving varies tremendously with the day and the baby. The formal, technical definition of a baby food serving is "however much your baby will eat." The point is that there is no absolute size or standardized amount of food that constitutes a serving for a baby. But just to give you a rough idea, the hypothetical average beginning eater's food serving probably falls somewhere between 1 and 4 tablespoons.

A major part of the Super Baby Food System is the preparation of ice cube-sized frozen vegetable cubes. For beginners, a food serving is generally ½ veggie cube to 2 veggie cubes. (Depending on the size of the cubes in your ice cube trays and how full you make them, each cube holds about 2 tablespoons, give or take a few teaspoons. I never said it was an exact system! So 1 food cube is about 2 tablespoons and ½ of a food cube is about a tablespoon.) Start by giving your beginning eater a food cube made by filling the ice cube about half way. If she wants another, don't worry, she'll let you know.

Another major part of the Super Baby Food System is the home-making of whole grain cereals, where dry uncooked grains are mixed into boiling water to cook. A food serving of homemade cereal for beginning eaters is ¼-½ cup of *cooked* cereal. This equates to 1-2 tablespoons of dry uncooked cereal, before it's stirred into boiling water (page 212). Of course, as your baby gets closer to her first birthday, serving sizes will become a little larger. A one year old may be eating ¾ cup (or larger) of cooked cereal on one sitting.

A beginner's food serving of yogurt is ¼-½ cup. Again, this is just to give you a rough idea. Give your baby as much as he will eat. But watch carefully for signals that he has had enough, and don't try to feed him more food after he loses interest.

Similar-Sized Food Servings

To balance your baby's diet among the food groups, keep food servings about the same size. For example, if your baby's vegetable servings are currently 2 food cubes, keep the fruit servings about the same size: 2 food cubes = 4 tablespoons = ¼ cup. Make cooked cereal servings twice the size of fruit or veggie servings, because cooked cereal is mostly water. For 2 veggie food cubes or ¼ cup fruit, an similar-sized cereal serving would be ½ cup of cooked cereal. (A half cup of cooked cereal is only a few tablespoons of ground dry cereal before it is mixed with water.) There's no need to become obsessive and use a scientifically-accurate scale to weigh servings, just approximate by eye-balling them.

REMEMBER: Keeping food servings similar in size will help to promote in your baby's diet a nice balance of nutrients from the different food groups.

Feeding Your Baby the Super Baby Food Diet Before 6 Months

Please read about the Super Baby Food Diet on pages 119-148. **Be sure to discuss your baby's diet with your pediatrician.** And remember that if her advice and mine conflict, please follow her advice. New knowledge about diet and nutrition is constantly being discovered. Your pediatrician will have the latest information on what is best for your baby.

Vegetables and Fruits

At this age, feeding your beginner the Super Baby Food Diet is a matter of making your own vegetables and fruits, instead of buying the commercial jars of baby vegetables and fruits. Instructions on how to prepare vegetables and fruits are given in Part II, beginning on page 178. For babies this young, I would suggest purchasing only certified organically-grown fruits and vegetables. Until your baby is 6 months old, remember to feed her only those foods listed for beginning eaters in the box on page 88 and use the Four-day Wait Rule (page 28). Please re-read the warnings about possible pesticides on some fruits and vegetables on page 13 and page 38.

Grains and Cereals

Until your baby is 6 months old, she doesn't have the proper enzymes to digest the whole grains in homemade rice and millet cereals. Feeding them to her may cause some digestive problems, like gas. The commercial boxed baby cereals are well-digested by a baby younger than 6 months, because they are processed and refined and not whole grain. It's up to your pediatrician and you whether you should feed them to your baby. These cereals are processed and I feel very strongly about feeding only whole, unrefined foods to a baby, which is why I chose not to give them to any of my babies.

Enough Iron is Extremely Important

If you also choose not to feed your baby iron-fortified commercial baby cereals and you are breastfeeding (and not using iron-fortified formula), make sure your baby is getting enough iron. Discuss iron supplement drops with your pediatrician. The iron stores with which babies are born begin to deplete as early as age 4 months, and possibly as early as 2 months for premature infants. If you'd like to go with commercial cereal because of the iron-fortification, check out the Earth's Best Brand (page 13). It is iron-fortified, but unlike the other top brands, it is organic and whole grain. Read more about importance of enough iron in your baby's diet beginning on page 69.

12. Feeding Your Super Baby at 6 Months

```
┌─────────────────────────────────────────────────────────────┐
│           INTRODUCE THESE FOODS TO YOUR 6 MONTH OLD           │
│                                                               │
│         homemade                      winter squash           │
│    single-grain cereals:           raw mild fruits:           │
│         brown rice                      papaya                │
│           millet                        mango                 │
│      rolled oats/oatmeal                pears                 │
└─────────────────────────────────────────────────────────────┘
```

Six months is a milestone in the development of your baby's digestive system, which now produces the enzymes necessary for the digestion of your own homemade whole grain cereals. At 6 months, cereals should be made with only one grain—don't start mixing grains together yet. There are instructions on preparing and storing homemade whole grain cereals in Part II, beginning on page 207. Your 6-month old is also able to eat the raw mild fruits listed in box above.

At 6 months, your baby is putting everything into her mouth that she can get her little hands on, which helps her to develop self-feeding skills. She may be able to feed herself a cracker and the soft strips of finger food listed under *The Rake* on page 79. Watch your baby carefully for gagging and choking, and please re-read the section *Choking Hazards*, pages 40-42. Although she holds her bottle and may hold a cup by the handle while trying to manipulate it, her skills are sorely lacking. If you have not already done so, please read the chapter *Mealtimes and Your Baby's Development* beginning on page 71. Offer her the teething foods suggested on page 80.

Food Consistency for Babies 6 Months Old

Your 6-month old is learning how to transfer food around within her mouth. She may now have a few teeth and you may notice within the next few months that she makes chewing motions when you feed her. But because she will not get her first set of molars until she is well into her second year, she will not be able to grind her foods for a long time. Foods for your baby of 6 months still should be made into a thin, very smooth, liquidy purée.

Daily Amount of Foods for Babies 6 Months Old

Your baby should be eating anywhere from 2 to 6 food servings a day. Each vegetable and fruit serving should be from 1 to 2 tablespoons, or ½ food cube to 1 food cube. Each cooked cereal serving should be ¼ to ½ cup. Sizes of food servings are discussed on page 92.

Daily Amount of Liquids for Babies 6 Months Old

Breast milk or formula is the top priority food. Your baby should be breastfeeding at least 5 times a day or drinking 32 ounces of formula a day. If your baby is not drinking this minimum amount, decrease the amount of solid foods you offer him.

Your baby should be drinking water after each meal and between meals. Limit your baby's water intake to at most 4-8 ounces (maybe more on hot days) per day in order to assure she is drinking enough breast milk or formula. Please read about water on pages 61-64.

Sample Daily Feeding Schedule for Babies 6 Months Old

Upon Awakening	breast/bottle
Morning	one or two food servings and breast/bottle
Noon	breast/bottle
Afternoon	one or two food servings and breast/bottle
Evening	breast/bottle
Bedtime	breast or bottle of cooled boiled water
Plus water after and between meals. If your baby still seems hungry, offer her a Super Snack in the evening.	

Feeding Your Baby the Super Baby Food Diet At 6 Months .

If you have not already done so, please read about the Super Baby Food Diet on pages 119-148. Please be sure to read about having enough iron in your baby's diet on page 69.

Vegetables and Fruits

Feed your baby certified organically-grown vegetables and fruits instead of the commercial jars of baby food. Instructions on how to prepare vegetables and fruits are given in Part II, beginning on page 178. Please re-read the warnings about possible pesticides on some fruits and vegetables on page 13 and page 38.

Super Porridge

You can give away those boxes of commercial baby cereals! Your baby can now eat healthy homemade whole grain cereals. Start with brown rice, which is one homemade cereal that is referred to in the Super Baby Food Diet as *Super Porridge*. Directions on how to make homemade Brown Rice Super Porridge are found on page 208 in Part II. After a 4-day wait (the Four-day Wait Rule, page 28) you can introduce Millet Super Porridge (page 211). Millet is a little round yellow whole grain with a naturally high protein content, which is packed with lots of other good nutrients for your baby.

13. Feeding Your Super Baby at 7 Months

<table>
<tr><td colspan="3" align="center">INTRODUCE THESE FOODS TO YOUR 7 MONTH OLD</td></tr>
<tr>
<td>

tofu

cottage cheese

homemade mixed cereals

hard-cooked egg yolk (not egg white)

</td>
<td>

asparagus

carrots

green beans

peas

summer squash

white potatoes

peaches

</td>
<td>

mild fruit juices/nectars, strained and diluted:
apple
apricot
grape
papaya
pear
peach
prune
maybe orange juice

</td>
</tr>
</table>

There are over a dozen new foods in the list above that you can introduce to your 7 month old. There just aren't enough days in the month to introduce them all, as you have to wait at least 4 days between new foods (the Four-day Wait Rule, page 28).

The experts don't agree on the ages to introduce foods. Some recommend that you wait until 8 months before introducing egg yolks and cottage cheese, so you may want to introduce these later in the month and concentrate on introducing the new veggies. Remember that the white part of the egg should not be introduced until your baby's first birthday because it is a common allergen (page 32). Whether you are feeding your baby hard-cooked egg yolks mixed into Super Porridge or scrambled egg yolk bits as a finger food, be careful to cook the yolk thoroughly to kill any possible salmonella (page 36). See how to store and cook eggs on page 266. Remember to follow the warning on page 267 about checking egg yolks thoroughly before feeding to your baby.

Tofu (also called "soybean curd" or "bean curd") is a great food for babies 7 months and older. Tofu is a cheese-like product made from soybeans. You may be aware of the nutritional and health benefits of soy products. The "health food" tofu has become so popular that it now can be found in most regular supermarkets. Tofu does not have to be cooked because it is made from cooked soybeans. See page 238 for how to store and freeze tofu. Mashed or puréed tofu can be mixed with your baby's fruit or veggies.

Or it can be added to homemade whole grain cereal to create a complete protein (see protein complementarity on page 513) meal for your little one.

At 7 months, your baby is ready for cereal mixed with fruit or vegetables. Try Brown Rice Super Porridge (page 208) with mashed bananas, or Millet Super Porridge (page 211) with sweet potato food cubes, or just about any combination.

Although your 7-month old is in the process of developing the pincer grasp, he may still have some time to go before he can handle small bits of finger food. Continue to feed him the finger foods listed on page 79 for 6-month olds. The rake, palmar, and pincer grasps are discussed in the chapter *Mealtimes and Your Baby's Development* beginning on page 71. Tofu is a very convenient finger food that can be served in strips or in small chunks.

Introduce Pasteurized, Diluted, Mild Fruit Juices at 7 Months

Please re-read the section about juice beginning on page 64. Your 7-month old probably will be awkward when it comes to drinking from the cup, so fill it with small amounts of water or diluted juice to minimize spilling.

Food Consistency for Babies 7 Months Old

Your baby's food should still be puréed or mashed to a smooth consistency, although it can be slightly thicker now than it was for a beginning eater. Purée your baby's food until it is the consistency of a thick cream.

Sample Daily Feeding Schedule for Babies 7 Months Old

Upon Awakening	breast/bottle
Breakfast	two or three food servings and breast/bottle
Lunch	two or three food servings and breast/bottle
Supper	two or three food servings and breast/bottle
Bedtime	breast or bottle of cooled boiled water
Plus water after and between meals. Offer 4 ounces of diluted fruit juice once a day.	

Daily Amount of Foods for Babies 7 Months Old

Babies at 7 months of age should be eating 2 meals a day, maybe 3. Each meal should consist of 2 to 3 food servings (see *How Large is a Food Serving?*, page 92). At each meal, your 7-month old should be eating a total of ½ cup or 4 ounces or more. Picture the amount in a small commercial baby food jar. See summary table for daily servings and portion sizes on page 58.

Fruits/Veggies: 3-4 servings per day, including 1 vitamin A fruit/veggie and 1 vitamin C veggie/fruit/juice serving. Each serving should be 1-2 tablespoons or ½ food cube-1 food cube. See list of vitamin C fruits/veggies on page 135. A vitamin A veggie is one of the Super Green Veggies or one of the deep yellow/orange vitamin A veggies/fruits listed on page 135. The Super Green Veggies are actually orange too, but their green color hides the orange. Make sure to feed your baby only those veggies/fruits that are age-appropriate, as listed in the summary schedule on pages 86-87.

Grains/Cereals: 1-2 cereal or grain servings per day. Each cereal serving should be 1-2 tablespoons dry cereal mixed with formula or breast milk. A serving of grains from cooked homemade Super Porridge cereal should be ¼-½ cup, equivalent to 1-2 tablespoons dry, ground grains before cooking.

Tofu: At least every other day, add 1-2 tablespoons of puréed or well-mashed tofu to Super Porridge to make a high protein cereal. Tofu is made from the soybean, therefore it forms complete high quality protein when it is mixed with the grains in Super Porridge. See protein complementarity, page 513.

Egg Yolk: Every second day or 3-4 times per week.

Dairy: 1 dairy serving every day or every other day. A serving is ⅓-½ cup yogurt and ¼ cup cottage cheese. Plus the breast milk/formula amounts stated in next paragraph.

Daily Amount of Liquids for Babies 7 Months Old

Breast milk or formula is still the main food for your baby. Your baby should breastfeed 5 times a day or drink 30-32 ounces of formula a day. If your baby is not drinking this amount, decrease the amount of solid foods. Your baby should be drinking water after each meal and between meals. Keep your baby's total water and juice intake to 4-8 ounces maximum per day (maybe more on hot days) to be sure your baby is getting enough breast milk or formula. Also, please read about water on pages 61-64.

Feeding Your Baby the Super Baby Food Diet At 7 Months

If you have not already done so, please read about the Super Baby Food Diet on pages 119-148. Please be sure to read about having enough iron in your baby's diet on page 69.

Super Porridge

At 7 months, you can make homemade whole grain Super Porridge cereals out of more than one grain. Try rice and millet, or rice and oats, or millet and oats. Directions on making these combined cereals are found in Part II, page 213. Remember to use only grains that have been previously introduced individually and checked for allergy using the Four-day Wait Rule (page 28).

Meat Alternatives (Protein)

At around 7-8 months, it is recommended that meat be introduced into a non-vegetarian baby's diet. The meat chapter begins on page 278. Instead of meat, the Super Baby Food Diet uses the healthier meat alternatives to supply protein: tofu, beans and other legumes, nuts, seeds, eggs, and dairy products. This month your baby is old enough to begin eating tofu, a soybean product. At 8 months, you can introduce ground nuts/seeds, tahini, and brewer's yeast and, at 9 months, legumes. Your baby does not need meat to get the protein he needs, the Super Baby Food Diet supplies more than enough. See the table on page 527 of the nutrition section for the amounts of protein in the Super Baby Foods.

14. Feeding Your Super Baby at 8 Months

INTRODUCE THESE FOODS TO YOUR 8 MONTH OLD		
apricot	*plums*	*tahini*
apple	*watermelon*	*finely ground nuts*
cantaloupe	*broccoli*	*finely ground seeds*
honeydew melon	*okra*	*brewer's yeast*
grapes (peeled and quartered, not whole grapes)	*cooked parsley*	*powdered kelp*
	wheat germ (if family allergy, wait until after 1 year)	*natural cheeses*
kiwi fruit		*powdered desiccated liver*

At 8 months, your baby's digestive system is maturing and you can introduce him to more and more foods. Don't slacken off and begin giving him too many new foods at one time. Continue to use the Four-day Wait Rule (page 28).

Your baby is more adept at the pincer grasp (page 79) and consequently at the self-feeding of finger foods. He also is chewing or, more accurately, "gumming" foods with his molarless gums. Be sure to give him small SOFT bits of finger food with a texture that can be easily and painlessly mashed with baby's sensitive gums. Offer him the teething foods suggested on page 80.

Sometime between now and your baby's first birthday, she will probably grab the spoon and attempt to self-feed. Ignore the mess, realize that your baby needs practice, and encourage your baby's efforts at self-feeding. Show her that you have confidence in her ability. If you have not already done so, please read the chapter *Mealtimes and Your Baby's Development* beginning on page 71.

Wheat and Other Foods Containing Gluten

The gluten contained in wheat, rye, and other foods is a common allergen, as discussed on pages 31-32. Some experts recommend waiting until your baby is one year old before introducing it, especially if a wheat/gluten allergy runs in your family. Discuss with your pediatrician whether you should introduce wheat germ, bread, and other products containing gluten this month.

Super Snacks

Somewhere between now and two months from now (age 8-10 months), your baby's food intake will increase substantially. But because your baby's stomach can hold only small amounts of food, she must eat frequently throughout the day to fill her nutritional and caloric needs. Super Snacks fill the void in her tummy between meals. Please turn now to page 131 and read more about Super Snacks.

Food Consistency for Babies 8 Months Old

Your baby's food should still be finely puréed. If your baby is easily eating this food, you can gradually decrease the added liquid for a thicker consistency. If your baby gags or chokes or spits out the food, you have made it too thick. At about 8-9 months, babies usually start on the commercial "junior" foods in the 6-8 ounce jars. On your next trip to the supermarket, note their consistency and copy it when you are puréeing homemade Super Baby Food.

Sample Daily Feeding Schedule for Babies 8 Months Old

Upon Awakening	breast/bottle
Breakfast	three food servings and breast/bottle or cup
Lunch	three food servings and breast/bottle or cup
Supper	three food servings and breast/bottle or cup
Bedtime	breast or bottle of water
Plus one or two Super Snacks, water, and diluted juice.	

Daily Amount of Foods for Babies 8 Months Old

See summary table for daily servings and portion sizes on page 58.

Fruits/Veggies: 4-5 servings per day, including 1 vitamin A fruit/veggie and at least 1 vitamin C veggie/fruit/juice serving. Each serving should be 2-3 tablespoons or 1-1½ food cubes. See list of vitamin C fruits/veggies on page 135. A vitamin A veggie is one of the Super Green Veggies or one of the deep yellow/orange vitamin A veggies/fruits listed on page 135. Make sure to feed your baby only those veggies/fruits that are age-appropriate, as listed in the summary schedule on pages 86-87. Some of the Super Snack finger food ideas listed in the box on page 293 can count as Fruit/Veggies.

Grains/Cereals: 2-3 servings or more of cereals or grains per day. Each cereal serving should be 1-2 tablespoons dry cereal mixed with formula or breast milk. Soon your baby will be eating more food at each meal— he now may be eating 2 cereal servings (2-4 tablespoons of dry cereal) in a single meal. Other foods that can count as grain servings are listed in the tables on pages 120 and 135. Be sure to feed your baby only those appropriate for his age, as listed in the summary schedule on pages 86-87. Finger foods and Super Snacks that can count as grain servings include whole grain baby crackers, whole grain bread pieces, Cheerios and other cereals for baby, and cooked grains. Any foods containing wheat/gluten (page 31) should be OK'd by your pediatrician first.

When your baby is 8 months old, she may be able to eat more Super Porridge at one meal—perhaps ½-¾ cup of cooked Super Porridge, which is equivalent to about 2-3 tablespoons dry, uncooked ground cereal grains. This counts as 2 grain servings in the Super Baby Food Diet worksheet on page 134.

Protein foods: 1-2 servings of meat alternatives or protein foods: tofu, tahini, ground nuts, ground seeds, and brewer's yeast (added to Super Porridge or yogurt for protein complementarity, page 513). Each serving size of ground nuts/seeds should be about 1 tablespoon before grinding, serving size of tahini should be ½-1 tablespoon, tofu should be 1-2 tablespoons, and brewer's yeast should be ½-1 teaspoon. Mix them in with Super Porridge or yogurt, or try some of the more simple Toddler Hors d'oeuvres Super Snack recipes with nuts/seeds beginning on page 293. Make sure your baby has been previously introduced individually to any ingredient in the recipe and watch carefully for choking.

Egg Yolk: Every second day or 3-4 times per week.

Dairy: 1 dairy serving every day or every other day. A serving is ½ cup yogurt, ¼-⅓ cup cottage cheese, or ½-1 ounce of grated bits of natural cheeses. Plus the amount of liquids below.

Daily Amount of Liquids for Babies 8 Months Old

Breast milk or formula is still the main food for your baby. Your baby should breastfeed 5 times a day or drink 29-32 ounces of formula a day. Your baby should be drinking water after meals and between meals. Offer 2-4 ounces of water per day, especially on hot days. Offer a few ounces of diluted fruit juice (½ water, ½ juice—see REMEMBER on page 66) and/or offer a few ounces of nut and seed milks. To be sure that your baby is drinking enough breast milk or formula, do not exceed 6-8 ounces (maybe more on hot days) of total juice, nut milks, and water per day. Please read about water on pages 61-64.

Weaning to the Cup

Starting any time now, you may want to start weaning your baby by gradually replacing mealtime bottles with cups of formula. The first bottle to be eliminated should be the bottle given with the mid-day meal, as discussed under the section *Gradual Weaning to the Cup* on page 78.

Feeding Your Baby the Super Baby Food Diet At 8 Months

If you have not already done so, please read about the Super Baby Food Diet on pages 119-148. Please be sure to read about having enough iron in your baby's diet on page 69.

Tahini

I love the convenience of tahini. Tahini is a super healthy spread made from ground sesame seeds (just as peanut butter is a spread made from ground peanuts) and is a very easy food to add into Super Porridge and yogurt. It is high in calcium, protein, and the healthy fat that your baby needs for proper development, especially brain development. For nutritional information and tips on tahini, read the chapter on seeds beginning on page 240.

Ground Nuts and Seeds

Other super nutritious Super Baby Foods that you can start adding to your baby's diet this month are seeds and nuts, especially flaxseed (or flaxseed oil), almonds, filberts, walnuts, and pumpkin seeds. You don't want your baby to miss out on the concentrated nutrition in nuts and seeds. Please read the chapter *Nuts, Seeds, and Sprouts* beginning on page 240. Whole seeds and nuts or even partial pieces of seeds and nuts are choking hazards for babies and toddlers, so you must grind them thoroughly in your blender as discussed on page 243. Feed ground seeds to your baby **immediately** after grinding, as they start becoming rancid as soon as their oils are exposed to the air. Another way to get these super foods into your baby's diet is via Nut and Seed Milks, discussed on page 67, but be sure that they do not decrease your baby's intake of breast milk or formula.

> **WARNING:** Be sure to get your pediatrician's OK before you introduce your baby to nuts and seeds, as they are high allergen foods. Please read about peanut allergies on page 32.

Brewer's Yeast

Brewer's yeast, torula yeast, or nutritional yeast are nutritional supplement powders or flakes that are high in protein, the B vitamins, trace elements, and other nutrients. If you flip through the nutrient tables (beginning on page 520), you will see that brewer's yeast is consistently one of the top suppliers for the major nutrients, especially the B vitamins and trace elements. Taking a few seconds to add a little brewer's yeast into your baby's morning Super Porridge gives it a super nutrition boost. Some yeasts are fortified with vitamin D-12, a nutrient which is sometimes lacking in *strict* vegetarian diets.

WARNING: Do not use the yeast for baking breads as a nutritional supplement. If you are not familiar with nutritional yeast, ask your natural foods store employee to help you find it.

Desiccated Liver and Powdered Kelp

You can begin giving your baby these two nutrition enhancers, which are discussed on page 274 and page 279.

Begin Using the Super Baby Food Daily Worksheet

Your baby is starting to eat a wide variety of foods. If you have not yet used the Super Baby Food Diet Worksheet on page 134, you can begin to do so at around this age. Remember that the worksheet is for a one-year old baby, so your 8-month old will be eating fewer servings than the numbers recommended in the bottom row labeled "Suggested Daily Servings." And she is not yet eating beans or legumes, except for tofu (from soybeans). But still, the worksheet will help you get into the habit of feeding your baby a balanced diet, with foods from each of the major food categories.

15. Feeding Your Super Baby at 9 Months

<table>
<tr><td colspan="2" align="center">INTRODUCE THESE FOODS TO YOUR 9 MONTH OLD</td></tr>
<tr><td>

Brussels sprouts
cauliflower
spinach
beets
greens
kale
eggplant
rhubarb
rutabaga
cooked onion
turnips

</td><td>

pineapple
finely chopped raw parsley

beans, split peas, lentils
and other legumes,
ground to a powder
and cooked,
or
cooked whole
and mashed with
skins removed

</td></tr>
</table>

Your baby's digestive system is almost as mature as an adult's, and you can feed him almost everything an adult eats. Kale is, in my opinion, the most super of the Super Green Veggies. I feed it to my baby at least every second day when it's in season. Buy two bunches at a time, because these and all greens shrink significantly when you cook them.

Your baby's pincer grasp (page 79) is developing and she is handling her finger foods very well. Your baby can now chew well and may be able to bite off a piece of food from a larger food. Continue to offer her strips of slices of banana, peeled wedges of ripe pears, peaches, and other fruit, strips of natural cheeses, cooked broccoli spears, peeled cucumber strips, and strips of toast. For other finger food and Super Snack ideas, see page 291.

If you have not already done so, please read the chapter *Mealtimes and Your Baby's Development* beginning on page 71. Continue to use the Four-day Wait Rule (page 28).

Food Consistency for Babies 9 Months Old

As your baby's eating skills develop, gradually make the purée consistency a little thicker by adding less liquid. Also, gradually increase the chunkiness of puréed food by using your blender or food processor on a slower speed and/or for less time. If you manually pulse the food (you don't need a special pulse button on your blender—just turn it on and off yourself), you can stop after each pulse to check for the right consistency.

Besides increasing the chunkiness of your baby's food, another way to slowly accustom him to coarser food is to add a finely minced food to a smooth purée. Try adding finely grated cooked vegetable to yogurt, or add a few teaspoons of grainy cereal to a smooth purée of vegetable. It is important that the chunkier food be very soft, so that your baby can chew them—"gum" them is more accurate—with his sensitive gums. If your baby gags or chokes or spits out the food, you have made it too thick or chunky.

Sample Daily Feeding Schedule for Babies 9 Months Old

Upon Awakening	breast/bottle
Breakfast	three food servings and breast/bottle or cup
Lunch	three food servings and cup of formula/breast milk
Afternoon Snack	Super Snack
Supper	three food servings and breast/bottle or cup
Bedtime	breast or bottle of water
Plus Super Snacks, water, and slightly diluted juice.	

Daily Amount of Foods for Babies 9 Months Old

You may notice an increase in your baby's appetite and in the quantity of food she eats. Beginning soon, if it hasn't already, a one-food-cube serving size will no longer be enough, and your baby will be able to eat 2, or even 3, food cubes. See summary table for daily servings and portion sizes on page 58.

Fruits/Veggies: 4-5 servings per day, including 1 vitamin A fruit/veggie and 1 vitamin C veggie/fruit/juice serving. Each serving should be 2-4 tablespoons or 1-2 food cubes. See list of vitamin C fruits/veggies on page 135. A vitamin A veggie is one of the Super Green Veggies or vitamin A veggies/fruits listed on page 135.

Grains/Cereals: 3-4 servings of grains per day. Each cereal serving should be 1-2 tablespoons dry cereal mixed with formula or breast milk. Soon your baby will be eating more food at each meal—he now may be eating 2 cereal servings (2-4 tablespoons of dry cereal) in a single meal. Other foods that can count as grain servings are listed in the tables on pages 120 and 135. Be sure to feed your baby only those appropriate for his age, as listed in the summary schedule on pages 86-87. Continue giving finger foods and Super Snacks that can count as grain servings: whole grain baby crackers, whole grain bread pieces, Cheerios and other cereals for baby, and cooked grains. Any foods containing wheat/gluten should be OK'd by your pediatrician first.

Your baby is probably now eating ½-¾ cup of Super Porridge in one sitting. A ½-¾ cup of all-grains Super Porridge counts as 2 grain servings in the Super Baby Food Daily Worksheet (page 134). Previously, Super Porridge has been made with all grains, but now your baby is old enough to eat Super Porridge made with a combination of grains and legumes, as discussed on page 109.

Protein foods: 2-3 servings per day of protein foods or meat alternatives: tofu; cooked pureed beans, peas, and lentils; ground nuts and seeds; and brewer's yeast. Add these protein foods to Super Porridge or yogurt for protein complementarity (page 513). A serving of brewer's yeast should be ½-1 teaspoon. A serving is 1-2 tablespoons of ground nuts/seeds or 1-2 tablespoons of ground beans (before cooking), and 2-3 tablespoons of tofu.

The legumes in ¾ cup of High Protein Super Porridge count as 1 legume serving, as discussed on page 109.

Egg Yolk: Every second day or 3-4 times per week.

Dairy: 1 dairy serving every day or every other day. A serving is ½ cup yogurt, ⅓ cup cottage cheese, or 1 ounce of grated bits of natural cheeses. Plus the breast milk/formula amounts stated in next paragraph.

Daily Amount of Liquids for Babies 9 Months Old

Your baby should breast-feed at least 3 or 4 times a day or drink 26-32 ounces of formula a day. Offer 2-4 ounces of water daily, especially on hot days. Offer 4 ounces of slightly diluted fruit juice, perhaps 3 ounces juice to 1 ounce water (see REMEMBER on page 66) and/or offer a few ounces of nut and seed milks. To be sure that your baby is drinking enough breast milk or formula, do not exceed 6-8 ounces per day (maybe more on hot days) of total water, juice, nut milks, and other beverages. Please read about water on pages 61-64.

Feeding Your Baby the Super Baby Food Diet At 9 Months

If you have not already done so, please read about the Super Baby Food Diet on pages 119-148. Please be sure to read about having enough iron in your baby's diet on page 69.

High Protein Super Porridge

This is the month we've been waiting for—the month that you can add beans and other legumes into Super Porridge, making it a complete high protein cereal! Beans and other legumes complement grains to make a complete protein (page 514) as high a quality as that from meat and dairy products. Chapter 24, page 214 has instructions on how to prepare and store High Protein Super Porridge. You have already begun adding tofu and ground nuts/seeds into Super Porridge made only from grains in order to increase its protein content (and because they are packed with nutrients for your baby). This month, with beans added into the grains before cooking, you are starting with a base of High Protein Super Porridge before you add any nuts/seeds or tofu.

Because of the beans, you can now write ¾ cup of Super Porridge into the Super Baby Food Diet Daily Worksheet on page 134 as 2 grain servings and 1 legume serving. In fact, your 9-month old baby is old enough to have the complete Super Porridge Main Meal outlined in the box on page 123.

Vegetables and Fruits

Instead of ice cube trays, you may wish to freeze larger portions of vegetables in other containers, such as empty yogurt containers. Fill them partially, make sure you cover them well, and freeze solid. It is important that their lids seal air tight. Use freezer tape around the lids if necessary, or cover with aluminum foil. You can also use the Nested Plastic Bag Freezing Method for these larger portions. Empty popsicle freeze molds also work if you leave out the stick and cover the tops well with aluminum foil.

16. Feeding Your Super Baby at 10 Months

INTRODUCE THESE FOODS TO YOUR 10 MONTH OLD

thinned peanut butter (the smooth kind, not the chunky kind)

other thinned nut butters

ground sprouts

whole grain pasta

homemade bulgur cereal

cooked whole grain cornmeal with the germ

raw and finely grated: carrots

greens summer squash sweet peppers

At 10 months, you can introduce your baby to nut butters. Peanut butter is not the only kind! You will find walnut butters (high in omega-3, see page 506), almond butters, cashew butters, and others at the natural foods store. Thick nut butters may cause your baby to gag, so it is important to thin them with milk, water, or even fruit juice. Delicious! Spread them on bread, crackers, and fruit pieces, as suggested in the Super Snack recipes beginning on page 291. See the tip on bonding with your child on page 292.

WARNING: Please read about peanut allergies on page 32.

Bulgur, a cracked whole wheat, should not be given if wheat allergy runs in the family. And even if you don't have a wheat allergy in your family, your pediatrician may advise you to wait until your baby is a year old before introducing any wheat products, such as pasta, which usually contains wheat flour. Pasta should be made from 100% whole grain flour, not the white/wheat flour that is typical in most, if not all, of the pasta at the supermarket. Read about whole grain pasta on page 225.

Continue to use the Four-day Wait Rule (page 28) with all new foods. If you have not already done so, please read the chapter *Mealtimes and Your Baby's Development* beginning on page 71.

Food Consistency for Babies 10 Months Old

Food should still be fork-mashed or puréed, but continue to gradually increase its thickness and chunkiness. By 10 months, your baby may be eating finger foods very well. Finger foods are becoming a larger part of her diet. Small pieces of plain soft-cooked whole-grain pasta are a good finger food, and they can be frozen in ½ cup portions using the Nested Plastic Bag Method. See page 225 for tips on how to freeze and thaw pasta.

Sample Daily Feeding Schedule for Babies 10-12 Months Old

Upon Awakening	breast/bottle
Breakfast	three food servings and breast/bottle or cup
Morning Snack	Super Snack
Lunch	three food servings and cup of breast milk/formula
Afternoon Snack	Super Snack
Supper	three food servings and cup of breast milk/formula
Bedtime	breast or bottle of water
Plus Super Snacks, water, and slightly diluted juice.	

Daily Amount of Foods for Babies 10 Months Old

You have probably noticed a big increase in your baby's appetite and in the quantity of food she eats. Servings now consist of 2 or 3 food cubes. See summary table for daily servings and portion sizes on page 58. In the next two months, your baby should gradually build up to amount of food in the Super Baby Food Diet summarized in the table on page 120.

Fruits/Veggies: 4-5 servings per day, including 1 vitamin A fruit/veggie and at least 1 vitamin C veggie/fruit/juice serving. Each serving should be 3-4 tablespoons or 1½-2 food cubes. See list of vitamin C fruits/veggies on page 135. A vitamin A veggie is one of the Super Green Veggies or one of the deep yellow/orange vitamin A veggies/fruits listed on page 135.

Grains/Cereals: 4 servings of grains per day. Follow instructions for Grains/Cereals for 9-month olds on page 108.

Protein foods: 2-3 servings per day. New proteins for this month are peanut and other butters, thinned to prevent choking. A serving is 1-2 tablespoons of peanut butter (before thinning) or other nut butter. See the other protein foods and serving sizes listed on page 108 (same as for 9-month olds).

WARNING: Please read about peanut allergies on page 32.

Egg Yolk: Every second day or 3-4 times per week.

Dairy: 1 serving per day of dairy or more. A serving is ½ cup of yogurt, ⅓ cup of cottage cheese, or 1 ounce grated bits of natural cheese. Plus the breast milk/formula amounts stated in next paragraph.

Daily Amount of Liquids for Babies 10 Months Old

Your baby should breast-feed at least 3 times a day or drink 24-32 ounces of formula a day. Offer 2-4 ounces of water daily, especially on hot days. Offer 4 ounces of slightly diluted or undiluted fruit juice (see REMEMBER on page 66) and/or offer a few ounces of nut and seed milks. To be sure that your baby is drinking enough breast milk or formula, do not exceed 6-8 ounces per day (maybe more on hot days) of total water, juice, nut milks, and other beverages. Please read about water on pages 61-64.

Feeding Your Baby the Super Baby Food Diet At 10 Months

If you have not already done so, please read about the Super Baby Food Diet on pages 119-148. Please be sure to read about having enough iron in your baby's diet on page 69.

Continue to give your baby Super Porridge made from the variety of whole grains, beans, and other legumes from the natural foods store.

The Super Baby Food System should now be a part of your daily life. You've developed your own schedule and make Super Porridge and frozen food cubes at regular, predictable intervals. Your baby may now be eating the number of servings recommended in the Super Baby Food Diet Daily Worksheet on page 134.

For the next several months and into toddlerhood, continue with the Super Baby Food Diet.

17. Feeding Your Super Baby at 11 Months

Foods to Introduce at 11 Months

Continue to introduce foods that your baby hasn't had yet using the Four-day Wait Rule (page 28).

Food Consistency for Babies 11 Months Old

Although you are still feeding your baby her main meals mashed or coarsely puréed, she is probably enjoying quite a bit of finger foods by now. Sit with your baby while she finger feeds and watch carefully for choking or gagging. Never leave her alone while she is eating.

Daily Amount of Foods for Babies 11 Months Old

Food requirements are similar to those of a 10 month old baby, but your baby may be eating a little more. See summary table for daily servings and portion sizes on page 58.

Daily Amount of Liquids for Babies 11 Months Old

Your baby should breast-feed at least 3 times a day or drink 24-32 ounces of formula a day. Offer 4 ounces of water per day (especially on hot days), and offer 2-4 ounces of undiluted or diluted fruit juice and/or a few ounces of nut/seed milk. Remember that you do not have to increase to 100% fruit juice—see REMEMBER on page 66. To be sure that your baby is drinking enough breast milk or formula, do not exceed 6-8 ounces (maybe more on hot days) of total juice, nut milks, and water. Please read about water on pages 61-64.

Your Baby's First Birthday

As your baby nears the end of his first year, you cannot remember what it was like in your previous life before kids. You feel that you are the luckiest person in the world to have him, and wonder what people without children do with their lives! Real joy in living truly comes from loving our children and watching them grow.

Have fun celebrating the end of this first wonderful year at your baby's first birthday party! Recipes for Super Baby healthy cakes and icings begin on page 345.

18. Feeding Your Super Toddler

INTRODUCE THESE FOODS TO YOUR TODDLER	
cow's milk	*tomatoes/tomato juice*
citrus fruits/juices	*strawberries, blueberries, and*
hard-cooked egg white	*other berries (not whole, cut into*
uncooked honey	*small pieces)*

Now that your baby is one year old, he is officially a toddler and will remain a toddler until he is three years old. Toddlers are curious little people that get into everything. They have discovered independence and want their own way, and if they don't get it—look out! It is rumored that the word "no" was invented by a toddler.

Toddlers are constantly testing the limit and mealtimes are no exception. Expect plenty of refusals. At mealtimes, you never know when he'll reject a food, even a food that he previously relished. He may adamantly refuse to eat the healthy foods he loved as a baby. When my little guy got to be about 16 months, he wouldn't eat plain Super Porridge anymore, I had to add several veggie cubes to it, which was fine with me. Try not to take food rejections personally, and continue to keep mealtimes pleasant and relaxing.

Your toddler can now eat just about anything you do, with the exception of the choking hazards listed on page 40. And, of course, don't feed him foods that are salty, spicy, sugary, or those that contain too much butter. Continue to use the Four-day Wait Rule (page 28). You may want to wait to introduce peanuts (see peanut allergies on page 32) until your child is three years old—discuss this with your pediatrician.

The Foundation Year for Future Food Preferences

Your baby's second year of life (from 1-2 years old) is THE most important time for establishing food preferences. What she learns to like now will probably stay with her for the rest of her life. Remember this when you are tempted to treat her with junk foods. Never use food as a reward, even healthy food; instead, substitute a smile, a hug, and a big kiss. And don't make deals to get your child to eat her veggies: "You can have the cookie if you finish your broccoli." In effect, you're saying "Cookies are better than broccoli and good children get to eat cookies."

How do you get her to eat only good foods? Don't have any junk foods in the house, or hide them and never let your toddler see you or anyone else eating them.

> **TIP:** If your toddler is refusing to eat healthy foods, let the time that lapses between meals be long enough so that your toddler is somewhat hungry for his next snack/meal. He'll be less fussy about what he eats.

After your child's second birthday, he will no longer be willing to try new foods as willingly as during his first and second years. To encourage him, place SMALL amounts of foods nicely arranged on his plate. A too-full plate is overwhelming to a child.

Cut your toddler's food into easy-to-eat pieces. Make healthy foods fun by using the food decorating ideas in the recipes part of this book on page 362.

Distract your child when you offer new or disliked foods. To change the focus away from the food, chat with him about his favorite things, such as the slide at the playground or his favorite television character.

Give your toddler as much control over her food choices as possible. But don't ask an open-ended question like "What do you want for lunch?" Give your child less latitude while still allowing her some control by asking a multiple-choice question: "Would you like apples or pears for dessert?"

Along with any new food, also offer a familiar food that your toddler likes.

If you get your toddler involved in food preparation, he will be more likely to eat it. Let him dump the cup of flour into the bowl, tear the lettuce, and wipe up the counter top. It's fun to let your child help, although it will take you three times longer for food preparation! Remember to be careful with sharp knives and other utensils and use safety precautions to prevent burns.

Keep offering new foods and don't be offended at refusals. Remember to keep mealtimes pleasant and don't start any battles.

Eating Skills

Please re-read the chapter *Mealtimes and Your Baby's Development* beginning on page 71, which has information on the eating skills your child will acquire during the toddler years.

While your toddler is eating, let her concentrate. Don't let her get distracted by a television set or other diversion; instead, use mealtimes to spend time with your toddler. You know what I mean if you've ever tried to spoon feed your baby a kiwi fruit while she's walking around the family room with Barney on the TV—it takes four times as long to finish it.

> **WARNING:** You should still not leave your child alone while she is eating. Always watch carefully for choking.

Toddlers' Tummies Are Still Small

Your toddler is still eating small amounts of food frequently throughout the day—probably 3 small meals and at least 2 snacks a day. Super Snacks continue to be a big part of your toddler's diet, and will be until your child is 4-5 years old. Although the average two-year old eats 5 times per day (3 meals, 2 snacks), some children eat as little as 3 times per day and others as often as 14 times per day! (When you feel that all you're doing is feeding and cleaning up after your toddler, think about those children's parents!)

A Decrease in Appetite at One Year

Your toddler's growth rate slows at about the time of her first birthday. Whereas she probably tripled her birth weight during her first year, she will gain only between 3 and 7 pounds during her second. The small weight gain during toddlerhood will produce changes in muscle mass and in the shape of the body, making your toddler look more like a child than a baby. Because she is eating less, it is important to make every bite count nutritionally. Remember: Never force her to eat or it might be the beginning of a lifetime of eating problems.

24 Ounces of Milk Per Day

Her bones will increase in length and density as calcium and phosphorus are deposited into them. Because of this bone mineralization, it is important to make sure that your toddler is getting enough minerals in her diet. She should continue eating or drinking 24 ounces or 3 cups of milk, yogurt, or other high-calcium and protein foods daily, although some experts hold that 2 cups per day are enough. (In nutrition part, see food sources for calcium, page 540 and for protein, page 527.)

Whole or Low-fat Milk?

Now that your baby is a toddler, he can begin drinking cow's milk, unless, of course, he has a milk allergy. Some experts suggest that you continue to feed him whole milk products, and no low-fat or skim milk products, until he is two years old. Other authorities say three years. If you are concerned about your baby's weight or cholesterol levels, you may want to switch to low-fat milk after his first birthday, but consult your pediatrician first. In general, a toddler's fat and cholesterol intake should not be greatly restricted. Please re-read the section *No Cow's Milk Until One Year* on page 60.

> **WARNING:** Be sure to get your pediatrician's OK before feeding your toddler the commercial milks for toddlers and older children. Some brands contain too much protein and not enough fat.

Iron is Still Important

Too much milk is not good for your toddler if it takes the place of other nutritious foods, especially foods high in iron. Iron continues to be an important nutrient through toddlerhood and milk is not a good source of iron. **Milk anemia** refers to the iron-deficiency anemia that occurs when a child's diet is lacking in iron because too much milk displaces iron-rich foods. Your toddler's diet should be balanced and consist of foods from all of the food groups, not just the dairy group, to supply the variety of nutrients his body needs.

Iron is a common deficiency among toddlers because they typically stop eating iron-fortified formula and cereals around their first birthday. Iron supplementation should be continued until at least 18 months. Ask your pediatrician how long to continue your child's iron supplements. Read more about iron on pages 69 and 549.

Food Serving Sizes for Toddlers

A general rule of thumb is to make your toddler's portion sizes equal to 1-2 tablespoons of food for each year of age. A two year old should get a 2-4 tablespoon portion, a three year old should get a 3-6 tablespoon portion, a 1½ year old should get a 1½-3 tablespoon portion, etc. If you cannot measure a particular food by tablespoon, give your toddler anywhere from ¼-½ of an adult's portion size. Toddler servings of cooked Super Porridge should be ¾-1 cup, which is equivalent to 3-4 tablespoons of dry, uncooked powdered grains and legumes.

Toddlers and Well-Rounded Diets—Fact or Fiction?

There's nothing unusual about a toddler refusing to eat. Some days she will refuse to eat all foods except one, and the next week she will eat a different one to the exclusion of all else. I never had any trouble with my toddlers refusing to eat their Super Porridge; in fact, they have always eaten it with gusto. Maybe I was lucky, but I think the trick is to start them on Super Baby Food right from the start and keep them on it. A toddler's ignorance of junk food is bliss for us parents! Concerned parents should know that toddlers do not need to eat very much to remain healthy:

Dr. Brazelton's Minimal Daily Diet for a Toddler

Dr. T. Berry Brazelton, on page 141 in his book, *Touchpoints* (see bibliography), defines a "minimal daily diet" for the second and third years (age 1-3 years, the toddler years) to be:

- one pint of milk (16 ounces, 2 cups, four 4-ounce servings or four ½-cup servings) or its equivalent in cheese, yogurt or ice cream (see page 127 for milk equivalents)
- two ounces of iron-containing protein (meat or an egg), or cereals fortified with iron
- one ounce of orange juice or fresh fruit
- one multivitamin to cover uneaten vegetables

T. B. Brazelton, TOUCHPOINTS, (page 141). ©1992 by T. Berry Brazelton, M. D. *Reprinted by permission of Addison Wesley Longman.*

According to Dr. Brazelton's minimum daily diet above, the Super Porridge Main Meal of the Super Baby Food Diet (see box on page 123) plus 2 cups of milk seem to be enough to meet a toddler's daily dietary needs.

TIP: Soup is a quick, easy, and convenient meal for your toddler. But although he is good with solid foods in the spoon, liquidy soup may be a problem. Try this: Use a strainer to collect the solid parts from the soup and place them in his bowl. Let him pierce them with his baby fork or eat them with his spoon. The liquid part of the soup can be poured into his cup for drinking.

Toddler Quirks

Many children don't like their foods to touch each other. If your child doesn't, oblige him by separating and spacing the food on his plate.

Toddlers may hold food in their mouths for hours.

Toddlers may want only one food for several consecutive days or weeks, and then abruptly refuse to eat that food for the next month.

Toddlers may get upset if you do not serve their food the way they are currently thinking that you should. For example, your toddler may be upset if you cut his bread in squares rather than in triangles. Or he may complain vehemently if you gave him juice in his Barney glass instead of his Winnie the Pooh glass. One day my little guy threw a tantrum when I put his spoon in his bowl instead of in his hand; after that, I never forgot to ask him where he wanted his spoon. Yes, we parents of toddlers learn to walk on eggshells. ☺

Toddlers are extremely active and need to move. After your baby has finished her meal, don't force her to remain at the dinner table listening to adult conversation if she doesn't want to.

House Rules

It is OK to establish and insist upon a few rules for toddlers who should know better. Some rules you may establish may be:

- No food throwing.
- No eating or drinking away from the table/high chair.
- No spitting.

When your toddler begins to act in ways that disturb you *with the intent to provoke you* rather than to practice skill development, it's time to put your foot down and show that you are the boss. Children need discipline, and they become insecure when you are not in charge. Show that you are serious by taking away the food immediately when established rules are broken. Be firm, but be in control and without anger. You can be kind and loving to your child as you discipline her.

Children Learn by Example

The best way to teach your children manners is to set a good example. Yelling and nagging is just not as effective. Children imitate the actions of adults, so act as you want your child to act. The old "do as I say, not as I do" doesn't work now and never did. If you wash your hands before a meal, he will too. If you say "please" and "thank you," so will he.

19. The Super Baby Food Diet

A Super Healthy Diet for Your Super Baby

The Super Baby Food Diet is an extremely healthy diet composed of only whole, natural foods. It is based on these major components: whole grain cereals, vegetables and fruits, yogurt and other dairy products, eggs, nuts, seeds, and legumes. Pediatricians and nutritionists agree that a semi-vegetarian diet (a lacto-ovo diet containing milk products and eggs) fulfills all of your growing baby's nutritional requirements.

You may recognize these foods as being those from the "new" food groups, the new "optimal diet" groups. The old food groups were meats, breads and cereals, milk and other dairy foods, and vegetables and fruits. The new optimal diet groups are similar, except that other high protein foods or "meat alternatives" have been added to the meat/protein group: legumes, nuts, and seeds. Compare the two food pyramids on pages 502-503. The meat alternatives usually contain much less pesticides, hormones, and other toxins than meats, and most of them do not have the sometimes fatal problem of bacterial contamination (E. coli, salmonella). Nuts and seeds contain the healthy unsaturated fats that your baby needs for development, especially brain development, without the gobs of the unhealthy saturated fats that meats have (page 504).

How Do I Keep Track of All the Foods My Baby Needs?

Please look at the summary table on the next page. The table lists the major food groups in the diet with a suggested minimum number of daily food servings from each food group. You may be wondering how a busy parent could possibly keep track of all these requirements. Well, the Super Baby Food Diet makes it very easy—I promise! Even your babysitter will think so. You will see how as you read through this chapter.

The Super Baby Food Diet

Food Group & Servings	Best Super Baby Food Sources and Approximate Portion Sizes for a One-Year Old
Grain Group: grains, cereals, breads, pasta 4 servings per day	½-¾ cup cooked whole grains ½ cup dry whole grain cereal (Oatios, Cheerios, etc.) ½ slice 100% whole grain bread ½ cup whole grain pasta or noodles 1-2 tablespoons wheat germ
Legume Group: beans, legumes, nuts, seeds 2-3 servings per day	⅛ cup (2 tablespoons) of dry beans/legumes or ¼ cup of cooked beans/legumes 1-2 tablespoons of ground nuts and/or seeds 1-2 tablespoons of nut butter or seed butter ½ cup of ground seed sprouts 1 ounce of tofu
Dairy Group: 4 servings per day for a total of 24 ounces or daily amount for child's age	½-¾ cup of milk: breast, formula, whole, 2%, or calcium & vit D fortified soybean or brown rice milk ½ cup of yogurt ⅔ cup of cottage cheese ¾ ounce of natural cheese
Vegetable/ Fruit Group 4-6 servings per day	1 or more Super Green Veggies 1 vitamin C fruit or juice ½ vitamin A (orange/yellow) veggie (or 1 every second day) 2 or more other vegetables and fruits Serving sizes of vegetables are 2-4 tablespoons or 1-2 food cubes. Serving sizes of fruits are ¼-½ of a fresh fruit, ½-1 cup of raw fruit pieces, or ¼-½ cup juice.
Egg Yolks 3-4 servings per week	½ hard-cooked egg or 1 egg every other day (yolks only for babies younger than 1 year) or a scrambled egg or egg yolk, cooked solid
Miscellaneous Nutritional Enhancers as often as once per meal	These nutritional enhancers can be mixed into cereal, yogurt, cottage cheese, and mashed veggies/fruits: brewer's (nutritional) yeast, flaxseed (linseed) oil, powdered kelp, blackstrap molasses, and foods listed as part of other groups above (wheat germ, mashed cooked beans, ground nuts/seeds, tahini, sprouts, tofu, and soybean grits/flour)

The Super Baby Food Diet Grows with Your Baby

The previous table shows the approximate portion sizes for a 12-month old baby. A younger baby will eat slightly smaller portions, a toddler will eat slightly larger portions. *The number of portions remains the same for all ages, it's the size of the portions that varies.* For example, a 6 month old baby may eat a ¼-cup serving of Super Porridge cereal, a 9-month old may eat ½ cup, and a 14-month old may eat a full cup. But, as the table says, all three babies should have 4 grain servings a day. The required portions from the different food groups help promote a balanced diet.

My Baby Doesn't Eat That Much!

You may be thinking to yourself, "Let's get real! No real-life baby eats 3 squares a day!" I hear you, and you're right. Most parents are lucky if their baby (or toddler) eats two good meals a day. In fact, many babies live on one good meal a day, one OK meal a day, breast milk or formula, and maybe a few snacks. If your baby is one of them, the Super Baby Food Diet is compatible with his eating habits. As you read the rest of this chapter, you will see that the Super Porridge Main Meal works as the one good daily meal, the yogurt meal can be the OK meal, and Super Snacks or the Third Meal can pick up any slack. The Super Porridge Main Meal of the Super Baby Food Diet also conforms nicely to Dr. T. Berry Brazelton's "minimal daily diet" for a toddler, which is shown in the box on page 117.

Two Well-planned Quick and Easy Meals per Day

The Super Baby Food Diet is based on two main meals a day, a few Super Snacks, and a third meal for older babies who eat more food. Even though I call them "main" meals, they are relatively small amounts of food compared to our adult-sized meals. Because babies stomachs are small, they do well when they eat small amounts of food—mini-meals and snacks—frequently throughout the day. The Super Baby Food Diet lends itself to this style of eating.

Each meal is very quick and easy to make, in fact, any given meal takes less than 3 minutes to prepare! Of course, this assumes that you have done some advance preparing and refrigerating/freezing of foods.

The first main meal is based on Super Porridge, the second main meal is based on yogurt, and the other meal and snacks vary from day to day. Super Porridge and yogurt, along with being extremely healthy foods alone, are great base mixtures to which can be added dozens of other foods, from puréed veggies to wheat germ and ground nuts/seeds. Keep yogurt and cooked Super Porridge ready in the refrigerator, and you can whip up a complete Super Baby Meal in minutes.

The next table is an example of a daily feeding schedule for a baby on the Super Baby Food Diet who at least 9 months old.

Sample Daily Feeding Schedule for the Super Baby Food Diet

Upon Awakening	breast/bottle
Breakfast	a main meal based on Super Porridge
Morning Snack	Super Snack
Lunch	a main meal based on yogurt
Afternoon Snack	Super Snack
Supper	a meal that varies from day to day
Bedtime	breast or bottle of water
Plus water after and between meals.	

A Healthy Diet Must Have a Variety of Foods

From the schedule above, it seems that the Super Baby Food Diet is the same foods every day. This is not true, because Super Porridge can be made from dozens of combinations of different cereal grains (brown rice, millet, barley, oatmeal, etc.) and legumes (soybeans, split peas, lentils, kidney beans, etc.). So Super Porridge is actually a large variety of foods, even though you cook it the same way no matter what grain and legume you choose.[1]

With regard to the yogurt meal, it is true that the yogurt stays the same from day to day. But it is good to eat yogurt every day, and some experts recommend it because of its superb health-giving properties. (See yogurt in appendix, page 252.) Even though the yogurt part remains the same, the yogurt meal is still varied due to the other foods and additions to the yogurt that change from day to day. Also, yogurt does not necessarily have to be made from cow's milk. Soy milks (fortified with calcium and vitamin D) and other non-dairy fortified milks can be used as a base for yogurt.

Super Porridge—The Super Baby's Super Cereal

You'll frequently see the cereal named *Super Porridge* in the Super Baby Food Diet. I call it "Super Porridge" because it is. Super Porridge is a cereal made from brown

---

[1] The only exception is Super Porridge with soybeans, as explained in Part II.

rice or other whole grains. Just as whole grains should be a major part of an adult's diet, Super Porridge is the foundation food of the Super Baby Food Diet. It is very easy to make—you can make 2-3 days' worth in about 10 minutes. Details are in Part II beginning on page 207. When your baby is 9 months old, you can add beans/legumes to the porridge to make it a complete protein baby cereal.

The Main Meal of the Day—Super Porridge

The mail meal of the Super Baby Food Diet is outlined in the next box. I feed my baby this meal in the morning at around 8-9 am, after I've gotten the older kids off to school. The baby can wait to eat his breakfast because the milk feeding he drank upon awakening tides him through the early morning.

The Super Porridge Main Meal

- ½-1 cup of Super Porridge cereal

- either one vitamin A veggie cube or 1 mashed hard-cooked egg yolk (depending on whether it's an egg yolk day) mixed into the Super Porridge

- ½-1 teaspoon brewer's yeast fortified with vitamin B12 mixed into Super Porridge

- 1-2 Super Green Veggie food cubes

- Vitamin C source (2-4 ounces of juice or ½ fruit)

- prescription vitamin drops and iron supplement drops

- maybe a pinch of kelp and ½ -1 teaspoon of desiccated liver (optional)

Preparation Time: 3-4 Minutes

The main meal includes egg yolk. The Super Baby Food Diet includes 3-4 egg yolks per week (egg yolks plus the whites when baby is one year old). Every second day, a mashed hard-cooked egg yolk (or whole egg) is mixed into your baby's Super Porridge.

TIP: A good way to keep track of when to include an egg is to go by the day of the week. In our house, Mondays, Wednesdays, and Fridays are "egg yolk days." Most weeks, my baby also gets a fourth egg during the weekend.

On the days that are not egg yolk days, a vitamin A veggie cube is included in the main meal in place of the egg yolk. Sweet potatoes and carrots are so high in beta-carotene that one food cube every two days, plus a daily Super Green Veggie, supplies all of your baby's vitamin A needs. (See vitamin A, page 529 in the nutrition section, which discusses why the beta-carotene from vegetables is not toxic.)

Preparation Instructions for Super Porridge Main Meal

This entire meal can be mixed in a single bowl, with the exception of the juice, of course. Start by removing a bowl of previously-cooked Super Porridge from your refrigerator. Remove the Super Green and orange veggie cubes from the freezer and push them into the porridge in the bowl. Thaw the porridge and cubes in the microwave on high for 1½-2½ minutes (or for the amount of time needed for your particular microwave oven). Meanwhile, while the microwave is going, peel and mash the egg yolk (you eat the white if your baby is not yet 1 year old). While mashing, look carefully at the center of the yolk to make sure that it is cooked solid (see salmonella warning, page 36). Prepare fruit or juice. Get the vitamin drops and iron drops ready. Get the brewer's yeast ready to be stirred into the porridge.

> **TIME SAVER:** I keep the brewer's yeast bottle (and other nutritional enhancers, such as the desiccated liver bottle and kelp shaker) in an easy-to-reach cabinet, so that it takes me only seconds to open and spoon them into the porridge on the counter directly below the cabinet.

> **TIP:** Keep your baby's vitamins on a surface that you can reach from the feeding area, but out of baby's reach. This way you won't forget them and have to jump up for them in the middle of the meal.

> **TIME SAVER:** When you are batch preparing veggie cubes, mix a few days' worth of Super Green Veggie cubes in with a few days' worth of vitamin A orange veggie cubes in the same small freezer bag. It's easier in the morning to find, open, and close only one freezer bag instead of two.

An Alternate Preparation Method

With above preparation, veggies are mixed in with the Super Porridge in the same bowl. If you prefer to feed your baby the veggies in a different bowl than the one with the porridge, so that your baby can enjoy the flavors separately, follow these preparation steps:

Warm Super Porridge from refrigerator in microwave for 45-60 seconds. Meanwhile, peel egg. Remove porridge from microwave. Thaw food cubes on high in microwave for 1-2 minutes. While veggies cook, mash egg (look closely to insure that it is cooked solid) and mix into porridge. Stir brewer's yeast into porridge. Prepare fruit or juice. Get vitamin drops and iron drops ready.

Vitamin & Iron Supplements
Should Be Given With the Main Meal

No nutrient works alone. Vitamin supplements work together with the nutrients in food to supply your baby's nutritional needs. Supplements should not be given on an empty stomach. If your pediatrician has advised you to give your baby prescription vitamin drops and/or iron drops, drop them into your baby's mouth in the middle of the Super Porridge Main Meal spoonfuls. Don't feed them at the end of the meal, or a coating will be left on the teeth. Or instead, you can mix the drops into the Super Porridge if you are confident he will eat it all.

Vitamin C and Iron Go Together

Vitamin C must be included in this main meal because it helps absorption of the iron from the egg, yeast, and porridge. To remind you of this, the column title in the worksheet on page 134 reads "Egg Yolk+Vitamin C." If your baby's vitamin drops contain vitamin C, you can leave out the fruit or juice from the main meal, especially if your baby is not old enough yet to eat the entire meal.

Brewer's Yeast with B12

Brewer's yeast, torula yeast, or nutritional yeast are nutritional supplement powders or flakes that are high in protein, the B vitamins, trace elements, and other nutrients. If you flip through the nutrient tables (beginning on page 520), you will see that brewer's yeast is consistently one of the top suppliers for the major nutrients, especially the B vitamins and trace elements. Taking a few seconds to add a little brewer's yeast into your baby's morning Super Porridge gives it a super nutrition boost. Some yeasts are fortified with vitamin B-12, a nutrient which is sometimes lacking in *strict* vegetarian diets.

> **WARNING:** Do not use the yeast for baking breads as a nutritional supplement. If you are not familiar with nutritional yeast, ask your natural foods store employee to help you find it.

Desiccated Liver Powder

If your baby is not a vegetarian, add a little desiccated liver powder (½-1 teaspoon) into the Super Porridge along with the brewer's yeast. It contains many trace minerals and iron, and the fact that it is meat will also help iron absorption. See page 279.

Kelp

Keep a salt shaker with kelp near the brewer's yeast and put just a pinch of it into your baby's Super Porridge each morning. See *Kelp* on page 274.

Don't Give Your Baby Milk with the Main Meal

What's obviously missing in the Super Porridge Main Meal? Milk. I don't recommend giving milk with this meal for two reasons. First, milk is very filling and your baby may not be able to finish eating the other foods. Second, some studies have shown that calcium binds with iron, and therefore decreases the iron available to your baby. Foods from the dairy group are the easiest to supply to your baby—it's as easy as pouring a glass of formula or giving a breastfeeding—and you can get the required amount in before the end of the day with no trouble.

The Main Meal Gets Your Baby Off to a SUPER START for the Day

In my opinion, if you've fed your baby a Super Porridge Main Meal this morning, you've already given her more good food and nutrition than that which exists in a whole day's worth of the typical American baby's diet.

Once you get some practice keeping Super Porridge in the refrigerator and Super Green Veggie food cubes in the freezer, you will realize how little time and money it takes to feed your baby a super healthy homemade diet. With the size of this chapter, you'd swear I was documenting a mission to Mars. It takes longer to read about how to make the Super Baby Food Diet's Main Meal than it does to actually make the meal!

After I give my baby the main meal each morning, I have a real feeling of accomplishment. I get this wonderful sense of security and fulfillment after he finishes eating, because I know that he's had almost all of his required nutrients for the entire day. I hope that you have the same experience with your baby every morning—the feeling that "I done good!" ☺

Once your baby has finished eating the main meal, you can coast for the rest of the day. Feeding your baby will consist of a super easy second main meal based on yogurt, a few Super Snacks, and maybe a third meal. These are described later in this chapter.

The Super Baby Food Diet Daily Worksheet

The Super Baby Food Diet Daily Worksheet on page 134 is an easy way to keep track of your baby's daily requirements for the food groups. Please look at it carefully, and compare it to the Super Baby Food Diet Summary Table on page 120. The worksheet and the table go hand-in-hand. Note two things:

1. the foods groups in the diet match the columns in the worksheet, and

2. the minimum daily servings in the table match the numbers in the bottom row of the worksheet labeled "Suggested Daily Servings."

Ignore the protein combo column for now. (The Super Baby Food Diet supplies your baby with more than enough protein, as shown in the protein table on page 527. Protein complementarity and plant foods that combine to form complete protein are discussed on pages 512-519.)

It's simple to use the worksheet. You could probably figure it out by looking at the sample menu and worksheet on pages 136-137. Just fill in the foods your baby eats during the day and place the number of food servings that each food supplies in the column under the proper food group heading. At the end of the day, total up the numbers and compare your totals with the minimum number of servings in the bottom row of the table.

REMEMBER: The worksheet is meant to insure that your baby is getting a proper balance of foods from the main food groups, so that there are no nutrient deficiencies in his diet. There's no need to be a slave to it. It is just a tool to help point out a possible weakness in the variety of foods you're feeding your baby.

The Dairy Column of the Worksheet

The bottom total for the minimum daily servings for the dairy column depends on your baby's age. Before your baby is one year old, he should be drinking the amount of breast milk/formula recommended for his age. After your baby is one year old, he should be drinking at least 24 ounces of cow's milk (or fortified soy milk or other equivalent milk product) to meet his calcium and vitamin D requirements.

Milk (Calcium) Equivalents

These milk products have the approximate calcium equivalent of ½ cup or 4 ounces of milk:

> ½ cup yogurt
> ⅔ cup cottage cheese
> 4 ounces tofu (calcium coagulated)
> ¾ ounce of natural cheese
> 1-inch cube of cheddar cheese
> 2 tablespoons of cream cheese
> ⅔ cup ice cream

For other food sources of calcium, see the calcium table in nutrition part on page 540.

Vegetables and Fruits Must Supply Vitamins C and A

One of the fruits/vegetables that you feed your baby each day must be high in vitamin C. Kiwi fruit, orange juice, and to a lesser extent, broccoli, kale, and the other foods listed in the vitamin C table on page 539 in nutrition part. Because vitamin C is a water-soluble vitamin, it must be supplied every single day, as discussed in the nutrition part.

Vitamin A (or more correctly, beta-carotene) must also be regularly included in your baby's diet and is found in sweet potatoes, carrots, broccoli, kale, and the other foods listed in the vitamin A table on page 529. Because vitamin A is fat-soluble, and therefore able to be stored in the body, it's OK to skip a vitamin A food cube once in a while. This is why it is OK to have a vitamin A food serving every second day and alternate it with an egg yolk, which contains some vitamin A. The Super Green Veggies that you feed your baby every day contain significant amounts of beta-carotene, as can be seen in the vitamin A table. If you give your baby two veggie food cubes, don't forget to double the numbers in the table, because the 2 tablespoon serving size used in the nutrient tables is equal to only a single food cube.

REMEMBER: Make sure that your baby is getting a nice variety of fruits and vegetables. For example, if he eats a lot of bananas and grape juice and no other veggies or fruits, he is probably not getting his nutritional requirements met. A variety of foods is one key to a healthy diet. There are columns specifically for vitamin A and vitamin C fruits/veggies in the worksheet on page 134 to help you keep track of these two important nutrients.

The Super Baby Food Group Quick Reference Table

The Super Baby Food Quick Reference Table on page 135 will help to remind you which foods fit into which food groups. Note that there is a box in the table for each column in the worksheet. Many of the foods fit into more than one food group. For example, flax seeds, tahini, and tofu contain some calcium (page 540); therefore, these foods help to fill the requirements for the dairy group, even though we don't count them there. Milk alone can be counted as a complete protein, but it fits best under dairy. You needn't be concerned with these overlaps because they insure that nutrient needs are being met. Be concerned only when requirements are not being met, according to the number of suggested daily servings in the bottom row of the table.

You have my permission to make copies for personal use (so you don't have to worry about copyright infringements) of the worksheet on page 134 and the reference table on page 135. The reference and worksheet are purposely juxtapositioned so that you can copy both together on one 8½x11 sheet of standard paper. If you find that the type is too small, or have trouble putting numbers in the correct columns, use the enlarge feature on the copier to make the worksheet bigger.

REMEMBER: Keep your completed worksheets for discussion with your pediatrician. Your pediatrician should be aware of and approve of the diet you are feeding your baby.

Writing the Super Porridge Meal into the Worksheet

The main meal is a very important part of the Super Baby Food Diet, therefore detailed examples on how to write it into the worksheet are shown on pages 136-139. The Super Porridge Meal is shown as the breakfast part of the worksheet on page 137. The identical breakfast part of the worksheet is shown enlarged on page 139 for easy comparison with the box on page 138. Note that the worksheet is an easier method of writing the same information in the box.

If you look at the full sample worksheet on page 137, you will see that the Super Porridge Main Meal makes significant contributions to those minimum suggested daily serving totals in the bottom row.

TIP: Ask your babysitter to write into the worksheet any meals s/he gives your baby, and you can easily keep track of his diet.

The Second Main Meal

The Second Meal Is Based on Yogurt

Give your baby yogurt almost every day as part of a second main meal. You can sometimes use cottage cheese instead of yogurt, which is very high in complete protein (page 527 shows that ¼ cup supplies 14 grams of complete protein), but it also has a lot of sodium (page 546). Yogurt is preferable because it contains the friendly bacteria so necessary for intestinal health. Yogurt's beneficial bacteria also promote the production of B vitamins in your baby's intestines. (There's more about the health benefits of yogurt beginning on page 252.) This, along with the fiber in the whole grains and legumes in their diets, may be the reason why my babies never got diarrhea or constipation. I realized this one day when my sons and I were watching television when a commercial was shown for the pink stuff used to treat diarrhea. One of my sons turned to me and said, "What's diarrhea?" It's been several years and they still have never experienced it, or constipation either. From what I hear about leaky diarrhea-filled diapers, I consider myself very fortunate.

While I'm bragging about my healthy kids, I'd also like to boast that they are very rarely sick. I was surprised when I read that the average child has 6 to 12 illnesses a year! In fact, my son once complained to me, "How come we never get to stay home sick like everyone else in our class does?" Well, I confess that we now play hooky occasionally to simply enjoy a day off from school—we can afford it! I claim that Super Baby Food Diet, with yogurt and Super Porridge from whole grains and legumes as its foundation foods, promotes super immune systems in children. Now, I realize that three kids is not a statistically significant number for a scientifically-accurate medical study, but I still say it's the Super Baby Food. Let some scientist prove me wrong!

Like Super Porridge, yogurt is great base to contain other foods and nutritional enhancers. Yogurt is a good source of complete protein alone, but mixing yogurt with some other foods increases the amount of complete protein (see protein complementarity, page 513). A yogurt-based lunch is also a great way to get the one or two daily servings of ground nuts or seeds into your baby's diet.

> **MONEY SAVER:** Homemade yogurt costs a small fraction of commercial yogurt. And it's so darn easy to make! See instructions beginning on page 256.

If Your Baby is Allergic to Milk

If your baby has a milk allergy, not to worry, your baby can still have the health benefits of yogurt. Buy yogurt made with soy milk or other milk instead of cow's milk. If you can't find this kind of yogurt, buy soy milk, brown rice milk, nut milk, oat milk, or some other non-cow's milk and make your own yogurt—it's just as easy as making yogurt from cow's milk.

A Quick and Easy Yogurt Meal

To make a meal out of yogurt for your little one, simply spoon about ½-1 cup of plain yogurt into a bowl. Add one or more of these:

½-1 teaspoon of well-ground flax seeds

avocado or avocado frozen food cubes (thawed first)

1 tablespoon tahini

1 teaspoon or more of ground pumpkin seeds or other seeds

1 teaspoon or more of ground almonds, walnuts, filberts, cashews, or other nuts

½ of a ground Brazil nut
   (see warning about too much selenium in Brazil nuts, page 552)

1 tablespoon of thinned peanut butter or other nut butter softened for a few seconds
   on low power in the microwave

½ cup ground sunflower seed sprouts

1-2 tablespoons wheat germ

1-2 vitamin A veggie cubes (sweet potato, carrots, etc.)

other veggie cube(s)

puréed or fork-mashed ripe banana, peach, kiwi, or other fruit

cooked beans, with skins removed and mashed or pureed, or frozen bean food
   cubes made from the same

blackstrap molasses

a jar or part of a jar of commercial baby fruit or veggie or no-sugar applesauce

Preparation time: 2-3 minutes

Preparation Instructions for a Super Yogurt Meal

First, place frozen food cubes, if any, in the microwave to thaw. Second, spoon any whole seeds or nuts into your blender container. Start the blender. Meanwhile, spoon approximately ½-¾ cup of yogurt into a bowl. Stop blender and mix the ground seeds/nuts into the yogurt. (Note that you grind only the nuts/seeds in the blender—don't put the yogurt in the blender, or some gets wasted and the container is more difficult to clean.) Add any other ingredients that need no preparation, such as tahini, wheat germ, etc. Last, mix the veggie cubes, which are finished thawing in the microwave, into the yogurt. If the veggie cubes get too hot, let them cool first before adding to the yogurt or the heat will kill some of the yogurt's beneficial bacteria. You may want to place the veggies in a separate bowl so that your baby can taste the individual flavors. If you use a second bowl, you can mix some of the ingredients from the box above into the yogurt and some into the veggies for more variety.

Yogurt Is a Great Base for the Healthy Fats Your Baby Needs

Almost every single day, I add a little ground flaxseed or flaxseed oil (which are the absolute best sources of the essential fatty acid omega-3, fish oil is not), and at least ½ food cube of avocado (which is another super source of the unsaturated fatty acids)

to my baby's yogurt. Babies need fats for proper brain development, and avocado, seeds, nuts, and nut/seed butters are the best sources of the healthy unsaturated fats. (See EFAs and flax on pages 505-507 in nutrition part.)

Writing the Yogurt Meal into the Worksheet

An example of how to write a yogurt-based meal into the worksheet is given on pages 136-137.

Super Snacks Are Real Food

With regard to a baby's or toddler's diet, the word "snacks" is a misnomer. We adults tend to think of snacks as sweet little bits of foods that we eat for enjoyment more than to assuage hunger or to provide nutrition. This is not true for your baby or toddler. Snacks should NOT be thought of as "extras" or "treats" for your baby, but as a necessary part of his daily diet that adds calories and nutrition. Snacks may provide your baby/toddler with 20%-25% of his daily calories and other nutrients. Because your baby's stomach is quite small, it cannot hold very much at one time, and therefore your baby must eat small amounts of food frequently throughout the day. Snacks fill the need for food in the time stretch between meals and should be as nutritious as baby's main meals. You shouldn't worry that snacks will spoil your baby's appetite for a meal, because snacks are small healthy meals! However, if your baby is hungry and it's near a main meal time, you may want to skip the snack and move the time of the main meal up.

> **WARNING:** The foods we consider snacks—potato chips, cookies, cheese doodles, candy—should be NO part of your baby's diet. Besides the obvious lack of any nutritional value, most of these snack "foods" are choking hazards for babies and toddlers.

Snacks should be offered at scheduled, predictable times every day and not at random. As hard as it is not to do this, snacks should not be given to a baby/toddler to keep him quiet while you're on the phone or because he is bored. Keep his favorite tape at the ready in the VCR or a favorite toy handy instead. Snacks should be eaten in the feeding area, as main meals are, because they ARE meals. Dr. Burton White, on page 152 of the 1990 edition of his book *The First Three Years of Life*, states "Frequent between-meal snacks more often than not accompany comparatively poor development. Furthermore, there are some indications that some cases of lifelong obesity have their roots in this rather common child rearing practice." (Incidentally, I highly recommend Dr. White's book—see bibliography. It believe it has helped contribute to all three of my children becoming geniuses. ☺)

Until your baby becomes proficient at feeding himself, you will be spoon-feeding him his main meals, which will give him most of his daily nutrition. Snacks should consist mostly of finger foods, to allow your baby to practice his self-feeding skills (page 79). Ideas for healthy Super Snacks are listed in the recipes beginning on page 291. Although the Super Snack list may not appeal to you as tasty snacks, remember that they are not meant to be treats or luxuries, but a necessary nutritional part of your baby's daily diet.

The Third Meal

All babies are different. A baby can begin eating three meals a day as early as 4 months or as late as 10 months. When your baby is ready for a third meal, you will be able to tell because he acts hungry! Here are some ideas for an additional meal.

Another Super Porridge Meal

For a second Super Porridge Meal, instead of mixing in yeast and a mashed egg yolk/vitamin A cube as you did in the main meal at breakfast, you can add any of the nutritional enhancers listed in the table on page 120 or the foods listed as additions to yogurt on page 130. Mix them into the Super Porridge bowl or feed from a separate bowl, so that your baby can taste them individually.

Sandwiches and Crackers

As your baby gets older, you can give him meals that require more advanced eating skills than Super Porridge that will supply him with as much nutrition. For instance, instead of using Super Porridge as a base for nutritional enhancers, spread the enhancers into a sandwich made from 100% whole grain bread or spread them on whole-grain crackers. For more information on how to buy bread, see page 224. The Whole Grains chapter (beginning on page 218) explains why it's so important to eat only 100% whole grain bread.

Sandwiches are quick and easy to make, especially if you use easy sandwich spreads like tahini, thinned peanut butter, yogurt cheese, other cheeses, prune butter, and hummus. Recipes for sandwich spreads begin on page 316, with a summary table on page 317. When I make sandwich spreads like hummus, I always make and freeze a batch using the Food Cube Method. One cube is the perfect size for a sandwich.

Buy 100% whole grain crackers from the natural foods store or make your own (see cracker recipes, page 332). Use the sandwich spreads or a dip like avocado dip (page 354) for the crackers.

Pasta

Whole grain organic pastas can be found at the natural foods store. Don't use pasta made from white wheat flour from the supermarket (page 225). Mix cooked, drained whole grain pastas with just about anything: easy-to-make homemade Super Pasta Sauce (recipe on page 334, store-bought jars are much too high in sodium), cheese, veggie food cubes, or even sandwich spreads. Sprinkle nutritional enhancers like ground nuts/seeds and a little brewer's yeast in the dish immediately before serving. Pasta is a dish that can be frozen in individual portions and thawed in the microwave for a quick and easy meal. (See page 225 for tips on how to freeze and thaw pasta.) Why pay so much money for the commercial brands of frozen dinners or canned junk made with refined flours and loaded with salt, sugar, and additives? Make a few extra portions and freeze them yourself (see Toddler TV Dinners, page 285). Pasta recipes begin on page 334.

Toddler Recipes

When your baby grows into a toddler, there are hundreds of easy recipes included in this book, some of which the rest of the family will enjoy as well.

A Sample Daily Menu

On page 136 you will find a sample of a full daily menu from the Super Baby Food Diet. It's for an older baby or toddler as you can see by the portion sizes. On the page opposite the menu (page 137), there is an example of how you would fill in the worksheet for the sample menu.

THE SUPER BABY FOOD DIET DAILY WORKSHEET

Date:_____

		Grains	Legumes	Nuts/Seeds	Dairy	Super Green Veg	Vitamin C Fruit/Veg	Vitamin A Fruit/Veg	Other Fruit/Veg	Enhancers	Egg Yolk + Vitamin C	Vitamin Drops	Iron Drops	Protein Combination
Breakfast														
Morning Snack														
Lunch														
Afternoon Snack														
Supper														
Other Snacks														
Actual Servings Eaten by Baby														
Suggested Daily Servings		4 +	1 to 2	1 to 2	24oz+	1	1	1/2	2	1 +	1/2	1	1	2 +

Quick Reference for Super Baby Food Groups

Whole Grains	Legumes	Nuts and Seeds
Super Porridge and other whole grain cereals whole grain flour whole grain bread whole grain pasta wheat germ Oatios/Cheerios whole grain muffins, crackers, bread sticks	Super Porridge made with legumes tofu soybeans/soy grits other beans lentils split peas soybean milk (peanuts are actually legumes)	ground flax seeds ground seeds ground nuts tahini other seed butters peanut butter other nut butters nut/seed milks sunflower seed sprouts and other sprouts
Super Green Veggies	**Vitamin C Veg/Fruits**	**Vitamin A Veg/Fruits**
kale broccoli greens (beet, turnip, dandelion, mustard, collard) Brussels sprouts asparagus Swiss chard okra peas (edible pod) spinach	orange/orange juice other citrus fruit/juice kiwi fruit papaya tomatoes cantaloupe strawberries Brussels sprouts broccoli sweet green peppers	sweet potatoes carrots pumpkin kale cantaloupe peaches, nectarines apricots winter squash mango spinach
Other Fruits/Veggies	**Dairy**	**Enhancers**
avocado, bananas apples, pears, plums pineapple, berries honeydew, watermelon green beans cabbage, cauliflower beets, turnips white potatoes tomatoes/sauce	cow's milk, whole or 2% yogurt, whole milk soy milk, fortified cottage cheese natural cheese See note about dairy column on page 127.	brewer's yeast flaxseed/linseed oil wheat germ ground nuts/seeds ground sprouts desiccated liver blackstrap molasses powdered kelp

Combine These Foods to Make Complete Proteins:

grains+beans/legumes	milk+seeds	milk+beans
grains+tahini	milk+peanuts	peanut butter+tahini
grains+brewer's yeast	milk+grains	potatoes+cheese

Sample Daily Menu of Super Baby Food Diet

Upon awakening	breast feeding or bottle of formula
Breakfast Preparation time: 3 minutes	¾ cup Super Porridge cereal made from whole grain millet and soy grits mixed with a mashed hard-cooked egg yolk and 1 teaspoon brewer's yeast 2 broccoli cubes ½ cup fresh squeezed orange juice prescription vitamin drops iron drops
Mid Morning Snack Preparation time: 1 minute	½ cup Oatios (the natural foods store equivalent of Cheerios) small, soft pieces of cooked carrot from the Super Snack Freezer Bag (page 292) breast feeding or ½ cup (4 ounces) formula
Lunch Preparation time: 2½ minutes	½ cup whole milk yogurt mixed with 1 tablespoon tahini and 1 teaspoon ground flaxseed avocado cubes breast feeding or ½ cup formula
Mid Afternoon Snack Preparation time: 1 minute	ripe kiwi fruit, cut into small pieces for finger food or spoon-fed directly from peel ½ slice whole wheat bread, broken into small pieces for finger food breast feeding or ½ cup formula
Supper Preparation time: 2 minutes	¾ cup Super Porridge cereal made from brown rice and lentils mixed with a small mashed banana and breast feeding or ½ cup formula
Bedtime	breast feeding or bottle of formula
Plus a 1-2 tablespoons water after each meal and between meals.	

See nutritional analysis of sample menu above on page 528 in the nutrition part of this book.

Example of Completed Super Baby Food Diet Daily Worksheet for Menu on Opposite Page

Meal	Food	Grains	Legumes	Nuts/Seeds	Dairy	Super Green Veg	Vitamin C Fruit/Veg	Vitamin A Fruit/Veg	Other Fruit/Veg	Enhancers	Egg Yolk + Vitamin C	Vitamin Drops	Iron Drops	Protein Combination
Breakfast	3/4 cup Super Porridge	2	1											1
	hard-cooked egg yolk										1			1
	brewer's yeast									1				
	broccoli cubes					1								
	orange juice						1							
	prescription vitamin drops											1		
	iron supplement drops												1	
Morning Snack	Oatios	1												
	carrots							1						
	4 ounces formula				4									
Lunch	yogurt				1									1
	tahini			1										
	flaxseed			1										
	avocado								1					
	4 ounces formula				4									
Afternoon Snack	kiwifruit						1							
	1/2 slice bread	1												
	4 ounces formula				4									
Supper	Super Porridge	2	1											1
	banana								1					
	4 ounces formula				4									
Other Snacks	8 ounce bottle in morning				8									
	8 ounce bottle in evening				8									
	Actual Servings Eaten by Baby	6	2	2	32+1	1	2	1	2	1	1	1	1	4
	Suggested Daily Servings	4+	1 to 2	1 to 2	24oz+	1	1	1/2	2	1+	1/2	1	1	2+

Compare the numbers in the box below with the numbers in the columns in the worksheet on the next page and note that they are consistent:

The Super Porridge Main Meal Supplies Foods From Almost All Major Food Groups

The Main Super Porridge Meal summarized in the box on page 123 supplies these food group requirements:

2 from **Grains** group (2 ¼-cup servings of cooked grains) from the Super Porridge. Keep in mind that a ¾ serving of Super Porridge contains ½ cup (2 ¼-cups) of cooked grains and ¼ cup of cooked legumes.

1 from **Legumes** group (a ¼-cup serving of cooked beans) from the Super Porridge.

2 or 3 from **Vegetable/Fruit** Group from the Super Green Veggie cube, the vitamin C fruit/juice, and the vitamin A veggie cube if it is not an egg yolk day. And technically, you can count the beans in Super Porridge as a vegetable—adding one more serving.

1 from **Eggs** if it's an egg yolk day.

1 or 2 from **Nutritional Enhancers** from the brewer's yeast and maybe the desiccated liver.

1 or 2 **Protein** servings: The grains + legumes in the Super Porridge combine to make complete protein, and the egg every other day is a second protein serving.

Iron is supplied mostly by the iron supplement drops, but there is also some iron in the egg yolk, brewer's yeast, desiccated liver, and the whole grains and legumes in the Super Porridge.

Milk or other foods from the **Dairy** group should NOT be given to your baby in this meal, because calcium binds with iron.

Directions on how to cook Super Porridge are given in Part II, page 207. But briefly, if your baby is 9 months or older and can have beans and other legumes, ¾ cup of cooked Super Porridge cereal is made with ½ cup of cooked grains and ¼ cup of cooked legumes, which is two ¼-cup grain servings and one legume serving.

Breakfast	
3/4 cup Super Porridge	2	Grains
hard-cooked egg yolk	1	Legumes
brewer's yeast		Nuts/Seeds
Super Green veggie		Dairy
orange juice	1	Super Green Veg
prescription vitamin drops	1	Vitamin C Fruit/Veg
iron supplement drops		Vitamin A Fruit/Veg
		Other Fruit/Veg
	1	Enhancers
	1	Egg Yolk + Vitamin C
	1	Vitamin Drops
	1	Iron Drops
	1 1	Protein Combination

Enlarged Main Meal Part of the Super Baby Food Diet Daily Worksheet

Advantages of the Super Baby Food System
An Advantage for You and the Rest of the Family

The Super Baby Food Diet is advantageous for meal planning for the rest of your family, too. You have made one or two very special meals for your baby during the day. By supper time, when your spouse comes home and the kids come home from school, you can concentrate on a meal centered around the rest of the family, and not your baby. Your baby can join the family table. The main meals and Super Snacks that your baby has eaten during the day have supplied the vast majority of your baby's daily nutrient requirements.

The Advantage for the Parent Working Outside the Home

I worked three days a week when my twins were babies. The Super Baby Food Diet fit in well with the daily routine, because I could get everything ready the night before. I started with a bowl of Super Porridge (already made and refrigerated) and put into it some Green Veggie cubes, brewer's yeast, and a mashed egg yolk or orange veggie cube, and put it back in the refrigerator. I also got a yogurt meal ready with some mixed-in nutritional enhancers, and transferred finger foods/snacks from the Super Snack Freezer Bag (see page 292) into a partitioned bowl. All of this took only 5 minutes. The babysitter knew that she was to give him vitamin and iron drops with the Super Porridge, as well as some orange juice. The babies were on a regular daily eating schedule of healthy Super Baby Foods, and the babysitter found it nice and easy to prepare the foods and feed them.

Shopping for the Super Baby Foods
The Supermarket has Everything You Need

You can buy everything you need for the Super Baby Food Diet from your local supermarket: brown rice, oatmeal, lentils, split peas, bags of dried beans, vegetables, fruits, eggs, yogurt, and milk. But, instead of shopping for your baby's foods at the supermarket, it's worth it to take a trip to your local natural foods store.

Get Thee to a Natural Foods Store

A natural foods store has foods that are much healthier for your baby, because they are grown organically. Who knows what long-term effects these supposedly safe pesticides will have on your baby (or you for that matter)? Your baby eats much more food per pound of body weight than we do, so pesticides get more concentrated in her little body (page 38). Organic rice and legumes are not much more expensive than those at the supermarket. Compare prices and you will see—it's only a difference of pennies per pound. If you don't know where your nearest natural foods store is, look it up in the Yellow Pages under *Health & Diet Food Products-RTL*.

Food Shopping Tips

🍠 Shop the inner aisles of the supermarket first and the outer aisles last. I spend a lot of time with coupons comparing prices of toilet paper and spaghetti sauce jars. To prevent broccoli from drooping and frozen juices from melting in my shopping cart while I'm doing math in my head, I don't put them in the cart until I'm done with the room temperature non-perishables in the inner aisles.

🍠 Run other errands first and save grocery shopping for last. That way ice cream won't be melting in the back of the minivan while you are stopping at the dry cleaners, at the car wash, and buying stamps at the post office.

🍠 Discard expired coupons from your coupon holder and clip new coupons immediately before a trip to the grocery store and they will be fresh in your mind when you walk those aisles. Valuable coupons about to expire will be discovered. Place them in a coupon pocket labeled *It's now or never!*, and check this pocket before leaving the store. This prevents the "Oh no! I had a coupon for that and it expired!" phenomenon.

🍠 Use the "bin inventory" method in your home to keep important items in stock. In a special storage bin or closet, place one bar of soap, one roll of toilet paper, one day's worth of diapers, and one of any non-perishable item that must be kept on hand at all times. When you think you've run out, you will be saved by the bin. Note: This method will not work if you do not immediately replace the item in the bin!

🍠 Does your baby make a meal of the grocery cart handle? Cut a 12-inch piece from a non-toxic plastic shower rod cover and wash with antibacterial soap and hot water. Snap it on the grocery cart handle. Your baby can chew on it instead of a handle containing germs from the hands of hundreds of people.

🍠 Save grocery receipts with computer-printed prices and item names. Use them to compare for best prices at competing stores.

Get Familiar with Your Local Natural Foods Store

If this is your first trip to your natural foods store, take a few minutes to check it out. (If you're already a regular customer, skip to the next section.) Walk up and down the aisles looking at the individual items. The box on page 143 gives an idea of the foods you can expect to see.

By the way, the kind of natural foods store I'm talking about is the local, one room Mom and Pop store, not the "pretend" health food big business store at the mall, which specializes in vitamin jars and cans of protein powders labeled with pictures of gleaming gigantic biceps. From my experience, the people at natural foods stores are knowledgeable in healthy foods and care as much about the quality of their food and your health as their profits. If you let them, they will get to know you and your family as family. One of my local stores let me walk out with $40 worth of unpaid groceries because I forgot my checkbook, trusting me to pay the next time.

Buy Brown Rice and Millet First

If you are going to follow the Super Baby Food Diet, here are the first foods that you should buy, and the order that you will need them as your baby grows: brown rice, millet, oatmeal/rolled oats, pearled barley, yogurt, tofu, eggs, juices, tahini, Oatios, pumpkin seeds, almonds, other nuts/seeds, brewer's yeast, wheat germ, lentils, split peas, beans, natural peanut and other nut butters (or nuts to make homemade nut butters), bulgur, non-degerminated cornmeal, whole wheat pasta, sunflower seeds for sprouting, and by now you're a pro and I don't have to tell you what to buy. Buy only the first two (brown rice and millet) your first time at the store, if you wish. Get the rest as you need them.

Buying Natural Foods Through Mail Order

If you can't get to a natural foods store, mail order is an option. Some mail order catalogs are more expensive than your local health food store, a price you pay for convenience. You can buy everything from natural peanut butter and tahini to organic whole grains and tofu through mail order. There are many natural foods catalogs. Here are just a few:

Diamond Organics, PO Box 2159, Freedom, California 95019 has vegetables, fruit, nuts and nut and seed butters, breads, whole grains, beans, oils, vinegars, juice, wine, and much more. Overnight delivery available. Toll-free phone: 888-ORGANIC (674-2642); fax 888-888-6777; www.diamondorganics.com.

Walnut Acres Organic Farms®, Penns Creek, PA 17862-0800 has fruits, vegetables, meat, poultry, fish, soups, stews, broths, pasta, beans, whole grains, nuts, seeds, nut and seed butters, beverages, and much more. Express delivery available. Toll-free phone: 800-433-3998; fax 717-837-1146; www.walnutacres.com

Harvest Direct®, PO Box 988, Knoxville, TN 37901-0988 has TVP®, tofu, and other soy products, grains, pastas, soups, meat alternatives, and more. Call for catalog: Toll-free phone: 800-8FLAVOR(835-2867); fax 423-523-3372; www.harvestdirect.com.

Under the Sun Natural Foods, PO Box 77, 1075 Winchester Road, Shady Valley, TN 37688 has good prices and a very nice selection of natural foods, including yeast for breads. Phone: 423-739-9266; fax 423-739-9300; www.undersunfoods.com.

Bio-Designs by Allergy Resources, see page 31.

Familiarize Yourself with These Items and Their Locations in Your Local Natural Foods Store

- organic dry whole grains: brown rice, millet, whole oats, oat flakes and oatmeal, quinoa, teff, triticale, barley, etc.
- whole grain flours and brans: whole wheat flour, soy flour, oat flour, rice flour, millet flour, oat flakes, etc.
- organic legumes: dried beans, peas, lentils, soy grits, etc.
- organic nuts and seeds, refrigerated: almonds, walnuts, flaxseed, etc.
- jarred and canned nut and seed butters, such as organic peanut butter, almond butter, tahini, etc.
- organic cow's milk, pasteurized and refrigerated
- yogurt made from organic cow's milk, organic soy milk, and other milks, refrigerated
- eggs from happy, free-running, no-hormones-added chickens, refrigerated
- tofu in sterile packages, refrigerated
- tofu in aseptic packages that need no refrigeration, which can be kept safely at room temperature for up to 10 months. Once opened, they must be refrigerated.
- commercial boxed breakfast cereals similar to those in the supermarket, such as Oatios® or some other Cheerios®-like cereal, whole grain corn flakes cereal, etc.
- nutritional enhancements, such as brewer's yeast (nutritional yeast), wheat germ, nonfat organic dry milk powder, desiccated liver, powdered kelp
- whole grain pastas, such as lasagna, elbow macaroni, and spaghetti made from whole wheat, brown rice, or other whole grain
- organic tomato, pasta, and other flavorful sauces, with no added salt, sugar, or hydrogenated oils
- boxes of non-cow's milk, such as soy milk, rice milk, Better than Milk, goat's milk, oat milk, and almond and other nut milks. These boxes can be kept at room temperature until the expiration date; they must be kept refrigerated once they are opened.
- snack-type foods, with no added sugar: whole-grain cookies, snack bars, fruit leathers, shredded coconut, and carob chips
- caffeine-free flavorings and flavored drinks, such as carob powder (a chocolate substitute), grain coffees, and natural teas
- books, including those on vegetarianism, nutrition, herbs, natural foods, and cookbooks (including the *Super Baby Food* Book)
- organically-grown fruits and vegetables
- organic baby foods, such as Earth's Best jarred fruits and vegetables, Earth's Best whole grain boxed baby cereals, and organic whole grain teething crackers
- environment-friendly laundry detergents and other household cleaning products

Each Meal Takes Only A Few Minutes to Prepare

Batch Cooking Is the Key

Why does it only take a few minutes to prepare an entire home-cooked Super Baby Food meal? Because you have previously cooked batches of baby food and stored them in baby-sized portions in your refrigerator or freezer. They are there, ready and waiting for you to grab them and pop them into the microwave, making you capable of whipping up a complete baby meal consisting of vegetables, a fruit, and a cereal or protein food in a few minutes.

"Aha," you're thinking, "there's the catch! I have to spend days cooking over a hot stove to prepare these foods in advance!" Not true at all. On page 7, there is a table summarizing the foods, their preparation time, and the frequency with which you have to prepare them.

Foods You Must Prepare in Advance

There are really only three categories of foods that must be advance prepared in large batches to save time: Super Porridge, frozen cooked vegetables, and hard-cooked eggs. That's it. Detailed step-by-step instructions for preparing and storing all of the Super Baby Foods are given in Part II of this book, but the box below contains a little information to give you an idea of how you would cook and store them. You just cannot buy these foods. There's no commercial baby food on the market that is as healthy as your homemade.

Super Baby Foods To Be Prepared in Advance

- ❧ **Super Porridge** is a cooked cereal made from 2 parts whole grain and 1 part beans or other legumes. It takes about 10 minutes to prepare 2-3 days' worth and keeps in the refrigerator for up to 3 days or in the freezer for 2 months. Preparation instructions start on page 207.

- ❧ **Hard-cooked eggs** take about 15 minutes to cook, but almost all of that time is waiting time while they boil. Once cooked, eggs keep in the refrigerator for only one week. See *How to Hard-Cook an Egg*, page 268.

- ❧ **Frozen food cubes** of cooked vegetables and fruits take the most time—about 20 minutes to an hour or more, depending on the amount you're preparing. But you only have to prepare them once every month or two. They keep stored in the freezer in plastic freezer bags for two or more months. Instructions begin on page 178.

The steps in the box on page 147 shows how you can prepare these foods in less than 30 minutes per week.

Foods Needing No Preparation in Advance

Other foods in the Super Baby Food Diet are fresh and require no cooking or advance preparation, and can be prepared in a minute or two immediately before serving. Some of these foods should not be prepared in advance, because of nutrient loss. For example, fruits are a main source of vitamin C, the most delicate of all nutrients. Preparing them a minute before your baby eats them helps maintain this unstable nutrient, which gets destroyed by air, heat, light, and water. Every minute after you cut open an orange or kiwi fruit means the loss of vitamin C. Other foods, like flax seeds, should not be prepared in advance because they get rancid in just a few hours.

Super Baby Foods That Need No Advance Preparation

- **Yogurt**, cheese, and other dairy foods: no preparation necessary, although you can make your own yogurt and save a bundle—see page 256.

- **Fresh fruit**: takes a minute or two to wash, peel, core, and mash. See page 197.

- Wheat germ, brewer's yeast powder, flaxseed oil, and other foods used as **nutritional enhancers**, which get sprinkled into other foods like Super Porridge and yogurt: no preparation necessary—just open the jar.

- **Raw nuts and seeds**: to prevent rancidity, kept them whole in the refrigerator, and then grind to a powder in the blender *immediately* before eating. The chapter *Nuts and Seeds* begins on page 240.

- **Tofu**: purée or mash and combine with other food, or use small chunks as finger food. See page 238.

- **100% whole grain bread**: no preparation necessary, except for possibly tearing into bite-sized pieces. Toasting destroys nutrients. For more information on how to buy bread, see page 224. The Whole Grains chapter beginning on page 218 explains why it's so important to eat only 100% whole grain bread.

Foods that You Can Batch Prepare in Advance, If You Wish

There are other foods you can make yourself in order to save money. But if you don't want to take the time, you can purchase them from the supermarket or natural foods store instead. They will be as healthy as homemade. Foods like yogurt, fruit leather, teething and snack crackers, and whole grain bread cost about one-third of store-bought if you make your own. The yogurt and fruit leather are cake to make yourself and I would definitely recommend it, but the crackers and bread take time. Someday if you're feeling especially domestic and Martha Stewart-like, you should try them. For directions on how to make homemade yogurt, see page 256; for fruit leather, see page 202; for homemade yeast breads, see page 226; for quick bread recipes, see page 320; and for crackers, see page 332.

The Super Snack Freezer Bag

Some Super Snacks, like diced cooked veggies, are foods that you probably don't want to make a little at a time. And if your baby is the only one in the house eating tofu, there's going to be a lot of waste because it will spoil in the refrigerator before your baby eats it all. So, to save time and food waste, I suggest that you batch cook and freeze some Super Snacks. Or, while cooking plain and unseasoned veggies for the family, dice a small portion and add them to your Super Snack Freezer Bag (page 292). For how to freeze tofu, see page 238.

Develop Your Own Super Baby Food System

As you become more practiced at making Super Baby Food, you will develop your own system. One of my kitchen sessions, which I do every few weeks, is shown on page 147. These kitchen sessions are meant to give you a quick overview of the time necessary to prepare the Super Baby Foods and an idea of the steps involved. The details on how to prepare all of the Super Baby Foods are in Part II.

Veggies Take the Most Time, But Are Cooked Infrequently

The veggies are the baby foods that have to be cooked least often because they keep for at least two months in the freezer. Obviously, the larger the batch of veggies, the less often you have to make veggie food cubes. Rarely, when I have a lot of energy, I go all out and do the multi-batch vegetable cooking session shown on page 195. Or, when one particular vegetable goes on sale at the supermarket, I take advantage and stock up on food cubes by cooking using an assembly line-type kitchen session similar to the one shown on page 196.

Hard-cook Eggs Once a Week

Because hard-cooked eggs keep for only one week in the refrigerator, I do them once a week on the same day of the week—Monday. That way I know when they've expired and should be thrown out (see tip on page 271).

Cook Super Porridge Once Every Few Days

Super Porridge keeps for only 2-3 days in the refrigerator so, unless you freeze it, it must be cooked two or three times a week. You may have to make it more often if you are blessed with twins, as I was! Although Super Porridge takes about 15 minutes to make, you can merge it into other household tasks so that it actually takes only a few minutes of your time, as shown in the kitchen session on page 148.

Simultaneous Preparation of the Three Types of Super Baby Foods to Prepare in Advance: Frozen Veggie Cubes, Super Porridge, and Hard-Cooked Eggs

Time for each step:	Steps for vegetables:	Steps for Super Porridge:	Steps for hard-cooking eggs:
3 minutes	Wash, chop veggies, and start cooking in microwave.		
30 seconds		Place water for Super Porridge on stove to boil.	
30 seconds			Place eggs in water on stove to boil.
3 minutes		Measure, mix, and grind in blender grains/beans and place by stove, ready to stir into water. Place whisk by stove.	
5-10 minutes wait while veggies cook	Get purée equipment ready.	When water boils, stir in ground grains & beans. Note time when porridge will be done. Stir Super Porridge frequently.	Eggs started boiling, set timer, get towel for drying eggs ready. Forget about eggs until timer sounds.
7 minutes	Veggies are done cooking and standing, purée and put in ice cube trays, cover well, freeze.	Keep stirring Super Porridge frequently.	
2 minutes		Super Porridge done. Pour into individual bowls, cover, and refrigerate.	
2 minutes			Eggs done. Run cold water into pot. Dry well, cover, and refrigerate.

Total time: 23-28 minutes.

Integrating Super Porridge into Your Daily Kitchen Routine

Super Porridge keeps in the refrigerator for 2-3 days, therefore every few days you must make a fresh batch (unless you freeze it). There's no need for it to take more than a few minutes out of your day, if you merge it into the household tasks that you're doing anyway. Plan on making Super Porridge when you are going to be hanging around in the kitchen for at least 10 minutes, because you should stir Super Porridge every couple of minutes to prevent scorching. I make Super Porridge while I simultaneously do my daily 15-minute "quick pick-up" routine. Here's how I fit it in:

Time Super Porridge Right and It Won't Take Any Time

1. Place water on the stove to boil. Remember to always use the back burners and to turn the handles toward the wall so that baby can't reach.
2. Measure and grind grains and beans in blender and place next to stove. Place whisk next to stove. Now everything is ready for when the water begins to boil.
3. While waiting the 5 or so minutes for the water to boil, I do a small "out of kitchen" task, such as: sort or start a load of laundry, pick up some of the toys that are scattered throughout the house, fix a bed, take out the garbage, make a quick phone call, etc. But don't get side-tracked and forget about the pot on the stove as I have done many times!
4. Return to kitchen and sprinkle the ground grain/bean powder into boiling water. If you use the same burner, the same pot, and the same amount of water, you will know exactly how long it will take for the water to boil and you can set a loud timer to signal you to return to the kitchen with perfect timing.
5. Reduce heat and keep stirring until it cools a bit.
6. Now's the time to do 10 minutes of kitchen tasks while stirring the Super Porridge every 2 minutes: hand wash the last meal's dishes or empty/load the dishwasher, make a batch of formula bottles, take an inventory of the food staples on page 287 so that you know what to buy on today's trip to the natural foods store, clip coupons, sweep the kitchen floor, wipe off the counter tops, do a quick clean of the refrigerator—throw old food out and wipe off a shelf, call Aunt Maggie and keep the cordless phone in one hand while you wipe down the top of the refrigerator with the other, etc.
7. Pour finished Super Porridge into individual bowls, cover well, and refrigerate.
8. Clean the pot.

Voila! Super Porridge for 2-3 days.

Part II

Preparation and Storage of the Super Baby Foods

20. Kitchen Equipment

Most of the equipment needed to make homemade baby food is probably already in your kitchen—bowls, knives, and ice cube trays. Use only stainless steel or glass pots and pans and not aluminum (see aluminum on page 556).

A Food Processor or Blender

You will need something that purées food. You must make vegetables and fruits very mushy for your little chewing-impaired sweetie pie. Blenders and mini food processors can now be found in local department stores for less than $20. If you have either of these, you're set. If you

have neither and can only afford one, I'd recommend the blender. It can do almost everything the food processor can do, but it's better at preparing liquidy foods, such as slushies and drinks with the consistency of milk shakes. Only four or five speeds are necessary on a blender—you don't really need an expensive, fancy blender. A pulsing feature, which promotes even blending by allowing food to redistribute between pulses, is nice but not necessary. You can alternately press a speed button and the off button to get the same pulsing effect manually.

WARNING: Be sure to read the use, safety, cleaning, and maintenance directions for your blender or processor completely before you begin to use it. Be sure that the manufacturer's instructions say that it is OK to grind dry ingredients in your blender or processor, such as brown rice, oatmeal, other grains, and whole nuts and seeds.

Mini-Blend Container

I very strongly recommend that you buy a mini-blend container for your blender. This little container holds about one cup or 8 ounces. It's easy to fill, empty, and clean, and makes grinding grains, beans, and other legumes for homemade Super Porridge cereals a dream! I use mine at least once a day and it's the best $5.00 I've ever spent. You can order one through the mail with a credit card by calling Oster/Sunbeam at 800-394-BEAM. They come in sets of two—it's nice to have two, but you can save a few dollars if you go in with a friend. If you have a blender brand other than Oster or Sunbeam, find your owner's manual and order one.

Mini-Blend Container

Manual Grinders

You can purée with a food mill, but because it's manual, it takes a lot more elbow grease than an electric blender or processor. I don't recommend those small white plastic baby food grinders for making large amounts of baby food. They sell for around $10, half the price of a good blender. I've used mine only once or twice.

> **TIP:** If you want a portable baby food grinder for the diaper bag, buy a tubular garlic press instead. The press will continue to be useful for pressing garlic and food decorating (great for making hair and more—see page 362) when you no longer make baby food. A small hand grater can also be used.

Steamer

If you don't have a steamer, buy one—it's worth it. Steaming vegetables retains much more nutrients than boiling them, and it takes less energy to steam vegetables than to boil them. My first steamer was like the one on the left below, one of the least expensive ones—about $5.00. I finally graduated to the top-of-the-line multi-level type on the right with a clear cover and matching steamer insert with heat proof handles.

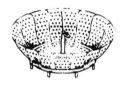

There are many other types of steamers. I never did experience the bamboo steamer. Grain steamers are discussed on page 222. Invest in a good steamer if you can afford it.

> **MONEY SAVER:** If you don't want to purchase a special steamer, you can always improvise a steamer by inserting a metal colander with legs, a flat-bottomed wire basket or strainer, or some similar heat-safe kitchen container with holes into a pot large enough to wholly contain it. Or place two aluminum foil pie pans with holes punched into them back to back on the bottom of a pot.

Microwave Oven

Once you've used a microwave oven, you can't live without one. You can now buy them for under $100. If you plan on purchasing one, look for one with digital timing (a keypad with numbers), instead of one with a round dial that turns. It's easy to accurately set the timer for short cooking times with a digital timer. You'll be setting that timer for 30 seconds quite often to warm small amounts of baby food. Choose a microwave with a built-in turntable, which promotes more even cooking. If you already own a microwave without a turntable, you can buy a separate turntable to place on the floor of your oven, or you can manually turn the food yourself during the cooking time.

A Strainer

If your baby is younger than 6 months, you may need a strainer or sieve for some foods, such as cooked fruits. Small seeds or bits of peel should be strained out for young babies in order to prevent choking or gagging. If you have a strainer, make sure it's in good shape. The metal wires should be unbroken and firm so that they won't break off into baby's food, and there should be no rust. Buy a strainer or sieve that is bottom shelf dishwasher safe even if you don't have a dishwasher. They tend to be more sturdy and you want to be ready just in case you do get a dishwasher some day. ☺

> **TIP:** Always rinse your strainer immediately after using to prevent food from drying on it. If you did let food dry on it, soak in hot soapy water and then scrub gently with a vegetable brush.

How to Strain To strain, use a rubber spatula (not a metal spoon which will put undo wear and tear on your strainer) to press the food through the holes in the strainer. For very fine straining, such as for baby juices and nut milks to prevent your baby from choking and so that the holes in the spout of your baby's training cup don't get clogged, I find that a yogurt strainer works well. Yogurt strainers can be purchased at kitchen stores and some department stores for the purpose of making yogurt cheese.

> **MONEY SAVER:** You can improvise a fine strainer for juices and nut milks by lining a colander with layers of cheesecloth, white paper towels, a clean thin kitchen towel, cloth diaper, coffee filter, or even a clean leg part from an old pair of pantyhose. If you don't have a colander, try using an aluminum pie plate with holes punched in it and place the cloth liner into the aluminum pie plate for fine straining.

Larger strainers can be used instead of a colander for rinsing beans and berries and can double as a flour sifter.

A Hand Grater

A small hand grater comes in handy when you are feeding a young child. It can be used to quickly grate cheese, raw carrots, apples, and other vegetables and fruits. Buy one that is dishwasher safe.

> **TIP:** When grating several food items, grate the softest food first. Subsequently grating harder foods will clean the softer foods from the grater holes. Use an old sterile toothbrush to clean your grater.

> **TIP:** If you do not have a food processor and want to grate carrots, cabbage, etc. for baby, you can use your blender. Place vegetables in blender, cover with sterile water, whiz until desired consistency, and pour grated veggies through sieve to strain water out.

Timers

Kitchen timers are life savers. The more you have, the better. Never put a pot on the stove without setting a timer. Although timers that make one beep are OK, I prefer the ones that don't stop beeping until I turn them off. (I sometimes miss one beep when I'm in the noisy laundry room or somewhere far off in another part of the house.)

An Organized Kitchen Saves Time, Money, and Energy

Clutter is the worst enemy of an organized kitchen. Get rid of it. If you are short on cabinet space (and who isn't?), place those items that you use once a year up into the attic. I put my ice bucket up there two years ago and haven't used it since—but I am using the cabinet space it freed up.

Kitchen items should be stored according to their frequency of use. The more often you use an item, the more easy it should be to grab. "Quick-grab" or "easy-access" kitchen spaces are those areas in your kitchen that are very convenient to reach: the front of an eye-level cabinet, the drawer next to the sink, the counter top in your most common work area, etc. Store infrequently-used light items in the upper cabinets and heavy items or fragile items in the lower cabinets. My bunny-shaped cake pan, which I use once a year if I'm lucky, is stored in the very back of the most hard-to-reach top shelf in my kitchen. However, my kitchen wipe-up towels—I seem to need a new clean one every five minutes when I'm in the kitchen—are stored in the big drawer between the sink and the refrigerator, which is the central part of the kitchen where I stand most often. (Wipe-up towels, discussed on page 159 in the next chapter, are a great help in keeping your kitchen clean.)

The quick-grab spots in your refrigerator and freezer are the door shelves and the front of the top main shelves. To prevent food waste, store leftovers with short shelf-lives where you'll be sure to notice them every time you open the refrigerator door. Seeing them will remind you to use them up.

Store perishable items following a consistent organization scheme that will rotate food to ensure that older food gets used first. My scheme is named the "book reading" method: left to right, top to bottom, front to back. Let's say you have 12 cans of tomato sauce with different expiration dates. The oldest can goes on the left side in the front row on the top layer. If you make a new batch of formula and still have two bottles leftover from the last batch, you should use the two older bottles first, of course. In our home, older bottles are placed on the left side of the refrigerator door shelf and everyone is instructed to "take from the left."

> **TIP:** If bottles keep toppling over in your refrigerator, place them in a cardboard carton six-pack holder or similar container to keep them together and upright.

Practical Improvisations for Kitchen Equipment

Just getting started and don't yet have a fully equipped kitchen? Here are some substitutes for commonly used kitchen items:

Rolling Pin. If you do not have a rolling pin, use as a substitute a liter bottle or a tall thin plastic bottle, a long can, a tomato paste or soup can, a potato chip can (any can should have no sharp edges), a wine bottle, a vacuum cleaner tube, or other sturdy or dense item shaped like a cylinder. A child's toy block shaped like a cylinder can be used for a very small rolling pin. To keep the dough clean and prevent it from touching items like your vacuum cleaner tube, place the dough in a plastic freezer bag or between two sheets of wax paper, or wrap the substitute rolling pin with wax paper.

Sifter. Shake flour through a strainer or sieve to sift it.

Strainer/Sieve. See money-saving tip on page 152.

Funnel. A funnel can be made from a plastic freezer bag with a hole cut in the corner, or a double piece of aluminum foil rolled into a cone shape, or from cutting off the top of a plastic liter bottle.

Cut here. ☞   Use top as a funnel. ☞

Yogurt Cheese Funnel. See page 254.

Steamer. See money-saving tip on page 151.

Disposable Dust Pan. An aluminum pie pan cut in half makes a quick and disposable dustpan. Sweep broken glass onto damp newspaper as described in the broken glass tip on page 38.

Pastry Bag. See page 376.

Colander. Use an aluminum pie plate with holes punched in it. Or use a large strainer/sieve.

More Ideas. The Homemade Baby Products chapter (page 466) and the section on Household Cleaning Solutions (page 476) have more ideas for household improvisations.

21. Kitchen and Baby Food Hygiene

Good Hygiene is Necessary to Prevent Food borne Illness

Food borne illness (commonly referred to as food poisoning) can be prevented if you follow the rules of kitchen and personal hygiene discussed in this chapter. Mishandling and improper storage of food in the home is the most prevalent cause of food poisoning. Babies and children are more susceptible than adults, so we must be very careful whether we are handling either our own homemade Super Baby Food or commercial baby foods.

Hand Washing—Yours and Your Baby's

Washing your hands is probably the most important thing you can do to keep baby food clean. Keep a pump bottle of antibacterial soap by the kitchen sink and use it frequently. When you wash your hands, rub the soap over every inch of your hands for at least 30 seconds, getting between your fingers, under your rings, and under your fingernails. With fingertips downward, rinse hands thoroughly under very warm water—the hottest you can stand. Dry with a clean paper towel or a freshly-laundered wipe-up towel (page 159).

> **REMEMBER:** When washing your hands, remember to thoroughly rinse off all soap so no trace of it ends up in baby's food.

> **MONEY SAVER:** Keep a spray bottle filled with water mixed with a few tablespoons of antibacterial dishwashing liquid near the sink. A few squirts on your hand or an a dish/pot that you are washing individually is more economical than a squirt of liquid at full concentration.

> **NOTE:** Some believe that over-using antibacterial soaps may cause super strains of bacteria (similar to the super strains of germs that have become immune to antibiotics).

Remember to repeat hand washing if you've touched yours or your baby's eyes, nose or mouth, sneezed into your hands, touched a pet or pet's dish, touched meat, eggs, or other raw animal products, and, of course, if you've gone to the bathroom or changed a diaper.

> **WARNING:** Cover any open cuts, especially those on your hands, with sterile adhesive strips or band-aids before feeding your baby.

When baby starts self-feeding, wash his hands thoroughly before each meal because you never know what he's been touching! Unlike adults who usually eat with utensils, baby's hands go directly into the food and into his mouth.

> **WARNING:** Puppies are wonderful! But be especially careful to wash your baby's hands thoroughly if she touches one. If she puts her hands in her mouth or eats with them before you wash them, she can get worms internally. Scary, I know. For a similar warning about the dangers of reptile-like pets, see page 36.

Use Antibacterial Dish Detergent

Antibacterial dish detergent is great because when hand-washing dishes, we sometimes don't use water hot enough to kill bacteria. Use hot water to wash and rinse dishes and dry with a freshly-laundered wipe-up towel.

> **TIP:** I hate hand-washing dishes—who doesn't? I find that I hate it much less if I have a pair of rubber gloves on. Then I don't mind putting my hands in mush and I can use very hot water without burning myself. Sprinkle a little cornstarch or baking soda into gloves to make them slide on and off easily. Use a warm hair dryer to dry the inside of rubber gloves, but watch carefully to prevent them from burning or catching fire.

Keep Your Sink and Faucets Clean

Use antibacterial soap, hot water, and an old toothbrush or vegetable brush to wash your kitchen sink faucets and sink interior daily. You don't want your clean hands to pick up germs from your sink faucets.

> **TIP:** Old toothbrushes are great for cleaning little nooks and crannies in blenders, hand graters, in the edge around the stove, electric can openers, strainers, garlic presses, etc. Run the toothbrushes through the dishwasher in the silverware basket to sanitize.

Cleaning Your Blender and Food Processor

Bacteria can hide in the cracks and crevices of your blender and/or food processor. It is important that you take them apart after every use and clean them. Use very hot water. If you have rubber gloves on, don't accidentally put a hole in them with the sharp blades. Thoroughly clean and dry each individual piece before re-assembling. As you know from reading the manufacturer's instructions, those large holes in the cutting blades are for the purpose of picking up the discs safely without touching the sharp edges that cut and grate.

> **WARNING:** Clean your blender soon after each use and never let it wait so long that food dries on the blades. If you simply cannot clean the blender right away, pour some hot tap water into it and let it soak until you can get to it. If you accidentally did let something dry in your blender so that it is impossible to clean off (orange pulp is the worst!), rinse as much as possible and then blend some water and ice. The cracked ice will blast it off.

TIP: To help get your blender clean before disassembling, place a little dish detergent in the blender with about a cup of hot water and optionally a ½ teaspoon of baking soda and run on low speed for 30 seconds. Use only a small drop of dish detergent, only one molecule, unless you want a kitchen full of suds! ☺

TIP: Blenders and food processors are loud. Buy a thick pad of rubbery plastic in a stationery shop for keeping office machines quiet, and place it under the blender to make it run more quietly. Or use an old computer mouse pad.

Cutting Boards

They used to say that the surfaces of wooden spoons and cutting boards were breeding grounds for millions of bacteria, and to use only plastic or metal. Now they say that bacteria do not grow on wood. Who knows! I still do not recommend wood cutting boards. Plastic cutting boards are supposedly safe when cleaned well. They should be discarded when deeply scarred because bacteria can grow within the cuts.

I use a small plastic cutting board with a claim on the label that will not dull knives. I wash it after every use in the dishwasher. It's small and takes little room. To prevent deep cuts, I place previously cut peels and other veggie/fruit parts on the plastic board under the food I'm currently cutting, so that the knife cuts into the peels instead of the board.

Meat Safety Deserves Special Attention

If you cut and prepare meat in your kitchen, please read the section *Handling Meat Safely*, beginning on page 279.

Important Safety Warnings

Please re-read the *Important Safety Warnings* chapter beginning on page 35. And make sure to read the bleach warnings on page 473.

Disinfect Kitchen Surfaces Often

You can buy disinfectant for kitchen counter tops and other kitchen surfaces, but it's cheaper and just as effective to use plain old chlorine bleach. A strong solution that will kill any germ in its path is 1 part chlorine bleach to 4 parts water. Let sit for 5 minutes and rinse. When it not longer smells, the bleach is dissipated and gone. Chlorine does give off toxic fumes in amounts well below recognized safety levels for adults. But I recommend that you disinfect only when the baby is not around and when you are in a well-ventilated kitchen.

WARNING: Never let chlorine bleach touch a metal sink or other surface or metal utensil. For metal surfaces, buy a special purpose disinfectant.

NOTE: Some experts insist that frequent household germ-killing is futile because it has such a short-term effect, and that the disinfectant treatment is more dangerous than the germs. Others claim that the only important preventative measure is frequent and diligent hand washing. Others believe that babies need to be exposed to germs to develop their immune systems. Still others recommend major household disinfection only if there is a contagious disease in the home. Ask your pediatrician for the latest advise, which I can't keep up with because it seems to change every month!

The Garbage

Regularly clean your kitchen garbage pail by taking it into the bathtub and washing it with disinfectant and hot water from the shower massage.

Hide your kitchen garbage pail in a locked cabinet for the next few years. If your baby is like mine, he loves to throw things like television remote controls and other expensive items into the kitchen garbage can. He also enjoys chewing on discarded banana peels and other food from the garbage. If you can't hide your garbage pail, replace it with one of those lock-able diaper pails available at any baby store.

WARNING: Plastic garbage bags are a suffocation hazard for toddlers; use paper until your baby grows older.

Dishwasher Tips

If you are fortunate enough to have a dishwasher, that's great! Use it to the max and follow these tips:

🍐 If you know you will soon be preparing a batch of baby food or formula bottles, load your dishwasher with everything you will need. Use the heat boost during the main wash cycle to kill every last germ. When the dishwasher finishes, it is the perfect time to prepare baby food or formula, when dishes, pots, bottles, nipples, ice cube trays, and utensils are freshly sterilized and still untouched by human hands inside the dishwasher. It also saves put away time—take the bottles and bowls from the dishwasher and use them right away. There's no need to put them away. They may never see the inside of a kitchen cabinet!

🍐 Pre-rinsing Is Not Necessary. It's not necessary to rinse off your dirty dishes before you put them in the dishwasher—it's just a waste of water. If you don't believe it, try just one dishwasher load with no pre-rinsing. You'll be surprised that the dishes get perfectly clean anyway. One time I remember being so exhausted that I threw half-full bowls of cereal into the dishwasher without any scraping at all. I dreaded opening the door after that wash cycle, but to my surprise and relief everything was perfectly clean! The only non-meat foods that you must pre-rinse, to my knowledge, are flax and chia seeds. Because they are mucigelatinous (you'll know what I mean if you eat them), they stick to everything, especially glassware. Rinse them off well and do so immediately after a meal, before they become hardened to the plate. See warning and tip on page 244.

🍐 Don't Use the Delay Option. If you have a delay option on your dishwasher, so that it starts in the middle of the night and not during peak electricity daytimes, you may not want to use it. Here's why: Water sitting in your pipes loses heat, which means that the water that fills your dishwasher at night is much cooler than water coming fresh from the hot water heater (unless you have midnight bathers in your home). This problem gets magnified the farther your hot water heater is from your dishwasher and the colder your basement is. The heat boost option during the main wash cycle helps to reheat the water, but it is best to have hot water for all wash and rinse cycles.

🐾 Run Hot Tap Water Before Starting. Immediately before you start your dishwasher, run tap water into your kitchen sink until it gets its hottest. This way the water cooled from sitting in the pipes won't fill your dishwasher. Turning up the thermostat on your hot water heater will make tap water hotter, but I don't recommend it. There's a danger of people, especially children, getting scalded in the shower or bath when your tap water is very hot. A temperature setting of 140°F is probably best for hot water in the kitchen and safety in the bathroom. However, please note that the American Academy of Pediatrics, whose main concern with water temperature is the prevention of scalding, suggests a setting of 120° or lower. Money Saver: While letting the tap water run until it gets hot, don't let it run down the drain, save it in jugs for watering plants or other purposes.

🐾 Dishwasher detergent becomes ineffective with exposure to air, so don't fill your dishwasher cups far in advance of starting the cycle. This is another reason that the delay option may not be a good idea. Fill the detergent cup that will be closed first and the open cup second. This way if you spill detergent on the door while filling the closed cup, it won't be wasted because you can count it towards the amount you need in the open cup. Decrease the amount you pour in the open cup by the amount you spilled..

🐾 **Warning:** Remember that dishwasher detergent is poison to babies/toddlers. Keep it out of baby's reach—both the bottle and the liquid in the cups on the open door of your dishwasher.

🐾 Use only detergent meant for dishwashers. Hand dish liquids will cause too many bubbles that may clog the drain and prevent the jets of water from doing their job. See recipe for homemade dishwasher detergent, page 476.

🐾 Load Carefully and Don't Overload. Your dishwasher will get your dishes clean only if the water jets can do their job. Make sure you don't place a big bowl or broiling pan in the way of baby bottles or any other dishes, or they will prevent the water from shooting at them and getting them clean. And don't overload your dishwasher, save the extra dishes for the next load. Tip: Load ice cube trays by placing them back-to-back and upright between the bars of the top rack of your dishwasher.

🐾 Dishwasher Baskets. I use two baskets on the top rack of my dishwasher to stop small items from flying around inside. I put everything from bottle caps to small plastic measuring cups in them. In my opinion, they are well worth the price, but if you'd rather not buy one, see the money saver tip on page 77.

🐾 Empty clean dishes from the bottom rack of your dishwasher first. Then if some trapped water spills from a dish/cup as you're emptying the top rack, no dishes on the bottom rack will get wet and have to be towel dried. Grab the silverware basket by the big handle and move it to the counter over the silverware drawer to save steps in emptying.

Wipe-up Towels Help Keep Your Baby and Kitchen Clean

The handiest thing you can have in your kitchen to keep it clean, whether or not there is a baby in the family but especially if there is, is a dozen or two of those cheap white terry cloth finger towels or wash cloths. You can buy them at the local X-mart store for around $3.00 a dozen. Or you can find similar cloths in large packages labeled "carwash cloths" in the automotive section of department stores. Make sure you buy only 100% cotton terry cloths. I use them to wipe up everything from my baby's face and hands to the kitchen counter tops and floor. There are always several clean wipe-up towels in a special kitchen drawer used only for the purpose of holding these towels, and everyone in the family uses them. Buy two or three dozen and you'll always have a fresh clean towel to dry your hands and for wiping up.

> **WARNING:** Sponges are breeding grounds for bacteria. Wipe-up towels are better—they can be used for many more purposes than sponges and are always clean because you wash them after every use. If you insist on using sponges, run them through the dishwasher on the top shelf. Or disinfect by soaking in ¾ cup of household bleach in a gallon of water for 10-15 minutes and then rinse them out very well.

You probably already use white cotton diapers as general-purpose wipes and spit-up rags for your baby. These are fine, but I find them too thin and large for kitchen use. Terry cloth wipe-up towels or washcloths are so much more absorbent. They are also small enough for single-use purposes, as you would use disposable paper towels.

> **TIP:** Buy different colors of wipe-up towels for different uses: yellow can be for wiping up kitchen counters and hand and dish drying, green can be for baby's bottom, white can be for baby's hands and face, etc.

> **REMEMBER:** You will want to wash them first before you use them, of course. Wash them and machine dry them *separately* the first time, because they will shed an incredible amount of lint the first time they are washed. (It's nice white lint, though. Use it to make play dough, see recipe on page 397.)

There are three reasons why these little terry cloth towels are so practical. One, you can use them to wipe up anything. They are so cheap that you don't care if they get stained or ripped. You can even use them on baby's bottom if you sterilize them afterward by washing them in hot water and bleach. Two, they'll save you money on paper towels. Three, their laundering cost is negligible, because you can add them into the washing machine with ANY other clothes or laundry. You can even wash them with a new red shirt, because you don't really care if they turn pink—they're rags.

> **TIP:** Even though they are rags, you can still extend their lives. When (not if) snags form in them, don't pull them, cut the threads instead. Do this also, of course, for your good terry cloth towels.

I do laundry at least every other day. In every load, there are several of these wipe-up towels. I usually wash my towels in hot water with bleach to sterilize them. Sometimes I don't have any other whites to wash them with, and it would be too energy inefficient to wash a few wipe-up towels in bleach and hot water in a large washing machine alone. So here's what I do to save water and energy. Place the wipe-up towels in the empty washing machine. Set the machine for hot water wash and the water level to low. Pour in detergent and bleach and begin the wash cycle. Let the machine go through the wash cycle and the first rinse and spin cycle, and then open the lid. The rags are now clean from a hot water and bleach wash (but not thoroughly rinsed) and are in the bottom of the washing machine. Now begin all over again from scratch for the rest of the laundry. Place the regular load of laundry into the machine with the wet clean wipe-up towels. Set the water temperature and level and add detergent according to the rest of the load. The towels will be washed again and finish the rinse and spin cycles with the rest of the load. From my experience, it seems that there is not enough chlorine bleach left on the towels after the first rinse and spin cycle to do any color damage to the other clothes, but you may not want to do this with clothing that is susceptible to color fading.

The only time you have to go through this procedure is when you feel that your wipe-up towels need to be sterilized in hot water and bleach, such as when you used them on baby's bottom or on the kitchen floor. Wipe-up towels used only on baby's face and kitchen counter tops probably don't need hot water and bleach, especially when you're going to dry them in a hot clothes dryer.

> **TIP:** An adaptation of this washing method can be done when you have clothes that should be washed in different cycles and different temperatures. Let's say you have two small bunches of clothes: one is more durable than the other and should be washed in hot water with normal agitation and lots of detergent in a long cycle, and the other bunch consists of more delicate clothing that should be washed in cooler water. Throw the durable bunch in the machine first with the full amount of detergent, set the water level to low and the water temperature to hot, and start the machine on a long-timed wash. When the machine is almost done with the wash cycle, set the water level to high and allow cold water to fill the wash basin to the top, making the water now warm or cool instead of hot. Then add the delicate clothes into the water and let them agitate for the short time left on the wash cycle. Both bunches get rinsed (in cold water) and spun dry together. In effect, you've done two different load types in one!

How Does Your Bacteria Grow

Small Amounts Are OK

Bacteria are everywhere! They are on your hands and skin, inside your mouth and nose, in meat and eggs, on the surface of fruits and vegetables, on insects, and worst of all, *bacteria are in the air* attached to dust particles. Food is constantly being contaminated with bacteria, which is why you must take such care in handling your baby's food. But these bacteria usually exist in small amounts, and because they are small amounts, they don't give us much trouble. It's when they grow and multiply into large amounts that they poison our foods and make us sick.

Bacteria Need the Proper Environment
To Multiply to Dangerous Levels

The environment must meet these four criteria to allow bacteria to multiply to dangerous numbers:

- **Moisture** Food must be composed of enough water (more than approximately 15%) for bacteria to be able to grow. Most foods do contain enough moisture, although some foods, such as dried fruits and flour, contain less than bacteria need.

- **Warmth** Food must be at the proper temperature for bacterial growth to occur, which is between 40° and 140°F. High heat kills bacteria, but cold only temporarily disables them, as discussed later in this chapter.

🍃 **Proper pH** Most fruits are too acidic and most vegetables are too alkaline to support bacterial growth. This is why you can leave fruits at room temperature to ripen. Meats, eggs, and other foods are in the proper pH range.

🍃 **Time** It takes time (2 or more hours) for bacteria to multiply and grow to dangerous levels. It may take as little as one hour or less in warm temperatures conducive to bacterial growth.

Food Preservation Methods Must Prevent Bacterial Growth

Methods of preserving food and protecting it from bacterial growth take advantage of one or more of the above bacterial needs. For example, dried food, such as dried apricots and beef jerky, have most of their moisture removed, enough so that bacteria cannot multiply. Freezing keeps food too cold for bacteria to multiply. Canning involves heating food to kill bacteria and packing it in bacteria-proof containers.

Storage Temperature Is an Important Bacterial Deterrent

It is very important not to leave food sitting out at room temperature for extended periods, because bacteria will grow rapidly in it. However, it does take time, possibly as long as 2 hours or more, for bacteria to multiply to dangerous levels and cause illness. That is why no one got sick at the last summer picnic from eating foods that sat outside on the tables. To be safe, do not leave food, especially baby food, at room temperature for more than a few minutes. Keep hot food hot and cold food cold.

Freezing Does NOT Kill Bacteria

As the thermometer figure on page 164 shows, temperatures higher than 165° Fahrenheit will kill most bacteria. It is important to note that cold temperatures 40° or lower, as in your refrigerator and freezer, only inactivate bacteria and temporarily prevent them from multiplying. *Cold does not kill bacteria.* When the temperature warms up, bacteria kick in and multiply at warp speed.

Shallow Containers are Best

To get food cooled as quickly as possible, store them in small and/or shallow containers. Deep or large containers may allow the food in the middle to remain at a bacteria-friendly temperature. Bacteria will have time to multiply before the middle food cools and will become alive again when the food is warmed. The ice cube trays used in the Super Baby Food Method are ideal for the quick-freezing of baby food to prevent bacterial growth—they are not only shallow, but the dividers between the cubes also help the food to freeze quickly.

Never Thaw Foods at Room Temperature

It is important not to let foods, especially meat, thaw at room temperature or in warm water. The outer layers can become warm enough for bacteria to multiply, even though the inside is still frozen. Thaw all foods in the refrigerator, where the outside layers will remain at a temperature too cool to allow bacterial growth. (Never marinate at room temperature—always marinate in the refrigerator.)

WARNING: Due to the possibility of bacterial growth, never refreeze food that has been frozen and thawed. Never cook baby food from frozen foods and re-freeze into food cubes.

Thaw Baby Food So That Bacteria Cannot Multiply

Puréed baby food must be handled very carefully to protect it from an influx of bacteria. Keep it cold right up to the minute before feeding your baby. Do not let it sit at room temperature for more than several minutes. Some baby food cookbook authors suggest thawing food cubes by taking them out of the freezer and letting them sit at room temperature for an hour before meal-time. I do not recommend this method, because it may give bacteria a chance to grow. Heating methods for frozen food cubes are discussed in the section *How to Safely Thaw Baby Foods*, page 175.

Safely Handling Baby's Food

Introduce as Little Bacteria as Possible

Minimize the introduction of bacteria into baby food by having all cooking equipment that touches the food whistle clean, including utensils, ice cube trays, blenders, counter tops, and your hands.

> **TIP:** Once you've cleaned utensils that will be used for baby's food, hide them from the rest of the family. If you put them in the silverware drawer, other family members (who may have forgotten to wash their hands) will touch them. Store them covered in a clean drinking glass in the back of a cabinet, or roll them up in a clean paper towel or wipe-up towel and hide them in the back of a drawer. Or store them in a new plastic storage or freezer bag. While emptying clean dishes out of the dishwasher, I always store a few spoons and other utensils that I plan to use for making baby food in a new plastic zippered freezer bag. Then I use that same bag for freezing the food.

Move food from cooking pan to refrigerator/freezer as quickly as possible to minimize the time that food is in the temperature range for fast bacterial growth. Cooking will destroy most bacteria, but it is inevitable that some bacteria will sneak into the food from utensils and other equipment or even from the dust in the air. To stop those bacteria before they begin to multiply, cool the food immediately after cooking. If you are concerned that the hot container will warm the inside of your refrigerator, set it in ice or cold water until it cools down a bit. Be careful with any hot glass container because it may crack if you put it on ice or cool it too quickly.

Dip with a Clean Spoon

Always use a clean spoon when removing food for baby from a large container. For example, when dipping yogurt or spooning cooked cereal out of a refrigerator container, use a clean spoon that has not come in contact with saliva or counter top bacteria. You don't want to introduce bacteria into the food.

> **MONEY SAVER:** To prevent food waste, use a clean spoon to take from the large container a small amount of food that you are sure your baby will finish, because you will have to discard any leftovers.

Bacteria Thrive at Room and Body Temperature

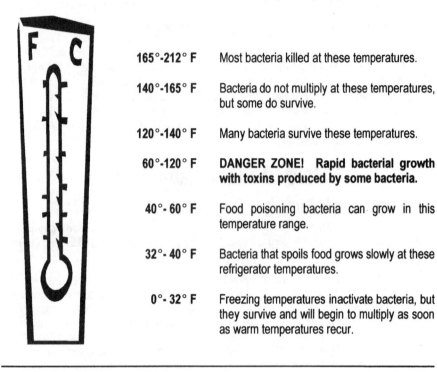

165°-212° F	Most bacteria killed at these temperatures.
140°-165° F	Bacteria do not multiply at these temperatures, but some do survive.
120°-140° F	Many bacteria survive these temperatures.
60°-120° F	**DANGER ZONE! Rapid bacterial growth with toxins produced by some bacteria.**
40°- 60° F	Food poisoning bacteria can grow in this temperature range.
32°- 40° F	Bacteria that spoils food grows slowly at these refrigerator temperatures.
0°- 32° F	Freezing temperatures inactivate bacteria, but they survive and will begin to multiply as soon as warm temperatures recur.

TIP: It's worth it to spend a few dollars on a refrigerator/freezer thermometer available at the local X-mart or kitchen store. Use it verify that your freezer's temperature is 0°F or colder. Do this by placing the thermometer in the front of your freezer near the top and leaving the door closed overnight or for at least 6-8 hours. If it reads higher than 0°F, lower the freezer's thermostat and check the reading again after keeping the door closed for 6-8 hours.

Use the same method as for the freezer to verify that your refrigerator temperature registers somewhere between 32°-40°F. As a general rule, try to keep your refrigerator as cold as possible without freezing the milk. The coldest part of most refrigerators is by the refrigerator coils or at the bottom (cold air sinks). A thermometer can find the coldest and warmest parts of your refrigerator—leave it overnight in each part and compare to find out which part is coldest.

WARNING: The freezer keeping times for foods stated in this book assume a freezer temperature of 0° F. If your freezer is warmer, the keeping times should be significantly shortened.

REMEMBER: To prevent bacterial growth, **keep hot foods hot and cold foods cold.**

If you take too much, you must discard any leftovers. It's OK if your baby doesn't eat all of the food—the days of the "clean plate club" are over. See the section *You Can Put Your Baby in a High Chair, But You Can't Make Him Eat* on page 53, which stresses to never force your child to eat. If you've taken too little and your baby wants more, don't worry, she'll let you know. Or you can ask her if she wants more (it's OK if she doesn't). You can then use a new clean spoon and take more out of the container.

With commercial baby foods, it's OK to feed your baby by spooning directly from the jar *if he is going to eat the whole jar.* Throw out leftover food in the jar if baby's saliva has been introduced into it. If your baby is going to eat only part of the food, use a clean spoon to dip out his portion and immediately replace the top and refrigerate the rest.

Baby Food Precautions

- **Baby food can be spoiled without necessarily smelling bad.** If you have any questions about the safety of a food that looks or smells strange, don't take a chance, discard it. Don't taste it to see if it's OK. **When in doubt, throw it out!**

- Do not keep baby food or juices, either opened commercial jars or homemade, in the refrigerator for more than one or two days.

- Any leftover homemade or commercial baby food or juice that has come in contact with your baby's saliva, because the spoon from your baby's mouth has been dipped into it or because your baby has drunk from the cup or container, must be discarded. The saliva's enzymes and bacteria will continue digesting the food or juice, breaking down the vital nutrients and causing it to begin to spoil.

- If commercial infant/baby/toddler cereal has been mixed with liquid, serve it immediately. Discard any leftovers and do not use them for another meal.

- Once frozen or refrigerated baby food/juice has been sitting at room temperature for more than a few minutes, do not re-freeze it or return it to the refrigerator. Bacteria from the air and other sources has been introduced into the food, even if your baby's saliva has not touched it. Its quality has deteriorated and bacteria may have started to grow to dangerous levels, making it unsafe for your baby to eat.

- Do not make baby food from frozen vegetables or other frozen foods and re-freeze it using the Food Cube Method. Baby food should not be frozen more than once.

- Never eat food that has mold on it. The mold you see is only the tip of the iceberg—poisons from molds form far under the surface and may not be visible. Don't cut off the moldy part of food and eat the rest. Throw away all of the food, even though only part of it is moldy.

- To prevent bacterial growth, never thaw baby food at room temperature (pages 162-163) and do not keep baby food in the danger zone for bacterial growth (see thermometer on page 164) for more than a few minutes. Follow all directions in the section *How to Safely Thaw Frozen Baby Foods* beginning on page 175. Follow all precautions in the chapter *Important Food Safety Warnings* beginning on page 35.

22. Methods of Freezing and Thawing the Super Baby Foods

Throughout this book are references to these freezing methods: the **Food Cube Method**, the **Tray-freeze Method**, the **Phantom Container Freezing Method**, and the **Nested Plastic Bag Method**. This chapter explains how to freeze foods using these methods, and includes other information about freezing and thawing foods.

TIP: Besides veggies and fruits, almost all other Super Baby Foods are freezable, including Super Porridge, tofu, yogurt, cottage cheese, egg yolks, pasta, wheat germ, sprouts, cooked beans (frozen whole or puréed in food cubes), juices, and homemade tomato sauce.

If you're not sure about the "freezability" of a food, check the appendix *Specific Fruits and Vegetables* beginning on page 424. You can also find several good books on freezing and preserving food at your library. See the bibliography. I especially like the one by Janet Bailey, entitled *Keeping Food Fresh*.

The Food Cube Method

Puréed, cooked vegetables are a large part of the Super Baby Food Diet. To save time and energy, cook and purée large batches of veggies all at once (directions begin on page 182) and freeze them in ice cube trays using the Food Cube Method. Most ice cube trays make food cubes that are about 2 tablespoons in volume, which happens to be the perfect size for a portion of baby food. You may wish to measure your ice cube capacity by using a tablespoon to measure water into one of the cubes. When your baby first starts on solid foods, she will probably eat only a tablespoon at a time, so you may want to fill your ice cubes only half way. As your baby's food servings grow, you can fill the cubes to capacity. Eventually, your baby will be eating 2-3 food cubes at a time.

MONEY SAVER: For a baby who eats very little, you may want to make food cubes using those tiny cocktail ice cube trays, which hold teaspoons instead of tablespoons.

The Two Steps to the Food Cube Method

The Food Cube Method involves two steps:
1) placing the food in ice cube trays and letting it freeze until solid, and
2) transferring the frozen food cubes into plastic freezer bags.

If you are in the middle of puréeing a big batch of baby food and you run out of ice cube trays, no problem. Use little paper cups. Or scoop the puréed food in little glops onto a tray and freeze using the Tray-Freeze Method, as discussed on page 170. Or use Styrofoam egg cartons, cleaned very, very well with very hot water and antibacterial soap. Cover well to prevent freezer burn and nutrient loss.

If ice cube portions are too small for the foods you wish to freeze, you can use slightly larger glops or larger containers, such as empty single-sized yogurt containers, butter or margarine containers, popsicle molds, or muffin or mini-muffin pans. Plastic containers should not be so flimsy that they will crack, and the tops must seal airtight. Reinforce the tops by using freezer tape to make them airtight.

REMEMBER: The puréed food in the ice cube trays should be frozen as quickly as possible. If you have the room in your freezer, do not stack the trays on top of each other. Warm trays will give heat to each other if stacked and will prolong freezing time. Try to place the trays separately in different parts of the freezer. If your freezer has a quick-freezing shelf, use it until trays are frozen, and then move to a regular part of the freezer.

Transferring the Cubes to Freezer Bags

After the food cubes are frozen solid, which may take 8-12 hours or overnight, transfer them to freezer bags. Use bags specifically made for freezing, not the thin plastic bags that look like freezer bags. I like the freezer bags from Hefty®, called "One-Zip®." They close very easily, but I sometimes have trouble opening them. The other type, where you have to match up the lines to zip shut, are sometimes difficult to close, but always open easily.

REMEMBER: Don't accidentally buy the "storage bags" instead of the "freezer bags." The packages look very similar and I once grabbed the storage type by accident when I was in a hurry and didn't read the box carefully.

Freezer bags usually come in two sizes—quart-size and gallon-size—but I suggest that you use only the smaller size bag. The last food cubes left in the bottom of the larger bags tend not to be very fresh, because it takes some time to use all the cubes in a larger bag. Also, it's easier to find space in a crammed freezer for a little bag.

TIP: If you are having trouble removing ice cube trays from the freezer because they are stuck to the shelf or other items in the freezer, place a sheet of waxed paper under them before freezing.

MONEY SAVER: When your are ready to make the transfer from ice cube trays to freezer bags, don't waste water by running it over the back of those trays to loosen the cubes. Let the trays sit on the counter for a few minutes. Thawing will occur around the edges just enough to allow the food cubes to easily pop out with a twist of the wrist or a whack on the counter. If you're going to do counter whacking, keep the aluminum foil cover on the tray to prevent the cubes from landing all over the counter or the floor and to keep them clean.

Place the food cubes in the freezer bag, but before zipping shut, remove as much of the air from the inside of the bag as possible. To remove air, follow these steps. Close the bag until it's almost shut, leaving it open about a half-inch at one end. Stick a drinking straw or one of those very thin coffee stirrer straws into the opening. Use your mouth (see warning below) to suck the air out of the bag through the straw until the bag shrink-wraps tightly around the food. Pinch the straw where it meets the zipper in order to keep the bag closed, pull the straw out, and quickly finish zipping closed the bag.

WARNING: Be very, very careful not to inhale any loose pieces of food while you're sucking the air out of the bag. I once choked on a crumb that I accidentally sucked down my throat. I know it sounds hilarious, but please be careful. Place a paper towel over the end of the straw or close your teeth tightly while sucking to block any small food pieces from flying down into your windpipe.

Label and Date Each Freezer Bag

The first vegetable you will probably cook and freeze for your baby is sweet potatoes. At first, there will be only one bag of sweet potatoes in your freezer. After your baby gets older and is eating a variety of veggies, you may gather quite a few bags. Even the keenest eye has trouble telling frozen carrot cubes from sweet potatoes, but you can usually smell or even taste them to tell (break off a piece with your clean fingers and taste, don't bite and leave saliva on the cube).

Label the bags with the name of the food, the date of freezing, and the date the keeping time expires. It depends on the specific food, but it is probably safe to say that veggie cubes will keep for at least two months. (See warning about freezer temperature and keeping times on page 164.) You probably will use your cubes up well before that time. An example of how you would label sweet potatoes, with a keeping time in the freezer of two months, is show on the right.

> *Sweet Potatoes*
> *Frozen:* 11/14/97
> *Expires:* 1/14/98

TIP: If your freezer bags have "built-in" labels, use them. They are less likely to fall off and get lost in your freezer.

TIP: If you're desperate for a freezer label, use a VCR tape sticker, a computer disk label, or even a band-aid.

You may have to retrieve baby food bags from the freezer several times per day, so keep them in an easy-to-reach place in the freezer. Being able to grab them quickly will not only save time and aggravation, but will minimize the time the door is open, preventing your freezer from losing its cool.

TIME SAVER: I mix together several days' worth of the orange and green veggie cubes and avocado cubes in the same freezer bag. It's easier every morning to find, pull out, and open ONE bag instead of THREE.

TIP: To get veggie cubes for baby's meals, you may be opening up a freezer bag two or three times a day. It soon becomes a real nuisance to be constantly sucking air out of freezer bags. To keep a large batch of veggie cubes fresh in your freezer without using your lungs three times a day, try this: Place a few days' worth of veggie cubes in a small freezer bag and close the bag without bothering to remove the air. The cubes get used up soon and don't get freezer burn—they stay fresh for several days even if you don't remove air from the bag. Store the rest of the big batch of veggie cubes in a large freezer bag and DO take the time to remove as much air as possible. These cubes will stay fresh because the bag is air tight. You need to open the big bag infrequently, only when the small bag runs out and you replenish the small bag with cubes from the large bag.

WARNING: Keep freezer bags or any type of plastic bag away from your baby/toddler—they are a suffocation hazard!

Re-use or Recycle Those Freezer Bags

Don't throw away those used freezer bags! Carefully wash them with hot water and antibacterial soap for re-use in the freezer or use for one of the many purposes listed below. Wash and re-use only the good quality freezer bags; throw out the flimsy sandwich bags.

WARNING: Never re-use bags that contained meat, poultry, fish, or eggs because of possible E. coli, salmonella, and other contaminants. The risk is not worth the savings. Carefully discard them where baby cannot reach them.

Besides re-using freezer bags in the freezer, they can also be used to: hold wet paper towels or wipe-up towels in the diaper bag for cleaning dirty faces and hands ✎hold wet/dirty clothes or diapers ✎hold a clean change of clothing for your baby ✎hold small muddy shoes for keeping your house or car carpets clean, or to place on adult shoes to keep from getting muddy—keep some bags in the trunk of your car ✎hold bottles that may leak or break in your suitcase ✎store fragile items in suitcase—surround item with cloth, place in freezer bag, blow up bag to inflate like a balloon and rubber band or zip shut air tight, store in suitcase ✎store older children's toys in (marbles, puzzles, jacks, etc.) to prevent small pieces from getting lost ✎store small pieces of *anything* in to keep them from getting lost ✎place between non-stick frying pans when stacking to prevent scratches ✎place milk cartons in to keep milk drips from messing up your refrigerator ✎hold food transferred from their original bags which got ripped ✎buy food in bulk and store in freezer bags ✎marinate foods in the refrigerator—turn often and you'll need only half the liquid ✎hold rarely-used kitchen utensils (corn cob holders, etc.) to keep them clean and together ✎use as a funnel or as a disposable pastry bag (page 377) ✎bags with tiny holes need not be thrown away if they will be used for non-waterproof purposes to hold large items that need not be kept sterile ✎keep an empty freezer bag in your purse at all times—fold it up until it's the size of a lipstick and wrap tightly with a rubber band.

TIP: If drawers start getting cluttered and messy with too many freezer bags, store them by wrapping them around paper towel or toilet paper tubes and securing them with rubber bands.

WARNING: Keep freezer bags or any type of plastic bag away from your baby/toddler—they are a suffocation hazard!

WARNING: Never use plastic bags with paint on them for food uses. Lead in the paint can get into the food. Recycled bread bags should not be turned inside out for this reason. Never use any bag with paint to cover foods in the microwave oven.

MONEY SAVER: Don't buy one of those expensive wooden racks sold in kitchen stores purposely for air-drying plastic bags. Make your own drying rack out of Tinker Toys® or by bending a clean wire hanger as shown in the picture on the right. Or stand a spatula, skewer (sharp end down), or other long utensil in a glass and hang the bag on it to dry. Or place a clean refrigerator magnet inside the washed bag and hang it upside down on the refrigerator to dry.

MONEY SAVER: Use the Food Cube Method for all freezable foods when you do not want to discard a small amount of clean leftovers. Often you open an entire can of some recipe ingredient and use only a small amount, such as tomato paste, stock, lemon juice, etc. Measure the leftovers into recipe-sized amounts and freeze in ice cube trays using the Food Cube Method or the Tray-Freeze Method. Tablespoons of frozen tomato paste can be dropped into sauces without thawing first.

TIP: What to do with extra ice cube trays when your baby grows and you're no longer making Super Baby Food? Use them as drawer organizers for small odds and ends.

The Tray-freeze Method

For berries or fruit chunks that you would like to easily retrieve *separately*, use the Tray-freeze Method. Line a tray or cookie sheet or anything clean, flat, and freezable with waxed paper. Arrange the chunks of fruit on the waxed paper so that they do not touch each other. Cover with foil or freezer wrap and place in the freezer. (If you use those flat, rectangular plastic storage containers with lids—you won't need waxed paper, and because they have a cover, you'll save on aluminum foil or plastic wrap.) When solidly frozen, remove fruit chunks from trays and store in plastic freezer bags. Later you can easily remove as many single pieces as you want because they won't clump together.

Puréed sweet or white potatoes can be frozen in ice cube trays using the Food Cube Method, or they can be rolled into little balls and tray-frozen. Beginning on page 293, there are many recipes for Toddler Hors d'oeuvres that tray-freeze very well.

TIP: Use a Styrofoam egg carton (cleaned very well with hot water and antibacterial soap) instead of a cookie sheet to keep ball-shaped foods separate during the initial freezing step. Cover well during freezing. Then transfer to freezer bags.

TIP: Use muffin tins to freeze broths and other liquids in pre-measured amounts for your favorite recipes. Cover well during freezing. Then transfer to freezer bags.

MONEY SAVER: Check out your local warehouse store or restaurant supply store for very large boxes of aluminum foil, waxed paper, and plastic wrap. You must buy a lot, but you will save a lot if you use a lot!

The Phantom Container Freezing Method

Supermarket TV dinners are expensive and contain too many sweeteners, sodium, and preservatives. Make your own TV dinners—a batch at a time—and freeze them yourself.

You will need a few containers to freeze homemade TV dinners. There are many shapes and sizes of plastic freezing containers, which can be found in most department stores and supermarkets. Invest in a few containers that are microwave, dishwasher, and freezer safe. They'll pay for themselves in no time. Buy those that are shaped for efficient storing, such as the flat ones that can be stacked to make the most of freezer space.

You're not limited to the number of containers you have if you use the Phantom Container Freezing Method. Here's what to do: Cook several servings of "TV" dinners. Good choices are macaroni and cheese, lentil stew, eggplant Parmesan, or almost any casserole. Spoon single servings into individual freezer containers. Freeze overnight until very solid. When frozen solid, take the containers out of the freezer and let them sit on the counter for a few minutes until the food thaws around the edges just enough so that you can pop it out of the container. The frozen food will maintain the shape as if there is an invisible or Phantom container surrounding it. Immediately place the block of food in a plastic freezer bag, or wrap well with two layers of aluminum foil. (Sounds just like the good old Food Cube Method, only for bigger servings.) Or use the Nested Plastic Bag Method (discussed next). Label and date and return to the freezer. The empty container is now available for other uses. When it comes time to eat the TV dinner, take the food block out of the bag or foil, place it back into the same container in which it was frozen, and heat it in the microwave as you would a store-bought TV dinner. If you are not in a hurry, thaw it in the container overnight in the refrigerator (never thaw food at room temperature). You will save energy re-heating it, and while it thaws it helps to keep the refrigerator cold.

You can place one or more side dishes of cooked vegetables, pasta, or other foods into the container with the entree, just as in supermarket TV dinners. It's OK if the container doesn't have individual compartments to keep the foods separated. With a large enough container and food that isn't too runny, the glops will stay apart if you're careful during handling. If the container is small or the foods are runny, they will probably run together. Some little (and big) people simply refuse to eat different foods if they touch or are mixed together. For them, use pieces of freezer-quality and microwave-safe plastic wrap or waxed paper to keep the foods separate in the container during freezing. To separate for serving, heat for a minute or two in the microwave until you can pull the foods apart. Then transfer them to a larger microwave-able dish with space between them to prevent their mixing.

TIP: Muffin pans—those with 12 cups—are great for keeping side dishes separate. As are popsicle molds. Save plastic containers from yogurt, butter, etc., and use freezer tape to make sure that they are airtight before using for freezing. But, by far, the best containers for homemade frozen TV dinners are the re-cycled ones you re-use from store-bought TV dinners! Ask friends who throw them away to save them for you.

Freeze soups in individual servings using the Phantom Container Method for up to 3 months. Pour soup into individual bowls, freeze, and pop out of bowl and into a freezer bag. Use the same bowl to re-heat and eat. Or, line a bowl with the freezer bag and pour soup into the bag and freeze. Reclaim the bowl when solidly frozen—the soup is already in the bag.

The Nested Plastic Bag Method

The Nested Plastic Bag Method is a method of freezing individual toddler-sized servings of finger foods and other foods, which saves you money on freezer bags. Simply nest several of the cheaper, lower quality sandwich bags inside a higher quality large freezer bag. Place individual servings of foods in the cheaper plastic sandwich bags, which cost a small fraction of plastic freezer bags. Then put the sandwich bags inside of a larger good quality plastic freezer bag. The sandwich bags keep the individual servings separate, and it doesn't matter that they are not freezer quality because they are inside a larger good-quality freezer bag.

WARNING: Don't put cheap plastic sandwich bags in the microwave, as they will melt into the food. Let the food thaw around the edges for a few minutes, remove it from the plastic sandwich bag, and transfer it to a microwave-safe container.

One application for the Nested Plastic Bag Method is in the freezing of Super Snacks. (See Super Snack Freezer Bag, page 292.) Keep diced carrots in one sandwich bag, chopped peaches in another, pasta pieces in another, etc. Or you can have a Frozen Fresh Herb Bag, where one sandwich bag contains dill frozen in ice cubes, another contains parsley, another oregano, etc. For how to freeze and thaw parsley and other herbs, see page 450.

I also use the Nested Plastic Bag Method to freeze cooked veggies for my older boys' lunches. I cook a batch of veggies and divide them into cheap sandwich bags containing half-cup portions, which I then place into a big good quality freezer bag. In the morning, I take one of the sandwich bags from the freezer bag and pack it in the lunch box. It's thawed and ready to eat by lunch time. (A small blue ice block keeps the food at refrigerator temperature to prevent bacterial growth.)

Important Rules for All Freezing Methods

Prevent Bacterial Growth

Whether you are using the Food Cube Method or one of the other freezing methods, use super clean equipment and utensils because although freezing retards the growth of bacteria, it doesn't kill them (page 164).

As soon as each ice cube tray or other container is filled with food that is to be frozen, don't let it sit at room temperature. Pop it into the freezer immediately. Get it cold as soon as possible to prevent bacterial growth.

> **TIP:** A few hours before you begin making frozen baby food cubes, especially if you're going to make several trays, turn your freezer thermostat down a notch to make the freezer colder than usual. Turn it down to -10°F to get it really cold. The food will freeze faster. A large amount of warm food may affect the foods already frozen in your freezer, so get your freezer nice and cold to prevent this.

Prevent Freezer Burn

Freezer burn occurs when air gets into the package and causes the food to dry up. You probably know how it tastes; it sometimes looks like pale gray spots. Before freezing, cover all food well with aluminum foil, freezer wrap, or place in a freezer bag and make it really airtight. Although freezer burn is not dangerous, it causes nutrient loss, and it dries and toughens the food and causes an off flavor.

Always use plastic and aluminum foil that is meant to be used in the freezer by carefully reading the label on the packages. Cheap plastic wrap or sandwich bags alone aren't heavy enough to protect frozen food. Do not re-use aluminum foil in the freezer, because the crinkles allow air to permeate into the food. Don't place aluminum foil directly on acidic foods (tomato sauces, pastes, etc.) for freezing or they may develop a metallic taste.

> **WARNING:** Some people contend that the only safe substance to place next to food is waxed paper, because aluminum foil and plastic wrap leave residues in the food. If you are concerned about this, you may want to place a layer of waxed paper between the food and an outer layer of aluminum foil or plastic freezer wrap.

> **TIP:** When doing a lot of re-arranging in your freezer, use oven mits to protect your hands from the cold.

> **REMEMBER:** Foods and liquids expand when they freeze. For those containers that have no flexibility, such as glass jars, remember to leave at least ½ inch of air space for expansion. Leave ½ inch of headroom on top of containers filled with liquid, or the liquid will expand and may come out the top during freezing.

> **TIP:** If you are going on vacation and live where power outages are a problem, place two ice cubes in a plastic bag in the freezer. Upon return, check ice cubes and if they are not still in the shape of ice cubes, you'll know there was a power outage. Freezer food may not be safe to eat.

TIP: Some foods in cooked recipes, such as pasta, vegetables, and grains become softer after being frozen and re-heated. If you find this, try undercooking the recipe a little before freezing it.

NOTE: You may find that my advice on freezing foods conflicts with the advice found in other cookbooks. This is so because other authors are concerned about the preservation of food texture during the freezing and thawing processes. For example, I say that you can freeze bananas, but others would disagree because, when thawed, bananas get mushy and darken. Although adults may not, your baby may like it that way! Some experts will tell you to cool the trays first in the refrigerator before putting them in the freezer. Cooling food before freezing reduces moisture condensation. The condensation (water) expands during freezing, breaks food fibers, and causes foods to be limp and soggy. With puréed baby food, we don't have to worry about this, so skip the refrigerator step, go directly from counter to freezer. You may have heard that before freezing most vegetables and some fruits, blanching is required. **Blanching** is the process of boiling food briefly and then quickly cooling it to stop the cooking process. Blanching sterilizes and cleans food before freezing. But more importantly, blanching stops enzymes from changing the food's composition (ripening it, decomposing it). Of course, we don't have to worry about blanching because our baby food's enzymes have been deactivated during cooking.

Freezer Space

A well-stocked freezer is more energy-efficient than a half-empty freezer, because the empty air space loses cold much faster than solidly frozen material when you open the door. If you don't have food to freeze to fill up your half-empty freezer, stuff it with newspaper. Even better, fill the empty space with empty clean milk cartons filled with water. The ice blocks that form will help to keep your freezer cold, especially if your electricity goes out for a while. Do leave some space for air circulation to keep your freezer working properly.

As your family grows, you are more likely to have the problem of too little, rather than too much, freezer space. You can make efficient use of your freezer space by using freezer containers that are of uniform size and square-cornered rather than round, because they will fit more tightly together. The method by which you freeze semisolid liquids in freezer bags can also save you some freezer space: Don't freeze them by initially placing them directly on the freezer shelf. They'll freeze into a roundish lump and may bulge into the wires of the freezer shelf. Instead, place the bags in the freezer on a flat surface (a cookie sheet, a piece of clean cardboard, etc.) and smooth their semisolid contents so that a somewhat flat, square shape is formed. Of if you want to get fancy, you can place the filled freezer bag into a box for a neat box shape. After the contents is frozen solid, you can then stack them compactly, directly on a freezer shelf. This method is good for pasta with sauce, stews, soups, and casseroles, because they have liquid and can be shaped into squares. Unfortunately, you don't have the flexibility to do this with baby food cubes in freezer bags, which have quite a bit of air space between them, unless you want to spend a lot of time packing the cubes individually so that they fit together like a tight jigsaw puzzle!

TIP: Here's a tip if you find yourself frequently searching for items in your freezer that aren't there, or find outdated frozen food that must be discarded and wasted. Keep an inventory list of freezer items taped to the freezer door. Update it every time you add food or take food out of the freezer. Besides preventing wasted food, this list also saves energy because you don't keep the door open looking for foods that don't exist.

How to Safely Thaw Frozen Baby Foods

"Safely" here has two meanings. First, baby food should be thawed in a way which prevents bacterial growth. Baby food never should be thawed at room temperature, and baby food should not be kept at room temperature for more than several minutes. Please be sure that you have read about bacteria on pages 161-163.

Second, "safely" means thawing baby food so that it is not too hot or too cold to be a danger to your baby. If it's too hot, it may burn your baby's mouth. If it is too cold, and therefore not thawed thoroughly, it may contain frozen food chunks that are choking hazards to your baby. (Food that is too cold may also "burn" your baby's sensitive mouth—see warning on bottom of page 80.)

Baby's Food Should Be Only Moderately Warm

Note that I have been using the word "thaw" here and not "re-heat." You want to just take the chill out of baby's food, you don't want to make it hot. Never feed your baby hot food! Your baby's mouth is much more sensitive to heat than your mouth, and food that does not feel hot to you may burn your baby. Baby's food should be only slightly warm, about the temperature of the body—98.6° F, like breast milk. When you touch the food, it should feel neither hot nor cold.

Stir Baby Food Thoroughly to Evenly Distribute Heat

Whether you're using the microwave or the stove top to thaw baby's food cubes, it is important that you make sure there are no heat pockets or "hot spots" anywhere within the food. It is very possible that one section of your baby's food feels cool or even cold, while other parts are dangerously hot and will burn your baby's mouth.

WARNING: *When warming baby food, always thoroughly mix before feeding to baby in order to distribute heat as evenly as possible. Be especially careful with foods heated in the microwave oven, which is notorious for its uneven heating of food. Stir completely and then test, test, test.*

Always Test the Temperature of Your Baby's Food

One way to test is to insert your clean finger into several areas of the bowl. Although you may be uncomfortable doing this, remember that it is certainly better than burning your baby's mouth.

> **WARNING:** Do not test the temperature of your baby's food by feeling the container. A not-too-hot container does not mean that the food contained within it is a safe temperature for your baby. Each part of the food must be temperature-tested directly.

Another way you can test is to touch each and every spoonful to your upper lip immediately before placing it in your baby's mouth. Although you may feel that sharing a spoon with your baby is unclean, some experts believe that normal bacteria from your mouth introduced into baby's mouth may actually help prevent cavities. But others do not agree and believe that bacteria from your mouth can cause cavities in your baby's mouth. Discuss with your pediatrician whether you should share a spoon with your baby. Of course, if you are ill, spoon sharing is not a good idea.

It is interesting that in some cultures, parents act as natural food processors: They chew food, remove it from their mouths, and feed it to their babies. The parent's saliva partially digests the food, making it easily digested by the baby.

Thawing Food Cubes in the Microwave

Many experts recommend avoiding the microwave altogether for thawing baby food because of its uneven heating. It's a fact that parents do, despite this recommendation, use the microwave because of its convenience. The microwave is the quickest and easiest way to thaw food cubes. And the short period of time it takes to thaw foods is excellent for retaining nutrients and preventing bacterial growth.

In using the microwave to thaw baby food cubes, the goal is to thaw each cube so that it has no icy solid chunks left in it, while keeping the food cool enough to be safe for baby's mouth. I'm so cautious that I microwave only until there is a little piece of frozen vegetable left in the middle of the cube. Then I mash the frozen chunk with a fork until it thaws.

Place the frozen cubes in a little microwave-safe bowl. I use Corelle® dishes—their little bowls are perfect for this purpose. Custard cups work well too, and so do the plastic dishes purposely made for babies. With experience, you'll know exactly how many seconds it takes to thaw a food cube, probably somewhere between 30 seconds and a minute. My old microwave takes 50 seconds on high to defrost each cube, but its wattage is much lower than the newer microwave ovens.

Baby's Food is Too Hot? How to Cool Food Quickly

If you accidentally make the food too hot and your baby is loudly complaining that she wants to eat NOW, add frozen food cubes and mix thoroughly to cool it fast. Or, try this: Scrape the food into a new cool bowl. The flatter the bowl, the more surface area on the food, and the faster it will cool. Place it in the freezer for a minute. Stir the food again thoroughly and it will be much cooler.

Thawing Food Cubes on the Stove Top

If you don't want to use the microwave, thaw food cubes on the stove top over low heat, or use a double boiler.

> **MONEY SAVER:** Save energy by warming two different veggies in the same pot by wrapping them separately in aluminum foil. This also saves time and water because you must wash only one pot instead of two.

Stove top thawing is a problem when it overheats the outside portion of the cubes in order to warm the inside. To avoid this use very low heat or a double boiler. This takes a while, so begin warming the cubes 15 minutes to ½ hour before mealtimes. Stir often while thawing.

Thawing Food Cubes in the Refrigerator

Food cubes can be thawed overnight in the refrigerator, where cold temperatures prevent rapid bacterial growth. This method may be the best alternative for parents who do not wish to use the microwave, either because they do not want the dangers of hot spots or because they are concerned that the microwave changes the structure of foods. It takes several hours for food cubes to thaw in the refrigerator, which is why thawing overnight might be the best way to thaw in the refrigerator.

> **WARNING:** Always be careful to check that cubes have been thoroughly thawed, and that there are no leftover frozen food chunks inside the cubes on which your baby can choke.

Although you might like your veggies warmed, your baby will probably be perfectly happy with them at refrigerator temperature. If so, you will save time, energy, and nutrients by thawing them overnight in the refrigerator and not warming them at all. However, warmed food does have more flavor. If you wish, you can warm your baby's food from the refrigerator by placing the container in a bowl of hot tap water for a few minutes, or by placing it in the microwave for a few seconds, or on the stove top over medium-low heat for a minute or so. As always, test for safe temperatures before feeding to your baby.

There is one disadvantage to overnight thawing in the refrigerator: You must discard puréed baby food from the refrigerator within a day or two. If you do not carefully plan the next day's meals, you may have to waste food by throwing it out. Baby food must be discarded after a day or two in the refrigerator because refrigerator temperatures only *slow* bacterial growth, they do not completely prevent it (as shown on page 164).

> **MONEY SAVER:** I've never found it necessary to use one of those hot water feeding dishes, whose purpose it to keep baby's food warmed during feeding. Baby's meals should last no more than 20 minutes, and food should never be kept at room temperature for lengthy periods. These dishes are not hot enough to thaw food cubes.

Never Re-Freeze Thawed Baby Food

Once baby food has been frozen and thawed, do NOT re-freeze it, discard it. Do not use frozen vegetables or other frozen foods for making frozen baby food cubes. Baby food should not be frozen twice.

23. Vegetables and Fruits

Vegetable Basics

This chapter explains the *general* steps for preparing vegetables. The appendix *Specific Fruits and Vegetables* (beginning on page 424) gives **specific** information on individual vegetables. For example, turn and look at the details for carrots on page 434. Included is how to choose the best carrots at the supermarket, when carrots are in season, cooking times, how old your baby must be to eat carrots, and other information about carrots. The fruits and vegetables in the appendix are listed in alphabetical order.

Buying Vegetables

In the best of circumstances, we would walk out the door of our homes to a beautiful, organic garden growing in the back yard and choose a healthy, ripe vegetable. To obtain the most nutrients, we would cook it or eat it raw immediately. This case is not true for most of us, but let's keep it in mind as the ideal to help us remember how to buy produce.

How to Choose the Best Vegetables

- Buy produce as free of pesticides as possible; certified organic is best. Pesticides affect small babies more adversely than adults, and become more concentrated in their little bodies. (For more information on pesticides, see page 38.)

- Buy produce that is local. It is likely to have less pesticides and hasn't lost nutrients during a long transportation process. Visit your local Farmers' Market or roadside stand.

- Buy domestic rather than imported produce. On average, imported produce contains pesticides several times the level of domestic produce. The FDA inspects less than 3% of shipments of imported food; therefore, imported produce is sometimes not checked to see if growers have met United States pesticide standards, which are generally more strict than standards elsewhere.

- If possible, buy vegetables that have ripened on the vine, not within a cardboard box. Unfortunately, economics dictates that to maximize profits, produce should be picked before it is fully ripe. Unripe produce is firmer, and therefore won't bruise as easily during the handling and transportation process. Even "vine-ripened" tomatoes are picked when they are still pink, before they turn ripe red.

🍃 Buy produce that is in season. It will be fresher and tastier. Cheaper, too. See peak times for each particular vegetable in the *Specific Fruits and Vegetables* appendix beginning on page 424.

🍃 As a general rule, the smaller the vegetable, the more tender and younger it is.

🍃 Once bought, get vegetables home from the store and into the refrigerator as soon as possible, as some nutrients are destroyed quickly if left sitting at room temperature or in a hot trunk. Run other errands, such as the car wash and the department store, first. The supermarket should be your last stop so that you can go directly home. If you can't get veggies home quickly, place them in a cooler in the trunk.

🍃 I highly recommend fresh, natural food or frozen food over canned food. However, if you choose to feed your baby canned vegetables, buy those which are all vegetables with no salt or additives. If you have vegetables with added salt, rinse them under the tap in a strainer to remove as much of the salt as possible. Sodium in canned foods is discussed on pages 545-547. Please read warnings about cans on page 37.

MONEY SAVER: When buying produce by the piece instead of the pound, such as broccoli, pints of berries, avocado, etc., use the supermarket's produce scale to see which weighs the most.

Be Gentle with Your Produce

Some vegetables and fruits look a lot tougher than they are. For example, pineapples look like they have tough skin, but it is actually very vulnerable to bruising. Damaging the skin of vegetables and fruits leaves them open to decay, which sometimes spreads very rapidly throughout the rest of the flesh. So be gentle with your produce, and treat it with tender, loving care.

Keep Vegetables Cold

Chemicals called **enzymes** cause a loss of nutrients and change the composition of vegetables, so that they rot. They convert sugar into starch so that, as time in storage passes, vegetables lose flavor and crispness. Have you ever tasted a pea picked fresh from the garden? It's actually sweet! Older peas are bland, tasteless, and all starch. Enzymes have converted virtually all their sugar. Cold temperatures slow down this enzyme activity.

Store Most Vegetables in High Humidity

Circulating refrigerator air is very dry. Protect vegetables from this dry air by placing them in plastic bags or in the vegetable crisper drawer of your refrigerator. Vegetables actually contain a lot of water (as human bodies do), and if this water dries up, nutrients get destroyed and taste is adversely affected. So keep your carrots from shriveling by leaving them in the plastic bag.

TIP: If you have a problem with *too much* moisture gathering in the vegetable drawer of your refrigerator, place a clean, dry sponge in the drawer to absorb the extra moisture. Or place several layers of white paper towels under produce to absorb moisture. Save paper towels by using newspapers or brown bag paper as bottom layers, but prevent newspaper ink from getting into produce by using several layers of paper towels on top. Optionally, sprinkle baking soda between layers to keep the drawer smelling fresh. Replace every week.

Some Vegetables Require a Cool, Dark, Dry Place

Some vegetables, such as pumpkins and potatoes, store well for months in a dry, dark, cool (about 45° to 50° Fahrenheit) place. If you don't think you have such a place, are you sure you thought of your attic (in winter, not in summer when it gets very hot), or a dark corner of your unheated garage, or even your basement (if it is not a damp basement)? A small thermometer can be used to monitor the temperature.

Freezing Is the Best Storage Method for COOKED Vegetables

Super Baby Food vegetables are most nutritious when cooked properly and eaten immediately. If this isn't possible, vegetables should be stored in a way that maintains the most taste and nutrients. Freezing is the best storage method and is, of course, also the most expensive method. Canning (or jarring) is popular because it's cheap, but most canned food is not nearly as tasty or nutritious as frozen. Drying is another method to preserve food. See page 202 for how to dry your dry your own fruit leather.

How to Clean Vegetables (and Fruits)

How to clean vegetables and fruits leaves me in a quandary. On one hand, I want to really soak and scrub them to remove as many chemicals as possible (on foods not grown organically) before they get into my little one's mouth. But on the other hand, the more I soak and scrub, the more nutrients get destroyed, especially the water-soluble vitamins. Personally, I'm more afraid of pesticides than vitamin-depletion, so I recommend lots of washing.

To Peel or Not to Peel

Whether or not you peel off the skin depends on the particular vegetable or fruit. See the specifics in the appendix. For example, see "Preparation for Cooking:" on page 434. It says that you can or cannot peel carrots, depending on their size. Keep in mind that a lot of the nutrients are in the skins, and scraping will cause them to be lost. Instead of spending time peeling carrots, I carefully scrub off the dirt with a vegetable brush or a clean nylon scouring pad. You may choose to peel instead, especially if the carrots are not organic and you are concerned about pesticides.

> **WARNING:** Avoid eating large amounts of orange peels or peels of other citrus fruits, as they may contain carcinogens (cancer-causing substances). Citrus rinds absorb pesticides, so try to buy organic citrus fruits only.

Peel any produce with a wax coating (apples, cucumbers, etc.), not only to remove the wax, but also to remove possible fungicides which are often used in combination with the wax. Peel produce with tough skins (apples, cucumbers, etc.) on which baby can choke. Remove the outer leaves of leafy vegetables (brussels sprouts, cabbage, lettuce) for baby. Then carefully wash the inner leaves while thoroughly checking for bad spots and insects.

MONEY SAVER: Don't discard those organic citrus peels—grate the rinds and freeze using the Nested Plastic Bag Method and use as flavorings in muffins, icings, and other recipes. See citrus zest on page 438.

Use Water and Soap

Most experts used to recommend cleaning vegetables and fruits with cold water, because warm water may soften them. Warm water also may cause a significant loss of nutrients and even the loss of some juice. However, the FDA recommends using warm water to wash produce for better removal of pesticides. I recommend using cold water for certified organic produce, and warm water for non-organic.

NOTE: Berries must be cleaned in a different manner than most fruit—see page 430.

Fruit and Vegetable Soaps

I recommend the use of one of the soaps specifically made to clean vegetables and fruits. In addition to the pesticides used on food crops not grown organically, other chemicals are added to prevent the pesticides from being washed away by rain. Soaps for veggies and fruits may help to cut through these chemicals and help to remove surface pesticides. Systemic pesticides—those absorbed by the plant during growth—cannot be removed by any amount of washing, which is why it is best to buy certified organic produce for your precious little one.

You will find these special fruit and vegetable soaps at your local natural foods store and in some supermarkets. If not, ask if they can order it for you.

WARNING: Make sure you use only soap that is meant to be used on food. Other soaps may leave a dangerous residue on food that will end up in your baby's tummy.

If you have vegetable/fruit soap: Spray each fruit/vegetable piece all over, covering every inch. Then let sit for at least 30 seconds. Or, follow the label directions.

Now take a vegetable brush and hold a piece under the water while gently scrubbing. For hard vegetables like un-peeled carrots, which have little crevices where dirt collects, move the brush up and down and side to side (as in brushing your teeth). Rinse well and be sure to remove all soap. Remember that all of this washing is causing nutrient loss. If you have organic produce, go light on the scrubbing—there are no invisible pesticides to worry about.

Wash All Produce

You may not be in the habit of washing fruits with thick peels that will not be eaten, such as oranges and bananas (see warning, page 13). But these have pesticides all over them and people have been touching them. So please don't forget to wash any fruit or vegetable that you will be giving your baby.

MONEY SAVER: Let your soapy water do double duty. Save soap and water by collecting the running tap water in the sink while you are washing produce. Use the second-hand water to wash fruits with peels that won't be eaten, like bananas and oranges.

If you're not going to cook the washed vegetables immediately, shake and lightly dry each piece with a towel and return them to the refrigerator as quickly as you can. Too much moisture may cause them to spoil. If you're going to cook them now, there's no need to dry them.

How to Cook Vegetables

When cooking baby food, your main concern besides safety should be that of nutrition. Negligent cooking techniques can destroy important vitamins needed for your baby's good health. Keep in mind that nutrients are destroyed by heat, air, light, and water. Water-soluble vitamins are lost when they leach into cooking water. Some vitamins are destroyed by the heat inevitable in cooking. Vitamin C is the most vulnerable vitamin, being both water-soluble and extremely susceptible to heat. Nature knew what she was doing when she put vitamin C into foods we eat raw, like citrus fruits.

Minimizing Nutrient Loss from Vegetables
During Preparation and Cooking

- Remember that nutrients are destroyed by heat, light, air, and water.

- Most vegetables need to be kept cold to retain their nutrients and stay fresh. Don't let them sit on the counter at room temperature, get them into the refrigerator as quickly as possible.

- Don't peel a vegetable or fruit if you don't have to. The peel contains concentrated nutrients and fiber. See warning about citrus fruit peels on page 180.

- Cut vegetables into the largest pieces possible. Cutting, chopping, dicing, and shredding cause nutrient loss due to exposure to air and warmth through the increased surface area. Make the pieces as uniformly sized as possible, so that each piece will take the same amount of time to cook. If you're cooking whole vegetables, such as potatoes, choose same-sized vegetables at the supermarket.

- Use as little water as possible during cooking. Water-soluble vitamins, such as vitamin C and the B-complex, leach into cooking water. Steam cook vegetables instead of boiling them. When steam cooking veggies, make sure that the bottom of the steamer is not submerged in the water, allowing water to touch the cooking vegetables. The steamer should be at least an inch or two above the boiling water. Keep the lid tightly closed to minimize the amount of steam that escapes. When steam goes, it takes nutrients with it and impedes cooking. In microwave cooking, use little or no cooking water. Most vegetables need only one or two tablespoons of added water to microwave cook. Vegetables with high water content need no added water. See instructions for each particular vegetable in the Specific Fruits and Vegetables appendix beginning on page 424.

- If you insist on boiling vegetables, simmer instead of boil as much as possible. Use no more than ½ inch of water in the bottom of the pot. Have the water boiling before you add the vegetables and simmer for as little time as possible.

- Don't use baking soda in cooking water, it destroys water-soluble vitamins.

🍃 Don't keep food warm—serve it right away. And don't leave leftovers at room temperature—refrigerate immediately.

🍃 Riboflavin, a B vitamin, is destroyed by light. Buy milk that is in opaque cartons rather than the transparent plastic or glass containers that let light shine in.

🍃 Light and warmth destroy vitamin C very quickly. Keep orange juice in a cold and dark place. Buy orange juice in opaque cartons in the refrigerator section of the supermarket. Or better yet, give your baby vitamin C by feeding him a fresh kiwi fruit or by squeezing him juice from a fresh orange.

🍃 Don't discard the water used for cooking vegetables—it contains valuable nutrients. Use it for puréeing baby's food. Or add it to a container in your freezer and use it for soups, stews, and in place of meat broth in recipes. It will keep frozen for up to 6 months. Or pour it over your pet's food or use it to water your plants when cooled.

Because vegetables for baby are just plain, unseasoned, whole vegetables with no fancy sauces or flavoring, cooking for baby is easy. It involves very little preparation and consists mostly of waiting while the vegetables cook. You just have to keep an eye on them while you do the rest of your kitchen chores.

How to Tell When a Vegetable Is Done Cooking

Cooking vegetables is a matter of timing. Vegetable cooking times vary due to moisture content, freshness, size, density, and age of the vegetable. The uniqueness of your stove and oven add to cooking time variability. Information on cooking times for specific vegetables can be found in the *Specific Fruits and Vegetables* appendix. Please take a moment and turn to the information on carrots on pages 434-435. Note that times for microwaving, steaming, and baking are stated. Use my recommended times as approximates and depend on your experience with your cooking equipment.

Because heat destroys some vitamins, a minimum amount of cooking time retains maximum nutrients, so test as soon as you think the vegetables might be done. You can always add cooking time if undercooked, but there is nothing you can do if they are overcooked. Test most vegetables for doneness by piercing them with a fork. The fork should slide in fairly easily. Whole vegetables, such as sweet potatoes and beets, should be soft all the way to the center. Leafy vegetables, such as spinach and kale, should look wilted, take on a brighter color, and be crisp tender to bite. (Crisp tender means that the greens are tender, but not so mushy that they don't crunch a little when you bite them.)

TIP: For future reference, make notes in this book on how much time it took to cook a particular vegetable. Every time you open your oven or lift a lid to test for doneness, heat escapes and energy is wasted, so write down the cooking times for your unique appliances. Add any other relevant details. I always write notes in my cookbooks, including specifics about my equipment, mistakes I don't want to repeat, and whether or not my family and I liked the finished product.

Methods of Cooking Vegetables

There are many ways you can cook vegetables: steaming, microwaving, baking, boiling, pressure-cooking, stir-frying, grilling, deep-frying, and, of course, not cooking them at all—eating them raw. Water and/or heat destroy vitamins; therefore, the best methods of cooking vegetables for your baby are those that have a minimum cooking time and use the least heat and water. Microwaving, steaming, and baking are best. Microwaving is excellent for nutrient preservation because it uses very little water and short cooking times. Steaming and baking are good because they use little water. Boiling vegetables in water causes a considerable loss of water-soluble vitamins. If you absolutely must boil, use as little water as possible: no more than ½ inch in the bottom of the pot. Have the water boiling before you add the vegetables and simmer for as little time as possible. Deep-frying vegetables, such as potatoes (French fries), should not even be considered. (See recipe for *French Fries-Not!* on page 302.)

Interestingly, eating vegetables raw is not always the way to get the most nutrients. Some nutrients become more available after cooking, such as the vitamin A in carrots.

Microwave Cooking

Microwave-safe containers. It is important to cook in microwave-safe containers. Glass and wood are usually safe in the microwave. Don't use any container with metal or put aluminum foil in the microwave (unless you're knowledgeable about shielding). Microwaves can't pass through metal. Containers with metal include dishes with gold or silver decorative paint. Many a time I've accidentally used a gold-banded plate and the sparks made me jump. Plastic is probably safe if it's dishwasher safe.[2] If you're not sure about a plastic container, test it this way: Fill it with a cup of water and microwave on high for a minute or two. If the water feels hot and the plastic does not, it is probably safe. If the plastic feels warm, it is not safe in the microwave and will melt at high temperatures. If you cannot fill a plastic dish with water to test it because it is too flat, don't heat it empty in the microwave alone. Place it in the microwave along with a cup with water. Then heat both for a minute or two on high and feel the plastic to see if it's hot. If so, then it's not microwave-safe.

Use only the plastic wrap, paper towels, and paper plates meant for the microwave. Before using plastic wrap, paper plates, or paper towels in the microwave, make sure that the label says they are safe for use in the microwave. Paper plates can be used as covers because they will not go limp or blow off the dish like wax paper or paper towels. Paper towels with colored designs should never be used in the microwave, use only white paper towels. Make sure that you do not use just any plastic wrap in the microwave, because it may melt into the food. Some people

---

[2] The authors of *The New Laurel's Kitchen*, an excellent book that should be part of every kitchen library, state on page 171 that "Until much more research has been completed, we strongly recommend microwaving only in heat-proof glass or lead-free pottery or china containers, rather than any plastic." See Robertson, Laurel in bibliography.

contend that you shouldn't use any plastic wrap in the microwave, and that it is safer to use as a cover a microwave-safe dish.

Standing time. Contrary to what you may think, microwaves do not cook "from the inside out" or "from within." In fact, microwaves penetrate at most 1½ inches of most foods. The microwaves cause the food molecules to vibrate, generating heat, which cooks the food. After the microwaves stop, the food continues to vibrate and cook. For this reason, food should be slightly undercooked. It is important to let the food stand for a short period of time after the microwave turns off. This standing time allows the food to finish cooking.

Microwaving Fresh Vegetables

- Microwave vegetables on high.

- Use as little water as possible when cooking vegetables. Water leaches some nutrients out of the vegetables and requires more cooking time.

- If possible, use a turntable to cook food evenly. If your microwave doesn't have a built-in turntable, you can buy a separate turntable to place on the floor of your microwave. If you don't use a turntable, turn the food frequently and stir often to promote even cooking.

- Cooking times will vary according to the size, moisture content, freshness, and age of the vegetable, and the wattage of your microwave oven. Cook for the shortest time possible and let stand. If you overcook the food, there's nothing you can do, but you can always add cooking time. Test for doneness by piercing with a fork. If not done, cook for one additional minute and test again. Repeat for one-minute increments, if necessary.

- Make notes in your cookbook to save testing next time.

- Microwave most vegetables in a covered container that will hold in the steam. Use the cover that came with the container. If you don't have a cover, use a microwave-safe flat dish or the heavy-duty plastic wrap specifically made for microwave cooking so that it doesn't melt into the food. Leave one corner open by turning the plastic wrap up. This "vent" will let steam escape and prevent an explosion. Be very careful when removing wrap so that you don't burn yourself. Open the end of the container farthest away from you in case steam shoots out. And use oven mits to protect your hands from burns.

- Some vegetables, such as whole potatoes, squash, corn on the cob, and sweet potatoes, can be cooked on the floor of the microwave oven with no container. (See particular vegetable in the appendix beginning on page 424.) Place at least two layers of paper toweling under them. Use only white paper towels—you don't need color seeping into your vegetables. Don't waste paper towels; if you're cooking one potato, use one paper towel folded in half to get two layers of toweling—not two whole flat paper towels. After cooking, you can use the same towels to wipe out the microwave.

- If you're cooking whole potatoes, beets, Brussels sprouts, eggplant, squash, tomatoes, or any other whole vegetable contained in a peel, pierce the peel several places with the tines of a fork. This will allow steam to escape during cooking and prevent explosions. Same goes for tofu dogs (and remember that hot dogs are not Super Baby Food).

> ❧ Always place the widest end of the food toward the outside of the oven and the smallest end toward the center. For example, arrange asparagus spears in the shape of wagon-wheel spokes with asparagus tips (small end) pointing toward the center of oven and bottom stalks (wide end) pointing toward microwave walls. Same goes for corn on the cob and whole potatoes. Remember that foods cook in the microwave from "out to in," so place the larger and more dense food parts toward the outer edges of the microwave.
>
> ❧ Shallow dishes are better for microwaving than deep dishes because they expose more of the food surface to heat. Containers with straight sides are preferable than sloped sides, because the sloped sides have a tendency to overcook on the edges.
>
> ❧ Microwave cooking requires less liquid than conventional cooking. To adapt your favorite recipes from conventional oven to the microwave, reduce the liquid ingredients to 75% of the amount called for in the original recipe. For example, if the recipe calls for one cup of water, reduce the amount to ¾ cup. Remember that steam is better retained in microwave cooking; therefore, covered dishes cook faster in the microwave. Subtract cooking time from your original recipes. Remember that it's better to undercook than overcook—you can always add cooking time.

The previous box has general rules for microwaving fresh vegetables. Read the instructions in the appendix *Specific Fruits and Vegetables* (page 424) for the cooking and standing times for each particular vegetable.

WARNING: Some people are concerned about the fact that cooking foods in the microwave is not natural and changes the structure of foods. If you have this concern, use another cooking method.

WARNING: There's always the danger of a child accidentally starting an empty microwave oven. Always keep a cup of water or a box of baking soda in the microwave when not in use. The baking soda will also help to eliminate odors in your microwave.

TIP: Never use abrasive cleansers or scouring pads in your microwave oven. Use a solution of one tablespoon of baking soda per cup of warm water for wiping clean the inside surfaces of your microwave. An easy way to remove dried foods from the walls of your microwave is to boil water in it for about 5 minutes. The steam will soften the dried foods, which will then wipe away easily with a soft damp cloth or sponge. Even easier: Wipe up spills immediately after they happen, before they dry and harden!

MONEY SAVER: Save energy and wipe out your microwave after you've boiled water to mix with baby's concentrated formula.

TIP: Some suggest this cleaning tip: Wet the inside walls of your microwave oven with a wet rag or a spray mister, run the microwave on high for 5 seconds, and wipe the walls down. I am hesitant to recommend this method because running an empty microwave may cause damage.

TIME SAVER: Keep a layer of microwave-safe wax paper on the bottom of your microwave or in the glass dish. Replace when it gets messy.

MONEY SAVER: To save a little money on energy bills, use the same glass dish to cook several bunches of veggies. When one bunch is finished cooking, spoon them out of the cooking dish and add more raw veggies to be cooked. You'll find that you can subtract a minute or two of cooking time for subsequent bunches because the dish is already piping hot. Also, cooking several bunches means you clean up only once, saving time, water and soap.

Steaming Method

I highly recommend steaming vegetables instead of boiling them, because steaming retains much more of the nutrients. Water-soluble vitamins, such as vitamin C and the B vitamins, leach out into cooking water. Vegetables come into contact with much more cooking water if you boil vegetables rather than steam them, thereby allowing a significant loss of nutrients.

Types of steamers are discussed on page 151.

TIP: The time it takes to steam vegetables is usually a few minutes longer than if you boiled them, because water conducts heat better than steam. So add a few minutes to the boiling time necessary to cook vegetables.

Steaming Fresh Vegetables

- Vegetables should be placed into the steamer so that they are no more than 2 inches deep.
- Stir or shake vegetables halfway through cooking time for even cooking.
- Place vegetables in steamer so that they are all at an even layer—don't have a big pile next to a small pile.
- If you are steaming whole vegetables, such as Brussels sprouts, place them in a single layer. Don't pile them up like a bucket of balls.
- To steam vegetables, place an inch or so of water into the bottom of a pot. The vegetables should be at least one inch above the water so that the water won't touch the vegetables when it is vigorously boiling.
- Bring the water to a full boil BEFORE placing the vegetables in the steamer into the pot.
- If the water starts to boil out, add more boiling water. If you are steaming a lot of vegetables, keep a separate pot with water boiling to replenish the water in the steamer when it gets low.
- Make sure the cover fits well on the pot to minimize the escape of steam into the air. Steam takes nutrients with it and the loss of steam impedes cooking.

Energy-saving Stove-top Cooking Tips

🙢 When boiling a measured amount of water, measure the water BEFORE boiling. Boiling water first and then measuring and discarding the excess wastes both water and energy.

🙢 To save energy, match the stove burner to the size of the pot as closely as possible or heat will be lost to the air.

🙢 Keep burner reflectors clean so they can reflect the heat efficiently. A no-scrub method of cleaning stubborn stains from metal reflectors is this: In a large pot, squirt some dishwashing detergent in water and stir until dissolved. Add burners and make sure they covered with water. Bring water and dishwashing detergent to a boil and boil the burners for about 5-10 minutes. Crusty black burned-on food will wipe off easily with a scouring pad.

🙢 Keep the lid on the pot when bringing water or other liquid to a boil. The liquid will boil faster and use less energy.

🙢 To save a little energy, turn off an electric burner a few minutes before the end of the cooking time. It will stay hot enough to finish the cooking. Likewise, turn off your oven a few minutes early.

Baking Method

Baking or roasting fresh vegetables preserves nutrients because little or no water is used. Some vegetables, such as sweet potatoes, can be baked whole. Simply pierce their skins and place directly on the oven rack or on a baking sheet. Some vegetables should be sliced and placed in a pan with a little water. For sliced vegetables, pack them tightly into a covered baking dish to retain moisture. Vegetables with high water content, such as zucchini, need no added water. Check the *Specific Fruits and Vegetables* appendix (page 424) for instructions on how to bake specific veggies.

WARNING: If your oven is within your toddler's reach, never turn it on until you make sure that it's empty and that your little one hasn't placed something in it! You may want to invest in a baby-proof oven lock, which you'll find in baby stores and catalogs.

MONEY SAVER: To save on energy bills, place a batch of vegetables in the same half-empty (conventional) oven you are using to cook dinner. Unfortunately, the same energy-saving method cannot be used with a microwave oven. When you put an additional food item into the microwave oven, you must add significant cooking time. In a conventional oven, you may have to add only a few minutes.

The Hybrid Cooking Method

You can partially cook food or thaw frozen food in the microwave oven and then finish cooking it in a conventional oven. Let's say you're going to use your conventional oven to bake a single cake. You can place 4 sweet potatoes in the microwave and partially cook them for 10 minutes. (See page 461 for full instructions on how to microwave potatoes.) While the potatoes are in the microwave, pre-heat your conventional oven and mix your batter. Then put the cake and partially cooked sweet potatoes in the oven together. In the 30 minutes that the cake needs to bake, you can simultaneously finish cooking the sweet potatoes.

Once you become aware of energy efficiency, a half empty oven will drive you crazy—keep potatoes and other foods on hand to cook when extra oven space is available. Freeze them for later eating.

How to Purée Vegetables

Your young baby cannot yet chew food, so you must purée it to a smooth lump-less consistency. To get this liquidy consistency necessary for beginning eaters, water must be added to the food mixture being processed. For most vegetables, use the water in which they were cooked, whether the water is from steaming, microwaving, baking, or boiling. This water contains valuable nutrients that have leached out of the vegetables during cooking.

Pour the water from the cooking pot into a container with a spout so that it will be easy to pour into the processor. I use a little glass measuring cup with a spout.

> **WARNING:** Never put very hot liquids in your blender, or hot moisture may become trapped and erupt when you open the lid.

I will use the term "processor" to refer to your blender, your food processor, your food mill, or whatever you're using to purée.

Place chunks of cooked vegetables into the bowl of the processor so that it's almost full. Make sure you leave some head room. Add a tablespoon or two of the cooking water.

> **TIP:** If you find that the sweet potatoes and other cooked veggies are too hot to handle while you're puréeing them, use a pair of those rubber kitchen gloves used for washing dishes. Then you can keep the gloves on for clean-up, when you can use really hot water without burning yourself.

> **WARNING:** Always keep your hand on the blender cover to assure that it doesn't come off and allow food to spew all over you and the kitchen. Do this especially when you have hot

food in the blender that could burn you. Your baby should be far away from a working blender (or even a non-working blender with its sharp blades) at all times.

Cover, keep your hand on the lid, and start the processor. Pour more water very slowly through the hole in the top of the processor until the food moves freely. If you're using a blender, use a rubber spatula to push the food into the blades, if necessary. Be careful not to let the spatula touch the blades.

> **WARNING:** Never use a metal utensil to push food into blender blades. This is dangerous and may ruin your blender's blades if it touches them by accident. If you don't have a rubber spatula, try using a plain old plastic straw. Be careful that no pieces of straw end up in baby's food!

If food pieces become lodged in the blades, stop the blender and wait for the blades stop completely before using your spatula to remove them.

Use the least amount of water necessary to get the consistency you need for your baby's age. For a very young baby who has just started on solid food, you must use quite a bit of water to get a very smooth texture.

> **MONEY SAVER:** Do you see how much water you must add to get this fine consistency? Makes you wonder how much of commercial jarred baby food is actually food and how much is water.

As your baby gets older, she can chew or actually "gum" chunkier food, for which you will, of course, add less water and purée for less time.

If you accidentally added too much water, simply add some more cooked vegetables.

> **TIP:** Next time you're at the supermarket, take a close look at the glass jars of baby food and note their consistencies. Copy their textures when making food for your baby at different ages.

> **TIP:** When it comes time that your baby can eat chunky vegetables, fill your food processor only halfway. This will prevent some food from getting over-chopped.

Fill the ice cube trays across the two rows (left, right, left, right) rather than down one long row. If you do not fill a whole tray, you will be able to use less aluminum foil to cover the food cubes.

As soon as you have filled an ice cube tray, cover well and store immediately in the freezer. Don't let it sit on the counter until you've completed all puréeing—get it cold as soon as possible.

> **WARNING:** You must be especially careful to keep any puréed baby food cold. Never leave it for extended periods at room temperature, because bacteria will thrive in it (page 164). The same is true for open jars of commercial baby food. Remember that bacteria grow in temperatures that are not too hot and not too cold—they love room temperature.

> **TIP:** My baby hates the loud noise my blender makes. I use an old computer mouse pad to help decrease it. A flat rubber drain stop or a plain damp towel will also help.

How to Store Cooked Vegetables

Refrigerating Small Portions

Store a portion or two of the food you just puréed in the refrigerator to feed to your baby within the next day. Cooked, puréed vegetables will not keep in the refrigerator longer than a day or two. Store them in a small covered microwave-safe bowl, and then you can just pop them into the microwave to re-heat. Freeze any cooked puréed food that you will not be using within the next day.

> **WARNING:** Do not store baby food that has been made from frozen vegetables or other frozen foods. For example, if you have bought some commercially frozen broccoli from the supermarket and cooked and puréed it for your baby, do not freeze it for future use. Discard any leftovers. Most foods should not be frozen more than once, especially vegetables.

Freezing—The "Food Cube" Method

Next to the processor containing the puréed food, place ice cube trays along with a spoon or little measuring cup (⅛ or ¼ cup size). Make sure everything is whistle clean, because although freezing retards the growth of germs in foods, it does not sterilize.

The puréed food can be poured into the ice cube trays if the consistency is very liquidy, just remove the processor bowl and pour into the trays. If the food is too thick to pour, scoop and pat into the cubes with your clean fingers.

> **TIME SAVER:** If you're puréeing a large batch of the same vegetable, you may have to fill your processor more than once. Don't waste time between refills scooping small amounts of vegetable from the bottom of the processor. Keep adding more food in on top and scoop out those last bits only once in the end when you're finishing up.

Freeze using the Food Cube Method as detailed on page 166. As soon as each ice cube tray is filled, immediately cover it and place it in the freezer.

While you're at it, you may want to freeze a few portions in little plastic containers with lids to be used when you go out for the day. Take them out frozen, place in a cooler with an ice pack to keep them at refrigerator temperature to prevent bacterial growth (see *Never Thaw Foods at Room Temperature*, page 162), and by meal-time they'll be thawed and ready. You can even use glass baby food jars, but remember to leave space for expansion. I don't recommend using glass, though, because it can break. If the glass cracks or chips, throw the whole thing out. You don't want little slivers of glass in your baby's digestive system.

> **WARNING:** See warning about opening glass jars on bottom of page 37.

> **MONEY SAVER:** Although they sell plastic covered containers in all sizes, even cute little 4-ounce ones, you really don't have to buy them. Instead, use single-size empty yogurt cartons, or margarine or cottage cheese containers. Use freezer tape around the lids to

make sure they are air tight. You can wash and re-use them or just throw them away after one use if you're on the road.

TIP: Make your food cubes a consistent size, then you'll know by experience exactly how much microwave or stove time is needed to thaw them.

When your baby is very young and needs a very smooth consistency, the cubes will have a lot of water in them and will freeze almost as solid as ice. As your baby grows and you make the cubes lumpier, they will be less icy and thaw and re-heat faster.

How to Batch Cook Vegetables

For Your Beginning Eater, Start by Making a Single Batch of Cooked Veggies

When your baby begins to eat solid foods, she will not eat much at all—only about a tablespoon or two a day. The first vegetable you will probably give her is sweet potatoes. (Other veggies, like carrots, spinach, broccoli, and others, should not be fed to very young babies because of the nitrates they contain. See warning on bottom of page 38.) Please take a moment now to read the information on sweet potatoes on page 461. Note how easy it is to make a month's worth of sweet potatoes for your baby! Wash 4 potatoes and prick with fork. Microwave potatoes for 14 minutes, let stand 5 minutes, cut them in half, scoop out the flesh, mash or purée them, and freeze in ice cube trays.

As your baby gets older and eats more, you can prepare two batches of veggies simultaneously. While the sweet potatoes are baking in the microwave, steam a batch of green beans on the stove top or purée a ripe avocado.

TIP: While you're cooking baby veggies, dice some snack-sized portions of finger food and replenish your Super Snack Freezer Bag (page 292).

For An Older Baby, 4 Batches a Month

As your baby gets older, you'll probably have to make about 4 batches of cooked veggies a month. Depending on the vegetable, a "batch" is approximately two ice cube trays. So a month's worth is about 8 trays—an average or 3 or 4 veggie cube servings a day.

Make One Batch Each Week=4 Batches a Month I usually keep up with my little one's veggie cube needs by making a single batch once a week. I save time and clean-up by combining baby food cooking with the cooking I do for the rest of my family. For example, when I make steamed broccoli for my family's dinner, I steam an extra bunch of broccoli in the same pot, purée it, fill 2 ice cube trays, and freeze it for the baby. Or if I'm baking a casserole in the conventional oven, I simply add another baking dish with vegetables for baby. The puréeing and freezing adds only an extra 10 or 15 minutes preparation time.

You may wish to stock up on Super Baby Food and make baby vegetables along with the other two types of baby foods that need advance preparation: cooked eggs and Super Porridge. If so, check out the sample session shown on page 147.

Or Make All 4 Batches Once a Month Occasionally, I dedicate the better part of one morning a month to the batch cooking of large amounts of baby veggies. On the day of the week when fresh produce has been delivered, I go to the supermarket and buy a month's worth. I run right home and get to work for an hour or two and make several weeks' worth of baby food. The more food I prepare at one time, the more time I save. It's similar to industrial mass production.

While one batch of produce is steaming on the stove and another batch is cooking in the microwave, I'm washing and preparing the next batch. If you've got a lot going on at once, there's no time to stand around and wait for something to get cooked. Your time is used very efficiently and you'll be amazed at how much you can get done in one or two hours if you do things in parallel. Also, you clean up only once at the end, another time-saver.

TIP: Before leaving for the supermarket, make sure your kitchen is clean and the counter tops are cleared off. Go through your refrigerator and freezer and throw out old food to make room for the new.

Advanced Batch Cooking

OK, so you've decided to spend the morning making a huge batch of Super Baby Food. It helps to decide which foods you're going to make before you leave for the supermarket. Super Green Veggies like broccoli and kale, and carrots or sweet potatoes for beta-carotene (vitamin A) should be regulars on your shopping list. The next example assumes you've decided to prepare a bunch of broccoli, 4 sweet potatoes, a bunch of carrots, and an avocado. It pays to think things through for a minute before you start cooking. Roughly estimate how much preparation and cooking time is needed for each food:

Broccoli:	Wash, minimally chop, and steam for 15 minutes. See page 431.
Carrots:	Wash, peel, slice, and then steam for 10 minutes. See page 434.
Sweet Potatoes:	Wash and microwave 14 minutes and let stand 5 minutes, for a total of 19 minutes. See page 461.
Avocado:	Ripe and ready. Wash. No cooking necessary. See page 426.

TIP: Always prepare and start cooking first the food that takes the most time.

The box on the next page shows one possibility for the order in which to do the kitchen tasks necessary to prepare and cook the four foods above.   Unless you consider yourself a lean, mean, cooking machine, the example will probably make your head spin. It's really not as difficult at it looks. Rest assured, you do not have to do all this cooking in one session! That's why I labeled it ADVANCED. It's rare when I do 4 batches at once—I usually do only 1 or 2 batches at a time.

In this example, about 8 trays or over 100 food cubes were made in less than 1½ hours. If your baby eats 2 cubes a day, that's 50 days' worth; if your baby eats 3 cubes a day, that's a month's worth.

A Vegetable Food Cube Assembly Line

It's a little easier to batch cook the SAME veggie in an assembly line-type method, as shown with broccoli in the box on page 196. When broccoli goes on sale for 69¢ a bunch, I stock up and buy enough for 2 months' worth of food cubes. In less than 1 hour, I transform 4 bunches of broccoli into approximately 120 food cubes. A 69¢ bunch of broccoli makes about 25 food cubes—**that's less than 3 cents per cube!**

TIME SAVER: If you have a friend who also makes homemade baby food, consider swapping food cubes for more variety.

If you have been able to successfully complete batch cooking sessions similar to those on the next two pages, consider yourself a black belt in Super Baby Food. ☺

Example of Steps Involved in
ADVANCED Multi-batch Vegetable Cooking

Time	Task
5 minutes	Arrange all necessary equipment on counter top.
1 minute	Place an inch or two of water in pot on stove to heat for steaming vegetables.
6 minutes	While waiting for water to boil, wash and chop broccoli and place in steamer. Water is now boiling, place steamer in pot and set timer for 15 minutes.
5 minutes	Wash sweet potatoes, pierce with fork, arrange on white paper towels in microwave and set timer to cook for 14 minutes. Keep an eye on timer, because you need to turn potatoes halfway through cooking time—or at 7 minutes.
10 minutes	Wash, peel, and slice carrots in preparation for steamer. During carrot preparation, turn sweet potatoes in microwave at 7 minutes.
1 minute	Timer goes off to indicate that broccoli is finished steaming. Remove from steamer and put in bowl to wait for puréeing. Wait to purée broccoli until it has cooled somewhat, so that you don't burn yourself.
1 minute	Add water to steaming pot, if necessary. It's easier to take a small glass with water to the pot, rather than bringing the pot to the sink tap.
1 minute	Place sliced carrots in steamer and place in pot after water starts boiling again. Set timer for 10 minutes.
0 minutes	Timer on microwave sounds, indicating that sweet potatoes are done cooking. Note time so that you will know when 5 minutes standing time has passed.
7 minutes	Purée broccoli and fill ice cube trays. Cover well with aluminum foil, and place in freezer.
7 minutes	Sweet potatoes are done standing. Cut sweet potatoes in half and scoop out flesh from skin. Purée, tray, cover, and freeze. During this step, timer interrupts indicating carrots are done steaming. Do step below and then finish sweet potatoes.
1 minute	Remove steamer with carrots from pot and place on counter to cool.
7 minutes	Purée carrots, tray, cover, and place in freezer.
7 minutes	If you have any energy left, do the avocado. Cut in half, scoop out flesh, purée, tray, cover, and freeze.
15 minutes	Clean up.

Total time: Approximately 1 hour and 15 minutes.

A Broccoli Food Cube Assembly Line

Time	Task
30 seconds	Coarsely chop the first bunch of broccoli.
2 minutes	Place cut broccoli in colander and wash well. A sink hose spray comes in handy for rinsing.
1 minutes	Place in covered microwave dish with a few tablespoons of water and start microwave to cook on high for 8 minutes.
2½ minutes	Coarsely chop the second bunch of broccoli and rinse in colander as you did the first bunch. Let it drain while waiting for its turn in the microwave.
5 minutes	While the first bunch of broccoli is cooking, get ready oven mits, large cooling/holding bowl, food processor or blender, slotted spoon, spouted cup, spoon or scoop, ice cube trays, and aluminum foil to cover the trays. At 4 minutes, or halfway through cooking time, stir broccoli in microwave.
1 minute	Microwave timer sounds indicating first bunch of broccoli finished cooking. Use oven mits (cooking dish is hot!) to remove from microwave oven and spoon cooked broccoli into cooling bowl with slotted spoon.
1 minute	Transfer second bunch of broccoli from colander to cooking dish, cover, place in microwave to cook on high for 7 minutes. (You can subtract 1 minute from 8 minute cooking time because the cooking dish is already hot.)
2 minutes	Coarsely chop and rinse the third bunch of broccoli in colander. Let it drain while waiting for microwave.
7 minutes	First bunch is in cooling bowl and is cool enough to handle now. Purée, spoon into ice cube trays, cover with aluminum foil, and place into freezer. During this step, stir second bunch of broccoli in microwave at about 4 minutes.
1 minute	Second bunch of broccoli is done cooking—transfer it from microwave to cooling bowl.
1 minute	Move third bunch from colander to microwave dish and start cooking for 7 minutes.
2 minutes	Coarsely chop and rinse fourth bunch of broccoli in colander. Let it drain while waiting for microwave.
7 minutes	Purée second bunch of broccoli, tray, cover, and freeze. During this step, stir third bunch of broccoli at 4 minutes.
And so on...	

Total time: Less than 1 hour for 4 broccoli bunches.

Fruits

We may consider fruits to be those produce that taste sweet, but fruits are actually the parts of plants that contain the seeds. Avocado, tomatoes, pumpkins, eggplants, rhubarb, and cucumbers are technically classified by botanists as fruits, not vegetables. All fruits grow above the ground on trees, vines, or shrubs. Fruits grown nearest the equator (bananas, figs, and dates) have a higher percent of natural sugar and are much sweeter than those grown in the temperate zones, because they get more sun exposure while growing. For the same reason, different parts of the same fruit are sweeter than others. The blossom end of orange is sweeter than the bottom because it gets more sun.

The best way to feed fruit to your baby is to take a whole, uncut, fresh, ripe piece of fruit from the refrigerator, wash, peel, and purée it, and feed it to her immediately. For older babies, peel and dice it into small pieces and serve immediately as finger food. (See warning about slippery foods, page 80.) Make sure the fruit is very soft and ripe to prevent choking. Minimize the amount of time fruit is exposed to warm room air and light to maximize the amount of nutrients retained, especially the very unstable vitamin C. Get the fruit from inside its peel to inside your baby as soon as possible!

Choosing Fresh Fruit

Buy fruit that is loose and not packaged in plastic, so that you can take a close look at each piece. In general, there should be no bruises, mold, cuts in the skin, or bad odor. You can't necessarily judge a fruit by its color. Sometimes color is important, and sometimes color means nothing. Did you know that green oranges are probably better than orange oranges? The appendix *Specific Fruits and Vegetables* (page 424) has information on each specific fruit, including how to choose them and how to tell when they are ripe.

Buy fruit that has begun to ripen a little in the store, in order to be sure that the fruit will, in fact, ripen. Fruit should feel firm, but not rock hard. Smell the fruit—if it smells slightly sweet, it's a sign that it has started ripening. Don't buy overripe fruit, even if it's on sale; many parts won't be edible. If you've no experience with fruit, I know that the ripeness tests in the appendix are not very objective. If you think you will have trouble determining subjective characteristics like "firm, but not hard" and "slightly sweet," don't worry. Take this book to the supermarket with you and test many fruits. With a little experience, you'll become a real expert.

It's All in the Ripening

Fruits should be ripe before we eat them. We don't let broccoli (a vegetable) get ripe, but we do let all fruits (including tomatoes) get ripe. Most mass-grown fruit arrives at the supermarket underripe and hard. If it hasn't fully ripened on the grocer's shelf, you must let it ripen at home. Some fruits, like bananas, will ripen no matter how green. But, some fruits will never ripen. I bought a few avocados that never ripened and remained hard for weeks, and I had to toss them. At the time, I didn't know to ripen them at room temperature and not in the refrigerator! Ripen most fruits by keeping them at room temperature out of direct sunlight, turning occasionally. For each commonly-used fruit, ripening instructions are given in the appendix *Specific Fruits and Vegetables*, page 424.

Fruit Ripeners

There is such a thing as a fruit ripener, which is nothing more than a plastic bowl with holes. If you use one, clean it often to remove invisible bacteria or molds, which can be passed from one batch of fruit to the next. A cheap, but just as effective, emulation of a fruit ripener is a simple paper bag punched with small holes or left slightly open. The holes will allow carbon dioxide and excess moisture to leave and oxygen to enter. It is interesting that ethylene gas, which is naturally produced by the fruit itself, helps the fruit to ripen. The fruit ripener or paper bag concentrates the gas around the fruit, which acts as a catalyst.

TIP: Try this if you want to speed a fruit's ripening: Place a very ripe piece of fruit, such as a black banana, in the same bag with hard fruit. It will emit lots of ethylene gas and cause quick ripening of the hard fruit.

Storing Fruit

Fruit should be kept uncut until needed. If fruit is cut, keep it tightly wrapped to prevent exposure to air. Most ripe fruit should be kept cold and in high humidity—so wrap it in plastic and/or put in the vegetable crisper to keep it from being exposed to the very dry air circulating in your refrigerator and freezer. Don't keep ripe fruit in light, especially direct sunlight. Light destroys vitamin C, therefore ripe fruit should be kept in the dark. This is why the light automatically turns off when you close your refrigerator door. I wonder how much vitamin C really exists in fruit juice that is packaged in clear plastic or glass bottles, which do nothing to stop light penetration.

Cleaning Fruit

To wash most fruits, follow the same instructions for cleaning vegetables on page 180. Berries must be cleaned differently, as discussed on page 430.

Refrigerating Fruit

See the appendix *Specific Fruits and Vegetables* (page 424) for the number of days each specific fruit will keep in the refrigerator. The storage times in the appendix are for whole, un-cut fruit. Most cut-up fruit and cooked fruit will keep for only a day or two, therefore any fruit that has been cooked and/or puréed should be kept in the refrigerator for only one day and then discarded. To prevent food waste, purée only one day's worth of fruit for baby, or freeze larger amounts using the Food Cube Method.

Freezing Fruit

It is best to feed your baby fresh, ripe fruit. However, you may wish to freeze fruits with short peak seasons, such as strawberries, so that they may be enjoyed year round. Frozen fruit tends to be soft and maybe even mushy when thawed because the moisture expansion within the fruit during freezing causes the cell walls to break. Your baby probably won't mind.

Fruit can be frozen raw—it doesn't need to be blanched or cooked first. Clean the fruit, cut into chunks, and let drip dry on paper towels. Follow the instructions in the *Specific Fruits and Vegetables* appendix, page 424.

There are several methods of freezing fruit. The Tray-freeze Method (page 170) is best if you would like to retrieve a few small fruit pieces from the freezer at one time. If not, and you do not mind if the fruit chunks clump together in one big blob, it is OK to freeze plain fruit chunks in an air-tight container with no liquid (this is called the "dry pack" method).

For light-colored fruits that loose their color and flavor when frozen, some experts recommend freezing fruit chunks in liquid (the "wet pack" method). The liquid, whose purpose is to keep the fruit from coming in contact with air and discoloring, is usually a syrup solution (which is nothing but sugar water) mixed with some ascorbic acid (vitamin C). In my opinion, baby food should not have added processed sugar, and you don't want to overload your baby with too much vitamin C. If you wish to use the liquid, I recommend that fruits be submerged and frozen in orange juice instead of the syrup solution. Orange juice, with its natural sugar and ascorbic acid (vitamin C), is a healthy alternative to sugar water. Of course, do not use orange juice if your baby is not yet old enough for citrus, use the Tray-freeze Method. Or if your baby is at least 9 months old, she is old enough for pineapple. Freeze fruit chunks under pineapple juice instead of orange juice. Simply place the washed fruit chunks in a rigid container and cover them with juice. The fruit pieces may float on top of the juice. To keep them submerged, place crumpled waxed paper or freezer wrap on top of the fruit chunks to keep them submerged under the juice so that they are not exposed to any air. Leave a little head room for expansion, cover tightly, and freeze.

MONEY SAVER: Instead of buying plastic containers for freezing fruit, use the empty waxed cartons from orange juice or milk that you would have thrown out. Wash them out well before using. If you wish, line the cartons with plastic freezer wrap or waxed paper.

Freezing Puréed Fruit in Food Cubes

To prevent discoloration of puréed fruit that will be frozen, mix a little lemon or pineapple juice into the purée before freezing. (If your baby has not yet been introduced to citrus fruits/pineapple, leave out the juice.) For freezing instructions on specific fruits, see the appendix *Specific Fruits and Vegetables* (page 424) or look up the fruit in the index.

How to Thaw Fruit

It is best to thaw fruit in the refrigerator for several hours or overnight. Follow instructions in *Thawing Food Cubes in the Refrigerator*, page 177. If you need to thaw fruit fast, thaw in microwave on lowest power for very short time periods, making sure that you watch very carefully so that you do not heat them. Or thaw on the stove top over very low heat or in a double boiler. Remember that heat and air destroy nutrients, so thawing fruit well-covered in the refrigerator is best. For specifics about berries, see *Thawing berries:* on page 430.

> **WARNING:** Fruit that has been frozen and thawed keeps for a shorter time than fresh fruit, so discard within 24 hours.

How to Cook Fruit

Before 6 months of age, it is best not to feed raw fruits to your baby (except for bananas and avocado). Cook fruits to make them soft and more digestible for your baby's immature digestive system. Cook fruits as you would vegetables (pages 182 -189) until they are tender and soft and then strain well (page 152) to remove the peels of fruits, which are choking hazards (page 40).

Canned Fruit

I recommend fresh, natural food or frozen food over canned food. However, if you choose to feed your baby canned fruit, buy those in their natural juices. If you have fruit that is canned in sugary syrups, rinse it under running tap water in a strainer to remove as much of the syrup as possible. Please read warnings about cans on page 37.

Too Much Fruit May Cause Diaper Rash

Please read the warning about diaper rash and too much fruit and/or fruit juice on page 27.

Dried Fruit

Food drying acts to preserve food because bacteria, molds, and yeasts cannot grow without sufficient moisture (page 161). The presence of mold on dried foods is an indicator that the food is not dry enough. Food drying is the process of dehydrating or removing most of the water from foods. Most fruits are more than 70% water, but it varies; strawberries are 90% water, apples are 84% and bananas are 65%. After drying, their moisture content drops to about 15-20%, causing them to significantly shrink in weight and size. In fact, it takes at least six pounds of most fresh fruit to make one pound of dried fruit.

Drying concentrates the natural sugars (and some nutrients) of fruits, which explains why dried fruits taste so sweet. Dried fruits contain a lot of sugar, natural sugar, but sugar just the same; therefore, you should prevent your child from eating limitless quantities. See warning about dental problems and dried fruit on page 48.

Drying foods causes significant nutrient loss, especially vitamins A and C, but some minerals are fairly well retained. Still, dried fruits are healthy snacks for our children, especially when compared to the sugar-laden empty-calorie junk that kids ask you to buy in the supermarket.

Dried fruits, such as banana chips and fruit leather, are good finger foods and snack foods for your baby or toddler. You must first chop them into small pieces and make them very soft by re-hydrating them (described later), so they are not a choking hazard.

> **TIP:** Dried fruit is easier to chop if it is cold—place in the freezer for about an hour to chill. Use kitchen scissors to cut into small pieces. To prevent sticking, rub butter on or oil-spray the scissors (or a knife), or dip them into hot water or granulated sugar. Chop dried fruits in your food processor a little at a time. If sticking occurs, try adding a few tablespoons of granulated sugar. Or try soaking them in cold water before putting them in your processor.

Dried apple rings (not rehydrated) are good for teething rings, but they must be very dry and hard so that your baby cannot bite off a piece and choke. They also must be large enough to not be a choking hazard (see measuring device on bottom of page 41).

You can buy dried fruits at the supermarket and natural foods store, or you can dry them at home yourself. The advantages of drying food at home are similar to those of making baby food at home: it saves you money, it gives you control over the quality of the ingredients, and it eliminates the need for preservatives. Your own home-dried fruits and fruit leathers are much healthier than most commercially dried fruits and rolled-up fruit snacks that may contain added sugar, partially hydrogenated oils, and chemicals.

> **WARNING:** Watch out for top-name brands that add partially hydrogenated oils (page 507) to their raisins and other dried fruits. Read the label carefully.

Food dryers are now available at department and kitchen stores and through mail order. Perhaps you've seen the infomercial! If you have a food dryer, you know how well they work for making dried fruits, dried herbs, beef jerky, and even dried flowers. If you don't have one, you can use your oven (conventional, not microwave) for making small amounts of dried foods. Your oven is not as reliable as a food dryer, or as energy efficient, but it gets the job done. My favorite book on food drying is by Deanna DeLong. Another excellent book that discusses food drying as well as food canning and much more is *The Big Book of Preserving the Harvest* by Carol W. Costenbader. Both are listed in the bibliography at the back of this book.

For instructions on how to dry parsley and other herbs, see page 450. For citrus peels, see page 438.

Storing Dried Fruit

The best way I've found to store dried fruit is the Nested Plastic Bag Method. Store individual servings in the inside bags with the air removed and place them in a stronger, thicker big freezer bag. This way, you can open the outer freezer bag without exposing the dried fruit to air. It is important to keep dried fruit from air, because it begins to absorb moisture from the air immediately, and moisture in dried fruit means mold. Store the bag in a cool (around 50°F), dry, dark place, and the dried fruit should keep for up to 2-4 weeks. At room temperature, it will keep for only about half that time. For longer storage, refrigerate for up to 2 months or freeze for 6 months to 1 year.

TIP: If raisins and other died fruit clump together, microwave them on high for about 10-15 seconds. Or place them in colander and rinse under hot running water.

Rehydrating (Plumping) Dried Fruit

You can eat dried fruit or use it in recipes as is, but you may find that it is more tasty and easier to chew if you "plump" or rehydrate it. You must rehydrate dried fruit for your baby to help prevent choking. Raisins, often "plumped" raisins, are a very commonly used dried fruit in recipes.

There are several ways to rehydrate dried fruit. Soak dried fruit overnight in water in the refrigerator to rehydrate. Or pour boiling water over dried fruit (1½ cups of boiling water per cup of dried fruit) and let sit until rehydrated. This may take as little as 10 minutes for small fruit pieces (raisins) to one or two hours for large fruit pieces (apricot halves). Plump raisins or other small dried fruit pieces by steaming them for 3-5 minutes over boiling water. Or plump small pieces in your microwave. Place dried fruit in a container and just cover with water. Microwave on high until water begins to boil. Let stand 5-10 minutes.

WARNING: Once dried food has been rehydrated, it spoils very quickly. Eat immediately or throw it away.

TIP: During baking, roll wet raisins and other dried fruit and nuts in flour before mixing into batter while using your fingers to separate the pieces. This helps prevent fruit pieces from sinking to the bottom of the batter.

MONEY SAVER: You're paying top dollar for the convenience of those little boxes of raisins. Buy in bulk and keep refilling the boxes. One pound of raisins = approximately 3 cups.

Fruit Leather

Take a stroll down the boxed snacks aisle at the supermarket and read the ingredients list on a fruit roll-type snack box. These dried fruit snacks, made with "real fruit" (as it so boldly states on the package), are nothing more than fruit leather with added sugar, hydrogenated oils, artificial colors and flavors, and other chemicals. Without coupons, the 6-ounce boxes cost about $2.19. That's about $6.00 per pound! We sure do pay a lot for packaging and convenience. Is the super hero on the package really worth it? If your kids think so, make them Fruit Leather Pinwheels (recipe on page 206) and I bet they'll change their minds.

One day I was puréeing fruit for fruit leather, and a 12-year old friend of my sons asked me what I was doing. When I told him, he surprisedly said, "What? You can make those?"

Fruit leather can be made from fresh fruit, thawed frozen fruit, or even drained canned fruits. If you're using fresh fruit, choose good quality, ripe fruits. Actually, slightly overripe fruit is also good for fruit leather, due to its full flavor and sweetness. Almost-black bananas and overripe juicy peaches are great for fruit leather.

Leathers can be made from fruits that are either raw or cooked. Cooking fruits causes nutrient loss, but the leathers made from cooked fruits are bright and glossy. Raw fruit leathers tend to look dull, but have more of a fresh-fruit flavor. Try making some of each and decide for yourself.

Food dryers sometimes come with a reusable plastic tray for making fruit leathers, or a tray can be purchased separately. Follow the directions for drying fruit leather in your food dryer's user manual.

How to Make Fruit Leather in Your Oven

Prepare a large cookie sheet or 10x15 flat baking sheet by lining it with plastic wrap. Tape the wrap under the cookie sheet on all four sides to prevent it from flipping over and covering the edge of the leather, preventing it from drying. Or instead of taping, wrap the plastic over the edges and underneath the sheet so that there is enough extra slack for the sheet to hold it down in place. If you don't want to use plastic wrap, you can just grease the cookie sheet with oil or a spray.

Wash the fruit well. You can peel the fruits, but it's OK to leave the skins on for fruit leather. Slice or chop the fruit and place in a food processor or blender to purée. To prevent discoloration, add a tablespoon of lemon juice if you wish. Purée, adding a minimum amount of water or juice, if necessary. Keep in mind that the more liquid you add, the longer it will take to dry. The **consistency** should be like that of molasses or thick applesauce. Two cups of fruit purée, give or take ¼ cup, is a good amount for a batch of fruit leather.

If you wish to cook the fruit, pour the purée into a saucepan and bring it to a boil over medium-high heat, stirring continuously. When it boils, keep stirring, turn off the heat, and let the purée simmer for 3-5 minutes. Let cool to room temperature.

Spread the fruit purée on the prepared cookie sheet until it is ⅛-¼ inch thick. Tilt and turn the tray or use a spatula to spread. Spread as evenly as possible so it will dry uniformly. Leave a border of at least 1-2 inches between the purée and the edges of the cookie sheet. Use two cookie sheets if you find you have too much purée. Or freeze the extra purée for drying another time; when ready to use, simply thaw, spread on sheets, and dry.

> **TIP:** You can make fun shapes while spreading the leather: circles or pancakes, teddy bear faces, clovers, hearts, etc. Use different colored fruit purées and garnishes (discussed later) and bring out the artist in you. Or wait until after it's dry, when you may find it easier to make designs out of already dried leather—see *Cutting Fruit Leather* on page 204.

Fruit Leather Drying Method 1: Place the tray in the oven with door slightly open. If you have an electric oven, leave the door open 1-3 inches. If you have a gas oven, leave the door open 6-8 inches. Keep the oven at 115-120°F. Dry for 6-8 hours. Then flip the leather over, pull off plastic wrap, and dry for another 6-8 hours.

Fruit Leather Drying Method 2: Place the tray in a preheated 175°F oven with the door slightly open for about 3 hours. If the bottom is not dry, flip and continue drying.

Fruit Leather Drying Method 3: Place the tray in a preheated 275°F oven with the door closed for 30-35 minutes. Then turn off the oven, leave the oven door closed, and let dry overnight or for at least 8-10 hours.

Fruit Leather Drying Method 4: You can also dry fruit leather in the sun, but it may take from 1-3 days, depending on the temperature and humidity. Protect it from insects by covering it with cheesecloth or netting. After it's dry, place it in a 200°F for 45 minutes before cooling and storing.

Fruit leather is finished drying when it feels tacky, but is pliable and will pull away from the plastic wrap. It is better to overdry than underdry. By the way, the dryer the leather, the longer it will keep; so if you want your leather to last many months, dry it until it is no longer tacky and completely dry.

> **TIP:** If you've accidentally let the leather dry too long and it has become brittle and crackly—not to worry! Break it up into little *leather chips* by hand or in the processor and use them as Healthy Extras. They are good as is, or rehydrate them (page 202). Use them as a flavor enhancer for cereal, yogurt, tofu, beverages, etc. And what possibilities leather chips are for Decorative Touches!

Rolling Fruit Leather

You can roll fruit leather to make it look like the boxed supermarket fruit roll snacks. Simply roll it up as you would a sleeping bag or jelly roll. The leather will be easier to roll if it is still slightly warm. You can roll it without removing the plastic, but for a small child it is probably better to roll it up without the plastic. You can place it on a piece of waxed paper and roll it. Then cut the roll into single snack-sized pieces that are about one inch wide. Cutting is easier if the leather is chilled first.

Cutting Fruit Leather

Instead of rolling, you can cut the slightly warm fruit leather into rectangular pieces and stack between strips of waxed paper. Or you can cut designs out of the leather and use them as Decorative Touches (page 362).

> **TIP:** There's nothing like fruit leather for cutting detailed shapes for Decorative Touches. You can easily spell out a child's name, or cut numbers for the age of the birthday child to put on the cake. Stencils can be used to make your letters and numbers professional. Use a clean utility knife or pizza cutter to make cutting easy, but first place the fruit leather on some waxed paper over old magazines or several layers of newspaper to protect your table top. Use a copy machine to copy your child's favorite picture from a book, then use the copy as a pattern to place over the fruit leather and cut the design. Or use the Simple Shapes on pages 367-368. Before drying, you can add food coloring (see page 364) to light colored fruit purée, such as apple or banana, for custom colors—like the purple of imaginary dinosaurs, or the green of Christmas trees.

Storing Fruit Leather

Place single servings of fruit leather in small plastic sandwich bags, remove as much air as possible, and tie a tight knot. Place the individual sandwich bags in a large plastic freezer bag. (This is the Nested Plastic Bag Method). Now you can open and re-open the large freezer bag without exposing the leather in the individual bags to air and moisture. Stored this way in a cool (around 50°F), dry, dark place, the leather should keep for up to 2-4 weeks. At room temperature, it will keep for only about half that time. For longer storage, refrigerate for up to 2 months or freeze for 3-4 months. Leather with garnishes or fillings should not be stored at room temperature, refrigerate or freeze them.

Fruit Leather Recipes

It seems that there are infinitely many combinations of fruits, flavorings, garnishes, and fillings for fruit leather. Apples are a favorite fruit for making leather, because their pectin content helps to thicken the purée. Some fruits, such as citrus fruits and blueberries, are too bland or juicy to be used alone. They should be combined with apples or other fruits to improve flavor and texture. Pears are best if they are not dried alone; combine them with apples or pineapple.

❧ *Fruit Combinations for Fruit Leather:*

These combinations of puréed fruit work well and taste good together in fruit leather:

apple-banana	banana-cherry	peach-blueberry
apple-strawberry	cherry-pineapple	peach-plum
apple-any berry	nectarine-pineapple	pear-apple
apple-apricot	nectarine-plum	pear-pineapple
apple-peach		strawberry-peach
apple-orange		strawberry-pineapple
apple-any fruit		
apricot-plum		

Tip: Add a crushed vitamin C tabled to a light fruit (peach, pear, banana, etc.) to keep it from browning.

❧ *The Easiest Ever Apple Fruit Leather*

Open a jar of applesauce, spread on the cookie sheet, and dry.

Variation: Add ¼ teaspoon of cinnamon into applesauce before drying. Or mix into applesauce a 4-ounce jar of baby fruit, such as peaches, apricots, prunes, etc.

❧ *Quick Strawberry Leather*

Thaw a package of frozen strawberries according to package directions. Purée in processor adding water or fruit juice until good consistency (page 203). Dry.

?? *Mango Leather*

Purée 2 cups of mango and dry.

?? *Pumpkin Leather Jack-O-Lanterns*

Open a 16-ounce can of pumpkin, stir in ½ cup of honey or maple syrup, and add ½ teaspoon of pumpkin pie spice. Dry. Cut into Jack-O-Lantern shapes and use garnishes and Decorative Touches for eyes, mouth, stem, etc.

?? *Fruit Leather from Canned Fruit*

Open a can or jar of fruit. Drain fruit and reserve liquid. Purée fruit in processor, adding only enough reserved liquid until good consistency (page 203). Dry.

?? *Flavoring Fruit Leather*

During blending, a teaspoon or more of honey or other sweetener can be added, if you wish, but it is not really necessary if your fruit is naturally sweet and ripe. Flavorings like lemon juice, almond extract, vanilla, and cinnamon, nutmeg, and other spices can also be added.

?? *Garnishing Fruit Leather*

Chopped nuts, raisins, shredded coconut, and other garnishes can be sprinkled onto fruit leather near the end of the drying period while it is still slightly sticky. The garnishes add a nice touch to leather cut into flat pieces. You can cut fancy shapes out of the leather and use garnishes to decorate. Or the garnishes can be rolled up into the leather, like jelly in a jelly roll.

?? *Fruit Leather Pinwheels*

These are the ultimate fruit leather snack! After the leather has dried, but is still slightly warm, spread a thin layer of filling over it, leaving an inch of margin around the edges. Then roll up jelly-roll style. Cut the roll into ½ to 1 inch pieces. Cutting is easier if the leather is chilled and stiff. For filling, use plain or sweetened tofu, softened cream cheese, softened peanut butter or other nut butters, tahini, yogurt cheese, a contrasting color jam or jelly. You can sprinkle garnishes over the filling and roll them in. Store the pinwheels in the refrigerator or freezer, not at room temperature. Children (and older folks) love the look of these pinwheels or spirals, and they are delicious!

24. Super Porridge Cereals:

THE Most Important Part of the

Super Baby Food Diet

Please turn to pages 502-503 and look at the Department of Agriculture's Food Pyramids, which indicate that grains and grain products should be the bulk of a healthy diet. The Super Baby Food Diet follows the guidelines of the Food Pyramid.

Super Porridge cereal is THE most important part of the Super Baby Food Diet.

Many parents who have used the first edition of this book have told me that they used this book to make only vegetables. Vegetables are only part of the Super Baby Food Diet. I encourage you to try making Super Porridge—it's very easy and, in my opinion, is the unique part of the diet that will make your baby super healthy. I have not done a scientific study, but it seems that babies who have not been fed Super Porridge get sick just as often as the "average" American baby—about 6 to 12 times per year. The parents who I know have made Super Porridge a major part of their babies' diets claim that their babies never or very rarely get sick. And they all claim that they NEVER have problems with diarrhea or constipation. The fiber in the whole grains and legumes of Super Porridge is necessary for colon health and overall health. So please include Super Porridge in our baby's diet—you and your baby will be happy you did.

> **TIP:** If you begin your baby on Super Porridge at 6 months and feed it to her every single day, she will probably continue to eat it well into the toddler years because she is used to it. Believe it or not, my son is now older than 3 years old and he still eats it every day! Here is his daily super healthy meal: Whole grains, legumes, brewer's yeast (yuck!), kale or some

other Super Green Veggie cube, and ½ an avocado cube. It doesn't taste good to me, but he eats it—no problem. He even asks for it! I'm keeping my fingers crossed that he will continue eating it forever. I force myself to eat his leftovers.

Super Porridge is a homemade baby cereal that, when cooked, looks very similar to commercial boxed baby cereal mixed with liquid. But unlike commercial cereal that is processed and refined, Super Porridge is a natural cereal made from unrefined whole grains. Whole grains are a very inexpensive source of super nutrition for your baby. These complex carbohydrates are a good source of trace minerals, such as chromium, copper, magnesium, manganese, selenium, silicon, zinc, and others.

Instead of starting baby on commercial rice cereal, you can start your baby on Super Porridge made from brown rice. However, your baby should be at least 6 months old before you give her Super Porridge, because her digestive system will then be mature enough to digest the whole grains.

You can buy brown rice at your supermarket, but your local natural foods store has organically-grown brown rice. Natural foods stores are discussed on page 140.

Storing Uncooked Whole Grains

Don't worry about buying too many whole grains—you'll use them before they spoil. Store dry, uncooked, whole grains in an airtight jar in a dark, cool cabinet and they'll keep for a year or more. Buckwheat groats and oatmeal are exceptions—keep them at room temperature for only one month or refrigerate or freeze them for longer storage—up to 6 months.

Insects love whole grains! Storing grains in sterile mayonnaise jars is a good way to protect them from the little varmints. Or use heavy plastic or metal containers. Grain bugs can chew through plastic bags, cardboard boxes, and wax paper coverings.

> **TIP:** Larvae of bugs are sometimes inside the grains—that's how they magically appear, even in tightly covered containers. If you have trouble with little grain bug specks, perhaps because you live in a climate of high heat and humidity. Try one of these preventative measures:
>
> ❧ Store grains in your refrigerator—if you have the room, or
> ❧ Place the grains in the freezer for 14 days to kill all insect larvae, or
> ❧ Heat the grains in the oven on cookie sheets or in shallow pans at 130°F for at least 30 minutes to kill the larvae, or
> ❧ Place a bay leaf or two into the grains, but be sure to remove the leaves and any leaf pieces completely before cooking. (Bay leaves are sharp and can cut your mouth and throat.) Enclose the bay leaves in cheesecloth or plastic netting to prevent pieces from mixing into the grains. Replace bay leaves after about one year.

Making Super Porridge from Brown Rice

Making Super Porridge is easy. First measure a cup of water on the stove to boil.

> **MONEY SAVER:** See energy-saving stove-top cooking tips on page 188.

WARNING: Be sure to read the use, safety, cleaning, and maintenance directions for your blender or processor completely before you begin to use it. Be sure that the manufacturer's instructions say that it is OK to grind dry ingredients in your blender or processor, such as brown rice, oatmeal, other grains, and whole nuts and seeds.

While the water is heating to a boil, measure ¼ cup of brown rice into your blender. Grind it very well, for about 2 minutes. Your blender makes a lot of noise, and it's hard to stand there listening to that motor go for so long, but please wait for the full 2 minutes. Even though the motor gets hot, rest assured that your blender is meant to work like this and the motor will not be damaged. I've used (and I mean used!) my Oster blender for 15 years now and it still works as if it's brand new.

WARNING: If you are grinding large amounts of grains and the motor sounds like it's laboring too hard, increase the speed. If it still doesn't sound right, grind smaller batches.

This fine grinding is necessary for your beginning eater. If your baby is a little older and eating chunkier food, you may have to grind for only 20-30 seconds to get the proper consistency. You know you're a pro at making Super Porridge when you can tell just by the sound of your blender when the grains are finished grinding!

WARNING: Your blender and food processor give off a lot of EMFs (electro magnetic fields), so don't stand very close to it. Step back a good foot or two while it is grinding.

When the cup of water starts to boil on the stove, turn the heat down to the lowest setting. Sprinkle the ground rice into the water while stirring briskly with a wire whisk. Cover the pot and keep it over low heat for about 10 minutes. Stir frequently with the whisk to prevent scorching on the bottom and to remove lumps. You will have to stir more frequently at first, when the pot is still very hot, than after it's had a few minutes to cool. When it's done cooking, it should look like the porridge in the next picture.

To prevent powdered grain from going all over the kitchen counter when you open the blender, unscrew the blender base from the blender container while holding it over the boiling water in the pot.

TIP: When you open the lid to stir the porridge, hold the lid over the pot so that the condensed steam will drip back into the pot and not on your stove top.

Adjust the Consistency, If Necessary

If your Super Porridge is too thick, thin it by simply mixing in a little breast milk, formula, or water. If it is too thin, add a little wheat germ, ground nuts, ground oatmeal, commercial powdered baby cereal, etc. Make sure that the thickener you use is age-appropriate, of course.

TIP: If you are making whole brown rice for the rest of your family, you can make Super Porridge from it by puréeing the cooked rice with an equal amount of liquid. See last method in the box on page 216.

How to Prevent Boilovers

There's a possibility that the cereal will boil over and make a mess of your stove. One way to prevent this from happening is to use a fairly large pot—the pot should be able to hold three times the volume of cereal. I use the Visions® cookware shown in the previous picture. It's made of glass, and boilovers seem to be more frequent with this cookware, because the glass gets hotter and stays hotter longer. To prevent boilovers, I move the pot totally off the burner immediately after I stir in the grains, and stir for about a minute until the electric burner cools down and the porridge stops boiling. Then I place it back on the burner with heat on lowest setting.

TIP: Use the same pot, same stove burner, same heat setting, and the same quantity of water/food and you will know the time and tricks necessary to cook the food quickly and perfectly. Or, use the same cooking dish and amount of food in your microwave every time and cooking/thawing Super Baby Food becomes very easy and efficient.

Refrigerate the Two Servings Immediately

After letting the cereal cook over low heat for 10 minutes, it's ready. One cup of water and ¼ cup of rice makes a little more than 1 cup of cereal, or 2 ½-cup servings. You may want to keep the cereal in the pot and refrigerate until mealtime, or you can divide it into two or three individual microwave-able bowls and refrigerate. Make sure you cover the cereal well so it won't dry up in the dry refrigerator air. Cooked Super Porridge will keep in the refrigerator for 2-3 days. If your baby is ready to eat now, make sure the cereal has cooled to a safe temperature before you feed it to her. (See *How to Cool Food Quickly* on page 176.)

Individual Bowls are More Convenient

When my Super Porridge is done cooking, I always pour it into separate bowls with lids before storing it in the refrigerator. When mealtime comes, I grab an individual serving and warm it in the microwave. This is easier than spooning out a portion and returning the pot to the refrigerator. It also saves space in your refrigerator—you can stack three or four plastic baby bowls with lids in a smaller area than a big pot would take. And emptying the cereal into bowls makes the pot immediately available for other uses.

Corelle® dishes are great for individual servings of Super Porridge. They do better in the dishwasher than the lidded plastic baby bowls, which are light and fly all over the place and are top-rack dishwasher safe only. I cover the bowls by placing a small Corelle dish over them, which believe it or not, seals tightly enough to keep the porridge fresh. The dish covers also make the bowls stackable, as seen in the picture on the right.

Corelle dishes can be used in the microwave and their flat dishes can be used as perfectly-fitting covers. The dishes and bowls stack compactly in the cabinet and in the dishwasher—an absolute must in my home. And you don't have to be gentle with them because they are break-resistant. Please know that I have no affiliation with Corelle and, to my knowledge, neither I nor my family own any Corning® stock. ☺ I just think their dishes are great for those who prefer practicality over fancy dinnerware.

Freeze Super Porridge for Longer Storage

If you wish, you can freeze Super Porridge in individual servings using the Phantom Container Freezing Method. It will keep for 2-4 weeks or longer. I usually don't freeze Super Porridge because it's so quick to make—I make it every 2 or 3 days and it's always ready in the refrigerator. Freezing changes the texture of the cereal so that it is a little rubbery, though it's fine after you mash it and add a little formula to it. I do occasionally reach into the refrigerator at baby's mealtime and find that I'm out of Super Porridge. Although it takes only 10 minutes waiting time to cook, it does take a while to cool, and my baby is not that patient. For these "emergencies" when I run out, I always keep at least one portion of frozen Super Porridge tucked away in the freezer. A few minutes in the microwave, and it's ready to eat.

Making Super Porridge from Millet

Millet is a super healthy whole grain cereal for your baby, and can be used instead of rice as a first cereal. Like rice, it is not likely to cause allergy and is easily digested. A grain of millet is much smaller than a grain of rice, so you must use a different portion when you make Super Porridge from millet. Instead of ¼ cup, which is actually 4 tablespoons, use a little less—about 3 tablespoons of millet.

Place a cup of water on the stove to boil and while it's heating, put 3 tablespoons of millet into the blender. Grind for 2 minutes or less. Follow the same directions as for rice: Whisk the millet powder into the boiling water and let it sit over low heat for 10 minutes. Whisk frequently to prevent burning and lumps.

Making Super Porridge from Barley

Your natural foods store carries organic pearled barley, or you can buy barley at the supermarket if you prefer. Use ¼ cup barley to 1 cup boiling water, as for brown rice, and cook it the same way.

Making Super Porridge from Oatmeal

Your health food store also carries whole grain oats, which look similar to brown rice grains. These, too, should be cooked the same way as Super Porridge brown rice. Most of us have probably never seen oat grains. We're more familiar with rolled oats (also called old-fashioned oats). These flakes are made from oat grains that have been steamed and flattened. They take about 15 minutes to cook. Quick-cooking oats are similar to rolled oats, but cook faster—in about 5 minutes—because they have been cut up before being steamed and flattened. Use the old fashioned rolled oat flakes (not the quick-cooking) to make Super Porridge. Whether you are using the oat grains or rolled oats in Super Porridge, cook them the same as you would brown rice—grind ¼ cup in the blender and cook the powder for 10 minutes.

The Smaller the Grain, the Less Grain You Use

With millet, it's 3 tablespoons of grains to 1 cup of water; with rice, it's 4 tablespoons or ¼ cup of grains to 1 cup of water. In general, the smaller the size of the grain, the less you use. This is because small grains pack more tightly and have less air space between them, making them denser so that you need a smaller measure of them. So when cooking other grains, compare them to the size of millet and rice and measure accordingly. Brown rice comes in three sizes: large grain, medium grain, and small grain. Use 1 cup of water for ¼ cup medium grain rice. The large grain rice would need a 1-2 tablespoons less water than the medium grain. The small grain rice packs denser and would need a few tablespoons more water than the medium grain.

> **REMEMBER: As a general rule of thumb for Super Porridge, use an amount of water equal to 4-5 times the amount of powdered grains/legumes**.

> **TIP:** When in doubt, use more water. If cereal turns out a little watery, just add a little ground dry oatmeal or wheat germ to thicken.

As Baby Grows, Double the Recipe

In no time at all, you'll find yourself running out of Super Porridge before the 2-3 day refrigerator keeping time is up. Then you can double the recipe. Boil 2 cups of water instead of 1, and double the volume of grains: ½ cup of grains for rice and the larger grains and 6 tablespoons of grain for millet and the smaller grains. This will yield a little more than 2 cups of cereal, which can be divided into 4 ½-cup individual servings or 3 ¾-cup servings. To save time and cooking, make enough Super Porridge to feed your baby for 2-3 days—the refrigerator keeping time of cooked Super Porridge.

Mini-Blender Containers

It's worth it to purchase a little blender container for grinding. One mini container holds one cup and has markings on the side for easy measuring, and it's **so much** easier to use than the big clumsy blender container. Mini-blend containers are also easier to take apart and clean than the big container. See page 150 for more info and how to order.

Batch Grinding in Advance

If you don't like grinding grains a quarter cup at a time every 2-3 days, you can grind a big batch of grains and store them in the refrigerator in a tightly closed sterile glass jar. The ground grains will keep in the refrigerator for up to a month. For example, you can grind a cup or two of brown rice all at once and store the powder in a clean mayonnaise jar in the refrigerator. When it comes time to make Super Porridge, boil a cup of water on the stove, and sprinkle 3-4 tablespoons of the already-ground powdered grain into the pot and cook for 10 minutes. Grinding in batches means you have to take apart the blender and clean it only once. Or if you don't have a blender, you can go to a friend's house and use hers to grind a whole batch and take it home.

TIP: Grinding is easier if you grind small amounts (about ¼-½ cup) at a time.

Super Porridge Made from Mixed Grains

When your baby is 7 months old, you can feed her cereals made from mixed grains. Simply mix any two grains together. For example, ¼ cup brown rice and 3 tablespoons of millet can be ground together in the blender and stirred into 2 cups of boiling water and cooked and stored as usual.

Super Porridge with Tofu, Cheese, or Egg Yolk

At 7 months, add hard-cooked egg yolk or a tablespoon or two of mashed tofu into cooked Super Porridge to make a high-protein Super Porridge. See protein complementarity, page 513.

High Protein Super Porridge

When your baby is 9 months old, he has arrived! At this age, he can eat the ultimate super duper Super Porridge—that which is made from a mixture of grains and beans/legumes. Super Porridge with beans is no more trouble to cook than Super Porridge made from plain brown rice—just mix some beans in with the grains, grind, and cook for 10 minutes. When beans are ground to a powder in the blender, no pre-soaking is necessary, and they cook in 10 minutes just as the grains do. Before grinding, pick through the beans and discard any that are cracked, malformed, or discolored. On rare occasions, you may also find little pebbles mixed in with the beans.

> **NOTE:** The only special treatment needed for Super Porridge with beans is when you add one specific bean—the soybean. If soybeans are included in the Super Porridge mix, you must cook for 20 minutes instead of 10.

As explained in the protein complementarity section, when approximately two parts grains are mixed with one part beans or other legumes, protein is formed that is as high a quality as that from eggs or meats. You don't have to be this exact, but if you want the very best proportions for maximum protein, use ⅓ cup rice or other grain and ⅛ cup lentil or other beans/peas/legumes. This mixture (equivalent to two cups of cooked Super Porridge) contains about 7.5 grams of complete protein.

High Protein Super Porridge Made from Mixing Grains with Legumes

To make 2 cups of high protein Super Porridge, mix in blender and grind:

⅓ **cup dry whole grains** (brown rice, millet, oatmeal, or any of the grains listed in the box on page 222) and

2 **tablespoons (⅛ cup) dried legumes** (lentils, soy grits, split peas, or any legume listed in the box on page 235)

This makes about ½ cup of powder. Stir powder into 2 cups boiling water, reduce heat to low, and cook for 10 minutes (20 minutes if soybeans are included), stirring frequently with whisk to remove lumps and prevent scorching. Refrigerate for 2-3 days or freeze for up to one month.

Your Natural Foods Store Is Full of Beans

That's a compliment. Newcomers probably never knew so many types of beans existed. Of course, you can buy beans and other legumes at the supermarket, but again, your natural foods store carries a wider selection and they are organically grown.

TIP: Finely ground bean flour, such as soybean flour or soy flour, can be substituted some of the regular flour in baking to boost the nutrition in the baked goods. See Super Flour on page 289.

To Save Time, Pre-Measure and Pre-Mix Grains and Beans/Legumes in Individual Containers

I have about a dozen mini-blend containers, which I fill with a variety of grain and bean combinations to make Super Porridge. As you can see in the next picture, I keep in my cupboard several bags of whole grains and several bags of beans/legumes. About once a month, when my mini-blend containers have been all used up to make Super Porridge, I pull out the grains and legumes. With an ⅛-cup measuring cup and a ⅓-cup measuring cup, I get to work mixing grains and beans/legumes into the containers all at one time. One container might have oats and kidney beans, another millet and lentils, etc. Or sometimes I put a tablespoon of rice, millet, and barley in the same container with 1 tablespoon soybeans, a few kidney beans, and a teaspoon of split peas to make ½ cup total—talk about mixed grains and beans!

I have several mini-blender containers because 12 years ago when I bought them, you had to buy them by the half-dozen, whereas today they sell them in sets of 2. If you would like to mix grains and beans like this, you don't need to use mini-blend containers—they're quite expensive (about $5 a piece). Instead, use paper cups or cheap plastic sandwich bags to hold the mixtures. Then, immediately before cooking, pour them into a mini-blend container and grind.

TIP: To make sure your baby is getting a variety of beans and grains, and that you're not feeding him the same ones over and over again, keep several types in your cabinet. Rotate them (as you would clothes in your closet) so that they are cycled through your baby's diet.

ned in this chapter on how to make Super Porridge are summarized
e the method that you find most convenient and the one that saves

Cook Super Porridge Using the
Method that Saves You the Most Time

There are several ways you can make Super Porridge:

- You can make 2-3 days' worth from scratch each time, measuring the grains and beans into the blender, grinding them, and stirring them into the boiling water to cook.

- You can proportion your whole grains and beans in several individual containers, and then grind immediately before cooking 2-3 days' worth and refrigerating. (I'm lacking in freezer and refrigerator space, so I use this one. The individual containers of pre-measured unground grains and beans, as in the previous picture, can be kept in the cabinet until grinding time.)

- You can pre-measure and grind a months' worth of beans and grains all at once and store the powder in sterile air-tight glass jars in the refrigerator. Then cook 2-3 days' worth at one time.

- You can cook a whole batch of Super Porridge once a month and store it in individual containers in the freezer (this takes a lot of freezer space) and then thaw one portion immediately before mealtime.

- And yet another way to make Super Porridge is to cook grains and beans whole as for adults, without grinding them in the blender, according to the directions in the next two chapters. Then purée the cooked grains and beans with liquid (water, breast milk, or formula). See the details on this method on page 223.

How to Make Super Porridge Thicker and Chunkier

I still give my 3-year old Super Porridge almost every single day. You're never too old for smooth, unchunky Super Porridge! As your baby gets older, you may want to make whole grain cereals a little chunkier to give your baby practice in chewing. Your baby might be ready for a thicker texture, but not quite ready for whole cooked brown rice and other grains.

The length of time for cooking grains depends on the size of the grain pieces and the hardness of the grain. The bigger the pieces of ground grains, the longer they take to cook. For example, brown rice Super Porridge is made from powdered grains and cooks in 10 minutes. Unpulverized whole brown rice cooks in 45 minutes as shown in the table on page 222. To make Super Porridge chunkier, do NOT chop the grains into bigger pieces and cook for 10 minutes or the cereal will contain gritty, hard pieces of uncooked grain. The correct way to make a more textured Super Porridge is to cook unground whole grains as directed in the next chapter, then purée the cooked whole grains in your processor with water or other liquid. For very smooth Super Porridge for a beginning eater, purée the cooked whole grains with an equal amount of liquid until you have a very smooth texture—the same texture as if you had ground the grains to a powder before cooking. (This is the last method listed in the previous box and on page 223.) For a more textured Super Porridge, thoroughly cook the grains whole and unpulverized as directed in the next chapter. Then add a little liquid and purée a bit. The cereal will have some texture and not be quite so smooth, but there will be no hard, uncooked pieces in it.

25. Whole Grain Super Baby Foods

Whole Grains vs Processed Grains

There is a enormous nutritional difference between whole grains and the enriched, processed grains used in most of America's food products. The word "enriched" means that more than a dozen natural nutrients have been destroyed during processing and a few synthetic ones (thiamin, riboflavin, niacin, iron, and maybe calcium) have been replaced in unnatural proportions. See the comparison table on the next page. (Enriched is different from "fortified," which indicates that nutrients have been added that were never there in the first place.)

Let's take whole wheat as an example. In the natural foods store on the grains shelf, you will see whole wheat kernels that look very similar to brown rice. If you were to dissect a kernel of whole wheat, you would find that it has the three parts pictured on the right.

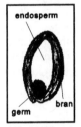

Whole Wheat Kernel

- the **bran** (as in wheat bran) is about 14% of the wheat kernel. It contains almost all of the fiber, some minerals, B vitamins, and a little incomplete protein. This layered outer covering of the grain is stiffer and harder than the inside of the kernel and offers it some protection against the outside world, as an apple peel protects the innards of an apple. It makes sense that the bran contains most of the fiber of the wheat kernel.

- the **germ** (as in wheat germ) is less than 3% of the wheat kernel, but it contains almost all of its nutrients, including vitamin E and unsaturated fatty acids or oils. The germ is the seed of the wheat plant and contains the stuff to grow new life. (See wheat germ on page 224.)

- the **endosperm** is 83% of the wheat kernel. It is almost all starch with minute amounts of nutrients. White flour is made from the nutritionless endosperm.

The whole wheat kernel, with its germ and surrounding support system, is actually the seed of the wheat plant. Plant it and it will grow; place it in water and it will sprout.

When whole wheat is ground into whole wheat flour, it contains the germ and the bran. But when whole wheat flour is refined into white flour, the germ and bran with all of their nutrients and fiber are removed. White flour is the stuff from which most commercial breads, rolls, biscuits, pretzels, muffins, cookies, cakes, and hundreds of other food products are made.

Comparison of Whole Wheat Flour, White Flour, and Enriched White Flour. Nutrients in ½ Cup

	Whole Wheat Flour	White Flour	Enriched Flour	% Removed In Refinement
calories	203.00	226.00	226.00	
protein	8.22	6.40	6.40	22%
fat	1.12	0.61	0.61	46%
carbohydrate	43.54	47.31	47.31	
fiber	1.26	0.15	0.15	88%
calcium	20.00	9.00	156.24	
iron	2.33	0.73	2.88	
magnesium	83.00	13.00	13.00	84%
phosphorus	208.00	67.00	67.00	68%
potassium	243.00	66.00	66.00	73%
sodium	3.00	1.00	1.00	67%
zinc	1.76	0.44	0.44	75%
copper	0.23	0.09	0.09	61%
manganese	2.28	0.42	0.42	81%
thiamine	0.27	0.07	0.49	
riboflavin	0.13	0.02	0.31	
niacin	3.82	0.78	3.66	4%
pantothenic acid	0.61	0.27	0.27	55%
vitamin B6	0.21	0.03	0.03	87%
folic acid	26.00	16.00	16.00	38%

In addition, 40% of the chromium, 89% of the cobalt, and 48% of the molybdenum is removed during refinement.

Note: Folic acid will be added to enriched flour beginning in 1998.

In 1998, food manufacturers will begin to add **folic acid** to enriched processed flour. Folic acid helps to prevent some birth defects, such as spina bifida and others. Folic acid is the B vitamin that the fetus needs in the first few weeks of pregnancy—usually before the woman knows that she is pregnant.

Why do manufacturers go through the trouble to remove the germ and the bran, after all, the process must cost them money? Because white flour has an indefinite shelf life. The oils contained in the germ make whole wheat flour go rancid and get bitter and spoil quickly. Refined white flour lasts forever, because it's virtually lifeless. And then, as if removing the germ and bran were not enough, food manufacturers go even further to strip white flour of any minute food value left in it by bleaching. Bleaching makes it very white and pretty.

Incidentally, the reason why wheat flour is so often used for bread products, rather than rye flour or some other flour, is because of its high gluten content. Gluten is the ingredient in flour that makes breads and bread products become soft and elastic and rise high. See *Home-Baking Whole Grain Bread* (page 226) for more information.

Keep Whole Wheat Flour Refrigerated

Whole wheat flour keeps only for about a week at room temperature, so refrigerate it if you don't plan on using it soon. And always refrigerate it on hot days. You can tell if whole wheat flour is fresh by tasting it. If it has the least amount of bitterness, it is spoiled. Breads made from whole wheat flour at your natural foods store are usually frozen. See the section *The Whiter the Bread the Sooner You're Dead* on page 224 for more on buying and storing whole grain bread.

BUYER BEWARE: Misleading Advertising:
"Wheat" does not mean "Whole Wheat"

If a package says "wheat flour," that does NOT mean whole wheat flour. White flour IS wheat flour—the nutritionless endosperm part of the wheat kernel. I believe that the manufacturer is hoping that the uninformed consumer will take "wheat flour" to mean "whole wheat flour." Manufacturers may also put in big letters on the package that a product is "Made from whole wheat." Well, there may be only a small amount of whole wheat flour in the product, while most of it is actually wheat flour (white flour). Read the ingredients list. Another trick of the food manufacturing trade is the use of the word *wholesome*. "Made from wholesome wheat flour" means that it's made from plain old wheat/white flour, which in my opinion, is not wholesome at all!

"Wheat bread" does not mean "whole wheat bread."

BUYER BEWARE: Nutritionists used to recommend that you eat dark bread, because it was made from whole grains. Then the food manufacturers caught on and added caramel coloring to their bread to make it a dark color, so that consumers would think it was healthier. Protect yourself by reading the ingredients list. One time in a Chinese restaurant, I asked for brown rice. The waiter informed me that their rice was brown after they added the dark colored sauce to the white rice. He just didn't get it.

Bread Is Not the Only White Flour Product

Beware that the typical American supermarket bagels, breakfast cereals, rolls, crackers, pretzels, spaghetti and other pasta products, buns, pizza crusts, pastries, cakes, cupcakes, and cookies are made from white flour.

WARNING: Read the ingredients list thoroughly and do not buy any bread or bread products containing hydrogenated oils. See page 507.

Other Whole Grains

White rice is to brown rice as white flour is to whole wheat flour. Degerminated cornmeal is to whole grain cornmeal as white flour is to whole wheat flour. The word *degerminated* sounds like something good, doesn't it? Take the germs out. Well, now we know that the germ is the staff of life, and foods that are degerminated might as well be labeled *denatured* and *denutrified*. *Enriched* is another word that makes white flour sound good, as discussed in the first paragraph on page 218. Even at the natural foods store, these food manufacturers' tricks are used. Make sure a product is labeled "whole millet flour," "whole cornmeal," "whole corn flour," "whole rye flour", etc.

NOTE: Cream of Wheat is not a whole grain cereal. Wheatena is.

Storing Uncooked Whole Grains

See page 208 for how to store whole grains before cooking.

How to Cook Whole Grains

Of course, grinding grains and making Super Porridge is one way to cook whole grains. But for older folks and for your baby when he gets old enough to eat food that is not puréed, grains are usually cooked without grinding them first.

Rinsing Grains Before Cooking

Some people recommend washing grains before cooking by rinsing them under cold running tap water. Rinsing causes a loss of B vitamins. I don't rinse mine, unless I can actually see surface grit, because I buy organic so I don't have to worry about pesticides, and I feel that the boiling water will sterilize the grains. If you would prefer, you can rinse your grains.

Cooking Grains on the Stove Top

Cooking whole grains is as easy as boiling water. Bring the recommended amount of water to a boil (see table on next page). Use a pot large enough to hold the grains and the water, with a little (or a lot of) headroom leftover. The heavier the pot, the less the chance of scorching. Sprinkle whole grains into boiling water. Stir once and only once. Cover the pot and turn heat down to lowest setting. Let simmer for recommended time. Do not stir again because you can damage the grains and cause the grains to cook unevenly and be gummy. Keep a close eye on the pot for the first several minutes, so that in case it starts to boilover you can quickly move it off the burner.

Variation: Another way you can cook whole grains on the stove top is to put the grains in water and then bring it to a boil. Cover the pot and turn heat down to lowest setting. Let simmer for recommended time in table. The grains will be creamier, as you would want for puddings. However, the grains are not as fluffy with this method, as when you boil the water before adding the grains.

Although you may have to wait up to 45 minutes or more for grains to cook, it is all wait time. That's why cooking grains is so easy—they require no attention.

MONEY SAVER: See stove-top cooking energy-saving tips in the box on page 188.

Grain Cooking Quick Reference

For each cup of dry grain:	Use this many cups of water:	And simmer for this many minutes:
amaranth	2	25
barley, pearled	2¾	40-45
brown rice	2	45
buckwheat groats	2	15-20
bulgur	2	15-20
couscous	1¾	4
kamut	2	50
millet	3	45
oatmeal/rolled oats	2	15
oats, whole	3	45-60
quinoa	2	15-20
rye berries	4	60
sorghum	3	45
teff	3	15
triticale	4	60
wheat, cracked	2	25
wheat berries	3	120

For cornmeal, see recipe for polenta, page 310.

TIP: Replacing some or all of the water with stock makes the grains much more flavorful. Or use milk, which will add to the nutrition and protein content. Or try undiluted tomato juice. You can also use apple juice or other sweet fruit juice, but replace no more than ⅓ of the water or the grains will be too sweet.

TIP: For a distinct flavor, toast grains for a few minutes in a heavy skillet on the stove top in a little butter. Then cook as discussed above.

Cooking Grains in the Oven

Grains can be baked in the oven. In a casserole dish, combine boiling water and dry grains in proportions in previous table. Bake, covered, at 375°F for 30-45 minutes or until water is absorbed. Or you can use your oven as a slow grain cooker. Mix grains with water (cold or boiling) in a covered casserole and bake at 200°F for 4 hours or more, until water is absorbed. Slow cooking at this low heat saves nutrients that would be destroyed at higher temperatures.

Grain Steamers

You certainly do not need to buy one, but if you already have a rice steamer, a vegetable steamer, or any food steamer, you can use it to cook whole grains. There are two basic types: metal units that look like crock-pots, and plastic units that cook by steaming alone. They all work well. Follow the instruction manual for how to cook rice in order to use the steamer to cook any other grain.

Cooking Grains in the Microwave

Cooking some grains in the microwave is faster than on the stove top. Although most grains can be cooked in the microwave, they require stirring and attention during cooking. It's much easier to cook grains on the stove top, with the possible exception of the few listed in the next table.

Grain Cooking Times for Microwave

To cook grains in the microwave, mix grains in a large bowl with recommended amount of water from the previous table. Cover bowl and place in microwave. Cook on high for time below. Stir every 2 minutes.

bulgur and other cracked grains	8 minutes
cornmeal	4½ minutes
oatmeal/rolled oats	5-7 minutes

Storing Cooked Whole Grains

Grains cooked whole can be kept refrigerated, covered well, for up to 5 days. Re-heat in the microwave on high for 30-45 seconds per cup of grains.

Cooked grains freeze well and will keep frozen for up to 3 months. Divide into individual portions and freeze using the Nested Plastic Bag Method. To re-heat frozen grains, transfer them out of the sandwich bag into a covered bowl in the microwave. Defrosting is not necessary. Add a tablespoon of water for each cup of grains. Microwave on high for 1-2 minutes for each cup of grains.

> **TIP:** Use leftover grains as an addition to soups to make them more hearty and to add a nutritional boost. Mix them with a little salad dressing. Make fried brown rice or other grain by sauteeing in a little oil with chopped onions/scallions, mushrooms, cooked peas, etc. See recipe, page 311. Make a quiche crust—see recipe on page 338.

Making Super Porridge from Cooked Grains

In the last chapter, dry uncooked grains were ground in the blender to a powder and then mixed with boiling water and cooked for 10 minutes. Super Porridge can also be made from grains that have been cooked whole with no grinding. First cook the grains as described in this chapter, cooking them in the proper amount of liquid from the *Grain Cooking Quick Reference Box* on page 222. Then mix the COOKED grains with ADDITIONAL liquid and grind in the processor until you have a smooth consistency. For the smooth texture needed for a beginning eater, use an amount of liquid equal to the amount of cooked grains and purée to a smooth consistency.

For example, let's say you have cooked some cooked brown rice for the adults in your family and you'd like to take some of the brown rice and make it into Super Porridge for the baby. For ½ cup of the cooked brown rice, add ½ cup of liquid (water, breast milk/formula) and grind in the blender or processor until smooth. For ¼ cup of cooked brown rice, use ¼ cup of liquid, etc. Use the same amount of liquid as cooked grains. If necessary, add more liquid during processing to get a smooth consistency.

As your baby gets older, she will be ready for a more textured and chunkier Super Porridge, but not quite ready to eat whole cooked unground grains (like the rice we eat as adults). When she's in this "in-between" stage, here's how to make a more textured cereal: Make Super Porridge as instructed in the last paragraph, but with less grinding. In other words, don't grind until the cereal is very smooth—leave a little chunkiness in it. As your baby becomes ready for even more texture and chunkiness, try adding less liquid and grind for even less time. Gradually decrease the liquid and increase the chunkiness until she can handle adult-style whole grains.

WARNING: The INCORRECT method for increasing chunkiness in Super Porridge is to follow the directions in the last chapter with less grinding. For grains to cook in 10 minutes, they must be ground into a powder. If you incompletely grind dry grains and leave big chunks of dry grain in the powder and cook for only 10 minutes, there will be hard, undercooked grain pieces in the Super Porridge. Therefore, the way to increase texture in Super Porridge for an older baby is to cook the grains completely as described in this chapter and then grind less and use less additional liquid. Please re-read page 217.

Wheat Germ

Wheat germ is actually the seed of the wheat kernel (page 218) and, like all seeds, is a super nutritious food. It is one of the parts of the wheat kernel that is removed when whole wheat is refined into white flour or wheat flour. You can buy wheat germ raw or toasted. Because of its oils, it is quite perishable and must be refrigerated or frozen in a tightly closed container. Toasting, although it reduces its nutrient content, will extend its shelf life for up to 6 months in the refrigerator. Toast your own raw wheat germ by spreading it thinly and evenly on an ungreased baking sheet and baking in a pre-heated 325°F oven for 15-20 minutes until lightly browned.

NOTE: Don't feed your baby wheat bran, oat bran, or other bran. See page 501.

The Whiter the Bread, the Sooner You're Dead

Every time I see an advertisement containing a sandwich made of glowing white bread I want to scream. It looks very pretty, but as discussed on page 218, it's a nutritional nightmare. Even worse are the breads that would be lily white but for the addition of caramel color to darken the bread, which tricks some consumers into thinking it's healthy.

While I'm on the subject of food advertisements, let me blow off some more steam here: How about those advertisements for "big kid nutrition," where they show a hot dog on a white flour roll with french fries and a cola beverage! Aarrggghh!

Anyway, try to buy bread at your natural foods store and read the label carefully. The first ingredient should be "whole wheat flour" or "whole some-other-grain flour" or "whole sprouted grains of wheat," etc. It will probably be in the freezer case. When you bring it home, keep it in the freezer until the night before you're going to use it, then switch it into the refrigerator where it will thaw in several hours. (If you forget the switch and need a quick sandwich, thaw a few slices in the microwave or toaster.) The loaf will keep for a couple of weeks in the refrigerator, whereas it would only keep for a day at room temperature. Be prepared to pay around $3.00 for a loaf of real bread, and remember that, in this case, you get what you pay for.

NOTE: Everything I have read about storing bread says that refrigerating bread hastens the staling process. But this certainly has not been my experience with the whole grain bread I buy from the natural foods store. If not kept in the refrigerator, it gets stale and hard within a day or two. The 100% whole grain bread I have occasionally bought at the supermarket does well at room temperature or in the refrigerator. Perhaps it's white bread that goes stale in the refrigerator.

MONEY SAVER: Don't discard the ends of bread if your family won't eat them. Use them as veggie burger buns. Or grind them into healthy whole grain bread crumbs (page 321).

Whole Grain Pasta

Whole grain pasta is an easy and convenient food for babies older than 10-12 months. Buy pasta at your natural foods store where you'll find it made from whole grains, such as whole wheat and brown rice. For babies with wheat allergy, use brown rice or other whole grain pasta. The typical supermarket pasta is made from white flour. Remember, if the ingredients list says "wheat flour," it's only white flour. See BUYER BEWARE on page 220. Spinach pasta has actually very little spinach in it, and is also usually made with wheat flour (white flour), so check the ingredients list. Whole grain pasta is an easy third meal for your baby, as discussed on page 132, and it freezes well. Pasta recipes begin on page 334.

Freezing and Thawing Pasta

Freeze pasta in individual portions using the Nested Plastic Bag Method or the Phantom Container Method. Although you can freeze plain pasta (as for finger foods), pasta freezes better if it is in sauce. Thaw pasta in the microwave. Re-heat stirrable dishes, such as macaroni and cheese, on high until warmed throughout, stirring halfway through cooking time. For non-stirrable food, such as lasagna, re-heat using only 50 percent or 75 percent power so that the edges don't dry up before the center becomes heated. You can also thaw and re-heat pasta by placing it in a strainer and dipping into boiling water.

Other Whole Grain Products

You will find many other products made from 100% whole grains at the natural foods store: muffins, English muffins, rolls, biscuits, bagels, pizza crusts, pie crusts, cakes, pita, hot cereals, and boxed breakfast cereals. Remember: The whiter the bread *product*, the sooner you're dead.

Home-Baking Whole Grain Bread

The saying "Bread is the staff of life" refers to whole grain breads, and not the nutritional disaster made from refined white flour found on the shelves of every supermarket in America. You can buy good quality breads, but they can be found only in natural foods stores; at least this is true in my neck of the woods. They are expensive, but in this case you get what you pay for. My family lives on a sprouted 7-grain bread that costs $3 a loaf at my local natural foods store, or on the comparable bread that I bake at home for about a third of that price.

As when you make own baby food, you can assure that only high quality, wholesome ingredients are used if you make your own homemade bread. No artificial preservatives are needed in the bread coming fresh out of your own oven. Most people consider it beyond the realm of their abilities to bake their own bread. For most of my life, I've had a fear of baking bread—not those quick breads that have baking powder or baking soda as leavening (rising) agents, but the breads that involve yeast and kneading and rising. Every-time I saw the words "active yeast" in a cookbook, my mind would automatically say "go to next recipe." But I've recently gotten into baking whole grain yeast breads, and it's not difficult at all. Of course, you can always buy a bread machine that bakes 100% whole grain breads!

If you'd like to learn how to bake whole grain breads by hand, I highly recommend that you buy or borrow from your local library some books on bread baking. My favorite is *The Laurel's Kitchen Bread Book A Guide to Whole-Grain Breadmaking* by Laurel Robertson and others (see bibliography). Maybe you do bake bread, but only with white flour, because your experience with whole wheat flour has been negative. (No one could eat my first whole grain loaves without breaking their teeth, so heavy and dense were they.) Perhaps you bake bread with SOME whole wheat flour (less than ½ or ⅓ of the flour) because that's what you thought was necessary to get light bread loaves. Good news! It IS possible to get light, delicious bread from 100% whole wheat flour if you follow the methods and tips in the next box.

Tips for Making Whole Wheat Bread

☙ When you knead whole wheat dough and want to reduce stickiness, add as little flour as possible to the kneading surface or your fingers—just a light dusting. Or use a little water instead of flour to reduce stickiness. Or don't use any flour or water and use a plastic kitchen scraper or spatula to scrape the dough off the kneading surface and your fingers. Too much flour is one of the most common causes of brick-hard whole wheat bread. It is better for whole wheat dough to be too wet than too dry. If you're used to baking with white flour, know that whole wheat flour will still feel tacky even after it has been thoroughly kneaded.

🏵 To get a good rise, the yeast must be fresh and of good quality. Also, make sure the liquid is at the right temperature for the yeast (110°F or the temperature stated in the packet instructions). The temperature of the warm rising place should be between 80°F and 90°F for a nice, slow, good rise. Also, a longer rising time or a little extra sweetener will increase the rise.

🏵 Use whole wheat flour that is as fresh as possible; it should be less than 2 months old. You can tell if whole wheat flour is fresh by tasting it—it should have no trace of bitterness. Whole wheat and other whole grain flours keep at room temperature for only about one week. If you won't use them by then, refrigerate for up to 2 months, or freeze for up to 6 months. If you really get into baking with whole grains, invest in a home mill to grind flour at home. There's nothing like a loaf of bread made with freshly ground flour. You can get freshly ground coffee beans at the supermarket. Maybe freshly ground flour will be available some day.

🏵 Use whole wheat flour of good quality, which you will find at your local natural foods store. The best flour for bread comes from HARD red spring wheat, because it forms a stronger gluten when kneaded. Buy flour with a high gluten content. Look for flour with at least 14% protein content. Buy only "bread flour" and not "all purpose" or "pastry flour."

🏵 To get a light loaf, you must knead whole wheat dough longer than white flour dough. When recipes call for 10 minutes of white-flour kneading, you may have to knead whole wheat dough for 15-20 minutes or even longer. Good things take time.

🏵 If your bread is dry or hard, try reducing the oven temperature or shortening the baking time. Also, try using a little less yeast.

🏵 If the top or edge of your bread has split or cracked, your oven temperature may be too high.

🏵 Replace a little of the whole wheat flour with gluten flour to increase the dough's elasticity and produce a lighter loaf. Gluten flour, made from wheat flour, is more than half pure gluten. Use this as a last resort, because gluten flour is processed.

🏵 When mixing the dough ingredients, add one teaspoon of baking powder or soda to the dry flour before mixing it with the yeast liquid. It will help the rising.

🏵 After all ingredients have been mixed and before the first kneading, sprinkle ¾ teaspoon of lemon juice or vinegar for each cup of flour in the recipe into the dough mixture to help increase its elasticity. Use no more than ¾ teaspoon per cup flour, or the acid will inhibit yeast fermentation.

🏵 These tips also hold for other bread products, such as buns, rolls, pizza crusts, pretzels, and breadsticks. Substitute all of that unhealthy white flour for 100% whole wheat flour in your favorite recipes.

About Yeast

Bread yeast is alive. It is a tiny plant, a fungus, which has been used for thousands of years to raise bread. When mixed with warm water, it becomes active, starts eating the sugar and flour, and produces gas (carbon dioxide) as a by product. Look closely at a slice of bread from your kitchen. Do you see those tiny air holes throughout the bread? That's what makes bread light and airy. The air holes are caused when tiny gas bubbles produced by yeast get caught and held within the bread. The bubbles are retained down in the dough when the dough's consistency is elastic enough to stretch and expand and encase the bubbles. Just as a balloon will stretch and expand and hold air, so will elastic dough. If a balloon is old and dry and not elastic enough, it will not hold the air and burst; if dough is not elastic enough, it will not be able to hold the bubbles within its structure. It is the retention of gas within the dough's structure that causes the dough to expand and "rise." As discussed later, kneading and gluten are necessary to make the dough elastic.

Non-yeast breads (quick breads), pancakes, muffins, cakes, cookies, etc., also have air holes. These bread products are too liquidy and thin or have a non-elastic consistency, which makes slow-working yeast ineffectual at raising them. Gas is instead produced by a chemical reaction among their ingredients. Baking soda (an alkali), when mixed with an acid (buttermilk, yogurt, orange juice, apple cider, molasses, etc.), will produce carbon dioxide gas. Baking powder is a mixture of baking soda (alkali) and an acid (cream of tartar, etc.) and will produce carbon dioxide when mixed with water and other liquids that produce a good acid/alkali balance.

> **TIP:** To test baking soda for freshness, mix a little with a few drops of vinegar or lemon juice. It should bubble. To test baking powder, mix a teaspoon with ⅓ cup of hot water. It should bubble.

> **MONEY SAVER:** See recipe for *Self-Rising Super Flour*, page 289.

Bread yeast comes in two varieties: *active dry yeasts* and *quick-rising yeasts*. Quick-rising yeasts multiply twice as fast and cut rising time in half. Active dry yeasts retain more nutrients and give the bread better flavor, so I use active dry yeast in bread recipes. Bread yeast can be purchased in packets or in cakes—one packet is equal to one cake. It used to be that one packet contained a full tablespoon of yeast, but in these days of constantly rising prices, a packet now contains only about 2 teaspoons. I guess manufacturers discovered that the new lesser amount has almost the same leavening power as a tablespoon.

> **MONEY SAVER:** It is much cheaper to buy yeast in bulk from the natural foods store (or Sam's Club, BJ's, or Costco) or from The Baker's Catalogue, PO Box 876, Norwich, VT 05055-0876 (call for a catalog at 800-827-6836). Store it in the refrigerator or in the freezer and it will be good for at least 6 months. You'll know if it is no longer good if it doesn't bubble when added to warm water.

> **WARNING:** Don't accidentally use brewer's, nutritional, or torula yeast. These yeasts, although I highly recommend them as nutritional enhancers, will not raise bread because their yeasts are dead.

The Major Steps in Making Yeast Bread Are:	Basic Whole Wheat Bread Dough Recipe
	(makes two loaves)
🐾 mix the dough ingredients	1 tablespoon active dry yeast
🐾 knead the dough	or 1 packet active dry yeast
🐾 let the dough rise	¾ cup warm water (110°F or temperature indicated on yeast packet)
🐾 punch the dough down	2 cups warm water
🐾 shape the dough into loaves	3 tablespoons honey
🐾 let the dough rise again	6 cups whole wheat bread flour
🐾 bake at 350°F	2 tablespoons oil
🐾 let cool	2 teaspoons salt
🐾 eat!	

Making 100% Whole Wheat Bread

Mix the Dough Ingredients Warm a cup under hot tap water and then measure ¾ cup warm water into it. When temperature is right, thoroughly stir in yeast. Put in warm place to proof for 5-10 minutes until bubbly. (If it does not get bubbly, your yeast is dead. Buy new yeast and try again.) Mix honey into the 2 cups warm water. In a large bowl measure 6 cups of flour and stir the salt into it. Make a well in the middle of the flour and slowly pour the honey water mixture into it. Then add the yeast water mixture. Stir dough with a wooden spoon, beginning at center and moving outward. Wet your fingers and hand-mash the dough until it is evenly mixed. The dough should be wet and sticky, but able to hold its shape. If it is too wet and runny, add another few tablespoons of flour. The dough should still be sticky, but not stiff. If it is stiff, making it difficult to squeeze, add one or two tablespoons more water.

Knead the Dough Dump the dough ball onto the kneading surface and knead for at least 20 minutes. Be careful about adding flour to the kneading surface to reduce stickiness. It is best to use a plastic kitchen scraper or spatula to scrape off dough that sticks to the kneading surface and your fingers. Your kneading will eventually reduce stickiness. If the dough becomes too stiff during kneading, add a little water to your hands.

Kneading is the process of rubbing dough particles against each other either by hand or by machine. (Now you know what that loud clacking sound is from your bread machine in the middle of the night.) Kneading by hand is what people are referring to when they say that making bread is a lot of work. The purpose kneading is to make the dough elastic. The component of the dough that becomes elastic during kneading is called *gluten*. Wheat flour (either white flour or whole wheat flour) is the flour that contains the most gluten, which is why wheat breads are so common. Other flours, such as rye flour, contain only small amounts of gluten that are not enough to make dough rise. Read the ingredients on a package of commercial rye bread and you will see that white or wheat flour is the main ingredient. Rye flour will be found lower on the list of ingredients, indicating that there is less rye flour than wheat flour in a loaf of rye bread.

Every baker has their own method of kneading. Some pound and throw the dough on the table; some push, pull, and fold; and some use their knuckles. Any method you like is good as long as you're mushing up that dough. Here's my method: Push on the dough ball with the palms of your hands using the weight of your torso, grasp the dough furthest from you with your fingers and fold it almost in half toward you, push down again, and then give the dough a quarter turn. Fold and repeat the sequence over and over again. When you first start kneading, be gentle during the first few minutes, and then get more vigorous.

When you knead, use a non-sticky surface, such as a wooden board, a marble tabletop, a Formica® kitchen counter top, or even a glass surface. Make sure that the surface is at a comfortable height, not so low that you have to bend over to knead and hurt your back, or so high that your elbows aren't at the right angle to give you leaning power. Most recipes tell you to knead for about 10 minutes. That 10 minutes actually means 15 minutes if you're taking it easy and barely pushing on the dough, or it means 5 minutes if you're angry about something and taking it out on the poor dough. If you need stress relief (and what new parent doesn't), kneading is a good and wholesome outlet. Speaking of wholesome, the first time I kneaded bread dough, I was surprised at how good and natural it felt, even though I had no idea what I was doing. It gets less fun after several minutes though, and I suggest you have something to think about or listen to, like music or the news on the television, to make the time go faster. Or chat with your children—it's good quality time and they'll look back and remember you as the virtuous Donna Reed-type mother. There are two times when I can't keep my eyes off the clock—when I'm on my exercise bike and when I'm kneading—but in both cases, I feel so good when I'm done!

Whole wheat dough will start out being sticky, but will gradually become less sticky and more elastic during kneading. Some recipes instruct you to generously flour the kneading surface and your fingers to reduce the stickiness, perhaps as much as one tablespoon for each cup of flour in the recipe. This is OK for white flour, but not for whole wheat. Too much flour is one of the most common causes of brick-hard whole wheat bread, so use as little flour as possible—only a light dusting. Or try using a little water instead of flour to reduce stickiness during kneading. I don't use any water or flour; instead, I scrape the dough off the kneading surface and my fingers with a scraper, butter knife, or whatever flat, straight (but not sharp) edge is available. The stickiness significantly subsides about halfway through kneading, but even after whole wheat dough is thoroughly kneaded, it will still feel tacky.

After you've been kneading for a while, you can check how far along you are by gently pulling the dough apart. Eventually craters will form over the surface and it will tear apart easily. Keep kneading until the dough becomes silky smooth and, when gently pulled apart, forms a very thin sheet or strand that doesn't tear. The dough will still feel tacky, but despite its stickiness, it will feel springy. When this happens, you're done kneading. Another indicator that dough is sufficiently kneaded is the appearance of little wrinkles on the dough's surface. With whole wheat, you must knead a lot longer than a white flour recipe instructs—perhaps twice as long. All good, healthy things take time. This 100% whole wheat recipe requires at least 15-20 minutes of kneading, so get ready for a good workout.

TIP: If you're not sure that you've kneaded enough, continue kneading for a couple more minutes. Although it is possible to overknead by hand, it takes a LOT of extra time. If you under knead by even a few minutes, your bread won't rise well. So err on the overkneading side. This is true only for hand kneading—If you're using a machine, overkneading is very possible.

For my first several loaves, I was never sure whether I kneaded enough. So I just assumed I was kneading strenuously enough, kneaded for the time suggested in the recipe, and added about 3 minutes. Since the loaves turned out well (after my first brick disaster, that is), I guess I did OK. Kneading is like anything else—with practice comes confidence, skill, and success.

Let the Dough Rise Place a teaspoon of oil in the bowl and turn dough to coat all surfaces. Cover with a warm, damp towel. Let rise in a warm place (80°F to 90°F is best for the yeast to do its work) for about 1½ to 2 hours until doubled in size.

Punch the Dough Down Take your fist and punch it right into the center of the dough. Whomp! You can leave the dough in the bowl if you like. The purpose of punching down is to remove air from the dough. You may hear a hissing sound as the gas escapes. After punching, fold the edges in toward the center and into the imprint of your fist. Knead the dough for a short time to squeeze more air out. You don't want big pockets of air in your bread; you want lots of little tiny holes for even rising. (We've all had slices of bread with huge holes.) Punching down also redistributes the yeast and gives it access to fresh dough to eat during the second rise.

It is during this short second kneading after punching down the dough that you would add any larger or chunky optional ingredients, such as raisins and other dried fruits, seeds or chopped nuts, cheeses, herbs, or sprouted grains. Or, you can flatten the dough, sprinkle bulky ingredients onto the dough, and roll up the dough jelly-roll style.

Shape the Dough into Loaves After you've punched down and kneaded a little, divide the dough into halves, and shape the dough into two loaves (or many pretzels or bread sticks or buns or pizza crust). Place the loaves into greased loaf pans or place the loaves on a greased flat baking sheet. Grease the pans with butter, not oil. Butter will form a nonsticky layer between the dough and the pan, whereas some of the oil may be absorbed into the dough and cause some sticking to occur. If you're using loaf pans, gently flatten the dough so that it covers the bottom of the pan. There should be room for upward expansion in the loaf pans. Or, use a slightly smaller loaf pan and fill it ⅔ full. The dough will rise so that it comes over the top of the loaf pan, making a nice mushroom shape. You may want to sprinkle sesame or poppy seeds, chopped nuts, rolled oats, slivered sauteed onions, or dry flour onto the top of the loaf after shaping, which will enhance the look and taste of your bread.

Let the Dough Rise Again Now that the bread is shaped and placed in pans or on a baking sheet, cover it and place in a warm place as before. Let it rise until doubled in size—it should take a little less time than the first rise. After this second rise, the loaves are ready to be baked.

Bake Place the loaves into a cold oven. Turn the oven on and set to 350°F. The smaller the loaves, the shorter the baking time, of course. And if you have very small pieces of dough, such as bread sticks or pretzels, the recipe will probably tell you to bake at a high temperature for a short period of time. A higher heat will cause a crisp outer crust, such as is common for bread sticks and pretzels. If the bread is far from being done baking and the crust is starting to burn or get too brown, cover the crust with aluminum foil (shiny side up) to slow its baking. You may want to cover all small dough pieces, like pretzels and bread sticks, with aluminum foil to keep them from burning.

Testing for Doneness There are several ways you can tell when the bread is finished baking. The bread will begin to pull away from the sides of the pan. A cake tester or other thin wire pushed into the thickest part of the loaf will come out clean. A toothpick can be used in small pieces of dough, such as buns. A tap on the bottom or top crust will produce a hollow thump rather than a solid-sounding thud, indicating the presence of light airy dough and the absence of thick raw dough. I like this very reliable method: Dump the loaf out of the pan upside down into your toweled hand. Insert a thin knife through the loaf from the bottom until it almost touches the top crust. It will pull out clean if the loaf is done baking. If you cannot tell whether the knife has raw dough on it or just moisture from steam, gently wipe it across the towel. The steam will wipe away and the dough will stay.

Let Cool It is important to cool each loaf thoroughly so that steam does not cause sogginess on the bottoms or sides. Take each loaf out of its pan and cool on a wire rack or anything that allows air to circulate underneath. Use an oven rack or the rack from a broiling pan, or just prop the loaf over two or three butter knives.

Store the Baked Bread Properly Unlike white bread, whole wheat bread will keep at room temperature for only a few days if placed in a ventilated bread box or wrapped loosely in a paper bag to allow for air flow to prevent mold. Let the bread cool completely before storing, so that it doesn't become soggy. Store it in the refrigerator tightly wrapped for 2 to 3 weeks. It will keep much better if you freeze it, even if you will be eating it within a few days. If you wrap it very well in aluminum foil, baked bread may keep for up to a year. Before freezing bread, it's a good idea to slice it so that you can easily remove a piece at a time and toast it—you practically need an electric saw to cut off part of a frozen loaf! Thaw frozen bread for about 4 hours at room temperature. Leave it in the aluminum foil, so that any ice crystals can be reabsorbed back into the bread. If you plan on eating it for breakfast, leave it out overnight. Or, thaw frozen bread by baking it in its aluminum foil for 15-20 minutes at 375°F, until the center is warm. Frozen bread keeps very well and tastes almost like freshly baked bread when thawed or toasted.

Good luck in your baking!

26. Legumes:
Dried Beans, Peas, and Lentils

Dried beans, peas, and lentils are called "legumes" or "pulses." Legumes come from plants that have pods. Legumes are second only to whole grains as our most important food source. Like whole grains, legumes are storehouses of vitamins, minerals, and fiber. Mixed with grains, they form complete protein, as discussed under protein complementarity on page 513.

How to Buy and Store Legumes

Choose legumes that are bright in color; dullness indicates age and long storage. They should also be uniform in size, so they will take the same amount of time to cook, otherwise some will be overcooked and some will be undercooked and tough. Look for beans with no tiny holes, which signify a bug infestation. Whole dried beans will keep for up to a year in a tightly covered container in a cool, dry place. *Uncooked* whole dried beans will keep indefinitely in the freezer.

Preparing Legumes for Cooking

Rinsing Beans

Before cooking, pick through the beans and remove any cracked, malformed, discolored beans and any pebbles or other debris. Place in a colander or strainer and clean by rinsing under cold-running tap water or the sink hose.

Slowly Rehydrating Dried Beans—The Overnight Soak

Before most dried are cooked, they must be rehydrated by soaking. (Lentils, split peas, and soy grits are exceptions.) The easiest and most energy-efficient way to soak beans is to place them in cold water that is at least 3 times their volume for 6-8 hours or overnight. Soak them in the refrigerator. (Some authors recommend refrigeration for soybeans only, but I recommend soaking all beans in the refrigerator, where cooler temperatures prevent fermentation and spoilage of all beans, especially during hot summer nights.) Cover the water and beans to protect them from the refrigerator air. After the soak, remove any beans that are floating on top of the water.

These beans were harvested prematurely, causing the beans to shrink within their seed coats. They may have molded and there might be dirt in the space under the seed coat.

TIP: To save washing a bowl, soak the beans in the same stainless steel or glass pot that you will cook them in.

The Fast Way—The Quick Soak Method

If you can't wait all night for your beans to soak, there's a quicker way. Boil water that is 3-4 times the volume of the beans. Drop the beans into the boiling water gradually, so as not to stop the water from boiling. Continue boiling all the beans for 2 more minutes, and then remove the pot from the stove. Cover and let it sit for at least one hour. The boiling process breaks the shells of the beans so that they absorb water faster. Because heat destroys nutrients, the Overnight Soak is preferred over the Quick Soak method. The Overnight Soak also saves energy.

MONEY SAVER: Some beans are sold as "quick-cooking" beans, meaning that they have been presoaked, redried, and packaged. These beans are usually more expensive, so why buy them when it's so easy to soak beans yourself? If you do buy them, cook them by following the directions on the label.

Cooking Beans

Now that the beans have been either soaked overnight or quick soaked, place them on the stove top. To help preserve nutrients, use the same water for cooking as for soaking for all beans except the soybean. To prevent bitterness in soybeans, drain the soak water and replace it with fresh water. Make sure that the beans are covered well with water. If the water is at a low level in the pot because the beans soaked it in, add more water. Place the beans over low heat (no need to boil first) and let them come to a simmer and cook for the recommended time. Beans do take a long time to cook, but, as with grains, it's all waiting time and your attention is not necessary until they are done.

Always cook beans by simmering, not boiling, because boiling will break the skins and cause the beans to separate. Boiling may also cause boilovers. Do not stir the beans while cooking or you may break the skins. Beans will have a firmer texture if you cook them uncovered. Cook beans in a covered pot for your baby, because they will be softer.

MONEY SAVER: See stove-top energy-saving tips in box on page 188.

Bean Cooking Quick Reference

For each cup of dried beans:	Use this many cups of water:	Soaking required?	Cooking Time
adzuki	4	yes	50 minutes
black or turtle	4	yes	1 hour
black-eyes pea	4	yes	1 hour
fava	4	yes	1 hour
garbanzo (chick pea)	4	yes	2 hours
kidney	3	yes	1½ hours
lentil	4	no	30 minutes
lima	4	yes	1 hour
lima, baby	4	yes	50 minutes
mung	4	yes	1½ hours
pinto	3	yes	1½ hours
soybean	4	yes	3 hours
soy grits	2	no	30-45 minutes
yellow or green split peas	3	no	40 minutes
white or Great Northern or navy bean (pea bean)	4	yes	1 hour

REMEMBER: Remember that tofu (page 238) is made from super nutritious soybeans. Tofu is a convenient no-cooking-necessary way to get beans into your family's diet.

For Quick Cooking, Freeze Uncooked, Soaked Beans

Beans soaked overnight can be frozen before they are cooked. Freeze them in small portions using the Nested Plastic Bag Method. Frozen beans will take only about 20 minutes to cook. This is because the freezing process breaks the strands that hold the beans together (similar to what happens in the Quick Soak method), which greatly shortens the cooking time.

How to Tell If Beans Are Finished Cooking

Test beans for doneness by tasting them. They should be firm, but tender, and smooth, not gritty. Another way is to blow on them, if they split, they're cooked. Squeeze one between your thumb and index finger. If the inside is hard, the bean is not finished cooking.

TIP: Gas is sometimes a problem with beans and babies (and adults). Introduce beans to your baby in small amounts, then feed him more when his body gets accustomed to them. If gas is still a problem, try this: Don't cook beans in the soaking water—discard it and use fresh water. Or change the water once or twice during soaking. Or replace the cooking water once or twice during cooking. Although this will decrease the nutrient content of the beans, it will also decrease the oligosaccharides in beans, which are the cause of flatulence.

Oligosaccharides are broken down to provide energy during the sprouting process, therefore flatulence is not usually a problem with sprouted beans. See Super Sprouts, page 245.

TIP: Although beans take a while to cook, sprouted beans take only 10 minutes to cook. See Super Sprouts, page 245.

WARNING: Some flavorings should not be added to beans before they are thoroughly cooked. Acidic foods (tomatoes, tomato sauce, lemon juice, wine, etc.) react with the seed coats' starch and toughens them. Calcium interferes with the cooking process, so do not add molasses or any other food containing calcium until beans are done cooking. Salt reacts with the seed coat and prevents liquid from being absorbed and toughens beans. Add any of these ingredients only when beans are finished cooking.

TIP: Flavor beans when cooking them for adults by adding chopped onion, minced fresh garlic, ginger, or other fresh herbs and spices to the beans' cooking water.

No Need to Pre-soak Soy Grits, Lentils, and Split Peas

These three are the legumes to use if you forgot the overnight soak, because you can cook them with no prior soaking. Soy grits are nothing more than coarsely chopped soybeans. I use them frequently instead of whole soybeans, which have to be soaked overnight and then cooked for 3 hours. You can cook these three legumes in the same pot with grains for complete protein (see protein complementarity, page 513), because they take approximately the same amount of time to cook. Of course, you can always mix any previously-cooked beans with any previously-cooked grains in the 1-part-bean-to-2-parts-grains ratio, but it's more trouble to cook them in separate pots for different lengths of time.

Let's say you wanted to mix brown rice and soy grits: put ½-cup brown rice (which will expand to 1 cup) and ¼ cup soy grits (which will expand to ½ cup) in a pot with 1½ cups boiling water (1 cup of water for the ½ cup of rice and ½ cup of water for the ¼ cup of soy grits). Turn the heat down and let simmer for 45 minutes and you've got a complete protein dish. Feed some to the family, purée a little portion with an equal amount of liquid for the baby (last method in box on page 216), and freeze any leftovers.

NOTE: Even though these three legumes do not have to be soaked, you can place them in a clear bowl and cover them with water for the purpose of finding the defective ones which will float to the top. This technique is called "culling."

Refrigerating and Freezing Cooked Whole Beans

Cooked whole beans, covered well, will keep only 3-5 days in the refrigerator. Beans spoil quickly, so freeze them using the Nested Plastic Bag Method in individual 1 cup or ½ cup portions for up to 4 months.

WARNING: The darker beans, such as black beans, stain light colored plastic. Use only discardable containers or containers that you don't care about staining.

Puréed Bean Frozen Food Cubes

Purée cooked beans in the processor and refrigerate for up to 3 days. Or use the Food Cube Method to freeze bean purée for up to 6 weeks. Add puréed bean food cubes to your baby's yogurt or mix with vegetables as a Healthy Extra (page 288).

Bean Flour

Bean flour, such as soy flour or soybean flour, can be used in recipes to increase the nutrient content (see Super Flour, page 289). Just as wheat flour is nothing more than ground up wheat kernels, bean flour is ground up dried beans. You can buy bean flours at the natural foods store. It takes a while to use up a bag of soy flour, so I suggest that you freeze it in pre-measured portions using the Nested Plastic Bag Method. When baking bread, muffins, or quick breads, grab a bag of ground bean flour and replace some of the flour in the recipe.

You can grind your own bean flours. A blender can be used to grind beans, but the powder is a little too coarse for flour. There are manual grinders for grains and beans that look like meat grinders, which cost about $50. These make a better flour than the blender, but it's still a little coarse. When I pull mine out of the cabinet, I grind many different grains and beans into flour all at once, and then freeze them using the Nested Plastic Bag Method. That way I only have to take it apart and clean it once. "TIP: A food grinder or pasta maker that won't stay firmly in place is a nuisance. Place a small piece of folded sandpaper, rough side out, between the clamp and table. Won't this scratch the table?" There are also electric grinders available at natural foods stores or through mail order, but they are, of course, more expensive than manual grinders. Some coffee grinders may work, but first check with the manufacturer to make sure that beans will not damage the unit.

Bean Equivalents

On pound of dried beans equals about 2½ cups of uncooked dried beans and about 6 cups, give or take ½ cup, of cooked beans.

Canned Beans. One 15-ounce or 16-ounce can of beans is approximately equal to 1¾ cups of drained cooked beans or about ¾ cup uncooked dried beans. Home-cooked legumes are easy and healthier and more economical than canned beans, but canned beans are better than no beans at all! Always rinse canned beans containing sodium well to remove as much salt as possible. Rinse beans in a colander/sieve/strainer under running tap water.

Tofu—A Most Convenient Bean Food

Tofu, also called "soybean curd" or "bean curd," is a product made from soybeans, which contains almost all of the nutritional benefits of the soybean. Like the soybean, it is one of the few plant products high in complete protein. Tofu contains some calcium and the numerous other nutrients found in soybeans. Tofu comes in three textures—soft, firm, and extra-firm. Firm tofu has excess water extracted, making it denser and easier to slice or cube.

You can now buy tofu at most supermarkets and at any natural foods store. Some tofu is packaged so that it has to be refrigerated—make sure that it is refrigerated in the store. Some tofu is packed in aseptic boxes that will keep unrefrigerated for up to 10 months. Once any tofu package has been opened, it must be refrigerated. I remember the good old days when blocks of tofu were sold in an open refrigerated barrel at my local natural foods store and customers would bag their own. But tofu is no longer sold that way, due to the liability of unfriendly bacteria. For your baby, be sure to buy tofu in sealed packages only.

Tofu (also known to small children as "toe food") is a great food for a baby older than 7 months. It does not have to be cooked, because it is made from cooked soybeans. Purée or mash it and add it to Super Porridge, fruits, veggies, yogurt, anything. Small tofu chunks or strips of tofu make great finger foods. See also Tofu Hors d'oeuvres recipe (page 294), Tofu McNuggets recipe (page 305), and other tofu recipes.

Refrigerating Tofu

You must store tofu underwater in the refrigerator. You might get away with an airtight container, but underwater is always good. The water must be changed daily. You may have seen this bumper sticker: *Have you changed your tofu's water today?* Treat it well and it will keep in the refrigerator for up to a week.

Freezing Tofu

Freeze tofu in its original carton. Or, freeze opened tofu in water. Freeze the whole block submerged in water, or place little chunks of tofu in ice cube trays, cover them with water, and freeze using the Food Cube Method for up to 2 months. Thaw overnight in the refrigerator. For quicker thawing, melt the ice cube in a bowl in the microwave on low power.

> **WARNING:** There are many brands of tofu, and some are firm, some are soft. Freezing changes the texture of some tofu so that it becomes rubbery. Before giving thawed tofu to your baby, make sure that it is not difficult to chew so that your baby will not choke.

> **TIP:** Steaming tofu causes it to develop a consistency similar to egg white. For people who would rather not eat eggs or for those with an allergy to egg white, try substituting steamed tofu for cooked egg white in potato salad and other recipes. Steam tofu for 7-12 minutes, depending on its firmness.

TVP®

TVP (texturized vegetable protein) is a food product that has been manufactured from soybeans (defatted soy flour) by the Archer Daniels Midland Company for more than 20 years. In canned and packaged foods, it is sometimes listed as the ingredient "hydrolized vegetable protein" or "textured soy flour." TVP is a low-sodium, low-fat food staple of many vegetarians and is used to add texture, complete protein, fiber and vitamins, especially vitamin B12 (found mostly in meat) to foods.

TVP comes in many sizes. The small granules are the quickest to reconstitute—simply pour ⅞ cup of boiling water over one cup of TVP granules and let stand for 5-10 minutes. Stir until all water is absorbed. For TVP slices or the chunk-sized TVP, pour one cup of boiling water over a cup of TVP and stir. TVP can be added dry to soups. Keep you hands wet when working with TVP to keep it from sticking.

Dry TVP will keep for months in a cool, dry cabinet. Once TVP has been reconstituted, it must be refrigerated and will keep in the refrigerator for a few days.

Reconstituted granules can be used in any recipe calling for ground meat (sloppy Joes, spaghetti sauces, chili, lasagna, etc.); larger chunks are good in stews, fajitas, kebabs, and pot pies. See TVP Barbeque Sandwiches recipe on page 314.

Sneak Beans into Recipes

For those older children who simply won't eat beans, you can still manage to sneak them into their diets. Substitute some bean flour for regular flour in baked goods, as in the Super Flour recipes on page 289. Mix a little bean flour into pancakes, muffins, and other baked goods. Mix mashed cooked bean purée or tofu into just about anything: sandwich spreads, sauces, gravies, veggie burgers, mayonnaise, salad dressings, omelettes, casseroles, milkshakes, soups, pasta sauces, and believe it or not, even puddings and ice cream.

27. Nuts, Seeds, and Sprouts

Nuts and Seeds Are Nature's Nutrient Powerhouses

Seeds are loaded with nutrients. If a seed is placed in the ground, it grows. If a seed is placed in water, it sprouts. Nature must have put a concentrated store of nutrients in the seed, which can grow a new plant with no soil and nothing more than plain water. The seed is the nucleus of a plant, the part that maintains survival of the species, the part that is most important to nature. If there is a variation and lack of nutrients in the soil, the other plant parts suffer at the expense of the seed. In infertile soil, the roots forage for every trace nutrient it can find in order to first form the seed. The seed is life itself.

I read once where if you are going to be shipwrecked on the proverbial desert island and you could choose only one food to take with you, you should choose sunflower seeds. They supposedly have every nutrient needed for human survival except vitamin C, but when sprouted they produce vitamin C. I am certainly not suggesting that your baby live on sunflower sprouts alone, but I do recommend that ground sunflower sprouts and other seeds be a regular part of your baby's diet.

> **WARNING:** Sunflower seeds are packed with nutrients, but they have a problem with rancidity. I suggest that you feed your baby only sprouted sunflower seeds—rancid seeds will not sprout, of course. See *Super Sprouts*, page 245.

Seeds Are More than Just Seeds

Whole grains are the seeds of grassy plants, such as wheat, millet, rice, etc. Nuts are the seeds of nut trees. Dried beans are seeds. Legumes are seeds. Plant them and care for them and they will grow into a whole new plant. You can also sprout nuts, beans, lentils, grains, and seeds in plain water and their nutritional value will be increased even more (see *Super Sprouts*, page 245). The healthiest foods for you and your baby are seeds, because they are living stores of nutrition.

It Just Doesn't Get Nutritionally Better than Seeds

Whole grains, beans/legumes, nuts, and seeds are the best natural sources of essential fatty acids, the healthy fats needed for your baby's brain development. They contain large amounts of protein, vitamin E, the B-complex, tons of other vitamins, minerals, trace elements, pacifarins (for the immune system), and auxones (to help build body cells and prevent premature aging).

So there you have it, the absolute optimum diet for human beings: whole grains, beans/legumes, nuts, seeds, fruits, and vegetables. I memorized that list, and whenever I stand in my kitchen thinking about dinner, I say to myself "whole grains, beans, nuts, seeds, fruits, and vegetables." For babies, add breast milk/formula, yogurt (even yogurt is alive with friendly bacteria), and egg yolks.

TIP: To get nuts and seeds into your family's diet, grind them and add them to pancakes, oatmeal, omelettes, casseroles, pasta sauces, and sprinkle them into cold breakfast cereal and milk. Also, see the recipes for nut/seed milks on page 67.

How to Buy Seeds

Fresh, Raw, Whole Seeds and Nuts

Go to the natural foods store. Supermarket seeds just don't cut it. If you think of nuts as the canned salted oiled nuts, and seeds as the bottled salted sunflower seed snacks, please change your thinking. At the natural foods store is a variety of fresh, raw, organically-grown seeds and nuts. It's easiest to buy them already hulled (with shell removed). Look them over to see if they are shriveled—a shriveled nut is a spoiled nut. If you are going to buy them in the shells, test for freshness by shaking. If they are loose in the shell and make a noise, don't buy them—they are shrunken and spoiled. Remember that this was also true of a spoiled bean, which floats to the top of the soak water because it had shrunk inside its outer coating and contains air space (page 233-234). A shelled nut (shell removed) should break in two when you snap it. If it bends instead of breaks, the nut is old.

TIP: Removing the shells from Brazil nuts is easy if they are first frozen. Freezing makes the shells brittle and the nuts come out whole instead of broken into pieces.

TIP: See page 493 for how to start a peanut plant.

Please read about peanut allergies on page 32.

Nut and Seed Butters

Your natural foods store carries a variety of nut and seed butters. Peanut butter is nothing more than ground peanuts and maybe some added non-hydrogenated oil to help make a smooth consistency. Walnut butter is ground almonds. Almond butter is almonds. **Tahini,** or sesame seed butter, is made from ground sesame seeds. I highly recommend that these nut/seed butters from the natural foods store be included in your baby's diet.

> **MONEY SAVER:** Use a small spatula to scrape every last bit of nut/seed butter out of the jar. You will be surprised at how much you would have wasted by throwing it away.

Homemade Nut Butters

It's easy to make your own nut butters. To make homemade nut butter, grind nuts in blender or food processor with a little natural foods store cold-pressed safflower oil (about 1 tablespoon of oil for each cup of raw nuts). Start by measuring ¼ cup of nuts and 1 teaspoon of oil and gradually add the rest of the nuts and oil.

> **WARNING:** Commercially made nut butters are closely scrutinized for mold that may contain aflatoxin, a carcinogen commonly found in mold. If you are going to make your own nut butters, use only the freshest nuts. Ask your health food store employee about the age of the nuts you plan to use.

Choosy Moms Choose Natural Peanut Butter

Try not to buy peanut butter at the supermarket. It contains added salt, sugar, and poisonous partially hydrogenated oils (page 507). Actually, it may now be possible to get healthy peanut butter at the supermarket. Read the ingredients list and make sure that the jar contains only ground organically-grown peanuts.

Natural Peanut Butters Separate

Because healthy, natural peanut butters (and other nut and seed butters) do not contain stabilizers, they separate and the oil gathers on top of the jar. If this doesn't happen, you should question that brand of butter. Use a butter knife to stir the butter. When you find it difficult and frustrating to stir the oil into the nuts, remind yourself that you are doing it for your baby's health. Know that, after it gets cold during refrigerator storage, you won't have to stir it again. The cold keeps it from re-separating.

> **TIP:** A few days before opening a new jar of nut/seed butter, place it on its side so that the oil will move. Turn the jar frequently. Keep the jar on the kitchen counter, where seeing it will remind you to turn it often to re-shift the oil. This turning will help pre-mix the butter before you open it, and make stirring easier for you.

Storing Nuts, Seeds, and Their Butters

Nuts and seeds must be kept refrigerated in a closed container to protect them from warmth and dry refrigerator air. Refrigerated shelled nuts will keep for 3-4 months, frozen they will keep for 8 months.

> **TIP:** If the nuts and seeds from the store are in clumsy containers, transfer them into the smaller-sized plastic zipper bags. They'll be easier to store in your refrigerator and take up less space.

My refrigerator has two crisper drawers. I devote one of them—the one that's supposed to be for meats—to the storage of nuts and seeds. The plastic zipper bags sometimes rip on the metal shelves inside the refrigerator and keeping them in a drawer helps protect them.

Seeds contain oils inside that go rancid quickly when exposed to air after grinding. *To prevent rancidity, seeds should be kept whole and refrigerated, and should not be ground in the blender until **immediately** before serving.* For more information about rancidity, see page 507.

Both nuts and seeds should be ground to a fine powder in the blender, not only to prevent your baby from choking on them, but also to promote the digestion of their many nutrients.

> **REMEMBER:** Once natural peanut butter jars and other nut and seed butter jars are opened, they must be refrigerated.

> **TIP:** Use peanut butter on your breakfast toast instead of butter or margarine. It's much more nutritious. Drizzle a little honey (for babies older than one year) or maple syrup over the peanut butter for an extra delicious treat.

Feeding Your Baby Nuts and Seeds

Introduce your baby first to tahini. Mix a little in his Super Porridge or yogurt. Then you can try raw almonds and pumpkin seeds—grind them and all nuts and seeds in the blender immediately before feeding them to your baby. Also good are peanuts or peanut butter, hazelnuts (filberts), flax seeds, and chia seeds. Flaxseed or its oil (also called linseed oil—the food grade oil, not the stuff found in turpentine) should be a part of your baby's diet every single day for EFAs (see page 505 in the nutrition part).

> **WARNING:** You know this, but I still want to say it: Never feed a baby or toddler whole (or even partially whole) seeds or nuts. They are choking hazards. Grind your baby's nuts and seeds in the blender or processor until they are a fine powder. Make sure there are no chunky pieces. Serve immediately before they become rancid.

Grind them for yourself and the older members of your family, also. Seeds and nuts must be chewed very, very well in order to get their nutrients, or they'll pass right through the body. This is especially true of the smaller seeds, like chia seeds, flax seeds, and sesame seeds. Eat them well-ground to get maximum nutrients. This is one reason why I recommend tahini—thoroughly ground sesame seed butter—for your baby rather than sesame seeds, along with the fact that it is so very convenient to add a spoonful into baby's yogurt or Super Porridge.

> **TIP:** If seeds and nuts clump in your blender while grinding, try adding a little flour to keep them moving.

> **TIP:** Again, I want to point out the convenience of the mini-blend container on page 150. I must use mine at least twice a day, and I know if I had to use the big container it would be a real inconvenience.

I find it a real inconvenience to have to eat seeds immediately after they have been ground to prevent rancidity. I do one grinding in the morning and use the breakfast meal to get them into my family's diet every day. Breakfast is convenient for me because everyone is together at one meal and the foods are very flexible. Ground seeds and nuts can be easily added immediately after grinding into cold cereals, omelettes, hot oatmeal, pancakes, waffles, or fruited yogurt. Then, after everyone has left for the day, I put the leftovers into my baby's Super Porridge.

> **WARNING:** Rinse nut/seed powder from bowls immediately after you're finished eating. Don't let them dry up or they become welded to the bowl. And don't ever let any flax or chia seed pieces get into your dishwasher or you'll be re-washing everything, especially the glasses.

> **TIP:** If you did let seed parts dry on a bowl, let the bowl soak for a while in plain or soapy water and they'll rinse right off. If seed parts are stuck on the lip of the bowl, nest it inside a bigger bowl, fill the bigger bowl so that the water covers the lip of the smaller bowl, and let it soak.

Nut/Seed Milks

Another way to get nuts and seeds into your children's diets is with nut/seed milks. Read about them on page 67. See recipes for Super Milks on page 359.

> **TIP:** Whole nuts and seeds are DELICIOUS when rehydrated! Soak them in water in the refrigerator overnight and enjoy them in your cereal in the morning or as a snack. Don't feed these whole nuts/seeds to your baby, though, because are choking hazards.

Super Sprouts

Whoever came up with the idea of the Chia Pet must have known their sprouts. Chia seeds are tiny, but they sure do grow! I actually bought one of those Chia Pets, which was displayed for impulse buyers near the checkout line in a local department store. The woman behind me commented to her friend, "Who would buy one of them?" before she saw that I had one in my cart. I pretended I didn't hear her and she pretended that she didn't know I heard her.

Sprouts can be added to salads, soups, sandwiches, omelets, beverages, and breads, or they can be eaten alone, with a little sweetener, or used as garnishes. Add sprouts to hot foods at the latest possible point in cooking. Remember that heat destroys nutrients. Add sprouts to soups at the last minute, just before serving. As with other foods, you must grind sprouts for a young baby. Your baby must be at least 10 months old before she can eat ground sprouts. Sprouts are great Decorative Touches (page 362) for your toddler's meals—they can be hair or a mustache or the green grass of home.

Sprouts are Super Healthy

Sprouts are nothing more than germinated seeds, in other words, seeds that have started growing into plants. As if seeds were not super nutrition-packed already, they actually increase in nutrient content when sprouted! According to biologists, plants are at their nutritional height when they are only a few days old—when they are sprouts. Sprouts take anywhere from two days to a week or two to grow, depending on the seed. They are packed with vitamins, minerals, enzymes, and other nutrients, and contain 3-5 times the vitamin C content of the seeds from which they grew. But they have less calories than the seeds because the sprouting process uses energy.

Sprouting, a method of indoor organic gardening, is one way you can have crisp, fresh vegetables at their prime. Even a big city apartment dweller can have freshly-picked baby plants (sprouts) every day. No worry about pesticides, insects, nutrient loss in transportation or on grocery shelves, soil depletion, diesel fuel, or delivery trucks. You've probably seen alfalfa sprouts at salad bars or at the supermarket, but they are not as fresh and tasty as those you can grow yourself at home.

WARNING: The authors of *Laurel's Kitchen* warn against eating large amounts of alfalfa sprouts.[3] They contain small amounts of a natural toxin (saponins), which do no harm unless eaten in large quantities. I recommend that you avoid giving your baby alfalfa sprouts altogether.

---

[3] Taken from page 121 in *The New Laurel's Kitchen*. See Robertson, Laurel in bibliography.

Sprouts are Fun, Fast, Easy, and Cheap

Let's take sunflower seed sprouts as an example. They cost a few pennies a serving, take two days to grow, and need only water and two minutes of your time a day. Believe me, you don't need a green thumb. Even I, whose house plants barely survive, have absolutely no trouble growing sprouts.

I suggest you start with shelled (shell is removed) sunflower seeds, because they sprout in only two days. Sunflower seeds are a super food, one which should be included regularly in the diet. However, unsprouted seeds very easily become rancid (see warning, page 240). In fact, I have a friend who got terribly sick from eating rancid sunflower seeds from a name-brand supermarket jar of the toasted, salted variety. Ever since then I have been cautious about eating sunflower seeds; however, I eat sunflower sprouts regularly—a seed that sprouts is not rancid. Let's see how very easy it is to do sprouts.

TIP: See *Learning About Seeds* on page 494.

How to Sprout

Buy a small amount of seeds at your natural foods store. The seeds that are salted and toasted in the jar on your grocer's shelf won't sprout. Do not sprout seeds for your backyard garden, which are often treated with fungicides. Make sure you buy only seeds that are *specifically for sprouting*. Store your seeds in the refrigerator until you're ready to sprout them.

For your first sprouting experience, take about ⅓ cup of sunflower seeds or, if you're starting with another seed or bean, use the amount of seeds suggested in the table on page 249. Pick through them and discard any split, discolored, or damaged seeds. And it's not unusual to find an occasional pebble mixed in with beans, so look carefully.

Wash the beans before soaking by rinsing in a strainer or colander under running tap water. Soak the seeds in water for several hours. Place them in the bottom of a clean quart glass jar—a 32-ounce mayonnaise or similar jar is good. Cover the seeds with cold water that is at least three times the volume of the seeds.

TIP: Add a few drops of liquid kelp or dulse to the soak water to increase the nutrient content of sprouts even further, if you believe that's possible. Your natural foods store folks have them.

Leave jar uncovered and unrefrigerated. Let the seeds soak for at least 6 hours, but no more than 12 hours—overnight is probably most convenient. In the morning, drain the water out of the jar without pouring out the seeds. You can do this by securing 2 layers of cheesecloth over the top of the jar with a rubber band or ring of a Mason jar. You can use nylon netting, stainless steel screen wire, a clean thin or threadbare white towel, a cloth napkin, a thin cotton diaper, a white paper towel, or anything clean and non-toxic that will let air and water in and out while keeping the seeds in the jar. I keep my sprout jars open without lids, because I use a small strainer (pushed concave into the top of the jar) to pour out the water and rinse.

WARNING: Remember to sterilize used cheesecloth or other cloth briefly in boiling water between sprout crops.

TIP: In the morning after an overnight soak, don't pour that soak water down the drain! Use it for beverages and soups—it contains valuable nutrients. (Soak water from beans must be cooked before drinking, so use it in soups and not in cold beverages.) Or make your houseplants or herbs happy by using it to water them—its nutrients fertilize them.

Now rinse the seeds well. Let cold tap water run through the cloth and into the jar. Swirl the jar to swish the seeds around in the water, but be very gentle—you don't want to break the tender shoots. Then pour out the water and repeat rinse once or twice again. The water may drain faster if you hold the jar at an angle rather than holding it straight upside down. Drain very well, so seeds won't get moldy; they should be kept moist, but not water-logged. Lay the jar on its side, or leave the jar at a slight angle so that the water can continuously drip out, but don't let the angle be so steep that the seeds are all crowded together at one end. Spread them throughout the length of the jar so that they form a thin layer and have room to sprout.

Let the moistened seeds sit in the jar until you rinse again. The jar acts like a little greenhouse for the seeds—a safe little garden where the seeds will sprout roots. However, don't leave the jar in direct sunlight because it will cook them. Remember that roots of plants grow underground, where it is cool and dark. Sprouts depend on you to keep them cool by rinsing and keeping them out of hot sunlight. Most seeds will grow either in the dark or in indirect light, but the ideal place is a dark, warm (70°F), humid place.

You need only rinse the seeds twice a day, maybe three times if the weather is very warm and dry. Don't wait more than 12 hours between rinses, because the seeds will dry up and die. Rinse your seeds whenever you think of it—morning, noon, and night is fine. If you work outside the home, rinse at dinnertime instead of noon. Don't worry, you can't over-rinse.

TIP: Keep your seeds where you can see them, so they aren't out of sight, out of mind. I keep mine near the kitchen sink, where I know I'll be throughout the day. I notice the seed jar often and take a minute to rinse them. Cover the jar with paper or dark cloth to keep the sprouts in the dark.

The hull, the outer covering of the seed that eventually falls off during sprouting, looks like an empty shell. The hull of a seed is similar to the bran of a grain and contains fiber. It is perfectly safe to eat. If you wish to clear out the hulls to give the sprouts more room to grow, place the sprouts in a bowl of water and the hulls will float to the top, where they can be skimmed off.

There are two types of sprouts—those that grow green leaves (alfalfa, chia, psyllium, clover, radish, cabbage, turnip, kale) and those that grow tails (sunflower, flax, lentil, soybean, garbanzo, other beans, wheat, millet, and other grains). A leafy seed is finished sprouting when it splits into a left and right leaf and its hull falls off. On the last day of sprouting leafy seeds or when the first sign of leaves appear, leave the jar by a window with natural indirect sunlight. Natural light will cause the seeds to photosynthesize and produce green chlorophyll and beta-carotene (vitamin A). A seed with a tail is finished sprouting when the tail is approximately the same length as the seed.

Sunflower sprouts take only two days to sprout. That means you can eat your sunflower sprouts after the morning of the third day. For example, if you soaked the seeds throughout Sunday night, you can eat them Wednesday morning. Leave them in indirect sunlight on Wednesday morning for a few hours and you'll be amazed at how quickly they turn green.

Large Bean Sprouts Must Be Cooked Before Eating

Most sprouts can be eaten raw, but large bean sprouts (soybeans, garbanzos/chickpeas, green pea, pinto, kidney, navy, etc.) must be cooked before eating because they contain harmful enzymes that inhibit the body's protein utilization. Eating them raw can cause digestive problems and nutrient deficiencies. Steam bean sprouts at least 10 minutes before eating to destroy the enzyme-inhibitors. Or, you can stir-fry them Chinese style. (See recipe for Sweet and Sour Sprouts, page 304.)

Storing Sprouts

When sprouts are finished growing, eat them immediately for maximum nutrition, or store for later use. Before storing, pick through the sprouts and discard any seeds that didn't sprout to prevent their decay from spreading to the healthy sprouts.

Refrigerate. When sprouts are finished growing, they can be refrigerated for up to a week, but the older they get, the less nutritious they are. You can store them in a plastic bag, but a glass jar will keep them fresh a day or so longer. Why not keep them in the jar used for sprouting? Pack them very loosely because if they get crushed they will decay quickly. Discard any that have lost their color or become slimy.

Freeze. Sprouts will keep frozen up to 2 months but may be limp and soggy when thawed.

Dry. Sprouts can be dried and ground into a powder for use as a nutritional enhancer and to replace flour in recipes. Place them on a cookie sheet in a conventional oven at 250°F for about 45 minutes until thoroughly dried. Then grind them in a blender and store the powder in a plastic bag or glass jar in the refrigerator, or freeze.

Diastatic Malt. This malt is made from hard wheat berry sprouts that have been dried. It is very sweet and can be used in pancakes, waffles, cereals, and breads, alleviating the need for other sweeteners. Use it as a sweetener when baking cakes, cookies, and other desserts by replacing some of the flour with this sweet malt—use about 1 part malt to 4 parts flour. To dry wheat sprouts for malt, place them in a 115°F oven for 8 hours or until dried. Then grind in blender. Take a taste—you'll be amazed at its sweetness.

WARNING: Do not eat tomato seed sprouts or potato sprouts (the ones that start as little eyes growing out of potatoes) because they are poisonous. Use seeds that are specifically for sprouting, because some seeds are soaked in fungicides and pesticides.

Seed, Grain, or Legume	Amount for Quart Jar	Sprouting Time	Optimum Length	Other Info
alfalfa seeds	2 Tbsp	4-5 days	1-2 inches	easy to sprout Do not feed alfalfa sprouts to baby— see warning on page 245.
almonds	½-1 cup	3-5 days	¼ inch	
chick-peas garbanzos	½-1 cup	3 days	½ inch	cook before eating (page 248)
lentils	½-¾ cup	3 days	½-1 inch	
millet	1 cup	3 days	¼ inch	bake into breads
mung beans	½ cup	2-3 days	2 inches	sprout in the dark
soybeans	⅓-1 cup	3 days	½ inch	rinse 4 or more times a day, cook before eating (page 248)
hulled sunflower seeds	⅓ cup	2 days	½ inch, but no longer than seed	very delicate, sprouts get bitter if sprouted too long
hard wheat berries	1½ cups	2-3 days	¼ inch	bake into breads; make diastatic malt

Flax and chia seeds don't sprout well in a jar—there are other ways to sprout them that are beyond the scope of this book. If you're interested, read *Sprout it!* by Steve Meyerowitz (see bibliography). He's known as "The Sproutman" and is probably the world's greatest expert on sprouting.

28. Yogurt and Dairy Foods

Cheese

Cheese is an easy and convenient baby food which, like milk and yogurt, is high in protein and calcium. Grated soft natural cheese and small lumps of cottage cheese are nice finger foods for your baby (see Super Snack box on page 291). Remember that babies needs fat, so buy whole milk cheeses for your baby.

TIP: Give your child small cheese cubes to drop into his soup to watch them melt.

Buy Only Natural Cheese

United States government standards require processed cheeses to be only 51% real cheese, so do not buy products labeled "processed cheese," "cheese spread," or "cheese food." Processed cheese has been altered for long storage life and many contain artificial colorings and preservatives. Buy only natural cheeses for your baby: Parmesan, Romano, Camembert, cheddar, feta, Monterey Jack, Swiss, provolone, mozzarella, farmer's, whole milk cottage cheese, ricotta, cream cheese, and many others. See also yogurt cheese on page 254.

When buying cheese, inspect the wrapper carefully for damage or stickiness and remember to check the expiration date. Avoid buying old cheese that looks dry or has cracks in it. The color should be uniform from center to edge. White cheeses (ricotta, etc.) become yellow as they get old. Look carefully for mold, which looks like white, blue, pink, or green flecks or furry patches. Avoid cheese with a greasy surface, which indicates that the cheese has been warmed.

Storing Cheese

Store natural cheese in an air-tight container, aluminum foil, or a plastic storage bag in the refrigerator. Cheese that comes in a rind should be kept in the rind until you are ready to use it.

WARNING: Discard any cheese with even the tiniest bit of mold on it. Experts say it's OK to cut off the moldy part and eat the rest, but I say *never* take chances with children.

Cheese can be frozen in an airtight plastic bag or container. Freeze cheese pieces separately in chunks no larger than ½ pound. Be ready for a change in texture: Firm cheeses may turn crumbly and soft cheeses may separate. Your baby will probably not mind the texture. Freeze cottage and ricotta cheese using the Food Cube Method. Freeze cheese for up to 4-6 months. Thaw overnight in the refrigerator and be sure to use thawed cheese within a few days.

Cheese Tips

- Cheese is easier to slice with a dull knife. Warm the knife under hot tap water for easier slicing.

- It's cheaper to buy cheese in bulk, grate it, and freeze it in small quantities in individual bags using the Nested Plastic Bag Method. If you hate shredding your own, you can buy already-shredded cheese in bulk and freeze. Soft cheeses (cottage, ricotta, etc.) can be bought in bulk and frozen using the Food Cube Method.

- Rub oil or butter on your grater or oil-spray it and grating cheese will be easier. The grater will be easy to clean, too.

- Soft cheese will be easier to grate if first placed in the freezer for 15-30 minutes.

- Small chunks of cheese can be grated with a garlic press.

- Use a potato peeler to make strips of cheese for hair (page 362) or other Decorative Touches.

- To prevent mold from forming, wrap a cheese block in white paper towels dampened with apple cider vinegar before placing it in a plastic bag to refrigerate. Periodically re-wet the paper towels with the vinegar.

- A sugar cube stored with hard cheese in the same container helps to prevent mold.

- Store cottage cheese, ricotta cheese, sour cream, and yogurt with the carton upside down in the refrigerator. The cheese pressing against the lid helps to seal it and keep the container air-tight, extending storage life.

- Block cheese dries out quickly if not properly stored. To rehydrate dried-out cheese, soak in buttermilk. Prevent cheese from drying out by rubbing cut edges with butter or oil or by oil-spraying the surface.

Nonfat Dry Milk

Nonfat dry milk is dried and concentrated pasteurized skim milk in a powder form. Fresh nonfat dry milk is odorless.

WARNING: Use only NONFAT powdered milk and not dry whole milk, because the cholesterol in whole or low-fat powdered milks has been damaged during the drying process, making it harmful.

Add the instant kind into baby's foods and beverages as a nutrition booster to add calcium and protein. Or use it to thicken homemade yogurt as described on page 259.

TIP: For older family members who don't need the fat in milk, mix a tablespoon of nonfat milk powder into a cup of skim milk to thicken it and make it more creamy.

Store an unopened box of nonfat dry milk in a cool dry place and discard after the expiration date. Once you open a packet, store it in an airtight glass container in the refrigerator and it will keep for weeks.

Nonfat dry milk also can be mixed with water in the proportions given in the directions (usually about 3 tablespoons powder to one cup of water) to make liquid milk that you can drink or cook with, but be warned that the flavor isn't near that of regular milk. Store the mixed liquid milk in an airtight container in the refrigerator and use within three days.

Yogurt

In this dairy chapter, I saved the best for last—yogurt! Yogurt has been around for thousands of years and is a Super Baby Food and a Super Adult Food. Yogurt is a good source of calcium, protein, phosphorus, potassium, riboflavin, vitamin B12, and pantothenic acid. It is said that yogurt has many health benefits, from preventing cancer and high blood pressure to curing vaginal yeast infections[4]. Yogurt has been shown to enhance the body's immune system by increasing the production of gamma interferons, which play a key roll in fighting certain allergies and viral infections.

Yogurt is a tangy fermented (curdled) milk that contains living bacteria. But unlike "bad" bacteria, yogurt bacteria cultures are friendly and very beneficial to health. Yogurt bacteria cultures, which multiply at body temperature, produce B vitamins in the intestines and attack harmful bacteria in the colon. Yogurt soothes stomach ailments and its cultures help digest casein, a milk protein. Yogurt helps restore the health-giving flora that naturally occur in the human intestines and helps to prevent gastrointestinal infections. In fact, Adelle Davis claims that babies who frequently eat yogurt have less diarrhea. Yogurt is easily digested and well-tolerated by babies and its protein is better assimilated.

Antibiotics, which unfortunately are prescribed like candy these days, kill friendly intestinal flora. People on antibiotics should eat two servings of yogurt a day, starting with the first dose and continuing until 10 days after antibiotic use has ceased. Antibiotics promote diaper rash, which is caused by the unfriendly bacteria that grow in the absence of these flora. Antibiotics also make your baby susceptible to thrush (a yeast which looks like a "whiteness" on the tongue) and other fungal infections, because they kill the good bacteria in the mouth too. If you are breastfeeding, your baby's infection may spread to your nipples causing redness, burning, and itching. Acidophilus powder (available at the natural foods store) mixed into your baby's

---

4

If you have a problem with vaginal yeast infections, try eating a daily cup of yogurt containing the *Lactobacillus acidophilus* culture for several months. There's a good chance that it will help.

formula once a day may help. Acidophilus is a healthy, intestinal bacteria also found in yogurt that is killed by antibiotics. If you are breastfeeding, the powder can be mixed into a little water and administered a few times per day. Get your pediatrician's OK before giving the powder to your baby. She may want to prescribe some anti-fungal medication for your baby.

TIP: Keep track of the doses of antibiotics that you give your child by posting a grid on the refrigerator door or somewhere in the house where you will be sure to see it several times a day. Let's say you are to administer to your child three doses of antibiotics per day for the next 10 days. On a sheet of paper, create a table with 3 columns and 10 rows. Label the 3 columns "Morning," "Afternoon," and "Night," and the 10 rows "Wed," "Thu," "Fri," ... or whatever the next 10 days are. After giving your child a dose, write the time in the table. The table will serve as a reminder and will be an accurate record of the time you administered each dose.

BOBBY'S ANTIBIOTIC				
		Morning	Noon	Night
1	Wed			
2	Thu			
3	Fri			
4	Sat			
5	Sun			
6	Mon			
7	Tue			
8	Wed			
9	Thu			
10	Fri			

Some people who cannot drink milk because of lactose intolerance can eat yogurt without any problem, because yogurt contains much less lactose than milk. The bacteria predigest the lactose. Lactose is a milk sugar that causes diarrhea and bloating in lactose-intolerant people. The active yogurt cultures create the enzyme lactase, in which lactose-intolerant are deficient. See page 33. People with milk ALLERGY should not eat yogurt made from cow's milk; however, they can have yogurt made from non-cow's milk, as discussed on page 129.

Plain low-fat yogurt can help reduce dietary fat by acting as a replacement in many recipes for sour cream, heavy cream, whipped cream, and buttermilk. It can replace all or part of the mayonnaise called for in a recipe. Yogurt can be used as an ingredient in dozens of recipes, from buttermilk pancakes to cheesecake.

How to Buy Commercial Yogurt

Commercial yogurt is exorbitantly priced. Before I started making my own yogurt, I cringed whenever I bought two 32-ounce containers of store-bought yogurt to make one mock cheesecake. Now, I make my own yogurt and instead of paying $4.36 for 64-ounces of commercial yogurt, I buy ½ gallon (64-ounces) of milk at $1.19 to make homemade and save over $3.00. The last section of this chapter contains directions for making homemade yogurt (page 256).

Buy Only Yogurt with Bacteria That Is Alive Carefully read the package and look for words like "live and active cultures." Commercial manufacturers sometimes pasteurize yogurt after culturing to increase its shelf life. Unfortunately, this heat treatment kills the beneficial bacteria. If you see words like "pasteurized", "stabilized", or "heat treated after culturing," beware that they are euphemisms for "all the good bacteria are dead."

Don't Buy Old Yogurt Fresh yogurt has "stronger" bacteria, which become less vigorous as the yogurt ages. Check the expiration date. Although UNOPENED yogurt can keep in the refrigerator up to 10 days past the expiration date, the cultures will be fairly weak by that time. If you're going to use commercial yogurt to start your own homemade yogurt, buy the freshest yogurt possible.

Buy Whole Milk or Low-fat Milk Yogurt for Baby Your baby needs fats and you should not restrict his fat intake until he is at least one year old. Also, the fat in yogurt helps make the friendly bacteria more hardy and healthy.

Buy Plain Yogurt with No Additives Avoid the yogurt with sugar, flavorings, gelatins, and artificial sweeteners. Besides the obvious reasons, these additives interfere with bacterial activity. Some commercial yogurts have fruit on the bottom, which you mix in, and some have pre-blended fruit already distributed throughout the yogurt. Some "farm-style" commercial yogurts come with a layer of yogurt cream on the top, which has a high fat content. Don't buy any of these. Buy only PLAIN yogurt and add your own flavorings.

Add Your Own Flavorings Commercially flavored yogurt usually contains excessive sugars and additives, which your baby doesn't need. Your baby will be happy with plain, unflavored yogurt, but use yogurt as a base for Healthy Extras. Flavor plain yogurt with any of the suggestions in the box on the next page. *Gently* stir or fold flavorings into yogurt, because if you stir too roughly, you will thin the yogurt. If convenient, the best time to add flavorings is immediately before eating; there is one exception—add dried fruit several hours before eating so that it softens, or soak the dried fruit to soften it and then add to the yogurt. If you're making homemade yogurt, add flavorings AFTER it's done incubating.

Freezing Yogurt

You can freeze yogurt in its original container for up to 6 weeks. If you can't use yogurt within 5-7 days, freeze it, well covered, in an air-tight container or by using the Food Cube Method. Yogurt bacteria grows like the bacteria discussed on page 161 and survives freezing temperatures.

Flavored frozen yogurt is all the rage now, but the commercial varieties are loaded with sugar and additives. Make your own frozen yogurt ice cream—see recipe, page 339.

Yogurt Cheese

Yogurt cheese is nothing more than yogurt with the whey (yellow-tinged liquid) drained from it. Yogurt cheese can be used as a healthy substitute for cream cheese and sour cream. To make yogurt cheese, use only plain, unflavored commercial or homemade yogurt with no gelatin added, which prevents the whey from draining out.

Place the yogurt into a container that will allow the liquid whey to drip through it. Yogurt cheese "funnels" can be purchased at kitchen and some department stores, but you don't have to buy one. Use a colander, strainer, or steamer and line it with a coffee filter, several layers of white paper towels or heavy white paper napkins, a double thickness of damp cheesecloth, a damp clean white towel cloth napkin, or a clean, unused damp cotton single-layer diaper. Place the colander over a bowl to catch the whey (the yellow-tinged liquid that drains out). Cover the colander with plastic wrap and place in the refrigerator. Let it drain for several hours in the refrigerator. Stir occasionally with a rubber spatula. The longer you let it drain, the thicker it will become. In a few hours the yogurt will have the consistency of sour cream; overnight it will resemble cream cheese. A pint of yogurt makes about one cup of yogurt cheese. Keep yogurt cheese refrigerated and it will keep for about one week.

TIP: Don't throw away that whey—it contains calcium and other nutrients. Drink it straight, use it in flavored beverages, as the liquid in muffins and other baked goods, and in soups and gravies.

WARNING: Yogurt cheese will become liquidy if you mix or beat it too hard, so be gentle when stirring it into recipes.

Home-Added Yogurt Flavoring Suggestions

Stir these flavorings into yogurt **gently** or yogurt will become thin and runny:

fresh fruit—apple, berries, peaches, pears, etc., chopped or puréed

frozen no-sugar-added fruits, chopped or puréed

natural jam or jelly

canned fruits, drained and chopped or puréed

jarred commercial baby fruit

applesauce

rehydrated dried fruit, chopped or puréed

crushed, well-drained, canned pineapple

blackstrap molasses

maple syrup

honey (for babies older than one year)

molasses

vanilla

wheat germ

lemon or lime juice

frozen orange juice concentrate, frozen pineapple juice concentrate, any frozen fruit juice concentrate

apple butter, prune butter, any fruit butter

well-ground nuts or seeds

thinned creamy peanut butter

thinned almond or any nut butter

thinned tahini or any seed butter

puréed cooked carrots or sweet potato (thaw a food cube or two)

finely-diced cucumber pieces

finely-chopped parsley

cinnamon

nutmeg

Healthy Extras (page 288)

For us mommies and daddies only, not baby:

butterscotch syrup

chocolate (or carob) syrup

chocolate chips

chocolate syrup/chips and peanut butter

instant coffee and sweetener

Jamocha (chocolate syrup and instant coffee)

chili or curry powder, chili sauce

Making Homemade Yogurt

Homemade Yogurt is Delicious!

You can tailor-make yogurt according to your individual taste. If you're missing out on the health benefits of yogurt and don't eat it because you don't like the tart flavor of store-bought, you absolutely must try making your own. Fresh—and I mean really fresh, as fresh as one day old—homemade yogurt is delicious, in that it has no tart flavor if made with new starter. You can add fresh puréed fruit, maple syrup, or any of the flavorings mentioned above, and it tastes like a sweet pudding, not like yogurt at all. If you like the tart flavor of yogurt, that's do-able too. Homemade does develop the tart taste after a few days in the refrigerator.

Homemade Yogurt is Cheap!

Commercial yogurt manufacturers do not want you to know how easy and cheap it is to make your own yogurt. In my local supermarket, the cost of 32 ounces of plain low-fat yogurt is currently $2.18. A quart of milk, to make 32 ounces of homemade yogurt, costs less than 70¢. An even greater discrepancy in price exists when you compare smaller quantities of yogurt; an 8-ounce single serving container of plain name-brand yogurt currently costs 59¢—that's $2.36 per quart. **Store-bought yogurt costs about 3 times that of homemade**, even when you consider the heat (gas or electric) necessary for making homemade.

Homemade Yogurt is Easy!

When you make yogurt, you actually breed friendly bacteria. You may not want to mention this to your older children who may refuse to eat "germs." Making yogurt entails heating (to sterilize) and cooling some milk, adding yogurt bacteria as a "starter," and letting it incubate (grow and multiply) in a warm place for several hours until it becomes thick and custardy.

Use Whole or Low-fat Milk for Your Baby

Yogurt can be made with almost any kind of milk. You can use whole milk, 2%, 1%, skim, pasteurized, homogenized, organic, raw, diluted evaporated, dry milk powder, cow's, goat's, water buffalo's (no kidding), and soybean milk. (A friend asked me about breast milk. I wouldn't do it, but who knows!) The thinner the milk, the thinner the yogurt; for example, skim milk yogurt is much thinner than yogurt made from whole milk. (Dried milk can be used to thicken yogurt. See *Optionally add dry milk powder...*, page 259.) For your baby, whole or low-fat milk is best, because a baby needs fat and the yogurt cultures remain more viable than in skim milk. Also, the fat content increases the assimilation of fat-soluble vitamins. Whole or low-fat milk yogurt is also more digestible than skim milk yogurt. If you're concerned that your baby has a weight problem, you can feed low-fat or skim milk yogurt to your baby after his first birthday if your pediatrician says that it is OK.

TIP: Try to buy only organic milk for yogurt making. They now sell organic cow's milk at natural foods stores and some supermarkets. Soy milk from the natural foods store is usually made from organic soybeans, but check to make sure before you buy.

Milk made from reconstituted dried nonfat, non-instant milk powder or evaporated milk can be used to make yogurt. (See nonfat dry milk warning, page 251.) Use boiled water cooled to 110-120°F and mix it with the powder or canned milk. Read the package directions for reconstitution and use a little more powder or canned milk than the directions call for. Use only fresh powdered nonfat milk—it should be odorless if it's fresh—and use only the non-instant kind. Check the expiration date on canned milk.

WARNING: Some authors say to use warm tap water to dilute dried or evaporated milk, because it's just the right temperature. Read page 63 to find out why you should NEVER use warm or hot tap water for drinking purposes.

If you're using powdered or evaporated milk and cooled boiled water, there's no need to scald the milk after it's mixed as is called for in the next section. The powder and canned milk should be sterile, and you boiled the water so it's free of bacteria too. Skip to the section *Cool the milk to incubation temperature...*, page 258.

Steps in Homemaking Yogurt

Briefly, the steps in making yogurt are:

1 Sterilize the milk to kill all bacteria.
2 Cool the milk to the incubation temperature for growing yogurt.
3 Optionally add nonfat dry milk for extra nutrition.
4 Introduce friendly yogurt bacteria (the starter) into the milk.
5 Let the yogurt bacteria incubate.
6 Refrigerate the finished yogurt.
7 Optionally add flavoring to the yogurt.

First Kill All the "Bad" Bacteria in the Milk by Scalding It[5]

When you buy milk, it is not sterile even though it has been pasteurized. After heating, a few bacteria are still left, and another few have been introduced during handling. That's why milk spoils if it is old, even if the carton is not opened.

Stove top scalding. Pour a quart of milk (or any amount) into a pot for heating on the stove. Use a metal spoon. You can use any pot, but glass, stainless steel, or enameled are best because they won't affect taste. Scald the milk, which means to heat the milk until it's *almost boiling*, when small bubbles form around the edges and steam begins to rise. This occurs at around 180°F-185°F Fahrenheit. I recommend the use of a

---

[5] Milk straight from the cow must be boiled for at least 10-15 minutes to kill all bacteria.

yogurt (or candy) thermometer to check the temperature. They can be purchased from kitchen stores, natural foods stores, and many department stores for under $3.00. Clip the thermometer on the pot and keep it submerged in the milk at least 2 inches while heating. Watch the red mark rise to 185°F. See page 164 for temperatures needed to kill bacteria.

> **TIP:** To verify the accuracy of your thermometer, place it in boiling water to see if it reads 212°F.

> **TIP:** To prevent the milk from scorching the bottom of the pot, heat the milk slowly and stir often. Scorching not only makes the pot difficult to wash, it also spoils the flavor of the yogurt. Use a double boiler, if you have one.

Microwave scalding. I don't suggest using the microwave because of its uneven heating problem (page 175). Bad bacteria can survive in cold pockets.

Jar-in-pot scalding. Here's another way to save washing a pot. Nest a thick, sturdy, heat-proof glass jar (I use a quart-size mayonnaise jar) with the milk into a pot of water on the stove top and bring it to a boil. Keep the thermometer submerged in the milk to watch for 185°F. The milk will not scorch and the pot won't get dirty because it contains only water. When the water boils, the jar will rattle loudly. You may want to place a small piece of cloth under the jar in the pot to stop the clacking.

> **MONEY SAVER:** After you remove the jar from the pot to let it cool, use the boiling hot water in the pot to sterilize utensils.

> **WARNING:** Make sure that you hands are super clean, along with any pots and utensils that will touch the milk. You don't want to introduce and incubate "bad" bacteria in the milk. Wash your hands in antibacterial soap. Use containers and utensils straight out of the dishwasher or wash them in very hot water and antibacterial dish detergent.

> **TIP:** If you have a dishwasher, wash the thermometer in it. When the cycle is finished, store the thermometer and a sterile spoon directly out of the dishwasher into a new plastic bag to keep it clean and ready for making yogurt. This tip is similar to the one on page 163.

After scalding the milk, you can remove any skin that forms on top, if you wish.

Cool the Milk to Incubation Temperature—about 112° Fahrenheit

Now that all the bacteria are dead and gone, cool the milk to a temperature that will allow yogurt bacteria to grow and thrive. Let it cool at room temperature, or place it in the refrigerator to speed the cooling. Keep a spoon in the milk for frequent stirring to evenly distribute the heat or use the thermometer to stir. Place the thermometer at an angle where it can be quickly and evenly seen with a peek into the refrigerator. The perfect temperature for growing bacteria is about 112° F. Keep the thermometer in the milk and watch it. It may take a good hour at room temperature to cool, so plan on sticking around the kitchen for a while. If you don't have a thermometer, place a drop of milk on your wrist; remember that your body temperature is around 98.6°F, so it should feel lukewarm. Another way you can test for 112°F is to put your clean little finger into the milk and slowly count to ten (one thousand and one, one thousand and two,...). If you have to pull out your finger because the milk is too hot, the milk must cool some more. You really don't need to be very accurate—actually any temperature between 90°F and 120°F is fine for incubating bacteria, but the closer you stay within 105°F to 110°F, the better.

Optionally Add Nonfat Dry Milk Powder for Extra Nutrition and to Thicken

You may at this time wish to add some nonfat dry milk powder to increase the nutritional content of the yogurt. The powder will also thicken the consistency of the yogurt. Nonfat dry milk powder is sterile, so you don't have to worry about it containing bacteria. Add about ¼ cup powder per quart of cooled liquid milk and mix very well. See nonfat warning, page 251.

Add the Starter

Now that the milk is at the right temperature, add the friendly bacteria culture—the "starter". One way to introduce yogurt bacteria cultures into the milk is to simply add some yogurt. The first time you make yogurt, you can use store-bought yogurt for your starter. Buy a small container of plain yogurt, but make sure that the label indicates that the yogurt contains live bacteria. Look for words like "live and active cultures." Also make sure that the yogurt is not too old. For each quart of cooled milk, gently fold in about 2 tablespoons of yogurt. The next time you make yogurt, you can use a few tablespoons from this first batch to start the next batch.

Let the starter yogurt sit at room temperature while the milk is cooling, so it will not be too cold when you add it to the milk. If you wish, take a little of the milk from the jar and mix it with the starter, and then add it back to the rest of the milk.

Another starter, which can be purchased at any natural foods store, is freeze-dried bacteria culture sold in packets. Although more expensive, this starter is more reliable than yogurt from a previous homemade or commercial batch.

Incubate the Yogurt and Let the Cultures Grow

Pour the milk from the pot into clean individual smaller containers (Pyrex bowls or custard cups are good). Or use a wide-mouthed jar or bowl. I like to use empty glass mayonnaise jars to hold my yogurt—they can be washed in the hot cycle of the dishwasher. Pre-warm the mayonnaise jars or containers immediately before you pour the yogurt mixture into them. Warm them by filling them with hot water, placing them on a wood stove, warming them in a 100° F oven, taking them from a warm dishwasher, etc. If you used the jar-in-pot method to scald the milk, you won't have a pot to pour from because you conveniently already have the milk in a jar of perfect temperature. Cover the yogurt during incubation so it's not open to the air, which always contains bacteria. Use the cover of the jar or place plastic wrap over the bowl.

Keep the yogurt warm during incubation. Place the yogurt mixture in a warm place to allow the bacteria to grow and the yogurt to thicken—for suggestions, see page 260. Remember that bacteria grow when the temperature is neither too hot nor too cold (page 164). Keep the temperature between 105° and 112° F, although yogurt bacteria will survive between 90°F and 120°F. The consistency and taste of homemade yogurt varies with the milk used and also with the temperature at which it was incubated. The lower the temperature, the sweeter the yogurt. The higher the temperature, the tarter the yogurt. But remember to keep the temperature in the range 90°F-120°F, or the bacteria will die from being too hot or become inactive from being too cold.

TIP: The first few times you make yogurt, babysit it. In other words, don't go out for the day or let it sit overnight. Be there so that you can check the temperature every hour or so.

Don't give up if you mess up your first batch of homemade yogurt. My first batch failed. When I told my older children with a feigned sad expression that "I killed my yogurt," they laughed hilariously. This I did by not realizing how darned long it took my oven thermometer to adjust its temperature reading. I turned up my oven temperature, the thermometer read 110°F, and I walked away thinking that the thermometer was finished adjusting. Half an hour later, I came back and was surprised that it read 150°F. Needless to say, that yogurt batch was ruined, but not all was lost—we used the hot milk to make cocoa.

TIP: If you're using your oven to incubate yogurt, pre-warm it before putting the yogurt into it and give the thermometer at least 15-30 minutes to adjust. That way you can be sure it's not hotter than it looks. See *Get to Know Your Oven Intimately*, page 264.

Warm Places to Grow Yogurt

Before you actually use a "warm place" to incubate yogurt, test its temperature by doing this: Fill a mayonnaise jar or a bowl with about a quart of warm water. Place the jar in the warm place for several hours. Keep your yogurt/candy thermometer dipped into the jar and check it about every hour or so to make sure the temperature stays within the range 90°F to 120°F—the closer to 112°F, the better. Once the warm place has been tested, you can confidently try it for incubating the real stuff.

Conventional oven. Wrap the jar of yogurt in a thick towel or yogurt towel bag (page 265) and place it in your oven on the lowest temperature (about 110° Fahrenheit). To monitor the temperature, I use a regular outside/inside air thermometer, because the oven should never get hot enough to go above the thermometer's maximum temperature mark and break it. You can use an oven thermometer, but the markings usually start at about 200° Fahrenheit—a temperature that will kill your yogurt. With an oven thermometer, you usually must estimate where the 110°F mark is. If you have only a yogurt or candy thermometer, place it in a bowl of water in the oven. Remember that your oven will be unavailable for cooking other food for several hours.

Conventional oven II. Instead of leaving your oven on throughout the incubation period, heat it periodically. First turn on your oven, heat it to 120°F, and turn it off. Keep an eye on the thermometer (hopefully you have a window so you don't have to open the oven door). When it drops near 100°F, turn on the oven for only a minute, and wait and watch the thermometer to see if it reads 120°F again. This is the method I must use with my electric oven, because if I leave it on continuously, even if it's set to the lowest temperature, it gets too hot and kills the yogurt cultures. It usually takes around 2 hours for my oven to drop to 100°F and need re-heating. If I'm going to let the yogurt incubate overnight, I certainly don't get up in the middle of the night to re-heat it. (Those of us with babies know what a luxury uninterrupted sleep is.) Instead, I set the "Timed Bake" to turn on automatically, let it heat for one minute, and turn off automatically. Keep the jar of yogurt wrapped in a thick towel or yogurt towel bag (page 265)to protect it from the variations in temperature inside the oven.

Conventional oven III. Keep the oven off completely. Use only the pilot light in a gas stove or the light bulb in an electric oven. The low heat generated will probably be warm enough. Don't use this method if it costs a fortune to replace your electric oven's light bulb.

Picnic cooler (the typical plastic insulated cooler that you take to the beach, or even a cheap Styrofoam one). Place the yogurt in a warm water bath (not your Jacuzzi, although it might work). Pour warm water (around 115°F) into a cooler so that it comes at least halfway up the jar containing the yogurt. Close the cooler tightly and don't peak too often—every time you open the cooler, heat gets lost.

Picnic cooler II. I make yogurt successfully by boiling a pot of water and placing it into an picnic cooler with the yogurt. The hot pot of water keeps it warm long enough for incubation. Use this method instead of the warm water bath and you don't have to pick up a heavy cooler to dump the water out. And if you are using jar-in-pot scalding, you can use the same water and pot.

The kitchen sink. If you don't have a picnic cooler, there's always the kitchen sink, the bathroom sink, or even the bathtub. Run a few inches of warm tap water (around 115°F) in the bottom of your sink so that it comes at least halfway up the yogurt container. You may want to cover the sink with towels, a carpet, a blanket, a newspaper, or whatever's handy to retain the heat. You may have to check every few hours to make sure the water doesn't get too cold. If it's unheard of in your house to make the kitchen sink unavailable for several hours, and this may be going too far, use baby's little bathtub to hold warm water. You get the idea—use just about any large container that will hold water.

The stove burner. Put a pot of water on the stove over the lowest heat setting. Place the jar of yogurt into the water. Make sure it doesn't get too hot. After an hour or two, my old electric stove brings the water temperature to 130°F, so I either have to watch it carefully and turn it on and off every so often, or use a double boiler.

An electric frypan. Fill it with warm water and set it to about 100°F-110°F. Place yogurt containers in the frypan and, if possible, place the pan's cover over them.

A crockpot. If your crockpot has only a low and high heat setting, it's probably too hot to incubate yogurt. Usually, a crockpot's low heat setting is 200°F and the high setting is 300°F. But if your have a rare crockpot where you can set the temperature, fill it partway with warm water, place the jar in it, and set it to between 110°F and 115°F. Verify with a thermometer that your crockpot stays at the proper temperature.

A warming tray. Use the kind that keeps foods warm at a party or the ones that keep baby food warm. Place a bowl with water on it and the yogurt jar in the bowl. If too hot, try putting layers of cloth towels between the tray and the bowl, but this wastes energy.

A heating pad. Wrap the yogurt in some thick towels or yogurt towel bag (page 265) and place on a heating pad on low setting.

A hot water bottle. A hot water bottle is another heat-source that can be placed in a picnic cooler or in a stock pot with the jar of yogurt. Wrap the pot in a large thick beach towel, blanket, carpet, or newspaper to help retain warmth.

A home-heating source. Try a radiator, wood stove, or heating duct. Wrap the yogurt in some thick towels or yogurt towel bag and place it on or near a home-heating source.

A major appliance. Try the top of your refrigerator or the top of the water heater.

Electronic equipment. Your TV, stereo, or other electronic equipment may be releasing enough heat to incubate yogurt. I think this worked several decades ago when vacuum tubes and transistors were state-of-the-art. Today's integrated circuits are just too energy efficient!

A wide-mouthed thermos. Wash it out with hot water and antibacterial soap and rinse very well. Pre-warm it by rinsing with hot water. Pour the yogurt mixture into the thermos, cover it, and leave it undisturbed for several hours. (You may have a problem with the formation of a vacuum within the thermos during incubation. The only way to know is to try it.)

Solar energy. Use the greenhouse effect to your advantage—place the yogurt in a hot car or in a sunny window.

Down. A sleeping bag, vest, or jacket may work to keep your yogurt warm and cozy.

Microwave-able neck warmers. Don't go out and buy one, but if you happen to already have one of those neck warmers that you heat for a few minutes in the microwave that stays warm for hours, try using it to incubate yogurt. Wrap the yogurt container in a thick towel or yogurt towel bag (page 265) and then surround with the neck warmer. Or use a homemade hot bag (page 417).

An electric commercial yogurt maker. As a last resort, you can always buy the appliance especially designed to incubate yogurt. This is too easy for those of us who like a challenge. Effortless and worry-free, you may find that it's worth it to buy one if you plan on eating yogurt every day, as you should.

The human body. While climbing a mountain, the heat from your body will keep a flask of yogurt at the right temperature.

Anywhere warm. You probably have the idea by now. Anything you can use to keep the yogurt at a comfortable temperature will do. You'll be surprised at what you'll find around the house.

Keep the yogurt still during incubation.

Place the yogurt mixture in a place where it won't be disturbed or have to be moved for several hours. Movement will cause the whey to settle out from the curd. Jiggling the yogurt will cause it to take more time to thicken, it won't ruin it.

Wait several hours until the yogurt is finished.

The yogurt will take anywhere from 4 to 12 hours to become thick and pudding-like. Test for doneness by touching the top with your clean finger. The longer you let it incubate, the more tart the flavor. If you make yogurt in your oven during the day, remember that your oven will be unavailable for cooking other foods for a significant stretch of time.

> **TIP:** Although it takes a lot of time to make yogurt, don't let that deter you. Yogurt making does not require constant attention, only occasional temperature taking that requires you to hang around the house for a while. This probably isn't difficult for those of us with new babies—most of us have happily dropped out of the jet set.

Refrigerate the finished yogurt.

Cover and refrigerate the finished yogurt for several hours before serving. The yogurt will keep in the refrigerator for 1 to 2 weeks. If you're going to use some of this current batch as a starter for your next batch, make sure that it is no more than 5-7 days old so that the bacteria is still strong. As with store-bought yogurt, the longer you store yogurt, the tarter it becomes. A yellow-tinged watery liquid, called "whey," forms on top of the yogurt. Pour it off to thicken the yogurt, stir it in if you want a thinner yogurt.

Optionally add flavoring or nutritional enhancers.

Follow the same instructions for flavoring commercial yogurt on page 254.

Experiment until you get the taste and texture you want.

The taste and texture of homemade yogurt depends on many factors: the milk used, the scalding method, the starter, the temperature during incubation, the stability of the temperature during incubation, the length of incubation time. Experiment until you find a yogurt that tastes best to you.

To thicken yogurt. Yogurt will thicken once it's refrigerated. Frequently pour off the whey, the yellow-tinged watery liquid that forms on the top of yogurt. If, after refrigerating, it's still too thin for your taste, next time try using a yogurt with more fat. Skim milk makes thinner yogurt than low-fat milk, which makes thinner yogurt than whole milk. Or, try adding powdered milk when you add the starter, as described on page 259. Or, "gel it." Add one packet (or one tablespoon) of agar flakes (page 275) or unflavored gelatin to the yogurt after it is finished and just before you place it into the refrigerator. First dilute the agar or gelatin in a few tablespoons of hot water, then mix it into the finished yogurt.

To increase/decrease the tart flavor. I personally do not like the tartness of yogurt. I like my yogurt thick and creamy, with no taste at all. Know that the longer the incubation time, the tarter the yogurt. Also, the longer the yogurt is stored in the refrigerator, the tarter it becomes. If your starter is tart, so also will be the yogurt. When my starter gets tart, I throw it out and use a new starter. The lower the temperature during incubation (but still within the range 90°F-120°F), the less sour the flavor of the yogurt. I let mine incubate for at most 5 hours at around 100°F to minimize its tartness. To decrease the tart flavor of refrigerated yogurt, add some lemon juice.

If Your Yogurt Didn't Turn out Right.

If your yogurt is much too runny, don't throw it out. Dissolve a tablespoon of agar (page 275) or unflavored gelatin in 4 tablespoons of warm water (use microwave to heat). Stir into the yogurt and refrigerate. Here is a list of problems that may have ruined your yogurt:

- You let it get too hot. Temperatures above 120°F will kill yogurt bacteria.
- You let it get too cold. Yogurt cultures become inactive at temperatures below 90-95°F.
- There were antibiotics in the milk. Most commercial milks should work, so this probably isn't the reason. If you think it may be, buy organic milk for making yogurt.
- Your starter may have been too old. Some advise you to begin with a new starter every month or so, although there is rumored to be yogurt alive today that's been passed down from generation to generation for hundreds of years.
- If your yogurt tastes sour and/or separates, your heat source may be a little too warm. Or too much starter was introduced into the milk—use a little less next time or incubate for a shorter time period.
- If you place yogurt into the freezer to cool it first, before placing it in the refrigerator, the consistency will be more even.
- If your yogurt tastes or smells strange, other bacteria may have taken up housekeeping in your yogurt. Toss it and start with a new starter. Make sure everything is scrupulously clean.
- Don't bake bread the same day or the day before you make yogurt. The yogurt may taste like bread yeast because it may pick up airborne yeast particles.

Get to Know Your Oven Intimately

Your oven is a good place to incubate homemade yogurt, let bread rise, and dry foods like fruit leather. But an oven that is too hot will kill the bacteria in the yogurt, the yeast in the bread, and will fry your foods instead of dry them. On days when you are not using your oven, learn about it by using trial and error to test how fast it heats. Figure out the exact number of seconds it takes to heat your oven to about 110°F. First put a thermometer into your oven—one that has markings as low as 100°F. Use a timer that is accurate to the second—the digital timer on your microwave or a separate digital timer works well. Close your oven door and set the timer for 60 seconds. Turn your oven off exactly when the timer beeps. Now watch the temperature inside the oven for the next few hours. See how hot it gets and how long it remains at 110°F. If 60 seconds wasn't long enough, try 90 seconds on another day. When you actually put the yogurt or bread in the oven, it will decrease the temperature, of course, which is OK. A slightly cooler oven will only prolong the process, and you can always adjust the temperature by turning the oven on for a few extra seconds.

Summary: My Easiest Yogurt Making Method

I wanted to give you complete detailed instructions on how to make yogurt, because you will use a lot of it if you're feeding your baby the Super Baby Food Diet. Making homemade yogurt will save you a ton of money. After years of trying to find the easiest, most effective, and "least dishes to wash" method of making yogurt, here's what I've come up with. It works every time with **my** refrigerator, **my** microwave oven, and **my** conventional oven. With trial and error, you will find the exact times for your equipment and find the easiest method for you.

1. Pour a quart of milk into a clean mayonnaise jar. I usually use organic soy milk enriched with calcium and vitamin D.
2. Nest the jar into a saucepan on the stove top with water that comes halfway up the side of the jar. Put a yogurt thermometer into the milk (not the water) and bring milk to 185°F. (If it clacks too much while heating, try putting a small towel under the jar.) From the refrigerator, remove the little jar containing the starter (see tip below) and let it warm to room temperature while milk is scalding and cooling.
3. When milk is 185°F, cover jar with lid and place in refrigerator to cool. Set my timer for 45 minutes, which is how long it will take in my refrigerator to cool to 115°F.
4. Place the spoon and other utensils in the scalding water in the sauce pan on the stove top in order to sterilize them.
5. When milk in refrigerator is 115°F, stir dry milk powder and starter into jar and replace lid.
6. Place jar in pre-warmed homemade yogurt towel bag (see below) and into pre-warmed oven. (I stick the towel bag in the oven while the oven preheats so that it will get pre-warmed with the oven.)
7. Five hours later, yogurt is firm. Move it to the refrigerator.

TIP: Before you begin to eat a freshly-opened container of yogurt, set aside a little of it to be used as a starter for your next batch of homemade yogurt. Save some of the yogurt by scooping 2 or 3 tablespoons into a small sterile glass baby food jar. Cover and keep in a cold spot in the refrigerator. Storing these tablespoons in a separate jar will keep it cleaner and insure that you won't eat all the yogurt and forget to save some to start your next batch.

Yogurt Towel Bag

Make a thick towel bag to fit around your yogurt jar: Take an old towel, fold it into several layers, and sew it into a pocket shape to fit the jar fairly snugly, similar to a sleeping bag. All parts of the jar are then covered neatly with several layers of thick toweling, so that the yogurt is kept at a fairly even temperature throughout many hours of incubation. The insulation of the towel bag prevents the yogurt from being too susceptible to outside hot or cold temperature fluctuations.

29. Egg Yolks

Eggs Are Not as Bad as They Are Cracked Up to Be

Perhaps the first thing you think of when you think of eggs is cholesterol. Well, it's true that eggs do have a lot of cholesterol, but remember that we are not restricting fats from your baby's diet. Your baby needs fats. Egg yolks are a very nutritious food for your baby; they contain vitamin A, 5 grams of complete high-quality protein, vitamin B12 (a problem nutrient for strict vegetarians), and many other nutrients. They contain about 6 grams of fat, of which 4 are unsaturated and 2 are saturated.

Egg white is one of the most common allergens among babies, and experts strongly recommend postponing their introduction until your baby is one year old. Cooked egg yolks can be introduced at 7-8 months.

> **WARNING:** Never eat raw eggs and never, ever feed them to your baby. See discussion on salmonella, page 36. Pasteurized egg white products are discussed on page 269, 273.

Separating Egg Yolks from the Whites

Crumbled bits of hard-cooked egg yolk and pieces of scrambled egg yolk are nice finger foods (see box on page 291) for your baby. To separate the yolk from the white of a raw egg for scrambling, place the raw egg in a small funnel nested in a cup. The yolk will remain in funnel and white will run into the cup. Or place the raw egg in the palm of your clean hand and let the white run off through your fingers. Most of us probably separate eggs by pouring the yolk back and forth between the two half-shells, but this method may cause bacteria from the surface of the shell to contaminate the raw egg.

Wash Eggs Immediately Before Cracking

Dangerous bacteria may lurk on the shells of eggs, which may contaminate the inside raw egg as it pours out of the shell. Therefore, wash the outside of the egg with warm water and antibacterial dish detergent (not dishwasher detergent). Rinse well. Do not wash eggs *before* storing, because you will remove the natural protective coating (called the "bloom") that helps protect against bacterial penetration through the pores in the shell. Therefore, leave the bloom on the egg as long as possible and wait to wash the shell until immediately before you're ready to use the egg.

> **WARNING:** As with meat, be scrupulously clean when working with raw eggs. Wash well with hot water and antibacterial soap anything that touched the eggs: your hands, pots,

dishes, utensils, the counter, etc. Follow all safety precautions for handling meat when you work with eggs—see page 279.

Buying Eggs

It is best to buy eggs from the natural foods store. Their eggs are from free-running, synthetic hormone-free, healthy, happy chickens who have not been forced to sit in a cage their whole lives, never to see the light of day. These eggs are more expensive, but they are worth it.

You might find it most convenient to buy large eggs, rather than medium or extra-large, because large eggs are the size used by default in most recipes.

Look for the expiration date on the package. To make things unnecessarily complicated, some packages have a Julian date instead of an expiration date. It is a number from 1 to 365 where 1 indicates January 1 and 365 indicates December 31. The Julian date is either the day that the eggs were packed or 30 days after the eggs were packed. Use eggs within one week after you bring them home. Although they may be OK for a month past the Julian date, their freshness diminishes.

TIP: The Egg Wiggle Test: Open the egg carton and gently turn each egg to make sure it moves freely. If it's stuck, the egg is cracked and the inside has leaked and dried.

How to Test for Freshness of an Egg

The words "fresh eggs" on the container mean only that they have been kept refrigerated since they came out of the chicken. Fresh eggs may not be fresh. To test for freshness, place an egg in a pan of water. If it sinks immediately, it's fresh. If it floats, it's too old to use. If it tilts, it's 3-4 days old; if it stands upright, it's about 10 days old. The movement of an egg under water is determined by the amount of air contained within the shell, which enters slowly over a period of time. The more air, the more the egg rises in the water. Old eggs have runny whites that flatten out in the pan, instead of thick whites that stand high. The runniness is caused by the thinning and breaking down of the white because of the release of carbon dioxide through the egg shell. Fresh eggs' shells are rough and chalky while old eggs' shells are smooth and shiny.

Never Eat Raw Eggs

Because of the risk of salmonella, you should never eat raw eggs, and you should certainly never risk giving them to your baby. As stated on page 36, even eggs with no cracks that are bacteria-free outside the shell can contain salmonella inside from the chicken's intestines. So washing an egg does not make it safe. Whether you are feeding your baby hard-cooked egg yolk or scrambled egg yolk, make sure that it is cooked through and solid, with no raw parts.

WARNING: Before feeding your little one a hard-cooked egg yolk, break it open with a fork and make sure that the yolk is solid all the way to the center. No part of the yolk should be undercooked because it may contain live salmonella.

How to Refrigerate a Raw Egg

Store eggs large end up, which is the way they come in the egg packs from the store. Keeping them large end up maximizes the distance between the air bubble inside the egg and the egg yolk, which is heavier than the white and sinks to the bottom. (Once cooked, it doesn't matter which side is up.) The large end of the egg is less likely to break if bumped.

> **WARNING:** Keep eggs refrigerated every minute! Do not let them sit out while you're making breakfast—return them to the refrigerator immediately.

Don't transfer eggs from the store container to the egg molds on the doors of old refrigerators. The door is usually the warmest part of the refrigerator, and eggs should be kept cold. The movement of the door may cause the eggs to form small invisible cracks.

Eggs must be kept covered when refrigerated to prevent a loss of moisture from the dry refrigerator air. Covering them also helps to prevent eggs from picking up odors from other foods.

With a baby that can't eat egg whites until her first birthday, you may find that you have many leftover egg whites. Make yourself an egg white omelette. Raw egg whites can be stored in the refrigerator, tightly covered, for about one week. (Raw eggs can also be frozen as discussed later.) Egg yolks can be refrigerated covered with water for up to 3 days. Place some cold water in an air-tight container and slide the yolks into the water unbroken. Cover the container well and refrigerate.

How to Hard-Cook an Egg

I've found that this method of hard-cooking eggs is less likely to cause cracks in the shell: Place the eggs in a saucepan and cover completely with cold water. Heat the water slowly over medium-high heat until it boils. Continue to cook the eggs in slowly-boiling water for 15 minutes. The water should be boiling, but not so rapidly that the eggs clack wildly and crack. After 15 minutes, plunge them into cold water to stop the cooking. (I just stick the stainless steel pot into the sink and run cold tap water into it. Don't do this with a hot glass pot—the cold water may cause it to crack.) Incidentally, quickly stopping the egg from cooking will make peeling easier.

There are other ways to hard-cook an egg. One is to slowly lower a raw egg into boiling water and continue to boil for 15 minutes. I always get a lot of cracks with this method. If cooking does cause a crack in one of your eggs, use it immediately.

> **WARNING:** Never cook eggs in their shells in the microwave or they will explode. When cooking an egg out of its shell in the microwave, you must first pierce the yolk to break it open, otherwise the yolk may explode. What a mess that would be!

Egg Tips

🐌 Many recipes call for room temperature eggs, but leaving eggs at room temperature for extended periods allows bacteria to grow. Instead, place eggs from the refrigerator into warm (not hot) water for 5-10 minutes immediately before using.

🐌 5 large eggs = 1 cup, 7 whites = 1 cup, 13 or 14 yolks = 1 cup
½ large egg is equal to about 1½ tablespoons

🐌 Many recipes call for whipped raw egg whites, which may contain salmonella. This is OK, as long as they will be baked or cooked at a high temperature that will kill all bacteria (page 164). For recipes that do not involve heating (such as egg nog, Caesar salad, etc.), raw egg whites can be replaced with a pasteurized egg white product. Ener-G® and Just Whites by Deb El Foods® are available at your natural foods store. If they are not on the shelf, ask the store employee to special order one for you.

🐌 While whipping egg whites, make sure you use a clean bowl because any oil or grease will prevent whites from rising. Make sure that all yolk has been completely removed. Remember that you should never eat raw eggs because of the danger of salmonella. Used whipped raw egg whites only in recipes where they will be cooked thoroughly to kill all bacteria.

🐌 To get the smoothest scrambled eggs, don't rush it. Start with a cold buttered frying pan and stir frequently while cooking slowly over medium-low heat. Add one tablespoon per egg of cream, evaporated milk, regular milk. For really creamy eggs, add ½ tablespoon of sour cream for each egg.

🐌 To prevent raw egg yolks from hardening on a plastic spatula making it difficult to clean, spray-oil or butter the spatula first.

🐌 Drop a raw egg on the floor? Use a baster to suck it up. Clean baster very well afterwards. Or, instead of the baster, sprinkle salt on the raw egg on the floor and wait 20 minutes and a paper towel will pick it up easily.

🐌 Add about one teaspoon of wheat germ for each egg before scrambling to increase nutritional content.

🐌 There's no major nutritional difference between white and brown eggs. The color of the shell has to do with camouflaging the egg from its natural predators.

🐌 It is common to add milk to eggs when scrambling them. Try orange juice instead, and see how you like the flavor.

🐌 Wet your fingers before handling whole raw eggs. It will give you a good grip and you will be less likely to drop them and make a mess!

🐌 To lessen the changes of breaking a yolk during cracking, hold the egg at an angle instead of straight while hitting it on the top edge of the pan or bowl.

🐌 Crack each egg into a cup first before adding it to a recipe. If the egg is spoiled, it won't ruin the entire recipe.

🐌 For easy peeling, tap the hard-cooked egg on all sides on the counter top. Roll gently between your palms to crackle. Pull the shell off beginning with the large end. Optionally, pull off shell while holding under cold running tap water. Another method is to crack the shell all over, insert a small WET spoon (baby has one) under the membrane and turn egg while prying the shell off.

🐌 For easy peeling of many eggs at one time, follow directions for *How to Hard-Cook and Egg* above. After boiling, pour off the hot water, and crack each egg with the back of a spoon. Cover eggs with cold water and keep running cold tap water into the pot until the water remains cool. Store pot in refrigerator for an hour or more to allow the water to get between the egg and shell. Peel and shells will come off easily.

🐌 Separate an egg (as instructed on page 266) and use the nonfat whites for your breakfast omelette. Cook the whole yolk for baby by simmering in water for 10-12 minutes. As always, break the cooked egg yolk open to look and make sure it is cooked through thoroughly with no raw parts.

🐌 Sliced eggs are great for Decorative Touches (page 362). If you have trouble with yolks crumbling while trying to get a pretty slice, try dipping knife in cold water first before slicing.

🐌 Add two tablespoons of vinegar per quart of cooking water to help prevent cracks in eggs. Or rub eggs with a cut lemon or lemon juice to help prevent cracking during cooking. If you still have trouble with eggs cracking while hard cooking, try piercing the large end with a sharp needle or pin before boiling. Hold upright and insert a sterile needle just a little (about ¼ inch) into the larger end of the shell. This will help air escape and help prevent cracking. Add vinegar to the cooking water to help seal hole and cracks.

🐌 Use a pastry bag or a clean freezer bag with corner clipped to stuff deviled eggs. Fill bag with stuffing and squeeze.

🐌 Deviled eggs look best when yolks are centered within the white. To help yolks stay centered, gently stir water and eggs for the first few minutes of boiling to set the whites. Also, the white will be stronger and will be less likely to break when stuffed. Store deviled eggs in a clean egg carton for traveling to parties.

🐌 Use the (cooled) cooking water from boiled eggs to water plants. The minerals that leached into the water from the egg shells make a very nutritious fertilizer. Place discarded egg shells into your watering can. Dry egg shells in the oven, pulverize them in the blender, and use the powder to fertilize houseplants.

🐌 See egg substitutes on page 273.

🐌 See stove-top cooking energy saving tips in box on page 188.

Storing Cooked Eggs

Eggs must be refrigerated both before and AFTER COOKING. Thoroughly dry each cooked egg with a clean wipe-up towel (page 159) and do so very gently, so as not to cause cracks. Refrigerate *immediately* after cooking to minimize the time the eggs are in the danger zone temperature range for bacterial growth (page 164). Bacteria in the air can enter the shell through minute invisible cracks, so get eggs cooled as quickly as possible after cooking to prevent bacterial growth. Plunging them into cold water after cooking helps to cool them quickly. Store cooked eggs in the refrigerator, well-covered, and, as with raw eggs, do not store in egg molds on the doors of old refrigerators. Eggs must be kept covered and cold, and the door is the warmest part of the refrigerator.

Keep cooked eggs no longer than one week. Use or discard hard-cooked eggs within one week after they have been cooked.

> **TIP:** I always hard-cook 4 eggs for my little guy on the same day of the week, Monday. If I crack an egg during cooking, he eats that one the same morning. He gets an egg yolk in his Super Porridge on Monday, Wednesday, and Friday (which my family and I call "egg yolk days") and maybe once during the weekend. Cooking eggs on the same day each week helps you to remember to discard them when they become a week old.

> **WARNING:** Don't eat eggs from Easter egg hunts. You never know how old they are or how well they've been kept cold.

Freezing Eggs

So eggs have gone on sale, and you took advantage and bought a gross. Good thing for you eggs can be frozen.

Freezing Cooked Egg Yolks Hard-cooked egg yolks can be frozen in a plastic freezer bag for up to two months. Hard-cooked egg whites become rubbery when frozen. Thaw frozen cooked yolks overnight in the refrigerator and use within one day. Do not refreeze.

Freezing Raw Eggs Whole Freeze only eggs that are fresh and are in an uncracked shell. First, do not freeze whole raw eggs in the shell, or they will expand and break the shell. Whites freeze well, but egg yolks gel and get sticky and thick unless you add salt or sugar. Break four whole raw eggs in a sturdy freezer container. Very gently mix the eggs so that the yolks break, or pierce the yolks to break them. Don't stir up foam or you'll have dry, freezer-burned eggs. Stir in ¼ teaspoon salt OR 2 teaspoons sugar or corn syrup for each four raw eggs. Use salt or sugar depending on how you will use the eggs when thawed. Leave no more than ½ inch of head room, cover well, label, and freeze for up to 6 months. You can also freeze the whole egg mixture using the Food Cube Method. Approximately 3 tablespoons is equal to one egg. Thaw (see below) and use scrambled, in omelettes, or in baking.

Freezing Raw Egg Yolks To freeze raw egg yolks, place the yolks in a sturdy freezer container and pierce them so that they break. Gently stir in ⅛ teaspoon salt or ½ teaspoon sugar or corn syrup for every four yolks to prevent coagulation. Freeze for up to 3 months. Approximately one tablespoon of thawed egg yolk liquid is equal to one egg yolk.

Freezing Raw Egg Whites Raw egg whites freeze well. No need to add anything to them. Freeze them using the Food Cube Method—one egg white per cube—for up to 6 months. Instead of cubes, you can freeze a whole bunch of egg whites in a sturdy freezer container with no more than ½ inch head room. Approximately two tablespoons of liquid egg white is equal to one egg white.

Thawing Raw or Cooked Eggs Thaw frozen eggs overnight in the refrigerator and use within one day. Do not refreeze.

What's That Green Stuff?

The green discoloration you sometimes see on the outer surface of a hard-cooked egg yolk may be unattractive, but it is harmless and you can safely eat it. It is caused by a chemical reaction between the iron in the egg yolk and the sulfur in the white. There are two things you can do to minimize it. Cook eggs in simmering water rather than water at full boil, and don't overcook them. Plunging eggs into cold water after 15 minutes of boiling will quickly stop the cooking.

Blood Spots

The blood spots you see occasionally when you break a raw egg are caused from small hemorrhages in the hen's reproductive tract. The egg is perfectly safe to eat. If you wish, remove the blood spot with the tip of a knife.

How to Tell a Raw Egg from a Cooked Egg

Spin it. A cooked egg will spin; a raw egg will wobble. Find out for yourself by comparing the movements of a spinning cooked egg and a raw egg.

> **TIP:** To keep track of which eggs are raw and which are cooked, keep them in separate containers in your refrigerator. If you're short on refrigerator space as I am, keep them in the same egg carton and mark the cooked eggs with a "C" using a non-toxic marker or crayon. Or, store raw eggs large end up and cooked eggs small end up, but you'll need good eyes with this method to tell which end is up. Or, store raw eggs on the right side of the container and cooked eggs on the left; remember that raw and right both start with "R." Some people can smell the difference between a raw and cooked egg. The most fun way to distinguish raw from cooked eggs is to put a few drops of food coloring and a little vinegar into the water while boiling to "color code" cooked eggs.

Egg Safety Hot-Line

For more information on the safe handling and storage of eggs, call the USDA. See page 280.

Egg Substitutes

Most commercial egg replacement products are nothing more than egg whites with no yolks and a small amount of other ingredients, such as vegetable oils, nonfat milk, emulsifiers, stabilizers, artificial colors, and others. For vegans, those who are allergic to eggs, or those who wish to cook without eggs for another reason, here are some homemade egg substitutes you can use instead of the commercial variety:

- For each egg to be replaced in a baked product, use one heaping tablespoon of soy flour or cornstarch plus 1½ tablespoons water. The soy flour is the more nutritious of the two.

- Use half of a mashed banana instead of an egg in muffins and cookies.

- In place of an egg, use one ounce of mashed tofu.

- Replace hard-cooked egg white in recipes like potato salad with steamed tofu. See tip on page 238.

- Instead of using eggs to bind ingredients in meatless loaves and burgers, use mashed potato, moistened whole grain bread crumbs, rolled oats, or tomato paste.

- Many recipes call for whipped raw egg whites, which may contain salmonella. This is OK, as long as they will be baked or cooked at a high temperature that will kill all bacteria (page 164). For recipes that do not involve heating (such as egg nog, Caesar salad, etc.), raw egg whites can be replaced with a pasteurized egg white product. Ener-G® and Just Whites by Deb El Foods® are available from your natural foods store. If they are not on the shelf, ask the store employee to special order one of them for you.

30. Miscellaneous Super Baby Foods

Kelp

Powdered kelp (which is actually a seaweed) can be purchased at your natural foods store. My family uses it instead of iodized salt as a source of iodine (see iodine on page 556. You may want to put just a pinch of powdered kelp in your baby's Super Porridge each morning. I keep kelp in a salt shaker—it's very convenient for sprinkling small amounts into foods. If you have the approval of your pediatrician, introduce kelp to your baby at 8 months, as stated on page 105. Please read about kelp and lead poisoning, page 559.

> **WARNING:** Some kelp may have a high arsenic content. Be careful about where you buy the kelp you feed to your baby.

Vegetable Oils

Typical supermarket brands of cooking oils are processed at high temperatures and have added chemicals. They are not at all natural, and have been processed, refined, deodorized, and bleached. Avoid them. And avoid margarines, which have partially hydrogenated oils (page 509). Be sure to read the label and avoid any oils containing BHT or BHA.

Flaxseed or flaxseed oil from the natural food store is a must for inclusion your baby's diet, as discussed at length in the nutrition section beginning on page 508. As for other oils, buy only cold-pressed, unrefined vegetable oil from the natural foods store. Olive oil is one of the least likely to be rancid. Natural, unprocessed oils should be kept under constant refrigeration to help prevent rancidity; they will get cloudy because of the lecithin they contain.

There are two camps when it comes to using fat for cooking and frying. Some experts claim that vegetable oils should NEVER be used for cooking or frying because heat causes them to become carcinogenic. They suggest using butter instead. Other experts don't agree with the use of butter because of its saturated fat.

WARNING: Never heat oil to the smoking point. It may ignite.

Homemade Oil Spray

Pam® and other commercial spray cooking oils are expensive, and they are nothing more than lecithin and alcohol. Save money by making homemade oil-spray with similar ingredients to those in commercial products (see the ingredients list on the can). Into a sterile spray or pump bottle, pour

½ cup of vodka or other flavorless alcohol from the liquor store (do NOT use rubbing alcohol)

2 teaspoons liquid lecithin (from the natural foods store)

Shake very well and use like Pam. Keep refrigerated. The vodka acts as an emulsifier to make the thick lecithin disperse easily. The vodka will evaporate during cooking, leaving only a thin coat of lecithin, which will prevent sticking and wash off easily.

Instead of the previous recipe, you can smear liquid lecithin directly on the pan, but you tend to use a lot of lecithin this way and it is thick and messy.

Variation If you are having trouble finding liquid lecithin, use 4 tablespoons granular lecithin (very easy to find) mixed into ½ cup corn oil. Mix thoroughly in your blender and keep the spray bottle refrigerated.

TIP: I have found that plain cooking oil (without alcohol) works just fine in a spray bottle as a Pam substitute. Or use a squeeze bottle and smear with a small piece of paper towel. As with all oils, keep refrigerated.

Cleaning the oil spray bottle The bottle containing homemade oil-spray does get messy. Clean it by emptying and filling with soapy, very hot water. Replace the spritzer and spray many times. Then fill with clear water and replace the spritzer again and spray many times to rinse out the soap. Repeat this rinsing with a fresh batch of clear water for a second rinse and again for third rinse until you are sure that all traces of soap have been rinsed away.

WARNING: If you spill vegetable oil, wipe it up with newspaper, paper towels, or other DISPOSABLE cloth. Never wash a rag or anything with vegetable oil in the washing machine with clothing, linens, or other items. Rancid oil will NEVER come out and it stinks. You will end up having to throw everything away, unless you want to wear them and lose all your friends.

Agar Agar

Did you ever notice the gelatinous goop that pools around chicken parts? That jelly contains the same ingredient in animal gelatin, which is made from the connective tissue in bones, hoofs, ligaments, cartilage, and tendons of animals. Gelatin is a substance which dissolves in hot water and solidifies in cold. We all have eaten or have at least seen Jell-O® gelatin—a dessert made from animal gelatin, artificial colors, and other ingredients.

Agar agar, also called "kanten," is a gelling substance made from seaweed (red algae). Unlike gelatin, it is not made from animal products and therefore is favored by vegetarians. Agar can be found at your natural foods store and comes granulated or flaked. Substitute 1-2 tablespoons (depending on the brand) of agar flakes for each tablespoon of gelatin or envelope of gelatin called for in your favorite recipes, or follow the directions on the package. Granulated agar is more "dense" and you need less of it: substitute ½-1 tablespoon of granulated agar for each tablespoon of gelatin. One tablespoon of flakes or ½ tablespoon of granules will gel one cup liquid. See more about using agar agar in Basic Vegetarian Gelatin recipe on page 351.

> **WARNING:** Don't add fresh pineapple, kiwi fruit, papaya, guava, ginger, or figs to a recipe with gelatin. It contains an enzyme called bromelin which will prevent the gelatin from setting, because it breaks down proteins (this is why it makes meat tender). There is no problem with canned pineapple, because the canning/heating process destroys the bromelin. Use agar agar instead of gelatin and there will be no problem with any pineapple, fresh or frozen.

Arrowroot

Arrowroot is a thickener derived from the tropical maranta plant root. It's more nutritious than cornstarch and does not have the raw flavor of whole wheat flour. Arrowroot is easily digested by infants and young children. One tablespoon of arrowroot will thicken one cup of liquid. Do not overstir, or mixture will become thin again. Use a little less arrowroot when substituting for flour in your favorite recipes, because arrowroot's thickening power is stronger than flour. Substitute two teaspoons of arrowroot for each tablespoon of flour. Like cornstarch, arrowroot should be mixed with enough cold liquid to make a paste before stirring into a hot mixture. Substitute the same amount of arrowroot for cornstarch in a recipe.

Blackstrap Molasses

You can buy blackstrap molasses at the natural foods store, and use it as a licorice-like sweetener in yogurt, baking, and beverages. I should warn you that many people do not like the strong taste of it.

Blackstrap molasses is actually a waste product from the refinement of table sugar, and it is the only sweetener that contains any significant amount of nutrients (except for diastatic malt, page 248). Besides other nutrients, most brands of blackstrap molasses are very high in iron, depending on the manufacturing process. Note how often blackstrap molasses shows up in the nutrient tables in Part III, page 522.

After opening the jar, store blackstrap molasses in the refrigerator.

> **TIP:** Blackstrap molasses is a slow as molasses in January. Try to buy a jar with a wide mouth, so that you can spoon it out instead of pouring.

> **TIP:** Wipe the lid and jar of blackstrap molasses, maple syrup, or honey with a damp towel before recapping to prevent sticking. Optionally, spritz the cap with oil-spray before recapping.

TIP: Before storing honey, maple syrup, and blackstrap molasses, place the jar on a plastic lid or inside a shallow plastic container or a used freezer bag. The jars tend to get sticky on the bottom, and the container will help keep your refrigerator shelves clean. After tightly capping, rinse stickiness off the whole jar under warm tap water.

TIP: When measuring blackstrap molasses and honey, warm the measuring cup by rinsing with hot water. The warmth will cause the sweetener to flow better. Or, if a recipe also calls for oil, use a measuring cup to measure the oil first. Use the same oil-lined cup to measure the sweetener—it will slide out freely.

WARNING: Blackstrap molasses, honey, and syrup are infamous for causing dental cavities. See warning about dental problems and sweets on page 48.

Honey

WARNING: Do not feed your baby honey or corn syrup until he is at least one year old, because of the possibility of botulism poisoning (see page 36).

Honey is just another sugar. It does have minute traces of nutrients, but not enough to mention. One advantage of honey over table sugar is that you can use less of it to get the same sweetness in recipes. (The health affects of too much sugar is discussed in the nutrition part under Simple Carbohydrates or Sugars on page 498.) Substitute approximately ⅔ cup honey for each cup of sugar called for in the recipe. If the original recipe does not contain any honey, reduce the baking temperature by 25°F to prevent over-browning. For each cup of honey substituted, add an extra ¼ teaspoon of baking soda to neutralize the acidity. Also, reduce the liquid in the recipe by about ¼ cup for each cup of honey. Honey substitutions in baked products are risky and, unless you are daring, substitute no more than half the sugar called for in the recipe with honey.

Honey doesn't spoil. Store honey at room temperature away from direct sunlight. Prevent water from getting into the honey, because moisture will cause mold to grow. You can keep it in the refrigerator, but colder temperatures will speed crystallization. Natural honey will eventually crystallize at room temperature. To re-liquify crystallized honey, place the open jar in hot water or in the oven at 250°F for several minutes and stir every few minutes, or in the microwave on high for a minute or more, stirring every 30 seconds. The time it will take to liquify depends on the amount of honey in the jar, of course.

Maple Syrup

Real maple syrup is also just another sugar, but it is more natural and healthy than the supermarket brands of "pretend" maple syrup, which are actually made from cheap corn syrup, preservatives, and artificial colorings. Real maple syrup must be kept refrigerated after the bottle is opened.

31. Meat

Meat is not a part of the Super Baby Food diet. Your baby will be perfectly healthy (and in my opinion, more healthy) on a vegetarian diet. The American Academy of Pediatrics and most pediatricians, registered dieticians, and nutritionists do not recommend a vegan (no animal products at all) diet, but they agree that a lacto-ovo diet (a vegetarian diet that includes dairy products and eggs), such as the Super Baby Food Diet, is safe and healthy for a growing baby. As can be seen by comparing the two food pyramids on pages 504 and 505, the Department of Agriculture agrees that meat can be replaced in the diet with the meat alternatives: legumes, nuts, and seeds.

People choose to eat a vegetarian diet because of a combination of several reasons: 1. As a group, vegetarians are healthier and get significantly less cancer, heart disease, and other illnesses than meat eaters. 2. Meat-eating contributes to world hunger; if you eat meat, you are eating for 17 people because the grains that are fed to animals raised for meat-eating can be fed directly to people. 3. Animals are sometimes raised and slaughtered in cruel conditions. 4. The acres of land used to raise cattle for food are a waste of water and other natural resources, and are a cause of the problems of erosion and soil depletion. 5. Some people go vegetarian to lose weight (in general, vegetarian diets contain less fat), feel better, and for various other reasons.

If you would like to know more, there are many good books on the subject of vegetarianism. If you need some motivation to become a vegetarian, read Barbara Parham's book *What's Wrong with Eating Meat?* (See bibliography.) That's the book that changed my diet. Be ready to change your eating habits if you read it, because you probably won't be able to enjoy eating meat again.

In order to make this book as complete as possible, I have included this chapter on meat for those readers who (no matter what I say! ☺) have decided to feed it to their babies. American society is ingrained with the idea that meat is necessary in a healthy diet, and some parents are afraid that their babies will not develop properly without meat in their diets. I understand. When I fed my twins a meatless diet more than a decade ago, my family made it clear to me that I was doing them wrong. They were genuinely concerned. It was hard enough to be a new parent of twins, never mind to have people tell you that you were deliberately hurting your children. Rather than have you feed meat to your baby with no guidelines at all, I have done some research on feeding meat to babies and included it here. I have to admit that I'm writing this chapter with no practical experience—the information here is nothing more than a conglomeration of the facts I've read from several other reliable and accurate sources.

Desiccated Liver

Desiccated liver is a powdered nutritional supplement made from dried liver. It is high in vitamin B12 (a nutrient sometimes claimed to be lacking in vegetarian diets) and other B vitamins. For those of you who are uncomfortable giving your baby a totally meatless diet, perhaps you will feel OK with no meat except for a little desiccated liver. You can introduce desiccated liver to your baby beginning at about 8 months (page105). Add ½-1 teaspoon to your baby's Super Porridge daily or several times a week to make up for whatever you feel your baby would be missing in a meatless diet. It tastes absolutely horrible and your baby may not mind at all, but most adults certainly do, which is why it should be added to foods in small amounts.

Meat

In my opinion, meat is dangerous to eat, or even to have in the kitchen. The deadliest food borne illnesses almost always enter the body through the eating of animal products, or from eating other foods (cantaloupe, lettuce, unpasteurized apple juice) contaminated by animal feces. Poultry carry salmonella and campylobacter, and raw shellfish have caused infection with Vibrio vulnificus. Ground beef is the most common source of E. coli (Escherichia coli O157:H7), which lives in the intestines of healthy cattle. When animals are slaughtered, E. coli organisms sometimes get thoroughly mixed into ground beef. The Department of Agriculture estimates that 500 people die per year (yes, die!) from eating meat (mostly ground beef) contaminated with E. coli. Thousands more get sick from eating meat every single day! These statistics are conveniently not mentioned in the "beef is real food for real people" television commercials. Blood (euphemistically called "juice") from meat containing E. coli and other bacteria can contaminate anything from cutting boards to other foods that it accidentally touches or drips on. Further information on E. coli is available from the National Center for Infectious Diseases, Centers for Disease Control and Prevention (CDC), 1600 Clifton Road, Mailstop C09, Atlanta, GA 30333.

Handling Meat Safely

If you prepare meat in your kitchen, make sure to wash thoroughly in very hot water with an antibacterial soap anything that touched meat or its juice, including your hands, utensils, cutting boards, etc. Be sure to use an FDA-registered antibacterial product and follow the instructions on the label. Or mix one tablespoon of chlorine bleach into one gallon of hot water to wipe surfaces clean. Allow surfaces to air dry. Utensils can also be sanitized by soaking in plain hot water (at least 170°F) for at least 30 seconds. Dishwashers working properly should reach this temperature. Keep a separate cutting board for meat than the board you use for produce and other foods, or cut meat on wax paper or parchment paper and discard immediately. (See more about cutting boards on page 157.) Wear rubber gloves when handling meat to protect cuts and abrasions on your hands from infection, and wash the gloves well with antibacterial soap product when done.

The Food Safety and Inspection Service (FSIS) is responsible for ensuring the safety of meat, poultry, and egg products. The FSIS is part of the United States Department of Agriculture (USDA). For more information about the safe storage and handling of meat, poultry, and eggs, call the USDA's Meat and Poultry Hot-line 800-535-4555 weekdays 10-4 Eastern Time. Recorded messages are available 24 hours a day. (In Washington, DC metropolitan area, call 202-720-3333.)

Safe handling of meat begins at the grocery store. In your shopping cart, keep meat, poultry, and fish away from produce, cans of food, boxes, and *all* other groceries. Bag meat separately from all other food items in its own plastic bag and tie the bag shut so that any leaking liquids will remain contained. Do not let the meat get above refrigerator temperatures for more than a few minutes (see page 164). Follow the shopping tips on page 141 and shop for meat last, so that it will remain cold as long as possible. Get meat home and into the refrigerator as soon as possible. If you cannot get home quickly (within about 45 minutes to an hour), keep a cooler with ice in your car to store the meat in to keep it cold. Keep meat and its liquids away from other food items in your refrigerator and freezer, as you did in your grocery cart. Put meat on a lower shelf where its liquids will not drip on and contaminate other foods.

If you suspect that vegetables or fruits have been contaminated by meat or its juices, soak them in this solution for 10-15 minutes: One teaspoon of bleach mixed into one gallon of water. The bleach should contain no sodium hypochlorite and no phosphorous. Then place vegetables and fruit into another clean bowl and rinse thoroughly by running tap water over them for at least 5 minutes.

Buying Meat for Baby

Do not buy frozen meat for the purpose of making frozen baby food cubes. To prevent bacterial contamination, foods should never be re-frozen.

WARNING: Never refreeze meat, poultry, fish, or any other food once it has been thawed.

Choose only fresh, natural meat. Ground meat should be bright red and as lean as possible. Do not buy dark red or brownish red meat. Do not buy bacon, which is high in saturated fat and low in protein. Do not buy ham that has been preserved with nitrates. Do not give your baby precooked luncheon meats because they contain salt, additives and fillers. Choose meat with the least amount of fat. Meat contains saturated fat (page 504), a type of fat that the immature digestive systems of infants do not handle well in large amounts.

Preparing and Storing Meat, Poultry, and Fish

Store raw or cooked meat in the coldest part of the refrigerator. A refrigerator thermometer can be used to find the coldest part—see page 164. Do not leave raw or cooked meat at room temperature for more than a few minutes.

WARNING: Meat contaminated with E. coli bacteria looks and smells normal. Therefore, you cannot assume meat is safe if it looks and smells OK.

Store raw meat and poultry in the refrigerator for no more than 24 hours before cooking. Be especially careful with ground meats. Do not cook food with interruption; partial cooking may encourage bacterial growth before cooking is complete. Before cooking, remove excess fat, cut lean raw meat into small individual pieces (see cutting boards, page 157), and be sure to cook meat very thoroughly so there remains no raw portions. Make sure that cooked meat has no pink parts (pink means that it's inadequately cooked). Juices should run clear. The inside should be hot. Fish should be cooked thoroughly until it is white, flaky, and separates from the bones easily. Purée the cooked meat/fish immediately, keep it at room temperature for no more than a few minutes, and freeze it immediately. Puréed food cubes of meat or fish will keep for up to one month in a freezer at 0°F or lower.

> **WARNING:** Be careful to remove all bones from meat, poultry, and fish, even from fish fillets which are supposedly boneless.

Use a meat thermometer to test that meat has been thoroughly cooked through. Internal temperatures of ground meat should reach at least 160-180°F in the center; ground poultry should reach at least 180°F in the center. Pre-cooked foods or leftovers should be reheated to higher internal temperatures—at least 5°F hotter. Meat cooked in the microwave should be checked in several areas near the center due to the uneven heating problem (page 175).

Cooked meat or dishes containing cooked meat should be stored in the refrigerator for no more than 24 hours. Discard any dishes containing cooked meat if they have been refrigerated for more than 24 hours, even if there is just the tiniest bit of meat in them.

Frozen Raw Meat

Raw frozen meat should be kept frozen no more than three months. Never thaw meat at room temperature or in warm water; thaw it in the refrigerator as discussed on page 162. Cook thawed raw meat within 24 hours. *Do not re-freeze into food cubes for baby.* Frozen meat that has been thawed and cooked should be eaten immediately or should be kept refrigerated. Do not keep meat in the refrigerator for more than one day. Discard from the refrigerator within 24 hours.

When to Introduce Meat, Poultry, and Fish

Poultry (chicken and turkey), beef, veal, and lamb can be introduced at 7-8 months; lean fish (flounder, sole, cod, catfish, haddock) at 8 months; pork, ham, liver, kidney, and fatty fish (tuna, halibut, bluefish, sardines, salmon) at 9 months; and shellfish (crab, scallops, shrimp, lobster) after one year because they are high allergy foods (page 33). As with other solid foods, meat should be puréed to a smooth consistency for young babies. Cooked meat can be coarsely ground or finely chopped for babies at about 10 months. Before feeding any meat/poultry/fish to your baby, get your pediatrician's OK.

> **WARNING:** Never give sushi or other raw fish, meat, or poultry to babies or children. Do not feed your baby fried fish or meat.

> **WARNING:** These fish have been known to be high in contaminants and should not be fed to infants or in large amounts to older babies: bluefish, carp, catfish, striped bass, and swordfish.

Meat Recipes

Mixed Meat Dinner

Make your own baby "mixed dinner" by cooking this mini meat loaf. Mix:

½ cup of fresh meat, ground beef, ground turkey, or a combination
½ cup grated raw vegetable
½ cup whole grain bread crumbs (page 321), wheat germ, or oatmeal or other dry grain pulverized to a powder in the blender, or a combination
1-2 tablespoons of soy milk, cow's milk, or tomato sauce

Press into loaf pan and cook thoroughly in a preheated 350°F oven or in the microwave until all meat is done. Purée for a younger baby or break into bite sized pieces and serve as finger food. Freeze for up to one month.

Finger Meatballs

Mix one part lean ground beef or pork with one part cooked mashed potatoes or raw rolled oats. Form into balls about an inch in diameter and place on ungreased baking sheet. Bake in preheated 350°F oven for at least 20 minutes until cooked through thoroughly. Or cook in skillet until cooked through. Drain off fat, cool, and serve to babies 10 months old or older as finger foods. Balls should not be windpipe-sized to prevent choking; never leave baby alone while eating. Do not leave at room temperature for more than a few minutes. Refrigerate and use within 24 hours or freeze for up to one month.

Help My Hamburger Quick

Ingredients:

1 pound of ground beef or ground turkey
1 medium onion, chopped
package of frozen vegetables blend (10-ounce)
16-ounce jar or can of spaghetti sauce
10 ounces of whole grain pasta, cooked

Over medium heat, sautee beef/turkey with onion until done. Add frozen vegetable blend and sauce and mix well. Cover and simmer for about 15 minutes until vegetables are done, stirring occasionally. Mix in cooked pasta.

Variations: Substitute all or part of the meat with reconstituted TVP, cooked beans, or canned beans. Leave out pasta and serve over cooked whole grains.

MONEY SAVER: Replace part of hamburger with cooked bulgur or cooked brown rice to improve your health and pocketbook. Ground nuts are great in meatballs, meatloaf, and burgers. Replace a quarter of a pound of ground meat with one cup of lightly sauteed, finely grated carrot, potato, or sweet potato, or a combination.

Part III

Recipes

32. Toddler (and Grown-Up) Recipes

Recipe index begins on page 569.

All of these recipes are designed around the following commandment:

Thou shalt spend the least possible amount of time in the kitchen and the most possible amount of time enjoying your beautiful baby.

Most of these recipes are super healthy for your baby or toddler and take only a few minutes of your time to prepare. There's not a fancy, two-dozen step, gourmet recipe in the bunch. The recipes are quick because they contain few ingredients—foods that are natural, whole, and minimally-processed. It's ironic that the healthiest baby foods are also the foods that require little or no preparation: fresh fruits, yogurt, cheeses and other milk products, cereals, raw nuts and seeds, and plain vegetables. Lucky thing for us busy parents that these plain, simple foods are the absolute best and most nutritious foods for our babies.

TIP: To make your kids feel special, name recipes after them. For example, the "Johnny Casserole" or the "Mary Broccoli Recipe." I once named a yogurt dip after one of my sons, and literally a year later (after I had long forgotten it), he remembered it was named after him. This is also a great way to get your kids to eat a healthy food that they don't particularly like!

Use The Batch and Freeze Method

There are a few recipes that have too many ingredients, take too many steps, and require too many mixing bowls and pans to be called simple. For these more involved recipes, I suggest that you make and freeze several batches. You've been making Super Baby Food for the last several months (I hope), so batch cooking and freezing is nothing new to you. There is a Toddler Hors d'oeuvres section in this chapter with recipes that are great for batching and freezing.

Toddler TV Dinners

Supermarket TV dinners are expensive and again, in my opinion, not worth the convenience. They're also high in sodium and loaded with junk—just look at the long list of unpronounceable ingredients. Why not make your own? When you're cooking, double or triple the recipe and freeze the extras to create your own homemade TV dinners. Do this for your family's meals as well as your toddler's meals, if you have enough freezer space. Luckily, toddler-sized meals don't take up much room in the freezer. And you don't have to invest a lot in freezer containers if you use the Phantom Container Freezing Method (page 171).

Toddler Take-Along Lunches

Don't buy those over-priced lunch packs that are nothing more than a few pieces of salty luncheon meat, crackers made from white flour, and candy pieces. The convenience of the packaging will ruin your pocketbook and our planet. (What will the food industry think of next!) Make your own by using a recycled Styrofoam egg carton cut in half, or for older kids an entire carton. Wash the egg cartons very well with hot water and antibacterial soap and, if you wish, line the cartons inside and out with aluminum foil. Put whole grain crackers, natural cheese slices, halved-grapes, and other Super Snacks into the egg holes. Cut the cheese slices and other foods into Simple Shapes (pages 367-368) or cut the foods into fun shapes with cookie cutters. You don't need to have a different food in each hole—alternate the foods to make it look like there is a nice selection. Cover with wax paper or aluminum foil to keep the foods in their bins. Add a napkin over the wax paper. Tape a picture inside the top of the egg carton so your child will see it when she opens the carton. A heart to remind your child that you love her will help make your child happy while she's away from home..

WARNING: Never use camera film containers for holding food. They may contain leftover chemicals. Little pill containers may be used, but your child must be old enough to understand that he should not eat food from any pill containers unless he has your permission.

Homemade Lap Table

Serve meals to sick children in bed on a cookie sheet or jelly roll pan on top of a homemade bed table. The pan's lip helps keep food and spills from getting onto the bed. Place a damp paper towel between the pan and dishes and glasses to prevent slipping, and then use the towel for face and hand cleanup at meal's end. (See Muffin Man Buffet, page 296.)

Make a homemade bed table from a cardboard box by cutting semi-circular holes in the bottom to fit over your child's legs. Cut one large hole for both legs or two holes for individual legs as shown in pictures on right. This table can also be used in the car as a writing desk. However, do not use the pan in the car—its hardness makes it dangerous in a car accident. Use wide tape and cloth strips to form a lip around the box edges to prevent crayons and other small items from rolling off.

Food Staples

Almost all of the ingredients in the recipes are staple foods that you should always have on hand in your kitchen. Many of them keep well at room temperature for extended time periods. Some, such as grains and legumes, store for up to a year. Because you don't have to worry about limited refrigerator or freezer space, or a short shelf life and wasted food due to spoilage, you can stock up when they go on sale. You may want to further increase your food savings by joining a food co-op (short for cooperative). A co-op is a group of people that go together to buy foods in bulk at reduced prices. Be aware that the group's record-keeping and food ordering will take some of your time, but the savings may be worth your while.

Keep on hand as many as possible of the food staples listed in the next box. If you haven't read the rest of the book, know that each of these food staples is discussed somewhere in this book , with details and instructions on how to prepare and store each one. See index for page numbers.

TIP: Running out of milk is a catastrophe in a house with a baby or toddler. For just this emergency, always keep a can of evaporated milk (not sweetened condensed milk, which is 40% sugar!) or some nonfat dry milk (page 251) on hand in the cabinet and follow the directions to reconstitute it on the label. Or, better yet, pick up a can of *Better Than Milk* from your natural foods store. Use it when you run out of fresh milk, or use it in place of fresh milk. Soy milk enriched with calcium and vitamin D is another type of staple milk. It will keep unopened in the aseptic box for months until its expiration date—so always keep some in the cabinet. Give your baby enriched soy milk to get him used to the taste, so that he will continue to drink it into adulthood.

Food Staples for the Well-Stocked
Super Baby Food Kitchen

- fresh fruit—ripe and ready to eat, especially vitamin C fruits like kiwi fruit and oranges, and vitamin C juices like orange juice
- frozen fruit—store-bought or home-frozen fruit chunks, or puréed fruit cubes in the freezer for snacks or for use in recipes
- fresh vegetables, especially the Super Green Veggies
- frozen vegetables—store-bought or home cooked and frozen vegetable chunks or food cubes
- bread, 100% whole wheat or other whole or sprouted-grain bread from the natural foods store
- Super Flour
- sandwich spreads such as natural peanut butter, hummus, tahini, cream cheese, and yogurt cheese—batch and freeze
- whole grain pasta and Super Pasta Sauce (page 334)
- natural cheeses, such as mozzarella, Swiss, and those in the list on page 250
- yogurt—store-bought with active cultures or homemade
- tofu—aseptically sealed tofu lasts for months at room temperature
- avocado—whole and ripe and/or frozen in food cubes
- milk—cow's milk, soybean milk, nut/seed milk, Better Than Milk
- nonfat powdered milk
- butter or natural cold-pressed, un-hydrogenated vegetable oil from the natural foods store
- raw/hard-boiled eggs from free-running, hormone-free chickens
- a variety of whole grains, especially brown rice, millet, rolled oats, teff, quinoa, and barley
- a variety of dried beans/legumes, especially soy grits or soybeans, lentils, split peas, and garbanzos
- boxed breakfast cereals, such as bite-sized whole wheat cereal and Oatios (the health-food store equivalent of Cheerios)
- healthy canned soups from the natural foods store or your own homemade frozen soups in individual servings
- your own homemade frozen toddler TV dinners
- blackstrap molasses
- maple syrup or honey (honey is for only babies older than 12 months old)
- raw almonds and other nuts and their butters
- raw seeds and seed butters—pumpkin seeds, flax seeds, tahini
- brewer's yeast
- lemon juice ice cubes
- parsley and other herbs—frozen fresh, frozen in ice cubes, or growing on your windowsill
- dried fruit—store-bought or home dried

Healthy Extras

In these recipes, you will frequently see the words "Add Healthy Extras." Healthy Extras are exceptionally nutritious "health foods," which you should feed to your baby as often as possible. (They look a lot like the food staples on the previous page.) Some of them, such as brewer's yeast, don't taste very good, but several of the recipes give you a chance to sneak them into your baby's foods without her noticing. Some of the Healthy Extras, such as wheat germ and ground oats, absorb liquid and cause the food to be a little dry. Add a little more liquid than is called for in the recipe to correct for them.

Healthy Extras to Add as Super Nutrition Enhancers

brewer's yeast (nutritional) yeast
wheat germ
ground dry oatmeal or rolled oats
tofu
yogurt
cooked crumbled egg yolk
shredded or diced raw vegetables (carrots, broccoli, celery, cabbage)
chopped fresh or frozen parsley
finely chopped sunflower seed sprouts
mashed (or whole for babies over 3 years) cooked dried beans or frozen puréed cooked bean food cubes
cooked soy grits
bean flour
ground nuts (almonds, walnuts, filberts, etc.)
nut butters (peanut butter, almond butter, other nut butters)
ground seeds (pumpkin, flax, chia, etc.) eat immediately
tahini and other seed butters
cooked brown rice or millet grains or any cooked whole grains
milks: breast, formula, Super Milks
instant nonfat dry milk

These Healthy Extras can double as sweeteners:

shredded or diced fresh fruits (apples, pears, kiwi, ...)
diced canned pineapple
chopped dried fruits, rehydrated (apricots, papaya, ...)
blackstrap molasses
mashed fresh or mashed frozen strawberries and other berries
concentrated frozen all-fruit juices
natural no-added-sugar all-fruit jams or jellies

Super Flour

Please make sure to read the chapter on whole grains (page 218), which discusses the nutritional difference between refined and whole grain flours. You can use plain whole wheat flour as Super Flour in any of the recipes, or you can add to the protein and nutritional value of Super Flour by mixing it with soybean flour and other nutritional extras. To make one cup of Super Flour, place the following ingredients into a one-cup dry measuring cup:

1 tablespoon soy flour
1 tablespoon wheat germ
1 teaspoon brewer's yeast

Top off the cup with whole wheat flour to fill the balance of the cup.

Or use the mixture below as Super Flour, which is a well-known formula devised by Dr. Clive McKay of Cornell University. The Cornell Formula is mostly white flour, but there's no law that says you cannot replace the white flour with whole wheat flour!

The Cornell Formula

To make one cup of Cornell Formula, place the following ingredients into a one-cup dry measuring cup:

1 tablespoon nonfat dry milk solids
1 tablespoon soy flour
1 teaspoon wheat germ

Top off the cup with unbleached, unbrominated white flour to fill out the balance of the cup. Or use my formula below for a home-enriched white flour. I add back the wheat germ and the bran that were removed during the refinement (page 218) of white flour:

Home Enrichment Formula for White Flour

Place the following ingredients into a one-cup dry measuring cup:

1 tablespoon wheat germ
1 tablespoon wheat bran or oat bran
1 teaspoon soy flour (optional)
1 teaspoon nonfat powdered milk (optional)
1 teaspoon brewer's yeast (optional)

Top off with unbleached, unbrominated white flour to fill out the balance of the cup. Make a cup for each cup of flour called for in the recipe. Or use part whole wheat flour and replace the other part of the flour in the recipe with the mixture above.

Self-Rising Super Flour

No need to buy self-rising flour. Make your own by putting 1½ teaspoons baking powder and ½ teaspoon salt into a one-cup dry measuring cup. Fill it to the top with Super Flour and level with a knife to make one cup total.

WARNING: Although soy flour is a great nutrition booster, which complements the wheat flour to form complete protein (see protein complementarity, page 515), it has a bitter taste. Don't add more than one tablespoon of soy flour per cup of recipe flour or its taste may affect your bread's flavor.

TIP: Whole wheat, germ, and bran absorb more liquid than white flour absorbs, so you may have to decrease the flour or increase the liquid in standard bread recipes by a few tablespoons. If you are replacing the white flour in a recipe with whole wheat flour, use a little less than is called for in the recipe, because it also will absorb more liquid.

WARNING: You can replace white flour with whole wheat flour in your favorite recipes, but whole grain flour tends to leave bread products flat and dense. I have been teased by my family and friends many times about being able to use my cakes and quick breads as doorstops. ☹ For these recipes, I have reluctantly resolved myself to replace ONLY PART of the white flour called for in the recipe with whole grain flour—no more than ⅓ to ½ —depending on the recipe. So before you go replacing all the white flour with whole wheat flour in a cake recipe for the school bake sale or your child's birthday party, make sure you've tested it beforehand.

Healthy Recipes for Commercial Food Products

Next time you are at the supermarket, take a look at the ingredients list of any boxed food product: salt, sugars, partially hydrogenated oils, artificial flavors, pesticides, coloring, wheat flour (same as nutritionless white flour), and other nutritional horrors. Then check the amount or weight in the box and the cost—an exorbitant price for a minute amount of junk food! Someone has to pay for all of that expensive advertising and attention-getting, environment-unfriendly packaging. Natural food stores have commercially boxed food products with healthier ingredients, but you are still paying high prices for their convenience. See if you recognize the familiar recipes with slightly modified brand names in the box of recipes below:

Cheese Driz Sauce (page 353) Instant Breakfast Drink (page 359) Flavored Yogurt (page 255) Frozen Yogurt (page 339) Tofutti (page 342) Cinnamon Sugar (page 355) Mustard Mayonnaise (page 352) Lemon or other citrus zest (page 440) Homemade Vanilla Extract (page 355) King Lion's Milk Bars (page 346) Honey Butter (page 317) Mixed Meat Dinners (page 282) Help My Hamburger Quick (page 282) Homemade Oil-Spray (Pam®) (page 275) Rolled-Up Fruit Snacks (pages 200-206)	Whereas commercial products use processed/white wheat flour, the recipes below contain only whole grain ingredients: Top-of-Stove Stuffing Mix (page 322) "Shake and Cook" Potato Coating (page 302) Popper Tarts (page 323) Pocket Sandwiches (page 319) Breakfast Flake Cereal (page 322) Nutty Grape Cereal (page 323) Croutons (page 322) Biscuit Mix (page 324) Italian Bread Crumbs (page 322) Cheesy Thins (page 334)

Super Snacks

Super snacks are an important part of the Super Baby Food Diet. They are healthy foods that add nutrients and calories. See *Super Snacks are Real Food* on page 131. Follow all instructions to prevent choking on pages 40-42.

Super Snacks—Finger Foods

SOFT pieces or wedges of ripe peeled and cored fruit: peaches, mango, papaya, watermelon, cantaloupe, honeydew, banana, pears, cucumber with seeds removed (See warning and tip about slippery foods on page 80.)

SOFT pieces of cooked, diced vegetables: broccoli florets, sweet potato sticks, or cooked white/sweet potatoes rolled into balls

raw carrot, grated fine (bigger carrot pieces are choking hazards, page 40)

small tofu chunks

beans cooked until very soft with skins removed

peas cooked until soft and smashed slightly with a fork (for older babies only)

Oatios or another brand of health food store equivalent of Cheerios

other whole grain and unsugared dry boxed cereal, but with no nut pieces or any hard pieces that can cause choking

crumbled egg yolk pieces, cooked solid (see page 266)

pieces of scrambled egg yolk, cooked solid (see page 266)

small pieces of soft cheese

small lumps of cottage cheese

cooked brown rice and other grains

whole grain crackers

well-cooked small pasta pieces

whole grain bread, cut into toast fingers or small pieces

a whole bagel makes a good teething ring

bits of French toast, cooked thoroughly so no raw egg (see page 266)

whole grain pancakes

Toddler Hors d'oeuvres (page 293)

Ripe, soft apple pieces or crackers topped with grated or sliced cheese and microwaved or broiled in the toaster oven to melt the cheese.

Any soft, ripe fruit, such as banana or apple, sliced and spread with thinned peanut butter or other nut butter. Mix freshly ground pumpkin and flax seeds into the nut butter before spreading.

Make a mash of any combination of ingredients above, form into small balls and other little shapes and serve as finger foods.

Follow all instructions to prevent choking on pages 40-42.

TIP: Use an egg slicer to slice pieces of finger food, like hard-cooked egg yolks and cooked mashed balls of food. A pastry blender will cut soft food into small pieces in no time. A pizza cutter can be used to quickly slice up whole grain bread, French toast, tofu, and fruits and veggies for baby. Be careful that food pieces are not windpipe size (see choking hazards, page 40). First cut round foods, such as bananas and hot dogs, lengthwise before slicing.

TIP: Bond with your child while he's snacking: Sit down with him and use a butter knife to spread the fruit slices with the nut butter *one at a time*, and hand each to your child. They like watching you prepare each piece and it makes you feel very nurturing.

TIP: Toddlers think it's fun to pull string cheese with you.

Batch Preparing and Freezing Super Snacks

Some super snacks, like Cheerios, need no preparation. But snacks like cooked vegetable pieces do, and they can be prepared in a large batch and frozen to save time and energy. Prepare and cook according to the directions in Part II. To prevent them from freezing together into one big clump, use the Tray-freeze Method and Nested Plastic Bag Methods of freezing foods. Actually, there's no need to cook snacks separately. Whenever you cook vegetables, save a few finger food-sized pieces and freeze for Super Snacks, as it says in the tip on page 192.

The Super Snack Freezer Bag

In my freezer, I have one large freezer bag known as **THE SUPER SNACK BAG**, which contains several inner plastic bags (Nested Plastic Bag Method) of batch-prepared Super Snacks: cooked veggie pieces, ripe fruit pieces, small tofu chunks in ice cubes, beans with skins removed, and bags of different Toddler Hors d'oeuvres (next page). When snack time comes, I pull out a few little food pieces and thaw them for a few seconds in the microwave. Or, instead of thawing them in the microwave, I remove several of them from the freezer bag the night before and place them in a covered bowl in the refrigerator. When it comes time for the babysitter or me to give them to the baby, they're thawed and ready.

TIP: Those infant feeding dishes with the separate compartments are perfect for storing one day's worth of different finger foods—soft-cooked carrot pieces for a morning snack in one part, an afternoon snack of diced peaches in another part, and shredded cheese in the third.

WARNING: Make sure that the food pieces are completely thawed, because frozen foods are choking hazards. Transfer them from the freezer to a warm part of the refrigerator THE NIGHT BEFORE, and they'll surely be thawed by snack time the next day.

WARNING: Once these little food pieces are thawed, don't keep them for more than one day in the refrigerator. Throw them out that same day.

All Snacks Can Be Batch Prepared and Frozen

It takes only a few minutes to prepare Super Snacks like tofu chunks (just cut them up) and ripe and soft fruit pieces (wash, peel, and dice), and you can prepare them immediately before feeding to your baby. But it will save time if you batch prepare and freeze them. Freezing them in batches may also help prevent food waste, because once a block of tofu is opened, or a large fruit is cut up, they must be eaten soon if they are stored in the refrigerator. Your baby probably doesn't eat enough to use them before they would spoil.

Toddler Hors d'oeuvres
(More Super Snacks)

Toddler Hors d'oeuvres are my favorite kids' snacks, because they are so nutritious and easy to make. Kids love them. They are actually more than snacks—serve them with a fruit and/or a vegetable and they make a meal. You can make a whole batch and refrigerate or freeze them, and then thaw for a minute or two in the microwave. Each of the hors d'oeuvres recipes can be refrigerated for up to one week or frozen for up to two months. Use the Tray-freeze Method and the Nested Plastic Bag Method. To make hors d'oeuvres, mix the ingredients and form into balls. Some need cooking and some don't.

> **TIP:** Wetting your hands to roll the sticky mixture into balls makes rolling easier. Or use a small melon-baller to make uniform-sized ball shapes. Flatten balls for a cookie shape.

How To Cook or Fry Hors d'oeuvres

Cook by baking on greased baking sheet in pre-heated 350°F oven for 10-15 minutes. Or you can cook hors d'oeuvres in a frying pan on the stove top for a few minutes, turning to cook all sides. Drain on paper towels to absorb some of the butter. (See Drain Tip, page 303.) Refrigerate or freeze.

Variation: Instead of balls, press the mixture into a baking pan, bake in preheated 350°F oven for 15-20 minutes, let cool, cut into bars, and refrigerate or freeze.

> **TIP:** A pizza cutter speeds the job of cutting out bars. Be careful that pieces are not windpipe size (see choking hazards, page 40).

Variation: Instead of bars/balls, make other shapes, such as triangles, stars, hearts, snakes, etc. Or flatten the mixture with your hands or a rolling pin (if you don't have a rolling pin, see tip on page 153), and use a knife to make Simple Shapes (pages 367-368) or use cookie cutters. You may wish to refrigerate before cutting for a firmer mixture that will cut more easily.

Make Your Own
Toddler Hors d'oeuvres Recipes

Recipes for Toddler Hors d'oeuvres follow, but you can see how easy it is to make up recipes of your own. Just mix together a few foods until you have a consistency that will form little cohesive balls. Refrigerate or freeze until snack time. Toddler Hors d'oeuvres are a great way to use up leftovers!

> **TIP:** Use a Styrofoam egg carton (cleaned very well with hot water and antibacterial soap) instead of a cookie sheet to keep Toddler Hors d'oeuvres separate during the initial freezing step. Cover well during freezing. When frozen solid, transfer to freezer bags.

Toddler Hors d'oeuvres

ᵃ Granola Hors d'oeuvres

1½ cups rolled oats
¼ cup wheat germ
¼ cup ground nuts
¼ cup nonfat dry milk
¼ cup melted butter or oil
5 tablespoons honey
1 beaten egg
¼ teaspoon vanilla
¼ teaspoon cinnamon
½ cup dried fruit

Mix all dry ingredients. Mix honey, oil, and vanilla into dry mixture. Add more honey moisten or dried oats to dry if necessary. Form into small balls. Bake or fry, making sure that egg gets thoroughly cooked.

Variation: To make granola bars instead of balls, press mixture into 8x8 baking pan. Bake at 350°F for 15-20 minutes, cool, and cut into bars.

ᵃ Nut Butter Hors d'oeuvres

¾ cup creamy natural peanut butter
¼ cup mashed cooked beans
2 tablespoons tahini or soft butter
¼ cup wheat germ
¾ cup crumbled shredded wheat cereal

Mix peanut butter, beans, and tahini in bowl and microwave for 2-3 minutes until soft and melted. Mix in wheat germ and cereal. Don't cook these balls. Drop mixture by tablespoons onto plate, aluminum foil, or waxed paper. Cover with plastic wrap and refrigerate until firm. Or freeze.

Variations: You can use almond butter or any nut butter in place of some of the peanut butter. In fact these balls are a good way to vary nut butters in your child's diet. The dry ingredients (the germ and cereal) can be mixed half and half or in any proportion as long as they add up to one cup. (Actually, you can use any quantity as long as you can form cohesive balls.) You can substitute part of the dry ingredients with ground oatmeal or ground

whole germ corn flakes. Ground seeds can replace some dry ingredients, too, but remember that ground seeds may get rancid in as soon as a few hours. The balls must be eaten immediately if they contain ground seeds. Make some with the seeds and eat right away and make the rest without and refrigerate or freeze.

ᵃ Cheese Hors d'oeuvres

1 cup grated natural cheese
½-1 cup Super Flour or wheat germ
2 tablespoons olive oil (optional)
water or milk

Mix, adding enough water or milk to make a good consistency. Fry or bake.

Variation: Replace some of the Super Flour with ground nuts or wheat germ.

ᵃ Cream Cheese Hors d'oeuvres

In large bowl, mix thoroughly:
1 8-ounce package of cream cheese, softened for a few seconds in microwave
1 teaspoon vanilla
2 tablespoons nonfat dry milk powder
1 tablespoon frozen orange juice concentrate, thawed

Form into 16 one-inch balls. Place about one cup of wheat germ in shallow ball and roll each ball until covered with the germ. Do not cook these. Keep refrigerated.

ᵃ Tofu Hors d'oeuvres

Drain one silken tofu packet (10½ ounces). Mash with:
½ cup whole wheat breadcrumbs
¼ cup ground nuts
1 tablespoon tamari

Eat uncooked or fry or bake as directed above.

ᵃ Whole Grain Neatballs

1 cup whole grains (rice or bulgur is good)
12 ounces of tofu, soft
½ cup whole grain bread crumbs (page 321)
½ teaspoon kelp powder or salt
1 teaspoon tamari

Mix all ingredients and bake as directed above.

⁂ Dried Fruit Hors d'oeuvres

Chop 1 cup of dried fruit (pears or prunes are good) in processor. Soak in ½ cup frozen juice concentrate overnight in refrigerator to soften. Mix with ¼-½ cup of ground nuts/seeds until you can roll into balls. Don't cook these. If you use ground seeds, eat immediately. I mix a few balls with ground seeds and serve right away. Then I make the rest with ground nuts and refrigerate or freeze.

Variation: Use wheat germ or ground oatmeal for all or part of the ground nuts/seeds.

⁂ Easier Dried Fruit Hors d'oeuvres

Mix ½ cup of finely chopped dried apricots or other dried fruit with 1 cup of peanut butter and ½ cup of chopped nuts/seeds. Don't cook these. Form balls and optionally roll to coat in shredded coconut.

Variation: Add a few tablespoons of wheat germ to the mixture.

⁂ Fresh Fruit Hors d'oeuvres

1 ripe mashed banana, or some
avocado or other mashed fruit
½ cup nuts
2 teaspoons honey
Do not cook. Form into balls and refrigerate or freeze.

⁂ Sweet Potato Hors d'oeuvres

Mix together:
flesh from 2 cooked sweet potatoes
1 beaten egg
2 tablespoons milk
Form balls and roll in
½ cup of whole wheat bread crumbs
(or wheat germ) mixed with
½ teaspoon fresh finely minced
parsley.
Bake or fry, making sure that egg gets thoroughly cooked.

Variation: Use 1 cup canned pumpkin or cooked carrot purée instead of puréed sweet potato.

⁂ Super Green Veggie Hors d'oeuvres

Follow recipe above for Sweet Potato Hors d'oeuvres replacing sweet potatoes with puréed cooked Super Green Veggie.

⁂ Raw Grated Carrot Hors d'oeuvres

Mix finely grated raw carrot with cottage cheese, tofu, or yogurt cheese until good consistency. Form into balls. Do not cook.

Variation: Use raw broccoli instead of carrots, or any other raw vegetable.

⁂ Red Lentil Hors d'oeuvres

Cook 1 cup of split red lentils (or other lentils) to yield 2 cups of cooked lentils. Fry 1 finely chopped onion in about 1 tablespoon butter on stove top until soft. Mix onions to lentils and add ¼ cup wheat germ. Form into balls (will be very sticky) and bake or fry.

Variation: Shape into patties or cutlets instead of balls, and fry. You can also use ground oatmeal instead of wheat germ.

⁂ Latke Hors d'oeuvres

Coarsely grate in food processor 1½ pounds white potatoes and 2 medium onions. Add 2 beaten eggs, ¼ cup wheat germ, ¼ cup fresh chopped parsley. Mixture will be wet. Bake or fry, making sure that egg gets thoroughly cooked.

⁂ Bean Balls

1 cup mashed cooked beans
½ cup ground nuts
whole wheat bread crumbs
Mix 3 ingredients above, using enough crumbs to make a mixture cohesive enough to be rolled into balls. You can cook these, but you don't have to.

heat Germ Balls

1 cup Super Flour
½ cup toasted wheat germ
½ cup vegetable oil
⅓ cup honey
1 beaten egg
1 teaspoon vanilla

Mix all ingredients well and roll into balls. Cover balls with wheat germ by rolling balls in shallow dish with about ½ cup of additional wheat germ. Bake at 350°F for 15 minutes, watching so they don't burn.

Honey Milk Balls

½ cup honey
½ cup creamy peanut butter
1 cup nonfat dry milk powder
1 cup ground rolled oat flakes

Mix all ingredients and shape into balls. Don't cook these.

"I Love You" Hearts

Mash a banana with 1 tablespoon lemon juice to help prevent discoloring and to add flavor. Color with red food coloring (beet juice is good, see page 364). Add enough dry Healthy Extras (ground nuts/seeds, wheat germ) to make a fairly stiff mixture. Divide into several parts and shape into hearts—use cookie cutters to make it easier. Don't cook these. Serve immediately or freeze. Tell your child that they are "I will love you forever, no matter what you do" hearts.

Monster or Cat Eyes

On a circular whole grain cracker, place a round slice of banana, and top with an olive slice.

Egg Burgers or Mini-Balls

3 hard-cooked eggs, mashed
½ cup cooked brown rice or other whole grain
4 tablespoons mayonnaise
1 teaspoon finely diced onion
½ cup whole grain cornflakes, pulverized in blender

Mix first 4 ingredients and shape into 4 burgers or other shapes, or make mini-balls. Roll in cornflakes to coat. Bake in pre-heated 425°F oven on greased cookie sheet for 10-15 minutes until browned. Burger shapes can be served on whole grain buns or bread.

Muffin Man Buffet

Make a meal more fun by serving it to your toddler in a muffin pan: cheese bits in one tin, Cheerios in another, fruit pieces in another, etc. A small drink in another tin gives it some support and makes it less likely to be spilled. A well-washed Styrofoam egg carton also can be used for a small buffet of snacks.

For more Toddler Hors d'oeuvres ideas, see Meatless Patties, page 313.

Fruits

See fruit leather recipes on page 205 and food drying on pages 200-206.

Super Healthy Two-Minute Meal

Mash an avocado and or banana and optionally add a little lemon juice. Add Healthy Extras, like wheat germ, ground nuts/seeds, and mashed beans for a complete meal.

I put this simple recipe here to remind you that as long as you have some Healthy Extras as food staples in your kitchen and bananas on the counter, you've got a very healthy meal that your child will love. Keep "whole grains, beans, nuts, seeds, fruits, and veggies" in mind as a constant reminder to add whole grains, cooked beans, and raw nuts and seeds to your child's food as often as possible.

Banana Pancakes

Mash or purée banana. Shape into small pancakes and dredge in ground nuts/seeds. Serve raw immediately.

Rolled-Up Fruit Snacks

See *Dried Fruit* on page 200 and read until the Fruit Leather recipes on page 206.

Broiled Fruit Wedges

Broil fruit wedges (apples, bananas, pears, pineapple chunks, peaches, orange wedges) under broiler about 5 minutes or until tender. Optionally sprinkle with lemon juice first. Serve plain or with yogurt/fruit topping.

‰ *Banana Sandwiches*

Slice banana in half lengthwise. Spread peanut butter inside and put banana slices (which act as bread slices) together to make a sandwich. These are a little messy, but fun to eat!

Variation: Apple sandwiches can be made with 2 apple slices or 1 cracker spread with peanut butter and topped with an apple slice. Or, instead of peanut butter, use another sandwich spread.

‰ *Broiled Bananas*

Peel banana and cut lengthwise and then horizontally into small pieces. Place on oil-sprayed baking sheet cut side up and sprinkle with cinnamon, nutmeg, and a little honey/brown sugar. Broil until warmed.

‰ *Healthy "Hot Dog"*

Spread one slice of whole grain bread with peanut butter. Place a small whole banana dog on the bread and fold bread up around sides of banana, so that it resembles a hot dog. Paint a face on the banana with extra peanut butter.

Variation: Use tahini or jelly/jam instead of peanut butter.

‰ *Apple Smiley Face*

Grate an apple in the processor. Mix with 1 tablespoon of peanut butter or other nut butter. Optionally add 1 teaspoon honey or maple syrup or blackstrap molasses and a pinch of cinnamon and/or nutmeg. Add Healthy Extras—grated carrots are good. Place on small plate and form into pancake-shaped face. Use Decorative Touches to form eyes, nose, hair, etc.

‰ *Baby Applesauce*

Wash two medium apples and peel, if you wish. Remove seeds and core, and chop. Purée in blender or food processor, adding just enough apple juice or water so that food moves freely. Add a little lemon juice, if you wish, to prevent darkening. Store, tightly covered, in refrigerator for up to one week, or freeze for up to 2 months. This recipe makes about 1 cup. Serve with Healthy Extras. If you wish, you can cook the apples after peeling and slicing and before puréeing. Microwave the apple pieces in covered dish with 1 tablespoon of water or juice for 2 minutes per apple. Pour apple pieces and water/juice into blender to purée—extra liquid will not be necessary.

‰ *Baked Apples*

Wash a few uniformly-sized apples. Remove the cores without cutting through the bottom of the apple. Leaving a little of the core in the bottom will prevent the stuffing from leaking out. Slit the peel in a few spots to prevent wrinkles. Stuff them with plumped raisins or dates, re-hydrated dried apricot pieces, and/or ground nuts or seeds. Optionally add a dash of cinnamon and/or nutmeg. It's not necessary, but add a teaspoon or two of maple syrup or honey if you wish. Press the stuffing firmly into the cored hole with your fingers or the back of a teaspoon. Dot a bit of butter on top of the stuffing, if you like. Place apples in a covered baking pan or dish with a little water or apple juice in the bottom to prevent scorching. If they are wobbly, slice a little off the bottoms to make them flatter and more stable, or place them in a muffin tin for support. Bake at 350°F for about 45 minutes or until tender. Toaster ovens are a nice appliance for baking a few apples. After baking, optionally add a bit of yogurt, whipped cream, or Mock Whipped Cream (page 344), and a dash of cinnamon, or vanilla ice cream on top of the apples. Or while bakes apples are still hot, top with a little honey to be absorbed by the apples—it will not get burned as it would when spread on top before baking.

Tip: Use the small side of a melon baller for easier apple coring.

Tip: Bake apples in muffin tins. Fill tins with a little apple juice or water first.

Tip: Bake apples in aluminum foil shaped into cups. Place foil cups in baking pan with water. Cups are disposable for picnics, etc.

❧ Microwave Baked Apples

Prepare and stuff apples as stated above. Prick the apples with a fork around the middle to prevent bursting. Cover and microwave on high for about 1½ minutes per apple (2 minutes if you are baking only one apple). Baste halfway through cooking time. If you have no turntable, turn apples once halfway through cooking time.

❧ Baked Stuffed Apples

These are very similar to baked apples, except instead of just removing the core of the apple, you also remove most of the fruit inside. In other words, hollow out the apple as much as possible with a spoon or a melon baller. Leave enough inside the apple so that it won't collapse—about ½ inch walls. First, cut a ½ inch slice horizontally off the top, so that you have access to the innards. Purée the apple pulp in your processor with ⅓ cup of tofu for each apple. Place mixture in bowl and add for each apple: 1 tablespoon of shredded mozzarella cheese, about ½ dozen raisins, and 2 tablespoons of cooked millet or other grain. Add just a pinch of cinnamon and nutmeg. Spoon mixture into apples and cover with apple tops. Cook same as Baked Apples above.

❧ Applesauce Custard

Preheat oven to 350°F. In blender, mix until smooth:
1 cup applesauce
½ cup pears or other puréed fruit or a four-ounce jar of commercial baby fruit (or more applesauce)
1 cup low-fat milk
4 beaten eggs
½ teaspoon cinnamon
Place in individual custard cups and top with a pinch of cinnamon. Set cups into shallow baking pan filled with hot water so it comes up 1 inch on sides of cups. Bake 50 minutes or until cake tester or toothpick comes out clean. Refrigerate, covered well, and eat within 2-3 days. Serve cool.

❧ Stuffed Peach Halves

Slice ripe peach in half and remove pit. Stuff with mixture of:
1 tablespoon peanut butter
1 tablespoon tahini
1 teaspoon maple syrup
2 drops vanilla
Variation: Use an apricot or a nectarine instead of peach.

❧ Dried Peach Millet Pudding

In processor, grind
1 cup dried peaches (or other dried fruit) into a powder.
In a baking dish, mix peaches with
4 cups milk
½ cup uncooked millet
¼ cup honey
Bake, uncovered for 2½ hours in preheated 325°F oven, stirring occasionally. Refrigerate and pudding will thicken as it cools.

❧ Strawberry Pizza

Preheat oven to 350°F.
For crust: Mix
½ cup wheat germ
½ cup ground oatmeal
1 beaten egg
1 tablespoon melted butter or oil
Press into bottom of a 9-inch pie plate; don't go up the sides. Bake crust for 10 minutes.
For filling: Mix
½ cup of yogurt cheese (or cottage cheese)
1 tablespoon of orange juice or other fruit concentrate.
Spread filling on crust.
For topping: Arrange fresh strawberries over filling into a design or shape or letter. Cut with pizza cutter. Keep refrigerated or freeze.
Variation: Replace strawberries with other fruit or use a mixture of fresh fruit.

❧ Melon Yogurt Bowls

Wash uncut whole cantaloupe (or honeydew or papaya). Cut cantaloupe in half (lengthwise or width-wise) and reserve the rind shells for later use as bowls. Scoop out seeds. Use melon baller to scoop out balls. Place melon balls into shell bowls with ¼ to

½ cup plain yogurt for each bowl. Sprinkle ground nuts on top. Serve immediately for maximum nutrients. Kids will love the natural bowls. If the bowls are rolling around and unstable, slice a little piece off the bottom to make it flatter. On picnics, bowls are also disposable.

⅜ *Pineapple Tubbie or Sailing Ship*

Like melon rinds, the pineapple shell makes a great natural bowl. We pretend it's a bathtub and the fruit purée is the bubble bath water. Put little plastic toy people or other cartoon characters in the tub and pretend they're bathing. To make the tubbie, wash and slice the pineapple in half lengthwise. You can leave its stem sticking out at one end or cut off the stem and stick it into the tubbie. (Your child will come up with some explanation for what the stem is.) Remove the flesh with sharp knife, leaving ¼ inch wall and floor. Be careful not to cut through the bottom of the shell. Discard the hard core part and use the tender flesh to make the fruit purée or diced fruit. Add other fruits to the tubbie if you wish.

⅜ *Canoes for Riding the Rapids*

Wash a banana well, that is, wash the peel of a banana. A slightly curved, shorter banana is good for this recipe. Make a vertical slit down one side of the unpeeled banana leaving about ½ inch uncut at each end. If the banana is curved, make the slit on the "upside" so that it's shaped like a canoe. Open slit and carefully scoop out the flesh. Fork-mash ½ of the banana and mix with ½ cup of mashed tofu, 2 tablespoons of ground seeds, 1 tablespoon of wheat germ, and honey to taste. Spread banana peel open gently and make bottom of canoe flat by pressing with fingers so that it will be stable, being careful not to rip ends. Return mixture to inside of banana. You can trim around the slit with a sharp knife to make the opening wider. Use the other half of the banana flesh to shape fish and rocks, roll in wheat germ, and place them around the canoe. These dangerous rocks must be avoided to prevent the canoe from breaking apart. Make oars out of carrot or celery sticks or anything else handy. Place small plastic toy figures (large enough not to be swallowed or choked on) in canoe or make your own out of Decorative Touches.

⅜ *Submarines Exploring the Deep*

Make the canoes in the last recipe, but close the slit after stuffing. You'll have to use a little less filling. Place a piece of banana on the top middle of the submarine as its periscope, and add a banana piece shaped like a propeller to the back. Leftover banana pieces can be fish, sharks, turtles, and octopuses. No need for missiles, because this is a peaceful voyage.

⅜ *Cold Fresh Fruit Purée Soup*

In a blender or food processor, purée fresh juicy fruits, such as cantaloupes, peaches, watermelon, kiwis, or honeydew. Put them in the freezer for ½ hour to make them really cold. Add a touch of lemon or lime juice. This soup can be served in natural melon rind bowls.

Variation: Add one tablespoon of plain yogurt for each ½ cup of "soup." Add Healthy Extras.

⅜ *Kiwi Health Cereal*

Dice or mash a kiwi with fork. Add cottage cheese, wheat germ, and a little honey or maple syrup. Add a pinch or two of brewer's yeast (whose bitter flavor will be hidden by the sweetness of the kiwi and honey) for an extra nutritional punch. The vitamin C in the kiwi works well with the calcium in the cottage cheese and the iron in the wheat germ. Instead of kiwi, you can use banana; instead of cottage cheese, you can use yogurt or yogurt cheese. Banana adds iron, but not much vitamin C, so serve with orange juice or some other high vitamin C juice.

❧ *Melon Baskets*

Carve a watermelon, cantaloupe, or other melon into a basket with a handle. Fill with melon balls, grapes, and other fresh fruit pieces.

Variation: Instead of a basket, design a whale out of a watermelon.

❧ *Dolphins in the Ocean Blue (Blueberry Bake)*

Grease a 2-quart casserole. In a large bowl, mix
  4 cups of blueberries
  2½ tablespoons arrowroot
  1 tablespoon lemon juice
Pour fruit mixture into casserole. In a large bowl, mix:
  1 cup Super Flour
  1 teaspoon baking powder
  1 tablespoon butter or oil
  1 cup milk
Pour over fruit mixture. Bake in pre-heated 400°F oven for 50 minutes until nicely browned.
Serve with yogurt topping: 1 cup yogurt mixed in blender with 2 tablespoons honey or maple syrup and enough blueberries to make the yogurt an ocean blue color. Place a small toy ship and/or dolphin on top or use blueberries or other Decorative Touches to draw them.

Variation: Instead of dolphins, let there be sharks. Stick triangular-shaped Decorative Touches into the topping to simulate shark fins, for a Jaws-like effect. Or for a more tame depiction of fish in water, use deep-yellow or orange veggie pieces to make goldfish in a pretty blue aquarium. Green veggies can be ocean turtles or seaweed. Or buy those commercial fish cracker snacks.

Variations for topping: Instead of blueberries, use strawberries and make a pinkish-red topping for a Valentine Cake. On top, make a heart-shape with strawberry halves for your special Valentine. Or you can make this any day as an "I Love You"

cake. Blueberries and strawberries mashed together make purple, like the color of imaginary dinosaurs.

❧ *Apple Crisp*

Preheat oven to 350°F. Blend using pastry blender or fork until flaky:
  ¾ cup Super Flour
  ½ cup brown sugar
  ½ teaspoon cinnamon
  4-6 tablespoons butter
Arrange 4 cups of peeled, cored, and sliced apples in an 8-inch square baking dish. Sprinkle mixture over apples. Bake for 60-90 minutes until apples are tender.

❧ *Avocado Cube Salad*

Cut small cubes of avocado and/or banana and/or tofu. Drizzle with a little lemon juice and honey (about 1 tablespoon per cup of cubes). My kids loved this as an outdoors summer afternoon snack.

❧ *Cucumbers and Yogurt*

Mix 1 tablespoon lemon juice into plain yogurt. Add sliced or diced cucumbers. Add Healthy Extras. Or use sliced cucumbers for dipping into yogurt mixture.

❧ *Easy Fruit Pastries*

Cream together 3 tablespoons melted butter, ¼ cup tofu, and ½ cup Super Flour. Chill dough in refrigerator until firm. Roll between waxed paper (see dough tip on page 332), making a 12x12 inch square. Cut dough into 16 squares. Place 1 teaspoon of fruit purée or jam in center of each square. Pull up the 4 corners of each square over the center and crimp edges together, encasing the fruit and forming an X. Bake in preheated 325°F oven for 18-20 minutes until edges become slightly browned.

Vegetables

◆ Frosty the Potato Man/Woman

Place two or three circular globs of mashed potatoes on a plate. Use a spoon or ice cream scoop to shape like a snowman. Use Decorative Touches to add a hat or hair, eyes, nose, mouth, buttons, scarf, and arms.

◆ Mr./Ms. Sweet Potato Heads

Slice 2 cooked sweet potatoes in half. Scoop out flesh, being careful to keep skin intact to be used as a bowl later. Mash flesh and mix with
    2 tablespoons yogurt
    1 tablespoon maple syrup or honey
    2 tablespoons orange juice
Replace mashed potato mixture into reserved skin bowls. Use Decorative Touches to make eyes, nose, mouth, hair, etc. Serve to children. For adults, you may have to reheat in oven or microwave.
Variation: Make mashed potato mixture by mixing flesh from the sweet potatoes with ¼-½ cup of puréed pineapple chunks.

◆ Super Potato Porridge

    1 raw potato, shredded in processor
    1 cup boiling water
    2 tablespoons fresh parsley (optional)
    1 tablespoon melted butter (optional)
Sprinkle shredded potato into boiling water, cover, and let sit 5-10 minutes. Add parsley and melted butter.

◆ Eggplant Pizza

Preheat oven to 350°F. Slice a small eggplant into thin (¼-inch) slices. Place slices on cookie sheet and cover with tomato sauce or pizza sauce and top with shredded cheese. Add other toppings if you wish. Bake 15-20 minutes until cheese is melted and lightly browned. Use spatula to place on serving dish.

◆ Tasty Eggplant Slices

Preheat oven to 450°F. Slice eggplant into ½-inch thick slices. Spread with tofu mayonnaise from the natural foods store. Sprinkle with wheat germ or whole grain bread crumbs, grated Parmesan cheese, and oregano. Bake on cookie sheet for 15 minutes.

◆ Cabbage Coleslaw

Shred some raw cabbage. For each cup of shredded cabbage, add:
    ⅓ cup of mayonnaise
    1 teaspoon lemon juice
    ½-1 teaspoon honey or maple syrup
    ½ teaspoon apple cider vinegar

◆ "Creamed" Cabbage

Finely shred 2 cups of raw cabbage (about ¼ of a small head). Cook, covered, in a pan over medium heat with 1 teaspoon of water and 1 tablespoon butter for 4-5 minutes until tender (or in microwave for 2-3 minutes). Remove from heat, stir in 3 tablespoons yogurt or yogurt cheese, cottage cheese, or sour cream and serve. Sprinkle with fresh parsley.

◆ Pineapple Flavored Cabbage

Over low heat in covered pan, cook sliced cabbage in pineapple juice (about ½ cup juice per half head of cabbage) until tender. Optionally add a tablespoon of butter or olive oil for more flavor.

◆ Carrot Salad

Shred a cup of raw carrot in the processor. Mix in 2 teaspoons lemon juice or orange juice and 2 tablespoons yogurt cheese or cream cheese. Add Healthy Extras.

◆ Zucchini Salad

Substitute shredded raw zucchini for carrot in the Carrot Salad recipe.

◆ Zucchini Cheese Slices

Place Swiss (or other natural) cheese on top of zucchini slices and slip under the broiler until cheese has melted.

ﾞﾟ *Zucchini Lasagna*

Preheat oven to 350°F. Cut a zucchini lengthwise into lasagna-size strips about ½ inch thick. Layer in baking dish with spaghetti sauce and cheeses. Bake uncovered for about 25 minutes.

ﾞﾟ *Acorn Squash Bowls*

Bake squash (see page 461). Scoop out flesh, being careful to keep rind intact. Add a tablespoon or two of orange juice, maple syrup, or honey into mashed flesh. Return mashed squash to acorn bowls. Add Healthy Extras.

ﾞﾟ *French Fries-Not!*

Don't deep fry potatoes in all that oil. Bake them instead. Pre-heat oven to 425°F. Cut up potatoes into uniform-sized quarters, eighths, French-fry shapes or 1/4-inch slices. You can peel them if you wish, but it's better to leave the peels intact because they contain many nutrients. Place the cut-up potatoes in a bowl and toss them with melted butter or olive oil. Use only one teaspoon of melted butter per potato. Spread buttered cut-up potatoes on a cookie sheet sprayed with non-stick cooking spray. (For slices, it's easier to spread melted butter onto baking sheet and coat each side with butter.) Bake for 20 minutes or more or until browned on all sides, turning and flipping for uniform cooking. If you wish, during last few minutes of cooking, turn on broiler and let potatoes broil for about 3 minutes, until light golden brown. Flip the chips and broil the other side. Optionally, sprinkle lightly with powdered kelp. Serve while still hot.

Variation: Use sweet potatoes instead of white potatoes.

ﾞﾟ *Whole Grain "Shake and Cook" Potato Coating*

Preheat oven to 350°F. Mix in bowl:
  3 tablespoons Super Flour
  1 tablespoon wheat germ
  ½ cup whole wheat bread crumbs
  2 teaspoons sugar
  1 teaspoon salt
  1 teaspoon Italian seasoning
  1 tablespoon olive oil

In plastic freezer bag, shake mixture with potatoes cut into ½-inch chunks. Place coated potato chunks on oiled baking sheet and bake for 30 minutes until brown. Store leftover mix in airtight container in refrigerator.

Read the tips about baking potatoes on page 302.

ﾞﾟ *Potato Skins*

From leftover baked potatoes, remove flesh. Brush olive oil on skins, cut into ½-inch strips, and sprinkle with a little salt, pepper, and optionally chili powder. Bake for 10 minutes at 400°F until crisp. Eat as snacks or crumpled over salads.

ﾞﾟ *Baked Potato Cubes*

Cube leftover baked potatoes into ½-inch cubes (leave skins on), toss in plastic bag with olive oil and herbs. Bake uncovered, flipping once or twice, at 425°F for about 45 minutes until crisp and golden brown.

ﾞﾟ *At-the-Ready Frozen Baked Potatoes*

Cut leftover baked potatoes in half. Scoop out flesh and mix with cheese, yogurt, chives, parsley, etc. Freeze using the Tray-Freeze Method. Check out the prices for these commercial flavored baked potatoes in the freezer section of the supermarket!

ﾞﾟ *Healthy Potato Chips*

Slice well-washed, unpeeled potato (about 1 pound) very thin using your processor or by hand. Spread one layer thin on a large buttered or oil-sprayed cookie sheet. Brush tops with oil. Bake in pre-heated 450°F oven for 8-10 minutes until lightly browned. Turn cookie sheet halfway through cooking for more even browning. Shake potato chips, while still warm, in paper lunch bag with 2 tablespoons of seasoning. Store in cool, dry place in plastic zipper bag.

❧ *Potato Pancakes*

Chop 2 raw medium potatoes and 1 small onion in your food processor. In bowl, beat 2 eggs. Place a lightly buttered or oil-sprayed frying pan over medium heat. Mix potatoes and onions into eggs and add 1 tablespoon of Super Flour into which ¼ teaspoon of baking powder was mixed. Use a quarter cup measuring cup or a tablespoon to spoon onto lightly greased pan over medium heat. Flatten with spatula. Cook 3 minutes on each side until lightly browned. Drain on paper towels. Serve with sour cream or yogurt cheese.

Drain tip: Rip up brown paper bags from the supermarket and place under paper towels as bottom layers for draining grease. Saves money on paper towels.

❧ *Sweet Potato Pancakes*

Make potato pancakes as in previous recipe, but use sweet potatoes instead. Serve with yogurt and/or applesauce.

❧ *Sunny Sweet Potato Cups*

Bake or microwave cook a sweet potato (page 463). Meanwhile, wash one whole orange. Slice in half and remove flesh, being careful to keep rinds intact to be used as bowls later. Purée cooked sweet potato and mix with 3 tablespoons orange juice squeezed from orange flesh. Spoon into reserved orange rind bowls. Use Decorative Touches to draw smiley face or other design on top.

❧ *Sweet Potato Salad*

> 4 large sweet potatoes, cooked and diced
> 1 onion, finely chopped
> ½ cup finely chopped celery
> 2 hard boiled eggs, sliced
> ½ cup mayonnaise (tofu mayo is good)

Mix together and refrigerate. Serve cold.

❧ *Pennies for Your Thoughts (Parsleyed Carrots)*

Toss 1 pound sliced, cooked carrots with
1-2 tablespoons butter
1 tablespoon lemon juice

2 tablespoons finely chopped fresh parsley

Play the game "A Penny for Your Thoughts" with your child. Every time your child eats a carrot slice—a penny, you have to tell him one of your thoughts: I think you're great! I'll always love you! What a lucky Mom/Dad I am to have a daughter/son like you! And every time you eat a penny, your child has to tell you her thought.

❧ *A-C-E-G All Children Eat Grass*

Cook greens according to one of the methods below. Place on a plate and pretend they are a green field of grass on a farm. Add little toy farm animals. Your toddler will love to pretend he's a cow eating the grass. But make sure you make it clear to him that he's not to eat the grass in the back yard!

Cooking Method 1: Thaw two or three green veggie cubes. Sauté over medium heat 2-3 tablespoons chopped onion and 2-3 tablespoons walnuts in 1 teaspoon olive oil or butter until soft. Toss sautéed onions and walnuts with cooked greens. Sprinkle with 1 tablespoon lemon juice and serve immediately.

Cooking Method 2: Thaw two or three green veggie cubes. Sauté ⅓ cup chopped onion in 1 teaspoon olive oil over medium heat until soft. Add ⅓ cup of sliced fresh mushrooms and sauté 2 minutes more. Decrease to low heat and add greens. Cook, covered for 2-3 minutes. Stir frequently and watch for burning. Add 1 tablespoon of Dijon mustard and cook and stir for 2 minutes more. Serve immediately.

Variation: An adult golf enthusiast can pretend with your toddler that they're enjoying a round of golf.

❧ *Spinach Loaf*

Preheat oven to 350°F. Combine:
> 2 cups cooked frozen chopped spinach
> one recipe white sauce (see page 334)
> 2 beaten eggs
> 1 sauteed onion, optional
> ½ to ¾ cup shredded cheese, optional

Pour into buttered casserole and bake 35-40 minutes until inserted knife comes out clean.

❧ Stuffed Froggies

Stuff half of a green pepper with Super Porridge or any Super Sandwich Spreads. Place upside down on a plate. Add eyes using a green olive sliced in half, legs shaped from the other half of the green pepper, and warts! Warts can be flax seeds or brown rice grains or any other small food pieces. If eyes and warts won't stick to the green pepper, wet the pepper with water or honey before sticking.

❧ Cream of Broccoli Soup

    2 cups milk
    1 cup chopped raw broccoli
    1 tablespoon butter
    1 cup vegetable stock or water
Blend in blender until smooth. In saucepan, bring to boil. Cover and cook over medium heat for 20 minutes, stirring frequently.

❧ Veggie Custard

Preheat oven to 350°F. Mix until very smooth by hand or in blender;
    4 egg yolks or 2 whole eggs
    ½ cup soy or cow's milk
    4 veggie cubes—thawed or ½ cup puréed vegetables
Place in four individual custard cups. Set cups into shallow baking pan filled with hot water so it comes up 1 inch on sides of cups. Bake 50 minutes or until cake tester or toothpick comes out clean. Refrigerate, covered well, and eat within 2-3 days. Serve cool.

❧ Veggie Marinade

In a small saucepan over low heat, mix in this order:
    ⅓ cup apple cider vinegar
    2 cloves crushed garlic
    1 teaspoon dried herbs or 1 tablespoon fresh (parsley, basil, dill, etc.)
    ½ cup olive oil
Let simmer very gently for 5 minutes. Remove from heat and set aside to steep. Meanwhile, lightly steam one pound veggies: broccoli, cauliflower, carrots, etc. Place in bowl or large freezer bag and mix with marinade. Marinate in refrigerator for at least an hour (overnight is good). Mix occasionally. Will keep for up to one week in the refrigerator.

Tip: Marinate foods in a plastic bag and turn often and you will need about half the marinade. Always marinate in the refrigerator, and never at room temperature to prevent bacterial growth.

Variation: Add some bite-sized tofu chunks or cooked chick peas and other large beans and let marinate with the veggies.

❧ Economical Vegetable Stock

Don't throw away the peelings from vegetables. Accumulate them in a freezer bag until you have enough to make a stock.

Sprouts

❧ Sweet and Sour Sprouts

Measure 1 cup of sprouts. Cook them by steaming over boiling water. The larger and thicker the sprout, the longer the steaming time. Steam slender sprouts, like alfalfa and radish, for only a minute or two; steam mung sprouts for about 3 minutes; and steam sprouts from large beans (soybeans, garbanzos, etc.) for 10-15 minutes to disable the enzymes. Meanwhile, mix together
    1 tablespoon olive oil
    1 tablespoon honey or maple syrup
    2 tablespoons apple cider vinegar
Pour mixture over steamed sprouts and mix well. Store in refrigerator for up to 3 days.

❧ Sprout Salad

Mix sprouts with grated carrots. Add mayonnaise, raisins, nuts, or any Healthy Extras.

❧ Sprout Omelette

For each egg, add about ½ tablespoon of milk. Cook until almost set, and then add sprouts—⅓-½ cup of coarsely-chopped raw sunflower seed sprouts per egg. Fold omelette in half encasing sprouts. Cook thoroughly so that no egg is left raw.

Variation: Add chopped raw, fresh tomatoes with the sprouts. Add grated or shredded natural cheese.

❧ Sprout Soup

For nutrition and flavor, add sprouts to homemade or canned soups.

Yogurt

❧ Yummy Yogurt

Don't buy the flavored commercial yogurts—they are too expensive and contain too much sugar. Flavor yogurt yourself by adding any of the flavorings suggestions in the box on page 255. For extra nutrition, add Healthy Extras, especially freshly ground nuts/seeds and eat immediately.

❧ Apple Cinnamon Yogurt

Add to 1 cup yogurt:
  ½ cup applesauce
  ¼ teaspoon cinnamon
  ½ teaspoon vanilla.

❧ Peanut Butter and Jelly Yogurt

Soften 2 tablespoons of creamy peanut butter for a few seconds in the microwave. Mix softened peanut butter and 2 tablespoons jelly into 1 tablespoon of milk to make it liquidy. Gently fold into plain yogurt.

Tofu

Tip: Tofu can be used in addition to or instead of cheese/eggs on pizza, in sandwiches, in omelettes, and in pasta dishes.

❧ Tofu Fingers

Preheat oven to 350°F. Slice tofu into strips. Dip into melted butter, milk, or water. Dip into and cover with a mixture of whole grain bread crumbs (page 321), wheat germ, Parmesan cheese, oregano, onion powder, and/or garlic powder. Bake on ungreased cookie sheet for 15-20 minutes, turning once. Or cook in microwave until heated through.

❧ Tofu McNuggets

Make previous Tofu Fingers recipe, except cut tofu into chunks or cubes instead of strips.

❧ Veggie Tofu

Mash together:
  2 tablespoons tofu
  1 thawed frozen veggie cube
  or 2 tablespoons mashed cooked veggie
Sprinkle on top:
  1 tablespoon shredded cheese (cheddar is good)
Microwave for 30-60 seconds until cheese melts or place under broiler to melt cheese.

❧ Cherry Tofu Cream

Mix 2 parts silken tofu with 1 part frozen cherries. Mix in blender with a little lemon juice.

❧ Maple Tofu Cream

Mix 4 parts silken tofu with 1 part maple syrup or honey. Mix in blender with a little lemon juice.

❧ Yummy Tofu

Most of the flavor suggestions for yogurt can also be used to flavor tofu. See box on page 255. Use silken tofu for a creamy smooth mixture. With tofu you do not have to be gentle when stirring. For extra nutrition, add Healthy Extras, especially freshly ground nuts/seeds and eat immediately.

❧ No-Cook Tofu Pudding

In blender or processor, mix until smooth:
  ¼ cup soy or cow's milk
  1 cup tofu
  2 tablespoons lemon juice
  1 teaspoon honey or other sweetener or to taste
  ⅛ teaspoon vanilla
Pour into bowl or individual containers, cover well, and refrigerate. Use within a day or two.

❧ Peanut Butter and Jelly Tofu

Make recipe for Peanut Butter and Jelly Yogurt on page 305 with tofu instead of yogurt.

❧ No-Bake Tahini Tofu Custard

1 10-ounce box tofu
¼ cup ground almonds
¼ cup tahini
¼ cup honey or maple syrup
1 teaspoon almond extract
Mix all in blender. Serve chilled.

❧ No-Bake Sweet Potato Tofu Pudding

½ cup cooked puréed sweet potatoes or thawed food cubes
2 cups silken tofu
1 teaspoon vanilla
½ teaspoon cinnamon
½ cup honey or maple syrup
Mix all in blender. Sprinkle with ½ cup ground almonds. Serve chilled. (To make a smaller amount, use 1 part sweet potato to 4 parts tofu and add the other ingredients to taste.)

❧ Scrambled Tofu

Mix about two tablespoons of mashed tofu with a ¼ teaspoon tamari/soy sauce. Optionally add an egg yolk or whole egg (the white part of the egg will help bind together). Mix together and fry in 1½-2 teaspoons of butter or oil.

❧ Fried Tofu

Slice a block (or part of a block) of tofu into rectangular slices. Press dry between clean towels. Dip in tamari/soy sauce or brush with a thin layer of Vegemite® (ask for it at your natural foods store). Fry slices in a thin layer of butter until brown. Optionally sprinkle with fresh parsley or oregano while frying.
Variations: Press tofu slices between clean towels and brown on both sides by frying in a mixture half honey and half butter/oil or in a mixture of butter/oil, honey, tamari/soy sauce, and a little ginger.
Note: Serve fried tofu alone or in sandwiches as you would a hamburger. Fried tofu can be stacked between layers of wax paper and frozen in a plastic freezer bag.

❧ Fried Tofu with Sauce

Make tofu sauce by heating
½ cup tamari/soy sauce
3 tablespoons honey
1 tablespoon fresh ginger
in saucepan and cooking over medium heat for 5-10 minutes until warmed through. Meanwhile, slice a block of tofu into 8 rectangular slices. Dredge in whole wheat bread crumbs to coat. Brown on both sides by frying in butter/oil. Pour sauce over fried tofu.

❧ Oven-Barbecued Tofu

Slice a pound of tofu into about 8 slices. Butter a lasagna (9x13) pan. Bake slices for 10-15 minutes. Flip and bake other side for 10 more minutes. Brush tops of tofu with barbecue sauce and bake 7-10 more minutes. Serve on whole wheat hamburger buns. You can also barbecue them on your outdoor grill instead of in the oven.

❧ Tofu-Carrot Salad

Grate a medium carrot. Add ½ cup or more mashed tofu and a tablespoon of lemon juice.

❧ Tofu Cheesecake

Preheat oven to 350°F. Mix ⅔ cup wheat germ with ⅓ cup ground nuts and press into a greased 9-inch pie plate to form the crust. In a small saucepan over medium-high heat, mix 3 ounces of agar (page 275) or unflavored gelatin with a 6-ounce container of fruit juice concentrate, such as orange juice or lemonade. Pour juice mixture into blender or food processor. Add:
1 pound tofu
1 tablespoon vanilla
¼ cup Super Flour
and blend until smooth. Pour into prepared pie shell and bake 25 minutes.
Variation: Make personal-sized cakes by lining individual muffin tins with cupcake liners. Press crust into each liner ⅔ up the sides. Pour tofu mixture into crusts and bake for 20-25 minutes. These freeze well.

❧ *Apple Tofu Custard*

Preheat oven to 350°F.
   1¾ cups applesauce
   1 10-ounce box silken tofu
   4 eggs
   1 teaspoon cinnamon
Mix all ingredients in blender. Pour into 4 or 5 custard cups. Sprinkle a little cinnamon on top of each cup. Place the cups into a baking pan filled with water 1 inch deep. Bake 45-50 minutes, until inserted toothpick comes out clean. Refrigerate, covered well, and eat within 2-3 days. Serve cool.
Variation: Replace ½ cup of the applesauce with a 4-ounce jar of baby peaches or apricots.

❧ *Hawaiian Tofu Stir Fry*

Cut a block of tofu into ½ inch cubes. Sprinkle with ¼ cup tamari/soy sauce. Drain and reserve juice from 1 can pineapple chunks. Cut 1 green and 1 sweet red pepper into triangle, square, and other shapes. Cut 1 onion into small wedges. Drain a small can of sliced water chestnuts.

In a small saucepan, whisk together ¼ cup apple cider vinegar and 2 tablespoons arrowroot or cornstarch, then mix in ¼ cup honey, ½ cup vegetable stock, and the reserved pineapple juice. Cook over medium heat until clear and bubbly while whisking continuously.

In large fry pan or wok, melt 4 tablespoons butter/oil on medium-high heat. Cook onion wedges for 2 minutes, then add tofu and cook for 1-2 minutes more. Add rest of ingredients, sauce last, and stir until heated through. Serve over cooked whole grains.

Eggs

See tips about eggs on page 269.

❧ *Monster or Cat Eyes Stuffed Eggs*

Slice 2 hard cooked eggs in half. Remove yolks and use a fork to mix yolks with
   ¼ teaspoon fresh minced parsley
   ¼ teaspoon apple cider vinegar
   ½ teaspoon prepared mustard
   2 tablespoons tofu mayonnaise
Stuff egg whites. Place olives in the middle of yolk mixture for irises of eyes. To stop eggs from rolling around, slice a bit of egg white off the bottom to flatten and make more stable. These "eyes" now look up at you!
Tip: Use a cake decorator to stuff eggs using pretty designs. Or mix stuffing for eggs directly in a freezer bag, remove air and zip bag shut, clip a corner, and squeeze stuffing into egg whites.

❧ *Sailboats*

Use recipe for stuffed eggs above and place small triangular cuts of cheese slices for sails.
Variation: Use a wedge of pie instead of a stuffed egg for the boat.

❧ *Egg McHeathy Muffin*

Preheat oven to 450°F. For each muffin, split a whole grain English muffin and place cut side up on a aluminum foil-covered and oil-sprayed baking sheet. For each muffin, beat together in a bowl:
   1 egg
   2 tablespoons of shredded cheese (cheddar is good)
   a little parsley, oregano, basil, or other fresh herbs or use ¼ teaspoon dried herbs for each muffin
   a pinch of powdered kelp or salt
   a pinch pepper

❧ *Green Eggs and No Ham*

Explain to your toddler that we don't eat Wilbur from Charlotte's Web. Scramble an egg with broccoli, kale, or other green veggie purée. Or use a well-drained thawed food cube. To thicken, add Healthy Extras with the consistency of powder, such as ground oats, wheat germ, or a pinch of brewer's yeast.

Tip: A drop or two of blue food coloring added to the yellow of an egg yolk will make green eggs.

❧ Eggs Florentine or Another Green Eggs and No Ham

Make a nest with a food cube or two of Super Green Veggies. Warm in microwave. Scramble an egg (solid through with no raw liquid) put it in the nest. Top with a sprinkle of fresh parsley and some cheese.

❧ Baked Egg Custard

> 4 eggs, well beaten
> ¼ cup maple syrup
> 1 teaspoon vanilla
> 2 cups milk

Mix first 3 ingredients. Heat the milk until it just boils and remove from heat. Pour hot milk slowly into other 3 ingredients, beating with whisk. Transfer to 6 well-buttered custard cups. Set the cups into a shallow pan of hot water approx 1 inch deep . Bake in pre-heated 325°F oven 45 minutes until inserted toothpick comes out clean and custard is set. Refrigerate, well covered, and serve cool. Eat within 2-3 days. Top with Mock Whipped Cream (page 344).

❧ Vanilla Custard

Preheat oven to 325°F. Combine:
> ⅔ cup nonfat dry milk powder
> 2 cup water

Then add:
> ⅓ cup honey
> 2 beaten eggs or 4 egg yolks
> 1¼ teaspoon vanilla

Pour into four custard cups set in a shallow pan of hot water 1 inch deep. Bake 50 minutes or until toothpick or knife comes out clean. Refrigerate, covered well, and eat within 2-3 days. Serve cool.

❧ Pumpkin Custard

Preheat oven to 350°F. Combine:
> 1½ cups pumpkin purée or canned pumpkin or sweet potato purée
> ½ cup honey
> 3 beaten eggs

> 1⅓ cups milk
> 1 tablespoon arrowroot or cornstarch
> 1 teaspoon cinnamon
> ½ teaspoon ginger
> ¼ teaspoon ground cloves
> ¼ teaspoon ground nutmeg

Pour into greased baking dish and bake for 45-50 minutes or until set. Refrigerate, covered well, and eat within 2-3 days. Serve cool.

Jack-O-Lantern: Use a circular baking dish and draw triangular eyes, nose, mouth, and stem with green-colored cream cheese or yogurt cheese.

❧ French Toast Sticks

Beat together:
> 2 eggs
> ½ cup apple juice OR milk
> ½ teaspoon vanilla

Pour mixture on small cookie sheet. Tear 2-3 slices of whole grain bread into pieces or sticks. Place the pieces in the mixture and wait until they completely soak up the liquid. Cook thoroughly on stove top in a greased or oil-sprayed pan so that none of the egg remains raw. Serve immediately with one of the Pancake Syrup Ideas toppings.

Variation: Instead of just tearing the bread into sticks, use cookie cutters to cut shapes out of whole grain bread.

❧ Banana French Toast

Mix one over-ripe banana with 2 eggs and ¾ teaspoon cinnamon. Add some milk if too thick. Use for French toast.

❧ Baked French Toast

Instead of cooking French toast on the stove top, bake in a preheated 450°F oven on a baking sheet. Place dipped bread on sheet and bake for about 8 minutes. Flip and bake for another 8-10 minutes until all egg has been thoroughly cooked through and no raw egg remains.

❧ Artistic Eggs

Plain scrambled eggs are unexciting. Use a baster or a clean squirt bottle to make designs for your toddler. The trick to prevent running is to let the liquidy egg mixture very slowly out of the baster and then wait until it starts to solidify. For your toddler, one egg mixed with a tablespoon of milk or apple juice is enough.

❧ Eggie in the Middle

Take a piece of whole wheat toast and cut a circle out of the middle with the rim of a can. Place it in a greased or spray-oiled non-stick fry pan. Take a spatula and flatten the bread down, especially at the rim edge of the circle. Pour a scrambled egg into its middle. The egg won't run into the bread if you firmed up the rim of the circle with the spatula. Flip the bread and egg with the spatula to cook the other side. I sometimes have trouble doing that, so I remove the bread and just flip the egg. You can use Decorative Touches to make a smiley face or other design on the egg.

Grains and Cereals

See ideas for leftover grains on page 223.

❧ Banana Super Porridge

Add a mashed banana into Super Porridge.

❧ Oatmeal Pudding

Cook oatmeal in milk instead of water. Add a little vanilla and sweetener to taste. Tastes like pudding!

❧ Oatmeal and Apples

Add 1 shredded apple to cooked oatmeal. Optionally add a teaspoon of maple syrup or other sweetener and a ¼ teaspoon of cinnamon.

❧ Hodgepodge Skillet Meal

Into a large skillet, stir in one food from each of the following four groups:

- Group 1. One cup of raw whole grain (rice, millet, etc) or pasta.
- Group 2. A can of soup (cream of potato, cream of mushroom, tomato soup, etc.) mixed with 1½ cans of milk or water.
- Group 3. ½ cup cooked beans or eggs
- Group 4. 2 cups cooked or raw veggies

Bring to a boil, reduce heat to low, cover pan, and simmer 30-45 minutes until grains are done. Stir occasionally. Optionally add ½-1 cup of cheese or tofu.

❧ Overnight Oatmeal

For the creamiest, most delicious oatmeal for breakfast, mix in a saucepan or microwave-able bowl:

1 cup oatmeal
1½ cups milk
¼ cup apple juice

Let sit overnight in the refrigerator. In the morning, it takes only a few minutes to warm and it is luscious! Optionally add fresh apple pieces for extra flavor and texture. And always consider adding Healthy Extras.

❧ Whole Grain Crockpot Breakfast

Before going to bed, mix together in crockpot:

2 cups whole grain (1 cup brown rice and 1 cup barley go well together)
2 peeled and chopped apples
½ cup chopped dried fruit or raisins
5 cups water
¼ teaspoon cinnamon

Cook overnight on low and serve in the morning with a little honey or other sweetener and some cow's or soy milk.

❧ Cinnamon Oatmeal

1 cup water
⅓ cup raisins
½ cup rolled oats
¼ teaspoon vanilla
½ teaspoon cinnamon
2 tablespoons tahini

In saucepan, bring water and raisins to a boil. Slowly stir in oats. Lower heat. Add vanilla and cinnamon and let cook for 10 minutes. Mix in tahini.

❧ Cinnamon Toast

Toast lightly a slice of 100% whole grain bread. Butter one side and sprinkle with cinnamon sugar (page 355). In oven or toaster oven, broil until sugar is melted and bubbly.

✿ Homemade Granola

Preheat oven to 350°F. Spread 5 cups oats in a 9" x 13" pan and heat in oven for 10 minutes. Meanwhile, combine in a bowl:
⅓ cup vegetable oil or butter
½ cup honey
1 teaspoon vanilla
1 cup coconut, sweetened or unsweetened
½ cup well-chopped nuts (almonds are good)
½ cup toasted wheat germ
1 teaspoon cinnamon
Mix into pan with oatmeal and bake for an additional 30 minutes, stirring frequently for even browning. After mixture cools, add:
1½ cups dried fruit (raisins, etc.)
½ cup sunflower seeds
Keep refrigerated in a tightly covered container.

✿ Dried Fruit Cereal

Into boiling water, add ¼ cup dried apple or other dried fruit for each ½ cup of dry grains. Cook as you would Super Porridge or whole grains.

✿ Pineapple Brown Rice

Cook 1 cup brown rice in 1½ cups water + ½ cup pineapple juice (instead of two cups water). When rice if finished cooking, stir in:
1 cup yogurt
1 can drained pineapple chunks or crushed pineapple
½ cup ground nuts (and/or seeds if you're going to eat it immediately)
Variation: Use another whole grain instead of brown rice and, of course, adjust water and pineapple juice amounts proportionately.

✿ Grain & Cottage Cheese Squares

Preheat oven to 400°F.
1 cup cooked whole grains
1 cup cottage cheese, puréed smooth in blender
1 tablespoon fresh chopped parsley
1 teaspoon finely minced onion
3 eggs, separated
Mix all ingredients except egg whites. Beat egg whites until stiff and fold into mixture.

Spread ½ inch thick in a rectangular buttered pan. Bake about 30 minutes.

✿ Polenta

Boil 2 cups water on stove. Slowly sprinkle 1 cup whole grain cornmeal into water while continuously whisking to prevent lumps. Turn heat to low and simmer for 10-15 minutes, stirring frequently. Serve with Honey Butter (page 317).
Variation: Before the last 5 minutes of simmering, add ½ cup of cheddar cheese and ½ cup of Parmesan cheese.

✿ Millet Loaf

Preheat oven to 350°F. You will need:
1½ cups cooked millet
2 cups cooked lentils
In 4 tablespoons melted butter/oil, cook ½ cup chopped onion for one minute. Add 2 cups coarsely chopped greens (spinach is good) and cook for another 2 minutes. Add millet and lentils. Add:
2 beaten eggs
2 medium apples, grated
1 tablespoon lemon juice
1 tablespoon parsley, fresh
Turn into oiled loaf pan and bake 35-40 minutes.

✿ Wheat-Nut Loaf

Preheat oven to 350°F.
1 cup ground nuts
1 cup wheat germ
1 cup shredded cheddar cheese
1 cup tomato juice, no salt
1 teaspoon brewer's yeast
2 beaten eggs
1 onion, finely chopped
Mix all ingredients and turn into greased loaf pan and bake 45 minutes.

✿ Whole Grain Stir-Fry

Sauteé in butter/oil ½ cup sliced carrots (or broccoli or other veggie) for 5 minutes. Mix in:
1 cup cooked grains
1 tablespoon tamari
2 teaspoons tahini
2 teaspoons fresh parsley
Sauteé 5 minutes more.

ও *Fried Rice*

Saute ¼ cup of finely chopped onions in 1 tablespoon of butter/oil. Remove from pan. Add more butter/oil to pan and saute 1 cup cooked brown rice. Add ⅓ cup cooked green peas and 1 beaten egg and continue to saute until egg is cooked through. You can double or triple this recipe. Serve with sprouts.

Variation: Replace some of onions with minced green peppers and/or celery.

ও *Bird's Nest*

Make a "bird's nest" by placing cooked brown rice or other grain or mashed potatoes or other puréed vegetable into a bowl. Using the back of a spoon, form a hole in the center. Place balls of Toddler Hors d'oeuvres (page 293) in the nest as "bird's eggs." Or spoon a different vegetable, a stew, a thick soup, or other food into the nest.

ও *Gilligan's Island*

Substitute your child's name for Gilligan.

On a dinner plate, place a mound of cooked dark grains, such as brown rice. Some mashed banana or a little butter (softened butter, peanut or other nut butter, or tahini or other seed butter) can be used to cement them together. Encircle the dark grains with lighter colored cooked grains/beans, such as barley, millet, or soy grits. Then surround the lighter colored grains with a light green or light blue colored (see food coloring on page 364) purée of mashed potatoes, mashed bananas, mashed white beans, yogurt, or other white food. The dark grain mound is the soil of the island, the light grain is sand on the beach of the island, and the green/blue food is the ocean. The grains could be puréed for young toddlers, or use Super Porridge. Use small broccoli stalks, celery sticks, and other raw or cooked green veggies for the island's trees and shrubs. Use Decorative Touches to make huts, boats, fish in the ocean, sharks, etc.

Variation: Instead of going through the trouble of three circles of dark and light grains and a colored ocean, use just one mound of grains/beans with a few green veggies poked in. It's Mom's or Dad's enthusiasm that makes it fun, not a detailed work of art.

Beans, Peas, Legumes

ও *Bananas about Beans*

Mash together two tablespoons (or one food cube) cooked puréed beans, lentils, or other legumes with ⅓ to ½ banana.

ও *Easy Bean Soup*

Purée 1½-2 cups of cooked beans (or a 15- or 16- ounce can of beans) with about a cup or so of broth for a thick and creamy soup base. Add another cup or two (or another can) of whole cooked beans, not puréed. Optionally add seasonings. Heat and serve.

ও *Easy Bean Chili*

Combine in large pot:
>   16-ounce jar of tomato sauce
>   16-ounces of stewed tomatoes
>   16-ounce can of red kidney beans
>   or 1½-2 cups of cooked beans
>   1 teaspoon blackstrap molasses
>   1 teaspoon sugar or honey (optional)

Let simmer for one hour, adding up to one cup of water as chili cooks down, if needed. Before serving, stir in until melted:
>   about two cups total of shredded cheese
>   (sharp cheddar is good) and/or crumbled
>   tofu

Variation: Replace some or all of beans with reconstituted TVP.

ও *Leftover Legume Loaf*

Preheat oven to 350°F. Mix thoroughly:
>   1 cup cooked legumes
>   1 cup wheat germ, ground nuts, or
>   whole grain bread crumbs
>   (page 321) or combination
>   1 cup liquid (milk, soy milk, or tomato
>   juice)
>   parsley, powdered or minced garlic,
>   onions, and other seasonings

Place mixture into loaf pan and bake about 30 minutes until firm.

❧ Garbanzo Loaf

Preheat oven to 375°F
   3 cups cooked garbanzos (chick peas), mashed
   ¾ cup chopped celery
   ½ cup chopped onion
   1 cup whole wheat bread crumbs
   ⅓ cup tomato sauce
   2 tablespoons Super Flour or wheat germ
   1 cup ground nuts
   3 tablespoons vegetable oil or melted butter
   3 tablespoons chopped fresh parsley or 1 tablespoon dry
   2 beaten eggs
Mix all ingredients and turn into greased loaf pan. Bake for 30 minutes or until set.

❧ Easy Soy Loaf

Preheat oven to 350°F.
   2½ cups cooked soybeans, mashed
   ¾ cup cottage cheese
   ¼ cup tomato paste
   2 eggs
   2 tablespoons vegetable oil
   1 teaspoon salt
   ½ cup wheat germ
Mix above and turn into greased loaf pan. Bake for one hour or until set.

❧ Layered Soy Cheese Casserole

Preheat oven to 375°F. In heavy saucepan, sauté one chopped onion in 3-4 tablespoons of butter/oil. Add to soft onion:
   2 cups cooked soybeans
   1 cup evaporated milk
   1 teaspoon ketchup
Stir and cook until heated through. Stir in:
   3 beaten eggs
Transfer half mixture to greased casserole dish. Layer over mixture
   ½ cup shredded cheese or cover with cheese slices
Layer other half of mixture over cheese. Place another layer of shredded cheese on top. Then sprinkle on top a combination of whole wheat bread crumbs and wheat germ. Bake for 40-45 minutes.
TIP: To re-heat casseroles without heating up the oven, place the covered casserole dish in a larger pan partly filled with water on the stove top.

❧ Easy Baked Beans

Preheat oven to 350°F. Place 4 cups drained, cooked beans into a large casserole dish. Mix in 2 cups barbeque sauce and 1 finely diced onion. Cover and bake for one hour, stirring occasionally, until beans are bubbly. Add a little water if beans start to dry out during baking.

❧ Garbanzo Snack

Preheat oven to 400°F. In bowl, toss COOKED garbanzo beans or canned garbanzos with olive oil and herbs. Use about 1 tablespoon olive oil and 1-2 tablespoons of herbs per cup of beans. Bake on cookie sheet until nicely browned and crispy. Serve hot. Refrigerate leftovers in airtight container. Re-heat leftovers before serving again—they are much better when eaten warm.

❧ Falafel (Garbanzo Croquettes)

   1¾ cups cooked garbanzos or a can of garbanzo beans (15 or 16 ounces) puréed or mashed well
   1 tablespoon wheat germ
   1 tablespoon bread crumbs
   1 egg, well beaten
   2 tablespoons fresh parsley
   ½ teaspoon cumin
Mix all and form into about 16 balls and flatten. Fry in a little oil three minutes on each side over medium heat. Serve with Lemon Tahini dressing, page 354.

Meatless Patties and Meatless Meals

Any of these patty mixtures can be formed into little **meatless balls** instead and served as Toddler Hors d'oeuvres.

Tip: Use the bottom of a very clean small can of tomato paste to make child-size patties. Trim whole grain bread end slices into circles the same size to make a child-size sandwich.

Tip: Use a melon baller or small scoop to make child-size patties and an ice cream scoop to make adult sized patties.

Tip: When freezing several patties, use plastic tops of yogurt, cottage cheese, margarine, etc. containers to separate and place in good quality freezer bag. Or separate with two layers of waxed paper pieces.

❧ *Protein Burgers*

Mix 1 cup cooked grains to ⅓ cup mashed beans/legumes.

Add a few tablespoons of any of these until you have the consistency of a hamburger patty:
  nut butter
  tahini
  beaten egg
  softened butter/oil
  whole wheat bread crumbs
  ground nuts/seeds

To flavor, add:
  minced onion/garlic or powder
  tamari/soy sauce
  barbecue sauce
  parsley/oregano

To cook: Fry in a little butter/oil, or bake in the oven at 350°F for 15-20 minutes.

❧ *Apricot Burgers*

In blender or processor, finely chop separately:
  3 dried apricots
  ½ medium carrot, grated
  2 tablespoons ground nuts
Mix above thoroughly with:
  1½ cups cooked brown rice, bulgur or other whole grain

  ¼ cup raisins
In blender, process together until smooth:
  1½ tablespoons tahini
  2 tablespoons maple syrup
  ¼ cup firm tofu
Stir into apricot mixture. Shape into 4-5 adult-sized or 6-8 child-sized patties, optionally dredge in whole grain bread crumbs (page 321), and broil on each side on oiled sheet in oven or on outdoor grill until heated through and browned.

❧ *Tofu Burgers*

  8 ounces firm mashed tofu
  1 medium minced onion
  2 tablespoons wheat germ
  2 tablespoons Super Flour
  2 teaspoons garlic powder
  2 tablespoons tamari sauce
Mix all ingredients above and shape into 4-5 adult-sized or 6-8 child-sized patties, optionally dredge in whole grain bread crumbs (page 321), and broil on each side on oiled sheet in oven or on outdoor grill until heated through and browned.

❧ *Avocado Soy Patties*

  1 medium avocado, mashed
  1 cup cooked soybeans, mashed
  ¼ cup cooked brown rice
  ½ cup minced raw onion
  1 tablespoon prepared mustard
  1 tablespoon tomato paste
  2 tablespoons wheat germ
Mix all ingredients and add enough whole wheat bread crumbs until your can form into patties. Fry patties in butter/oil until browned.

❧ *Lentil Burgers*

  2 cups cooked lentils, mashed
  1 beaten egg
  2 cups cooked millet
  1 chopped onion
Mix above and form into patties, adding whole wheat bread crumbs if necessary. Dip into milk and then roll in whole wheat bread crumbs or wheat germ. Fry in butter.

❧ *Riceburgers*

  1 cup brown rice
  3 tablespoons minced onion
  2 tablespoons chopped green peppers
  3 tablespoons chopped celery
  1 beaten egg

¼ rolled oats
¼ cup wheat germ
1-2 tablespoons Super Flour
Mix all ingredients except Super Flour. Add enough Super Flour until good consistency for patties. Makes 8 adult-sized or twice as many or more toddler-sized patties. Dust with more wheat germ, then fry on both sides in a little butter/oil. Optionally, melt a slice of cheese on top of each patty.

๒ Tofu and Grain Patties

Preheat oven to 400°F. Mix in a bowl:
1 cup mashed tofu
1 cup cooked whole grains (cooked brown rice is good)
½ cup minced celery
2 cloves garlic, minced
1 tablespoon brewer's yeast
1 tablespoon peanut butter
2 tablespoons tamari
½ teaspoon olive oil
½ teaspoon sage
Shape into about 10 child-sized patties or 6 adult-sized patties. Coat both sides of patties by dredging in whole grain flour or wheat germ and bake on well-greased baking sheet 25-30 minutes until golden brown, flipping patties halfway through baking.

๒ Soybean Steak

In blender/processor, mix:
1½ cup cooked soybeans
¾ cup cooked whole grain (rice, etc.)
½ medium onion
Add:
½ cup wheat germ
¼ cup oat or wheat bran
¼ cup whole grain cornmeal
1 beaten egg
2 teaspoons tamari sauce
½ teaspoon powdered kelp
1 teaspoon brewer's yeast
Mix all and shape into balls or 4-5 adult-sized patties or 6-8 toddler sized patties. Freeze between wax paper.

๒ Potato Burgers

Here's a use for those leftover mashed potatoes. Form into patties. Dip into beaten egg and then whole grain breadcrumbs. Let sit in refrigerator for one hour. Fry until brown on both sides and serve immediately.

๒ TVP Barbeque Sandwiches

Reconstitute 1 cup TVP granules with ½ cup boiling water and let sit 5 minutes. Sautee one medium finely chopped onion in 1 tablespoon water or broth until onion is clear. (Optionally add 1-2 cloves of garlic and sautee one additional minute.) Add reconstituted TVP and stir. Add enough of your favorite barbeque sauce to get the proper consistency for sandwiches. Heat through over medium-low heat and serve on whole grain buns or bread using Stuffed Bun method (page 318).

๒ Quick TVP Sloppy Joes

Rehydrate one cup TVP with ⅞ cup boiling water. Add a 16-ounce can of sloppy joe sauce. Heat through over medium-low heat and serve on whole grain buns or bread using Stuffed Bun method (page 318).

๒ TVP Skillet Meal

In large saucepan or skillet, pour a can of tomatoes (28-ounces) with juice. Crush the tomatoes. Add 2 cups water and bring to a boil. Meanwhile, mix:
1 cup of whole grain pasta (elbow macaroni is good)
1 cup dry TVP
2 tablespoons dried onion
6 tablespoons fresh parsley, chopped or 2 tablespoons dried parsley
1 tablespoon fresh oregano, chopped or 1 teaspoon dried oregano
1 teaspoon dried thyme
When tomato mixture boils, add mixture above and reduce heat. Cover and simmer 15-20 minutes, stirring occasionally, until pasta is tender. Add hot water if necessary. Optionally, during last 5 minutes of cooking, add some grated carrot or other fresh veggie or a cup of frozen peas.

๒ Vegetarian Hot Dogs

Grind in blender:
1 cup cooked garbanzo beans
1-2 slices of bread
egg replacer equal to 1 egg
¼ teaspoon garlic, minced
¼ teaspoon red peppers, diced
½ teaspoon salt

pinch of pepper
Shape into about 10 hot dogs and chill for at least hour. Deep fry until browned and serve with mustard and relish as you would meat hot dogs.

Sandwiches

❧ *Super Quick Mini Jelly Roll*

Take a slice of untoasted whole grain bread. Remove crusts. (Use crusts for Whole Wheat, page 321.) Flatten with a rolling pin or with the palm of your hand. Spread with all fruit no-sugar-added jelly or jam. Roll bread up as you would a sleeping bag. (If it is too difficult to roll up the bread because it too thick, try using a rolling pin (page 153) to make it thinner.) Stab with a plain or fancy toothpick to keep from unrolling. (Be careful and watch small children with toothpicks.) Instead of, or in addition to, the jelly, use peanut butter, cream cheese, tahini, hummus, or any sandwich spread. One of the sandwich spreads should be a colorful jelly so your child can see the swirl.

❧ *Quick No-Rise Pizza Crust*

Mix in this order:
1½ cups Super Flour
2 teaspoons baking powder
½ teaspoon salt
½ cup soy or cow's milk
3-4 tablespoons oil
Use fork to mix. Knead gently to finish mixing for only 10-12 strokes. Shape and roll to fit greased pizza pan. Add toppings (see recipe for Economical Pizza Sauce on page 355) and bake in preheated 425°F oven 15-20 minutes. Make several pizza pies and freeze.

❧ *Easy, No-Cook Vegetable Pizza*

Lift handset of telephone and dial local pizza place that delivers. Order a pizza with mushrooms or other vegetable topping. Wait 30 minutes or until doorbell rings. Pay delivery person. Eat and enjoy.
Tip: Save pizza box for crafts projects.

❧ *Super Quick Pizza Bread*

On a slice of untoasted or slightly toasted whole grain bread, spread tomato, spaghetti, or pizza sauce. Sprinkle with shredded mozzarella cheese. Toast in toaster oven or under broiler for a few minutes until cheese melts. This happens fast, so watch carefully.
Variations: Add a few canned or fresh mushrooms before broiling or sprinkle with Parmesan cheese. Add a dash of fresh or dry oregano into the sauce before spreading.

❧ *Super Quick Garlic Bread*

Follow the Super Quick Pizza Bread recipe above, but brush bread with olive oil or melted butter instead of sauce. Sprinkle with shredded cheese and minced fresh garlic or garlic powder.

❧ *Bagel Ferris Wheel*

Slice a whole grain bagel in half. Slice a small piece off the outer edge of the bagel, making a flat edge on which the ferris wheel can stand. Fill the bagel with a Super Sandwich Spread. Use Decorative Touches for passenger cars, which stick half way out of the spread.

❧ *Never a Plain Old Sandwich*

Don't just cut a sandwich in half, be imaginative! Cut a heart-shaped sandwich to tell your little one you love her. Or let her decide on a shape. Does she want a star, a circle, a triangle, an oval, a parallelogram? She's never to young to start learning geometry! Cookie cutters will work well on fairly flat sandwiches. If your whole grain bread is too thick, cut each slice into two thinner slices to make a flatter sandwich. It's easier to slice bread like this if it's slightly frozen. Or use only one slice of bread and place a cheese slice on it. Cut it into shapes and then microwave or broil to melt cheese. Cut a bread slice into a heart shape, spread with red jelly and give your heart to your toddler. Cut a sandwich into 9 square blocks and use raisins or re-hydrated dried apricot pieces to play tic-tac-toe, or any small food pieces can be used. These blocks can also be stacked into a brick wall. Or, leave the sandwich uncut and open-faced and use sticky peanut butter as a canvas for a picture created with Decorative Touches.

Sandwiches are more fun if made with two different slices of bread, such as one slice whole wheat and one slice of rye. Or don't use bread at all and make a sandwich with a whole grain tortilla, bagel half, or pita bread or even a rolled up lettuce leaf.

❧ Freezing Sandwiches

I have to get up at 6 am to get my kids off to school on time. It's so nice when I don't have to make their lunch sandwiches, because I previously made and froze them—batch and freeze to the rescue again! Most frozen sandwiches placed in lunch boxes in the morning thaw and are ready to eat by lunch time. If a sandwich is quite thick, move it from freezer to refrigerator the night before to insure thawing by lunch. At home, the babysitter can remove the chill by placing it in the microwave for 30 seconds to 1 minute in the microwave, or in the toaster oven or under the broiler. Some elementary schools and day care centers have microwave ovens for the children's food.

Sandwiches made with these fillings can be frozen for up to 2 months: peanut butter, jelly, cream cheese, hummus, prune butter, tuna salad, mashed banana, yogurt cheese. Use day-old bread and spread the butter/peanut butter on the insides of both slices to prevent a wetter filling, like jelly, from making the bread soggy. In other words, don't place jelly directly on the bread, separate with a layer of peanut butter. Or place a slice of cheese between wet filling and bread.

Do not freeze egg salad (it gets rubbery), tomatoes (they get mushy), or salad veggies (they go limp). Ketchup freezes well, as does mustard and pickle relish. Mayonnaise separates and curdles unless you mix it with cream cheese or a similar spread; it should be no more than one third of the mixture.

Freeze sandwiches using the Nested Plastic Bag Method, and the sandwich will be in its bag, ready to go into the lunch box. When mass-producing and wrapping sandwiches, use a spatula to slide sandwiches into sandwich bags. Or wrap individual sandwiches in aluminum foil.

Tip: When making several sandwiches with butter, mix a little milk into softened butter with a small whisk to decrease saturated fat content and save money.

Tip: Prevent soggy lunch box sandwiches. When packing a sandwich for lunch, keep tomatoes, pickles, and other soggy ingredients in separate plastic bags and have the diner place them on the sandwich immediately before eating.

Super Sandwich Spreads

All sandwich spreads must be kept refrigerated. Or freeze them using the Food Cube Method for up to 2 months. Thaw one or two cubes in the microwave and your sandwich spread is ready for spreading. (The assembled sandwich can also be frozen, as discussed in the previous section).

Tip: Keep little packets of ketchup, mustard, etc. from fast food restaurants for lunch box sandwiches. Store salt and pepper in portable shakers by filling drinking straws and twisting ends up.

Tip: Yogurt cheese (page 254) and cream cheese in sandwiches are great places to hide Healthy Extras.

See more spread recipes under Condiments on page 352.

❧ Tofu Cream Cheese

Mix together:
> ½ cup tofu, press between towels to drain very well and then mash
> 3 ounces cream cheese
> 1 tablespoon yogurt cheese
Add Healthy Extras.

SUPER SANDWICH SPREAD COMBINATIONS

Combine one or more of these ingredients:	with one or more of these sweet ingredients:
yogurt cheese	mashed banana
tofu	shredded apple or other fresh fruit
cream cheese	no-sugar added fruit jelly or jam
shredded natural cheese	concentrated frozen orange or other juice
cottage cheese	drained crushed canned pineapple
ricotta cheese	honey
peanut butter	apple butter
any nut butter	prune butter
tahini or any seed butter	rehydrated dried fruit, such as raisins, dates, figs, apricots, and pineapple
mashed avocado	powdered dried fruit
puréed cooked beans	mashed sweet potato
mashed cooked egg yolk or whole egg	shredded or mashed carrots

And add one or more of these: ground nuts ground seeds (eat immediately) ground sprouts chopped fresh parsley or other herb	If too thick to spread, add a little milk or fruit juice.

ᨀ Egg Salad Spread

Mix a crumbled hard-cooked egg with 1 tablespoon of mayonnaise and a tablespoon of any or all of the following: diced celery or onion, fresh parsley, tofu, and mashed beans.

ᨀ Egg-less Salad Spread

Mix together:
1 pound tofu, crumbled
¼ cup tofu mayonnaise
2 teaspoons prepared mustard
¼ teaspoon garlic powder
1 green pepper, minced
1 celery stalk, finely chopped
½ medium onion, minced
½ teaspoon tamari

ᨀ Super Butter (Mock Margarine)

Mix equal parts softened butter with a good quality cold-pressed non-hydrogenated oil from the natural foods store.

ᨀ Honey Butter

You can buy commercial honey butter, but the price is ridiculous. All you have to do is mix one part honey into two parts softened butter. Your kids will love it. Refrigerate or freeze using the Food Cube Method.

ᨀ Homemade Peanut Butter

See page 242 for how to make peanut butter, almond butter, and other nut butters.

❧ Honey Peanut Butter

Make honey butter with peanut butter instead of butter.

❧ Parsley Lemon Butter

Mix:
    ½ cup softened butter
    2 tablespoons lemon juice
    1-2 teaspoons finely minced fresh
    parsley

❧ Herb Butter

Beat fresh herbs from your kitchen window garden into butter. Use 3-4 tablespoons of finely minced fresh herbs (or 1 tablespoon dried herbs) for each ½ cup (4 ounces) softened butter. Try one of these: basil, dill, chive, marjoram, tarragon, and, of course, parsley. Make a big batch and freeze for up to 6 months.

❧ Churn Your Own Butter

Into a 32-ounce mayonnaise or similar jar, pour one pint of heavy whipping cream. The jar must have a lot of head room for shaking. You can add a little salt too, but it is not necessary. Shake for 15 minutes or more until you hear the solid pieces hitting the sides of the jar. Strain through sieve to get solid butter parts. Place pieces into ice cube trays or molds (page 385). Refrigerate.
Variation: Add fresh herbs before molding.

❧ Prune Butter

Your kids will love this sweet high-fiber spread on whole grain bread or crackers.
    1 cup pitted prunes
    ½ cup apple juice
    1 tablespoon orange juice
    ¼ teaspoon vanilla
Combine all ingredients in saucepan. Simmer over low heat for about ½ hour, stirring frequently. Cool and purée in processor until smooth. If too thick add a little more apple or orange juice. Keep refrigerated in an airtight jar.
Variation: Mix cooked prune butter with a little butter.

See tip on baking with prune butter, page 455.

❧ No-Cook Prune Butter

In blender, mix until smooth:
    8 ounces (1⅓ cup) soft pitted prunes
    ⅔ cup frozen apple juice concentrate,
    thawed in refrigerator
    ¼ teaspoon vanilla (optional)
Keep refrigerated in air-tight jar.

❧ Easy Apple Butter

Make apple butter by simply reducing applesauce. Place about 1 cup applesauce (optionally add a dash of cinnamon) in a saucepan and bring to a boil. Turn heat to low and simmer, stirring occasionally, until desired consistency is reached. Yields about ½ cup.
Variation: Instead of applesauce, use puréed fresh fruit to make pear, pineapple, blueberry, mango, papaya, peach, pear, or plum butter.

❧ Avocado Spread

Mix equal parts mashed avocado and mashed banana. Add 1 tablespoon lemon juice for each cup to prevent darkening.

❧ Garbanzo Cream Cheese Spread

    1 cup cooked garbanzos, well mashed
    3 ounces cream cheese
    ⅓ cup tofu
    ½ cup celery, minced very fine for
    toddlers
Mix all ingredients. Makes about 2 cups.

❧ Mr/Ms Sunshine

Place a scoop of sandwich spread in the middle of a canned pineapple ring. Use Decorative Touches to make facial features on the spread.

❧ Fruit Flowers

Instead of the pineapple ring in the previous recipe, arrange apple, orange, pear, or other fruit wedges around the scoop of spread, making a flower-like picture.

❧ Stuffed Buns

Stuff an un-cut bun jelly doughnut-style by cutting a hole in the top and piping sandwich filling inside. This method also can be used for Sloppy Joes to make them less sloppy.

❧ *Hummus*

This spread is super healthy and combines tahini, chick-peas, and whole grain bread to make complete protein (page 521). It's also super delicious and one of my favorites. Purée until smooth these ingredients in the blender/processor:

1 cup cooked chick-peas
2 tablespoons tahini
2 tablespoons lemon juice
1 tablespoon olive oil
2 t minced fresh parsley

Optionally add ½ clove pressed garlic or a pinch of garlic powder (not garlic salt).

❧ *Hummus from Canned Chick Peas*

1 15- or 16-ounce can of chick peas/garbanzo beans (equivalent to a little less than 2 cups home cooked)
6 tablespoons lemon juice
½ cup tahini
1 tablespoon olive oil
2 cloves pressed garlic (optional)

❧ *Orange Hummus*

3-4 cups cooked garbanzo beans
½ cup orange juice
¼ cup tahini
3 garlic cloves, crushed
1 teaspoon kelp or salt
1½ tablespoons apple cider vinegar
½ teaspoon paprika
½ teaspoon ginger
½ teaspoon coriander
½ teaspoon cumin
½ teaspoon dry mustard
¼ teaspoon turmeric

Process all above until smooth in food processor. Add more orange juice if necessary. Stir in:

3 scallions, finely minced

❧ *Tofu-Nut Butter Spread*

Mix in blender:

1 cup tofu
½ cup peanut butter or other nut butter
2 tablespoons maple syrup
Healthy Extras

❧ *Banana-Lemon Spread*

Add a little lemon juice to mashed banana. Use about 1 teaspoon per ½ cup mashed banana. Simple and good with crackers.

❧ *Dried Fruit Spread*

Mix dried fruit and a little water in the blender until spreadable consistency. Dates and figs are good.

❧ *Flying Saucers*

Make your child's favorite sandwich on whole-grain English muffins or rolls. Name different sandwiches after planets; for example, peanut butter and jelly is from Pluto, yogurt cheese and prune butter is from Mars, etc. Ask which planet your child would like his sandwich from today. You soon develop a repertoire of personalized recipes especially for your child.

❧ *Pocket Sandwiches*

Don't buy the commercial frozen pocket sandwiches—make your own for quick breakfasts, lunches, or snacks.. For each pocket sandwich, take about two tablespoons of whole grain bread dough (homemade or commercially bought) and roll it out flat. (See dough tip on page 332.) Top with fillings, such as shredded Monterey or other cheese, cooked broccoli or other veggie, etc., or make a pizza flavored pocket sandwich with mozzarella cheese and tomato sauce/paste. All fillings should be thoroughly cooked before stuffing and drain the fillings well so that the sandwich will not be soggy. Roll dough up and pinch the sides down to contain the filling. Bake according to dough directions. Refrigerate or freeze. Thaw and warm them in the microwave for about 30 seconds or in the toaster oven.

Quick Breads

See how to bake yeast bread on page 229.

ᏪᲬ *Apple Surprise Bread*

Preheat oven to 350°F. Grease a 9x13x1 pan and arrange on the bottom:
    1 apple or pear, sliced
In a large bowl, mix dry ingredients:
    2 cups Super Flour
    ¼ cup wheat germ
    ¼ cup bran
    1 teaspoon baking soda
    1 teaspoon baking powder
Then add to dry ingredients:
    ½ cup ground nuts
    1 apple or pear, grated
In a small bowl, mix wet ingredients:
    2 beaten eggs
    1 cup milk
    1 tablespoon melted butter/oil
    1 teaspoon vanilla
Make well in dry ingredients and pour in wet ingredients. Mix until combined, but do not overmix. Bake at 350°F for 30-35 minutes. Let cool before icing. For icing, mix 1 cup yogurt with 3 tablespoons maple syrup or 2 tablespoons honey and drizzle over cool cake.

ᏪᲬ *Zippity Zucchini Bread*

Preheat oven to 350°F. Mix in this order:
    2 cups Super Flour
    1 teaspoon baking soda
    ½ cup melted butter/oil
    1 beaten egg
    1 8.75 oz. can of crushed pineapple, not drained
    ½ cup plumped raisins
    ½ cup grated zucchini
Pour into greased loaf pan and bake 60 minutes, until toothpick or cake tester comes out clean. Cool loaf on wire rack to prevent sogginess.

ᏪᲬ *Banana Nut Bread*

Preheat oven to 350°F. Mix wet ingredients in one bowl:
    1 beaten egg
    3 medium ripe bananas, mashed
    3 tablespoons melted butter/oil
    3 tablespoons honey
    2 tablespoons frozen orange juice concentrate
    1 teaspoon vanilla
Mix dry ingredients in another bowl:
    1½ cups Super flour
    1 teaspoon baking soda
    a pinch of salt
Mix wet ingredients into dry ingredients and add ¾ cup chopped nuts (walnuts, filberts, and almonds are good). Bake 50-60 minutes.

Variation: Replace all or some of the nuts with sunflower seeds.

ᏪᲬ *Awesome Orange Bread*

Preheat oven to 325°F. Mix in this order:
    3 beaten eggs
    ½ cup melted butter/oil
    1 cup orange juice
    2¼ cups Super Flour
    1 teaspoon baking soda
    1 teaspoon baking powder
    2 teaspoons cinnamon
    1 cup chopped nuts
Bake in greased and floured 9x5 loaf pan 50-60 minutes until cake tester or toothpick comes out clean. Cool on wire rack. Serve with topping of ½ yogurt cheese and ½ orange juice concentrate or with Orange Topping (page 350).

ᏪᲬ *Corny Corn Bread*

Preheat oven to 350°F.
    1 cup whole grain cornmeal
    ⅔ cup Super Flour
    ½ cup nonfat dry milk
    2 teaspoons baking powder
    2 beaten eggs
    1 cup yogurt
    3 tablespoons melted butter/oil
Mix all ingredients and place in a 8-inch square baking pan. Bake 30 minutes until lightly browned. Cut into 16 or 20 squares.

❧ *Honey Corn Bread*

Preheat oven to 400°F. Grease a 9-inch loaf pan. Mix these dry ingredients:

1¾ whole grain cornmeal from the natural foods store
½ cup Super Flour
2 tablespoons wheat germ
1 teaspoon salt
3 teaspoons baking powder

Mix these wet ingredients in another bowl:

2 beaten eggs
2 tablespoons vegetable oil or melted butter
2 tablespoons honey
1 cup milk

Combine wet and dry ingredients. Bake 25 minutes or until done.

❧ *Peanut Butter in the Bread*

Preheat oven to 350°F. Grease a 9- inch loaf pan. Thoroughly mix wet ingredients:

¾ cup peanut butter
1 cup milk
½ cup honey

Mix dry ingredients in separate bowl:

2 cups Super Flour
1 tablespoon plus 1 teaspoon (4 teaspoons) baking powder
½ teaspoon baking soda
¾ teaspoon salt

Combine wet and dry ingredients and bake for 45 minutes.

❧ *Banana Bread*

Preheat oven to 350°F. Mix wet ingredients:

1½ cups mashed ripe banana
¼ cup oil
½ cup honey
1 teaspoon vanilla
1-2 beaten eggs (optional)

Mix dry ingredients:

2 cups whole wheat flour or Super Flour
½ cup wheat germ
1 teaspoon baking soda
1-2 teaspoons baking powder (optional)

Add dry ingredients into wet, then fold in:

½ cup chopped walnuts

Bake in oiled loaf pan for about an hour.

Bread Products

The supermarket is infamous for its bread products made from white wheat flour (see page 218 for difference between processed flour and whole grain flour). The natural foods store is THE place for buying bread products, but they tend to be a little expensive. You can save quite a bit of money by making your own following the recipes in this section.

Besides this section, whole grains are found all throughout the recipes, such as *Whole Grain "Shake and Cook" Potato Coating* (recipe in Vegetable recipes on page 302) and *Whole Grain Bread Pudding* (recipe in Dessert recipes on page 342). Make sure you read about Super Flour on page 289.

❧ *Homemade Whole Grain Bread*

See page 226.

❧ *Whole Grain Bread Crumbs*

Don't throw away bread crusts and the end slices from whole grain bread. Save them in a paper bag in the cabinet until they get stale and hard. Then break them into small pieces and whiz them in your blender or food processor to make whole wheat bread crumbs. Or put them in a plastic bag and crush them with a rolling pin (page 153) and you'll have more control over the coarseness. Store in a tightly-covered jar in your kitchen cabinets. Three slices will make about one cup of crumbs. I think they taste fine, but if you find that the breadcrumbs taste like stale bread, try drying fresh bread on an unoiled baking sheet in a single layer at 300°F until completely dry and lightly browned. Let cool completely before pulverizing.

❧ Whole Grain Italian Bread Crumbs

To each cup of whole grain bread crumbs in previous recipe, add:

2 tablespoons grated Parmesan cheese
½ teaspoon dry oregano
½ teaspoon dry basil
1 tablespoon dry parsley
½ teaspoon garlic powder
½ teaspoon sugar (optional)

Store in plastic bag or airtight container in refrigerator for up to two months or until expiration date on cheese label, or freeze.

❧ Bread Crumb Substitutes

Crackers, uncooked rolled oats/oatmeal, whole grain corn flakes, or any dry cereal whirled in the blender make cracker crumbs, which can substitute for bread crumbs in recipes. Or use plastic bag/rolling pin method.

❧ Whole Wheat Breadsticks/Croutons

Cut up slightly dry whole grain bread into narrow rectangular strips for breadsticks or into cubes for croutons. Lightly coat with melted butter/oil and herbs, or if you find it easier, coat with butter and herbs before cutting bread into strips or cubes. I find that the easiest way to coat cut bread is to shake everything together in a plastic bag. Use about 1 tablespoon of butter/oil and 1 teaspoon of dry herbs per ½ cup of bread. Optionally add ½ teaspoon of seasoning per ½ cup of bread, such as garlic powder or onion salt, grated Parmesan cheese, etc. On large baking sheet in a single layer, bake 300°F for about 10-15 minutes or microwave on medium power until they dry. Stir during cooking for even drying. Let cook completely and store in airtight container or storage bag in the refrigerator for up to two months or freeze using the Nested Plastic Bag Method for up to 6 months. Shake before using.

Tip: Don't throw out leftover bread or the bread ends that no one will eat. Freeze them in a freezer bag until you have enough for a batch of croutons or breadsticks.

❧ Whole Grain Top-of-Stove Stuffing Mix

Save bread ends, crusts, and leftover bread to make this economical and healthy stuffing mix. Preheat oven to 350°F.

2 cups of cubed dry/stale bread
1 teaspoon dry parsley flakes
1 tablespoon bouillon powder or 1 bouillon cube
1 tablespoon dried minced onion
2 tablespoons dried minced celery
½ teaspoon thyme
½ teaspoon pepper
pinch of powdered kelp
1/4 teaspoon sage

In bowl or plastic bag, mix all ingredients. Double or triple recipe if you wish. Store in refrigerator for up to three months or in freezer for up to one year.

To cook: For each cup of stuffing mix, stir in ¼ cup water and 1 tablespoon olive oil or melted butter. Toss well and warm on top of the stove, in the microwave, or bake at 350°F in oven until warmed through.

Variations: Per cup of stuffing mix, add 2 tablespoons plumped raisins, 2 tablespoons canned mushrooms, 2 tablespoons chopped or ground walnuts or other nuts, and/or a tablespoon of Worcestershire sauce.

❧ Homemade Whole Grain Breakfast Cereal Flakes

Boxed breakfast cereals are overpriced and sometimes contain unhealthy ingredients and preservatives. It's easy and much cheaper to make your own using the whole grain flours found at your local natural foods store. Choose from whole wheat, millet flour, oat flour, whole corn flour, etc. Or use Super Flour as described on page 289. If your family is used to a high-sugar cereal, begin by making homemade cereal with high sugar content and gradually decrease to the recipe below. Or completely leave out the sugar altogether for toddlers and those lucky folks who have not developed a sweet tooth.

2 cups of whole grain flour or Super Flour
½-1 teaspoon powdered kelp or salt
½ cup honey, maple syrup, blackstrap molasses, sugar, or other sweetener (optional)

approximately 2 cups water

Mix ingredients together, adding water slowly as the last ingredient until you have the mixture of a thin paste. Butter a cookie sheet or spray with oil. Pour mixture onto sheet while shaking to distribute over entire surface of sheet. As soon as you have enough to cover the cookie sheet as thinly as possible, stop pouring. If you've poured too much, simply return the excess back into the mixing bowl. Bake in pre-heated 350°F for about 15 minutes until dry and lightly browned. Peel off cookie sheet, let cool, then break into pieces that look like commercial corn flakes. Or you can break into designs and shapes.

ᴥ Homemade Breakfast Nutty Grape Cereal

Mix in a bowl until smooth:
 3½ cups Super Flour or whole wheat flour
 1 cup brown sugar
 2 cups yogurt, buttermilk, or sour milk
 1 teaspoon baking soda
 ¼ teaspoon kelp or salt
Spread on two greased cookie sheets. Bake for 25-30 minutes until golden brown. While still warm, grind a bit in processor or grate by hand using the large holes.

ᴥ Whole Grain Popper Tarts

Mix ingredients below for dough.
 2 beaten eggs
 ¼ cup olive oil
 2 tablespoons melted butter
 ¼ cup + 2 tablespoons honey
 2 cups Super Flour
 2 teaspoons baking powder
Chill for one hour. Roll dough into a six 8x12 inch rectangles. (See dough tip on page 332.) These rectangle will be folded in half to make 8x6 inch pastries. Spread about a tablespoon of filling (jam, jelly, strawberry preserves,...) on one half of the rectangle, leaving room for sealing edge. Fold in half, enclosing filling by crimping edges with a fork or pastry wheel. Bake in preheated 350°F oven for about 20 minutes. Let cool. Make a frosting by mixing:
 2 tablespoons honey or confectioners' sugar
 1/4 teaspoon vanilla

 1 tablespoon milk
Dribble a design on each tart with frosting. Store using the Nested Plastic Bag Method or wrap individually in aluminum foil. Refrigerate for up to one week or freeze for up to three months. You can also double or triple this recipe to make 12 or 18 pastries instead of six.

To re-heat: Re-heat in toaster for 2 minutes (or 4-5 minutes if frozen). In microwave, heat each tart on high for about 1 minute (or 2 minutes if frozen).

Variation: If your family likes a particular commercial toaster tart, read the ingredients list and experiment to create a healthier, cheaper homemade version.

ᴥ Quick Breadsticks

Makes about 16 sticks. Mix dry ingredients:
 1 cup Super Flour
 ½ cup oat or wheat bran
 ½ teaspoon baking powder
In another bowl, mix wet ingredients:
 1 beaten egg
 4 tablespoons melted butter/oil
 ¼ cup of water
Make well in dry ingredients and mix in wet ingredients. If dough is too dry, add water; if too wet, add flour or bran. Keep dividing dough in halves until you have 16 balls. Roll into sticks about ½ inch in diameter. After shaping, you can optionally wet them with a mixture of one beaten egg mixed with 2 tablespoons of water and roll them in sesame seeds or wheat germ. Place on greased baking sheet and bake in pre-heated 350°F oven for 20 minutes, until crisp and golden-browned. Cover with aluminum foil, shiny side up, for softer bread sticks. Store in an air-tight container.

ᴥ Whole Grain Soft Pretzels

In a large mixing bowl, mix:
 1 cup Super Flour
 1 tablespoon canola oil
 1 cup apple juice (not concentrated)
 1 tablespoon active dry yeast or 1 packet active dry yeast
Beat with electric mixer for 3 minutes. Add:
 1 cup Super Flour
Knead 10-15 minutes adding a little water or flour for good consistency. Roll about 16 pieces of dough into long snakes and

form into pretzel shapes. Place pretzels on oiled baking sheet and let rise for 30 minutes. While waiting for oven to preheat 450°F, beat one egg in a small bowl and brush beaten egg over pretzels. Optionally sprinkle with coarse salt or kelp granules. Bake 14-16 minutes or until pretzels become a nice golden brown. Let cool a little before eating to prevent mouth burns.

❧ *Whole Wheat Buttermilk Biscuits*

Preheat oven to 425°F. Sift together:
 1¼ cups whole wheat flour
 ¾ cup unbleached, unbrominated white flour from the natural foods store
 2 teaspoons baking powder
 ½ teaspoon baking soda
 1 teaspoon salt
While mixing, slowly add:
 ¾ cup buttermilk or milk
 ¼ cup oil (safflower or corn)
Knead about two minutes. Roll out to ½-inch thick. Use 2-inch biscuit cutter to cut out a dozen or more biscuits. Bake on buttered or oil-sprayed cookie sheet for 12 to 15 minutes, watching carefully for burning at end of cooking time.

❧ *Whole Grain Biscuit Mix*

 4 cups Super Flour
 1 teaspoon salt
 ½ cup oil
 ⅔ cup instant nonfat dry milk
 3 tablespoons baking powder

❧ *Whole Grain Master Baking Mix*

 2 cups whole wheat flour
 2 cup unbleached white flour
 1 cup wheat germ
 3 tablespoons baking soda
 ¾ tablespoon salt
 ¾ tablespoon cream of tartar
 2 tablespoons honey
Cut in until consistency of cornmeal:
 1 cup vegetable shortening
Add:
 1 cup dried milk
Store in tightly-covered container at room temperature or in refrigerator.
To use: In bowl, beat together:
 1 cup milk
 1 beaten egg

1½ cups master baking mix
Use for pancakes, waffles, etc.

❧ *Whole Wheat Popovers*

Popovers rise because of trapped steam and not leavening agents such as baking powder. Preheat oven to 450°F.
 1 cup whole wheat flour
 1 cup unbleached, unbrominated white flour
 2 tablespoons honey
 4 egg whites
 2 cups milk
Generously grease 12 muffin tins (do not use paper, popovers will stick). Hand beat the eggs and gradually stir in the milk. Mix ingredients and fill tins ⅓-½ full. Bake for 10 minutes in pre-heated 450°F oven. Reduce heat to 350°F and continue baking for 15 minutes. To prevent falling do not open the oven until end of cooking time, or the hot air inside the popovers that is raising them will escape and cause the popovers will collapse. Popovers should be nicely browned before you take them out of the oven, under-baking will cause them to collapse. When done baking, immediately prick popovers with fork in several places to let the steam escape to prevent sogginess. If popovers stick, run a knife around the edge and use more grease on the tins next time. Serve with jam, honey, or cheese. Or split and stuff with scrambled eggs. Freeze popovers in an airtight freezer bag for up to 3 months; heat by placing frozen popovers on an ungreased baking sheet in a preheated 450°F oven for 10-15 minutes.

Super Muffins

Tip for filling muffin tins: Use a small measuring cup tins for uniform sized muffins. If you have an ice cream scoop with a lever, all the better, the batter comes out of scoop easily. Or put batter into a clean milk carton for easy pouring, especially if you are using mini-muffin tins. Do not fill tins more than ¾ full or you'll have flat tops. For beautiful rounded muffin tops, grease tins only halfway up the sides.

Tip for oiling muffin tins: Use a pastry brush and oil or melted butter to stick-proof each muffin tin. Or a crumpled piece of paper towel to grease the tins. Or oil-spray. Run a knife around the edges of muffins before removing.

Prevent pointy muffins: Do not overmix muffin batter or muffins may be pointy. Stir until batter is moistened and lumps will disappear during baking.

Surprise Muffins: Place a surprise in the middle of each muffin, which your child will discover while eating it. Ideas: a chunk of pineapple, a soft cooked and pitted prune or piece of plumped dried papaya or apricot or other plumped soft dried fruit, a peeled piece of apple or pear, glop of peanut butter, carob chips, banana chunk, or anything that would not be a choking hazard.

Don't Warp Your Muffin Tins: The recipes here require the use of muffin tins for baking. If you find that you don't have enough batter to fill all of the tins in the pan, and some must be left empty, fill them halfway with water. This will prevent the muffin pan from burning or warping.

Mini-muffins These recipes will make 12 regular sized muffins. You can make 2-3 dozen mini-muffins instead—kids love things their own size. Bake mini-muffins a few minutes less and watch carefully for burning.

Batch and Freeze

Save time by doubling the recipe to make two batches of muffins and freeze one. Freeze muffins in a single layer in a large freezer bag for up to 3 months. Thaw overnight in refrigerator and heat in microwave for about 15 seconds or in a 325°F oven loosely wrapped in foil for about 10 minutes.

❧ Heart Shaped Muffins

Make "I love you" muffins for your child by placing aluminum foil between the paper muffin cup and the metal muffin tin to form the muffin into the shape of a heart. Crunch the foil into a ball the size of a marble so that it will cause an indentation on top. Crunch foil into rectangular shapes to push in sides on bottom to form point. Exaggerate the heart shape by decorating with frosting in a heart shape.

Aluminum foil shaped into ball goes here

Two foil rectangular shapes go on sides to form point

Variation: Bake muffins in clean tuna cans and various other empty food cans. Butter or oil-spray well to prevent sticking.

❧ Bunny Muffins

Make muffins into bunnies by adding eyes, ears, nose, and whiskers using Decorative Touches.

❧ Muffin Frisbees

Slice leftover muffins horizontally into thin circles and bake like cookies in the oven or toaster oven until lightly brown or toast both sides by broiling. Spread with butter or jam.

❧ Orange Juice Muffins

Preheat oven to 425°F.
In large bowl, combine the dry ingredients:
    1½ cups Super Flour
    3 T wheat germ
    1 teaspoon baking soda
    ¼ teaspoon cinnamon
    ½ cup raisins
In a small bowl, combine the wet ingredients:
    2 eggs, beaten
    1 cup orange juice
    2 tablespoons melted butter/oil

Blend the wet ingredients into the dry ingredients and do not over mix. Pour into greased or lined muffin cups. Bake 15 minutes or until a toothpick or cake tester comes out clean. Serve with Orange Topping (page 350) for an Overly Orangy Taste.

ぺ *Eggless Apple Muffins*

Preheat oven to 350°F.
Mix dry ingredients in large bowl:
  2 cups Super Flour
  ½ cup rolled oats
  2 teaspoons baking powder
  1 teaspoon baking soda
  ½ teaspoon cinnamon
Mix wet ingredients in a small bowl:
  1 23-ounce jar applesauce
  ½ cup yogurt
  2 tablespoons molasses
  ½ cup plumped raisins
Mix wet ingredients into dry. Pour into greased or lined muffin cups. Decorate with ground nuts. Bake 25-30 minutes.

ぺ *Polenta Mini-Muffins*

Preheat oven to 350°F.
  1½ cups water or stock
  ½ cup whole grain cornmeal
  2 beaten eggs
  ½ cup shredded cheddar cheese
  ½ cup yogurt
  ¼ cup shredded cheddar cheese
Bring water or stock to a boil on the stove. Slowly add cornmeal into boiling water or stock, stirring continuously with whisk to remove lumps. Thicken by cooking over medium heat for 5 minutes, stirring constantly. Remove from heat. Stir in the beaten eggs, ½ cup cheese, and yogurt. Spoon into 24 greased or lined mini-muffin cups. Sprinkle ¼ cup cheese on top of muffins. Bake 18-22 minutes until firm. Let cool slightly before removing from pan. Serve with tomato sauce.
Variation: Add a little mashed beans to the mixture before baking.

ぺ *Pizzazzy Pizza Muffins*

Preheat oven to 400°F.
Combine dry ingredients in a large bowl:
  1¾ cups Super Flour
  2 teaspoons baking powder
  1 teaspoon baking soda

  1 tablespoon fresh oregano or 1 teaspoon dry oregano
Combine these wet ingredients:
  1 beaten egg
  ½ cup homemade tomato sauce
  1 cup yogurt
  ½ cup shredded mozzarella cheese
Mix wet ingredients into dry. Pour into greased or lined muffin tins. Place a slice of tomato on top of each muffin. Sprinkle more shredded cheese on top of tomato slice. Bake 20-25 minutes.

ぺ *Banana Nut Muffins*

Preheat oven to 375°F.
Mix dry ingredients in large bowl:
  1¾ Super Flour
  ½ teaspoon baking powder
  ½ teaspoon baking soda
  1 teaspoon cinnamon
  ½ cup ground walnuts
Mix wet ingredients in small bowl:
  2 beaten eggs
  ¼ cup yogurt
  2 tablespoons melted butter/oil
  ¼ cup maple syrup
  1 tablespoon lemon juice
  3 small mashed ripe bananas (about 1 cup)
  ½ cup plumped raisins
Mix the wet ingredients into the dry ingredients. Pour into greased or lined muffin tins. Decorate each muffin with a walnut on top (not for babies/toddlers, whole nuts are choking hazards). Bake 20 minutes or until golden.

ぺ *Peanut Butter Muffins*

Preheat oven to 350°F.
Mix in this order:
  2 beaten eggs
  ¼ cup creamy natural peanut butter
  ¼ cup mashed banana
  ½ cup thawed apple juice concentrate
  1 cup milk
  ½ cup melted butter/oil
  2½ cups Super Flour
  1½ teaspoons baking powder
  1 teaspoon baking soda
  1 cup finely chopped peanuts
Pour into greased or lined muffins tins and bake 15 minutes.

❧ *Cholesterol Killing Bran Muffins*

Preheat oven to 425°F. Combine these dry ingredients in a large bowl:
  2 cups oat bran
  ¼ cup wheat germ
  1 teaspoon cinnamon
  1 tablespoon baking soda
Combine these wet ingredients:
  ½ cup evaporated skim milk
  ¾ cup frozen apple juice concentrate
  1 beaten egg
  2 tablespoons maple syrup
Mix wet ingredients into dry.
Add:
  1 unpeeled apple, cored and finely grated
  ⅓ cup ground/chopped nuts
Pour into greased or lined muffin tins and bake 18 minutes. These muffins will not rise much because of all the bran, so don't worry that they will seep out of the muffin tins.

❧ *Easy Bran Muffins*

Preheat oven to 400°F. Mix these dry ingredients in a large bowl:
  2 cups Super Flour
  1 cup wheat or oat bran
  2 tablespoons baking powder
  ¾ teaspoon salt
In a separate bowl, beat together:
  2 eggs
  2 cups milk
  ½ cup applesauce
  ½ cup molasses or honey
  ⅓ cup blackstrap molasses
Combine wet and dry ingredients. Pour into 8 greased or lined muffin tins until ¾ full and bake 15 minutes, until nicely browned.
Variations: Add raisins or other dried fruits.

Wonderful Waffles

I used to buy the commercial, expensive, chemicalized, white flour frozen waffles with imitation blueberries from the supermarket. Yes, I let myself get roped in by those darn coupons. When my son started asking me to buy more, I became aware that he was eating sometimes three or four a day! I decided to invest in a waffle iron, which paid for itself in no time. Every few weeks I pull it out and make and freeze dozens of Super Flour waffles with real blueberries. I no longer have to cringe when I see him reaching into the freezer. Frozen waffles are just one more overpriced commercial food whose price is not worth the convenience, once you've made use of the batch and freeze method. Waffles will keep in the freezer for up to 6 months. For waffles that you know will be frozen, you may wish to slightly undercook them.

Tip: Before freezing waffles, cool *completely* on wire racks. Heat directly from freezer (without thawing) in toaster, or toaster oven at 350°F for 5 minutes, or in the microwave on high for 7-10 seconds per waffle (They won't be as crisp from the microwave as they would from the toaster or oven.)

❧ *Wonderful Waffles*

Separate 2 eggs.
Mix in this order:
  2 beaten egg yolks
  1¾ cups milk
  2 cups Super Flour
  1 tablespoon plus 1 teaspoon baking powder
  ½ cup melted butter/oil
Beat egg whites until soft peaks form. Fold into other ingredients. Bake in preheated waffle iron until steam stops and waffles are golden brown.
Tip: I use oil-spray or a butter spray and spray the waffle iron between waffles.
Variations: Add 1 shredded apple or a 1 cup frozen blueberries (no need to thaw) or other berries. For other possible additions, see Pancake Additions Ideas, page 329.

Tip: Use an old sanitized toothbrush to clean batter from crevices in your waffle iron.

Tip: To keep your waffle iron clean, make waffles that are slightly small and then they won't "overflow" and make a mess. Use the same scoop or measuring cup until you know the exact amount to make a perfect waffle with your particular waffle iron.

❧ Waffle Pizza

Onto cooked waffles, smear peanut butter and jam or jelly for the pizza sauce. Add Decorative Touches, such as slices of banana for pretend pepperoni, etc. Make a smiley face pizza.

Crepes

❧ Whole Wheat Crepes

(makes one dozen)
Crepes: Beat 2 eggs in a bowl. Add:
    1½ cups skim milk
    1 cup Super Flour
Mix with whisk or in the blender to remove lumps. Heat a small non-stick skillet or crepe pan over medium heat. Lightly butter or spray pan with vegetable oil. Remove pan from stove top, quickly pour ¼ cup of batter to thinly coat bottom of pan. Turn and tilt pan to even out batter and made the crepe as circular as possible. Pour any excess off and back into bowl. After about a minute, when dry on the top and brown on the bottom (check by peeking under edge), flip. Cook the second side for about 30 seconds until blotchy brown. Place finished crepe on wire rack to cool while you make the next crepe. Stack cooled crepes on a plate. Cooled crepes will not stick together as readily as warm crepes. Re-grease pan before cooking next crepe, if necessary.

Variation: Add ½ teaspoon of cinnamon to crepe mixture. And/or replace a tablespoon of Super Flour with wheat germ.

Filling: There seems no end to the possibilities for crepe filling:
    yogurt cheese
    cottage cheese
    shredded cheese
    Prune Butter (page 318)
    applesauce
    any puréed fruit
    jelly, jam, or marmalade
    re-hydrated dried fruit
    any fruit mixed with any cheese
    soft-cooked vegetables
    Healthy Extras
Topping:
    Mock Whipped Cream (page 344)
    plain yogurt
    yogurt mixed with jam, sweetener, or puréed fruit.

Batch and Freeze: Double the recipe and freeze using the Tray-freeze Method.

Pancakes

❧ How to Cook Pancakes

Don't overbeat the batter, stop stirring once the ingredients are moist (a few lumps are OK) or your pancakes will be tough. Adjust batter by diluting with milk or other liquid if too thick and adding flour if too thin. Heat griddle or skillet until hot. Its temperature is just right when a few drops of cold water dropped on the griddle will jump and sizzle. If the griddle is not hot enough, the water will just lie there and boil; if it is too hot, it will instantaneously evaporate. To prevent pancakes from sticking, add butter/oil after frying pan is hot. Pour a small amount (about 2-3 tablespoons) of batter onto the griddle until the pancake is the size you want. Make even smaller pancakes for your little ones. Cook about 2 to 3 minutes or until the surface is filled with bubbles and the underside is slightly brown. Raise the edge of the pancake with the spatula to test if it is firm and brown. If so, flip and cook the other side 1 to 2 minutes more. Do not flip again or the pancake will be tough. Do NOT use the spatula to press down the pancake (it feels so right to do this, doesn't it?) or it will be heavy.

Tip: Your child will love watching you make pancakes. If you have an electric frying pan, cook them at the table. If not, let your child have a high seat a safe distance away from the stove.

Tips: Mix pancake batter in a large measuring cup or a wide-mouthed pitcher instead of a bowl for easier pouring. Or put the batter into a clean milk carton—it's spout makes for easy pouring. Or use a squeeze bottle for more control when pouring batter for pancake art. Sometimes it's easier to use scissors to cut fun shapes (page 367) out of plain circular pancakes. Mom and Dad can eat the scraps.

Tips: Substitute room temperature club soda for liquid in these recipes for a fluffier pancake or waffle, but use immediately and do not store. Or separate eggs and mix yolks into rest of batter. Last, whip egg whites until stiff and fold gently into batter.

Variation: For fruity tasting pancakes, try substituting orange juice for the milk in pancake batter. Optionally add a tablespoon of citrus zest (page 438). Or use peach nectar instead of orange juice and add ½ cup chopped soft and ripe fresh peaches.

❧ Pancake Additions Ideas

Add any of the following to the Basic Pancake recipe:

> ½ cup of frozen or fresh blueberries or strawberries (no need to thaw frozen berries first, see bottom of page 430)
> thinly sliced pieces of an apple or other fresh fruit
> seedless grapes sliced in half
> raisins
> carob chips
> dates
> dried apricots or other dried fruit
> chopped walnuts or other nuts

Or replace some of the milk with another flavorful liquid: crushed pineapple, or apple, orange, or other fruit juice.

❧ Batch and Freeze Pancakes

I think pancakes are a lot of trouble to make, maybe because I make a mess that takes time to clean up, so I make a big batch and freeze the leftovers. Pancakes freeze well if you cool them completely on wire racks before freezing. Freeze them in freezer bags between sheets of waxed paper for up to 3 months. To re-heat, place frozen pancakes single layer on a baking sheet in a 325°F oven or toaster oven for 7-10 minutes, or microwave each pancake individually on high for about 20 seconds.

❧ Pancake Syrup Ideas

For Heaven's sake, don't give your precious children the pretend maple syrup sold in supermarkets. It's nothing more than corn syrup and caramel coloring. Serve real maple syrup, even though it's expensive. If you use the shot glass idea (see below), you don't use much syrup at all. Another nice topping for pancakes is fruit jelly—use a brand that contains no added sugar and is all fruit. Liquify it by adding a bit of water and maybe maple syrup or honey or melted butter/oil. For large breakfasts, create a selection of flavored pancake syrups by adding a few tablespoons of different jellies or jams to separate containers of maple syrup. This is a good way to use the last bit of jelly left in the jar—heat the jar a little and the jelly will come right out. Try plain applesauce, or a purée of banana with applesauce, using some added apple juice or water to thin it. Or, make your own syrup with fresh fruit: Blend fresh fruit and a little water or juice in the blender. You can buy fruit syrups at the natural foods store, but you can make your own for ⅓ the cost. Yogurt makes a nice base for a pancake syrup. Add a couple of tablespoons of frozen concentrated orange juice, honey, or other sweetener and/or jam and/or a few drops of vanilla or almond extract. Cooked prunes and yogurt (2 tablespoons yogurt per prune) makes a delicious pancake spread. Add some blackstrap molasses to any syrup as a nutritional enhancer, but go light with it because it has a strong taste. Sprinkle some fresh strawberry or banana pieces over the pancakes for an extra special touch—get them from your Super Snack Freezer Bag (page 292). Serve syrup warmed in the microwave for extra flavor and to prevent cooling the pancakes.

❧ *Have a Shot of Syrup*

If I let them, my kids would pour an entire quart of maple syrup over one pancake. I confess, even I would love to use lots of maple syrup. But REAL maple syrup is expensive, and too much sweetener is not good for anyone. Here's a way to use maple syrup so that you get maximum taste from a minimum amount. Fill a shot glass halfway with maple syrup—this takes only about 1 tablespoon! Dip pancake forkfulls (cut thin so that they will fit) into the shot glass so that only the tip of each forkfull gets covered with maple syrup. Place on tongue, syrup first, to get a full syrup flavor from only a small drop. When you're finished eating your pancakes, you'll be surprised at how little syrup you actually used. If you don't have a shot glass, use any small, shallow container with a thin circumference. The tiny dipping cups for sauces or butter in restaurants are great. Take home the plastic ones, but don't take the metal ones! If you don't have anything else, shape aluminum foil into little syrup dippers.

❧ *Dried Fruit Syrup*

Combine ½ cup dried fruit and ½ cup water in a saucepan. (If you have a real sweet tooth, use fruit juice or concentrated frozen fruit juice instead of water.) Bring to a boil and simmer for 20 minutes. Cool. Then whip in a blender, adding water very slowly until mixture reaches syrup consistency. (This will take anywhere from ½ cup to 1½ cups of water, depending on the dried fruit.) Store in refrigerator or freeze using the Food Cube Method. Warm in microwave before serving over pancakes.

❧ *Blackstrap Syrup*

Combine ½ cup blackstrap molasses, ½ cup honey, and 1 teaspoon vanilla in blender. Keep refrigerated.

❧ *Pancake Flour Alternatives*

In the Basic Whole Grain Flour Pancake recipe below, try substituting oatmeal for some of the flour. Or, try using some cooked whole brown rice grains, or millet grains, or other whole grains. Cooked mashed beans or bean flour mixes well into pancakes, too. Pancakes are a good way to use leftover cooked grains and beans that are getting old in the refrigerator.

❧ *Basic Whole Grain Pancakes*

Mix in this order:
  2 cups Super Flour
  2 teaspoons baking soda
    OR 2 teaspoons baking powder
  2 lightly beaten eggs
  2 cups milk
  2 tablespoons oil or melted butter
  Healthy Extras
Follow directions for How to Cook Pancakes.
Tip: Pancakes are a great way to get ground flax and pumpkin seeds and nuts into your child's diet. Grind into powder, sprinkle in to batter, and eat immediately.

❧ *Peanut Butter and Jelly Pancakes*

Spread a pancake with peanut butter and jelly. Roll up like a sleeping bag. Your toddler can eat these with her hands.

❧ *Banana Pancakes*

  1 cup Super Flour
  ¼ cup wheat germ
  ¼ cup oat or wheat bran
  ½ cup cooked millet or brown rice
  ½ cup milk
  ½ cup mashed bananas
  2 beaten eggs
  1 tablespoon melted butter/oil
Mix ingredients and cook.
Variation: Slice bananas lengthwise and then crosswise into small pieces. Pour pancake batter into pan, quickly add sliced bananas in a design. Flip pancake and finish cooking. Add ground nuts/seeds.

❧ *Personalized Picture Pancakes*

Pour Basic Whole Grain Pancake batter onto griddle. Place Decorative Touches, such as blueberries, walnuts, etc., into the cooking batter to make a smiley face, a heart or other shape, or your toddler's initials. Finish cooking the pancake. Place on your child's plate with the best-looking side facing up. If your decorative touches are hidden inside the pancake and can't be seen, next time remember to either gently push then down into batter or let them float above the batter.

❧ *Teddy Bear Pancakes*

Pour batter to make a regular pancake. Then pour two small circles on top of the pancake for the bear's ears. Finish cooking. You can add Decorative Touches to make eyes, nose, and mouth.

Tip: Use clean empty food cans with both ends opened and removed as molds for perfect circular pancakes.

❧ *Gingerbread People Pancakes*

Pour pancake batter into gingerbread people shapes.

❧ *"What's in a Name" Pancakes*

Spell your child's name in pancake batter. Simply pour the batter so that it forms the letters of your child's name, using a baster or cake icing applier with large-holed tip for more control. Finish cooking. Place it on the plate so that it is right side up, not backwards, of course.

❧ *Smiley Face Pancakes*

On skillet ready for cooking pancakes, drop two eyes, a nose, and a smile. Let cook for just a few seconds. Then pour a circular pancake over them. Flip and your pancake will smile at you.

Variation: If your child will enjoy it, you can do a sad face, a mad face (sloped eyebrows and straight line mouth), a surprised face (open mouth), etc.

❧ *ABC Pancakes*

Shape pancakes into letters and numbers. Do free-hand or use cookie cutters.

❧ *Great Pumpkin Pancakes*

1 beaten egg
1 cup canned pumpkin
2 tablespoons blackstrap molasses
½ cup Super Flour
½ teaspoon baking powder
½ teaspoon pumpkin pie spice
Mix in bowl and cook. Top with a mixture of yogurt and orange juice concentrate.

❧ *Bunny Pancakes*

Use the Great Pumpkin recipe above and substitute puréed cooked carrots for the canned pumpkin.

❧ *Nutty Millet Pancakes*

1 beaten egg
1 cup milk
3 tablespoons melted butter/oil
2 cups millet flour
1 tablespoon baking powder
1 cup chopped nuts
Add more milk if too thick.

Variation: Add 1 cup reconstituted dried fruit or fruit purée.

❧ *Oat-Yogurt Pancakes*

2 beaten eggs
2 tablespoons melted butter/oil
1 tablespoon maple syrup
1 cup yogurt
1 cup rolled oats
¼ cup wheat germ
Add more wheat germ if necessary. Mix in bowl and cook.

❧ *Brown Rice Pancakes*

2 cups cooked brown rice
1 cup yogurt
1 tablespoon lemon juice
¼ cup Super Flour or wheat germ
milk
Mix all ingredients, adding enough milk to pour for pancakes. Makes 6.

Crackers

☙ *The How To's of Cracker Rolling*

Cracker dough should not be kneaded, as is bread dough. It is best to have all ingredients, except eggs, at room temperature before mixing the dough. The cracker recipes below require that you roll the dough very thin—from 1/16 to ⅛ inch thick. It is important that you roll the dough to a uniform thickness, to promote even baking. The thinner you roll the crackers, the crisper they'll turn out after baking. Use a good rolling pin, and roll the dough on a cold, smooth, flat surface, such as a Formica® counter top. Flour the surface with a couple of tablespoons of flour. Roll the dough *gently* from the center of the dough out, flipping occasionally. Use a little more flour if the dough is sticking. Place the entire flat dough sheet on a baking sheet. Use a pizza cutter, a sharp knife, or an unused hair comb to cut *almost* all the way through the dough. The baked crackers will break easily at these score lines. You can also cut the dough into separate crackers before placing on the baking sheet. Or, cut the dough into squares, rectangles, circles, etc. To make a nice edge around each cracker, press lines into the edges of each cracker using a fork. Before baking, prick several holes in each cracker *all the way through* the dough with a fork. These air holes are not really for decoration, their purpose is to help the crackers to stay flat during baking. Of course, you can always poke holes so that they make a design.

Dough Tip: Rolling out dough is easier if you roll it on wax paper. To keep the wax paper from sliding around, place a few drops of water between the paper and the countertop. If you do not have a rolling pin, see tips on page 153.

☙ *Preventing Sogginess in Crackers*

After baking, it's a good idea to cool the crackers on a wire rack before storing to prevent sogginess. After they are completely cooled, store in an airtight container in a dry, cool, dark place. Include in the container a few grains of dry rice—these will absorb moisture and help keep the crackers crisp. (A few grains of dry rice in your salt shaker will help keep it flowing freely.) If the crackers are stale or smell bad, throw them out. If they become soggy, but have no odor and taste OK, you can save them. Dry them by cooking for 3-5 minutes in a preheated 300°F oven and they will keep for another week. Or microwave them on high for 30 seconds. Fresh crackers stored in airtight canisters or plastic bags will keep for up to 3-4 weeks at room temperature, up to 3 months in the refrigerator, and up to 6 months in the freezer.

You can add seeds (sesame are good) as a garnish to your crackers before baking. To insure that the seeds stick to both sides of the crackers, sprinkle some seeds on the rolling surface. Place the flat, pre-rolled dough over them, sprinkle some on the top of the cracker dough, and gently roll to press them into both sides of the dough. See Bread Crumb Substitutes, page 322.

☙ *A Dozen Quick Crackers*

Preheat oven to 350°F. Mix in a bowl:
    1 cup Super Flour
    ¼ teaspoon salt
    4 Tablespoons cold-pressed canola oil
        from the natural foods store
Gradually stir in 3-4 tablespoons very cold water until the dough is the consistency of pie crust. Refrigerate dough for an hour to chill. Roll very thin to ⅛-¼ inch thickness. Use pizza cutter to cut dough into rectangles, triangles, and other shapes. Prick air holes with fork all the way through the dough. Bake on oiled baking sheet for 10-15 minutes until lightly browned and crisp.

☙ *Whole Wheat Teething Crackers*

For babies older than one year.
Preheat oven to 325°F.
    2½ cups Super Flour
    ½ teaspoon salt
    1 tablespoon honey
    1 beaten egg

½ cup milk

Mix all ingredients together. Add more milk, a tablespoon at a time, until the dough forms a cohesive ball. Roll thicker than other crackers (about ⅜ inch thick). Use pizza cutter to almost cut through dough to from rectangular shapes crackers, approximately 3x1½ inches. Prick air holes in each cracker with a fork completely through the dough. Bake until very dry—about an hour. Cool on wire rack. If crackers are not hard, return to oven for 5-15 minutes.

⮞ *Applesauce Crackers*

Preheat oven to 350°F.
    1 cup Super Flour
    ½ cup plus 1 tablespoon applesauce
    4 tablespoons melted butter/oil
Roll and bake for 10 minutes. Flip each cracker over and bake for another 5-10 minutes.

Variation: You can make these crackers into twist shapes. Cut rolled dough into rectangular strips, about 3x½-inches. Hold the strip with two hands by the ends, twist in opposite directions, place on baking sheet and gently press the ends down onto the sheet to prevent unwinding. Bake.

⮞ *Oatmeal Wheat Germ Crackers*

Preheat oven to 325°F.
    ¾ cup oatmeal
    ¾ cup wheat germ
    ½ teaspoon salt
    1 tablespoon honey
    ¼ cup softened butter/oil
    3 tablespoons milk
Mix all ingredients together. Add more milk, a teaspoon at a time, until the dough forms a cohesive ball. Bake 15 minutes. Flip and bake for an additional 5-10 minutes.

⮞ *Peanut Butter IN the Crackers*

Preheat oven to 325°F.
    1 cup Super Flour
    2 tablespoons melted butter/oil
    2 tablespoons softened peanut butter
    ¼ cup milk
Combine ingredients. Add extra milk, a teaspoon at a time until a soft dough is formed. Knead 5 minutes and roll until

⅛-inch thick. Use pizza cutter to cut almost through dough to form rectangular shaped crackers. Prick air holes in each cracker with a fork completely through the dough. Bake about 12 minutes or until lightly browned. Cool on wire rack.

⮞ *Tahini Crackers*

Preheat oven to 325°F.
    1 cup Super Flour
    2 tablespoons tahini
    2 tablespoons melted butter/oil
    2 tablespoons water
Combine ingredients. Add extra water, a teaspoon at a time until a soft dough is formed. Roll until ⅛-inch thick. Use pizza cutter to almost cut through dough to from rectangular shaped crackers. Prick air holes in each cracker with a fork completely through the dough. Bake about 10 minutes or until lightly browned. Cool on wire rack.

⮞ *Millet Crackers*

Preheat oven to 350°F.
Mix in this order:
    2½ tablespoons melted butter/oil
    1½ teaspoons honey
    4 tablespoons water
    ½ cup raw millet, ground to a powder in blender
    ¾ cup Super Flour
Add more flour, a tablespoon at a time until good dough consistency. Knead for a few minutes and roll until ⅛-inch thick on buttered baking sheet. Score with a knife in diamond shapes. Bake about 20 minutes or until lightly browned. Cool on wire rack.

⮞ *Whole Grain Cheese Thins*

Mix in this order:
    1 cup Super Flour
    ½ teaspoon salt
    ¼ teaspoon paprika
    2 cups grated Cheddar cheese
    2 tablespoons oil
    2 tablespoons melted butter/oil
Shape into roll and refrigerate overnight in wax paper. Slice very thin, shape into fish or crescent designs as with commercial cheese thins, and bake on greased or oil-sprayed cookie sheet in pre-heated 350°F oven for about 10 minutes, watching carefully at end of baking time for burning. Store in airtight

container for up to two weeks in a cool, dark cabinet. Use in soups or for dipping.

❧ *Cheesy Thins*

Combine with your fingers or a pastry blender until dough consistency:

¾ cup Super Flour
½ cup extra sharp Cheddar or Swiss cheese or combination, grated
2 tablespoons butter, grated

Use only high quality cheeses. Knead about 30 seconds only and chill in refrigerator until firm. Roll very thin. Cut into strips 2½ inches long and ¾ inch wide. Bake in pre-heated 400°F oven for 5 minutes, watching carefully for burning. Makes about 30 thins.

Pasta

Cooking Pasta: Save some energy by experimenting with pasta cooking. Bring water to a rapid boil. Add pasta and turn off heat. Let stand for a 15 minutes or until done.

Leftover Pasta: Refrigerate leftover pasta, covered well. If pasta sticks together, boil for just one minute or two. Use leftover pasta the next day—sauté in a little butter/oil and garlic. Delicious! See tips on freezing and thawing pasta on page 225. Or use leftover pasta for breakfast. For breakfast, mix with scrambled eggs, veggies, cheese, and/or tofu to make Macaroni and Scrambled Eggs.

Tip: Make whole grain pasta often. It's healthy and inexpensive. And pouring boiling water down drains helps to keep them clear, as discussed on page 479.

Tip: Let cold tap water run in the sink while you are pouring off boiling water from pasta. It may help prevent steam and splashes from scalding you.

❧ *Super Pasta Sauce*

Most commercial spaghetti sauces have too much sodium. Make your own by mixing plain tomato paste (read label and make sure that there is no added salt) with the amount of water specified on the label. Add your own fresh herbs, such as oregano and parsley (page 452), and even shredded cheese and other Healthy Extras. Freeze

using the Food Cube Method or the Phantom Container Method.

Tip: Cut off both ends of a tomato paste can and freeze. Store in a small freezer bag. Cut off a slice when needed. Remember never to refreeze any food that has previously been frozen, due to possible bacteria contamination. If using a thawed frozen tomato paste to make sauce, do not refreeze the sauce. Keep refrigerated and use within 24 hours.

❧ *Quick Super Pasta*

Cook some whole grain pasta. As a sauce, thaw a few Super Pasta Sauce food cubes (previous recipe) or vegetable food cubes or both. Add some cooked beans (whole or mashed) or cooked soy grits to the sauce. Heat sauce on the stove or in the microwave. Or don't heat at all, the heat from the pasta will warm it. Pour sauce over cooked, drained pasta. While pasta and sauce are still hot, sprinkle with shredded mozzarella or other natural cheese and let cheese melt. Or melt cheese by placing dish in the microwave for several seconds. Serve immediately. There's no end to the Healthy Extras you can add to a pasta dish. This is another meal you can freeze as individual TV dinners using the Phantom Container Freezing Method.

❧ *Easy Macaroni and Cheese*

1 cup cooked whole grain pasta
¼ cup grated natural cheese
¼ cup cottage or ricotta cheese
1 teaspoon butter
2-3 tablespoons of milk

Mix all ingredients. Heat on stove top or in microwave until cheese and butter melt. Add a sprinkle of wheat germ on top.

❧ *White Sauce*

Mix together with whisk or fork in saucepan:

2 tablespoons melted butter/oil
2 tablespoons arrowroot
1 cup milk
1/8 teaspoon pepper (optional)
1 teaspoon salt (optional)

Stir constantly over low heat until thickened. After sauce has thickened, cook for an additional minute.

Tip: Macaroni and Cheese can be frozen using the Nested Plastic Bag Method or Phantom Container Method in individual toddler-sized portions.

❧ Macaroni and Cheese Bake

Cook 8 ounces whole wheat elbow macaroni. Preheat oven to 375°F. Beat together:

> 2 beaten eggs
> 1 cup milk

Make alternate layers in a greased, 2-quart casserole:

> cooked macaroni and
> 2 cups of grated natural cheese
> (Mozzarella, Swiss, Cheddar, etc.)

Pour egg/milk mixture over layers. Bake for 40-45 minutes.

❧ Blender/Stove-top Macaroni and Cheese

Cook 8 ounces whole wheat elbow macaroni. Mix in blender:

> 1½ cups milk
> 1½ cups shredded cheese or an 8 ounce package
> 2 tablespoons arrowroot or unbleached white flour
> ½ teaspoon powdered kelp or salt
> 1 tablespoon oil or melted butter

Put cooked macaroni in large frying pan and pour blender mixture over macaroni. Cook over low heat, stirring frequently, until thick (about 5-10 minutes). Sprinkle top with whole grain bread crumbs or wheat germ and place under broiler until browned and crunchy.

❧ Homemade Egg Pasta Noodles

> 3 beaten eggs
> 1 tablespoon oil
> 1½-1¾ cups whole wheat flour

Add beaten eggs to oil. Mix with flour until you have a stiff dough. Knead for 3-5 minutes. Roll out with rolling pin until very thin. (See dough tip on page 332.) Let dry for 1 hour. Cut into strips. Cook immediately in boiling water for 4-5 minutes or freeze.

❧ Spinach Noodles

Make same as homemade egg noodles, but replace one of the eggs with a small food cube of finely puréed spinach or other Super Green Veggie Cube.

❧ Tofu Lasagna Roll-Ups

Cook 1 package of whole wheat lasagna noodles (about 8 noodles) and rinse under cold water. Meanwhile, get ready:

> 2½ cups tomato sauce
> 2 cups shredded mozzarella cheese

Mix:

> 1 cup mashed tofu
> ¼ cup grated Parmesan cheese

On each cooked noodle, spread a thin layer of the tofu mixture and about 2 tablespoons of tomato sauce, then sprinkle with some shredded cheese. Roll up the noodle jelly-roll style and place it on its side in the baking pan so that you can see the spiral from the top view. When finished with all the noodles, pour the rest of the sauce over them and sprinkle with the rest of the mozzarella cheese. Bake, covered, in a preheated 350°F oven for 30-45 minutes. Freeze leftovers.

Tip: You may wish to cut the noodles in half to make them shorter, so that the spirals will be toddler size.

❧ Alfredo Pasta

In blender, mix until smooth:

> one part milk
> four parts cottage cheese
> two parts grated Parmesan
> fresh dill and/or parsley (approximately 1 tablespoon per two cups of cheese or to taste)
> nutmeg to taste
> black pepper

Toss with hot wholewheat pasta.

❧ Mushroom-Tofu Sauce

Over medium heat, sauté ½ cup onion and ½ cup mushrooms in 1 tablespoon butter or olive oil. Optionally add 1 clove garlic and sauté for an additional minute. Turn heat down to low. Meanwhile, blend tofu (about 1 cup) in processor. Add 1 teaspoon Worcestershire sauce and ⅓ cup vegetable stock or water to processor. Mix tofu mixture into pan and stir until warmed through. Serve over cooked pasta or grains.

Casseroles

Tip: Save time in the kitchen by making two casseroles and freeze one using the Phantom Container Freezing Method. Thaw overnight in refrigerator. As a general rule, an unthawed frozen casserole should be cooked about twice as long as a thawed one. To test a casserole for doneness, insert a butter knife in the middle of the casserole, leave for 10 seconds, remove and feel for heat. If knife is cold, continue cooking.

◄ *Easy Bread Casserole*

Mix in this order:
    1 cup whole wheat bread crumbs
    1¼ cups milk
    1 large beaten egg
    ½ cup cheese
    1 tablespoon or more wheat germ
    and/or ground nuts
Bake in pre-heated 375°F oven for 30 minutes.

◄ *Cheery Cheese Casserole*

Preheat oven to 375°F. In large bowl, mix in this order:
    3 beaten eggs
    ½ cup oil or melted butter
    ½ cup soy or cow's milk
    1 cup cottage cheese
    2 cups grated jack or cheddar cheese
    1/4 cup Super Flour
    1/4 cup wheat germ
Pour smooth mixture into buttered casserole dish and bake for 40 minutes until set.

◄ *Lentil Stew*

    2 tablespoons olive oil
    2 cups chopped onion
    1 sliced raw carrot
    ½ cup diced celery with leaves
    2 tablespoons minced garlic
    3½ cups broth
    1 pound dry lentils
    ½ cup uncooked medium pearl parley
    16-ounce can crushed tomatoes
    1 teaspoon salt
    ½ teaspoon pepper
    ¼ teaspoon oregano

1 package frozen chopped spinach
Sauté onions, celery, and garlic in oil for 8 minutes. Add 8 cups water, the broth, lentils and barley. Cover, bring to a boil, reduce heat and simmer 1 hour or until very tender. Add crushed tomatoes, carrot, and seasonings. Bring to boil, reduce heat, and simmer uncovered for 5 minutes. Add spinach and stir to separate. Simmer another 5-7 minutes. This recipe freezes well. Use for Toddler TV Dinner. Sprinkle this stew with lots of Parmesan cheese and it's even more delicious!

◄ *Easy One-Dish Casserole*

Preheat oven to 300 degrees. Mix in a covered casserole dish:
    ½ cup uncooked lentils
    ¼ cup soy grits
    ½ cup whole grains (millet, brown rice, etc.)
    1 small chopped onion
    3 cups vegetable broth
    1 tablespoon parsley
    ½ teaspoon sweet basil
    ¼ teaspoon oregano
    ¼ teaspoon thyme
    1 teaspoon garlic powder
Bake, covered, for 90 minutes. Add shredded or grated cheese on top for last 15 minutes of baking.
Variation: This recipe can also be cooked in a crockpot.

◄ *Tofu, Rice, and Parsley Casserole*

Preheat oven to 350°F. Mix in blender:
    1 cup milk
    1 cup tofu
    ½ cup sharp cheese
    1 egg
    1 large onion
    one bunch fresh or frozen parsley
    1 green pepper, in large pieces
Grease a casserole dish and add 2 cups cooked brown rice or other grain. Pour mixture from blender over rice and bake covered for 45 minutes.

❧ Quick Broccoli-Rice Casserole

Preheat oven to 350°F. In bowl, mix in this order:
    1 beaten egg
    ½ cup milk
    ½ cup grated cheese
    2 cups leftover brown rice
    1 cup broccoli, finely chopped
    1 chopped onion (sauté first if you wish)
Mix all and turn in buttered casserole dish, cover, and bake for 45 minutes.

❧ Kale - Rice Casserole

Preheat oven to 325°F.
    2 cups cooked brown rice or other grain
    1 bunch raw kale, washed and chopped
    ½ cup shredded cheddar cheese
    ¼ cup fresh parsley
    2 beaten eggs
Mix above ingredients and press into greased baking dish. Top with this mixture:
    ¼ cup whole wheat bread crumbs
    ¼ cup wheat germ
    3 tablespoons melted butter/oil
    ¼ cup Parmesan cheese
Bake, uncovered 40 minutes.

❧ Sweet Potato Loaf

Preheat oven to 350°F.
    5 tablespoons melted butter/oil
    ½ cup orange juice
    ¾ cup cooked mashed sweet potatoes
    1 beaten egg
    1 cup ground oatmeal
    ¼ cup wheat germ
    1 teaspoon pumpkin pie spice (page 355)
    ½ teaspoon baking powder
    1 teaspoon vanilla
    2 tablespoons blackstrap molasses
    ½ cup ground or chopped nuts
    Add a little more orange juice if your loaf is too thick.
Mix ingredients above in one bowl. Pour mixture into greased loaf pan. Bake for 40-45 minutes, until cake tester or toothpick comes out clean.

❧ Easy Cheese Strata

Preheat oven to 350°F. Butter a 9x13 pan and arrange 6 slices of whole grain bread in bottom of pan. Cover with cheese slices or sprinkle with about 2 cups of shredded cheese. Layer another 6 slices of bread over cheese. In bowl, beat 3 eggs and mix in 3 cups milk. Pour egg mixture over bread/cheese layers. Bake uncovered for 45-50 minutes or until lightly browned.
Variation: Add leftover chopped cooked veggies as a layer. Sauté first if you wish.

❧ Sweet Potato Casserole

Place cooked purée from two sweet potatoes into a large bowl. Add 1 beaten egg and ½ cup yogurt. Mix well with mixer or potato masher; don't use a blender or food processor. Stir in 2 tablespoons fresh parsley. Optionally add Healthy Extras. Place into greased baking dish and bake in preheated 350°F oven for 35 to 40 minutes until browned. You can make the casserole ahead and refrigerate—but add about 12 minutes to baking time.

❧ Eggplant Parmesan

Preheat oven to 350°F.
In a shallow bowl, mix these dry ingredients which will make approximately ½ cup:
    ¼ cup Super Flour
    1 tablespoon Parmesan cheese
    1 tablespoon wheat germ
    1 tablespoon whole wheat bread crumbs
    1 teaspoon parsley.
In another bowl, mix wet ingredients:
    a tablespoon of milk
    1 beaten egg
Slice raw eggplant into ¼ to ½ inch slices. Wet both sides of each slice by dipping in wet ingredients. Then dip into bowl of dry ingredients to coat each side with flour mixture. Grease a large baking pan. Layer coated slices into the pan. Cover each layer with tomato sauce and sprinkle with Parmesan cheese. Cover the pan tightly and bake 35-45 minutes until eggplant is tender when pierced with fork. Turn off the oven. Sprinkle top with mozzarella cheese and return pan to oven. Let sit for 5 to 10 minutes until mozzarella is nicely melted. Serve or freeze in individual TV dinners using the Phantom Container Freezing Method.

❧ *Grain Quiche Crust*

Preheat oven to 350°F. Beat 2 eggs in a bowl. Add 3 cups total of cooked brown rice, millet, or other whole grain. Grease a pie plate (9-inch, preferably glass). Press grain/egg mixture into pie plate to that it covers the bottom and up the sides. Bake 15 minutes. It will bake further when you put in the quiche filling and bake in the oven—cover with foil to prevent it from burning or becoming too hard. (If you're going to use this crust in a pie that does not require baking, bake it for 25 minutes instead of 15.)

❧ *Potato Quiche Crust*

Preheat oven to 425°F. Grate 3 cups of raw potato. Mix with a tablespoon or two of oil. Press into 9-inch pie pan and prebake for 15 minutes until it just starts to brown. Add quiche filling and bake. Because of this thick crust, you can probably reduce the number of eggs in your quiche recipe to 3 eggs.

❧ *Rice and Cheese Crust*

Preheat oven to 425°F. Combine:
   2 cups cooked brown rice
   1½ ounces of grated cheese
   1 beaten egg
Pat into greased pie tin and prebake for 15 minutes.

❧ *Broccoli Cheese Rice Quiche*

Prepare crust (see recipe above). Preheat oven to 350°F. Arrange in bottom of crust:
   1 cup cooked chopped broccoli florets
   1 cup shredded natural cheese (Swiss and mozzarella are good).
In separate bowl, mix:
   4 beaten eggs
   1½ cups milk.
Pour over broccoli and bake in preheated 350°F oven until firm. Let stand 15 minutes before serving.

❧ *Tomato Quiche*

Prepare crust (see recipe above). Preheat oven to 375°F. Arrange in bottom of crust sliced tomato (1 large or two small tomatoes). Sprinkle on tomato slices:

   1 teaspoon oregano
   1 teaspoon sugar
   ½ cup chopped onion
   1 cup shredded cheese
Mix in separate bowl:
   2 beaten eggs
   2 tablespoons wheat germ
   1 cup evaporated milk
Pour over tomatoes and bake for 45 minutes or until set. Let stand for 10 minutes before serving.

Frozen Treats

Tip: Popsicles can be very messy. Poke the stick through a small paper plate, a plastic lid, or a coffee filter to catch the drips. Or, for a deeper drip catcher, use a paper cup cut short. Wrap a napkin around the stick under the plate or cup to absorb the liquid that will seep through the hole.

❧ *Healthy Sundae Topping*

Thaw one of your frozen baby fruit cubes to use as a topping on ice cream. Or use a jar of baby prunes, pineapples, or some other sweet fruit.

❧ *Creamsicle*

Mix frozen vanilla yogurt or ice cream mixed with thawed frozen orange juice concentrate.

❧ *No-Added Sugar Popsicles*

Just try to find popsicles made from 100% real fruit or fruit juice at a reasonable price in the supermarket or natural foods store. It's so easy and cheap to make your own! You can buy popsicle molds, use ice cube trays, or buy little paper cups. They have 3-ounce or 5-ounce paper cups with cute designs that are sold as disposable bathroom cups. For sticks, use wooden popsicle sticks—recycled (boil to sterilize) or purchased or buy small plastic spoons. Making popsicles could not be easier—just fill the cups, place the sticks in, and freeze! To make sticks stand centered and upright, place them into popsicles after about an hour of freezing, when they are partially frozen. Use the same tip on page 167 for loosening ice cubes to remove popsicles from molds.

If using paper cups, you can unmold using that tip or just rip them off.

Use plain fruit juice or concentrated fruit juice mixed into plain yogurt or vanilla flavored yogurt. Fresh fruit pieces (or even cooked veggie pieces) mixed into fruit juice or yogurt makes a popsicle more interesting. Be careful-watch little ones for choking! Or make layered popsicles by pouring small amounts of fruit juice/yogurt into molds and letting it freeze before another layer of a different color is added on top. Insert fruit pieces between the layers. Have your child decide on the layers and flavors.

Framed Personalized Picture Popsicles

Use a small, flat, shallow, freezable container for each popsicle. (I sometimes use small paper boxes lined with freezer wrap.) Fill halfway with plain yogurt sweetened with honey or maple syrup and a little lemon juice. Freeze until semi-solid, but still mushy. Remove from freezer and push small berry pieces or other Decorative Touches into the yogurt to "draw" a design or a name. For really detailed pictures or words (that require higher resolution!), you can use small candy sprinkles or silver balls or dried fruit chopped well in the blender. Insert a popsicle stick into the yogurt without ruining the picture (this takes skill). Place into freezer and let freeze solid. Remove and cover design with a clear fruit juice, such as white grape or apple juice or even plain water. Make the juice layer as thin as possible, so it won't become cloudy and hide the picture. Freeze again until solid. The opaque yogurt acts as the background and frame for the picture, the juice acts as a clear glassy cover. If you need the containers, remove the popsicle and place in a freezer bag, as in the Phantom Container Freezing Method.

Tip: To make a young (or not so young) house guest feel special, make a personalized popsicle before their arrival. Make one for each guest at a birthday party.

Homemade Frozen Yogurt

Freeze plain yogurt in a flat shallow container, well covered, until mushy (about one or two hours). Remove from freezer and mix well with whisk or fork. Add flavoring: about ¼ cup of sweetener and ½-1 cup mashed fruit for each cup of yogurt. Try fork-mashed strawberries and/or bananas. (You need a lot of flavoring because sweetness is hard to taste when in frozen foods.) Mix well and return to the freezer until firm.

Variation: For us chocoholics, not our babies, add as flavoring ¼ cup chocolate syrup to a cup of yogurt. After adding flavoring, freeze in popsicle molds or in paper cups with popsicle sticks for individual servings.

Frozen Yogurt Loaf

Mix yogurt with flavorings and freeze in a plastic-lined loaf pan. When solid, transfer to a freezer bag. For a quick snack, cut off a slice, let stand at room temperature for about 10 minutes to soften a bit before eating.

Yogurt Milkshake

Add 1 cup milk to at least ½ cup frozen yogurt. Fork mix or use blender and serve immediately.

Variations: Add frozen fruit for an extra sweet taste. Add an ice cube or two to make it super cold. For an adult mocha shake, add 2 tablespoons chocolate syrup and 2 tablespoons decaffeinated coffee to 1 cup milk and ½ cup plain frozen yogurt.

Yogurt Cheese
See page 254.

Mock Ice Cream

Purée frozen bananas in blender or food processor. Add orange juice, honey, and/or vanilla to taste.

Ring Around the Ice Cream

Place a bit of Mock Ice Cream (previous recipe) in the middle of a canned pineapple ring. Use Decorative Touches to make a smiley face or other picture.

Variation: Instead of a pineapple ring, use a ring of cantaloupe or honeydew. Slice melon in half and remove seeds. Use sharp knife to cut all the way around the inside, very close to rind. Slice to make rings.

❧ Fruit Freeze Pops

1 6-ounce can frozen orange juice
concentrate
¾ cup strawberries
⅓ cup water

Mix in blender. Pour into paper cups with popsicle sticks. Freeze.

Variation: Replace strawberries with a banana.

❧ Push-Up Pops

My son discovered squeeze pops at a friend's house and now insists on eating "the cold long, long lollipops." So I bought a box of the commercial unhealthy, artificially colored and flavored sugar water push-up pops, making sure they were pasteurized. This was solely for the purpose of obtaining the plastic containers. You, too, can buy and re-use these containers for healthy freeze pops for your child. Cut the tops off them, pour out their contents, rinse them out with very hot water, and use a tiny funnel to pour natural, no-sugar added pasteurized fruit juice into them. The natural foods store has a great selection—try watermelon or pina colada! If your child complains that they don't taste as good as the commercial brands, make them just a bit sweeter by adding a little honey or maple syrup. (After filling the containers, I considered taping them shut, but was concerned about my son eating that glue on the tape, so I just leave the containers opened.) Place the filled pops into a very tall plastic cup to keep them upright and prevent spillage. Keep the filled freeze pops in the cup and place into the freezer for a few hours until they freeze solid. Then transfer them to a large air-tight freezer bag. You can re-use the containers over and over again if you wash them between each use with very hot water and antibacterial dish soap. Rinse well to get every last trace of soap out!

❧ Fruit Ice Milk

In blender, blend 1 cup fruit (blueberries, peaches, strawberries, or other fruit) with 2 cups of milk (cow's or soy). Pour into shallow tray, cover tightly, and freeze until mushy. Remove from freezer and mix with electric mixer, fork, or whisk until smooth. Optionally, add more fruit chunks or Healthy Extras. Place back in the freezer until frozen.

❧ Frozen Fruit Cream

½ cup evaporated milk
package of frozen fruit

Blend in processor until smooth. Freeze in paper cups with popsicle sticks.

❧ Homemade Ice Cream Sandwiches

Make your own ice cream sandwiches by placing Mock Ice Cream (page 339), frozen ice cream, or yogurt between two large, flat homemade cookies. Freeze until solid using the Nested Plastic Bag Method.

❧ Ice Cream Soda

Place a scoop or two of ice cream in a bowl or cup. Pour some Mock Soda Pop (page 357) over the ice cream. Serve immediately. Optionally cover with Mock Whipped Cream (page 344).

Variation: In place of ice cream, use Mock Ice Cream (page 339) or frozen yogurt or any frozen sweet food, such as frozen fruit chunks.

❧ Watermelon Alphabet or Artwork Popsicles

From a whole watermelon, slice a circular piece about 1-inch thick from the center of the melon where the circumference is greatest. With a sharp knife, cut out shapes or your child's initials. Insert a popsicle stick up through the bottom. Freeze using the Tray-freeze Method. These popsicles are very drippy and are best eaten while wearing a bathing suit!

❧ Real Fruit Sherbet

This is too easy. Simply blend frozen fruit (store-bought or your own frozen fruits) in the food processor or blender until smooth. Frozen melon balls are great for this. So are frozen strawberries and blueberries. Optionally add into blender some frozen fruit juice concentrate (about 1 tablespoon for each cup of fruit), or a little orange and/or lemon juice. The mixture is very thick and it may be necessary to open a stir a few times and add a little juice or water. Sprinkle Healthy Extras on top. Or you can freeze the fruit in individual cups to have Italian Ice.

Variation: Freeze fruit sauces instead. See recipe on page 353.

❧ Fruit Slushy

In blender, mix fresh fruit with ice cubes. Add ice cubes gradually until desired consistency.

❧ "Creamy" Fruit Slushy

Blend together:

- ½ cup unsweetened apple juice or any fruit juice
- ½ cup low-fat plain yogurt
- 1 teaspoon maple syrup or blackstrap molasses
- 2 ice cubes

Blend very well, adding more ice or water to desired consistency.

Variation: Instead of juice, you can add fruit pieces, such as strawberries, bananas, or blueberries. Or you can add re-hydrated dried fruit, such as papaya and apricots.

❧ Strawberry Fruit Ice

In blender, mix 1 cup water or juice with 1 cup fresh strawberries or other fruit until smooth. Optionally add a teaspoon of lemon juice. Freeze using the Food Cube Method. Take what you need, chop until smooth in blender or food processor. Serve in shallow bowls. Sprinkle Healthy Extras on top.

Variation: Use just about any other fresh or frozen fruit.

❧ Lunch Box Slushy

Freeze strawberry fruit ice or any fruit ice in small lidded containers or empty single serving yogurt containers. Cover well before freezing. In the morning, put in lunch box (next to a food or drink that should be kept cold). By lunchtime, your child has slush!

❧ Fruit Juice Snowballs

Crush ice in blender to make snow. Use ice cream scoop to shape like snowballs and place in bowls or shallow glasses. Pour (very cold) fruit juice over snowballs.

Variation: For a sweeter, thicker topping, use frozen juice concentrate diluted with a little water. Use paper cups instead of glass for a refreshing outside summer snack.

❧ Quick Vanilla Ice Cream

Mix 2 tablespoons cream or milk with 2-3 tablespoons honey and ⅓ teaspoon vanilla. Stir into 2 cups crushed ice from blender. Eat immediately.

❧ Non-Dairy Ice Cream

- 8-12 ounces of tofu
- 1 frozen sliced banana
- 1 tablespoon honey
- ¼-½ cup fruit juice or water

Mix in blender for about a minute until creamy. Place in freezer container and optionally stir in frozen fruit pieces, such as strawberries, blueberries, etc. Freeze for 30 minutes before serving.

Variation: Make your own recipe. Add ground nuts, a tablespoon of tahini, and/or other Healthy Extras. This is a good way to use up leftovers.

❧ Frozen Fruit Crunch

In a blender, mix ⅓ cup milk with 2 tablespoons frozen fruit concentrate. Add 2-4 ice cubes gradually until desired consistency.

❧ *Frozen Banana Pops*

Cut bananas in half lengthwise and then width-wise to make 4 banana quarters. Stick popsicle sticks in the widest end. Roll in honey, maple syrup, fruit juice concentrate, or fruit juice to coat. Then roll in a mixture of dry ingredients, such as chopped or ground nuts, wheat germ, finely chopped dried fruit. unsweetened coconut, or mini-chocolate chips.. Freeze using the Tray-freeze Method.

Variation: Coat with chocolate or carob syrup before rolling in dry ingredients, or spread bananas thinly with peanut butter or tahini before rolling.

❧ *Tofutti*

Mix 1 box tofu with ½ cup fruit juice concentrate or to taste. Freeze in plastic cups.

Desserts and Dessert Toppings

Tip: Whiz regular granulated sugar in the blender on high to make superfine sugar.

Tip: Make brown sugar from white sugar mixed with a little blackstrap molasses—one or two tablespoons molasses to a cup of white sugar. It's more nutritious and cheaper too! Freezing prevents brown sugar from hardening. If brown sugar has hardened, use a cheese grater to scrape off what you need, or whiz in blender. Or sprinkle hardened brown sugar with a little water and warm it in a 200°F oven for a few minutes, then crumble with fork or whiz in the blender. Place a slice of bread or an apple slice into container and hardened brown sugar will soften in a few days.

Tip: Freeze leftover whipped topping by glopping it onto cookie sheets and using the Tray Freeze Method.

❧ *Parfait Buffet*

Allow your child to be "in charge" by having him make his own parfait. Or you can make it under his direction; it's quicker and much less messy. The choices in the buffet could include yogurt; sliced, diced, or puréed fresh fruits and veggies or thawed food cubes; ground nuts and seeds, soft peanut butter and other nut or seed butters; grated cheeses; wheat germ; cooked grains and legumes; raisins and other dried fruits; and Mock Whipped Cream (page 344). You certainly don't need all of these! In fact, too many may allow your child to assemble some stomach-turning combinations. Your child will feel just as special if you allow him to direct your parfait construction with only two or three ingredients—"Which one do you want on the bottom? Is that enough? ..." You should, of course, use a tall transparent plastic (or glass if you are brave enough) container so that your child can see the layers he created. A Parfait Buffet is a good way to use leftovers.

❧ *Instant Blender Whole Grain Bread Pudding*

1 cup whole grain bread crumbs (see recipe on page 321)
¼ cup cream or milk
1 teaspoon lemon juice
2 tablespoons raw apple, diced
2 tablespoons diced dried apricots or raisins

Grind in blender and serve. Add a little more milk if too thick.

❧ *Baked Whole Grain Bread Pudding*

Preheat oven to 350°F. Combine in 2 quart casserole dish:

8 slices whole grain bread, crusts removed and cubed
1 can evaporated skim milk (12 ounces)

Let stand for 10-15 minutes until milk is absorbed. Meanwhile, combine in a small bowl:

2 extra large eggs
1 egg white
1 cup milk
½ cup honey
1 teaspoon vanilla
½ teaspoon cinnamon

Stir ½ cup plumped raisins or other dried fruit into bread and milk mixture. Pour egg mixture from small bowl into casserole. Bake 45 minutes or until set. Serve warm with Mock Whipped Cream (page 344).

❧ *Edible Play Dough*

2 tablespoons creamy peanut butter
2 tablespoons honey
approximately 4 tablespoons instant powdered milk (dry, do not mix with water)

Mix and knead until dough-like consistency. Add a little water to thin or milk powder to thicken. Roll into balls, shape into snakes, make your child's initials, flatten and out into any shape you want. Use Decorative Touches to decorate. And then EAT! Make each guest at your child's birthday party feel special: Place her edible initials on her party plate to mark her place at the table.

❧ *Play Dough Cookies (Marizipan Cookies)*

These cookies can be shaped (as you would play dough) and then baked and eaten. Preheat oven to 300°F. Mix:

1 cup butter or margarine
½ cup sugar
¼ teaspoon almond paste
2½ cups Super Flour (use mostly white flour)

Cream first three ingredients and add flour. Divide into several batches and color. Let children mold into shapes using Decorative Touches. Bake for 25-35 minutes depending on size of shapes. Watch very carefully so they don't burn. Remove smaller shapes if they are done, leaving larger shapes to continue baking.

❧ *Stained Glass Cookies*

These cookies are a lot of fun to make with your children! The melted hard candy give these cookies a stained glass look. They can be placed on the tree as ornaments or given as gifts from our child.

Use a sugar cookie dough for this recipe. Or use this recipe: In large bowl, blend together:

½ cup softened butter
1 cup sugar
1 beaten egg
1 teaspoon vanilla

Combine dry ingredients in another bowl:

2½ cups Super Flour
½ teaspoon baking soda
¼ teaspoon salt

Add dry ingredients into butter mixture. Add 4-6 tablespoons water as you mix them together until a stiff dough forms. Cover and chill in refrigerator for at least one hour. Meanwhile, use about one pound of hard candy (life savers, lollipops, etc.) and crush them in a sturdy plastic bag until granulated. Use a can, rolling pin, or something hard (page 153) to crush the candy within the bag. Roll chilled dough into snakes the thickness of a pencil and shape into stars, bells, Christmas trees, circular ornaments, and other shapes. Bake on cookie sheets lined with aluminum foil or parchment paper in preheated 350°F oven for 10 minutes or until very lightly browned. Remove from oven and fill shapes with crushed candy—fill up completely to the top of the cookie dough. Bake 3-4 minutes, watching carefully so you can remove from the oven immediately after candy has melted. Don't let candy bubble. Optionally decorate by pushing different colored candy pieces or other decorative candies into the melted candy. Let cool completely before removing from foil/parchment paper.

❧ *Oatmeal Raisin Cookies*

Preheat oven to 375°F. Grease two cookie sheets. In large bowl combine:

1 cup whole wheat flour or Super Flour
¾ cup wheat germ
½ cup rolled oats
1 tablespoon baking powder
2 teaspoons cinnamon

In blender/processor, process at medium or low speed until dried fruit is finely chopped:

1 cup apple juice concentrate
¼ cup oil
1 egg
¾ cup dried fruit (raisins, apricots, prunes, etc.)

Pour blender mixture into bowl of dry ingredients. Stir together. Drop by heaping teaspoons onto cookie sheets one inch apart. Flatten with back of fork. Bake 8-10 minutes, watching carefully to prevent cookies from becoming crispy and brown. Let cool slightly and place in plastic bag to prevent cookies from becoming hard. Let cool completely before closing bag.

❧ *Crunchy Apple Crisp*

Apple mixture: Wash, peel, core and slice thinly 8 large apples. Mix with:

    3 tablespoons honey
    3 teaspoons lemon juice
    1 teaspoon of cinnamon

Place apple mixture into a 9-inch square baking dish. The apples will really fill the dish, but will shrink during cooking. Preheat oven to 350°F.

Oat topping: Combine

    1 cup rolled oats
    ¼ cup Super Flour
    ¼ cup wheat germ
    ¾ cup chopped walnuts
    1 teaspoon cinnamon

Then combine ¼ cup melted butter or oil with 6 tablespoons of maple syrup or honey and mix with oat topping mixture. Sprinkle oat mixture over apples. Bake 45-50 minutes until top is lightly browned and apples are soft. If oat topping begins to burn before apples are cooked, shield with aluminum foil. Serve topped with Mock Whipped Cream (page 344) or Mock Ice Cream (page 339).

Variation: Replace apple mixture with this peach mixture:

    2 pounds of sliced frozen peaches
    2½ tablespoons of lemon juice
    3 tablespoons honey
    ¼ cup of melted butter or oil

Oat topping remains the same as above.

❧ *Cheesecake*

Preheat oven to 375°F. Make a graham cracker pie shell by whizzing whole grain honey graham crackers from the natural foods store in the blender to make 1 ½ cups crumbs. Mix crumbs with 2 tablespoons of melted butter/oil and 3-4 melted concentrated fruit juice. Press into 9 inch pie pan and bake for 7-8 minutes. Meanwhile, combine:

    2 beaten eggs
    1 cup (8 ounces) combination of cream cheese and/or cottage cheese
    ½ cup honey
    ¼ cup nonfat dry milk powder
    2 teaspoons vanilla
    2 tablespoons lemon juice

Pour mixture into crust and bake at 375°F for 30 minutes. Refrigerate for at least 45 minutes before eating. Top with fresh strawberries or other fruit.

Variation: Add to filling ground nuts or a small can of crushed pineapple.

❧ *Peanut Butter Pudding*

Mix in blender:

    one small mashed banana
    ½ cup yogurt or tofu
    ½ cup natural peanut butter
    1 teaspoon maple syrup or honey
    ¼ teaspoon vanilla.

Process until smooth, pour into individual cups, and refrigerate until cold.

Variation: Replace all or part of the peanut butter or tofu with tahini, almond butter, or other nut/seed butters.

❧ *Mocked Whipped Cream*

Here are healthy alternatives to the expensive supermarket whipped cream products, which have lots of sugar and preservatives.

Tip: Poke beaters through a sheet of wax paper before inserting into mixer base. The wax paper covering the bowl will help prevent messy splatters.

Tip: To whip a small amount of cream, use a sturdy cup and only one beater of your electric mixer. As always, make sure the ingredients, cup, and beater all very cold for better whipping. For sweetened topping, confectioners' sugar makes more fluff than granulated. Evaporated milk will whip, but with more work than heavy cream with its high fat content. For best results, freeze milk in ice cube tray until ice crystals just begin to form. Using an ice cube tray will allow the center of the milk to get colder then a bowl would.

Tip: For a special touch that requires only a few seconds, sprinkle whipped topping on desserts with a little powder that has color: cinnamon, carob or cocoa powder, colored sugar, nutmeg, powdered kelp, etc.

⋅ *Mock Whipped Cream I*

Process at high speed until peaks form:
  1 cup cottage cheese
  1 tablespoons unsweetened pineapple
  concentrate
  1 tablespoon lemon concentrate
Serve immediately.

⋅ *Mock Whipped Cream II*

Add equivalent of one pasteurized egg white
(page 269, 273) to a thoroughly mashed
banana. Use an electric mixer and beat until
mixture stands in peaks. Add ½ teaspoon
vanilla and 1 tablespoon honey or other
sweetener. If you wish, add coloring
(page 364).

⋅ *Mock Whipped Cream III*

Put one cup ice water in your blender.
Slowly mix in one cup nonfat dry milk and
blend until consistency of whipped
cream—about 5 minutes. Serve
immediately.

⋅ *Brown Rice Pudding*

In a saucepan over medium heat, heat to
boiling:
  1 cup cooked brown rice or other
  cooked whole grain
  1 cup milk
  1 cup applesauce
  ½ cup raisins
Reduce heat to low and add:
  ½ cup chopped nuts
  2 teaspoons tahini
Cook over low heat for 20 minutes.
Remove from heat and stir in
  1 tablespoon vanilla.
Serve with yogurt topping:
  1 cup yogurt mixed with
  2 tablespoons honey or maple syrup
Sprinkle with a dash of cinnamon and/or
nutmeg.

⋅ *No-Cook Brown Rice Pudding*

Mix together:
  2 cups cooked brown rice or other
  cooked whole grain
  1 cup chopped pineapple, drained
  ¼ cup dried fruit, chopped (raisins,
  dates, prunes, apricots, etc.)
  ½-¾ cup yogurt, plain
  ¼ cup ground nuts (optional)

grated coconut (optional)
Mix together and refrigerate at least 2 hours
before serving.

⋅ *Tofu Icing*

In blender, mix:
  1 pound of tofu
  ½ cup maple syrup or other sweetener
  1-2 tablespoons tahini
  1 tablespoon vanilla
  2-3 drops almond extract
  ⅛ teaspoon nutmeg
  ¼ teaspoon kelp or salt

⋅ *Yogurt Icing*

Mix thick yogurt cheese with honey, maple
syrup, puréed fruit, or concentrated fruit
juice to make a healthy alternative to sugary
cake icings.

⋅ *Powdered Milk Icing*

  ½ cup softened butter or oil
  ½ cup honey
  ¼ cup maple syrup
  1 teaspoon vanilla
  1 cup nonfat dry milk powder
  1-3 tablespoons water
Mix first three ingredients and slowly add
milk powder while mixing. Add water, a
small amount at a time, until desired
consistency. Please read warning about
using only NONFAT milk powder on
page 251.

⋅ *Pineapple Cream Cheese Icing*

Mix in blender/processor:
  1 package (8 oz) cream cheese
  ¼ cup frozen pineapple juice
  concentrate or canned crushed
  pineapple
  ¼ cup ground cashews and/or other
  nuts
Variation: Use any fruit juice concentrate.

✒ Apple Juice - Cream Cheese Frosting

1½-2 teaspoons unflavored gelatin or agar
½ cup apple juice concentrate divided into 2 tablespoons and 6 tablespoons
16 ounces cream cheese
2 teaspoons vanilla
½ cup finely chopped dried fruit (raising, apricots, prunes, etc.)

In small saucepan, stir 2 tablespoons of thawed juice concentrate into gelatin and let stand two minutes. Heat to boiling and stir to dissolve. Meanwhile, in blender or processor, mix the rest of the ingredients until smooth. Beat gelatin mixture into cream cheese mixture until well-blended. Refrigerator for 30-60 minutes until frosting begins to set, and use to frost the cake.

✒ Mock Cream Cheese Frosting

2 cups ricotta cheese
3 tablespoons honey
1 teaspoon vanilla

Whip until smooth in blender and chill in refrigerator immediately. When cold, use as frosting.

Variation: Replace part of ricotta cheese with yogurt cheese or tofu.

✒ Cream Cheese Frosting

Blend equal parts of butter, cream cheese, and honey. Add a touch of vanilla.

✒ The Easiest Cream Cheese Icing

Mix cream cheese and honey together. Use about 2½ tablespoons of honey for each 4 ounces of cream cheese.

✒ Lemon Sugar Drizzle

Mix the juice of one lemon with ¼ cup of sugar/honey and drizzle immediately over cake.

✒ No-Fail Party Cake Frosting

In large bowl, mix with an electric mixer:
6-ounces cream cheese
4 tablespoons butter
1 teaspoon vanilla

When smooth, gradually beat in:
4 cups sifted confectioners' sugar.

Sifting prevents lumps. If you don't have a sifter, sift by shaking sugar in a strainer or sieve over bowl while adding to mix. Tint with food coloring. Enough for one 9-inch round double layer cake or one 9x13 sheet cake.

✒ Nut Frosting

½ cup ground nuts (almonds are good)
¼ cup olive oil or melted butter
¼ cup honey

In saucepan, heat oil and honey until they almost boil. Remove from heat and stir in nuts. Spread on cake (good for carrot cake) and place under oven broiler for a minute.

✒ King Lion's Milk Bars

Here is a homemade version of one of the expensive health food store candy bars:
¾ cup peanut butter
1 tablespoon brewer's yeast
1 teaspoon honey
3 tablespoons sugar
1 cup instant nonfat dry milk

Mix ingredients above with your hands (because it is so thick and dry). Shape into candy bars or balls. Dip bars into about ½ cup of melted sweetened carob chips plus 1 teaspoon canola oil. Dry on waxed paper.

Variation: Add raisins or other dried fruit, ground nuts and seeds, or coconut.

✒ Dried Fruit Bars

Preheat oven to 375°F.
1 beaten egg
½ cup melted butter/oil
¼ cup honey
¼ cup orange juice
1½ cup Super Flour
1 tablespoon wheat germ
1¼ teaspoon baking powder
1 cup dried fruit (dates are good)

Mix ingredients in bowl in the order above, adding dried fruit last. Press into square pan. Bake 25 minutes or until lightly browned.

❧ Bunny Birthday Cake

In medium saucepan, bring to a boil:
    2½ cups grated raw carrots
    1 cup plus 2 tablespoons of frozen apple juice concentrate, thawed
Lower to simmer, cover, and cook 15-20 minutes or until carrots are tender. Purée in blender or processor until smooth. Add:
    1½ cups dried fruit (raisins, apricots, prunes, etc.)
and process until fruit is finely chopped. Let cool. Preheat oven to 350°F. Grease two 9-inch square cake pan and line with wax paper. In large bowl, combine dry ingredients::
    2 cups Super Flour or whole wheat flour
    ½ cup wheat germ
    2 tablespoons baking soda
    1 tablespoon ground cinnamon
Combine wet ingredients:
    2 eggs
    4 egg whites
    1 tablespoon vanilla
    1¼ cup apple juice concentrate
Add wet ingredients into dry ingredients and beat until well mixed but don't overbeat. Fold in carrot purée from blender and
    ¾ cup unsweetened applesauce
Bake 35-40 minutes. Cool before frost with cream cheese icing.

❧ Bunny Cake

Grease and flour a 9x13 baking pan. Preheat oven to 325°F. Use whisk to beat until foamy (about 1 minute) in a large bowl:
    4 eggs
    ½ cup melted butter/oil
    ¾ cup pineapple juice concentrate
    ½ cup orange juice concentrate
Add to bowl:
    1½ teaspoons cinnamon
    1¼ cups grated carrot
    2 cups Super Flour
Hand beat for 3 minutes. Sprinkle 1 tablespoon baking soda into the mixture and mix by hand for exactly 30 strokes. *Immediately* pour into readied baking pan. The mixture will seem like it's foaming. Bake for 30 minutes until toothpick or cake tester comes out clean.
Tip: For more nutrition, dust a cake pan with wheat germ instead of white flour.

❧ Easy Carrot Cake

Preheat oven to 350°F. Grease and flour a 9x13 baking pan. In large bowl, mix ingredients in this order:
    2 beaten eggs
    ½ cup olive oil
    ½ cup honey
    ½ teaspoon cinnamon
    1¼ cup grated carrots
    ½ cup ground nuts
    1¼ cups Super Flour
    2 teaspoons baking powder
Bake 25-30 minutes. Good with Nut Frosting or almost any cream cheese icing.
Tip: For scratch cakes with lots of dry ingredients, open a few new large plastic storage bags. While measuring dry ingredients into the bowl, also measure them into the plastic bags. Store in a cool dry place or in the refrigerator. Next time you make your scratch cake, you have the mixed, measured, dry ingredients ready and waiting.

❧ Healthy Honey Cake

Preheat oven to 325°F. Grease a flour a loaf pan. Mix together in this order:
    1 beaten egg
    3 tablespoons melted butter/oil
    ¾ cup honey
    ½ cup milk
    1½ cup Super Flour
    ½ teaspoon baking soda
    ¾ cup ground almonds
Bake for 45 minutes until loaf begins to pull away from sides of pan.

❧ No-Egg Dried Fruit Squares

On stove top or in microwave oven on low power, melt:
    1 cup frozen apple juice concentrate
    ¼ cup butter/oil
Stir in:
    ½ cup raisins
    ½ cup dried apricots
Let sit for 10 minutes. Meanwhile, in large bowl, combine dry ingredients:
    1¼ cups Super Flour
    ¼ cup ground nuts
    1½ tablespoons baking powder
Slowly stir juice-butter mixture into dry ingredients, until just blended. Pour into greased 8-inch square pan. Bake in a preheated 325°F oven for 30 minutes, until

a cake tester or toothpick comes out clean. Slice into 16 squares.

✵ Nutty Rattle Snake

Grind 1 cup nuts (almonds, cashews, filberts, walnuts,...). Mix with:
½ cup honey
4 tablespoons softened butter
1 teaspoon vanilla
Roll dough into a snake shape. Place two small nut pieces for the snake's eyes. Wrap in waxed paper and refrigerate overnight. Place chilled roll on ungreased baking sheet. Shape chilled dough into wavy snake with raised "head" and "rattler tail." Bake in preheated 350°F oven for 8-10 minutes or until browned. Place on white paper towels to absorb excess oil and allow to cool before serving. Refrigerate.

✵ Slithery Snake Snacks

Mix together in this order:
2 cups ground nuts
1 cup ground pitted prunes
1 beaten egg
1 cup of honey
Shape into slithery slimy snakes. Bake in a preheated 375°F oven on a buttered cookie sheet for about 10 minutes. Refrigerate.

See recipe for Edible Play Dough on page 343, which can also be used to make snakes and other creatures.

✵ Almond Cupcakes

Preheat oven to 325°F.
½ cup almond butter/oil
1½ teaspoons almond extract
1 teaspoon vanilla
¾ cup honey
1 cup milk
2 beaten eggs
1 cup Super Flour
2 teaspoons baking powder
½ cup ground almonds
Mix ingredients in a bowl in the order given, reserving 2 tablespoons of ground almonds. Pour into 12 greased or lined muffin tins. (See tip for filling muffin tins, page 325.) Sprinkle reserved almonds on top for garnish. Bake 25-30 minutes until toothpick comes out clean and tops are a golden brown.
Tip: Instead of frosting cupcakes on top, slice them in half and frost the cut edges

making a cupcake "sandwich." Use in lunch boxes to prevent icing from sticking to wrap.

✵ Mori-Nu® Dairy-Free Pumpkin Pie

Preheat oven to 350°F.
1½ packages (about 16 ounces) of Mori-Nu Tofu (Silken Firm, Firm, or Extra Firm)
2 cups canned or cooked pumpkin
⅔ cup honey
1 teaspoon vanilla
1 teaspoon pumpkin pie spice
1 unbacked 9" pastry crust
Mix tofu in blender or processor until smooth. Add other ingredients and blend well. Pour into a 9" deep dish pie shell. Bake for about one hour. Filling will be soft, but will firm up as it chills. Chill and serve.

✵ Easy, Healthy Pie Crust

Mix in a pie pan:
1½ cups Super Flour
⅓ cup oil
6 tablespoons ice water
Prick with fork and prebake 10-12 minutes.

✵ Granola Pie Crust

Pulverize 2 cups granola in blender or food processor. Mix with 3 tablespoons apple juice. Press into pie pan and prebake at 350°F for about 10 minutes.
Variations: Instead of granola, pulverize whole grain honey graham crackers, breakfast flake cereal, or whole grain cookies. Instead of apple juice, mix with no-sugar added jam or preserves, concentrated frozen fruit juice, or jam-flavored or honey-flavored yogurt.

❧ No-Bake Mini-Cream Pies

You can make a few of these mini-pies and refrigerate for up to one week, or make lots and freeze them for up to two months. These make great little healthy lunches or snacks. Thaw them overnight in the refrigerator or for several seconds in the microwave before serving.

Containers: Butter or oil-spray 24 mini muffin tins.

Crusts: Mix:

½ cup wheat germ
½ cup ground nuts (almonds or walnuts are good)
¼ cup melted butter/oil

Press crust mixture into containers to form crusts that go ¾ up the sides.

Filling: Mix:

½ cup of mashed avocado
½ cup of yogurt cheese
1 teaspoon lemon juice
¼ cup honey or maple syrup

Spoon mixture into crusts.

Topping: Sprinkle top with ground nuts and/or wheat germ. Or place a small dollop of jelly or jam or a fresh strawberry or other berry on top. Or, make a happy face or other design with Decorative Touches.

After mini pies are assembled, cover well and freeze until solid. When frozen, remove pies and place in freezer bags.

Filling Variation: Instead of avocado, use all yogurt cheese, or use all cream cheese, or use a mixture of cream cheese and yogurt cheese and mashed avocado.

❧ Peanut Butter Fudge

4 tablespoons honey
½ cup peanut butter
1 cup nonfat powdered milk (not instant)
¼ teaspoon vanilla

Mix well and press into pan lined with waxed paper. Refrigerate until firm and cut into squares.

❧ Peanut Butter Carob Fudge

Make peanut butter fudge as in previous recipe, replacing ½ cup of powdered milk with carob powder (or, for adults, cocoa powder or a mixture of both).

❧ Nut Banana Bites

3-4 ripe bananas
½ cup crushed wheat squares cereal
1 tablespoon peanut butter or other nut butter
1 tablespoon honey
1 teaspoon carob powder

Mash all together and roll into bite-sized balls.

❧ Apple Honey Candy

Bring 1 cup applesauce and 1 cup honey to a boil in a saucepan. Add 1 package gelatin or 1-2 tablespoons agar and mix well. Add 1 cup ground nuts. Place in 8x8 pan and refrigerate for 24 hours. Use cookie cutters or cut into one inch squares. Optionally, decorate with a mixture of colored sugar (page 366) and ground nuts.

❧ Peanut Butter Cookies

Preheat oven to 375°F. Mix these ingredients in this order:

2 beaten eggs
1 mashed ripe banana
2 tablespoons melted butter/oil
1 teaspoon vanilla
½ cup natural creamy peanut butter
1 cup Super Flour
½ teaspoon baking powder
½ teaspoon nutmeg
1 cup chopped peanuts or other nuts

Mix well. Drop by teaspoonfuls onto greased cookie sheets. Flatten by making criss-cross perpendicular lines with a fork . (Let your toddler help by making the lines.) Bake 6-8 minutes until lightly browned. Cool on rack. Makes at least 2 dozen.

Tip: For an easy cookie topping that gives a nice taste and glaze, spread a thin layer of jelly over the cookies before baking.

Tip: If you're short on cookie sheets, use a broiler pan or other large shallow baking pan. Flip upside down and use the bottom.

Tip: Remove a baked cookie stuck to the pan by sliding dental floss under it.

Tip: Roll cookie dough into a sausage shape for easy cutting of uniformly shaped cookies. Or freeze dough in large juice can. Thaw at room temperature 15 minutes before pushing up and slicing, using the can's edge as a cutting guide.

Tip: Press cookies flat with the bottom of a drinking glass. Dip glass in sugar before pressing each cookie.

❧ Oatmeal Cookies

Preheat oven to 325°F. Mix in this order:
    2 beaten eggs
    ½ cup oil
    ¾ cup honey
    ¼ cup blackstrap molasses
    1 teaspoon vanilla or almond extract
    2 tablespoons wheat germ
    1 cup nonfat dry milk
    3 cups rolled oats
Drop teaspoon-sized amounts two inches apart on buttered or oil-sprayed cookie sheet. Bake 10-12 minutes or until browning begins around edges.

Tip: You may enjoy the flavor of oatmeal cookies more if you bake the oatmeal before you start. Sprinkle oatmeal evenly on a cookie sheet and bake at 300°F for about 10 minutes. Use as ingredients for cookies and other recipes.

❧ Pear Date Sandwich Bars

Preheat oven to 350°F. Mix together:
    1 cup puréed pears (or baby food pears)
    2 eggs
    ⅓ cup melted butter/oil
    1½ cups Super Flour
    1 cup rolled oats
    2 teaspoons baking powder
Spread into two buttered 8-inch square baking pans or one 9x13 pan. Bake 20 minutes until lightly browned. Cool on wire racks. Cut cake into bar-sized pieces. Make sandwiches by spreading date filling between two pieces.
Date Filling: Process pitted dates in blender or food processor, adding enough water to make spreadable consistency.
Variation: Instead of pears, you can use applesauce or other puréed fruit. Instead of date filling you can use Prune Butter (page 318).

❧ Orange Topping

Place ¼ cup orange juice in the freezer to make it ice cold. Mix in blender the cold orange juice, 1 teaspoon frozen orange juice concentrate until smooth. Add ½ cup nonfat dry milk powder and blend until stiff. Add Healthy Extras. Yields about 1 cup. Serve immediately over muffins or cake and keep refrigerated or freeze.

❧ Maplenut Yogurt Topping

    1 cup plain yogurt
    2 tablespoons maple syrup
    2 tablespoons ground walnuts or other nuts or seeds
Stir ingredients and serve immediately. Good on pancakes.

❧ Watermelon Pudding

    2 cups puréed watermelon, seeds removed
    1 tablespoon arrowroot
    1 tablespoon frozen orange juice concentrate
    ½ teaspoon vanilla
    3-4 tablespoons honey or maple syrup
In saucepan, heat all ingredients to almost boiling. Turn down heat to low and stir until thick. Refrigerate and serve cold.

❧ Applesauce Pudding

In saucepan over low heat stir 1 cup applesauce with 1 tablespoon arrowroot or cornstarch. Stir constantly until pudding-like consistency.
Variation: Use any fruit sauce.

Gelatin/Agar Agar

❧ *Healthy Juice Gelatin*

Make gelatin from fruit juice, not the commercial stuff which is sugar and chemicals. Save money by buying unflavored gelatin in bulk—it keeps indefinitely. One tablespoon of gelatin (equal to one packet) will gel two cups of liquid. For juice gelatin, mix one tablespoon (one packet) of dry gelatin into one cup of cold juice and let sit for one minute. Add one cup of boiling juice and stir until dissolved. Pour into mold or individual cups and refrigerate until gelled.

Variation: Let gelatin gel a little until it is the consistency of raw egg white, then add fruit pieces.

Gelatin Tips: If you are not using a colorful juice (such as apple juice which makes brown gelatin), you may want to add food coloring for a brighter color.

To prevent lumping, always mix gelatin first with cool liquid and let stand one minute to let the granules separate (even though a recipe may say to add boiling water directly to the dry gelatin.)

For a sweeter gelatin, replace one quarter cup of fruit juice with 2 tablespoons of concentrated fruit juice.

When serving pudding or gelatin at a child's birthday party, pour into muffin tins double-lined with paper muffin cups. Then serve by placing on the child's paper plate. Baby food jars are a nice size for a single serving of gelatin.

Speed the gelling process by placing gelatin in the freezer for 30 minutes and then placing in the refrigerator.

Freeze individual gelatin servings in yogurt containers and place in your child's lunch box. Gelatin will be thawed by lunchtime.

Before turning a gelatin mold out onto a plate, wet the plate with cold water so that it will be easy to move the mold and center it on the plate.

Unmold by sliding a knife between the gelatin and the container to break the vacuum. Then submerge the mold up to its edge into a bowl of hot water for about five seconds. Hold the wet plate upside down firmly over the mold, flip, and jerk once. The mold should fall onto the plate. Good luck.

❧ *Basic Vegetarian Gelatin*

Gelatin is made from animal products, agar agar is made from seaweed (page 275). One tablespoon of agar agar will gel 1-2 cups of liquid, depending on the brand. Follow the directions on the label or mix two tablespoons of dry agar agar into two cups fruit juice. Bring to a boil, reduce heat, and simmer for 5 minutes. Refrigerate until set in individual containers or mold.

❧ *Juicy Vegan Cloud*

Stir two tablespoons agar agar (page 275) into ½ cup orange juice in a medium bowl and let sit for 1-2 minutes. Meanwhile, bring ½ cup juice to a boil and stir until dissolved. Stir in one cup of cold soy milk. Refrigerate until set.

❧ *Juice Blocks*

To make jiggly gelatin blocks, simply add twice as much gelatin (one tablespoon per cup of liquid) for a more firm gelling. To make a 9x13 mold, sprinkle four tablespoons (four packets) dry unflavored gelatin into one cup of cold juice. Wait 1-2 minutes. Add three cups of boiling juice and stir until dissolved. Pour into 9x13 pan and refrigerate until firm. Cut into blocks, use cookie cutters, or cut freehand into Simple Shapes (pages 367-368).

❧ *Dinosaur DNA*

If you've seen the movie Jurassic Park, you may remember the mosquito fossilized in sap. Make gelatin bars with raisin or prune pieces inside, which could be cut and shaped to look like flying insects. Place a "mosquito" in each gelatin block. For a less creepy dessert, place a piece of candy or a small non-toxic plastic toy favor into each block.

❧ *Jiggling Jelly Worms*

Make recipe for Juice Blocks in a shallow baking dish. Submerge large straws in the mixture so that they fill with the gelatin.

(Place jars on top of the straws if they float to keep them submerged.) Refrigerate overnight or for 6-8 hours to let gelatin become very solid. Remove straws, and use a rolling pin (page 153) from the end of each straw to push out the worms.

❧ Gelled Orange Slices

Wash an orange and cut a small hole in one end. Hollow out the orange thoroughly. Prepare Juice Blocks recipe with orange juice and pour into orange shell. Refrigerate until very solid. Use a sharp serrated knife dipped in very hot water to cut orange into slices and serve. These slices make a hit at birthday parties.

❧ Fruit Yogurt Mold

Dissolve 1 tablespoon gelatin into ½ cup orange juice in a saucepan. Wait one minute and heat over low heat or in the microwave for 30 seconds. Add two tablespoons honey. Stir an additional ½ cup cold orange juice into gelatin-juice mixture. Into one cup yogurt, mix ¼ cup all-fruit jelly. Add yogurt and jelly to orange juice mixture and stir well with fork or whisk. Pour into mold and let set in refrigerator.

❧ Fruit Frappé

Dissolve 1 tablespoon gelatin in ¼ cup cold water and heat water until hot. Let cool in freezer for a few minutes. Place 1 cup fruit (or canned crushed pineapple in its own juice) in blender with 1 tablespoon of lemon juice. Add a 6-ounce can of frozen orange juice concentrate and keep blending. Add ice cubes one at a time while blending until good consistency. Serve immediately.

❧ Cantaloupe Gelatin Planet

Wash uncut whole cantaloupe (or honeydew). Cut off a circular slice of rind from the stem end of the cantaloupe to use as a lid. Discard seeds. Use melon baller to hollow out cantaloupe and make melon balls. Invert melon and let drain. Make gelatin using agar (page 275) or by following directions on box of unflavored gelatin using orange juice instead of water. Fill hollowed out cantaloupe. Pour any extra

gelatin into another container. Refrigerate. After gelatin is slightly thickened, add melon balls. Return to refrigerator to finish gelling. Replace "lid" on cantaloupe planet and serve. If the bowls are rolling around and unstable, slice a little piece off the bottom to make it flatter. Let your kids eat the oceans, lava, rock layers (the melon balls are big rocks and they have teeth as strong as lions, or their mouth is a front loader or other construction machine). If they are into gross and disgusting, see page 366 for suggestions on creepy crawlies that you can place in the gelatin.

❧ Orange Peel Moons

For smaller servings of planet innards, use hollowed out oranges or lemons instead of melons in the Cantaloupe Gelatin Planet recipe above.

Condiments, Sauces, Seasonings, and Dips

Tip: If you are using dried herbs in these sauces, place them in hot water for just a moment and drain, and they'll be fresher, greener, and have more flavor. Before using dried herbs in any recipe, roll them with the palms of your hands to crumble them and this will bring out more flavor.

Tip: To get stubborn ketchup flowing from the bottle, release the vacuum by sticking a drinking straw, knife, etc. into the center.

Syrups: For healthy natural syrup recipes that can be used on pancakes, ice cream, fresh fruit, etc., see *Pancake Syrup Ideas* on page 329.

❧ Mustard Mayonnaise

Don't buy mustard mayonnaise—make your own by mixing mustard and tofu mayo in a proportion that suits you. Begin with 1 tablespoon mustard to ½ cup mayo and experiment from there. See also recipes for Honey Butter (page 317) and Super Sandwich Spreads (page 317).

❧ Mustard Butter

As with mustard mayo, you can save money by making your own mustard butter. Blend about a tablespoon of prepared mustard with ½ cup of softened butter. Melt over cooked veggies or use to fry scrambled eggs. Delicious!

❧ The Easiest Cheese Sauce

Place a slice of cheese or shredded cheese pieces over vegetables and either microwave for 30 seconds, or place in 450°F oven, or under the broiler until the cheese has melted. Another easy cheese sauce is a can of condensed cheese soup from the natural foods store mixed with 1/4 cup milk. Pour over cooked vegetable pieces such as broccoli or cauliflower.

❧ Cheese Driz Sauce

Mix in your blender/processor in this order:
  ½ cup warm water
  1 teaspoon liquid lecithin
  ¼ teaspoon powdered kelp
  12-ounce package of shredded natural cheese at room temperature (sharp cheddar is good)
Gradually add a small amount of instant nonfat powdered milk until consistency is similar to commercial Cheese Whiz®. Refrigerate in airtight glass jar.

❧ Fruit Sauces

Instead of the very common applesauce, make sauces from bananas, blueberries, cherries, strawberries, mangos, papayas, peaches, pears, pineapples, and plums. Simply purée the peeled, cored, fresh fruit in the blender. Or you can use canned or frozen fruit. Fruit sauces are used in some recipes in this book. For the easiest fruit sauce of all, use baby food fruit in jars.

❧ Thickened Fruit Sauce

  ½ cup frozen concentrated fruit juice
  2 tablespoons water
  1 tablespoon arrowroot
  1 tablespoon lemon juice
Cook above ingredients in saucepan, stirring constantly with fork, over medium heat until arrowroot dissolves and mixture begins to thicken. Add:

  2 cups chopped fresh fruit or frozen fruit, thawed
Stir and continue cooking over low heat for 10 minutes. Use over ice cream, in yogurt, and in cottage cheese.
Variation: Instead of fruit juice concentrate, use a mixture of half honey and half water.

❧ Nut Sauce

Blend in processor until smooth:
  ½ cup nuts
  ¼ cup water or more
  1 teaspoon maple syrup
  ¼ teaspoon vanilla
Use in yogurt, cottage cheese, and Super Porridge, and mixed with cooked, puréed veggies.

❧ Mock Cream Sauce

Blend equal amounts of cottage cheese and vanilla flavored yogurt. Use over fruit pieces or as fruit dip.

❧ Tofu Sauce

Saute in 2 tablespoons of butter/oil:
  1 medium onion, chopped
  1 block tofu, cubed
Add:
  2 cups well-cooked mashed beans
  2 tablespoons parsley
and enough water (¼-¾ cups) to make a sauce. Serve over cooked grains. Freeze leftovers.

❧ Shake It Up Baby Salad Dressing

Place into clean baby food jar:
  3 tablespoons olive oil
  1 tablespoon apple cider vinegar
  1/4 teaspoon prepared mustard
  herbs (parsley, basil, dill,...)
Place lid tightly on jar and shake well.

❧ Cottage Cheese Dressing

  3 tablespoons cottage cheese
  3 teaspoons olive oil
  3 teaspoons apple cider vinegar
  1 teaspoon lemon juice
  ¼ teaspoon oregano or dill
  pinch of garlic powder
Blend until smooth.

❧ Lemon Tahini Dressing

1 teaspoon olive oil
¼ cup lemon juice
¼ cup tahini
½ teaspoon dry parsley or 2 teaspoons fresh parsley
½ teaspoon dry oregano or 2 teaspoons fresh oregano
1 clove minced garlic (optional)

Mix well and store in covered jar in refrigerator. Refrigerate until cool before serving.

❧ Yogurt Dip

In blender, mix:
6 walnut halves, ground
1 tablespoon olive oil
1 clove garlic
1 cup yogurt
2 teaspoons lemon juice.

❧ Avocado Dip

Mix mashed avocado with an equal amount of cottage cheese or tofu. Optionally add Healthy Extras. The avocado skins can be used as cups to hold this dip. Use it for dipping anything from whole-grain bread sticks to carrot sticks. Or use as a spread in sandwiches, on whole-grain crackers, celery sticks, or fruit pieces.

❧ Guacamole

Mash together a ripe avocado and 1 teaspoon mayonnaise, ½ teaspoon salsa, and 1 teaspoon lemon juice. Optionally add a pinch of kelp or tamari/soy sauce or maple syrup. Mix well. Use chilled as a dip for fresh vegetables or whole-grain crackers or bread sticks, or as a sandwich or cracker spread.

❧ Tofu Dip I

Mix in blender until smooth:
8 ounces tofu (first press between clean towels to remove as much moisture as possible)
1 tablespoon lemon juice
¼ teaspoon dry mustard

❧ Tofu Dip II

Mix in blender until smooth:
½ pound tofu
4 tablespoons apple cider vinegar

3 tablespoons olive oil
1-2 teaspoons tamari

Variation: Add a few teaspoons of minced onion and/or grated cheese and/or parsley, basil, chives, dill, Italian herbs, onion powder, paprika, garlic powder.

❧ Cream Cheese Dip

4 ounces softened cream cheese
½ teaspoon vanilla
2 tablespoons honey or maple syrup
water

Mix first three ingredients in processor or by hand and slowly add water, a tablespoon at a time, until desired consistency.

❧ Pineapple Cottage Cheese

Drain ½ cup canned shredded pineapple and mix it into an 8-ounce container of cottage cheese. Refrigerate.

❧ Tofu Mayonnaise

Mix in blender until smooth:
8 ounces tofu
1½ tablespoons lemon juice
2 tablespoons apple cider vinegar
1 teaspoon tamari/soy sauce
4 teaspoons safflower oil
½ teaspoon dry mustard
2 cloves pressed fresh garlic

❧ Mock Ricotta Cheese

1 pound firm tofu
5 teaspoons sugar
½ teaspoon salt or kelp
2 tablespoons lemon juice or 1 frozen cube (page 440)

Mix until consistency resembles cottage cheese. Use in stuffed shells, manicotti, and lasagna or other layered casseroles.

❧ Mock Sour Cream I

Mix recipe above for mock ricotta cheese in blender until very smooth.

❧ Mock Sour Cream II

In blender mix
½ cup yogurt
1 tablespoon fresh lemon juice
Slowly blend in
1 cup cottage cheese

❧ *Mock Sour Cream III*

¾ cup low-fat or nonfat cottage cheese
⅓ cup yogurt cheese
¼-½ cup plain low-fat yogurt
1 teaspoon lemon juice
minced fresh chives or other herbs

Blend cottage cheese in blender until smooth. Gently fold in yogurt cheese and enough plain yogurt until desired consistency is reached. Add herbs.

❧ *Easy Mock Sour Cream*

1 cup cottage cheese
1 tablespoon milk or yogurt
2 tablespoons lemon juice

Blend until smooth.

❧ *Cinnamon Sugar*

Don't buy cinnamon sugar in the supermarket spice section. Save money and make your own by mixing 2-3 tablespoons powdered cinnamon into each cup of sugar or colored sugar (page 366) or 1-1½ tablespoons cinnamon into ½ cup of sugar.

❧ *Vanilla Sugar*

Buy a package of vanilla beans at the natural foods store and place them (however many there are in the package) in an airtight container with a pound of granulated or confectioners' sugar. Let sit for at least one week at room temperature in the airtight container. Shake or stir every few days. The same vanilla beans can be used repeatedly for this purpose for up to 6 months.

❧ *Pizza Seasoning*

Combine well:
2 tablespoons dried oregano
1 tablespoon dried basil
1 teaspoon onion powder
¾ teaspoon garlic powder

Add about a teaspoon of mixture to each cup of tomato sauce or next pizza sauce recipe.

❧ *Economical Pizza Sauce*

Mix a 15-ounce can of tomato sauce with a 5-ounce can of tomato paste and add flavorings above.

❧ *Pumpkin Pie Spice*

Mix in proportions that suit your own taste buds. If you don't know where to start, try:

2 parts cinnamon
1 part nutmeg and/or allspice
½ to 1 part cloves
½ to 1 part cinnamon (optional)

❧ *Homemade Vanilla Extract*

NEVER buy imitation vanilla, which is made of artificial flavorings, or vanilla flavoring, which is a combination of real vanilla and imitation vanilla. Real or pure vanilla extract is more expensive, but it's worth it. You can save money by making your own. Vanilla and some other flavorings are mostly alcohol—read the ingredients list and you'll see. Soak vanilla beans from the natural foods store in vodka (or brandy). Use anywhere from 2 to 4 vanilla beans—whatever size package the health food store sells. The more beans, the stronger the vanilla flavor, of course. Split the beans with a sharp knife vertically without cutting in half, making sure that any small seeds are captured on wax paper. Place beans and seeds into a small glass jar with about ¾ cup of vodka. A 6-ounce baby food jar is the perfect size. Chop the beans lengthwise so that they'll fit in the jar. Let age in a dark cabinet for at least two weeks, shaking occasionally—at least every few days. The longer it sits, the stronger the vanilla flavor, of course. As you use your vanilla, keep replenishing the jar with more vodka. This homemade vanilla will not be as dark as store-bought. Vanilla beans should be replaced every 6 months.

See previous recipe for Vanilla Sugar.

Beverages

For any of these drinks, add a bendable straw and a garnish on the side of the cup, such as a triangular pineapple piece or a citrus fruit circle or wedge. For *older children*, use as a beverage stirrer a short celery stick with its top leaves or a cucumber stick. (Strings in celery are choking hazards.) Your kids will think it's fancy. Garnishes (not celery) can be cut and frozen using the Tray-freeze Method. Cut slits in garnishes before freezing to easily slip on cup. Many of these beverage recipes call for fruit juice. Your local natural foods store has a smorgasbord of natural fruit juices, from coconut to kiwi juice. Try them all and use any of them in these recipes.

Sweeteners: Many of these beverage recipes call for sweetener. Use honey, maple syrup, rice syrup (available at natural foods stores), or frozen apple juice concentrate or frozen concentrate for pineapple juice or grape juice or any no-sugar added fruit juice.

Add thickness: Any of the drink recipes below can be made thicker by adding a tablespoon or two of nonfat dry milk powder. Please read warning about using only NONFAT milk powder on page 251.

Tip: Here's a tip to keep beverages cold in the lunch box without diluting them with melted ice. The night before day care or school, place your child's plastic drink container in the freezer with ½-1 inch of fruit juice in the bottom. It will freeze overnight into a big ice cube that will keep your child's juice cold until lunchtime. As it melts, it will not dilute the juice. You can, of course, do this with milk or other beverage. If the plastic container has a straw that can't fit into the container because of the block of ice on the bottom, try freezing the container on its side, so that the block of ice doesn't shorten the length of the inside space of the container.

Tip: To prevent juice or other beverage from getting diluted from melting ice cubes, enclose ice cubes in a plastic bag and place in pitcher so that melted water won't dilute the juice. Or forget the plastic bag and make ice cubes out of the juice itself.

❧ Mineral Water

In a quart jar, place:
> ½ cup organically-grown raw almonds with skins
> ¼ cup organically-grown rolled oats
> ¼ cup organically-grown raisins
> 1 tablespoon blackstrap molasses (optional)

Let soak in the refrigerator. Strain and keep refrigerated. Discard after 2-3 days.

The water absorbs minerals and iron from the food. The almond skins contain an enzyme that will help protect babies/toddlers from getting worms. Use the strained out almonds, etc. for older family members' cereals and salads. This Mineral Water recipe is adapted from page 45 of Gena Larson's *Better Food for Better Babies*. See bibliography.

❧ Lemonade or Limeade

Squeeze the juice of one lemon or lime into a glass. Add 1½ tablespoons sweetener. Fill with water and ice. Drink immediately for maximum vitamin C. Or use lemon/lime ice cubes instead of fresh fruit. Thaw by microwaving 1-2 minutes on high first before adding to honey, water, and ice. Or better yet, let the lemon ice cubes thaw naturally in the water. Or, for real convenience, freeze ice cubes made of 2 tablespoons lemon juice plus 1½ tablespoons honey for "instant lemonade" cubes.

Tip: To keep pesky bugs out of kids' outside drinks, prevent spilling, and keep drinks colder, use a lidded cup with a straw. Or cover the top of a plain cup with aluminum foil and poke a straw through the foil.

❧ Fruit Soy Milk

> 1 cup soy milk
> 1 banana
> ½ cup orange juice
> ½ cup pineapple juice
> 1 tablespoon honey
> 1 tablespoon wheat germ
> dash of kelp

Blend all ingredients.

๊ *Purple Barney Milk*

Mix 2 parts milk or yogurt with 1 part purple grape juice.

๊ *Easy Orange Whip*

Mix on high speed in blender equal parts orange juice and milk (soy or cow's) and serve immediately.

๊ *Mock Soda Pop*

Mix 1-2 tablespoons of frozen fruit juice concentrate into 1 cup no sodium seltzer water or club soda. Add a few ice cubes.
Variation: Mix 1 part fruit juice to 2 parts seltzer water/club soda.
Variation: Mix equal parts fruit juice and no sodium seltzer water.
Tip: Run water over ice cubes before placing into carbonated beverages to reduce foam.

๊ *Mock Cream Soda*

Mix 1 teaspoon honey and ½ teaspoon vanilla into 1 cup of club soda.

๊ *Yahoo Yogurt Fruit Drink*

Here's a delicious way to get yogurt into your toddler. Mix equal parts plain yogurt and apple or other fruit juice. Optionally add a little lemon or orange juice.
Variation: For a thicker, creamier shake, add some fresh fruit or use yogurt cheese and use blender to mix.

๊ *Banana Yogurtshake*

Mix ½ cup of yogurt or milk (try soy milk) and frozen banana chunks (about ½ banana) in blender. Optionally add any of these:
  1 teaspoon lemon juice
  chunks of other frozen fruit (strawberry is great)
  a dash of vanilla
  a little sweetener
Add milk if too thick.

๊ *Tofu Yogurt Smoothie*

In blender, mix
  ½ cup silken tofu
  1 small banana
  2 teaspoons lemon juice
  ½ cup yogurt
  1 tablespoon sweetener
Add water or fruit juice if too thick.

๊ *Apricot Prune Smoothie*

Soak in refrigerator overnight:
  2 tablespoons dried apricots
  1 cup prune juice
In morning, mix in blender with
  1 cup yogurt
  1 teaspoon lemon juice
  1 tablespoon sweetener

๊ *Any Fruit Milkshake*

Blend in blender:
  1 cup cold milk (cow's or soy)
  ¼ cup nonfat powdered milk
  1 cup frozen fruit (strawberries, blueberries, peaches, or other fruit)

๊ *Melon Juice*

  1 cup cold melon pieces (cantaloupe, watermelon, honeydew)
  1 teaspoon lemon juice or lemon juice ice cube
  1 tablespoon sweetener (optional)
  2 ice cubes
  approximately ¼ cup of water
Mix all in blender. Slowly add more water, a tablespoon at a time, until desired thickness is achieved.

๊ *Watermelon Crush*

Mix in blender ½ cup watermelon pieces with seeds removed, ½ cup strawberries, and a few ice cubes.
Variation: Replace fruits with (or add) pineapple or cantaloupe chunks.

๊ *Thick Fruit Drinks*

Mix part applesauce or any fruit sauce (see page 353) and fruit juice. Try applesauce and pear juice, pineapple sauce and grapefruit juice, and pear sauce and papaya juice.

๊ *Carotene Cocktail*

This drink is high in beta-carotene.
  ¼ cup of sweet potato purée (or two thawed food cubes)
  1 tablespoon of frozen orange juice concentrate
  ½ cup milk or mixture of milk and yogurt
Mix all in blender. Slowly add more milk, a tablespoon at a time, until desired thickness.

Variation: Instead of sweet potato, use carrot purée or canned pumpkin or a mixture of all three.

❧ Fruit and Veggie Shake

In blender, mix orange juice with chunks of carrots, broccoli, and/or other raw vegetables.

❧ Molasses "Coffee"

Stir 1 tablespoon blackstrap molasses into a cup of warm water. Add milk/cream if desired.

❧ Kids' Tea

See recipe under citrus zest on page 440.

❧ Instant Powdered Coffee for Kids

Thoroughly mix ¼ cup blackstrap molasses into one cup wheat or oat bran. Spread on large cookie sheet and bake in 300°F oven, stirring occasionally, for 25 minutes or until browned and dry. Break up clumps with fork. Store in refrigerator in air tight container. Use as you would instant coffee.

❧ Veggie Beverage

Mix in blender:
    1 cup nut/seed milk (page 359)
    2-3 carrot cubes

❧ Fancy Fruit Party Punch

Open a 10 or 16-ounce package frozen strawberries, remove about half of them, and replace the other half in the freezer. To make fancy ice cubes, mix in blender:
    1 cup cold water
    ¼ of a 6-ounce can orange juice concentrate (3 tablespoons)
    ¼ of a 6-ounce can pineapple juice concentrate
Pour mixture into 12 muffin tins or popsicle molds. Drop strawberries into the tins and freeze until mushy. Place mint sprigs, orange slices, or celery leaves into the mushy ice cubes as garnishes so that they stand vertically and partially stick out of the cubes. Return to freezer and let freeze solid. These are the ice cubes for the punch. You may also use food coloring to make different colored fancy ice cubes.
Mix in the blender:

the other ¾ of the orange juice and pineapple juice concentrates
the other ½ of the frozen strawberries from the freezer
1½ cups of cold water.
Pour blender mixture into punch bowl and add:
    2 more cups of cold water
    the fancy ice cubes
    orange slices and whole strawberries as garnishes
    32-ounce (quart) bottle of chilled ginger ale
Makes about 12 6-ounce servings before the ice cubes melt. If you need a few more servings, add more ginger ale.

Variation: Use a loaf pan, a small rectangular pan, or bundt cake pan to freeze one big ice cube instead of 12 little ones. With the larger surface area, you can spell a child's name with Decorative Touches or make some interesting design. Partially freeze until mushy, place designs into the mush, then freeze solid. Or wash and freeze a cluster of grapes still on the vine and use as a garnish in the punch bowl. Or fill very clean balloons with water, freeze, and float in the punch bowl. Put colored water in the balloons and use rubber bands to shape like a teddy bear or mouse ears and freeze on cookie sheet. Cut off balloons with knife. Be careful and discard balloon parts—they are choking hazards for young children.

❧ Healthier Hot Chocolate

The commercial mixes are made up of mostly sugar! Make your own mix by combining 4 parts nonfat dry milk powder to 1 part unsweetened carob powder or cocoa powder. To serve, mix 3 tablespoons into heated water and add 1 teaspoon of honey or other sweetener or to taste. Mix with whisk or fork to remove lumps. And a marshmallow melting on top now and then will not hurt too much!

❧ Non-Dairy Hot Chocolate

    1 cup soy milk heated slowly in a saucepan or microwave oven
    1 teaspoon cocoa
    1 teaspoon honey or to taste
Mix with whisk or fork to remove lumps.

Variation: Use almond milk, oat milk, or other non-dairy milks available at your local natural foods store. Or use your own super milk from the recipes below.

❧ Instant Breakfast Drink

Mix in blender:
1 cup milk
½ cup instant nonfat dry milk
1 teaspoon vanilla
1 tablespoon sweetener

Variation: Add two tablespoons carob powder for a carob-flavored drink. Or add fresh fruit pieces or dried fruit pieces for a fruity-flavored drink.

Super Milks

The Super Milks here are super nutritious, but should not decrease your baby's intake of breast milk, formula, or cow's milk, which is your baby/toddler's main source of calcium, vitamin D, and protein. Make sure your baby is getting the recommended amounts of milks. Use Super Milks in addition to regular milk.

Straining Nut Milks: A fine strainer is needed to remove the powdery pulp in blended nut milks so they will not clog bottle nipples. A yogurt strainer works great to remove the pulp, or see the method to strain juices and nut milks explained on page 152.

❧ Nut/Seed Milk

⅓ cup *organic* nuts or seeds (cashews, almonds, sesame seeds, are good)
1 cup water

Rinse nuts and seeds and let soak in water overnight before blending. This will begin the sprouting process, increase the nutrients in the water, and soften the seeds/nuts for better blenderizing. In the morning, liquify in blender. Shake well before each use. You can strain this milk, but don't discard the pulp—it's full of nutrients. Use it in adult family members' cereals and salads. The milk will keep in the refrigerator for up to 3 days.

❧ Nut Milk

Grind in blender ⅓-½ cup organic nuts to fine powder. Slowly add 1 cup cold water. Good nuts to use are raw cashews and blanched almonds. (Blanch almonds by pouring boiling water over almonds, let stand for two minutes, and drain. Remove skins by pressing each almond between your thumb and index finger and popping the nut out of its skin.)

❧ Parsley Sprout Milk

1 cup organic sunflower seed sprouts or other organic sprouts
4 tablespoons fresh parsley, organically-grown
1 cup water
1 tablespoon maple syrup
1 tablespoon wheat germ
½ teaspoon brewer's yeast

Liquify in blender and strain.

❧ Warm Super Milk

Boil 1 cup water. Place in blender with
1 tablespoon nuts
1 teaspoon flaxseed
1 teaspoon pumpkin seeds
1 tablespoon blackstrap molasses or other sweetener

All ingredients should be organic. Blend until smooth. Shake or stir before sipping and drink immediately.

Variation: Optionally add one or more of the following:
1 teaspoon carob or cocoa powder
1 teaspoon peanut butter
1 tablespoon strawberry jam or other fruit jam
1 teaspoon tahini
½ teaspoon lecithin granules (available at your natural foods store)
pinch of cinnamon

❧ Super Easy Soy Milk

In blender, combine
½ cup silken tofu
1½ cups milk or water

Homemade soy milk made with water has little calcium and vitamin D and no vitamin K. You can buy soy milks at your natural foods store. Make sure you get a brand that is enriched with calcium and vitamin D.

❧ *Tahini Milk*

Liquify in blender:
    3 tablespoons tahini
    1 cup water
    1 drop almond flavoring (optional)
    1 tablespoon honey or other sweetener to
    taste (optional)

❧ *Raisin-Sweetened Milk*

Place organic raisins in milk and let soak for 2-3 days in the refrigerator. Use about ½ cup raisins for each cup of milk. Strain. You can use the raisins in cereal, but they will have lost of lot of their taste.

❧ *Molasses Milk*

Stir 1 tablespoon blackstrap molasses into milk.

❧ *Warm Oat Milk*

    1 cup cold water
    1 tablespoon organic rolled oats
    1 tablespoon organic sunflower seeds
Mix ingredients and place over medium heat for 5-10 minutes. Then turn heat down to low and let simmer for another 15 minutes. Liquify in blender. Add 1 tablespoon sweetener (honey, blackstrap molasses, maple syrup) or to taste.

Recipes in other parts of the book:

Part IV

Fun Stuff!

33. Food Decorating

Decorative Touches

Toddlers think it's lots of fun when you make playful, decorative food. Decorating takes only seconds, but it makes your child feel very special. Some recipes in this chapter, such as *Apple Smiley Face, Stuffed Froggy, Pineapple Sailing Ship, Mr./Ms. Sweet Potato Head*, and *Personalized Picture Pancakes* call for eyes, noses, legs, and other body parts.

> **WARNING:** All Decorative Touches should be age appropriate; for example, babies younger than one year should not eat honey or egg white. Be sure to follow all the precautions to prevent choking on pages 40-42.

For eyes: use cooked sliced eggs—the whites can be the whites of the eyes, add olive slices for irises, or try sliced kiwi fruit, cooked beans, peas, halved grapes, or anything round or oval.

For nose: use raisins, strawberries or other berries, small round carrot or cucumber slices, mushroom pieces, pumpkin seeds, or carob chips.

For mouth: use softened rehydrated dried fruit pieces, an orange section, tomato wedge or semi-circular green pepper slice, a line of raisins, a crescent-shaped apple section or ½ cucumber slice with rectangular teeth cut out jack-o-lantern style.

For hair: use millet grains, corn kernels, mashed beans, or cooked crumbled egg yolk for blonde hair; tomato pieces and curly carrot peelings for red hair. To make curly carrot peelings, peel large strings from carrot and place in ice water—they will curl in a few minutes. Or peel strings with a vegetable peeler from a block of cheese (see cheese tips on page 251). Try cooked brown rice, wheat germ, or ground raisins for dark hair, or use a vegetable peeler to peel strings of chocolate/carob from a candy bar. For green hair, use sprouts and broccoli florets. A regular garlic press or a tubular garlic press (see picture on page 151) is great for making hair: squish colored tofu, colorful veggies, or other food through the holes and you will get spaghetti-like strands that can be hair, a beard, a mustache, animal fur, etc.

For arms and legs: use whole wheat pretzel pieces, small celery or carrot sticks, long slices of other veggies or fruits, pasta pieces, or thin long pieces of whole wheat bread or crusts.

For deer antlers, dog legs, cat whiskers, elephant tusks: use pieces of curved whole wheat pretzels or elbow macaroni.

For sails on sailboats and geometric designs: use cheese slices or fruit leather cut into triangles and other shapes.

For cement: use mashed bananas, mashed beans, and cream cheese make good glues for holding decorative food pieces together.

Glaze: use honey for a glaze that looks like windows or stars.

Pasta (whole grain) is a great Decorative Touch, with its multitude of sizes and shapes. Elbow macaroni can be used for eyebrows, nose, or mouth. Spaghetti or fettuccini can be used to draw lines, circles, and other shapes. Soak them in water with food coloring to tint them.

Cooked **grains**, such as brown rice, can be molded before serving. Place rice in a well-buttered mold and cover the top with plastic or foil. Place a weight (a full unopened can or other heavy item) on top and store in refrigerator for at least one hour before unmolding and serving.

Tofu and **cheese** slices can be cut with cookie cutters into fun shapes. Or use a sharp knife to make your child's initials or other favorite shapes. Create snowpeople, "molecules," and silly creatures from tofu and cheese chunks and marshmallows. Give your child small cheese cubes to drop into his soup to watch them melt.

Whole grain **bread pieces** or crusts, toasted or untoasted, can be shaped into just about anything. Use scissors instead of a knife for easier cutting, or cut with cookie cutters. Use leftover bread pieces for Whole Wheat Bread Crumbs, page 321.

The ultimate food for making Decorative Touches is **fruit leather**. See page 205 for recipes.

Supermarkets carry a huge variety of candy, which can be used as Decorative Touches: licorice whips and strings, candy fish, M&M's®, and fruit snacks in all shapes and sizes. Buy only for special occasions, because these are definitely not Super Baby Foods!

> **TIP:** Use old mustard squeeze bottles for more control when decorating food. Strawberry jelly in a squeeze bottle is my favorite. It takes only seconds to write a child's name on an open-faced peanut butter sandwich. And toddlers love to decorate their own sandwiches!

Special Days. Make Valentine's Day special by adding red food coloring to milk, or to batter for making heart-shaped pancakes. Make green milk and clover-shaped green pancakes on St. Patrick's Day. Alternate red and green pancakes in a stack of Christmas morning pancakes. Use your child's favorite color on his birthday or on any day to make your child feel special.

Special Dishes. Serve food to your toddler on "special" dishes, such as leftover party plates or plain paper plates cut into fun shapes, disposable containers from TV dinners or fast food meals, and rarely-used specialty dishes, such as those for corn on the cob. See also Muffin Man Buffet, page 296. Serve a glob of flavored tofu, cottage cheese, yogurt cheese, super sandwich spreads (page 317), etc. in an ice cream cone just for fun! Or in a hollowed-out orange half or cantaloupe half. Or roll up a spread in some romaine lettuce or in a whole grain tortilla. Also see recipes for a Bird's Nest (page 311) and Gilligan's Island (page 311).

Picnics. Your child will love a picnic—indoors or outdoors. For indoor picnics, make a big fuss and lay a tablecloth on the living room carpet. Pack a basket or cooler with everything including napkins and utensils. Outdoor picnics can be as close as your porch or back yard. If the ground is damp, place a tarp, shower curtain, or ripped flat plastic bag under a blanket. ☛Buy a sale-priced leftover twin-fitted sheet with a colorful pattern to use as a picnic tablecloth; the fitted ends can be stretched over a picnic table to prevent blowing in the wind. Or make a regular tablecloth blow-away-proof by sewing pockets in the corners and placing rocks or other heavy objects in the pockets to weigh it down. ❧Take along damp wipe-up towels in a plastic freezer bag for easy clean-up. ❧Instead of packing six condiment bottles, use a muffin tin or a clean egg carton to hold ketchup, mustard, mayonnaise, pickles, relish, sliced onions, etc. and seal with foil. ❧Use a clean egg carton to hold plums, apricots, and other easily bruised small items. ❧Instead of bowls that must be cleaned and carried back home, use scooped out melon halves, orange halves, coconut halves, etc. ❧Line food bowls with aluminum foil or plastic wrap so you won't have to wash them. ❧Protect your drinks from insects by using cups with tops or by covering the cup with foil and sticking a straw through the foil. ❧Pack charcoal briquettes in cardboard (not Styrofoam) egg cartons. Light the cardboard carton with the briquettes still inside for no-mess charcoal cooking. ❧No need to buy blue ice packs if you wet large sponges, freeze until solid, and place them into water-tight small freezer bags in your cooler. When the picnic is over, use them to clean up. ❧Instead of blue ice, fill clean paper milk cartons with water or juice and freeze, and drink when melted. ❧Or freeze water in plastic containers, pop out these huge ice cubes (the larger the ice cube, the longer it takes to melt), and place in large freezer bags and into the cooler. ❧The more full the cooler and the less you open the lid, the longer it will stay cold. Cover the cooler with a light blanket and place it in the shade. Re-read the *How Does Your Bacteria Grow* section beginning on page 161.

Food Coloring

For tinting anything from mashed potatoes to yogurt or cream cheese, and for "painting" pictures on flat foods used as canvases, such as bread and pancakes, use these foods for colorings:

Blue: mashed blueberries, red cabbage leaves, sunflower seed hulls.

Red and Pink: tomato sauce, ketchup, mashed strawberries, cherries, cranberries, red cooking water from beets (reduce by boiling for a really concentrated red color), food cubes of puréed beets. Be careful, beet stains are impossible to get out of clothing, plastic containers, wood, etc.

Green: green water from cooking kale, spinach, and other greens (reduce by boiling), mashed honeydew for light green.

Orange: mashed sweet potatoes, cantaloupe, orange pulp and peels.

Yellow: mashed millet, acorn squash, corn, orange peels, pomegranate rinds, onion skins.

Purple: blackberries, elderberries, mixed mashed blueberries and strawberries (as in imaginary dinosaurs). See more about color mixing on the next page.

Brown: walnuts, filberts, and other brown nuts, almond skins (see Nut Milk recipe on page 359 for how to remove skins). For arts and crafts projects that will not be eaten, instant coffee makes a nice brown color.

A convenient food coloring is jelly or jam. Orange marmalade, red strawberry jam, purple grape jelly, just take your pick from the shelf.

In a pinch, drink mixes, such as Kool-Aid®, sweetened or unsweetened, can be used to color cake icing and other food.

>   TIP: When you cook, remember to reserve a few tablespoons of the "food colorings" listed above. Freeze them in ice cubes and have a special food coloring freezer bag.

Commercial Food Colors

Instead of using natural food colors, you can always buy commercial food coloring! I suggest using the paste food colors, because they are much more economical than the drops. They are very concentrated and last forever because you need so little—use a toothpick to scoop out the tiniest bit of paste to color a large batch. The pastes also make colors that are much darker and brighter than the food coloring drops. They can be found in kitchen stores and arts and crafts stores. Look for the 2-ounce Wilton® Primary Colors pack with four ½-ounce jars of these colors: lemon yellow, Christmas red, sky blue, and brown. It's all you need if you use color mixing.

Color Mixing

green = yellow + blue

orange = red + yellow

purple/violet = red + blue

turquoise = blue + a little yellow

pink = red + white

gray = black + white

navy blue = blue + black

black = brown + blue

brown = orange + green = blue + red + 2 yellow

For black icing, mix chocolate icing and blue food coloring.

WARNING: Be very careful with any food colorings! Some of them make stains which are impossible to get out of clothing, furniture, carpets, etc.

A Little Decorative Color Goes a Long Way

Some children need just a little coaxing to eat their food. If your child won't drink his cow's or soy milk or mashed potatoes, try adding a drop of food coloring. Purple dinosaurs and blue dogs often eat foods like this.

Let your child "paint" his sandwich with a small bowl of milk with added food coloring. Give him a sterile toothbrush, new paintbrush, or cotton swab to dip in the colored milk and paint his sandwich, pancake, waffle, etc.

>   TIP: Teach your children about mixing primary colors by using food-colored water. Mix red water and yellow water to make orange, etc. Don't leave the room to answer the phone, as I did, or when you come back all of the water in the glasses will be black! Mix on a cookie sheet to minimize the mess, or in the bathtub. Or do the no-mess color mixing projects on page 386.

TIP: Make colored ice cubes with water and food coloring. Place two primary colored cubes in a little bowl and let them melt and mix into a secondary color.

Colored Sugar

Commercial colored sugar is expensive. Make your own by mixing some regular granular table sugar in a plastic bag with a bit of food coloring. Work the color through the sugar with your fingers until it is uniform. Use to decorate cookies, cakes, etc. For more control when decorating, place colored sugar in a salt or spice shaker and cover most of the holes with tape. You can also use colorful sweetened drink mixes as a sugar-type decoration for cakes and cookies.

Gross and Disgusting

Some kids love gross and disgusting. Make insects out of raisins, dates, and dried prune pieces. Use scissors to cut slits, separate, and you have insect heads and wings. Rub a little butter or use oil spray on scissors to prevent sticking. Raisins are the perfect size for black houseflies and carpenter ants, prunes are good for large crawling insects, like scorpions. Place a slit raisin in gelatin to make the fossil in Jurassic Park. Earthworms can be rolled out of mashed beans or softened cheese. Other gory things can be bought at the supermarket, like those candy worms.

TIP: Whenever you are cooking, keep toddler food decorating in mind, and put aside in the freezer any food pieces that would be good Decorative Touches. For instance, when chopping fresh fruit or cooking elbow macaroni, freeze a small amount for use in future food decorating. Use the Nested Plastic Bag Method and have a special freezer bag just for Decorative Touches.

Simple Shapes

It is obvious by the way I drew the simple shapes on the next two pages that you do not have to be a professional artist to create patterns for decorating your child's food. I made them by simply tracing *the edges* of pictures in children's books and coloring books. Details, such as faces and inside lines, can be added into the shapes by copying them from the pictures (see the lines drawn in the barn shape on the next page). Simple shapes also can be taken from the hundreds of cookie cutter shapes available in kitchen stores, and from pictures printable from the Internet at children's websites. Another source for simple shapes is scroll saw pattern books. Look for them at hardware stores and at your local library. Children's books, cookie cutters, and scroll saw pattern books also contain special patterns you can use for the holidays.

As long as your child recognizes a shape, she won't care how perfectly you drew it. She'll think it's great fun!

Simple Shapes

34. Let's Have a Party!

Toddler Parties

All aspects of children's parties depend on the age of the children, of course. Here are some general rules for toddler parties. The number of guests to invite should be equal to the age in years of the children. A one-year old baby should have another baby as a guest, a two-year old should have two guests, a three-year old three guests, etc. Some say that you can add one guest to the previous numbers, for example, a three-year old can have four guests. All parents should stay for the length of the party for children under three. Three or over, *some* parents should stay. Parties for children under 3 years should last no more than 60-75 minutes; for ages 3-5, about 90 minutes; and for school-aged children, about 2 hours. Schedule the party around the kids' nap times, when they will not be tired and cranky. Plan on starting with games and activities, then serve the food, and last open the presents. But one must always be flexible when dealing with toddlers!

Make it Yourself

There's no need to buy expensive commercially-manufactured party invitations, party favors, paper plates, cups, napkins, etc. for your child's party. Think up a theme for your child's party according to her current interests—purple dinosaurs, trucks, crayons, lions, blue dogs—and go with it.

Personalize and Decorate Accessories. Each child at your party will feel special if you personalize EVERYTHING with their names. Party hats, placemats, goody bags, cups, plates, favors, balloons, etc. For decorating, use non-toxic crayons, markers, colored glue, sponge paints, glitter, bright-colored feathers, pom poms, sequins, beads, buttons, small candy, pieces of aluminum foil, ribbon, stickers, pictures cut from magazines, children's artwork, fabric pieces, Christmas tree garland and icicles, etc. The more colorful and sparkly, the better.

> **WARNING:** Safety first. Watch for small toys and treats that may be choking hazards and any plastic (wrap, bags, etc.) that can suffocate small children. Be especially careful of pieces of broken balloons, which are one of the most common causes of choking and suffocating. Dispose of broken balloons immediately. Watch for ribbons, string, etc. that can strangle. Always use non-toxic crayons, markers, etc. for decorating. And do the parents of your guests a favor—use only washable markers, crayons, glue, etc.

Homemade Invitations. Design your own invitations with your child's help by using construction paper and decorating them yourself with crayons, markers, glitter, fabric pieces, dried flowers, etc. ⏵Write invitations with invisible ink (page 388) and include directions on how to make the ink visible in order to read it. ⏵Inflate balloons, write party information (time, date, place, etc.) on the balloon with marker, deflate, and mail to guests. ⏵Make "puzzle" invitations by writing information on colored cardboard, cutting into a few jigsaw-style pieces, and mail. ⏵Make paper dolls or hearts or snowflakes and use as invitations. ⏵If the "theme" of your party is magic, make an invitation by cutting a rabbit shape out of white paper, a top hat shape out of black paper, and taping the hat to the rabbit so that the rabbit's ears are peaking over the hat. The rabbit should look like it's coming out of the hat. Write the party information on the rabbit behind the hat. Be creative with other party theme invitations. ⏵Use yours or a friend's computer, color printer, and clipart. ⏵Copy your baby's birth certificate or birth announcement and use as the front of the invitation, fold, and write party information inside announcing that "Now I'm one year old!"

Homemade Party Hats. Make your own party hats by cutting a cone shape out of an 8 x 12 sheet of colored construction paper, roll, and tape closed. Use an existing party hat as a pattern or practice with old newspaper until you have the correct pattern. Personalize and decorate—yarn, ribbons, streamers, garland, Christmas tree icicles, etc. can come out the hole in the top of the hat. Glue a stripe of cotton or aluminum foil around the bottom of the hat. ⏵Give each guest a crown hat made from aluminum foil over cardboard. ⏵A clean egg carton cut through the middle of each egg cup makes a great party hat resembling a crown when decorated. ⏵Bake Styrofoam cups upside down on an ungreased cookie sheet in a warm oven until the rim curls out and up, making a perfect party hat to be personalized and decorated. ⏵Buy painters' hats for less than $1 a piece and decorate.

Inexpensive Prizes and Party Favor Ideas. Crayon cookies (page 390). ⏵Fill empty toilet paper rolls with treats/toys, wrap in colorful paper, and tape ends sausage-style. Personalize with each child's name. ⏵Use paper lunch bags in pastel colors (less than 2¢ each at X-mart) as going-home goody bags. Decorate and personalize them. Fold the top down, punch two holes, and tie ribbon through the holes to close, or use a candy cane horizontally threaded through the holes to close. ⏵Or nest the lunch bags for strength and make baskets with handles out of yarn, plastic, or cardboard. ⏵Make individual party baskets by threading colorful ribbon through supermarket green plastic strawberry baskets. Add a ribbon handle. ⏵Use decorated paper cups with ribbons as handles as favor holders. ⏵Homemade paints. ⏵Wrap in pretty ribbon some homemade rolled-up fruit leather (page 202) or Fruit Leather Pinwheels (page 206) ⏵Small puzzles or other child-safe items from the 99¢ store. ⏵Watch for 75% off sales on holiday items (Christmas, Valentine's Day, etc.) and buy a bunch of cheap small gifts for under a dollar. Save them for your next party. ⏵Line a Frisbee® with a paper plate. Write child's name on the frisbee to use as a place marker. ⏵Homemade Silly Putty® (page 398) in a plastic Easter egg. ⏵On a small tree, hang the previous eggs or other small favors. Let each child pick one off the tree to take home at the end of the party. ⏵See more ideas under Homemade Toys section on page 408. ❧The Oriental Trading® Company has inexpensive toys that are perfect for party favors. Call 800-228-2269 for a catalog.

Other Party Accessories. Make place cards out of unlined pastel-colored index cards folded in half and decorated, or out of paper cut into the shapes of dolls, trucks, or other Simple Shapes (pages 367-368). ❧Paint some clean, nicely-rounded rocks with each guest's name and use as place markers. ❧Print each child's name with your color printer in a decorative font. Laminate with clear adhesive paper. Use as a place marker and give as a take-home gift at the end of the party. ❧Write names on party favors or goody bags and use as place markers at the table. ❧Write names or initials with icing on cupcakes or cookies. ❧Use helium-filled balloons with guests' names written with felt-tip markers tied to the backs of chairs, or tape non-helium filled balloons to the chairs or table or place them in cups, so that they stand straight at each child's place. ❧Make a smiley-face straw for each guest by cutting a 3-inch circle out of construction paper, Styrofoam, or plastic lids. Draw a face on the circle and punch two holes—one in the forehead and one in the chin—to push the straw through. Straws can be used as place markers. ❧Dip paper cups in honey and then in colored sprinkles or colored sugar to decorate the rims of the cups. ❧Freeze alphabet cereal spelling each guest's name into clear or colored ice cubes. Or freeze a small candy into a cube. The color of the candy can be associated with a small grab bag gift.

Party Tablecloths. Use the Sunday comics taped together as a party tablecloth. Tablecloths should be short and not hang off the sides too low, so that the kids won't pull them. Make your own placemats out of construction paper, cardboard, an old blanket or cloth tablecloth. Supply markers and/or crayons for each guest to decorate his placemat. Or cover the table with heavy white paper (found at office stores) for kids to color. Or have all guests draw on a big tablecloth as a souvenir for your child, and continue to use that same tablecloth at birthday parties as a tradition from year to year.

> **TIP:** Decorate by attaching streamers to the walls with either toothpaste or rubber cement. The toothpaste wipes off easily, and you can use your fingertip to rub and roll the rubber cement into little balls that will fall off the wall. Always test on an inconspicuous spot first to make sure that wallpaper and paint won't be damaged.

Party Arts and Crafts. Instead of loot bags filled with expensive sugar and plastic junk, have the children take home arts and crafts projects they made at your party. Very young children do better playing by themselves with crafts more so than in a structured game. ❧Give each their own crayons. ❧Give each child their own homemade play dough (page 395) in yogurt cups or small freezer bags. Include cookie cutters and a plastic knife. ❧Let children build with blocks and homemade big blocks (page 410). ❧Make homemade cookies as a project during the party and let the children take turns mixing, kneading, using cookie cutters, and decorating the cookies with icing and sprinkles. (Cookie cutters dipped in warmed vegetable oil make cleaner cuts and the cookie dough doesn't stick.) Or make the cookies before the party and let the children decorate them. ❧Make Edible Play Dough (recipe on page 343) or Shape and Bake Play Dough cookies (recipe on page 343). ❧Make jewelry by stringing pasta, beads, etc. on shoe laces or dental floss, or make *edible* jewelry by stringing Cheerios, minimarshmallows, dried fruit pieces, olives, etc. on licorice strings. ❧Paint each child's face with homemade face paint (page 389). ❧Homemade stickers (page 391). ❧Homemade binoculars or kaleidescopes (page 413). ❧Seeds planted in yogurt cups. ❧One of the No-Mess Color Mixing Projects on page 386. ❧Trace with marker or chalk each child's silhouette on a large sheet of paper using sunlight or a spotlight to cast a shadow. Let each child color in their face and clothing. Or trace their shadow on a big sheet of black paper, cut it out, and glue it to a big sheet of white paper. ❧Buy a large bag of sterile play sand and color it yourself (page 394). Let the children make sand art creations in plastic bottles (page 394). ❧See more ideas under Homemade Toys section on page 408.

Party Games. Toddler games should last no more than 10-15 minutes. Pin the tail on the purple dinosaur or another favorite character with cotton balls and double sided tape or clear tape turned in on itself—much safer than pins. Be aware that some children do not like to be blindfolded—suggest that they close their eyes and cover them with their free hand. ❧Instead of Musical Chairs, try Musical Plates and use paper plates for children to stand on when the music stops. Take away the disappointment after each music stop by giving the losing child a small party favor. ❧Make your own piñata by stuffing and decorating a paper bag with a big smiley or grumpy face ☹. ❧Play pickup sticks with long dry spaghetti. Color by dipping in food-colored water. Let dry thoroughly before using to play. ❧A feely game where children are to guess what's in a bag by feeling with their hands and without looking. ❧Use white flour to make lines on grass as boundaries for ball games. ❧Play "hide the bear" by having one child leave the room. Hide a stuffed bear or other toy somewhere in the room. When the child returns and is searching, the other children help her find the bear by clapping loudly when the child is near the hidden bear and softly when farther away. ❧Have a scavenger hunt with search cards made from magazine pictures or clip art from your computer. ❧Plan more activities than you can possibly do in the party time—better to be safe than to have a bunch of bored toddlers on your hands!

Outside Parties. If you don't have a big back yard fit for a party, why not have the party at the local playground? Or at the public swimming pool? (Make sure a specific person knows s/he is responsible for watching children at all times. Drownings occur when everyone thought someone else was watching.) Save money by packing a big picnic (page 363), so you do not have to buy food from the refreshments stand. ❧For your backyard, borrow toddler sliding boards, seesaws, and other toys from friends. Sand boxes are messy, but fun! Warn parents to dress themselves and the children in easy-care play clothes. Inexpensive sand box toys can be used as take-home party favors. ❧Scatter several non-helium balloons about the yard and let the toddlers soccer kick them about—what fun! ❧Give each child a little paper cup with a bit of homemade bubble solution (page 398) and wands for blowing bubbles cut out of plastic or Styrofoam. ❧Have a scavenger hunt for plastic eggs with a treat inside, non-toxic flowers, homemade Silly Putty® (page 398), or other small toddler-safe toys. Keep plenty of extras aside to give to those children who didn't find many. ❧Collect autumn leaves of different colors and seal them sandwich-style between two sheets of wax paper with an iron (medium heat or a little hotter). Along with the leaves, seal crayon shavings (page 390), glitter, confetti made from colorful construction paper, and a piece of colored paper with the child's name. ❧Take the kids on a nature walk and have them gather nuts, pinecones, twigs, flowers, and grass for making mosaic wreaths (page 393). ❧Line up decorated boxes with holes in the bottom so kids can use their feet Fred Flintstone-style to puff puff chug chug around like a long choo choo train. ❧The kids can get dressed up in aluminum foil astronaut suits with paper towel tubing air hoses and take off for the moon in a small wading pool. ❧A winter party can consist of back yard sledding, tobogganing, and snowman and snowwoman building, followed by hot cocoa and cake. ❧A summer party can include body painting in bathing suits (see page 389), running through a back yard sprinkler, ice cones with a choice from different flavored syrups, and bubble blowing (page 398).

The Menu. It should be simple and child oriented. A birthday party is a time to be somewhat flexible about serving sugary foods. You don't want your child disappointed or embarrassed by "yucks" from the guests. Start with Super Snacks (page 291) and maybe add individual toddler-sized pizzas, cookie cutter-shaped sandwiches, crackers with spread, and other easy-to-hold foods. See Edible Play Dough recipe on page 343. Avoid serving food that causes serious stains; for example, choose apple juice over grape juice. See Fancy Fruit Party Punch recipe, page 358. Serve one of the fun gelatin recipes on page 351.

> **TIP:** Serve semiliquid food, such as gelatin, pudding, or custard, in small paper cups. Or double-line muffin tins, fill, and place on each child's plate.

> **TIP:** Save several weeks' worth of the colorful Sunday funny papers to spread under the party table for easy cleanup.

Party (or Any Day) Cakes

Every day is a party when you have children! It doesn't take much time or artistic talent to bake a cake that is fun.

Individual Cakes

Instead of one large cake, you may wish to serve cupcakes. They are all the same size (and therefore "fair"), and because they are precut and ready to be served, they are especially convenient for preschool and day care centers. Decorate each cupcake with one letter and spell "HAPPY BIRTHDAY MICHAEL" by arranging on a tray. Serve ice cream cup cakes. Fill flat-bottomed ice cream cones halfway with cake batter and

place on a baking sheet. Bake the same time as cupcakes—at 350°F for about 20 minutes. Let cool before icing. Or, serve with a scoop of ice cream over the cake. Because of the cones, there are no wrappers to throw away.

Instead of cupcakes, make individual rectangular cakes cut from a regular-sized cake. For example, if choo choo trains are the theme of the party, place a "train car" cut from a loaf pan cake at each child's place and connect the cars around the table with train tracks made of licorice whips. In front of the birthday girl, place both the engine (either Thomas the Tank Engine or the Little Engine that Could) and the caboose.

Carefully cut a hole in the bottom of each already-baked cupcake and insert a small surprise toy wrapped in plastic into the middle. Be sure the children don't bite into the toy.

Cake Tips

- If you must cut a cake still warm from the oven, use unwaxed dental floss instead of a knife and you will cause less damage.

- Dip a knife into boiling water before cutting a cake and less damage will be done to the frosting.

- A toothpick is too short to be a good cake tester. Use a stick of dry spaghetti.

- Before cutting a cake into one of the shapes on pages 378-382, freeze the unfrosted cake for easier and cleaner slicing and handling.

- If a cake is too high in the middle, take a slightly smaller dish or flat pan and gently press it down into the cake to flatten. Place a sheet of wax paper between the dish and cake to prevent sticking.

- To cut a few pieces of cake and store the rest so that it doesn't get dry, cut the cake in half and take the pieces from the inside. Push the two halves together (similar to the football on page 380) and the cut edges of the cake will stay moist. A slice of bread placed over the cut edge will keep it fresh. Hold bread in place with toothpicks.

- Do not over-beat a cake batter. It will mix too much air into the cake, which may cause the cake to crack while baking.

- Before greasing the pan, place your hand inside a small sandwich bag to keep it clean. Dust the cake pan with dry cake mix or cocoa instead of flour.

- To measure ½ cup of butter or solid shortening, add ½ cup water to a measuring cup and add chunks of butter/shortening until the water reaches the one cup mark. Pour out the water.

- Decrease fat in baked goods by replacing butter/oil with prune butter, see page 457.

- Separate the batter for a white cake into two or more separate bowls. Add different colored food coloring to each bowl for a multi-colored cake. Make two different colored layers or gently swirl the batters together for streaks of color.

- To make cake come loose from the pan, set it on a damp towel immediately after taking it out of the oven. To loosen a stuck cake (or cookies), hold a hair dryer to the bottom of the pan or place the pan over a low flame for 5-10 seconds. Invert the cake carefully and it will fall out.

- A cake will be easy to remove if you line the pan with a piece of wax paper sized to fit the bottom of the pan. Place the wax paper under the bottom outside of the pan and trace the perfect size and shape before cutting. Grease the pan and both sides of the paper before pouring in the batter. When the cake is done baking, the cake will turn out of the pan easily. Peel the wax paper off immediately. If the paper sticks because you let it cool, brush the paper with warm water and wait a minute and it will peel off cleanly.

🐾 When taking a cake to a party, don't use a plate that will have to be washed and returned. Cut a plate out of cardboard and cover with aluminum foil. For round cakes, use an old 33 rpm lp record covered with clear plastic wrap as a nostalgic conversation piece.

🐾 If you've burned a cake, turn it upside down, cut off the burned parts, and use frosting to disguise the damage and reshape it. Freeze it first to minimize the problem of crumbs getting into the icing or use the first tip in the next box.

🐾 Place raisins, other dried fruits, and nuts in hot water or heat them briefly in the oven before mixing into the batter. This will prevent them from sinking to the bottom. Roll frozen berries in sugar to unclump them and to uniformly distribute them in the batter. Dip banana pieces in fruit juice before adding to cakes and pies to prevent them from burning.

🐾 Granulated sugar ground in the blender can serve as confectioners' sugar.

Cake Frosting Tips

🐾 Loose crumbs are a problem with cake decorating, especially if you are going to be cutting up your cake to form fancy shapes. When frosting the sides of cut pieces of cake, first brush with a pastry brush to remove most of the loose crumbs. Then paint the edges with some preserves and let dry. Or do a *crumb coating*: Frost with a very thin base coat of frosting, let dry thoroughly, and put a regular layer of frosting on top. The crumb coating will help prevent crumbs from getting into the top layer of frosting and will help fill in cake imperfections.

🐾 The thicker the frosting, the more mistakes you can hide underneath. Use lots of frosting to hide the seams in the cakes on pages 378-382.

🐾 In a pinch, sweetened or unsweetened drink mixes can be used to color frosting.

🐾 Don't buy colored sugar for decorating cakes. Save money by coloring plain granulated sugar (see page 366).

🐾 Frozen cakes are much easier to work with than cakes at room temperature. Defrost for several hours before serving.

🐾 Press cookie cutters gently into the frosting and use the lines as a guide while you are piping with decorative frosting. Do this on the sides of the cake as well as the top, for example, horses on the side of a merry-go-round cake. Use one color to outline the cookie shape and another to fill the shape in with color.

🐾 For a nice touch, sprinkle cake frosting with colored sugar or sweetened colorful drink mixes. Or create a design with the sugar or drink mix by using stencils (page 385). Place over dry icing, coat frosting through stencil with honey, and sprinkle with colored sugar or sweetened drink mix. Use damp paper towel or vacuum cleaner to pick up waste sugar scattered on the stencil.

🐾 Add a pinch of baking soda to frosting and it should keep moist and prevent cracking.

- If you accidentally put too much food coloring into your mixture, sop it up with a paper towel before mixing.
- Use a portable hair dryer to speed drying of on-cake frosting.
- If frosting hardens in the bowl while you are working, place the bowl of frosting within a larger bowl of hot water to keep it soft and workable.
- Place the cake on a plate with strips of wax paper around the edges while frosting. When you are finished frosting, very carefully remove the wax paper by gently pulling the strips sideways. The plate will be clean and frosting-free.
- For a quick cake frosting, sprinkle the cake with chocolate chips during the last minute or two of baking. As the chips soften, spread with a flat knife.
- Whipped cream, flavored with honey or maple syrup, makes a quick and easy frosting, but it must be kept refrigerated and does not freeze well.
- For a quick cupcake frosting, place marshmallows on the cupcakes during the last 3 minutes of baking. They will melt and form a nice white frosting.
- An easy fancy topping can be obtained by placing a doily with a large pattern over the cake and sprinkling with powdered sugar. Carefully remove the doily to expose the pattern. Stencils (page 385) or a homemade pattern can also be used.
- It's easier to dip and twist cupcakes into a soft frosting than to frost the cupcakes with a knife. Brush crumbs off the cupcakes first.
- With a cake for someone that loves frosting, split each cake layer in half and add extra layers of frosting. Remember that you will need double the amount of frosting. While frosting, stick dry spaghetti through the layers as you add them to hold them in place until the frosting sets. Be sure to remove all spaghetti sticks when finished.
- If the cake filling is different from the frosting, leave at least ½ inch around the edges of the filling so that it doesn't bleed into the frosting.
- Place a small juice glass in the middle of a bundt cake and fill with flowers, lollipops, candy canes, etc.
- Make a disposable pastry bag with a sheet of wax paper. Twist into a cone shape and secure the top with a piece of tape. Fill with frosting, fold down the top of the cone, and snip off the pointed end to pipe the frosting. Or use a freezer bag instead. Fill with frosting, push frosting into a corner of the bag, and then cut off a bit of the corner. To prevent waste, use a pencil or similar object to roll up the bag and squeeze out every last bit of frosting.
- Pipe a design with melted chocolate or carob. First pipe onto a sheet of wax paper, place in refrigerator until solid, then peel off the wax paper and transfer the chocolate to the cake. Melt chocolate by microwaving chocolate chips/squares on low power in a microwave-able plastic bag. The bag can double as a pastry bag, as in the previous tip.
- Fill pastry bags easily by first placing the bag inside a large jar and folding the top of the bag down over the jar's rim. Spoon in frosting.
- Place plain prepared whipped topping in the pastry bag for a quick and easy frosting. For a flavored whipped topping, add a little chocolate syrup or other flavored syrup into the topping.

❧ Use a mustard squeeze bottle, a clean squeeze bottle from non-toxic white glue, or a new clean syringe to pipe decorative frosting for writing on a cake.

❧ Use a fork or a new, unused, wide-toothed comb to make stripes in frosting. Use a spatula for smoothing.

❧ Melt chocolate and pour onto wax paper in a thin layer and refrigerate until solid. Use an exacto knife to cut Simple Shapes (pages 367-368). Or pour melted chocolate into cookie cutters on wax paper in thin layer. First butter or oil-spray the cutters for easy removal.

❧ Make chocolate curls or carob curls with a vegetable peeler (refrigerate chocolate for easier peeling) and use in cake decorating.

❧ Decorate cake tops with real flowers (non-toxic) dipped in honey and pressed with white superfine or colored sugar.

❧ Add chunkiness to a frosting by mixing in chopped nuts or small colorful candies.

❧ Oil-spray plastic wrap before placing it over a cake and it will not stick to the frosting.

❧ Use a toothpick to trace in text or decorations in the frosting. Draw freehand or use stencils. Correct mistakes by smoothing the frosting and re-picking. When your design is perfect, follow the lines while piping the decorative frosting. Similarly, you can copy a picture from a magazine or coloring book onto a cake. Place wax paper over the picture and trace the picture into the wax by scratching lines with a pencil or other pointy object. Move the wax paper onto the top of the frosted cake, and with the tip of a sharp knife or toothpick, transfer the pattern onto the cake by piercing a dot pattern through the lines on the wax paper and into the frosting. Keep paper in place by sticking toothpicks or dry spaghetti sticks around edges to hold it while you are piercing. Pipe frosting onto the cake while "connecting the dots." Color the picture with different colored decorative frostings, homemade colored sugar (page 366), or colored coconut (use same method to color coconut as with sugar).

❧ Pyrex® has a well-designed plunger-type small cake decorator that costs about $5.00. It is made of clear plastic so that you can see how much frosting is left inside. The five cake decorating tips (and a pastry filler) are designed to be stored inside so they won't get lost. For a reference, I cut off the part of the instructions on the package with the pictures of each tip and the design it creates and keep it inside along with the plastic tips.

❧ Clean cake decorator tips by first soaking them in a small cup with hot water and soap. Then place the tips in a strainer and rinse well under hot-running tap water.

❧ **Birthday Candle Tips:** To hold birthday candles on top of the cake, use life savers, large gumdrops, or small marshmallows as candle holders. Do not eat if candle wax dripped onto them. (To keep marshmallows from drying out, freeze them.) If candles are thin or small and fall over easily, try sticking toothpicks into their bottoms to hold them stable in the cake. Keep a careful count to make sure that all toothpicks are removed before eating. Use a piece of dry spaghetti to light birthday candles. Light the inner candles first and then the outer candles. Freeze birthday candles before using and they will burn slower and drip less.

❧ See recipe for No-Fail Party Cake Frosting, page 346.

Cakes from a Square Pan and a Round Cake Pan (8 or 9 inch)

"I Love You" Heart

Cut the circular cake in half and place it on two sides of the square cake as shown here. Ice with white icing and use red icing to outline and accentuate the heart shape.

Your child will love a cake made to look like her. Use her skin, eye, and hair color, and draw her favorite shirt on the body. Add candy jewelry or buttons. There's no limit to what you can do with this cake!

Your Child

For the sun, use yellow and orange icing. To get the bottom of each triangle to fit well around the circle, trim it so that it has a curve to match the outer curve of the circular face:

For the bunny rabbit, cut two ears out of the square cake and use the round cake for the face. Use white icing for fur, pink icing for ears and nose, and blue icing for eyes and whiskers. Instead, a 9 x 13 cake pan could be used for this bunny rabbit cake. Make a **Kitty Cat** cake similar to this bunny by making triangular ears and longer whiskers.

Bunny Rabbit

For the rocket, slice the round cake in half for the top and bottom of the rocket. The right-most figure's white lines and circles can be in navy blue and the rest can be a gray color to emulate metal. Add a leftover triangular piece as the pointed top and waves of icing or whipped cream at the bottom for exhaust.

Rocket Ship

Cakes from Two Round Cake Pans 8-inch or 9-inch

Push two circular cakes together, removing a piece as shown on the right to shape them into the number 8 for a child's eighth birthday party. Remove two semicircular pieces of cake to make it look like a 3 for your toddler's third birthday party. Or make a snowman/woman by adding black eyes, mouth, and buttons and a carrot nose. Or draw an 8 onto the cake to make it look like a race track and put small toy cars on the track. Or make it into a guitar. If your child just got glasses, place the 8 on its side and make it look like a pair of eye glasses with pipe cleaners as the sides of the glasses. Pipe cleaner legs can transpose the 8 into the friendly ant from *Honey, I Shrunk the Kids*. Or turn the 8 sideways and trim it to look like a butterfly with pretzel sticks for antennae. Two circular cakes separated can be made to look like bicycle wheels, with licorice sticks, pipe cleaners, or bendable straws cut and decorated to look like the rest of the bike.

Add six cupcakes and make the two circular cakes look like a teddy bear or a Panda bear. Cut one cupcake in half for the ears and use the sixth cupcake for a long, three-dimensional nose.

Cakes from A Single Round Cake Pan

Spider

This spider can be made from a single layer or double layer round cake. If you wish, draw a friendlier face making the eyebrows curved, rather than making them V-shaped as illustrated here. Use licorice, pipe cleaners, or bendable straws for legs.

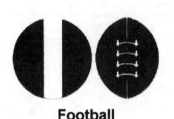

Football

Remove a rectangular strip of cake from the middle of a round cake and push the edges together. Use brown icing for the ball and white icing for the threads. For real authenticity, write the brand name of your child's football on the cake and add an air hole dot for pumping up the football.

This shape can easily be made into a **FISH**. Use the middle cut out piece to shape fins and a tail.

Keep your eyes open for everyday things with a circular shape. Decorating a circular cake can be as easy as drawing a smiley face.

Cakes from 9 Inch by 13 Inch Cake Pans

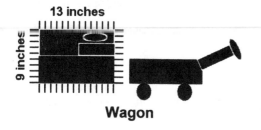

Wagon

For the wagon, only one color is necessary. But it looks nice if you make the body red and the handle and wheels another color.

For kite, cut out triangles as shown. Use different colored icings to make the skeleton of the kite and leftover cake to make the bows. Use yarn, string, pipe cleaners, icing, or licorice to connect the bows.

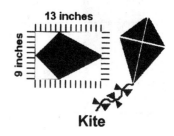

Kite

Van

For the van, cut a triangle in front of the windshield and cut around the wheels on the bottom. Use at a different-colored icing to draw in the windows and hubcaps. Yellow as the body color makes this van a school bus.

For the fire truck, cut out the rectangle and then use a soup or tomato paste can to cut out the wheels. Use a different colored icing to draw in the windows, ladder, and compartment.

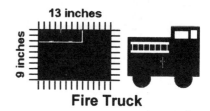

Fire Truck

13 inches

9 inches

Kitchen Window

For this kitchen window, no cutting is necessary. Draw in the curtains, window panes, etc. You may find cookie cutters helpful for other things seen out your kitchen window.

9 inches

13 inches

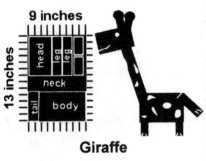

head | leg | leg
neck
tail | body

Giraffe

For this giraffe, use yellow icing for the fur and green or blue icing for the eyes, nose, and spots.

Make a **Puppy Dog** by shortening the neck, lengthening the legs, and making the ears triangular. When slicing, extend the legs into the neck part, as illustrated in layout on right:

Puppy Dog

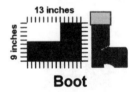

tail | neck | head
body | leg
leg
ear | ear

Make this boot by putting whipped cream at the top for the foam lining. Use the color of your child's boots. Or frost it red for a Christmas-y Santa Claus boot.

13 inches

9 inches

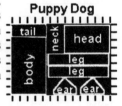

Boot

A square two-layer cake can be decorated with licorice whips to look like a wrapped present, or like a baby alphabet block, or a die. Slice a roof diagonally and create a three-dimensional house, or cut a slant in the front of a square cake to make it resemble the windshield of a three-dimensional car. Make a square cake into a hot air balloon: For the basket, slice a square of cake from the middle of a square cake and place within it small toy people. Attach a helium-filled balloon to the cake with string and let it the balloon float above the cake basket.

35. Arts and Crafts

Arts and crafts are educational and fun! They stimulate your child's imagination and creativity. Your child improves her eye-hand coordination, manual dexterity, and learns colors, shapes, numbers, textures, and volume. Help your child learn by talking with your child as you are playing. Name the shapes and colors. "That's a nice red circle you drew!" "You have two yellow crayons." "There's lots of dark blue paint left in the cup." "Put the big blue triangle next to the little orange rectangle."

> **TIP:** Proudly display your child's artwork on the refrigerator by attaching it with toothpaste or rubber cement. The toothpaste will wash right off and the cement will rub into balls that fall off. Your child will be happy that you think so much of his work.

Your Child's Art Decoration and Crafts Box

You can spend a fortune in the arts and crafts department at the local mega-toy store, but you don't have to. Now is the time to start collecting articles for future arts and crafts projects with your toddler. Find a large, sturdy cardboard box and toss into it any item that might possibly be considered an "art decoration." For example, buttons, bits of yarn, ribbon, and string, old greeting and Christmas cards with pretty pictures, pretty wrapping paper, and the entire list under mosaics on page 392. Ask a local department/furniture store if you can have their old wallpaper and fabric books. Use the inside of toilet paper rolls to keep yarn, ribbon, and the like from tangling. Use a piece of tape or cut a slit in the tube to secure the ends. Frayed ribbons can be made new again by trimming off the fray or dabbing the ends with some clear nail polish. Before discarding old clothes, remove buttons, lace, etc. Buy glitter in bulk to save money and place into a salt shaker or cheese shaker for easy sprinkling. Block some holes with nail polish or tape if the glitter pours out too fast.

Keep containers that may come in handy for craft projects: plastic containers and their tops, tops of laundry detergent bottles (they make great paint cups), spray can tops with indentations (for stamping), baby wipe containers, film cannister containers for organizing small items, and squeeze bottles from ketchup, mustard, dishwashing soap, contact lens saline solution, and Elmer's glue.

Take a walk around an arts and crafts store and note the materials and the prices. Or look at prices in arts and crafts mail order and toy catalogs and add shipping and handling. This will give you ideas on materials you can start collecting in your child's arts and crafts box. Read through this chapter to see how usually-discarded household items can be used to make crafts projects. There's even a recipe for a play dough whose main ingredient is clothes dryer lint (page 397)! Keep your eyes open at garage sales for arts and crafts materials.

Arts and Crafts Accessories

Child-sized Table. At a garage sale, I purchased for $15 a large, very sturdy, Formica-topped oval kitchen/dining table with wooden legs. We cut the legs to the length of a child-sized play table (I took a measuring tape to Toys R' Us). My children have constantly used this large table for their arts and crafts projects. It's currently being used to hold a wooden train set. All for only $15!

If you don't have the room for a large permanent table, how about this: On the top of a round or rectangular laundry basket, place a piece of ½ inch thick plywood so that it extends about a foot beyond the basket on all sides. Remove slivers by sanding and optionally paint it. The table is portable and can be stored easily when not being used. The laundry basket can be used for toy storage.

An old coffee table is also good for a child-sized table, if it has no sharp or pointy parts.

Painting smock. A large adult-sized t-shirt can be used to protect your child's clothing during paint projects. Or make a waterproof apron from an old sanitized shower curtain (machine wash in hot water and bleach). Or cut a hole in the top of a pillowcase for your child's head and two holes in the sides for her arms. Use the tops of old socks to protect your child's sleeves.

Grab an old shower curtain, some duct tape, and a pair of scissors and make plastic bibs for baby (and yourself!). Use a friend's bib as a pattern. Shower curtains are good material for making an apron to protect your child's clothes while she paints at her easel. A button down man's shirt worn backwards makes a good bib for Mom or Dad. Buy a plain shirt, and use patterns to sew on fancy animal and other shapes.

Drop cloths. Protect your floor from paint by covering with a tarp, an old waterproof tablecloth, shower curtain liner, linoleum remnant, layers of brown grocery bags, or an old window shade. Protect your table top by having your child paint and play with play dough and glitter in a jelly roll pan or large baking sheet. The lip helps to prevent paint jars and crayons from rolling to the floor.

Paint palettes. Use clean Styrofoam trays from the supermarket or fast food restaurants, foil baking trays, margarine lids, or plain aluminum foil as disposable paint palettes. Cut them in the shape of an artist's paint palette. Glue small milk jug lids into place around the palette to hold each different color of paint. Cut a child-sized thumb hole. Your child will love to pretend he's an artist—like the one Corduroy met in the laundromat. The separate compartments of clean Styrofoam egg cartons or muffin pans can be used to hold paints. A paper plate can be used as a handy disposable palette for paint mixing—place a dab of each color around the edge and your child can mix colors in the middle.

Paint brushes. Cotton swabs make great disposable paint brushes—use one for each color. Old toothbrushes can also be used. Store paint brushes in a long potato chip can— brush end up, so as not to flatten the brushes. Keep the droppers from liquid vitamins and medicine—they are fun to paint with. So are food coloring bottles. Cleaned empty roll-on deodorant bottles make good tools to roll paint onto paper—use soft fibrous paper or paper towels for best results.

> TIP: Don't wash those dirty brushes. Wrap them in foil and stick them in the freezer. Let them thaw at room temperature for an hour or two before the next painting project. Place hard paintbrushes in hot vinegar to soften. Then wash with mild soap and water.

Paper. Buy paper in large rolls from your office supply store. Or ask a local business office to save computer paper for you. Use white shelf paper or the glossy side of freezer wrap for finger painting—it's much cheaper than finger paint paper. Brown grocery bags can also be used for painting.

Stencils. Make your own stencils with an exacto or utility knife. Cut them out of clean Styrofoam trays, lids from margarine tubs and other plastic tops, backs and fronts of cereal boxes, cardboard, etc. Trace designs and shapes (see Simple Shapes on pages 367-368) with non-toxic washable marker before cutting. Make a stencil with your child's name.

Molds. Save fancy assorted candy trays. Candy molds can be purchased at crafts and kitchen stores. Watch for candy molds, cookie cutters, and fancy cake pans at garage sales. Molds can be used for play dough, crayon melting, and the other activities in this chapter.

Frames. Pick up cheap framed pictures at garage sales, throw away the pictures, and keep the frames for your child's artwork or your family pictures. Glue small pieces of fabric or used fabric softener sheets on the back/bottom of each frame to protect the wall/furniture from scratches.

Easels. Drawing and writing on vertical surfaces is extremely important for your toddler's hand development, and for the development of hand-writing and other fine motor skills (page 74). Your three-year old should use an easel or other vertical surface for writing/drawing activities on a daily basis. If you don't want to buy a commercial toy easel, make a homemade easel from a cardboard box by cutting it diagonally as shown in the picture. Reinforce the corners and edges with packing tape. Cover with decorative adhesive paper, self-sticking floor tiles, or a plastic rectangular drop ceiling sheet from the hardware store. Use it as a table top easel by lying it on the cut edge. Or make it into a standing easel by attaching it to a tripod or by using another large cardboard box as its base. Toddlers can also get practice writing vertically (upright prehension) on wall blackboards and by bathtub finger painting (page 401) and coloring with soap crayons (page 401) on the bathtub wall. Let your child paint your house with plain water and a clean paintbrush. The water makes the house a darker color. Until the paint dries, your child will think he's actually painting.

Blackboard. Did you know that blackboard paint exists? It does—in black and green—for about $6.00 a can. If your arts and crafts store doesn't have it, ask them to order it for you. Make a huge, cheap blackboard for your child with a 4 x 8 sheet of Masonite. Follow directions on can: Go outdoors and spray one coat, let dry, spray another coat, and let dry for at least 48 hours before writing on it with chalk. Nail some wooden trim or a border on the bottom as a chalk tray to hold chalk and erasers/cloth. Keep blackboard clean by washing occasionally with plain white vinegar. After washing with vinegar, let board dry completely or overnight before using again.

> **WARNING:** Do not let the flour, plaster of Paris, or any of the ingredients for play dough or the other recipes in this chapter get into your kitchen drain. They'll block it like cement. Also, do not flush them down the toilet or compost them. Discard extra ingredients in the garbage. An empty milk carton is good for holding this waste, or follow the disposal instructions on the package.

Painting and Coloring

Three Bottles of Paint Do it All

This section has recipes for homemade paints. All of them require an ingredient I call "paint color." There are many different paints on the market: acrylic, watercolor, poster paint, tempera, etc. My recommendation is to buy *non-toxic, WASHABLE* tempera paint, either powder or liquid. Again, I am stressing the *WASHABLE* for obvious reasons! I prefer the liquid tempera over the powdered tempera because it's easier to use. It is most economical to buy only three large bottles of the primary colors—red, blue, and yellow—and mix to create non-primary colors. See the Color Mixing box on page 365. You might also want to buy bottles of white, brown, and black liquid tempera. The bottles will last quite a while and you can use them in most of the recipes in this section.

Food colors (either the drops or the paste) can also be used as "paint color," but be warned that they stain. See *Commercial Food Colors* on page 365.

> **TIP:** Use words like "light" blue, "dark" blue, a "little" more, a "lot" more, etc. while talking to your child when you are mixing colors.

No-Mess Color Mixing Projects

Let your child learn about color mixing by this method of no-mess finger painting. Onto a white paper plate, squirt liquid tempera paint in the three primary colors (red, blue, and yellow) into three puddles about the size of silver dollars. The puddles should be positioned like the three points of a small triangle. Cover the paint with clear plastic wrap. Let your child push the colors together by stroking the plastic wrap to mix the paint. Secondary colors (orange, green, and purple) will emerge like magic! Remove the plastic wrap, let paint dry, and proudly hang your child's abstract artwork.

Another no-mess color mixing project can be done with Jello®. Make three different colors of Jello—blueberry, strawberry, and lemon (or any three flavors, as long as you have blue, red, and yellow). After the Jello is solid, take a dollop of each color and place in a freezer bag. Remove air and zip shut; you may wish to place tape over the zipper for extra strength. Give the bag to your child and let him smoosh the Jello together. Eat when finished!

No-Mess Brush Painting

Do you think "Oh no!" when your child says he wants to paint? Here's how to minimize the work and the mess. Cover the table with newspaper and take out your three bottles of liquid tempera paint (red, blue, yellow). Use a clean empty Styrofoam egg carton and mix a different color in each cup. When your child is finished with his artistic endeavors, throw away the egg carton and the newspaper for quick clean up. A muffin pan can be used instead of an egg carton, but it will need to be washed.

Milk Water Paint

Mix nonfat powdered milk with an equal amount of water and add paint color. Or use evaporated milk (right out of the can) and add paint color. Optionally mix in a little cornstarch, arrowroot, or white flour to thicken. Discard after one use. Instead of milk, plain old tap water can be used.

Window Paint

Mix equal parts water and clear mild dishwashing liquid (not dishwasher detergent, which is toxic) and add paint color. Try this as a paint for windows—it wipes off easily with a *dry* paper towel.

Shiny Paint

Use white glue (Elmer's) with added paint color to paint, and it will shine when dry.

Puffy Paint

Mix equal parts white flour, water, and salt. Place into squeeze bottles, add paint color, and shake well. Let your child squeeze paint. When dry (this takes hours or days), this paint will be puffy with a nice three-dimensional look and sparkle, especially on dark construction paper! Makes great snow and snowpeople. This paint can also be used with a brush or dribbled onto paper with a spoon instead of a squeeze bottle.

Egg Yolk Paint

What to do with the unused raw egg yolk when a recipe calls for only the white part of an egg? Mix raw egg yolk with half as much water (two parts yolk to one part water). Add paint color. Make sure your child does not eat this paint—raw eggs may contain salmonella (page 36).

Spin, Drip, Dribble, Double, Roll, Shake, and Blow

Place a paper plate or circular sheet of paper on a phonograph turntable, a lazy Susan, cabinet turntables, or a dish. Spin at low speed and let your child hold a marker or paintbrush or squeeze a stream of paint on the turning paper. Circles will emerge.

ᵉ⃨Drop some different colors of watery paint on a sheet of paper and hold vertically so the paint dribbles down, but turn sheet before it goes off the edge. Or blow gently to make a paint trail. ᵉ⃨Have your child paint on half a sheet of paper, fold, and press together firmly to help teach your child the concept of symmetry. ᵉ⃨Line a round cake pan with paper, place a marble in paint, and let your child tilt the cake pan so that the marble leaves a line of paint. Do the same with another color. ᵉ⃨Line a bottle with paper, cover beans with paint, and shake the beans inside the bottle to create a splatter painting. ᵉ⃨Dip a straw into paint, stir, place close to paper, and blow gently.

Bubble Painting

In a cup, mix equal parts water and mild dishwashing liquid (not dishwasher detergent, which is toxic) and add paint color. Use a straw to blow until bubbles froth up a bit over the cup. Gently lay a paper on the bubbles. Let paper dry and you have nice sheet of stationery, a greeting card, or wrapping paper.

Invisible Ink

Use a cotton swab to draw or write on a piece of white paper with lemon juice and let dry. Hold over a heat source, such as a toaster or 100 watt light bulb, or hair dryer. Your invisible message will appear. Milk can be used instead of lemon juice as ink. Or use 1 teaspoon of baking soda mixed into 2 teaspoons of water.

Snow Painting

Fill a spray bottle with water and several drops of food coloring. Let your child spray paint designs on the snow outside.

Watercolor Paint

Collect small bottle tops to hold these paints. Mix a tablespoon each of white vinegar, baking soda (will foam), and light corn syrup. Add ¼ cup cornstarch and mix well. Separate into bottle caps and mix in paint color. Let dry thoroughly (depending on the size of the bottle caps, this will take hours or days) and use as you would commercial watercolor paints. Optionally glue caps to a piece of cardboard cut into the shape of an artist's palette.

Finger Paint

Mix ¼ cup cornstarch and 2 cups of cold water and boil liquid until thick. Optionally add a few drops of dishwashing liquid (not dishwasher detergent, which is toxic) to make cleanup easier. Pour into about 6 separate containers and add paint color. Let your child finger paint directly on a Formica top, a cookie sheet, on white shelf paper (much cheaper than finger paint paper), or on freezer wrap (the glossy side). Dampen paper with a sponge first. This paint can also be used for brush painting. A clean plastic wide-toothed comb can be used to draw lines in the paint.

Finger Painting with Salt

Pour salt into a cookie sheet and let your child "finger paint" in it. Or use colored salt (page 394). Teach your child the correct method of forming letters and numbers in the salt.

Pudding and Cream Finger Paint

Make some vanilla pudding and divide it into separate containers with paint color. Edible food coloring instead of tempera paint makes this pudding edible! Use a cookie sheet for quick clean-up. Or use shaving cream with optional color added as a quick finger paint. (I picked up some for sensitive skin for less than a dollar—well worth the quiet time while my three-year old painted!) Let your child stand in the bathtub and paint the inner wall, then just rinse off.

Ice Cube Painting

Mix washable tempera paint or food coloring into water and freeze in ice cube trays (regular or cocktail size). Let child paint on paper by drawing with these melting ice cubes.

Face Paint

Mix 2 tablespoons cornstarch and 1 tablespoon solid white shortening (double the recipe if you need a lot) and separate into muffin tins or a clean egg carton. (Another recipe: 2 tablespoons cornstarch plus 1 tablespoon water plus 1 tablespoon cold cream. Or you can just use plain cold cream or baby sun screen lotion.) Tint with food coloring. Add a bit of water if too thick. For beards and mustaches, add cocoa for a brown color. Use corn syrup to "glue" cotton onto your child's face. Cotton balls can be found in pastel colors now, or tint them yourself by soaking them in colored water and letting them thoroughly dry.

> **WARNING:** If you are going to buy commercial face paint, avoid buying the brands that contain ferro cyanide as an ingredient. Check the label.

For fake blood for clothing, Halloween bandages, or skin, mix corn syrup with a little red food coloring. Be careful, because this mixture will stain.

Body Paint

Add non-toxic, washable, powdered tempera paint to non-irritating baby shampoo and smooth on body. Let your child run through sprinkler to rinse it off, or rinse it off in the bathtub.

Chameleon T-Shirt

On a plain white 50% polyester-50% cotton t-shirt, trace a picture from your child's coloring book with permanent black fabric marker. Let your child use washable markers to color in the picture. Wash the shirt to remove the coloring and the shirt is ready to be re-colored.

Sponge Painting

Buy cheap sponges, foam pieces, or use your old cosmetic sponges and cut them into shapes for sponge painting. Use Simple Shapes (pages 367-368) or your own ideas—chunky designs with minimal detail are best. Put paint in shallow bowls, the flat lid of an egg carton or take out fast-food container, or in a clean Styrofoam meat or other tray. Dip sponge in paint and lift straight up. Make greeting cards out of plain paper, and gift wrapping paper out of brown grocery bags. Glue thin sponges onto empty film canisters or children's blocks so that your toddler can hold them easily. Small sponge/foam pieces can be held with spring clothes pins, safety diaper pins, or the back of an old cassette tape case.

Re-cycled Crayon Cookies

Save all broken crayons and crayon pieces in a special can or container—you'll have plenty of them! Renew them by melting together into "cookies" by using muffin pans. Insert two paper muffin liners into each muffin tin, or use one foil muffin liner in each tin. Remove paper labels from crayons and sort by similar colors into muffin cups until ½-inch deep. (Do not fill more than half way.) Bake in 200-250°F degree oven. Crayons should melt in about 5 minutes. Crayon wax is flammable, make sure it doesn't get too hot and start smoking—remove immediately as soon as crayons have melted. You can mix the melted crayons with a toothpick for more uniform color or leave as is for a unique pattern of colors. Cool before removing paper muffin liners. These crayon cookies are great for rubbings (see below).

Variations: Mix in glitter for sparkle crayons. Make multi-layered crayon cookies by letting one layer of melted crayons cool before melting another different-colored layer on top. Make "chunky" cookie crayons by dropping unmelted crayon pieces into a layer of melted crayons. Instead of sorting similar colors, place a variety of different colors in the same muffin tin. Chop or grate the crayons before melting for a more uniform multicolor pattern. Instead of muffin tins, use candy molds for fancy shaped crayon candies, but make sure that your child knows that he is not to eat these! Use the containers from supermarket manicotti for molds to make huge crayons for little hands to easily grasp.

More Uses for Broken Crayons

Make **crayon shavings** by using a small pencil sharpener, a vegetable peeler, a food grater, or a sharp knife. Seal shavings between two sheets of wax paper with a warm iron until the shavings melt. Thread string through the top of the wax paper and hang in a window as a "stained glass" light catcher. ❧Use melted crayons as sealing wax for homemade stationery. ❧Melted crayons can be used to decorate Easter eggs (page 419) or plain Christmas ornaments. ❧Use melted crayons as an ingredient in the homemade candles (page 404).

Artwork with Crayons

To make crayon **rubbings**, place a sheet of paper over coins, cookie cutters, leaves, a piece of wood, or anything "bumpy." Have child rub crayons over the paper until the pattern comes through. ❧Have child draw with crayons on a sheet of paper and then paint over it. When the paint dries, the crayon lines show through. Use white paper and white crayons to write an invisible message. Paint over it and the secret message shows through.

Stamping

Besides sponges in the previous example, stamps can also be made out of art gum erasers, rubber erasers, large pink erasers, cork, Styrofoam, or shoe insoles (the smooth latex side). Oily dirt on erasers can be removed with an emery board. Stamp in paint as with sponges or use a stamp pad—they now sell washable-ink stamp pads. Potatoes are great for stamping. Cut off an end from a whole potato, then use an exacto knife or a paring knife to cut a shape into the flesh about ¼ inch deep. Or push a cookie cutter into it. Remove excess flesh around outer edge of design, so that the design is raised. Stamp as with sponge painting above. Slice an apple horizontally and stamp with it for a star shape. (Yes, the shape around the seeds in the middle of an apple looks like a star.) Slice an apple vertically for an apple shape, on top of which your child can stamp leaves. Other produce that produce interesting stamps are: onions, mushrooms cut vertically or the underside of mushroom caps (remove stem carefully), oranges or other citrus fruit cut horizontally to show sections, green peppers, corn on the cob—just roll it in paint and then on the paper or cut corn on the cob crosswise so a circular shape will be stamped, cucumbers, radishes lengthwise with greens left on, and broccoli florets for tree shapes. Practice stamping first on scrap paper.

Stickers

Kids love to lick stickers. Make your own sticker glue (at least you'll know what they are licking). Ingredients:

  1 tablespoon (1 packet) unflavored gelatin
  1 tablespoon cold water
  3 tablespoons boiling water
  ½ teaspoon light or white corn syrup
  ½ teaspoon lemon extract (or cherry or peppermint extract)

Sprinkle gelatin in cold water and wait one minute. Add boiling water and stir until dissolved. Thoroughly mix in corn syrup and extract.

(You can use the recipe above or this recipe: mix 2 tablespoons boiling water with 1 tablespoon flavored Jell-O® or Royal® gelatin.)

Brush onto decorated homemade stamps (made from non-toxic paper, paint, and markers) and let dry thoroughly. Have fun licking and sticking. Store glue in baby food jar in refrigerator for 3-4 weeks. It will gel, place jar in hot water to liquify before using again.

A non-lickable sticker glue is nail polish. Brush on the back of stickers or homemade stationery, stick, and allow to thoroughly dry.

Homemade Sticker Book

Laminate construction paper or old wallpaper pieces with clear adhesive paper. Staple in center and fold together like a book. Have your child save all his stickers (homemade or not) in this homemade sticker book.

Mosaics and Textured Art Materials

Mosaics are pictures or designs made from inlaying small bits of material onto a background. Your child (with your help) can create these textured pictures by gluing to paper or cardboard a combination of any of the following:

uncooked rice
raw oatmeal
any other uncooked grain
dried beans and peas
Cheerios and other cold breakfast cereals
unpopped or popped corn
sand, colored or left natural
glitter
salt, colored or white
pieces of aluminum foil
bits of torn paper (toddlers like to tear paper)
bits of torn tissue paper
bits of brown bag paper
bits of torn tissue or paper toweling
feathers
fake fur pieces
bits of cotton
bits of fabric
yarn, lace, rickrack
pieces of Styrofoam egg carton
crushed egg shells, white/brown or colored leftovers from Easter eggs
seeds: watermelon, pumpkin, apple, etc.

twigs and bark pieces
grass clippings
green carrot tops
pieces of leaves, especially autumn leaves
toothpicks
tiny sea shells
pasta, such as macaroni and spaghetti
sugar cubes
instant coffee granules
tea leave pieces from inside a tea bag
pipe cleaners
small colored beads
pieces of broken crayons or crayon shavings
small bits of colored hardened play dough
small pebbles
small decorative rocks
clean, colored gravel, like that used in the bottom of fish tanks
string, colored or plain
plastic bottle tops
bits of wire or bent paper clips (for older children only)
pennies

Instead of glue, mosaics can be made by pressing materials into play dough spread very thin to cover the bottom of a foil tray, paper plate, Styrofoam tray, or shallow cardboard box.

White rice is good for rain, salt for snow, cotton balls pulled thin are good for clouds, brown rice for dirt at the play ground, and sand for a sand castle or beach scene. Torn paper and fabric can be used for houses and other main objects in your child's picture. Yarn, string, and cotton can be used for hair or fur. Bottle tops and coins can be used for wheels or eyes on a those huge faces your child is always drawing. Twigs can be used for trees, with beans as fruit on the trees.

Have your child work in a large cookie sheet to minimize spilling to the floor. Cleanup will be easier because you can just dump the contents of the cookie sheet into a large plastic storage bag for next time. Take a simple picture from a coloring book without too many details and lines. Instead of coloring it, make a mosaic out of it. Work with one section of the picture at a time and let the glue (Elmer's is good) dry before working on the next adjacent part.

A young toddler can use cookie cutters to create simple glitter mosaics. Fill a shallow dish with glue and have her dip the cutter in the glue. Then "stamp" the cookie shape onto the paper. Sprinkle glitter or salt on the glue. Let dry and shake off. Use an old salt shaker and fill it with glitter or colored salt or sand for easy sprinkling. An empty mustard bottle or similar container, with the tip enlarged with scissors (snip a little off the tip), is good for slightly larger materials, such as rice.

Dry pasta, dry grains, string, cotton, egg shells, and paper can be colored by placing in water colored with food colorings. Baby food jars are good for holding colored water. When you have the correct hue, strain and save the colored water to use again. Let colored pieces dry thoroughly on paper towels over layers of newspaper. (Remember that newspaper ink comes off easily and dirties anything it touches.) Dry pasta can be shaken in a plastic bag with a few drops of food coloring; let dry thoroughly before using. Save colored egg shells from Easter time for mosaics (see page 419 for how to color eggs). Place dry shells in a plastic bag and crush with a rolling pin (if you don't have a rolling pin, see page 153). Color sand and salt using the same method discussed for coloring sugar on page 366.

Shadow Boxes

A nice background on which to glue is a shallow box, which has its own built-in frame. Examples are a handkerchief box, tie box, shoe box cover, circular top from an ice cream bucket. For a miniature shadow box, use a sardine can, tuna can, or a can from canned pineapple. Optionally paint the box first. After the shadow box is finished, you can spray with clear laquer as a nice finishing touch. If you wish, cover the box with clear plastic wrap taped down in back of the box. (Remember to keep plastic wrap away from your child—it's a suffocation hazard.) Or use a small toy box and other box that has a clear plastic top to display the inside contents. A paper clip or string can be attached to the back of the box for hanging on a wall, or tape a strip of sturdy paper or cardboard on the back to act as a brace for displaying on a table top. These make great gifts FROM your child.

Mosaic Wreaths and Mosaic Signs

Cut cardboard (pizza boxes) into a wreath shape and glue on pine tree branches, pine cones, red and green bows, etc. for mosaic wreaths. Have your child make a sign as a personalized gift to a loved one with the pieces: "Bobby loves Grandma Mary." Use twigs to form your child's name on a smooth piece of wood—"Melissa's Room." So much nicer than painted plastic, and your child can say that she made it herself!

Sand Art

Don't buy colored sand, make it yourself. Put some sterile sand in a freezer bag and add some paint color. Food coloring drops or dry tempera paint are good, but not the tempera paint that remains white until you wet it. Or crush some colored chalk in a freezer bag or with a mortar and pestle and use as color. Work the color through the sand with your fingers until color is uniform. Another way to color the sand is to put sand in a small jar and pour colored water over it until sand becomes the desired color. Let color set for at least 15 minutes before pouring through a paper towel-lined strainer/colander. Spread colored sand on newspaper and let it dry thoroughly. ☙Your child can make sand art on paper with the colored sand. Draw a design on a sheet of paper or use a paper with a pre-drawn design, such as those in coloring books. Draw over the design with white glue thinned with a little water, sprinkle sand on the glue, and let dry. (Or dip cookie cutters or stamps in undiluted glue to make designs.) Do multi-colored pictures by working with one color sand first, let glue dry, and then another color sand. Add glitter and other art decorations.

Bottled Sand Art

You probably have seen these bottles with multi-colored layers of sand in them. Sprinkle a layer of colored sand to cover the bottom of a transparent jar. (Old decorative jars or candle holders are perfect.) Then sprinkle another color of sand on top of that layer. Pencils, pipe cleaners, or toothpicks can be used to make "mountains" and several adjacent pokes make "waves." Tip the jar for slanted layers of sand. When the jar is full (no air space on top), seal lid tightly. These make nice gifts from your child to loved ones.

Salt Art

Same as previous Sand Art but use regular table salt instead of sand. Of course, you cannot wet salt in order to mold and work with it.

Paper Maché

Thoroughly mix equal parts white flour and water (or you can use equal parts white glue and water). Dip newspaper strips into mixture and drape damp newspaper over an inflated balloon (but not the knot) or a bowl (first smear with petroleum jelly) several layers deep. (Or you can smooth on dry newspaper strips and then paint with the mixture to dampen.) Patient people can let each layer dry before adding another. Let dry throughly before popping the balloon or before removing the newspaper from the bowl. Decorate with paint, glitter, or textured art items (page 392).

Play and Modeling Doughs

Play Dough

There exist many recipes for homemade play dough, but I found this one to be the easiest (you don't have to cook it), the cheapest (only flour and salt and maybe oil as ingredients), and one which contains ingredients that you are likely to have in your kitchen. The oil makes the dough more pliable and easier to work with, but I found that it makes the dough a tad sticky. Make a batch with and without the oil and compare.

Ingredients:
  2+ cups white flour (non-self rising)
  ½ cup table salt (iodized or plain)
  1 cup hot tap water
  1 teaspoon cooking oil (optional—makes dough more pliable)
  glitter (optional—for a sparkly play dough)

In large bowl, mix flour and salt. Slowly mix in water (and oil) while stirring. When stirring gets difficult, use your hand to knead in the bowl. When you get all the flour off the sides of the bowl and have one neat dough ball, dump it out and continue kneading until desired consistency. You may have to add quite a bit of extra flour (¼-½ cup or more) until the stickiness disappears. The entire stirring/kneading process takes about 5 minutes. Divide into three balls (or however many different-colored dough balls you want). Use paint or food coloring to color the balls as directed below; if you wish, you can just leave the balls un-colored. Store at room temperature using the nested plastic bag method. Cheap sandwich bags will keep the different colored dough balls separated within a good quality large zipper bag. You can also store the dough in panty hose eggs, empty commercial play dough containers (from discarded play dough that has dried up), yogurt cups, or other air-tight containers to prevent it from drying out. This dough is so cheap to make, you won't even care when your child lets it sit out and dry up! Tape a piece of the dough to the top of an opaque container to indicate the color dough inside. If you store the dough too long, the water will separate out, so have your child play with it frequently. If it becomes watery and sticky after being stored for many weeks, simply knead in more white flour until the consistency gets back to normal again.

Coloring the Dough. Poke a deep hole with your finger into the top of the dough ball and place color in the hole. I find liquid washable tempera paint with the flip top lid easiest for this purpose. Squirt about ½ teaspoon into each fist-sized dough ball. The more you use, the brighter the color, of course. Knead color into dough ball until it is uniform.

> **TIP:** If you are making a single color dough, you may find that it's easier to add the paint color to the water before mixing with the flour and salt.

When color mixing, liquid tempera is the easiest paint to work with. For example, if you're trying to get a "Barney purple" color and it's too red, just add a drop of blue and knead. Instead of liquid tempera, you can use regular food color drops, concentrated paste for cake icing (which makes really nice bright-colored dough), or powdered tempera. It does take a lot of kneading to get a uniform color. Powdered tempera is most difficult to knead to a uniform color, but is great if you want a marbleized look. After sitting for a day, the color will get uniform, deeper, and brighter. To knead in un-washable color, wear rubber gloves or you'll have funny-colored hands until after they've been through several showers, baby baths, and dishwashings. Don't get the paste under your fingernails or on your tablecloth or clothes or it will stain. Kool-Aid® makes great smelling dough coloring. Use the unsweetened soft drink mix to which you have to add sugar. One .23 ounces (.65 grams) packet that makes 2 quarts will brightly color a fist-sized ball or about one cup of play dough. Make sure your child knows that they are not supposed to eat the dough. Jello®, paprika, kelp, cinnamon, instant coffee, and cocoa (dissolved in a little water first) can also be used in a pinch as a dough coloring.

Play Dough Tools. Let your child use these tools for molding and cutting homemade play dough. Heavy-duty plastic knives, forks and spoons. For cutting circles: all sizes of plastic cups, bottle caps, spray can tops, laundry detergent tops, camera film canisters, and cardboard toilet paper cores or paper towel cores. Cookie cutters (flour/oil-spray to prevent sticking). A plastic ruler or plastic lid cut in half for a dough scraper. Unsharpened pencils for hole poking and line pressing. A garlic press for making spaghetti, hair, animal fur, plants, and birds' nests with little eggs made from small balls of dough. Kitchen spatulas for flipping play dough pancakes. A rolling pin, tall thin plastic bottle, cylindrical toy block, tomato paste/soup can or potato chip can (with no sharp edges) for flattening the dough (place dough between wax paper to prevent sticking). Children's scissors to cut the dough. Children's stencils or stampers for impressions. Measuring cups—learn about volume by filling them inside (unmolding is easier if oil-sprayed/floured first) or press dough around the outside to make different sized play dough bowls. Pizza cutter and cheese grater, but only with an adult's close supervision. Press the cheese grater on dough for indentations like those on citrus fruit and strawberries. Oil-spray your Formica table to help prevent sticking. To help keep dough off the floor, let your child play with the dough in a large baking/cookie sheet with a lip. Place dough in a freezer bag and let your child knead and squish it—no mess!

Permanent Play Dough Sculptures. If your child has made a creation that she wants to keep, leave it in the open air for a few days to dry and harden. Or place in a 200°F oven for an hour or more to speed drying. The color will lighten considerably when the dough dries out. The hardened sculpture can be painted or decorated with markers when dry. Brush on clear (or colored) nail polish or lacquer for a glossy shine. After drying, glue on buttons for eyes, glitter, fabric scraps, grass, cotton, beans/peas, etc., or push these items into the dough creation before it dries. If pieces fall off, simply glue them back on. Make Christmas tree ornaments and snowpeople for your family or as gifts. Swirl two different colored play dough snakes together for a barber pole affect. Put tape or glue fabric on the bottom of these sculptures so they do not scratch yours or Grandma's fine wood furniture.

Hand Prints and Foot Prints. Roll play dough flat and have your child place her hand on it. Trace your child's hand and carefully trim with a plastic knife. You have a play dough hand. ⇨Make a plaque with your child's hand and/or foot prints. Place a thick layer of play dough in a round pie plate. Have your child press her hand and/or foot to make an impression. (You can also do this with your pet's paw or make fossils from leaves, seashells, etc.) Write your child's name with a toothpick and decorate for a nice circular wall plaque. Use pencil or straw to poke a hole ½ inch from the top for a string to hang the plaque on the wall, or insert a paper clip into the dough in the back near

the top. Let the dough dry hard. Create a square plaque with a foil pan and place your child's hand print on one side and footprint on the other, and place your child's name and date in the middle.

You can also make the above plaques with plaster of Paris instead of dough. See warning about drain clogs on page 386. They sell kits for this, but why buy them when it's so easy! Follow directions on the box or mix one cup plaster of Paris with ½ cup of water and 2 tablespoons of white household glue. Double for a larger plaque. Optionally add pink or blue paint color. Measure plaster into one bowl and mix water and glue together in a separate bowl. Pour water/glue mixture into plaster and mix until smooth. Press your child's hand/foot in when the plaster is "almost" hard. Poke hole on top for hanging or insert paper clip. These make great gifts for the grandparents.

Bread Dough for Modeling

Remove crusts from white bread. Mix bread with white glue—about one tablespoon glue for each slice of bread. This is messy, but keep kneading until smooth. Add paint color. This dough will keep in an airtight bag in the refrigerator for a few days. Mold into shapes. Attach dough pieces together by gluing at point of contact. If dough dries up while you work, add a few drops of warm water and knead. Paint finished piece with white glue (or equal parts of water and white glue) for extra strength and to prevent from cracking while drying. This dough will dry as hard as a rock in several days and is good for making beads and jewelry for older children or as gifts—use a toothpick to make holes for stringing. Attach dough to parts of old, broken jewelry for making earrings, bracelets, etc., or epoxy together when dough is dry. When dry, you can paint or cover with clear or colored nail polish. A decorated or personalized pendant necklace makes a nice gift from your child—"Bobby loves Aunt Linda."

Clothes Dryer Lint Play Dough

Finally a use for all that dryer lint! Ingredients:

    3 cups dryer lint
    2 cups warm tap water
    ⅔ cup white flour

1 teaspoon antiseptic (Listerine®, Bactine®, or generic brand)
In a pot, moisten the lint with the water and add the antiseptic. Stir in flour until lumps are gone. Cook over low heat, stirring constantly until dough sticks together and peaks form. Dump onto newspapers and let cool. Use as paper maché and mold over bowls, boxes, balloons, etc. and allow to dry for several days.

WARNING: Dryer lint is extremely flammable. Read warning on page 481.

Gak (Homemade Silly Putty®)

Mix equal parts liquid laundry starch (shelved with the laundry detergents in the supermarket) and Elmer's white glue (not school glue) and optionally some paint color. The more you knead it, the better it gets. Store in air-tight plastic Easter egg or baby food jar. Use as you would commercial Silly Putty®—play with it on wax paper, bounce it, stretch it, and pick up pictures from the comics (but first store it overnight to let it set or it will just stick to the newspaper). If putty hardens, knead with a little warm water. Keep this putty off clothes and the carpet!

Gooey Weird Stuff

Mix three parts cornstarch with approximately two parts water in a bowl and roll it between your hands until it forms a ball. Is this ball liquid or solid? Let the water evaporate and you will have cornstarch, which you can use next time. Try different proportions of cornstarch to water.

Bubbles

Super Bubble Solution

Mix together gently to prevent froth:
½ cup room temperature tap water
1 Tablespoon + 1 teaspoon Joy® concentrated dishwashing detergent
Do NOT use dishwasher detergent or laundry detergent because they are toxic.

Optionally add one of the following "bubble strengtheners:"
1 teaspoon light corn syrup
OR 1 teaspoon plain table sugar
OR ¼ teaspoon glycerin
OR ½ teaspoon vegetable oil

Optionally add a drop or two of food coloring. If you're making this for a big bunch of kids, just mix 1 part Joy with 8 parts water.

Our favorite dishwashing liquid is lemon scented Ultra Joy®, which we found to be a good brand for bubble making. It also has a nice scent. Dawn® and other brands of grease-cutting dishwashing detergents work well also. Bubble strengtheners allow the bubble to grow larger and last longer, but our tests showed that they really didn't make that much difference. Depending on the ingredients, some bubble solutions get better with age and some don't last very long, so save the leftovers just in case yours ages well.

WARNING: Make sure your child knows that he is not to drink any bubble solution.

No Tears Bubble Solution

¼ cup part baby shampoo
¾ cup room temperature tap water
3 tablespoons light corn syrup (optional)
Mix, blow, and enjoy!

Bubble Solution Containers

To hold the bubble solution for dipping, use a paper cup, a pie pan, a cake pan, or a cookie sheet for super big bubbles.

TIP: Blow bubbles at picnics, while waiting for the parade to start, or while waiting in lines at theme parks. It will keep the kids entertained and also the people around you!

Bubble Blowers

Use these household items to make bubbles:

a slotted spatula or spoon
a baby bottle ring
a drinking straw (cut the tip diagonally)
a plastic strawberry basket for lots of little bubbles
a funnel or a cut-off top of a plastic liter bottle
a paper clip shaped into a circle (be careful with young children)
a wire hanger shaped into a circle (optionally wind a string around the wire to help hold the bubble solution)
plastic 6-pack holders
the rim of a plastic carton cut off with scissors
a juice can and other cans with no rough edges
an apple corer (watch sharp edges)
a potato masher
a whisk
a ring from your finger (that you don't care about losing)
a clean hair curler
a key ring
a new clean fly swatter
an empty tape dispenser core from the office
contact paper with different shaped holes poked into it
your fingers shaped in the OK sign
a bubble pipe made from a straw and a camera film container
several straws bunched and taped together
any child-safe item around the house with holes that won't get soggy

Bubble Blowing Tips

Get the blower dripping wet with bubble solution and blow gently and slowly. But too slowly or too fast means no bubbles at all. Try varying the speed of blowing and your child will discover that faster blowing makes many small bubbles and slower blowing makes a few large bubbles. If bubble sticks to blower, flip or turn blower slightly to break the bubble off. The more moisture in the air, the better for bubble blowing, so blow your bubbles early in the morning or at night. Cold, wet weather is best; immediately after a rain or on the porch during a rain is ideal.

> **WARNING:** Do not place bubble blowing containers or blowers in the dishwasher to clean. I stupidly put ALL of the items we used for testing our bubble recipes in one dishwasher load and it took me forever to get rid of the mountains of bubbles!

Super Bubbles

Form your hands together into a cylinder shape, cover with solution, and blow! ✒Cut a hole in a Styrofoam plate as shown below on left and dip it into another Styrofoam plate filled with bubble solution. ✒Thread 2½ feet of string through two straws and tie string to complete a circle as shown below. Make super bubbles by moving plate or straw contraption through the air in a large sweeping motion, with an occasional brief pause during the sweep. Practice until you get just the right speed.

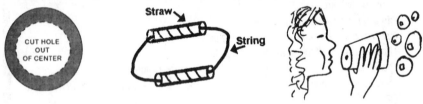

Use different sized paper or Styrofoam cups (use fast food milkshake container for big bubbles), poke one or more holes in the bottoms of the cups or cut the bottoms off completely, and blow through the top as shown above on the right.

Bathtub Fun!

Bathtub Colored Water

Add a few drops of food coloring to your child's bath for a fun-colored water! Here's the place you can have your child do color mixing—much smarter than on the kitchen table! See tip on page 365.

> **TIP:** After you've filled the tub, run cold water for a few seconds to make the faucet cool. A hot faucet may burn your child.

Bathtub Finger Paint I

Shaving cream makes a great finger paint for the bathtub walls. Add a few drops of coloring if your bathtub is white.

Bathroom Finger Paint II

Pour 3-4 tablespoons of Bon Ami® non-abrasive household cleanser into a paper cup. (Bon Ami is non-toxic.) Add enough water to make a thick paste. Add a few drops of food coloring and mix thoroughly. Let your child "paint" the shower and bathtub walls. This paint rinses off easily.

> **TIP:** Finger painting and writing on the bathtub walls with soap crayons help to develop the same muscles used for drawing on easels. See page 385.

Bathtub Soap Crayons

Mix about ½ cup of soap flakes (available at natural foods stores, some supermarkets, or make your own by grating a bar of mild soap) with 1-2 tablespoon very hot water, dropping water in slowly while stirring. Stir well, which is difficult because the mixture is very thick. Divide into small bowls and mix in food coloring until you have the desired tint. Place into molds and smooth and pat with fingers. Molds can be plastic candy molds, boxed candy or cookie trays, trays from frozen food manicotti or ravioli trays, ice cube trays, etc. Let dry until very hard. This may take as long as a week or more, depending on the humidity. Let your child have fun drawing on the tile wall, the side of the bathtub, or on herself!

Bathtub Aroma Therapy for Baby and You

Into a net bag or cheesecloth, place lemon peels, orange peels, or other citrus peels. Let water run through the bag while the tub is filling. The peels' oils are good for baby's skin. "Sniff! That smells so good!"

When I was little I had a problem with skin rashes. I remember my mother giving me oatmeal baths. Place some plain raw oatmeal into a terry cloth bag or a nylon stocking and hold it under the running water as the tub fills. Leave the bag in the tub to continue releasing the skin-soothing liquid.

> **MONEY SAVER:** See bath tips and recipes for homemade bath accessories, page 473.

Water Play

Bathtub play is fun as well as educational. The understanding of mathematics begins when your child realizes that some things are bigger than others. Graduated-size stacking /nesting cups help develop this concept. She eventually discovers that one volume of liquid is greater than another. The concept "some things are bigger than others" eventually applies to numbers in the abstract. Understanding continues to evolve into more complex mathematical concepts: the water in two of these cups exactly fills this bigger cup. The sum of these two numbers is equal to this number. Water play also helps your child develop the concept of conservation. If you are interested, look up "conservation" in an introductory psychology textbook.

Bathtub Toys

Temporarily recruit these items from your kitchen for use as bathtub toys:

plastic bowls
plastic or paper cups
cream cheese and yogurt containers
scoops (from laundry detergent, well washed)
measuring cups
lightweight plastic pitchers
egg poacher parts
funnels
a baster (teach toddler how to fill and empty it)
a dropper from liquid vitamins/Tylenol®
plastic colanders and sieves
all kinds of plastic and squeeze bottles
corks
an old rubber glove with holes in the fingers
clean milk cartons
foil pans with or without holes poked into them
a small plastic watering can for plants with a long spout and maybe holes that sprinkle
Styrofoam cups, egg cartons, clean meat rays, fast food take out containers and any other Styrofoam items—Styrofoam is great for the bathtub because it floats
large laundry detergent bottle tops (wash well)
sponges (clean and sterile) make great bathtub blocks
clean sandbox toys

Make your own toy water tiles by sealing pictures, colorful paper shapes and letters, etc. between two layers of clear Con-Tact® paper. Press to seal all around the edges to make them waterproof. Also, some coasters and placemats (if too large, cut into pieces) stick well to wet walls.

If you dare, give your child some empty trigger spray bottles for squirting. Use instead of squirt guns—no need for ANY kind of guns as toys for children.

WARNING: Watch carefully for sharp points that may poke an eye and for small pieces that may break off your homemade toys. Do not leave babies/toddlers alone with Styrofoam toys. Pieces easily break off and are choking hazards. And, of course, never, never leave a child alone in a bathtub for even a minute.

TIP: Teach your child to play near the inside wall of the tub to minimize flooding. Place a large towel or throw rug against the bathtub where it meets the floor to sop up the inevitable splashes and spills. Air it dry after each bath.

Squeeze a squeeze bottle and make a fountain. Poke several holes in the top of a plastic jug to make a sprinkler. Let your child stop the flow of water and feel the water pressure when she places her fingers over the holes. Poke different sized holes in plastic containers to demonstrate that water comes out of larger holes faster than smaller holes. A smaller volume of water pours when there are less holes in one bottle than another bottle with a greater number of equal-sized holes.

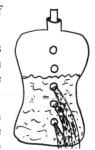

Your child will learn about gravity if you punch a line of holes vertically down a plastic bottle so that the water stops pouring from the upper holes as the water level goes down. See figure on the right.

Poke a single hole in the bottom of a squeeze bottle and fill with water. Ask your child: When you close the top of the squeeze bottle and stop air from entering from the top, why does the water stop pouring out the hole on the bottom?

Dry Water Play

Your child can "water play" without getting wet. Give her grains of dry rice and other grains, dried beans, corn kernels, etc. on a cookie sheet. She can shift and pour the grains between different-sized measuring cups, spoons, and other unbreakable containers. Count the beans/grains to discover that larger containers hold more beans than smaller containers, and that the same container will hold more of a smaller bean than a larger bean. If they spill on the floor, vacuum them up with a nylon stocking over the end of your vacuum cleaner nozzle. Turn off the vacuum while holding it over the cookie sheet to allow the grains to spill back out onto the sheet. Fill a child's small wading pool with bird seed for an indoor sand box.

Beach and Sand Box Toys

Many of the bathtub toys listed on the previous page are also good for the sandbox or beach. ❧Spoons of all types and sizes can be used as scoops for sand, and even an old shoe horn. ❧Use a Bathtub Toy Bag (page 473) or a pair of panty hose to carry beach toys and collected sea shells and rinse them or dunk them to remove the sand. ❧Make a pail out of a plastic liter bottles by cutting them 6 inches up from the bottom, poking holes near the top, and attaching a rope handle. The top piece can be a funnel or a scoop with a handle. ❧An underwater viewer can be made from cutting both ends off a clean milk carton and covering one end with plastic wrap. Glue around the edges or use a rubber band or duct tape for extra strength. ❧Or use a plastic bottle with a clear bottom as an underwater viewer. Cut off the top and sand any rough edges to prevent your child from getting cut. ❧Who cares if you forget these toys and leave them at the beach—just make more! ❧Have fun watching a homemade volcano erupt in the sandbox while your child learns a little chemistry. Place a small cup or tomato paste can inside a sand mountain and pour vinegar into the cup. Add a tablespoon of baking soda and watch out! ❧Make a sprinkler out of a two liter plastic bottle. Cut a few slits into one side of the bottle. Insert the end of a hose into the bottle and tape it closed with duct tape. Have fun running through the spray.

Miscellaneous Crafts and Recipes

Tinted Glue

Stir some paint color (page 386) into Elmer's white glue and transfer into a clear plastic container, such as a Sue Bee® honey squeeze jar. Use it to make textured paintings. Add glitter for sparkles.

Homemade Paste

Run out of Elmer's glue? Here's a substitute you can whip up in a pinch. In a saucepan, mix one part white flour with two parts water. Slowly bring to a boil over low heat. Then keep stirring until mixture is thick and shiny. Let cool and store in a tightly-covered container. Tint with paint color if you wish.

Homemade Candles

Melt crayon pieces (page 390) and mix with paraffin or melted white pillar candles (which are much cheaper than paraffin). For scented candles, add a drop of oil scent, but no more than a few drops or candles will smoke. These ingredients are available at arts and crafts stores. Make your own wicks by soaking heavy twine or braided cotton string for at least 24 hours in this solution: Two or three tablespoons borax and one tablespoon table salt stirred into one cup warm water. Hang straight and let dry for 3-4 days before using. Roll wicks into a ball and store for later use. Using quart milk cartons or cardboard juice cans as disposable molds, pour in melted wax. Optionally add small pinecones, dried fruit, etc. and arrange them near the edge of the mold so they will be seen within the wax. Into the sides of the candle, press gold and silver studs and stars, available at craft and fabric stores for use in denim jeans. (Decorate cheap commercial candles with these studs to make them more expensive-looking.) Get more candle-decorating ideas from examining department store candles, or look in the candle making books at your local library.

> **WARNING:** Be very, very careful with hot wax and lighted candles! Kids can help by choosing colors and decorations, but should not do any of the actual candle making. Let them watch from a safe distance.

Sidewalk Chalk from Plaster

To make this chalk, use a disposable plastic spoon or wooden stick, a disposable bowl such as a margarine tub, and disposable molds. Don't dispose of plaster down your drains—read warning on page 386. Place some plaster of Paris into small paper cups. Mix water into plaster until all plaster dissolves (you will need about an equal amount of plaster and water, or maybe a little less water than plaster). Optionally add paint color (liquid or powdered tempera is good). Mixture may get warm while mixing. Let dry thoroughly for several days. Tear off paper cups and you have chalk! Use this chalk only on the sidewalk or driveway, not on your blackboard.

Instead of paper cups, use disposable molds. Good disposable molds are frozen manicotti trays from the supermarket, toilet paper cores with duct tape or aluminum foil on one end, or pieces of wax paper rolled up around the plaster mixture and taped closed. Line molds with wax paper for easy removal. After pouring mixture into molds, tap gently on a counter to release any air bubbles. Let dry for several days before popping out of molds.

Draw a hopscotch game board on the driveway, or draw highways for large toy dump trucks and other vehicles, or a driving path for tricycles and child-sized cars. Rinse clean with the garden hose or wait for it to rain.

> **TIP:** Place wide tape around one end of the chalk to keep little hands clean and to prevent chalk from breaking when it is dropped.

Eggshell Sidewalk Chalk

For each chalk stick, you will need shells from about six eggs. Wash six egg shells thoroughly so that no raw egg remains and let dry completely. Pulverize egg shells to a powder in your blender. In a bowl, mix one teaspoon of white flour with one teaspoon of hot tap water to form a paste. (For colored chalk, add some food coloring to the water before mixing with flour.) To flour/water mixture, add powder from eggshells (about one tablespoon) and mix well, using the back of a spoon to mash together. Roll mixture and shape like a stick of chalk. Roll stick up in a strip of paper toweling. Let dry for three or more days. Peel off toweling. Use this chalk on sidewalks and driveways only, not on blackboards.

Embroidery and Stringing Toys

Threading encourages fine motor development (page 74). When I was young and foolish, I actually spent $10 on a lacing toy that was nothing more than a piece of cardboard with holes in it and some shoe laces (just in case one of my kids wanted to be a world-famous brain surgeon someday). Make your own sewing cards out of paper plates, cardboard, part of a cereal box, Styrofoam trays, plastic margarine tub tops or similar plastic tops, etc. Leave them as they are or cut them into letters, numbers, or other Simple Shapes (pages 367-368) to help your child with shape and letter recognition. Or use a not-too-detailed picture from a coloring book; trace onto thick paper or poster board or glue onto cardboard or plastic to make it sturdier. Punch holes around the edge or form a design with a hole puncher (or a hammer and nail for the plastic tops). The needlework creation can be personalized and given as a gift from your child: an "M" for Aunt Mary or "I love Aunt Mary" for an older child with a longer attention span and more patience. Reinforce around each hole with nail polish if you wish.

For the string, use a long shoe lace or a long piece of yarn. (Be careful with young children, lace and string are strangulation hazards.) Put a dab of nail polish or melted crayon/candle wax or some Elmer's white glue on the end of the yarn to make a stiff "needle," or wrap a small piece of clear tape around it. Tape the other end to the back of the tray.

Instead of a flat surface, your child can have fun lacing through a green plastic strawberry basket from the supermarket. Use different colored yarns, or braid several yarns together for a thicker and more colorful lace.

Yarn can be used to string beads together, either store-bought or the beads you home-make from the Bread Dough recipe on page 397.

For the Birds

It's hard to tell who likes these homemade bird feeders more—the birds or the kids! (My son asked me one day if birds grew from bird seed. ☺) Help your child make a bird feeder for your family or as a gift for someone else. Wash a half-gallon milk carton and cut square windows into the sides. Optionally add a perch: a pencil, wooden dowel, chopstick, or tree stick/branch. 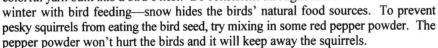 Place glue on the perch and poke it through the side of the carton near the bottom. Poke two holes in the top and string/yarn it to a tree or porch, where you can watch and enjoy. Smear the string with petroleum jelly to keep the squirrels away. Fill with bird feed, apple pieces, suet, etc. Or fill with nesting paraphernalia: string, pieces of yarn, hair, pet fur, etc., but not clothes dryer lint, which stays soggy in bird nests. You may be able to spot some of your colorful yarn built into a bird's nest! Be consistent throughout the winter with bird feeding—snow hides the birds' natural food sources. To prevent pesky squirrels from eating the bird seed, try mixing in some red pepper powder. The pepper powder won't hurt the birds and it will keep away the squirrels.

Bird Baths Instead of a milk carton, use a plastic liter bottle and cut similar side holes. Plastic keeps forever and these bottles can hold water and be a miniature hanging bird bath. A trash can top placed in a small depression in your back yard works great as a bird bath. Be sure it's away from bushes and other places where bird predators may hide. And change the water every single day to prevent mosquitoes from laying eggs in it. Do NOT place oil on the water to keep mosquitos away; oil on birds' feathers will remove the natural insulation and water repellence and the birds will die. Keep your child away from the bird bath to prevent drowning.

Here are some other ways to feed the birds: Place a shallow plastic margarine tub, aluminum foil pie pan, or other shallow container on a windowsill or hang from a tree. ❧Spread a mixture of peanut butter and bird seed (peanut butter alone can choke birds) on and between the scales of a pine cone, and hang. ❧Hang a corn cob by puncturing into the ends with a cut wire coat hanger. ❧Spread a toilet paper or paper towel tube with peanut butter and roll in bird seed. Tie it to the tree with string/yarn through its center. ❧Buying bread at a day-old bread store to feed your bird friends might sound like a good idea, but birds need insects and seeds for fats and energy to stay healthy and keep warm. Buy black oil sunflower seed in 50-pound bags from a feed store. Or, make homemade suet by mixing 4 parts of cornmeal to one part white shortening, one part peanut butter, and one part flour. Keep refrigerated. ❧Hang suet in a green strawberry basket or a nylon onion bag. ❧String a garland of popcorn and hang it on a tree. ❧Spear an overripe orange or grapefruit half on a tree branch; remove after two days. ❧If the wind blows away the birdseed, smear peanut butter on the bottom of the container. Then place the birdseed in and "glue" it down with the peanut butter. ❧And, of course, there's always the absolutely no-fuss method of throwing bird seed directly on the ground!

Crystal Gardens

Why buy the crystal garden kits when the idea behind them is so simple? Fill a clear glass container with water, stir salt or sugar into the water until it is saturated and the water will absorb no more. Let it sit somewhere for days where it can be watched and where it will not be moved. It should be kept perfectly still. As the air evaporates the salt/sugar will form crystals and cling to anything dangling in the water. Use as danglers: pipe cleaners, rubber bands, paper clips, or string hanging from a pencil suspended over the glass. Shape a pipe cleaner into a little four-legged animal and place it under the solution in the jar. Crystals will form on it as the water evaporates.

Homemade Toddler Toys and Gifts

Toddlers are wonderful! They don't care how much you paid for something. They don't care if their sheets match their curtains. Give them your time and they'll have fun fun fun! Peek-a-boo is hilarious. Cuddles are wonderful and free. Your child will not remember the fancy expensive toys your bought her, but she will remember the time you spent loving her and playing with her.

Before you buy *anything,* look carefully at what it is. If you can make it safely, why buy it? One of the most ridiculous toys I've ever seen advertised in a toy catalog was a puppet show front for a doorway priced at $60 plus shipping! For goodness sake, buy a cheap shower curtain rod, cut it to the width of a door, and throw a blanket over it. Do they think we are willing to buy anything? It seems the more society develops, the less independent and self-sufficient we become, and the more we think we have to "buy" things. Commercial baby food is a prime example!

Sixty dollars is a lot more than sixty dollars when you consider it's coming out of your pay after all necessary expenses. I explained this once to my sons after they said, "Well, it only costs $20!!" Just because you might be lucky enough to take home $300 per week after taxes, that doesn't mean you have $300 a week to play with. After rent/mortgage, utilities, food, clothes, etc., etc., etc., there isn't a whole lot left. Sixty dollars might be two weeks' worth of after-tax and after-necessity pay.

> **NOTE:** Happiness does not come from "stuff," especially if it puts you in financial bondage. If money seems to be too important in your life, do yourself a favor and read Joseph R. Dominguez's excellent book *Your Money or Your Life.* See bibliography.

I believe that garage sales are the greatest things ever invented. I've picked up beautiful almost new sweaters for 50¢, toys for a fraction of what I'd pay at the local toy mega-store, and hundreds of other bargains that I'd love to use up these pages bragging about. My whole home is decorated in "Early Flea Market." Who needs expensive electronic toys that speak the alphabet when your child touches a button! A parent is perfectly capable of saying the letters as a child points to them in a book picked up for 25¢ at a thrift shop or borrowed from the library for free! You get the point: Don't waste the money that you work so hard for on stuff that you really don't need.

Don't let some minor damage on used items deter you from considering buying them or accepting them as hand-me-downs. Call or write the manufacturer and ask if you can get repair parts. There is a catalog of replacement parts for Fisher-Price® toys called the "Bits and Pieces" catalog. Get one by calling 800-432-5437 or faxing 716-687-3494. First be sure that any used or older toy or children's product is safe by calling the CPSC (page 16) and the JPMA (page 16).

Toy pieces get lost, but you can help minimize this by keeping a box labeled *Lost and Found* in your home. Place any unidentifiable part (a jigsaw piece, a spring, a screw, a part to a game or toy, etc.) found around the house into this box. When you discover a part is missing to some toy, you might get lucky and find it in the *Lost and Found* box.

A little cleaning and paint can fix up worn-looking toys. Toddlers don't notice, but older children will appreciate a new looking toy. Plastic gets dirty, but it doesn't get old. Clean it thoroughly with a toothbrush and cotton swabs to get in every little crack and it will look as good as new. You'll be doing your pocketbook and our environment a favor by cleaning and re-using those huge plastic toys (Little Tikes® and the like) that last forever.

Don't discard used baby clothes and toys. Save them for your next baby or for a friend, or give them to charity. Used baby clothes can often be fixed to look like new. Small tears, stains, and bleach spots can be hidden with decorative patches (see Baby Clothes on page 467).

Homemade Toys

Make your own **bean bags** from small stuffed toys found at garage sales by removing the stuffing, filling with beans, and sewing shut. (First bake dried beans for 20 minutes in a 250°F oven to kill insect pests and prevent sprouting.) Or fill with buttons instead of beans for a nice clicking noise. Or fill stuffed toys with something heavier (like marbles) and make them into bookends. Place non-stick bathtub appliques on the bottom to make them hold the books better. Very cute in a baby's nursery!

Remove the stuffing from medium-sized stuffed toys and use as **puppets**. If you sew, zigzag the slit to reinforce it. As a puppet stage, cut a window from a large cardboard box, decorate with crayons/paint/markers, and use an old shower curtain or fabric scrap as a curtain. Or, as stated earlier, use a shower curtain rod cut to fit a doorway and drape a blanket over it. Paper puppets can be made by glueing laminated pictures onto tongue depressors or popsicle sticks.

Mobiles are expensive. Make your own by hot-glueing or taping two triangular plastic hangers together at right angles. Suspend colorful small toys, pictures of human faces, etc. from the hangers using short pieces of dental floss (not more than 4 inches) and hang on the crib so that your baby can see it. Make sure you design the mobile from your baby's point of view, and not that of a standing adult's viewpoint. A mobile should be about one foot from your baby's face. Change the toys periodically.

WARNING: Mobiles are dangerous to older babies. For safety, mobiles should be removed from cribs as soon as your baby begins to reach for the objects with his hands. Also, your baby will get frustrated if he is trying to grab something he cannot reach.

Traveling checkers games and other **traveling games** can be homemade with some fabric, markers, and velcro to keep the pieces in place.

Always have on hand some clear mailing/packing tape that is two inches wide. Use it to repair books, laminate artwork, etc. Or use clear adhesive-backed covering (Con-Tact® paper). Remove air bubbles by pricking with a pin and flattening. Use clear packaging tape on the corners of new toy/game boxes to reinforce them, keep them new looking, and prevent them from falling apart.

Make **books** out of magazine pictures, pictures of family members, etc. with adhesive backed paper and two-inch clear packaging tape. Cut out numbers, shapes, letters, etc. Make a personalized story book by replacing the text with your child's name, address, phone number, friends' names, etc. Replace the faces in the pictures with your child's face. Or cut a long rectangle from poster board and fold it into one of those accordion-style books, decorate with pictures, and laminate. Sew your own cloth books with fabric hand-decorated with permanent markers.

Make your own half and half books for matching heads with bodies by cutting each page in half horizontally. Place a picture of your toddler's head so that it fits on an animal's body and your child will think it's hilarious. See figure on the right.

Make simple **shape puzzles** from Styrofoam trays. Press cookie cutters into the Styrofoam and cut with a sharp knife or exacto knife, or copy Simple Shapes (pages 367-368). Make your own jigsaw puzzles by glueing magazine pictures or a child's artwork onto cardboard (t-shirt insert cards are good for this). Laminate with clear adhesive paper and cut jigsaw pieces with scissors. Make a puzzle from a blown-up picture of baby. Glue the picture to cardboard, laminate with clear adhesive cover, and cut into jigsaw pieces. This is a great gift for relatives, who can put it together with baby when she visits. Huge floor puzzles can be made from large cardboard boxes.

If you surf the Internet, there are many web sites with **pictures for coloring** that you can print out. Do a search for these keywords: color, pictures, children, crafts, etc. You can also find free games and lots of other ideas for children's fun. Visit my website http://www.superbabyfood.com, which has links to children's fun pages.

Make your own **recordings** on cassette tape of books that your child loves. Say "turn the page" or ring a bell so your child can follow in the book with your voice. Use a tripod and your camcorder to make video recordings of books from the library. You can personalize the tapes any way you wish: Change the main character's name to your child's name, change the town's name to your town, add a "Good night, Bobby! I love you!" at the end. And don't forget to check out the children's VCR and cassette tapes that you can borrow for free from your local library.

Let your child practice writing his numbers by printing them in the blocks of an old calendar.

Make big toy **blocks** by cutting the tops off two clean half-gallon milk cartons. Push the open ends together by placing one inside the other; this closes the ends and adds strength to the blocks. Optionally glue them together. You can then decorate the blocks with adhesive paper— a brick-like pattern is ideal. These large toy blocks are great for making walls, castles, cages, and forts. For older children, visit your local lumberyard and ask for small scraps of child-safe wood—smooth with sandpaper to prevent slivers. Optionally decorate with non-toxic paint or stickers. Don't use pressure-treated lumber, the chemicals on it might be a danger to your child. Make huge toy building blocks by stuffing grocery bags with newspaper, taping them shut, and optionally decorating. Sew fabric over blocks of foam to make large soft blocks.

Instead of buying a snake with different **textured fabrics** for baby to feel, make your own by sewing fabric scraps together and stuffing. Do not stuff with dryer lint—it's extremely flammable (see warning, page 479).

To make a noisy **rolling toy**, cut off the tops of two clear plastic bottles and push the bottle bottoms inside each other. Glue together with epoxy cement. Before glueing, place small items (bells, old keys, balls, etc.) in the bottles that will make noise when rolled across the floor. Use the cut-off tops of the bottles as toy megaphones or kitchen funnels. Tape noisy items inside a small plastic box for your child to shake and rattle.

Use an clean empty ice cream tub as a space helmet for future astronauts. Cover with aluminum foil and cut eye and mouth holes. Or make another **mask** out of the tub. Add a paper towel tube and let your child be an elephant. My two-year old walked around for days with a plastic bowl on his head as a hat. It just doesn't take much to entertain a toddler!

Kids love to play **dress up**. Fill a box with old clothing, purses, wallets, hats, bicycle helmets, shoes and boots, etc. Remove strings and small objects that can choke or strangle.

Objects of graduated size help your child begin to understand mathematics (see *Water Play* on page 401). Give your child plenty of different sized containers to use for stacking and **nesting cups**. Let her play with your pots and pans and their lids.

Cut a hole opposite the handle of a large plastic jug. Use it to hold Legos® and other small toys. Or use it as a scoop to catch balls. The handle can be hung on a belt as a handy container while berry picking. Kids love to walk around with a **container** on their belts.

Make a safe **ball** for throwing inside the home by stuffing a sock with old pantyhose and sewing it shut. Or enclose a tennis ball in a thick sock. Buy a Nerf® ball at a yard sale. Sew velcro strips on a sock ball and an old oven mitt to make a homemade version of the commercial sticky mitt game.

Stuff socks with beans and make a **bean toss game** out of a piece of plywood. Cut holes in the wood and use paint to label each hole with the number of points.

A **bowling** game can be made from ten plastic liter bottles filled with a little water or sand to add weight.

Make a child-size neighborhood with **houses** made from large appliance boxes. (If you have no new appliances, ask your local major appliance store for donations.) Cut out swinging doors and windows with shutters. Use packaging tape to strengthen. Don't forget a large garage for your child's riding toy and smaller garages for those big toy dump trucks. Practice interior decorating with white glue and wallpaper remnants, fabric scraps, and decorative contact paper. Tell your child it's OK to color on these walls. Buy cheap leftover remnant self-stick floor tiles. For more adventure, make child-size forts and castles. Use smaller boxes to make doll houses.

Let your toddler **shovel** snow with a dustpan.

Paint an old sheet, shower curtain, or non-shag carpet remnant with **roads**, train tracks, buildings, etc. and buy some small cars, trucks, and other vehicles at garage sales. Or buy some fabric with a car and building design on it. Sew loops around the edges or attach curtain rings for quick pick-up. Gather the loops and hang the fabric, cars still inside, on a wall hook.

Use your child's baby bathtub as a doll's toy tub. Buy a toy baby crib at a yard sale and sew a new-looking toy baby quilt, crib bumpers, and pillow from pieces of an old pretty baby-colored quilt. Making a **doll set** will cost you pennies, buying it will cost you a small fortune. If an old doll's eyes look dull, brighten them up with a little dab of paint.

Play **makeup** can be made by mixing food coloring (red for lipstick and blue for eye shadow) into petroleum jelly. Use mom's old makeup containers or bottle caps for containers. Be careful not to stain clothes or furniture.

Plastic fruit pieces from garage sales, boxed cereals, and other non-breakable items from your kitchen cabinets are great for pretend **grocery shopping**. Your child's baby stroller can be the grocery cart and a toy cash register can be placed in your living room on the coffee table check-out.

Toddlers will hold **cards** easily if you fold a plastic margarine lid in half and staple to hold it folded. Insert cards around the semicircle.

Make a miniature **golf** course in your back yard by burying cans up to their edges as golf holes. Punch holes in cans for rain drainage.

On an old flat sheet, use permanent colorful markers to write letters and numbers. Have your child jump on the number or letter that you call out. For an older child call out several numbers/letters in sequence so your child has to jump on them in order. Graduate to "**jump spelling**" words.

Make a homemade drop-in **shape sorter** toy by cutting holes in the top of a box or plastic container to match the shape of your child's blocks and other items. Cut the top off a plastic jug, turn upside down, and you have a good "box" into which you can cut the shapes. Or use a cylindrical baby wipe container, or a empty ice cream tub. Make sure shapes for sorting are not small enough to be choking hazards—see choking hazard measuring devices on page 41.

I searched for a simple reference sheet with the **alphabet** on it at toy stores for days, until I realized that I could just make one myself with my word processor and color printer! My son sat on my lap as we watched the Wheel of Fortune. As each letter was called, he found it on the printout. He learned his letters this way and practiced counting as Vana turned the letters over.

Use your computer to make **flash cards** with clip art; put one picture on each flash card with the word printed under it. Make flash cards with numbers and the corresponding number of balls or other small countable pictures. Make a printout with your child's name, address, and phone number, laminate it with clear packaging tape or adhesive-backed paper, and practice reading and writing with it. Or use paper plates to make flash cards. Child can throw a successfully-read plate like a frisbee. There's no end to what you can do with flash cards if you have a scanner or digital camera; family members, pets, places, and personal items can be made into flash cards.

Write your child's name an cardboard with white glue or puffy paint and let dry thoroughly. Let your child trace the **tactile letters** of his name with his finger.

Make your own "open the door" **alphabet** toy out of two layers of poster paper. On the bottom paper, glue magazine pictures or draw pictures beginning with each letter of the alphabet. Place other poster paper on top with the letters of the alphabet written on the flaps that will open to expose their corresponding pictures beneath. Cut holes like flaps or shutters for your toddler to open. Pictures can be periodically changed to expand baby's vocabulary. If you are making this as a gift, enclose extra more advanced replacement pictures. Laminate the pictures, if you wish, so they will endure more wear and tear.

Personalize your child's wooden rocking chair, table, and other in-home articles by painting his name on them with stencils and permanent non-toxic paint. Do not personalize backpacks, articles of clothing, etc. that the child will wear in public. A child abductor might call your child by name to gain his trust.

Sew a pocket onto your child's pillowcase to hold teeth for the **tooth fairy** and the money she will leave.

Sale-priced leftover pillowcases with bizarre designs or cartoon characters may be just what your child would love to use as a **laundry bag**. Plain pillowcases can be decorated with markers and your child's name. Add velcro strips to the pillowcase opening and use as a self-closing toy storage bag.

When your toddler is older, teach him how to sort beads/buttons by colors and shapes into a clean Styrofoam egg carton. Count as you sort. Or use laundry detergent lid cups for **sorting**. (Laundry detergent is toxic so wash them out well first—let them run through the washing machine with a load of wipe-up towels.) Write a number on each cup and let your child count while placing that number of items into the cup.

Make a **lava bottle** by mixing equal parts oil and colored water in a baby food jar or a clear liter bottle. Fill the jar completely so that there is no air in it. Let your child shake and rock it and observe that oil and water don't mix. Hot glue the jar before screwing on to prevent spills. Add glitter inside and decorate the outside of the jar by drawing fish shapes with markers, or paste on small fish shapes (see Simple Shapes, pages 367-368) cut from construction paper. If the oil gets cloudy, let the bottle sit for a few days until it clears.

Make a **piggy bank** from an empty coffee can. Glue pink felt around the can and add eyes and ears. Cut a slit in the plastic top for coin insertion.

Noisy **maracas** can be made by placing dry rice, lentils, beans, macaroni, etc. into paper lunch bags. Blow up the bags and secure with rubber bands. Optionally decorate bags. Or sandwich the rice between decorated paper plates and tape or staple all around the edges. First add a cardboard "handle," if you wish. Or fill cardboard tubes from paper towels or toilet paper.

Make **binoculars** by placing a rubber band around two toilet paper tubes. Decorate. Cover one end with small colored beads sandwiched between plastic wrap and you have a **kaleidoscope**.

Make a **game spinner** by writing the numbers 1 through 4 on a round or square plastic lid. Separate into four pie pieces with lines and color. Punch a hole through the center and insert a small pencil. Play a game by having your child spin the lid. Your child must then count while placing that many items in a cup, taking that many steps, jumping or spinning around that many times, or giving you that many kisses and hugs. Keep the spinner in the diaper bag and use to entertain while waiting in line or at a table in a restaurant.

Make a game out of **setting the table**. Draw a place setting on a large piece of paper to be used as a pattern.

A fringed vinyl tablecloth can be a "**magic carpet**" for your child, and it can also help protect your carpet from toys like play dough and silly putty.

A caterpillar-to-butterfly **viewer** container can be made out of a milk carton. Cut windows in the carton similar to those in the bird feeder on page 406. Stretch and tie a pantyhose stocking over it. Don't forget to place food and water in the carton before tying shut.

A large plastic jug with the top cut off can be used as a **fish bowl**. Add rocks and gravel.

Plant a **tree** for baby. Take his picture by it every year. Decorate it on holidays.

Make a **growth chart** for the wall from sturdy colorful paper to measure baby as she grows. Shape it like a giraffe's head and neck and color in the details. Some parents make marks on a wall to keep track of their child's growth. If you move to a new home, you can take the chart with you—you can't take a wall with you!

Make a "Watch-Me-Grow" **sidewalk** for your home by adding a small block of concrete each year. Imprint your child's hand prints and footprints in each new block. Have him write his name and the year in the blocks. Your child is the Hollywood movie star in your cement sidewalk.

Keep a **journal** of your baby's development. I know you are busy, but keep it handy next to your bed at night and update it every few days. I did this for my twins and they really enjoy when I read it to them now that they are older. Your baby will eventually begin to talk and say the most adorable things, which you can remember forever by recording in this journal.

> **TIP:** Teach your children to say "thank you" as soon as they begin to talk. No matter how close the family member, ALWAYS have your child mail or hand deliver the gift-giver a thank you card. If she cannot write yet, let her draw a picture or a scribble as a thank you. When she does start to write her own thank you notes, don't correct her spelling. It's so much cuter and more meaningful when it's obviously her own work.

Homemade Gifts FROM Your Toddler

When Grandpa's birthday comes along, don't run out and buy a tie from your child as a present. Have your child make him a gift. Your child will be so proud of his work! He will never learn the joy of giving if he hands Grandpa the tie that you bought. When in the process of making the gift with your child, discuss the person who will receive it and how they will use it and enjoy it. "Uncle Sam is really going to like this ornament! He can hang it on his wall by the mirror and look at how pretty it is!"

Below is a gift that my young sons created for their grandmother. The obviously un-edited story was written by one of the twins and the picture was drawn by the other. I did not help them except when they asked me how to spell the few words within the text that are spelled correctly. I framed it and it is still displayed prominently in the proud grandma's living room today for friends and family to enjoy. Doesn't the necessary cryptography make it so much more interesting?

to: grama regina
from: john

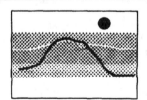

DRAGUNS

once thare was a dragon that livteed in the mistymiuntns one night that thar was a storm and that night the dragn kame done frume thernowtin and the dragon lade an egg and the egg hatched the dragon went up to the moutn but the muther rord so he went bake down agen so he hid and never was sene

ilestrated by Fred

Reprinted with permission from the author and illustrator.

Ideas for Homemade Gifts

Through this chapter I've mentioned many art and crafts creations that would make great gifts from your child. If possible, choose gifts that your child is capable of completely making herself. If you have to help, tell the receiver details about the work your child did. "Kristi painted this part by herself to match your kitchen—she knew that you liked blue!" Say it so that your child can hear it, and watch her smile and glow with pride.

Other homemade gift ideas: A miniature herb or fruit plant garden. See how to grow them yourself beginning on page 490. ✿Homemade herb vinegars in pretty bottles (page 452). Do not homemake flavored oils, as there is a risk of botulism poisoning. ✿Homemade Cinnamon Sugar or Vanilla Sugar or Homemade Vanilla Extract (recipes on page 355) in decorated baby food jars. ✿"Sand Art" Baked Goods. In a fancy decorative glass jar, do sand art (page 394) with the dry ingredients for a brownie or other baked goods recipe. Tie the recipe and baking instructions onto the bottle with pretty ribbon. ✿Homemade bird feeder (page 406) . ✿Homemade scented candles (page 404). For the holidays, use appropriate colors and decorations. ✿Pomander Balls. ✿A homemade calender. Make 12 copies (one for each month) of a grid with days and dates. Bind them with 12 family pictures, your child's artwork, or pictures from magazines or flower catalogs. ✿Desk organizer sets made from decorated boxes and soup cans with no sharp edges. Make some matching decorated stationery, notepads, and post-it notes. A desk caddy can be made by cutting the tops off four milk cartons, glueing or taping them together, cutting them at a slant, and decorating. ✿Magazine holder made from a cardboard box cut diagonally and decorated. ✿Decorated rocks make good paperweights. Larger rocks make good doorstops. ✿Napkin rings. Cut two-inch sections from a paper towel tube and decorate with adhesive paper or color. Your child will be so proud when they are used to hold napkins at the holiday table. ✿A napkin holder or a coupon holder (with dividers) from a decorated tissue box. ✿Buy a cheap plain apron and oven mitt and have your child decorate them. Or make an apron/mitt by sewing them out of fabric lined with an old bath towel or mattress pad. ✿Make a placemat for a special person on a special occasion by sealing between clear adhesive paper your child's picture with a special message written on colored paper— "Happy Father's Day! I love you!" or "Get Well Soon Aunt Jean!" Or make a placemat with your baby's picture. ✿A laminated picture collage. ✿Refrigerator magnets made from cheap magnets decorated with family pictures, artwork, or anything from the list under Textured Art on page 392. Or attach a photo to one of those magnetic stickers that are sold in craft and hardware stores. Or cover over a magnetic sticker given to you as an advertisement for the bank or your insurance agent. ✿A decorated diaper pin to be worn as jewelry. I proudly wore the one my son gave me into teach one day. The students just loved it—they thought it was adorable. ✿When giving gifts, keep in mind the person's hobbies and interests. If grandma knits, make her a knitting needle holder from a decorated coffee can. ✿If grandma golfs, make a golf towel from a plain towel decorated with fabric paint/markers. ✿If she exercises, make wrist sweat bands from the tops of old thick socks and decorate with markers. ✿If she sews, make a pincushion by using a pretty fabric to cover a bar of soap. Or stuff the fabric with steel wool (keeps needles and pins sharp) or dried coffee grounds and sew it shut. ✷For an avid reader, make personalized bookmarks from pretty fabric with a small tassel or from laminated artwork. Glue fabric or artwork to a paper clip and the bookmark will not fall out of the book. Or make a bookmark with your child's picture above the words "I'll save your place" laminated between two sheets of clear adhesive paper. ✷For a gourmet cook, shape a wire hanger into a recipe book holder and decorate. Add a piece of glass or plastic or a clear page from a photo album to protect cookbooks from food splats. Copy your favorite recipes and make into a homemade cookbook. Or put together an "ethnic cooking kit," for example, a wok, Chinese cookbook, sesame oil and other Chinese ingredients, chopsticks, Chinese soup spoons. Or an Italian cooking kit with rare-shaped pastas, Italian spices, Parmesan cheese grater, etc. ✷For a gourmet coffee drinker, make yummy chocolate spoons. Use sturdy silver or gold plastic spoons and dip in good quality melted chocolate. Add flavoring to melted chocolate, such as almond extract, peppermint, kahlua, etc. Dip generously so that a puddle gathers in the bowl of spoon and so that there is chocolate part way up the handle. Let dry with handles on the edge of a cookie sheet lined with wax paper. Optionally drizzle over the dry chocolate melted white chocolate to decorate. Package each spoon in plastic or a plastic sandwich bag tied with a ribbon and label with the flavor. My kids made these for a professor who gave them free computer lessons. He collected gourmet coffees for years and absolutely loved these gift spoons! ✷Candied tea stirrers can be made by dipping plastic spoons in peppermint- or lemon- or cinnamon-flavored hard candy melted over low heat with a little light corn syrup. ✷For us chocoholics, make chocolate coated pretzels. Dip half of each pretzel in the chocolate and let dry, then dip the other half. Or use pretzel sticks. Or dip homemade cookies halfway in chocolate. ✷Make a snake for preventing under-door drafts by stuffing the leg of an old pair of adult pants. Decorate with fabric scraps and buttons for eyes. ✷Wind chimes made from decorative tin cans, string, and a wire hanger. ✷Homegrown herbs dried and packaged in decorated baby food jars tied with pretty ribbons. ✷Homemade cookies or other treats packaged in a decorated coffee can. ✷Assortments of nuts and other foods packaged into supermarket TV dinner compartmentalized trays, wrapped and decorated with plastic wrap and ribbon. ✷Decorated baby food jars filled with potpourri from home-grown flowers. ✷A set of coasters made from matching decorated plastic lids (rim side up) with a matching spoon rest. Or make coasters out of small tiles. Glue fabric or felt to the bottom to protect furniture from scratches. ✷Give aroma therapy by growing some fragrant plant in a pretty mug. See page 492. ✷A drawer sachet made long for a uniform fragrance throughout the drawer. Enclose potpourri or home-grown fragrant flowers in a fabric piece rolled into a sausage shape and tied on the ends with pretty ribbons. ✷A padded hanger sachet with perfume spritzed on the inside layers of batting. Cover with silk fabric and keep it from slipping off the hanger by attaching ribbons to the fabric and the hanger hook. The ribbons and fabric can match the color of the plastic hanger. This is a pretty and practical gift for pre-school teachers, babysitters, etc. ✷For someone who enjoys word puzzles, collect crosswords, jumbles, etc. from the newspaper and glue into a homemade puzzle book. Place solutions in the back of the book. ✷Make an umbrella stand by stacking and taping four or five large cans with all ends cut out except the one on the very bottom of the stack. Optionally, hot glue the bottom of the stack of cans to a block of wood for stability. Decorate. ❧A jewelry case made from a sturdy box covered with pretty fabric or quilted fabric and lace. ❧An eyeglass case made from a potholder folded in half. Sew together on the "hook" side, so it can be hung on a convenient hook. Let your child decorate it. Or make a case from part of an old purse lined with soft fabric and decorated. ❧Buy a cheap picture frame and decorate with jigsaw puzzle pieces, sea shells, hard candy, autumn leaves, and other items listed under textured art on page 392. Give it a shellac finish. Use bridal fabric for a wedding picture frame. Glue fabric or felt to the back/bottom of the frame to protect walls/tables from scratches. Prevent wall pictures from slanting by putting a small piece of masking tape on the wire where it hangs on the nail. ❧A wall plaque with baby's hand print and foot print (see page 397). ❧A homemade video for far away friends entitled "A typical day in the life of Melissa Smith." ❧Videotape a special party or event and borrow a friend's VCR to make a copies to give as gifts. ❧Make a food basket for friends in the hospital and save big $$. Have your child help you pick out fruit and other snacks at the grocery store, arrange them in the basket, and enclose in pretty plastic wrap. Tie closed with a ribbon. Add a personalized homemade get well card. ❧For a friend who is bedridden due to illness or pregnancy, make a large fabric holder with plenty of pockets that can be hung on the bed or side table. Fill the pockets with accessories, such as fragrant skin lotion, tissues, comb, eye glasses, paperback books, non-perishable snacks, get well cards, TV guide, TV remote control, etc. ❧For a baby gift, buy a cheap wicker basket and paint it baby blue or pink. Fill it with baby accessories, the baby announcement or newspaper announcement laminated, etc. Or instead of a wicker basket, weave blue, pink, or yellow pastel-colored ribbons through a laundry basket to hold the baby gifts. Or use a baby bathtub. ❧Have your child make a "New Baby Journal" as a new baby gift. Place into it the baby announcement or newspaper announcement, pictures of Mom pregnant, a picture of the hospital room with flowers, a picture of the nursery, etc. The cover can be decorated with used baby announcement cards. ❧A belt or tie holder from a piece of wood and golf tees, painted and personalized. ❧For long-time warmth on cold nights, make your loved one a "hot bag." Sew cheap, uncooked white or brown rice into denim or terry toweling. (First kill all bug larvae in the rice as described in the tip on page 208.) To warm, heat in the microwave for about two minutes and shake to distribute heat. Place the hot bag next to cold feet in bed to keep them snugly warm. Optionally make a drawstring machine-washable cover. Neck warmers, fanny warmers for football games, and hand-warmers can be made this way also. If you are really going to make a lot of these as gifts, check out the price of whole feed corn at a farm supply store—it will probably be a lot cheaper than rice.

Homemade Cards and Gift Wrap

Why pay several dollars for a card and wrapping paper when your child can make his own? Paint, color, stamp, sponge paint, or bubble paint to decorate plain white shelf paper, or plain 8½ x 11 sheets taped together, or brown paper grocery bags. ❧Twist bows out of ribbons or make ribbons and bows out of glittery colorful decorated paper to match the gift wrap. Curl strips of wrapping paper using scissors as you would curl a ribbon. Mix paper strips with matching ribbon to create a professional-looking bow.

❧Protect bows from being crushed by placing a plastic green strawberry basket over them. ❧Make matching gift tags out of extra pieces of wrapping paper, or from white cardboard, pieces of old greeting cards, or t-shirt/underwear cardboard inserts. Save last year's Christmas cards and use the pictures as decorative gift tags. ❧Make a matching personalized decorated greeting card out of sturdy paper. Create a textured card using old greeting card pieces and the items listed for creating mosaics (page 392). Or use your computer and clip art or, better yet, use your own computer artwork and text. Use commercial pop-up greeting cards or children's books to give you ideas for your own homemade pop-out cards. So much nicer and more thoughtful (and cheaper) than purchased sentiments! ❧Add some aroma to your greeting cards by gluing fragrant plant pieces (page 492) to the card. ❧Use sticks of chewing gum to form the child's name or initial to decorate a package. Or use candy cane sticks, chocolate kisses, or other individually-wrapped candy pieces to decorate the package in the shape of a star or other Simple Shape (pages 367-368). Or use coins (cleaned so that they shine) and new dollar bills to design a pattern. Or use buttons, old jewelry, or other textured art materials (page 392) to create a design. ❧Create snowflakes or Christmas tree shapes from contrasting paper or fabric and glue onto Christmas wrapping paper. ❧Wrap a package in the shape of a Hershey kiss with aluminum foil. The gift tag can be shaped like the paper coming out the top. ❧Wrap a toy jump rope around a child's wrapped present as you would a ribbon. ❧Enclose within a thank you card a picture of your child wearing or playing with the gift. ❧Wrap a baby gift in a receiving blanket held together with colorful diaper pins. Wrap a wedding present in a bath towel. ❧Attach a rattle, small stuffed toy, or other baby item to the wrapped package. ❧Re-use wrapping paper by ironing it on the wrong side. The heat will help to remove tape. When gift wrapping, use as little tape as possible so it can be removed more easily. Strategically place holes in wrap where a bow can be placed to camouflage the hole. Iron used ribbons to straighten them or use a curling iron to freshen used bows. ❧Re-use commercial greeting cards you have received by wiping a cotton swap with bleach over any handwriting to remove it. ❧Measure the size of the wrap you need by encircling the largest part of the box with a piece of string and adding a few inches. ❧Use an old road map as wrapping paper. ❧Wash out an empty potato chip bag, turn it inside out and you have a beautiful silver bag in which to wrap a small gift. ❧Use nice magazine pages to wrap small gifts. ❧Or buy cheap odd-lot wallpaper to wrap gifts. ❧Make beautiful textured wrapping paper by melting crayon shavings onto the paper. Place shavings on paper, cover with a sheet of waxed paper, and iron to melt. Place a sheet of brown grocery bag between the iron and the wax paper to protect the iron. ❧Use the colorful Sunday comics as wrapping paper. ❧Wrap a present in a colorful pillowcase. Or sew a drawstring fabric bag for an odd-size gift. ❧Sometimes it's cheaper to buy fabric for gift wrapping instead of paper gift wrap! And it can be used over and over again. The receiver can consider it part of the gift if he sews. Trim raw edges with pinking sheers or zig zag sew to prevent fraying. Or use leftover fabric scraps sewn into a quilt-like pattern as gift wrap. The same special family "birthday bag" can be used repeatedly for birthday presents. ❧Use other unusual material as gift wrap: cellophane, white bridal veil netting, tinted plastic food wrap, etc. You don't need wrapping paper if you decorate a plain white gift box. ❧Don't buy those commercial gift bags when you can make your own by decorating a plain bag and adding ribbon handles to it. ❧For gifts too large to wrap, make a paper trail the receiver must follow to find the present. Or lay string throughout the house. Or leave written clues as to where the present can be found. Or wrap a small piece of the too-large present, for example, just the horn of a bicycle. Or wrap a picture of the present. ❧Wrap a noisemaker in the box with the present to prevent someone from guessing what the present is. For example, enclose dried beans in a small plastic container so that they will make noise when shaken.

Valentine's Day Cards

Have your child create a finger-painted picture for a special someone with white, pink, and red hearts on colored construction paper. ❧Heart-shaped stamps (page 391) and heart-shaped sponges for sponge painting (page 390) are easy to make. ❧Make heart-shaped laminated placemats for the kitchen table or office desk with construction paper and clear adhesive-backed paper. Have your child date it and sign it with "I love you, Mommy." ❧Make a mobile for hanging the valentine's cards your child has received.

Easter Crafts

No need to buy special Easter egg coloring kits. Color hard-boiled eggs or empty eggshells. To blow raw parts out of eggshells, poke small holes into each end with long needle, use the needle to break the yolk, blow out the raw parts into a bowl, clean the inside of the shell well and let thoroughly dry. For each different color: Into ¾ cup hot water, stir in one tablespoon white vinegar and some food coloring (page 364). Use slotted spoon, rubber gloves, or kitchen tongs to remove eggs when they reach desired color. Let dry and optionally polish with vegetable oil on disposable towels (see warning, page 275). ❧Place tape on part of eggs and dip in coloring solution until desired color. Leave the covered parts white or dip and color again with a lighter color. ❧Decorate colored eggs with non-toxic paints, markers, stickers (page 391), tiny candies and sprinkles attached with gel icing in the tiny tubes, spatter paint with a toothbrush, etc. Glue cotton on eggs for bunny tails and colored toothpick pieces for whiskers. ❧Make marbleized eggs by wrapping plain eggs in onion skins or strips of a man's old silk tie. Tightly wrap in a piece of old pantyhose and tie ends. Hard-cook in boiling water, cool, remove hose and onion skin/silk. ❧Paint melted crayon wax/paraffin over small herb sprigs. ❧Into a cup of boiling water, grate colored crayon wax. Add (colored) egg and stir gently while melting wax is adhering to egg. Seal with clear acrylic or nail polish on blown eggs that will not be eaten. ❧Decorate eggs by sponge painting (page 390) with small bits of sponge/foam held with spring clothes pins, safety diaper pins, or the back of an old cassette tape case. Paint half the egg and let dry thoroughly before painting the other half. ❧Make pretty Easter baskets by threading colored ribbon through green plastic strawberry baskets. ❧Make nests with baby chicks by dipping cotton balls into yellow-colored water. Let dry thoroughly. Place shredded paper into one section of a Styrofoam egg carton. Place yellow cotton ball as chick's head. Draw eyes with a marker and glue a small orange beak cut out of construction paper. ❧Make an Easter tree from budding branches gathered from outside placed in a vase. Hang plastic eggs and other Easter decorations from the branches. ❧Use a cotton ball and baking soda to make Easter bunny footprints leading up to your child's hidden Easter basket, so he could follow the trail to find it.

> **WARNING:** Remember that, because of bacterial growth, hard-cooked eggs should be kept refrigerated at all times, and eaten or discarded after one week (page 271).

Christmas Crafts and Gifts

Stockings can be hung by the fireplace much cheaper if you make your own. Buy fuzzy red and white cloth to sew stockings or Santa hats, or buy cheap undecorated stockings/hats. Write children's names with Elmer's glue and green glitter. These make nice personalized Christmas gifts. ❧Make glittery paper snowflakes and stick onto windows with dabs of toothpaste. ❧Create Christmas placemats by arranging last year's Christmas cards on stiff paper and laminating with clear adhesive paper. ❧Make pinecone ornaments by rolling pinecones in Elmer's glue and then in glitter. Or make ornaments from pinecones that look hand painted: Place very large pinecones in water until they close up. Dry the outside with paper towels and spray paint or glitter paint them. It helps to hang them with dental floss while painting them. When they completely dry and reopen, it will look like you took the time to hand paint only the tips. ❧Make a snowy Christmas globe with a baby food jar. Hot glue small figurines or ornaments inside the lid cap before filling with water and glitter. Or, instead of water, use white/light corn syrup for a thicker liquid. Hot glue/rubber cement the lid before tightly capping. Display upside down on waterproof surface (just in case). ❧Make decorative snow: mix ½ cup liquid starch into a cup of soap flakes or granular detergent and add a few blue drops of food coloring. Use as decorative snow to dab on the tree with a paintbrush. Colorful decorative sprinkles, sequins, or glitter add a nice final touch. ❧A Christmas wreath made from a wire hanger tied with strips of green plastic garbage bags is both inexpensive and waterproof. Add bright red Christmas bows. ❧Make homemade holiday candles (page 404) in pretty metal Christmas boxes bought for 75% off after Christmas last year. ❧Make a Christmas gift for the kitchen by sewing a Christmas kitchen towel into a stocking and stuffing with a set of kitchen utensils. ❧Insert a toilet paper roll with candy or small toys and wrap sausage-style with Christmas wrap and ribbon. ❧Make a frozen pond with a garage sale mirror or aluminum foil and plasticine, pine sprigs, cotton, small toy ice skaters, and decorative snow. Make bushes and trees from the tips of branches from the Christmas tree or fir cones—dab with glue and sprinkle with salt, which will look like snow. Use glue or melted wax to keep things in place. ❧Build a village under the tree with small boxes and the like. Pieces of masking tape can be made to look like shingles. Sandpaper makes good roads and driveways. ❧Use a man's shoe and dip it in a shallow container of baking soda to make Santa's footprints in the carpet.

Homemade Ornaments Make delicious smelling ornaments with a dough mixed from a 4.12 ounce jar of ground cinnamon (or 1 cup bought in bulk at the natural foods store) and ¾ cup commercial applesauce (homemade applesauce is too watery). Dough should be stiff. Optionally add glitter. Roll dough between waxed paper until very thin (about ¼ inch thick). Use cookie cutters or cut Simple Shapes (pages 367-368). For hanging, use a straw to make a hole near the top. Let air dry on wax paper for a few days until hard. Decorate. Do not eat. ❧Each visitor to your home can choose an ornament off your tree to take home. One advantage of giving your ornaments away, besides the joy of giving: You will have less un-decorating to do after Christmas. ❧Make a bird cage tree ornament by wrapping string dipped in white glue around an inflated balloon. Let dry thoroughly, pop balloon, and insert a toy bird into the cage. ❧"Hand" ornaments can be made by tracing your child's hand on a piece of paper. Use as a pattern to cut a hand shape from green and red felt. Glue green and red hands together back to back and decorate with glitter, rick rack, etc. Make one of these hand ornaments each year to see how much your child's hand has grown. ❧Make antique-like paper ornaments by gluing pictures from last year's Christmas cards back to back. Punch holes around the edge and lace together with yarn. ❧Make a Christmas tree (see figure on the right) by gluing together paper towel tubes sliced into one inch segments. Glue a small ornament in each segment, paint it green, and add glitter. Instead of cardboard tubing, use baby food jars. ❧A "baby's first Christmas" ornament can be made from a plain clear glass ornament (available at craft stores). Clean by removing cap and soaking the glass part in bleach. Use cotton swabs to dry the inside and it will gleam! Make a laser copy of baby's picture (optionally add name, birth weight and length, etc.) and laminate it. Or use a regular picture of your baby, laminated. Cut it into a circle a little smaller than the ornament, roll it up and insert into ornament. It will unroll and flatten. Tie a blue or pink ribbon around top of ornament. Ornaments can also be made from these clear ornaments by filling with iridescent cellophane, potpourri, etc. Instead of clear glass ornaments, use baby food jars for a comedic touch.

> **TIP:** Put breakable ornaments with metal hooks near the top of the tree out of baby's reach. Use only baby-safe ornaments on the bottom of the tree attached with *short* (less than 3 inches) pieces of yarn or string. (Still there was trouble in my home when a short piece of string got tightly wrapped around my son's finger and turned it blue!) Or, place the entire Christmas tree in the playpen or behind a baby gate in the corner.

Halloween

Homemade Costumes Buy a large stuffed bunny or teddy bear at a garage sale for a few dollars, remove the stuffing (this is really, really messy) and use it as an adorable costume for your little one. ❧Jogging suits are perfect as a base for Halloween costumes; they keep kids warm and they can be worn after Halloween is done. A bunny costume can be made from a white suit and fluffy cotton balls for a bunny tail, a dalmatian from a white suit with black fabric circles tacked on or black contact paper stuck on and ears tacked to the hood, Spiderman from a red suit with black accents, a skeleton from a black suit with white bones tacked on, a skunk costume from a black suit with a fake fur stripe down the hood and back. ❧Make a snowman by stuffing a white suit until round. Add black coal buttons, an orange cone made of construction paper as a nose, a scarf, a broom, and a black top hat. ❧A tin man from the Wizard of Oz can be made from a grey sweatsuit covered with a brown paper bag with cut out head and arm holes. Glue aluminum foil all over the bag. Make a hat from a funnel or a cut-off top of a plastic liter bottle covered with aluminum foil, and thighs and calves from plastic liter bottles with both ends cut off and covered with aluminum foil. Add an aluminum foil axe and a red heart clock. ❧Use aluminum foil to make your child a silvery Hershey Kiss® candy. As a hat, use a foil-covered funnel or cut-off top of a plastic liter bottle with a long white sheet of paper with "Hershey" written on it coming out the top. ❧Make an M&M® candy costume out of a size-too-big Onsie®, stuffed so baby looks circular. Add matching leggings and tack a large white "M" on her tummy. ❧Make a homemade Tigger from a bright orange sweatshirt with a hood a few sizes too large. (Visit the thrift store to find the orange sweatshirt.) Add ears, tail, a white chest, and stripes with a black marker. Finish the details with face paint. ❧Pin purple and/or green balloons all over your child's clothing to make him a bunch of grapes. Multicolored balloons make a jelly bean costume, mark them with "M"s for a bunch of M&M candies. ❧A pretty party dress with glitter crown and yard-sale costume jewelry makes a beautiful princess costume. A white dress with glittery veil made from white netting makes a traditional bride costume. ❧Cardboard boxes make robots, traffic lights, road signs. Add paper plates as wheels for cars, trucks, busses. My twins went as a matching clothes washer and dryer one year made from same-size cardboard boxes, complete with dials and stickers with energy efficiency numbers. ❧Another year they went as a set of salt and pepper shakers made from long shirts with hoops in their bottoms and stuffed (to make them stand straight up) paper chef's caps with large dots on top to make them look like shaker tops. ❧Another year, it was a pair of dice made from cardboard boxes painted white with black dots. A black eye liner pencil added more dots on their faces. Twins are fun. ☺ ❧Wrap your child in a tube of stiff colored paper to make him look like a Crayola® crayon. Look at a crayon and decorate the costume with the logo and the name of the color ("yellow orange," "sky blue," etc.). Add a cone hat made from the same paper. ❧Make your own holiday costumes from scratch by using newspapers to design a pattern before cutting the fabric. ❧Make a magic wand by attaching a star to a straw—add glitter to the star. ❧Masks can be made from brown paper bags or round paper plates with eye holes and decorated. ❧Plain masking tape or colored electrical tape can be made into long green or red fingernails. ❧Add matching gloves and face paint (see recipe, page 389) as final touches to all costumes. ❧Consider making the clothing flame retardant (page 481). ❧Glue or sew reflector tape on the costumes of children who will be outside in the dark.

Halloween Treats and Decorations ❧See jack-o-lantern tips on page 460. ❧Make a jack-o-lantern cake from a bundt cake with orange icing. Place a flat-bottomed ice cream cone upside down in the center for a pumpkin stem and cover with green icing. Decorate front with triangles of green icing for the jack-o-lantern's face or use green jellies. Use mini-bundt pans for individual jack-o-lantern cupcakes. ❧For black icing on Halloween treats, mix chocolate icing and blue food coloring. ❧To prevent other parents from worrying about the safety of your trick-or-treat snacks, place an address sticker on each treat you give to halloweeners. ❧Make small ghosts by covering round lollipops with a napkin/tissue and tying a piece of yarn around the "neck." Draw a face on the napkin. ❧Make ghosts from cheesecloth (as you would paper maché, page 394). Dampen cheesecloth with diluted school glue and drape over a balloon (place balloon in a plastic cup or lid to stabilize), leaving a long flowing tail. Let dry overnight, paint a face on the ghost, and display on a table or hang from the ceiling. ❧Light your sidewalk for trick-or-treaters by lining it with brown paper bags cut with jack-o-lantern faces. Fill the bottom with a few inches of sand and place a lit candle in the middle of the sand. Watch these carefully so mischievous kids don't burn down your neighborhood.

Part V

Reference
and
Appendices

A. Specific Fruits and Vegetables

This appendix contains information on specific fruits and vegetables, such as how old your baby must be to eat them, when they are in season, and the details on how to choose them, store them, and how to cook them. See tip and warning about freezer temperature on page 164. The foods are listed in alphabetical order.

For Acorn Squash, see Squash, Winter

Apples

Apples can be served as a sweet dessert that does not cause a quick rise in blood sugar levels as other sweet desserts do. Although apples are not found much in the vitamin and mineral bar chart tables in the nutrition section of this book, they do contain modest amounts of many vitamins and minerals. They are abundant in pectin, a fiber found on the apple peel and just below, which is known for its cholesterol-lowering effects. Whenever possible, eat apples unpeeled. And remember, "An unpeeled apple a day keeps the doctor away." Unfortunately, apple peels are choking hazards for babies and toddlers (page 40).

Note that apple *juice* does not lower cholesterol. How does juice differ from cider? Apple **cider** is fresh-crushed apple in season. Apple **juice** is pasteurized and bottled for a long shelf-life. "Clarified" apple juice is filtered to remove all pulp. See warning about E. coli in unpasteurized apple juice and apple cider on page 65. Vinegar is made from the fermentation of a sugar. Wine vinegar is made from grapes. Apple **cider vinegar** is made from fermented apple cider. Use plain white vinegar for cleaning, and apple cider vinegar for eating—it's much healthier than plain vinegar. Store cider vinegar in a cool dry place for up to 6 months, or according to the expiration date. See how to make apple cider vinegar below.

Apples are known as "Nature's Toothbrush." Pack an apple in your child's lunch box and instruct her to eat it last. It doesn't replace brushing, but it helps clean the teeth and massages the gums.

Equivalents: 3 medium apples = 1 pound = 2½ cups peeled and sliced.

Baby must be at least: 8 months for peeled raw grated apple. At least 3 years old for unpeeled, because apple peels are choking hazards (page 40). See apple juice on page 64.

In season: Available year round; peak for Cortland, October to January; for Empire, October to April; for Granny Smith's, April to July; for McIntosh, Newton Pippin, and Red Delicious, September to June; for Golden Delicious and Spartan, September to May; for Idared, Rome Beauty, and Winesap, October to June.

Choosing: Choose apples that are smooth and not shriveled. Bruises seriously affect apples, so check carefully for small depressions in the skin. Apples should be very firm and not yield when pressed. Be especially careful to check for firmness in large apples, which age more quickly than small apples. Small brownish or tan freckles on the skin are OK. Try to buy unwaxed apples. Wax used on produce is supposedly safe, but it may contain pesticide residues.

Several years ago, there was a big scare about the pesticide, alar, used on apples. To qualm any of your fears, confirm with your grocer that alar has not been used on her apples. Alar is no longer used on apple crops, and it is unlikely that there are any apples with alar still left in storage.

Ripening and storing: As apples ripen, they become sweeter. Some varieties, such as Granny Smiths, stay more sour or tart than others. If apples are too firm or sour, ripen at room temperature for a day or two and they will ripen quickly. Place ripened apples in a plastic bag in refrigerator. Apples keep in the refrigerator very well, up to two to four weeks before they begin to soften. Apples will keep longer if they don't touch each other—but who has the room! Soft apples can be eaten raw, but they are better for baking or applesauce.

Freezing applesauce: Freeze unsweetened applesauce using the Food Cube Method for up to 2 months.

Tip: Don't throw those apple cores away, see air freshener tip on page 482.

Recipes: See recipes for applesauce, baked apples, and more on page 297.

Drying: See page 205 for Easiest Ever Apple Leather Recipe.

Making apple cider vinegar: Make apple cider vinegar with your child. Cut up a peeled apple, blenderize it, strain out the juice. Place juice in jar in a warm place (not in refrigerator). First bubbles will form and alcohol ("hard" cider) will be produced. In about one week, bacteria will change the hard cider into vinegar. To be on the safe side, don't drink or taste it. See how to make herb-flavored vinegars on page 450.

Growing: Grow an apple tree. See Johnny Appleseed in the appendix *Your Kitchen Window is a Green Mine*, page 492.

Apricots

Baby must be at least: 8 months.

Equivalents: 8-10 medium apricots = 1 pound fresh= 2 cups sliced; 1 pound dried apricots = 3 cups.

In season: Available May to August; peak June and July.

Choosing: Buy juicy-looking, plump apricots with a uniform golden-orange color. Skin should have a little give when pressed and should not be hard or shriveled. Blemishes will not affect the flavor if the skin is not broken. Avoid firm fruit and those that are pale yellow or have a greenish tint.

Ripening and storing: Keep at room temperature for no more than two days in a loosely-closed paper bag until ripe (soft but not mushy). Store in refrigerator in a plastic bag for up to 3 days after ripe, or place in a clean egg carton.

Serving: Peel with vegetable peeler. Purée for young babies. For older babies, peel and dice soft apricot pieces and use as finger food.

Freezing: Peel and purée and freeze using the Food Cube Method. Or freeze in chunks using the Tray-freeze Method. Apricots will keep in the freezer for 10 to 12 months.

Dried apricots: It takes 6 pounds of fresh apricots to make 1 pound of dried apricots, which really concentrates the sweetness and nutrients. Dried apricots are nutritional snacks eaten as is, or they can be ingredients in other dishes to add a natural sweetness. Dried fruits should be eaten in moderation because of their concentrated sugar. See more about dried fruit on page 200.

Asparagus

Asparagus is one of the Super Green Veggies.
Equivalents: 12-16 stalks = 1 pound = 3½ cups pieces.
Baby must be at least: 7 months.
In season: Available February through July; peak April through June.
Choosing: Buy asparagus loose so that you can take a close look at each piece. Select asparagus whose tips are closed and compact. The stalks should be brittle, straight, firm, not limp, and almost totally bright green. The stalks also should be perfectly round, not angular, and with no vertical ridges. Fatter is better: The thicker the stalk, the more tender.
Storing: Get them into the refrigerator quickly, as room temperature rapidly deteriorates asparagus. Remove any rubber bands. The bottom should be kept damp: wrap the ends in wet white paper towels and place in a plastic bag in the refrigerator. Or, if you have the refrigerator room, store them upright in a container with their ends in water, as you would a bunch of flowers. They will keep for up to 3 days.
Preparation for cooking: Don't throw away half your asparagus. Cut off only the very tough bottom inch or so and peel the stalk as you would a carrot. It's difficult to find asparagus without sand or grit. To clean, soak in cold water for 30 minutes and then rinse thoroughly.
Microwave: Place tips toward the center of the container and the stalks outward to promote even cooking. For one bunch or one pound, use 3 tablespoons of water. Cover and cook on high for 4 minutes. Rearrange and cook 3 minutes more. Let stand, covered, for 2 minutes.
Steam: Steam whole asparagus for 10 minutes, cut asparagus pieces for 5 minutes.
Freezing: Freeze using the Food Cube Method or Tray-Freeze Method for up to 2 months.

Avocados

Avocados are a great first food for your baby. They are an excellent source of unsaturated fatty acids and have a higher proportion of this "good" fat than any other fruit except the olive. Yes, they are actually fruits, even though they are commonly thought of as vegetables. Try using mashed avocado as a "vegetable butter," a replacement for butter that can be spread on crackers or sandwiches.
Equivalents: 1 medium avocado = 1 cup.
Baby must be at least: 4 months.
In season: Available year round; peak December through May.
Choosing: When selecting avocados, look carefully for damage, which shows up as soft dark spots in the skin. Tan-colored patches are OK. When picked up, an avocado should feel heavy for its size. If you're not going to eat the avocado for a few days, select an avocado that is firm, but not rock hard, and ripen it at home. If you plan on eating it immediately, select a ripe avocado as described next.
Ripening: Firm avocados will never ripen in the refrigerator—let them sit at room temperature for up to 6 days. Place them in a brown paper bag to speed ripening. Avocados are ripe when they yield to gentle pressure and feel soft all over. Another way to test for ripeness is to gently squeeze the whole avocado with all five fingers. (Using all five fingers prevents bruises.) If the flesh feels like it is separating from the seed, the avocado is ripe. As avocados ripen, the skin becomes a darker green. Still another way to test for ripeness is to insert a toothpick in the stem end. If it moves easily, the avocado is ripe. Avocados are easy to peel when they are ripe; the peel is hard to remove when avocados are underripe.

Storing: After ripened, store the whole avocado in the refrigerator in the vegetable crisper for up to two weeks. Your very young baby will certainly leave you with avocado leftovers. Store cut avocados by leaving the skins on and keeping the pit in the uneaten portion. You can brush the fruit part with lemon juice (if baby is old enough for citrus) to keep it from turning brown. It's OK to eat the brown part, but you can easily scrape it off with a knife. Wrap tightly in plastic wrap and store in the refrigerator.

Freezing using the Food Cube Method: The easiest way I've found to freeze avocado in food cubes is this: Take a sharp knife and cut avocado in half crosswise so that you have two "cups." Remove the huge seed. Use a spoon to scoop out flesh from peel and place on a flat dish. Use a fork to mash flesh on dish. Spoon into ice cube trays and pat flat with your clean fingers. Freeze for up to 3 months. I suggest that you give your baby 1-2 tablespoons or ½ to 1 food cube every day for some of the fatty acids she needs for brain development.

Growing: Start an avocado plant. See page 492.

Bananas

Bananas are God's gift to parents (second to the baby, of course). They are one of the easiest, handiest baby foods—simply peel, fork-mash, and feed. I'll never understand why parents pay a fortune for jarred baby bananas when fresh are so easy. Because they are prepackaged in their own peels and require no cooking, they can be thrown in the diaper bag at the last minute for an instant traveling baby snack. Mashed bananas are one of the most versatile ingredients in homemade baby food. You can add almost anything to mashed bananas—yogurt, cream cheese, cooked cereal, ground sprouts, nutritional yeast, and any of the Healthy Extras (page 288). Your baby will love these combinations because the bananas give them a naturally sweet taste. Nutrition-wise, bananas are known for their high level of potassium and fiber, and contain fair amounts of many other nutrients. See warning about fungicides and bananas, page 13. See *Wash All Produce*, page 181.

Baby must be at least: 4 months.

Equivalents: 3-4 medium bananas = 2 cups sliced = 1½ cups mashed.

In season: Available year round.

Choosing: Select bananas with no bruises. The entire peel should be intact with part of the stem still attached. Bananas are a rare fruit in that they actually ripen better *off* the tree. It's OK to buy bananas in any stage of ripeness, from totally green and unripe to totally yellow with black flecks. However, the more ripe, the more easily the banana will bruise, so be gentle. Red bananas are generally larger than yellow bananas and take a little longer to ripen, but they taste the same. The skins of red bananas take on a deeper color as they ripen. Avoid bananas with a dull, grayish color, which means they have been stored in cold temperatures and will never ripen.

We eat dozens of bananas in our house each week. I buy some that are all yellow with brown specks (ripe), some with green tips (slightly underripe), and some totally green (very underripe). As they yellow and ripen, they get eaten. In rare cases where some are around long enough to turn black, they get baked into healthy, delicious breads or muffins.

Ripening: Ripen bananas by leaving them uncovered at room temperature. People like bananas at different ripeness stages. Some like them slightly underripe (yellow with a little green at the stem), and some like them very ripe (all yellow with black flecks). Feed your baby *very ripe* bananas, because that's when they are at their nutritional height and mash very easily. Their starch has turned to sugar and is easily digested.

Storing: When bananas are at just the right stage of ripeness, place them in the refrigerator to keep them at that ripeness stage. Their peels turn black in several hours, but their flesh remains unchanged and they will keep in the refrigerator for up to 6 days. Unpeeled bananas stored in an airtight plastic bag or jar in the refrigerator will last even longer. If you do not have room in your refrigerator, but want to slow the ripening of bananas at room temperature, place them in a plastic bag with as much air removed as possible (see page 168 for how to remove air).

Storing a partially peeled banana: Your baby will probably be able to eat only part of a banana at first. Eat the rest yourself. Or, partially peel the banana, uncovering only the amount your baby will eat. Remove part of the banana and replace the peels by wrapping them around the cut part of the leftover banana. Store in the refrigerator with a piece of plastic wrap on the open end. (I use a plastic sandwich bag twisted tight and a rubber band to hold it in place.) The cut will darken, but it is OK to eat.

Freezing banana purée: Yes, you can freeze bananas! That's fortunate for those of us who bought too many at the 29¢ a pound sale or who let their bananas get black. Just fork-mash or purée and freeze in ice cube trays. You can add 1 tablespoon lemon juice (if baby is old enough for citrus) for each cup of banana to prevent darkening. Bananas will keep frozen for up to 3 months. When thawed, they'll be mushy—perfect for your little one or as an ingredient in baked goods. For Mock Ice Cream (page 339) or milk shakes, peel, cut in large chunks, and freeze using the Tray-freeze Method to keep the chunks separated.

Freezing whole bananas: Bananas can be frozen whole for up to 6 months. Place them whole and within their peels inside a large airtight freezer bag. To use, thaw completely in the refrigerator. Then slice off the stem and squeeze the mushy banana flesh out through the hole.

Beans, Edible Pod: Snap, Green, Yellow, or Waxed

For dried beans, like soybeans, navy beans, kidney beans, etc., see page 233. This section covers beans with edible pods, including green beans.

Baby must be at least: 7 months.

Equivalents: 1 pound of green beans = 3 cups fresh = 2½ cups cooked.

In season: Available year round; peak May through October.

Choosing: Select beans that are brightly colored green or yellow with as few brown spots as possible. Brown spots can be cut away because they are bruises and not decay. Pods should be smooth, thin, and well-filled, but with no ridge and no bulges, which indicate that the beans are too mature. They should be stiff, so that they would snap easily, and not wilted or flabby. Pick beans of uniform size for even cooking.

Storing: Store in a plastic bag in the refrigerator for up to 4 days.

Preparation for cooking: Snap or trim ends (it's really necessary to trim only the stem end), but leave small beans whole. Cut very large beans in two.

Microwave: Add 3 or 4 tablespoons of water for each pound of green beans. Cover and microwave on high for 8 minutes, rearranging once or twice during cooking time, and let stand, covered, for 5 minutes.

Steam: Steam for 9 to 12 minutes.

Freezing: Freeze using the Food Cube Method or Tray-Freeze Method for up to 2 months.

For Beet Greens, see Greens

Beets

Grated beets can be fed to your baby raw. Cooked beets are tasty and very colorful. They can be used as a decorative touch or even a food coloring (page 364) in baby's food. Beets stain, so use a good bib when feeding your baby beets. Be aware that several hours after your baby eats beets, her stool will be quite red in color. I panicked the first time I saw the red during a diaper change—my first thought was blood! See *Poop Panic!* page 27. Beets are a good indicator of the time it takes food to pass through your baby. ☺

Warning: Beet stains are impossible to get out of cloth, plastic containers, and wood.

Baby must be at least: Cooked, 9 months; raw and grated, 10 months. See warning about nitrates, page 38.

Equivalents: 6 medium beets = 1 pound = 2 cups sliced.

In season: Available year round; peak June through October.

Choosing: Beets are sold with or without their green tops. The tops, called "beet greens," should be fresh-looking, thin-ribbed, and deep green, with no brown or red edges, and with no trace of slime. If they are a little wilted, the flavor of the red root should not be affected, because the greens rapidly deteriorate while the root remains good. (Beet greens are edible, see page 442.) Beets without their greens should have at least ½ inch of stem left on top and their bottom roots should be at least two inches long. The bulbous root should have a lush, deep-red color and smooth, firm skin with no cuts or soft spots. Roots should have no scaly areas or circles on the top and they should be a good globular shape (round), and not elongated. Buy small to medium-sized beets, as large beets tend to be tough with inedible, woody cores.

Storing: As with other root vegetables, immediately remove the greens so that they do not pull moisture from the root. Leave an inch or two of stem on the root, or it will bleed during cooking. See greens (page 442) for information on how to store beet greens. Don't remove the bottom roots. Store beets in the refrigerator in a plastic bag for up to 10 days.

Preparation for cooking: Scrub well under cold-running water.

Microwave: Prick beets with fork. For a pound of beets (about 6 medium-sized), add ¼ to ½ cup of water to the microwave dish. Cover and cook 16 minutes. Let stand, covered, for 5 minutes.

Steam: I don't recommend steaming. It takes about 60 minutes!

Boil: Simmer whole beets for two hours. Peels will easily come off and juices will be better retained in whole beets.

Bake: Wash thoroughly, wrap all beets in one large sheet of aluminum foil and bake at 400°F for 90 minutes to two hours—the larger the beets, the longer the baking time.

Peel and purée: After cooking beets, remove stems. If you wish, slip off peels under cold running water before puréeing.

Freezing: Freeze using the Food Cube Method or Tray-Freeze Method for up to 2 months.

Growing: See how to grow a beet plant, page 493.

Blueberries and Strawberries

Fresh blueberries are a nice finger food for babies over 3 years old. Don't give whole blueberries to younger babies—they are a choking hazard (page 40). Purée or mash them for babies from 9 months to a year of age and make sure there are no large peels. Blueberries might be helpful if your baby (or you) has diarrhea.

Baby must be at least: 9-12 months for mashed raw blueberries or strawberries. Three years or older for whole blueberries because they are a choking hazard. Blueberries are a common allergen and your pediatrician may want you to wait until your baby is one year old (some say two years old) before you introduce them to your baby.

Equivalents: 1 pint berries = 2 cups.

In season: Blueberries: Available May through September; peak June through August. Strawberries: Available March through September; peak April through June

Choosing blueberries: Select those that are firm and plump, dry but not shriveled, and with no decay (caused by too much moisture). Avoid light-colored blueberries or those that are green or have a reddish tinge. A dark blue color with a silvery sheen (a natural protective coating) indicates good flavor. Don't buy watery, soft, or moldy blueberries because they are overripe.

Choosing strawberries: Select strawberries that are firm, plump, lustrous, moist-looking, those that smell sweet, and those that are completely deep red. Leaf caps should be attached and fresh. Avoid strawberries that are greenish or with large uncolored areas, dull, shrunken, shriveled, bruised, soft, or those with dry, brown leaf caps. Don't go by the nice berries on top—make sure you check all berries in the bottom of the container. The container should not be stained or sticky—check the bottom. Don't buy those in large containers because the bottom ones definitely will be crushed.

Cleaning and storing berries: Blueberries, strawberries, and other berries bruise very easily and you must treat them gently. Immediately remove decayed, moldy, or bruised berries before the damage spreads to other berries. Ideally, berries should not be washed until you are ready to use them. But, I wash them before they go into the refrigerator so they are ready to grab for quick snacks. (It's against my kids' religion to wash fruit.) Berries are best cleaned by placing them in a colander or large strainer and dipping them in water or gently spraying them with the sink hose or slow-running tap water. Don't soak berries because their juice will be replaced with the water through osmosis. Let the berries drip dry for a short while and then place them back into the container they came in—usually a green plastic basket or a perforated cardboard container. Or place them in a colander. Don't layer them too deep or the bottom berries will be crushed. Cover them well with plastic wrap. Whereas blueberries will keep for a week or maybe even two, strawberries may get moldy within a day or two. One way you can prolong strawberries' keeping time is to wash them and let them dry completely. Then place them in a glass jar with an airtight screw top lid, place a paper towel over them in the jar to absorb moisture, tightly close the jar, and refrigerate. Leave strawberries' green caps on when you store them—open areas in strawberry flesh left from ripping out the caps will decay rapidly. Clean strawberries by rinsing them well *before* removing their stems or they will become soggy.

Tip: To prevent berry juice from dripping in your refrigerator, place the container on a flat bowl or dish. To remove berry stains from your hands, rub with lemon juice.

Freezing berries: Pick berries over, wash them, and freeze in a plastic freezer bag or in a rigid container, or use the Tray-freeze Method (page 170). Leave a little head room (½ inch) in any rigid container for expansion. Label and date them. Blueberries are great for freezing and will keep frozen for up to a year. Remove leaf caps from strawberries after washing and before freezing. Strawberries will keep frozen for up to 6 months.

Thawing berries: In general, see *How to Thaw Fruit* on page 200. Frozen berries in a plastic bag can be thawed by placing the bag in a big bowl of cold water for 10-20 minutes—move them around a bit during thawing. (This bowl method can't be used to thaw big pieces of fruit, because it would take too long at room temperature for them to thaw. Foods should never be thawed for more than several minutes at room temperature—see page 162.) To use frozen berries in pancakes (blueberry pancakes) or muffin recipes, there's no need to thaw blueberries or strawberries first. Simply add the frozen berries to the batter.

Drying: See recipe for Quick Strawberry Leather, page 205.
Berry baskets: Don't throw out those green plastic strawberry baskets. Nail them to the inside of a cabinet and use to hold small packets. Use them to hold soap, scouring pads, or sponges. Make them into a dishwasher baskets (page 77). Use for children's arts and crafts: Easter baskets (page 419), party favor holders (page 370), bubble blowers (page 399), lacing toys (page 405), and bird feeders (page 406).

For Butternut Squash, see Squash, Winter

Broccoli

We all know how good broccoli is for us. This Super Green Veggie, a good source of vitamins A and C, calcium, and many other nutrients, should be a regular food in your Super Baby's diet. Your baby should have a Super Green Veggie serving every single day, and broccoli is one that is available year round.
Equivalents: 1-pound head of broccoli = 2 cups florets.
Baby must be at least: 8 months for cooked broccoli.
In season: Available year round; peak October through May. The plants do well in cool weather.
Choosing: Select medium-sized bunches with small, tightly closed green buds that crowd together tightly. Stalks should be slender and feel firm, but not too tough and woody. Stalks should also be tender, especially in the upper portion toward the florets. Any leaves on the stalk should be fresh and not wilted and brightly colored green. Avoid bruised or wilted broccoli and broccoli whose buds are spread instead of tight. Do not buy broccoli with yellow flowers in the buds, as they indicate age. The more yellow, the less desirable the bunch is. Avoid those with any soft slippery spots. Also, use your nose. If the broccoli has a strong odor, pass on it.
Storing: Refrigerate unwashed in plastic bags for up to 3 days. Dolores Riccio, author of *Superfoods* (see bibliography), says that a better way to store broccoli "is to treat it like a bunch of flowers. Slice off the ends of the stalks and stand them in a pitcher with about two inches of water, loosely cover the head with a plastic bag, and refrigerate." She recommends that we eat broccoli 4 to 5 times a week. I almost agree. We and our babies should have at least one of the Super Greens (page 135) every day—it doesn't have to be broccoli.
Preparation for cooking: While rinsing, use your fingers to open florets so that water flows between them and gets them really clean. Broccoli sometimes causes gas in babies (and adults). To prevent gas, slightly undercook broccoli. Undercooking maintains the green chlorophyll, which counteracts gas-causing sulfur compounds. Trim off any tough part on the bottom of the stalk—leave about 3 or 4 inches under the florets. You can cut the broccoli lengthwise into spears or crosswise leaving the florets whole. If the florets are too large, cut them into pieces so they'll fit in the steamer. If you will be cooking only the florets for baby, cut the stems very close to the florets and they will separate automatically into individual florets. Broccoli florets cook faster than the thick stalks, so slash the entire length of the stalks 5 or 6 times to cause them to cook as fast as the florets. You can eat the stalk and the leaves. The leaves cook very quickly, as other greens do. Pull them off and save them. Then throw them into the pot for the last minute or two of cooking.
Microwaving: Place broccoli stalks in a dish so that the florets are in the center. Sprinkle a tablespoon or two of water over them. Cover and microwave on high for 6 minutes if the pieces are small and 8 minutes if the pieces are large. Rearrange or turn dish halfway through cooking time if you do not have a microwave turntable. Let stand, covered, for 4 minutes.

Steaming: Place broccoli in steamer, stalks on bottom, florets on top. Steam for about 15 to 20 minutes for large pieces and about 8 to 10 minutes for smaller pieces.
Freezing: Freeze using the Food Cube Method or Tray-Freeze Method for up to 2 months.
Buying frozen broccoli: Short spears are best; they are mostly florets. Whole spears are next best. Broccoli cuts contain too many stalks, and chopped broccoli is almost all stalks. I always put frozen veggies into a strainer or colander and run them under water for a few seconds to remove that frosty covering which sometimes gives them an off flavor. Do not use frozen broccoli for making baby food cubes. Never re-freeze a food that has been previously frozen (see *Never Re-freeze Thawed Baby Food*, page 177).

Brussels Sprouts

Brussels sprouts are a Super Green Veggie.
Baby must be at least: 9 months for cooked Brussels sprouts. Never feed your baby raw Brussels sprouts.
In season: Available year round; peak September through March.
Choosing: Select small Brussels sprouts whose leaves are tight, firm, and bright green. They should feel heavy for their size. Avoid those with bruises, worm holes, or yellow leaves that are soft, wilted, or puffy. If they are packaged, you'll have to look very carefully for insect damage (tiny holes in the leaves). Large Brussels sprouts are coarse with a strong flavor and odor. Buy the smallest ones you can find. Check that the stem is not cut too close, otherwise the outer leaves will fall off during cooking.
Storing: Pull off any yellow or yellowish-green leaves. Place in plastic bag in refrigerator for up to 3 days. Use as soon as possible or their flavor will be too strong.
Preparation for cooking: Don't overcook Brussels sprouts or they will get mushy and have a strong flavor. Trim the stems off the bottom. Cut two slashes into the bottom perpendicularly (like a cross) and this will help them cook evenly.
Microwave: For each pound of small, whole Brussels sprouts, add a tablespoon of water to the cooking dish. Slice large sprouts in half. Cover and microwave on high for 6 minutes, stirring halfway through cooking time. Let stand, covered, for 3 minutes. Test stem end for doneness.
Steam: Steam whole for 15 to 20 minutes until stem end is done.
Freezing: Freeze using the Food Cube Method or Tray-Freeze Method for up to 2 months.

Cabbage

Baby must be at least: 18 months for cabbage because it tends to cause digestive problems. See page 43.
Equivalents: ½ head = 1 pound cabbage = 4½ cups raw, shredded = 2½ cups cooked.
In season: Available year round; peak October through May.
Choosing: Cabbages are sold with or without their outer leaves, called wrapper leaves. Inside the wrapper leaves is a head that is very firm, spherical, tightly packed, and a very pale green—almost colorless. Wrapper leaves should be crisp and fresh, with no signs of wilting or decay. If the wrapper leaves have been removed, make sure that the inner head is fresh, moist, and hard, not puffy, and feels heavy for its size. Inspect the base of the cabbage to ensure that the leaves are firmly attached to the stem and that there is no separation from the stem. There should be no splits. Avoid cabbage with discolored veins. Use your nose; fresh cabbage does not have a strong cabbage odor.
Storing: Remember that the more you cut vegetables, the most nutrient loss from air exposure, so don't shred the cabbage until you're ready to use it. If shredded cabbage is exposed to air, especially warm air, it loses lots of its vitamin C. Store whole cabbage in a plastic bag in the

refrigerator for up to two weeks. If you use only part of the cabbage head, keep the unused section in one piece and store tightly wrapped in the refrigerator for up to two days.

Preparation for cooking: Cabbage is rich is vitamin C, which is destroyed by heat, so cook for as short a time as possible. Pull off any wilted outer leaves, but only if badly wilted because the outer leaves are richest in nutrients. Cut in half lengthwise and remove the inner core. Cut into wedges or shred. Shredding cabbage allows for a shorter cooking time. Cabbage contains sulfur compounds which causes cooking odors—keep a tight lid on to minimize the smell.

Microwave: Place wedges so that the wide ends are outward. For each pound (about ½ head), add 2 tablespoons of water. Cover wedges and microwave on high for 6 minutes; if you shredded the lettuce, 4 minutes. Turn once halfway through cooking time. Let stand, covered, for 3 minutes. Double cooking time if using a full 2-pound medium head, which is about 9-10 shredded cups.

Steam: Steam wedges for about 15 minutes.

Stuffed Cabbage: To prepare cabbage for stuffed cabbage, first cut out core of whole cabbage with a sharp knife. Then submerge head in boiling water and let cook for 5 minutes. Then move it to a bowl of cold water. Or, wash and dry a head of cabbage and freeze, uncooked, in a large plastic bag. When thawed, the leaves are easy to pull off and use for stuffed cabbage. Who really has time for stuffing cabbage, anyway? Get the same taste results by baking shredded cabbage and the stuffing in layers in a baking dish.

Freezing: Freeze cooked cabbage using the Food Cube Method or Tray-Freeze Method for up to 2 months.

Cantaloupe

The orange color of the cantaloupe means a high beta-carotene (vitamin A) content. Cantaloupes are also a good source of vitamin C, potassium, magnesium, B-vitamins, and more.

Baby must be at least: 8 months.

In season: May through October, peak June through August.

Choosing: When a good, ripe cantaloupe is harvested, the stem comes off in a nice clean break. Look at the stem end. There should be a smooth, shallow, circular depression with no jagged edges. There should be no stem remaining. The opposite (blossom) end should give slightly when pressed. A cantaloupe will feel springy if you squeeze it gently between your palms. Be careful, though, cantaloupes are not strong, even though their peels are thick. The webbing should be course, thick, dry, raised, and look "three-dimensional," not flat. The background under the webbing should be yellow, not green. Gently shake the melon, if you hear sloshing inside, pass on it. Buy cantaloupes that are oval (or, less desirable, round), with no flat or dented sides. Avoid those with bruises or off-color spots, because the damage probably goes into the flesh. The stronger the cantaloupe scent, the riper the cantaloupe. But don't buy an overripe cantaloupe, which smells too sweet, feels soft and flabby all over, and has a bright yellow color, because it will be tasteless and watery.

Storing: If necessary, ripen at room temperature for 2 or 3 days. It will get no sweeter, but it will get softer and juicier. Store ripe, whole cantaloupe in a plastic bag (to keep the smell from other produce) in the refrigerator for about a week. Cut cantaloupe, when tightly wrapped and refrigerated, will keep for only a day or two. Leave the seeds in halved melons for longer freshness.

Freezing: Cut into slices or use a melon baller. Place in a rigid freezer container and cover with orange juice—its vitamin C content will prevent darkening and flavor changes. See *Freezing Fruit*, page 199. To keep melons submerged under juice so that it is not in contact with the air, try placing crumpled waxed paper or freezer wrap in the container. Leave a little head room.

When completely thawed, melon is mushy, so serve to adults when still a little bit frozen for better texture. Different melons (cantaloupe, honeydew, watermelon) can be mixed in the same freezer container and will keep in the freezer for 10 months to a year.

Tip: Use an ice cream scoop or large spoon to remove seeds from halved melons.

Carrots

Carrots are loaded with beta-carotene, a form of vitamin A that is not toxic, even in large doses. Don't believe anyone who tells you not to feed your baby too many carrots (within reason, of course) for fear of vitamin A toxicity. In fact, you should give your baby a vitamin A veggie every day. It's the vitamin A from animal products and vitamin pills that causes toxicity. See Vitamin A, page 529, for more information. The beta-carotene in carrots is made more available to the body by cooking. Also, grating raw carrots makes the beta-carotene more available. Carrot juice has the most available beta-carotene. Raw carrots are said to lower cholesterol levels. You can't go wrong—eat them raw, cooked, or juiced!

Baby must be at least: 7 months for cooked carrots, 10 months for finely grated raw carrots. See warning about nitrates, page 38.

Equivalents: 6 or 7 medium carrots = 1 pound = 3 cups shredded.

In season: Carrots are available year round. They are at their peak in the summer.

Choosing: Carrots are sold "topped" (green top stems removed) in plastic bags. You may also find carrots complete with their bushy green tops. If you buy them this way, cut off their tops immediately to prevent them from pulling moisture out of the orange root. Select carrots that are clean and bright orange, indicating large amounts of beta-carotene. Buyer beware: Sometimes carrots are packaged in orange-tinted plastic bags that may hide pale carrots. In this case, check for freshness by bending them. They should be firm, not flabby or shriveled, and have no decaying spots or splits. Smaller carrots are sweeter and more tender. Large, thick carrots may have tough, woody cores. But instead of the overpriced carrots labeled "baby carrots" in the supermarket, go for the small to medium-sized regular carrots—they're tastier. Avoid carrots with green spots, for they will taste bitter. Green discoloration or "sunburn" in the orange stem is a sign that the carrots have been left in sunlight (sunlight helps plants produce green chlorophyll).

Storing: Carrots need cold temperature and high humidity. Store in the refrigerator in a plastic bag with air holes, which helps to retain moisture and protect from the refrigerator's dry air. The air holes helps air circulate to prevent terpenoid (creates a bitter taste in the carrots) from forming. Keep carrots away from fruit, if you can, because the ethylene gas from the fruit will also cause terpenoid to form. Make sure to remove their green tops immediately to prevent sap from flowing into them, taking nutrition and flavor with it. Fresh carrots will keep in the refrigerator for up to two weeks. And good news—they keep their nutrients when properly stored.

Preparation for cooking: Nutrients are most concentrated in the peels of carrots and just below. You don't have to peel or scrape young or small carrots if you give them a good scrubbing with a vegetable brush. Older, bigger carrots are probably better peeled.

Microwaving: Slice into ½ inch pieces. For each pound (6 to 8 medium carrots) add 3 tablespoons water. Cover and microwave on high for 10 minutes. Stir halfway through cooking time. Let stand, covered, 3 minutes.

Steaming: Steam whole carrots 15 minutes; carrot slices about 10 minutes.

Baking: Large carrots can be baked in the oven. Scrub them and leave whole and unpeeled. Bake at 350° for 30 to 40 minutes.

Freezing: Freeze puréed carrots using the food cube method for up to 2 months.

Growing: Grow a carrot plant. See how on page 493.

Cauliflower

The off-white florets (called the "curd" because it looks like curd) are usually sold surrounded by some green outer leaves. Cauliflower contains vitamin C, potassium, fiber, and the B-vitamins. Watch your baby for signs of gas after you feed her cauliflower.

Baby must be at least: 9 months for cooked cauliflower.

Equivalents: 1½ pounds = 2 cups cooked.

In season: Available year round; peak September through November.

Choosing: The curd should be clean, creamy white, heavy, firm, dense, and tightly crowded together. If it has a yellow tinge or has begun to spread and is loose, don't buy it because it's old. The florets can be either smooth or bristly, but not too granular or rice-looking, and they should not easily crumble if you scratch them. Avoid cauliflower with a lot of brown or black spots on the florets; if there is just a little bit, you can trim it off and the rest is OK to eat. The outer leaves should be fresh and crisp. If the leaves drop off, don't buy that head. It's OK if there are a few green leaves growing out of the curd if they haven't begun to flower.

Storing: Store the head wrapped in plastic in the refrigerator for about a week. Use as soon as possible, as old cauliflower develops a strong taste and odor. Raw florets cut from the head will keep for only one day. Cooked cauliflower keeps in the refrigerator for up to 3 days.

Preparation for cooking: Turn the head upside down, remove all leaves, and use a knife to cut out most of the center stalk. Cut florets in large pieces. Although most people throw away the leaves, you can actually eat them cooked or raw. Cook them with the cauliflower or separately. Instead of cutting up the head, you can leave it whole. To get rid of any insects, soak head down for at least ½ hour in cold water, to which has been added about a teaspoonful of salt. Then rinse thoroughly. However, I suggest you simply cut it into florets and check carefully for bugs. The soaking leaches out nutrients and the longer cooking time required for the whole head destroys more nutrients. Cauliflower contains sulfur compounds which causes cooking odors—keep a tight lid on to minimize the smell.

Note: It is best to undercook cauliflower; overcooking makes it mushy and the flavor too strong.

Microwave: For a whole head: Place stem down with florets up in dish. Add 2 tablespoons water, cover, and microwave on high for 10 minutes. Halfway through cooking, flip head so that florets are down and stem is up. Let stand, covered, for 5 minutes. For cut up florets: Add 2 tablespoons water for 1½ pounds (about 1 medium head), cover, and microwave on high for 5 minutes. Rearrange or stir halfway through cooking time. Let stand, covered, for 5 minutes.

Steam: Steam florets for 10 minutes, whole head for 20 to 30 minutes.

Boil: Boil florets for 12 minutes.

Tip: To prevent cauliflower from yellowing while boiling, add one or two tablespoons of milk to the water first.

Freezing: Freeze using the Food Cube Method or Tray-Freeze Method for up to 2 months.

Celery

Baby must be at least: 7 months for cooked celery, 10 months for very finely grated raw celery. Make sure there are no hard celery pieces, because they are choking hazards. *Remove all strings from celery.* Never give a baby celery with strings—strings are also a choking hazard. (See *Choking Hazards*, page 40).

Equivalents: 1 stalk = ½ cup diced.

In season: Available year round.

Choosing: Select a bundle of medium length and thickness with green, fresh top leaves or only slightly wilted top leaves, which have no sign of yellow. The ribs should be very crisp, brittle, and rigid, ones that will snap easily. The ribs should have a good glossy green color: light, medium, or dark green is OK depending on the variety. Remember that more green means more vitamin A. Don't buy limp, rubbery, lifeless celery with any brown or gray discoloration on the stalk or rust-colored marks near the base. Gently open the bundle to check that the insides of the stalks are fresh-looking and smooth with no holes or off-color patches. Feel the insides with your fingers and don't buy if there is roughness or puffiness.

Storing: Do not remove leaves for storing. Store in paper bags in the refrigerator. Or wrap in white paper towels, then store tightly-wrapped in plastic bag in refrigerator for up to two weeks. If you have the refrigerator room, place the stalk end in a shallow bowl of water (like flowers in a vase) and cover with plastic.

Preparing: Pull the stalks from the bundle. Trim off the leaves, wash very well, and use fresh to flavor soups, salad, or stew. Or dry the leaves and make into a powder by rubbing through a sieve; use powder as a flavoring. Trim the bottom of the stalks. Clean each stalk thoroughly with a vegetable brush, rinsing well. Whole outer stalks are best for cooking; tender, inner stalks are good for salads or eating raw. Celery can be finely diced for use as a Healthy Addition for older children. *Remove all strings from celery for baby.* Remove the stalk's tough part and strings with a vegetable peeler. Or remove strings from outer stalks by using a knife to pull strings from the top to the bottom and throw them away. Or remove strings by snapping the stalk about an inch from the top and while it's still partially attached, pull down the length of the stalk pulling the strings out. Celery strings, as well as hard slices of celery or hard celery pieces, are choking hazards for babies and toddlers (page 40).

Microwave: Add 3 tablespoons water to 4 cups of 1-inch slices. Cover and cook on high about 10 minutes, stirring halfway through cooking time. Let stand, covered, 3 minutes.

Steam: Whole ribs for 20 minutes, 1-inch pieces for 10 minutes.

Freezing: Freeze using the Food Cube Method or Tray-Freeze Method for up to 2 months.

Tip: If your recipe calls for fresh parsley and you're out of it, use celery leaves.

Cherries

Baby must be at least: 9 months for finely sliced raw cherries, or 1 year if an allergy runs in the family. Do not feed whole cherries to children under 3 years old, see choking on page 40.

Equivalents: 1 pound fresh cherries = 2 cups pitted.

In season: May through August; peak June and July.

Choosing: Select firm, plump, and glossy cherries that are not shriveled or soft. Color is very important in determining freshness and sweetness. In sweet cherries, look for a brightly-colored mahogany (like cherry wood), deep-reddish brown, purple, or even black surface; dullness is a sign of age. Sour cherries are lighter red; they should have a bright, uniform color. Avoid cherries without stems, as the empty hole opens the cherry to decay. The stems should be fresh-looking, not dark or dry. Look very carefully for decay, which can be camouflaged by the dark color of the cherries. To help detect decay, look for leaking spots and mold.

Storing: Clean and store cherries as you would berries, as instructed on page 430. Don't wash until ready to use. Place in the refrigerator in a plastic bag for up to 4 days.

Freezing: Wash first. Then de-stem and remove pits (use a specially-made cherry pitter, the top of a vegetable peeler, or other makeshift utensil, such as a paper clip or pen holder) and freeze for up to 10 months. Label and date them.

Citrus Fruits and Juices
(Oranges, Lemons, Limes, Grapefruits, and Tangerines)

Citrus fruits are a super source of vitamin C. A good way to get the vitamin into your baby is fresh squeezed orange juice. Vitamin C is very unstable and is lost quickly with exposure to heat, light, or air, so you must squeeze and feed immediately. The body uses vitamin C within a few hours, so it's best to give a little portion of vitamin C foods to your baby several times a day, instead of one big dose, as discussed under vitamin C in the nutrition part, page 539.
Baby must be at least: 12 months for citrus fruits/juices or earlier with your pediatrician's OK. Oranges are a common allergen, so watch your baby carefully for an allergic reaction.
In season: Available year round; peak depends on variety.
Choosing: Citrus fruits are not picked until they are mature, so you don't have to worry about unripeness. The most important factor in selecting good citrus fruit is feel. Oranges, grapefruits, lemons, limes, and tangerines should all feel firm and heavy for their size. Their peels should be smooth and fine-grained; large pores are not good. Rough, shriveled, or wrinkled peels mean the fruit probably will have thick skin and be pulpy and not juicy. Avoid fruit with soft spots or mold. Non-organic citrus fruits are often waxed and sprayed with fungicide, so wash very well with warm water (page 181), even if you are not going to eat the peel.
Storing: Store citrus fruits in a plastic bag or the vegetable crisper. They will keep for at least two weeks. Small citrus fruits can be stored in a clean egg carton.
Freezing: Citrus fruits can be frozen whole in plastic freezer bags for later squeezing. Wash well first.
Oranges: Some variety of oranges are available all year. Valencia oranges are available all year; peak April through October. Navel oranges are available October through April. When choosing oranges, don't be concerned with color. Green or orange doesn't determine freshness or ripeness. Unfortunately, manufacturers gas green oranges to color them orange to meet uninformed consumers' expectations. All fruit dyed this way must, by law, be advertised as having "Color Added." Brown spots on the peel are fine and usually indicate a good orange.
Grapefruit: Available year round; peak January through June. 1 medium grapefruit = ½ pound = 1 cup sections. You'll find grapefruits that are either white or pink—they taste the same. The pink color comes from beta-carotene (vitamin A), so pink grapefruit is better than white from a nutritional standpoint. Judge a grapefruit by its skin—thin skins probably mean a nice juicy fruit. Pass on those with thick skins, rough or wrinkled skins, or deep pores. Choose grapefruits that are firm, but not hard, and with thin skins that are springy to the touch. Grapefruits should be well-rounded and flat, not pointed, at both ends. The color and look of the skin is not important.
Lemons: Available year round; peak March through September. The peel of the lemon should be oily or glossy, thin, and yellow. If it has a green tinge, all the better; it's very fresh, has a good flavor, and will store longer than a yellow lemon. Choose small to medium-sized lemons, as larger lemons tend to be thick skinned and less juicy. Buy those that are least pointed on the ends. Check the stem end for soft spots, mold, decay, or discoloration. Lemons store in the refrigerator for a month or more, so keep some handy to flavor everything from iced tea to yogurt. See below for how to freeze lemon juice cubes.
Limes: Available year round; peak June through August. Persian limes should have shiny green peels; Key limes should have light yellow peels. Limes should be glossy, firm, and have no dark patches. When limes begin turning brownish yellow, use them fast. Freeze lime juice as lemon juice below.
Tangerines: Available October through April; peak November through January. Tangerines are easy to peel. Select lustrous, glossy tangerines that are deep-yellow or orange, almost red,

not pale yellow or greenish. They don't have to feel very firm, but don't buy those that are too soft.

Commercial baby orange juice: If you've read about vitamin C, you know that warmth and light destroy this very unstable nutrient. I wonder how much vitamin C remains in the clear glass jars in which commercial baby orange juice is sold. The glass lets in light and these jars are stored at room temperature, not in the supermarket's refrigerator section. And look what you're paying! The 4 ounce jars are selling at my local supermarket in 1998 for 35 cents—that's over $5.00 a half gallon. It is much more economical, natural, and nutritious to buy fresh and squeeze it yourself. See warning on page 65. Or, if you don't want the inconvenience of squeezing your own, buy the half gallon cartons of pasteurized orange juice in the refrigerator section of the supermarket. The containers keep out light and they are also kept cold.

Squeezing your own citrus juice: To get the most juice from citrus fruits, roll them on a hard surface before squeezing to break the inner tissues. Some recommend warming them in hot water, in the oven, or in the microwave for a minute or keeping them at room temperature for a while before squeezing to increase the amount of juice, but warmth destroys vitamin C. So keep citrus fruits cold until immediately before serving. A medium-sized orange will yield about 1/3-1/2 cup of juice; a lemon, about 3 tablespoons; a grapefruit, about 1 cup; and a lime, 1½-2 tablespoons of juice. Refrigerate fresh-squeezed juice for up to 2 days. Remember to protect from air and heat to minimize vitamin C loss. **Tip:** If you need only a few drops of juice, use a fork to prick a small hole in the peel and squeeze a little out.

Freezing juice: You can freeze fresh-squeezed (or non-frozen commercial) juices. Do not re-freeze concentrated fruit juices. Juice can be frozen in cubes and then transferred to plastic bags, as in the Food Cube Method. Cubes will keep for up to 3 months. **Tip:** Buy fresh lemons (or limes) when they are on sale and squeeze and measure tablespoons of their juice in ice cube trays. Transfer the pre-measured recipe-sized lemon juice cubes into plastic freezer bags, where they will be ready to thaw for your favorite recipes. **Tip:** Concentrated frozen fruit juice is often used as a healthy sweetener in recipes. Buy in bulk, proportion frozen juice into recipe-sized amounts without letting the juice thaw, and freeze in small containers or use the Nested Plastic Bag Method.

Citrus zest (dried citrus peel): Zest is the colored part of the peel and doesn't include the white pith, which has a bitter flavor. Don't pay for the expensive supermarket varieties when it's so easy to make your own! Choose citrus fruit with thick peels, such as Navel oranges. Use only organic fruit for citrus peels in recipes—see warning, page 180. Wash and scrub the fruit well, peel off the zest diagonally, which is easier than straight up and down. Remove any white part and chop finely. Dry by spreading out in a single layer on an ungreased baking sheet for 20 minutes in a 200°F oven or overnight at room temperature. Store in a small airtight jar in the refrigerator (baby food jars are a nice size) or freeze. A medium orange will yield 2-3 tablespoons grated zest; a medium lemon will yield 2 teaspoons ; a medium lime will yield 1 teaspoon grated zest. These are great for flavoring your herbal tea. Or stir into plain hot water for a beverage or kids' tea. If you wish you can grind into a powder in the blender.

Tip: Use a vegetable peeler to remove peels without white rinds. Grating is easier while the fruit is still whole and uncut. Freeze citrus peels for easier grating.

Granulated zest: Combine the lemon zest from one lemon (about 2-3 teaspoons) with 1-2 tablespoons of granulated sugar and grind to a fine powder in the blender. Store as you would zest above. Great in herbal tea!

Tip: The smell of citrus is clean and delicious! See *Bathtub Aroma Therapy for Baby and You* on page 401 and *Air Fresheners* on page 482.

Grow a citrus fruit plant: See appendix, page 492.

For Collard Greens, see Greens

Corn (Sweet Corn, Maize, Zea)

Corn gives us so many things: cornmeal, cornstarch, corn oil, and livestock feed (made from the cobs). Its tall corn stalks give us paper and much more. The instant an ear of corn is picked, it quickly converts its sugar to starch. Every minute counts. At room temperature, half of corn's sugar gets converted to starch in one day. Heat or cold stop the conversion, so rush home from the store and either eat, boil, or refrigerate the corn immediately. (Scientists supposedly have come up with a new variety of corn that doesn't convert its starch to sugar so quickly, but we've yet to see it.)

Baby must be at least: 18 months, because corn tends to cause digestive problems. See page 43. Whole corn kernels are choking hazards (page 40).

Equivalents: 1 medium ear = ½ cup kernels.

In season: Peak May through September. Fresh corn is definitely one vegetable that you should buy only when in season.

Choosing: The husks of corn should be green, moist, snug, and flexible, not yellow, wilted, or rigid. The bottom stem end should also be green and moist, not dry and brown. Don't buy husked corn (corn with green husks removed), unless it is refrigerated, and really not even then. The silk should be moist, golden yellow, not brown, and free from decay and worm damage. Peel back the husk and make sure the kernels are tightly packed together and neither oversized or undersized. Kernels should be plump and juicy, not shrunken or shriveled. If you dare, stick one with your thumbnail—it should break easily and squirt a thin, milky juice. The rows of kernels should be even and close together with no space between them. Yellow or white, don't rely on color for freshness, but yellow corn has more beta-carotene (vitamin A) than white. Very dark yellow, though, indicates old corn.

Storing: Don't! Use it the same day you buy it. If you can't use it the same day and must store, keep husks on and wrap ears in damp paper towels and refrigerate in a plastic bag for no more than a day or two. Or cook the corn as soon as you bring it home, cool it quickly in cold water, and store it in plastic bags in the refrigerator for up to 3 days.

Preparation for cooking: Remove husks and all of the silk.

Tips to remove silk: To remove silk, rub from top to bottom with a damp paper towel. Another method is to use a vegetable brush or a sterilized toothbrush in a downward motion. If it is still difficult, brush under running water.

Cooking tips: Your baby doesn't need sugar or salt added to cooking water, and besides, salt hardens the kernels. A teaspoon or two of lemon juice in the cooking water will keep corn a nice yellow color.

Cooking fresh corn off the cob for your toddler: Remove corn from the cob by standing the cob on end and using a sharp knife to cut off a few rows at a time from top to bottom. Do not cut deeply—too near the cob. Then use the back of the knife to scrape the germ off the cob and into the pot. See the nutritional importance of the germ, page 218. Cook the kernels, covered, with a little milk or formula over medium-high heat for only about 3 minutes. Then purée and freeze using the Food Cube Method for up to two months.

Tip to remove corn kernels: Use a clean shoehorn to remove kernels from the cob.

Oven roasted unhusked corn: Preheat oven to 450°F. With husk still on corn cobs, thoroughly wet under running water. Bake in oven for 45 minutes, turning occasionally. Protect hand with oven mitt and turn with corn tongs. Remove husk and enjoy! No pans to wash.

Microwaving unhusked corn: An easy way to cook corn on the cob is to place it, unhusked, on two layers of white paper towels in the microwave. No water is needed because the husk is still on and will retain moisture. To microwave one ear, lay it in center of oven; two ears, place side by side; three ears, shape in a triangle; four ears, shape in a square; five ears, place four of the five side by side and the other one at the end of the other four; six ears, four side by side and one at one end of the four, one at the other end. Cook on high 3 minutes for each ear, turning once halfway through cooking time. Let stand for three minutes.
Another way to microwave unhusked corn: It's more difficult to remove silk while corn is hot after cooking. Try this. Pull back husks carefully. Remove silk. Replace husks and tie with string or wrap each ear in plastic wrap to keep husks in place. Then microwave as directed above.
Microwaving husked corn: If your corn cobs already have the husk removed, place in a dish with 1 tablespoon water per ear and cover the dish. (Or wrap each ear individually in heavy duty plastic wrap.) Cook on high 3 minutes for each ear, turning once halfway through cooking time. Let stand for 3 minutes.
Steam: Steam husked corn on the cob in one layer for 10 minutes.
Bake: Wrap unhusked ears with aluminum foil and bake in 350°F oven for about 40 minutes.
Boil: Boil one inch of water (or half water and half milk) in a large pot. Drop corn on the cob, husks and silk removed, into boiling water one ear at a time so as not to disturb the boiling. Cook for 4 to 6 minutes. **Tip:** If you have pot with a colander insert (page 151), use it so you won't have to remove each cob individually with tongs. The corn can then be drained easily over the sink.
Corn on the cob for baby: Babies cannot bite whole kernels off corn cobs as we do, but they can still enjoy sucking half-kernels of corn on the cob. Cook corn on the cob using one of the methods above and let cool. Remove part of each kernel from the cob by slicing down each row halfway through the kernels. Let your baby suck out the juicy milk and germ.
Tip for buttering corn on the cob: Don't rub a butter stick directly on the cob, it wastes too much and is messy. Use a pastry brush and melted butter for a thin coat. In a pinch, the leaves on top of a celery stick will work, but not as well as a brush. For your large barbeque party, fill a tall thin bottle with hot water and a stick of butter. When butter melts and floats to the top, slowly dip an ear of corn into the bottle so that it gets coated with a nice layer of butter.

Cucumbers

Baby must be at least: 18 months for raw puréed cucumber, because cucumber tends to cause digestive problems. See page 43.
Equivalents: 1 medium cucumber = 1½ cups sliced.
In season: Available year round; peak May through August.
Choosing: Select small or medium cucumbers that are dark green, solid and firm all over, slender, even-shaped, and have many small lumps on their skin. Whitish tips are OK. Avoid mushy cucumbers with shriveled ends and overgrown cucumbers, which are puffy, large, dull-looking, and possibly yellowed—these will taste bitter. It is almost impossible to find non-organically-grown cucumbers that are not waxed. Wax used on produce is supposedly safe, but it may contain pesticide residues. If you remove the wax by peeling, you also remove a lot of the vitamin A. Don't peel if the cucumber is young and has very tender skin. Use finely diced cucumber as a Healthy Extra (page 288). Or slice them lengthwise or crosswise for older children to dip into yogurt.
Storing: Store wrapped in a perforated plastic bag or unwrapped in the vegetable crisper for up to a week. Wrap cut cucumbers well before placing in the refrigerator or other foods will pick

up their odor. Sliced, wrapped cucumbers or cucumbers in dressing keep in the refrigerator up to 3 days.

Freezing: Don't.

Purée: Peel, scoop out seeds with a spoon or knife tip, and purée in a blender. Serve immediately and don't freeze.

Tip: To remove seeds from a large cucumber, peel and cut in half lengthwise. Then remove seeds with a melon baller, or run the tip of a teaspoon down the center of each half. Use cucumber sticks as "stirrers" in beverages.

For Dandelion Greens, see Greens
For Edible Pod Beans, see Beans, Edible Pod

Eggplant

Baby must be at least: 9 months for cooked puréed eggplant. Do not eat raw eggplant.

Equivalents: 1½ pounds = 2½ cups diced.

In season: Available year round; peak June through September.

Choosing: Select small, firm, shiny, tight, smooth, rich purple eggplant with only a small scar on the blossom end. An eggplant should feel heavy for its size. Press gently on the skin—it should cause a dent that immediately springs back when you release. If you can't dent it, it's too young; if it doesn't spring back, it's too old. Avoid those with dark brown or rust-colored spots or those with shriveled tips or cracks.

Storing: Keep in cool place (about 50°F) up to one week. If your house is too warm, keep it in a plastic bag in the refrigerator for only a few days. If stored longer than that, it will probably look good, but it will taste bitter. Cut eggplant can be stored, well-covered, in the refrigerator for up to 2 days.

Preparation for cooking: Do not eat raw eggplant. It's up to you whether you want to eat the peel or not. You should buy only small eggplant, but if you have a large one, you probably should peel it. If eggplant is to be cooked for a long time, don't peel it; for a short time, peel it. It's easier to remove the skin of an eggplant after it has been cooked. Do not undercook eggplant as you would other vegetables. Many cookbooks will tell you to soak or salt the eggplant to remove bitter juices. Avoid doing this, because it leaches out the water-soluble vitamins. Instead, buy small eggplant, which are more likely to be sweet and tender. If you already have a large eggplant, it may not cook well because it contains too much water. To draw out the bitter juices, slice and sprinkle both sides with salt. Let sit for 30 minutes, rinse very well to remove the salt, and dry with paper towels

Note: Eggplant absorbs oil like a sponge, so never fry it unless you want to eat a lot of fat..

Microwave: For whole eggplant: Pierce skin with fork to prevent explosion. Place on at least two layers of white paper towels. Microwave on high for about 12 minutes, turning halfway through cooking time. Let stand 3 minutes. For cut-up eggplant: Cut eggplant into uniform pieces. Add about 2 tablespoons water to dish. Cover and microwave on high for 5 to 6 minutes, stirring halfway through cooking time. Let stand, covered, 2 minutes.

Steam: Cut into uniform pieces. Steam for 15 to 20 minutes.

Bake: Slice in half lengthwise. Place on buttered cookie sheet with cut side down. Bake in preheated 350°F oven for 30 minutes.

Freeze: If you like, add a little lemon juice (if your baby is old enough for citrus) to puréed eggplant to keep it from discoloring. Freeze cooked eggplant using the Food Cube Method for up to 2 months.

For Grapefruit, see Citrus Fruit

Grapes

Baby must be at least: 8 months for cut up grapes. Never feed a baby whole grapes–she can choke (See choking hazards on page 40). Peel them and slice them into quarters. See warning about slippery foods on page 80.

Equivalents: 1 pound of grapes = 2½ cups.

In season: Available July through March; peak July and August.

Choosing: Select grapes that are bright, dry, and plump. Avoid shriveled, leaky, wrinkled, or damaged grapes. They should have a good, bright color for their variety. Red grapes should be good and red, but the seedless, common green grapes, to be sweetest, should have a yellowish cast. The grapes should be of good color around each stem and stems should be pliable. Grapes do not ripen off the vine, they must be ripe when picked. They don't get sweeter or juicier either. To test for freshness, pick up a bunch of grapes by the top stem and jiggle it very gently. The grapes should stay firmly attached. The more grapes that fall off, the older the bunch.

Storing: Remove any damaged grapes and store in a plastic bag in the refrigerator for up to 5 days.

Freezing: Freeze only the seedless grapes, unless you want to take the time to remove the seeds. Wash grapes and remove stems. Freeze in a freezer bag. For my older children, I keep frozen grapes in an open container on the freezer door, for easy grabbing. They don't have time to get freezer burn because they disappear so fast. Kids love these nice little refreshing snacks throughout the hot summer days. Whole frozen grapes are for older children only, they are choking hazards for babies and toddlers (page 40).

Growing: See how to grow a grape vine, page 492.

For Green Beans, see Beans

Greens

These Super Green Veggies include beet greens, collard greens, dandelion greens, kale, mustard greens, sorrel, spinach, Swiss chard, and turnip greens. Light green iceberg lettuce is a nutritional waste of time—go for the dark, leafy greens. Buy at least 2 bunches at a time when making baby food cubes because they shrink a lot during cooking. You can use the dandelion greens from your back yard, but make sure that they are totally organic and have never been sprayed with chemical fertilizers or weed killers. The dandelions I've cooked up from my back yard tasted very, very bitter.

Baby must be at least: 9 months for cooked greens, 10 months for finely chopped raw greens. See warning about collard greens and nitrates, page 38.

In season: Beet greens, June through October; collard greens, dandelion greens, kale, and mustard greens, January through April; sorrel, July through October; spinach, all year, peak in April and May; Swiss chard, July through October; turnip greens, October through March.

Choosing: Buy greens that are loose and not in plastic bags. Greens are very short-lived, so you should be able to have a good, close look at each leaf. Leaves should be young and tender with no thick veins, bright green, crisp and not wilted, insect-free, and have no bruises, decaying spots, or slime. Don't buy greens with yellow, red, or brown spots. Beet greens should contain red color. Swiss chard stems should be thick and white or red. Dandelion greens should have

part of the root still attached. If the supermarket regularly squirts a wet mist on the greens, check them carefully for dark or decaying spots, as wet greens rot quickly.
Storing: Rush home from the supermarket and cook and freeze greens the second you walk in the door. If you must store, wrap them in white paper towels and place in plastic bags in a cold part of the refrigerator or the vegetable crisper. Use them fast—within a day or two. Greens are tough to get into a plastic bag: turn the plastic bag inside out and with your hand inside the bag, grab the greens and turn bag right side out while enclosing the greens.
Preparation for cooking: Discard leaves with a lot of yellow or decay. Trim off any thick stems and small blemishes *before* cooking—stems are much more difficult to remove after cooking. If you wish, coarsely chop into uniform pieces. Wash each leaf under cold running tap water. For leaves with a lot of sand, such as spinach, wash them this way: first swish them in a sink full of *lukewarm* water to send sand to the bottom of sink. Drain the sink, making sure all sand is cleaned out. Refill sink, this time with *cold* water, swish, and drain again. Repeat with *cold* water until no sand is left in the sink. The more curly the leaves, the more places dirt could hide, and the more thoroughly you should wash them.
Preparing kale: Kale is a Super Duper Green. Get your baby used to the flavor and stir a kale cube into your baby's Super Porridge as often as possible! To prepare kale, swish in a sink full of cold water. Remove stems before cooking. Here is the best method I've found from my experience de-stemming countless numbers of kale leaves. (If I had a nickel for every kale leaf I've prepared for my babies, I wouldn't have had to write this book! ☺) First fold the leaf in half along the stem line. While holding leaves in your right hand, use left hand to hold the stem on the bottom and rip upwards using your right hand in a "hinged palm-up" motion from bottom to side. On large and long leaves you will have to move your right hand up and rip several times to get the whole stem off. Discard the stem in your left hand. Then use both left and right hands to rip leaves into smaller uniform pieces. (If you are left-handed, change left hand to right hand and vice versa in these instructions.) I feed my baby a LOT of organic kale and I usually batch cook three kale bunches at a time, so I had to find a quick and efficient way of ripping kale apart from its stem. It is important that you remove the stem BEFORE cooking, because it's more trouble to remove after cooking—even if the kale is not hot.
To reduce flavor: Greens have a strong flavor, which some babies dislike. If your baby refuses to eat greens, try steaming or microwaving them *uncovered*, which will reduce the strong flavor. Cooking uncovered does cause nutrient loss, though. Instead, to hide the strong flavor of greens, try mixing them with a more pleasant tasting food, such as mashed banana. I reduce their strong flavor by mixing only one food cube with a full cup of Super Porridge.
Microwave: Place washed greens in dish and cover. Don't add water, the rinsing water still left clinging to leaves is enough for cooking. Microwave on high about 7 minutes per pound. Stir halfway through cooking time. Let stand, covered, for 2 minutes.
Steam: Steam whole leaves 5 minutes; pieces 3 minutes.
Tip: Greens like spinach are sometimes too soggy for adults after cooking. Remove excess liquid by squeezing between two dinner plates.
Raw greens: Greens can be used in salads and in place of lettuce on sandwiches. However, for these purposes, use only very young, small, tender leaves.
Freezing: Purée and freeze using the Food Cube Method for up to 2 months. As you purée cooked kale, it will have the consistency of tiny hard flakes in dark green water. Push the purée against a spoon to squeeze off as much water as possible and then spoon into ice cube tray. The "drier" the kale, the less ice cube trays you'll need. If it's too dry in your baby's Super Porridge, add a little milk to the Super Porridge. When you are done puréeing, scrape and pour

what's left in the processor into a strainer and you may get enough for a whole new cube. I actually FORCE myself to drink the leftover green water! My life insurance company gives me a discount because of this! ☺ I call it "self-flagellation for good health."

Honeydew Melons

Baby must be at least: 8 months
In season: Available year round; peak June through October.
Choosing: Ripe melons should have a creamy white, ivory, or pale yellow color, even on the underside, and a faint and pleasant scent. Mature honeydews have a light velvety feel to their rind. Don't buy a slick, bald feeling melon—it's too mature. A ripe melon has a slightly soft blossom and stem end. The stem will not necessarily be smooth. Avoid those with punctures in the rind or water-soaked areas, and those with a greenish white or white color. Gently shake the melon, if you hear sloshing inside, pass on it. Buy large honeydews that are at least six inches in diameter and weigh at least five pounds. A cut melon's flesh should look soft and juicy and have a pleasant scent, even through the plastic wrap.
Storing: If necessary, ripen at room temperature away from sunlight for up to 4 days. It will get no sweeter, but it will get softer and juicier. Store ripe, whole melon in a plastic bag in the refrigerator for about a week; store cut melon for up to 5 days. Leave the seeds in halved melons for longer freshness.
Freezing: Follow directions for freezing cantaloupe, page 433.
Tip: Use an ice cream scoop or large spoon to remove seeds from halved melons.

For Kale, see Greens

Kiwi Fruit

Kiwi fruit is a funny-looking brown, fuzzy, egg-shaped fruit with beautiful insides. The bright green flesh, little black seeds, and cheesecake-like center can be used as Decorative Touches (page 362) in many toddler meals. Kiwi fruit is a good source of vitamin C and babies love its natural sweet taste. For a quick and easy snack, I grab a cool, ripe kiwi out of the fridge, wash it, cut it in half, and use a spoon to feed my baby right out of the peel. Don't be surprised if you see the little black seeds in your baby's diaper! See *Poop Panic!* page 27.
Baby must be at least: 8 months for peeled kiwi fruit, peels are choking hazards.
In season: Available year round, peak June through March.
Choosing: Select fruit that is plump with no bruises. A ripe kiwi yields to gentle pressure and feels soft (as a ripe peach does), but not mushy or spongy. In the store, it will probably still be firm, so you must ripen at home. Make sure it is evenly firm with no soft or shriveling spots.
Storing: Ripen at room temperature out of sunlight, turning fruit occasionally. Refrigerate ripened kiwis in plastic bag or vegetable crisper for up to one week.
Serving: Cut in half and scoop out flesh and edible seeds. Mash with fork and serve immediately before the vitamin C is destroyed by air, light, and warm temperature. Kiwis are quite watery—you may want to mix with a thickener, such as or ground dry oatmeal or wheat germ. For older babies, you can slice or dice the fruit and serve as finger food. Peel first to prevent choking. See warning about slippery foods on page 80.
Freezing: Peel kiwis with vegetable peeler. Purée and freeze using the Food Cube Method for up to 2 months. You may want to add a little lemon juice (if your baby is old enough for citrus) to prevent darkening. You can also freeze kiwis sliced, diced, or left whole. Follow directions for freezing cantaloupe, page 433.
Kiwi and gelatin: See warning on page 276.

For Lemons, see Citrus Fruits

Lettuce

Besides fiber and a little vitamin A, tasteless anemic-green iceberg lettuce is a nutritional waste of time for your baby (and you). Go for the greens, dark greens, instead. I include it here only for completeness. Romaine lettuce is more nutritious than iceberg.

Baby must be at least: 10 months for finely diced lettuce.

In season: Available year round; peak May through July.

Choosing: Iceberg leaves should be crisp, bright, and light green, but not pale. The head should give slightly when squeezed; it should be firm, but not hard. Don't buy iceberg lettuce if it is irregularly shaped or if the leaves are brown at the tips. Romaine lettuce is more oval than iceberg and darker green. Its leaves are looser and not so crisp. Buy lettuce that is being refrigerated in the store and not stacked up on a middle display box at room temperature. The latter may last only a day once you bring it home.

Storing: Do not remove leaves for storing. Store lettuce in paper bags in the refrigerator. Or wrap in white paper towels, then store tightly-wrapped in plastic bag with air holes or lettuce crisper in refrigerator for up to one week. Lettuce is tough to get into a plastic bag: turn the plastic bag inside out and with your hand inside the bag, grab the head of lettuce and turn bag right side out while enclosing the lettuce. Tear lettuce for salads immediately before serving—not before storing—to retain maximum vitamin C and to prevent wilting.

Preparation: Don't discard the outer (wrapper) leaves if they are undamaged, as they have most of the nutrients. Remove core of lettuce by cutting it out. Or, better than cutting (cutting causes brown spots): Hold the head with its core end down and smack it sharply on the counter to loosen the core, and then twist the core and pull it out. Wash leaves by rinsing under cold running tap water, letting water flow between leaves. Shake off water, drain well or dry with clean towels. **Tip:** Line a colander with nylon net for rinsing lettuce. Then just lift out netting and squeeze gently to drain.

Freezing: Don't.

Tip: Never put salt on lettuce—it will toughen it and wilt it. To keep salad really fresh, nest your empty salad bowl inside a slightly larger bowl containing water and freeze. Both bowls should be freezer-safe, of course. Weight down the inner bowl so it will not float on the water in the larger bowl. The ice layer that forms between the two bowls will keep the salad in the inner bowl cool and crisp.

Tip: To prevent greens from becoming limp, place a small inverted bowl/saucer at the bottom of your salad bowl so that excess water will collect under it. For picnics, first put salad dressing on bottom under the bowl (after the salad has drained well and you have poured off the water) and toss immediately before serving. You won't need to pack the salad bottle and bring it home.

Tip: When using oil and vinegar as a salad dressing, first pour on the vinegar and second the oil, otherwise the oil will just slide off the lettuce.

Tip: Use old spice jars or baby food jars to hold salad dressing for travel, or individual sandwich bags tied closed and placed inside a large freezer bag— similar to the Nested Plastic Bag method without the freezer. Do NOT use 35mm film canister to hold any food, because they contain residues of dangerous chemicals.

For Limes, see Citrus Fruits

Mangoes

Besides being delicious (and expensive), mangoes are nutritious with their vitamins A (orange color indicates beta carotene), C, and D. Mangoes are antiviral; mango juice poured into a test tube with live viruses actually deactivates them.

Baby must be at least: 6 months.

In season: Available May through August; peak June and July.

Choosing: Select fresh-looking, plump mangoes with a pleasant fragrance and smooth, undamaged skin. They should be at least 5 inches in diameter. Choose those with the fewest possible black spots, where the damage will move into the flesh when the fruit is very ripe. When ripe, mangoes are orange-yellow or red and feel soft. You can buy them firm and partially green and ripen them at home, but don't buy them completely green, as they may not ripen.

Storing: Ripen, uncovered, at room temperature out of direct sunlight before storing. Store ripened fruit in a plastic bag for up to 3 days.

Peeling: With a sharp knife, slash the peel. Over a bowl, slowly tear back the peel and scoop out the flesh. Or slice completely into the fruit to the pit and divide into two half bowls. Scoop out flesh. Purée for young baby. Give diced pieces to older baby (see warning about slippery foods on page 80. Serve immediately to prevent air and warmth from destroying the vitamin C.

Freezing: Peel, pit, purée, add a little lemon juice (if your baby is old enough for citrus) to prevent discoloring if you like, and freeze using the Food Cube Method for up to 10 months.

Fruit leather: See recipe for mango fruit leather, page 206. Delicious!

Mushrooms

Unless you're a mushroom expert, don't eat mushrooms from your backyard. Some very pretty harmless-looking white mushrooms grow wild, but contain poisons. Mushrooms are widely-thought to have no nutritive value, but they do contain potassium, fiber, and the B vitamins. They also contain a good amount of the trace mineral (germanium) found in garlic with antiviral and antitumor properties.

Baby must be at least: 9 months for cooked mushrooms. Raw mushrooms and raw mushroom pieces are choking hazards and should not be given to a baby under 3 years old (page 40).

Equivalents: ½ pound of fresh mushroom = 2 cups sliced.

In season: Available year round; least in August; peak October through June.

Choosing: It's better to buy loose mushrooms than packaged mushrooms, so that you can get a good look at them. Select clean, firm, young, small- or medium-sized fresh mushrooms that have a uniform color of white, off-white, or light tan. The caps should be bright, smooth, and tight around the stem, revealing little or none of the gills (paper thin tissue under the cap). Gills should be light tan or pink. Avoid mushrooms that are slimy, shriveled, spongy in texture, discolored, bruised, or pitted. Don't buy mushrooms that are bleached (label must inform you of this) or those with preservatives. As mushrooms mature, their caps open and expose more of the gills, and they get darker in color. Mature mushrooms have a stronger flavor, which some people prefer. You can buy mature mushrooms, but they will have a shorter storage life, of course.

Storing: Mushrooms are mostly water. This is one vegetable that you should not store in plastic wrap because they will get soggy. Don't wash them before storing; clean immediately before using. Place in refrigerator in an open container, such as the cardboard container they came in or a folded back open paper bag, and cover loosely with a wet paper towel wrung half dry to keep them from shriveling. They should keep for up to 3 days. Or, cook and cover mushrooms and store in refrigerator up to 4 days.

Raw mushrooms: Don't feed raw mushrooms to your baby as a finger food. They are slippery and hard to chew. Your baby may swallow one whole before she gets a chance to chew it; therefore, they are a choking hazard (page 40).

Preparation for cooking: Do not peel mushrooms. Remove any tough stems. Never soak mushrooms, for they absorb water and become waterlogged. To clean, wipe gently with a wet paper towel or a sterile soft toothbrush (no need to buy a fancy mushroom brush). Or, rinse quickly under running cold tap water and drain between paper towels. If some mushrooms are much larger than others, cut in half lengthwise for a more uniform size for cooking.

Microwave: Add 2 tablespoons of water for each pound of mushrooms. Microwave, covered, on high for 5 minutes. Stir halfway through cooking time. Let stand, covered, for 3 minutes.

Steam: Don't steam mushrooms, as the mushrooms' moisture will drip out the holes into the boiling water.

Saute: Clean and slice or chop mushrooms. Place 2 or 3 tablespoons of butter for each pound of mushrooms in a heavy frying pan over medium-high heat. Add mushrooms and saute, uncovered, for 3 or 4 minutes, stirring so that the butter coats the mushrooms. If mushrooms get too hard, next time try sauteing over a higher heat.

Bake: Bake, covered, for 15 minutes in a pre-heated 350°F oven.

Freezing: You can freeze whole raw mushrooms without blanching. They'll lose their texture and won't be good to eat raw after thawing, but they will be good for cooking. Cooked mushrooms with their pan juices (puréed or not) keep in the freezer for up to 2 months. To use up leftover mushrooms before they go bad, purée and freeze them using the Food Cube Method. Use in soups, stews, sauces, etc.

Tip: An egg slicer is great for quickly slicing mushrooms into uniform pieces.

For Mustard Greens, see Greens

Nectarines

Nectarines can be used in any recipe in place of peaches. Their hue indicates a good beta-carotene (vitamin A) content and they also contain some vitamin C.

Baby must be at least: 5 months for cooked nectarines, 7 months for raw puréed.

Equivalents: 3 or 4 medium nectarines = 1 pound = 2 cups peeled and sliced.

In season: Available June through August; peak in July.

Choosing: Select plump, smooth nectarines with a bright color. Color hues (red, yellow, tan flecks, or even green spots) are not good indicators of ripeness. Look for a bright color and avoid dull fruit. Unfortunately, the brightness may come from a wax coating. Wax used on produce is supposedly safe, but it may contain pesticide residues. They should feel slightly soft along the seam. Don't buy dull, hard, wrinkled, or shriveled fruit or fruit with soft spots, mold, or broken skin. Use your nose and buy only fruit that has a sweet fragrance.

Storing: Ripen, if necessary, at room temperature for up to 3 days. Store ripened fruit in a plastic bag in the refrigerator for up to 5 days. If cut, store tightly wrapped in refrigerator for at most 2 days. If you wish, to prevent exposed cut flesh from darkening, rub it with lemon juice (if your baby is old enough for citrus).

Freezing: Wash and peel nectarines with vegetable peeler. Remove pit, purée, and freeze using the Food Cube Method for up to 2 months. You may want to add a little lemon juice (if your baby is old enough for citrus) to prevent darkening. Or, you can freeze nectarine halves.

Wash, peel, remove pit, place in rigid container and cover with orange juice (if your baby is old enough for citrus) to prevent darkening. Leave a little head room for expansion. See *Freezing Chunks of Fruit*, page 199. Nectarine chunks or halves will keep in the freezer for up to a year.

Okra

Okra is a Super Green Veggie used more for thickening than flavoring. Its gluey, syrupy juice typically is used to thicken soups and stews, such as the Southern gumbo and Creole stews. Okra combines well with tomatoes and corn. It has good amounts of vitamins A and C, along with other nutrients. Okra can be eaten raw in salads.

Baby must be at least: 8 months for cooked okra.

Equivalents: 22-28 pods = 1 pound = 5 cups.

In season: Available year round in the South; peak June through October.

Choosing: Select small, crisp, bright-green okra pods that are less than 4½ inches long—ideally from 2 to 3½ inches. Their tips should bend with very slight pressure. Avoid those that are flabby, wilted, pale, tough, woody, stiff, or those with hard bodies. Don't buy those that are pitted or those with black spots.

Storing: Store okra in the vegetable crisper or in an open plastic bag in the refrigerator for up to 3 days. Make sure there is no moisture on the okra and that it is very dry before you put it in the plastic. Any water on the skin will turn it slimy. Cooked okra can be stored, covered, in the refrigerator for up to 4 days.

Preparation for cooking: Too much contact with water makes okra sticky, so rinse lightly and quickly, using a vegetable brush to remove the fuzz. Don't peel okra. Cut off the stems carefully, so as not to pierce the pods. Leave small pods whole. Slice larger pods in half. Don't overcook okra; it will become slippery and gummy. Brass, iron, tin, or copper cookware will discolor okra, but it will be safe to eat.

Microwave: Add 2 tablespoons of water per pound. Microwave, covered, on high for 6 minutes. Let stand, covered, for 3 minutes.

Steam: Steam whole okra for 15 minutes.

Bake: Bake in aluminum foil for 30 minutes at 350°F.

Freeze: Purée and freeze using the Food Cube Method for up to 2 months.

Onions

Baby must be at least: 9 months for cooked onion, and 18 months for raw onion. Raw onion might cause digestive problems—see page 43.

Equivalents: 1 medium onion = ¾ cup chopped or sliced.

In season: Available all year.

Choosing: Select onions that are firm, hard, bright, and shiny. The outer skin should be dry, papery, and crackly. Check under the skin for dark, moldy areas. Examine the neck closely—it should be small, tightly closed, firm, completely dry, and free from decay. Avoid spongy, soft onions or onions with hollow woody centers. Don't buy onions that are sprouting, those with green sunburn spots, and those with any wet spots. Buy onions loose, so that you can examine each one. Or buy them bagged in netting, but make sure you check each one for decay, because one bad onion spreads its decay to the others.

Storing: Store in a cool, dry, place with good air circulation for up to 2 weeks. Spread onions out in a single layer and store in one of those wire mesh hanging baskets, which allow for air circulation. Or use an old clean pair of pantyhose. Onions will store loose, not in plastic bags, in the refrigerator for up to 2 months, but they pass their odor to other refrigerator inhabitants. Onions that have been cut, if wrapped tightly in plastic, will keep in the refrigerator for up to

3 days. To prevent odor from getting into other foods, store cut onions in a glass jar with an airtight screw lid; they will keep a few days longer stored this way. Cooked onions in a tightly covered container will keep in the refrigerator for up to 5 days. Do not store onions near potatoes, because each releases gasses that shortens the others' storage life. **Tip:** Rub butter over the cut part of an onion before storing in the refrigerator to keep it fresh longer.

Preparation for cooking: Wash, peel off outer skin, and cut out any damage. Leave small uniform-sized onions whole, or cut large onions into halves, quarters, or slices. To prevent the center of the onion from "telescoping" (poking out during cooking), cut a small X into each stem end.

Microwave: Add no water. Microwave in covered dish for about 6 minutes per pound. Let stand, covered, for 5 minutes.

Steam: Steam whole onions for 30 minutes,

Bake: Remove outer skin from whole onion. Bake for 30 minutes until outside is crisp and inside is tender.

Freezing: Onions don't need blanching before freezing. Peel and chop onions—use your processor to chop to save tears. Freeze them in plastic freezer bags for up to 1 year. Many recipes call for only a little chopped raw onion. Chop and freeze leftover onion to use for these recipes. You may want to pre-measure by tablespoon, ½ cup, or whatever measure your favorite recipes require. Freeze pre-measured amounts using the Nested Plastic Bag Method.

Eating raw onions: If you find that raw onions are too strong, slice and separate into onion rings and soak in cold water for about one hour.

Dried onions: Slice onions paper thin and separate into rings. Spread on baking sheet and let dry in a 275°F oven for about 45 minutes until they are dry and lightly browned. Chop and refrigerate in an airtight screw-top glass jar and they will keep for up to one month. Use in recipes as you would dried onions.

Tips for less tears: Tears are caused by the release of a gas (propanethial-sulfur oxide which turns into sulfuric acid in the air) into the air when you tear the onion's cell walls. To prevent your eyes from tearing, wear your swim or ski goggles or wrap-around sun glasses. Start slicing at the top of the onion and cut off the root end last. Or, peel them under cold running water to dilute the gas before it gets released into the air—you will lose some nutrients this way and raise your water bill. Or, keep rinsing only your hands under running water. Refrigerate onions to make them cool before peeling to slow down the gas. Keep your mouth closed tightly while peeling. Work under your kitchen's exhaust fan. Or try holding an unlit match between your teeth; the match's sulfur with react with the gas and help reduce tears. Or use your food processor instead of cutting onions manually.

For Oranges, see Citrus Fruits

Papaya

The orange-colored flesh of the papaya indicates its high beta carotene (Vitamin A) content. Papayas are loaded with vitamin C.

Baby must be at least: 6 months.

In season: Available year round; peak April through July.

Choosing: Select fruit that is smooth, well-shaped, unbruised, unbroken, and at least half yellow with as little green as possible. Avoid fruit that has any soft spots or is mushy or shriveled. You will probably find papaya in the market unripened and firm. Let it ripen at room temperature for up to 5 days. Ripe papaya turns all yellow, has a pleasant fragrance, and becomes soft like a ripe peach, so that it yields to gentle pressure.

Storing: Store ripe papaya in a plastic bag in refrigerator for up to 2 weeks.
Serving: Cut in half lengthwise and remove seeds for baby. (The seeds are edible. You can grind them in the blender until they are the size of coarsely ground pepper and add them to drinks or salad dressings.) Mash some papaya and serve immediately to your baby, before the warmth and light in the room destroy the vitamin C.
Freezing: Remove black seeds and follow directions for freezing cantaloupe, page 433.
Papaya and gelatin: See warning on page 276.

Parsley

Parsley, too often used as a decorative garnish to be dismissed with the dirty plate, should be eaten, and eaten often! This herb is a powerhouse of nutrition, rich in vitamins A, C, and iron. Herbs are easy to grow in your kitchen. See *How to Grow Herbs on Your Windowsill*, page 488. You can just snip some fresh leaves off the living plant with clean scissors (can't get any fresher than that!) for use in omelets, cereals, etc. Always add parsley to cooked dishes immediately before the end of the cooking time; cooked parsley tastes bitter. In your favorite recipes, substitute 1 tablespoon chopped fresh herbs for 1 teaspoon dried herbs. In other words, 3 parts fresh herbs equal 1 part dried herbs.
Baby must be at least: 8 months for cooked parsley, 9 months for finely chopped raw parsley.
In season: Available year round; slight peak October through December.
Choosing: Fresh parsley comes in flat leaf and curly leaf varieties. Either way, buy only crisp, fresh, bright green leaves and never those that are yellow or brown. Avoid parsley that has watery areas or is wilted.
Preparation for storing or freezing: Discard tough stems. Cut off any damaged, yellow, or wilted leaves. Rinse well under running tap water. Gently shake to remove most of the water.
Storing: Wrap prepared parsley in white paper towels and refrigerate in plastic bags for up to 4 days.
Freezing parsley (and other herbs): Prepare as above and pat dry with white paper towels. (You don't have to blanch herbs before freezing. You can blanch for 10 seconds, if you wish, but why destroy nutrients when you don't have to?) Make sure the leaves are very dry so they won't stick together when frozen. You can freeze fresh herbs whole, cut into large pieces, or chopped into small pieces. Place them into the freezer in airtight freezer bags or foil. When needed, cut off the amount you want and immediately put the rest back into the freezer. Freeze for up to a year. (To prevent basil leaves from losing color, dip in boiling water for 2-3 seconds before freezing.)
Another way to freeze fresh herbs: Chop or purée herbs and place in ice cube trays, cover with water and freeze. Then pop the herb cubes into a plastic freezer bag, as in the Food Cube Method. Freeze for up to 4 months. Frozen cubes can be dropped, unthawed, into stews or soups to flavor and add nutrients. Or, let frozen herb cubes sit in a strainer over a bowl or glass until the ice melts. For quicker thawing, melt the ice cube in a saucepan on the stove top or in a bowl in the microwave and pour through a strainer.
Herb vinegars: Make your own herb-flavored vinegars by placing fresh, clean herbs (not basil) in apple cider vinegar in a tightly-covered airtight screw-top jar in the refrigerator. Make sure the jar and top is sterile before filling. It's ready for use after 2 weeks. Strain. Keep refrigerated.
Drying parsley and other herbs: Dried herbs are concentrated fresh herbs. Drying causes the same flavor concentration in herbs as it does in fruits (see page 200). 1 teaspoon of dried herbs is equal to 3 teaspoons of fresh herbs, so be careful about adding dried herbs to your recipes. Adding too little is no problem, you can always add more; but if you add too much, you've blown it.

To dry herbs, such parsley, oregano, sage, basil, mint, and others, rinse them and gently shake off excess water. Herbs can be dried in bunches by hanging them leaves down with the stems tied together like an upside-down bouquet. This will allow the essential oils in the stems to flow into the leaves, making them more flavorful. To prevent the herbs from getting dusty while drying or getting broiled in the sun, and preventing leaves from falling all over the floor, place the bouquet upside down in a paper bag. Cut several holes or slits in the bag for air circulation. Tie the paper bag closed at the stem end of the bouquet. Let it hang in a warm, dry place for up to 3 weeks, until the leaves are so dry that they will crumble.

Herbs dry much faster in your conventional oven, of course, than they do hanging upside down in a paper bag. Pre-heat your oven to 175°F. Spread herbs loosely on a dry cookie sheet and place in oven. Wait two minutes and turn the oven off. Let the herbs sit in the oven with the door closed for about 8 hours or overnight. (If you have a gas oven, you can use only the heat from the pilot light to dry your herbs. Place the cookie sheet in the oven and let them dry for several days.)

When dry, remove the leaves from the stems and store them tightly covered in a small glass jar away from air, light, and heat. You can crush the leaves before storing, but their oils keep better if you leave them whole; crush them just before using for maximum flavor. Store them in a dry, cool, dark place in glass jars. Don't use paper or cardboard containers, because they will absorb the essential oils and the herbs will be tasteless. I like to keep my dried herbs out in the kitchen, so I wrap aluminum foil around the glass jar to prevent light from penetrating. Keep dried herbs away from any heat source: stoves, refrigerators, etc. The glass jars should be as small as possible, no bigger than the 4-ounce glass jars of baby food. The larger the jar, the more flavor loss from frequent opening to the air. Use a small piece of masking tape on the bottom of jar to label with date.

Herb butter: See recipe on page 318.
Growing: Grow parsley and other herbs in your kitchen—see page 488.
Tip: Chew parsley after a meal—it is a delicious and natural breath freshener.
Tip: If your recipe calls for fresh parsley and you're out of it, use celery leaves.

Peaches

Baby must be at least: 5 months for cooked peaches, 7 months for puréed raw peaches.
Equivalents: 4 medium peaches = 1 pound = 2 cups peeled and sliced.
In season: Available May through September; peak July and August.
Choosing: Select firm or slightly soft peaches with a nice fragrance. Pick peaches that have a good shape with a seam that is easily distinguishable. Avoid peaches that are very hard or very soft or those with flattened bruises, which mean inner decay. Color is important. Peaches should have a yellow or cream-colored background, and most varieties also have a red blush. Don't buy peaches that have any green color.
Storing: Ripen at room temperature for a day or two, until the peaches feel soft and yield to gentle pressure. Ripe peaches will have a strong and sweet scent. Store ripe peaches in plastic bags in the refrigerator for up to 5 days. Store cut peaches tightly wrapped in plastic in the refrigerator for one or two days. A little lemon juice (if your baby is old enough for citrus) rubbed on the cut flesh will prevent darkening.
Tip: Peaches are easier to peel if you use a potato peeler. Peaches are naturally fuzzy, but commercial peaches are usually defuzzed by a brushing process.
Freezing: Peel ripe peaches using a vegetable peeler. Remove pit, purée, and freeze using the Food Cube Method. Or freeze peach halves following directions for nectarines, page 447.

Pears

Pears are a good source of fiber and a fair source of vitamins C, B, A, and iron.
Baby must be at least: 5 months for cooked pears, 6-7 months for raw.
Equivalents: 3 medium pears = 1 pound = 2 cups peeled and sliced.
In season: Available year round, peak August through November, depending on variety.
Choosing: In general, pears are usually sold green and turn yellow as they ripen. Select pears that are plump and firm, but not hard. Make sure that the areas around the stem and blossom ends are not weak. Avoid pears that are wilted or shriveled, for they are immature and will never ripen. To be sure that pears will ripen, buy those that are a little soft, indicating that they have already begun the ripening process. Don't buy pears with soft spots or those that look dull. Try to get pears that haven't been waxed. Wax used on produce is supposedly safe, but it may contain pesticide residues. Color is important: Bartlett (this summer pear is probably the most common) should be pale to rich yellow or dark red, peak availability is July through November; Bosc pears should be greenish yellow to brownish yellow background with differing intensities of reddish blush; Comice pears should be light green to yellow green or dark red; Winter Nellis should be medium to light green. In the one case of the d'Anjou variety, color does not indicate ripeness.
Storing: Ripen at room temperature for up to 5 days, until they become soft and yield to gentle pressure. Store ripe pears in a plastic bag in the refrigerator for up to 5 days. Store cut pears wrapped tightly in plastic in refrigerator for a day or two. If you wish, rub cut flesh with lemon juice (if your baby is old enough for citrus) to prevent darkening.
Freezing: Freeze and purée pears that are still a little firm, before they turn completely soft. Peel, remove core and seeds, and purée flesh. Add a little lemon juice (if your baby is old enough for citrus) to prevent darkening. Pears will keep in the freezer for up to one year.

Peas (Green Peas or Shell Peas)

The peas in this section are those where the pod is not edible. See Beans, page 428 for green beans and other edible-pod peas. Also, see dried split peas in the legume section on page 233.

Peas are very perishable and quickly turn from sugar to starch, so eat them as soon as possible. Don't remove them from their pods until the last possible minute. Peas right from your backyard garden, when shelled and eaten immediately after the picking, are sweet and delicious. I find shelling them tedious. My family eats fresh peas very rarely—only when they come straight from a relative's or our home garden. However, my baby eats dried split peas as part of his Super Porridge very frequently.
Baby must be at least: 7 months for cooked puréed peas. Whole peas are a choking hazard until at least age 3 years (page 40), but whole peas smashed lightly with a fork make a nutritious finger food for older babies.
Equivalents: 1 pound of pods = 1 cup shelled peas.
In season: Available March through November; peak March through June.
Choosing: Select crisp, bright green pods that are filled with peas, but not bulging. Avoid those that are flat, dull, bloated, light green or yellowed, gray-spotted, mildewed, or wilted, even just a little wilted. Buying frozen peas (the "petite" ones are best) is an option, but do not use these for frozen food cubes (see *Never Re-freeze Thawed Baby Food*, page 177). Canned peas, which are completely tasteless, should be outlawed.
Storing: Eat them the same day you buy or pick them. If you must store, refrigerate in pods in a plastic bag for up to 4 days. Store cooked peas in refrigerator for up to 4 days.

Preparation for cooking: Remove peas from pods. Place in colander or large strainer and rinse under tap water.

Microwave: Add 2 tablespoons for each cup of shelled peas (one pound of peas in pod yields about 1 cup). Cover and microwave on high for 5 minutes. Stir halfway through cooking time. Let stand, covered, for 3 minutes. For small quantities of peas (less than ½ cup), you may use a little butter instead of the water if you wish.

Steam: Steam peas (removed from pods) 8 minutes.

Freezing: Freeze puréed peas using the Food Cube Method or Tray-Freeze Method for up to 2 months.

Tip: Remember that boiling causes a great loss in nutrients, but if you choose to boil, cook the peas IN the pods. The peas will come out of the pods during boiling and you won't have to manually remove the pods.

Peppers
(Bell Peppers, Sweet Green Peppers, Sweet Red Peppers)

The peppers you feed to baby are the sweet green or sweet red ones, not the hot peppers! By the way, all peppers start out green and turn to another color (or stay green) when ripe. Peppers are a good source of that unstable nutrient, vitamin C. It is better to serve them to baby puréed or diced *raw* because cooking destroys this vitamin.

Baby must be at least: 10 months for finely grated sweet peppers.

Equivalents: 1 large bell pepper = 1 cup chopped.

In season: Available year round; slight peak May through October. This vegetable is OK to buy out of season—the vitamin C content is great for preventing winter colds.

Choosing: Select firm peppers with bright color that feel heavy for their size. Look for glossy, thick, smooth skins. Buy only peppers with their stems still on. Try to find peppers without that darned wax coating, which causes accelerated bacterial growth inside peppers. Also, wax used on produce is supposedly safe, but it may contain pesticide residues. Avoid soft, flabby, wrinkled, wilted, cracked, or spotted peppers or those with thin, flimsy walls. Look carefully for soft watery spots, which reveal decay underneath.

Storing: Don't keep peppers at room temperature. Place immediately in refrigerator in a plastic bag or put them in a paper bag in the vegetable crisper. Keep for not more than 5 days. Wrap cut pepper tightly in plastic and refrigerate for up to 2 days.

Preparation: Wash and remove stem. Slice lengthwise and remove seeds, membranes, and pith. (The pith is the soft, spongy core in the center.) If you cut carefully, the seeds and pith will come out in one piece. Purée pepper for young baby, or dice it well for an older baby. Slices of green or red peppers are great for Decorative Touches on toddler food. Or stuff pepper halves with ground nut/seed and cheese mixtures for older children.

Freezing: No need for blanching diced or sliced peppers before freezing. Purée and freeze raw peppers using the Food Cube Method, or slice or dice peppers and freeze using the Nested Plastic Bag Method. Freeze for up to 6 months.

Tip: When you are chopping up one green pepper, chop up an extra one or two and freeze using the Nested Plastic Bag Method for future use in soups, stews, and other recipes.

Tip: Before baking stuffed peppers, rub skins with olive oil to prevent them from splitting.

Tip: When freezing green peppers whole, as for stuffed peppers, slice off tops, remove seeds and membrane, blanch, and freeze peppers nested one inside the other to save freezer space.

Pineapples

Pineapples are fun! They also contain a good amount of vitamin C and manganese.
Baby must be at least: 9 months.
Equivalents: 1 medium pineapple = about 3½ pounds = 3 cups peeled and diced.
In season: Available year round; peak March through July.
Choosing: Select the largest pineapple possible; it will give you more fruit. Buy only those pineapples that are plump, firm, glossy, and bright. Don't buy pineapples that are a dull yellowish-green, as they may never ripen. Spikes (leaves on top) should be fresh-looking and green. It is important that the fruit have a strong, sweet fragrance—a sour or fermented smell means it's overripe. Soft or dark spots or bruises are a sign of decay, which will spread rapidly underneath. The pips, or eyes, should be flat, glossy, and slightly separated. Avoid pineapples whose eyes are either pointy or sunken.
Ripening: Leave the pineapple at room temperature for up to 2 days to get it softer and juicier. When the pineapple is ready to be eaten, the spikes will pull out easily. The mature unripe pineapples are green and turn yellow and orange and become softer and juicier as they ripen. A ripe pineapple will sound solid, not hollow, if you thump your finger against it. (Some disagree that these signs of ripeness are accurate. They suggest that you buy only pineapples with a label guaranteeing ripeness and flavor.)
Storing: Store whole pineapple in a plastic bag in the refrigerator for up to 5 days. Cut pineapple keeps longer than whole pineapple. Place pieces in an airtight bag or container for up to one week. (Yes, cut pineapple lasts longer than whole pineapple.)
Preparation: Here's an easy way to cut up a pineapple. Slice lengthwise into quarters. Use a knife, preferably curved, to slice core off top of each quarter. Slice the edible flesh from the peel. Discard the core and peel. Purée or dice the flesh. A medium-sized pineapple yields about 3 cups of diced fruit. See recipe for Pineapple Tubbie or Sailing Ship (page 299) for another way to cut up a pineapple. If you wish to use only part of a pineapple, slice it whole starting from the bottom, and peel and core each disc individually. Cover the cut end of the pineapple very well before refrigerating.
Tip: Wear an oven mitt while slicing pineapple for a good "unpicky" grip.
Canned: Although I usually don't recommend canned food, *unsweetened* canned pineapple is a nice treat for baby, and it's a fair source of vitamin C. It can be added as a natural sweetener to yogurt, cottage cheese, tofu, etc. Transfer opened canned pineapple to a glass dish, cover tightly, and it will keep in the refrigerator for up to one week. See more about canned foods on pages 37 and 200.
Freezing: Freeze the purée from fresh (not canned) pineapple using the Food Cube Method or freeze diced pineapple pieces covered in their own natural juice. See *Freezing Chunks of Fruit*, page 199. For a better texture, serve thawed pineapple to adults while it is still a little bit frozen.
Growing: Grow your own pineapple palm plant. See page 492 in the appendix *Your Kitchen Window is a Green Mine.*
Pineapple and gelatin: See warning on page 276.

Plums and Fresh Prunes

Fresh prunes and plums are almost the same fruit. One difference is that fresh prunes are "freestone"—the pit pulls out easily from fresh prunes, as peach pits do. It's no easy job to remove the flesh from a plum pit. It really hangs on! Another difference is that fresh prunes don't ferment during the drying process, which is why dried prunes are so common. Also, fresh prunes are firmer, sweeter, and more acid than plums.

Baby must be at least: 8 months.

Equivalents: 8 medium fresh plums = 1 pound = 2½ cups pitted.

In season: Peak July through August.

Choosing: Choose fruit that is brightly colored for their variety. They should be firm, not too soft and leaky and not too hard and wrinkled. Feel the skin—it should be slightly soft and yield to gentle pressure. Don't buy dull or bruised fruit.

Storing: Ripen firm fruit at room temperature for a day or two. Store ripe fruit in a vegetable crisper or plastic bag in the refrigerator for up to 5 days.

Preparation: Wash, peel, remove pit, and purée.

Freezing: Freeze purée using the Food Cube Method for up to 3 months. Add a little lemon juice (if your baby is old enough for citrus) to prevent darkening, if you wish. You can freeze plums or fresh prunes whole in their peels in plastic bags for up to 3 months. Before thawing whole frozen fruit, dip in cold water for 15 seconds and rub off the peels—they'll come off easily. Thaw and serve.

Tip: Replace butter/oil with prune butter. Prune butter—a thickened prune purée—can be substituted in equal amounts for butter or oil in baked goods. Substitute up to ¾ of the butter/oil called for in the recipe with prune butter and you will still have a nice texture in the final product. Prune butter goes especially well in brownies and other recipes with cocoa powder, dark muffins, quick breads, cakes, and cookies. You can buy prune butter, also called "lekvar," in your supermarket or natural foods store. Or you can use jarred baby prunes instead of prune butter, but they are usually more expensive. Or you can make your own—see recipes for Prune Butter and No-Cook Prune Butter, page 318.

Potatoes, White

The potato is a tuber, not a root vegetable. To preserve as much as possible of the high vitamin C content, cook potatoes in their skins. As usual, nutrients are found in large amounts in the skins and just underneath. By the way, potatoes can be eaten raw, and their vitamin C is intact since no cooking has destroyed it, but eat raw potatoes immediately after you cut them, because they oxidize very rapidly. Serve cooked potatoes puréed (for adults, they are called mashed) with a little yogurt or cottage cheese (made smooth in the blender) instead of high-fat sour cream. Potatoes aren't fattening; it's the butter, sour cream, and other fatty flavorings that we add to potatoes that are fattening. Avoid dehydrated instant potatoes, which are almost vitamin C-less and have chemical preservatives added.

Baby must be at least: 7 months for cooked white potatoes.

Equivalents: 1 medium potato = ½ pound.

In season: Available year round.

Choosing: Don't buy the red potatoes, because they may be dyed and/or waxed. Wax used on produce is supposedly safe, but it may contain pesticide residues. The "new" potatoes are harvested when they are young, and therefore their skins are thin and easily torn. Buy uniform medium-sized (½ pound) baking or general purpose potatoes that are firm, unshriveled, relatively smooth, and fairly well-shaped. Give the potato a gentle squeeze—its skin should fit tight. There should be very little peeling, eyes, and sprouts, and no deep cracks or sticky or decaying spots. One bad potato spoils the others, so fish around and do a careful check of all potatoes in the bag. Don't buy potatoes with green discoloration. Green patches caused by sunlight have a chemical called solanine, which is similar to nicotine and toxic in large doses. Green patches caused by artificial light, rather than sunlight, are not poisonous, but how do you know which light caused the green? Don't take a chance and avoid potatoes with any green spots. Don't buy a potato with black eyes, which indicates that the potato was accidentally frozen. Look for dirty potatoes—potatoes grow underground and naturally come out dirty. If they have been commercially washed, they are sometimes more expensive and may have absorbed water and lost nutrients. (Some disagree: They say to buy clean potatoes, because dirt harbors microorganisms. Use your own judgement.)

Storing: Don't wash potatoes until just before use because moisture will cause decay. Unlike most other vegetables, do not store potatoes in plastic. Store potatoes in a paper bag or something that will allow air circulation and moisture release. Or use a leg from an old clean pair of pantyhose. Store unwashed potatoes in a cool (about 50°F), dry, dark place for up to 2 months. Make sure you keep them completely out of natural sunlight to prevent greening. If you store them at room temperature, do so for no more than 2 weeks. Don't store potatoes near onions, because each releases gasses that shortens the other's storage life. If you refrigerate potatoes, let them sit for a day or two at room temperature before using. Refrigeration changes the starch in potatoes to sugar; room temperature will change the sugar back to starch. Leftover cooked potatoes will keep in a tightly closed container in the refrigerator for up to 5 days. Some say to place peeled potatoes in cold water to prevent darkening, but I disagree because this causes nutrients to leach out. Instead, store cut or peeled potatoes in an airtight plastic bag, removing as much air as possible using the method described on page 168.

Preparation for cooking: Scrub with vegetable brush under cold water. Remove any damaged areas, and eyes and sprouts, which are toxic. Cut away the green areas; don't worry, the solanine in the green area doesn't "spread" into the surrounding white area.

Microwave: Pierce potatoes in several places with a fork. Place potatoes on at least two layers of white paper towels. If cooking more than 2 potatoes, arrange like a star or wagon-wheel spokes. Place the larger ends of the potatoes toward the walls of the microwave. Microwave on high 5 minutes for first medium-sized potato and an extra 2½-3 minutes for each additional potato. Turn halfway through cooking time. Let stand for 5 to 10 minutes. If potatoes turn out shriveled, you've overcooked them.

Steam: Steam 30 minutes for whole, unpeeled potatoes; 8 minutes for ½-inch slices.

Boil: Boil enough water to cover potatoes. Place washed, whole, unpeeled potatoes in boiling water, cover pot, and cook for 20-30 minutes until tender.

Bake: Scrub and wash the skin and dry with a white paper towel. You may wish to rub a little butter on the skin to keep it soft and prevent cracking during baking. Pierce potatoes in several places with a fork. Place on baking sheet or directly on oven rack. For a medium sized potato, bake at 325°F for 1½ hours; at 400°F for about 50 minutes to an hour; at 450°F for about 45 minutes. Potatoes are done if they feel soft when pressed or when a fork goes into the center easily. A metal kebab skewer inserted through a whole potato lengthwise will cut its baking time in half. Or use the metal prongs sold at kitchen stores for baking potatoes. A potato boiled for 5 minutes will bake in half the time. It is not true that a potato wrapped in aluminum foil will bake faster. Foil slows down the heat transfer from the oven and does not allow the peel to get crisp. Use aluminum foil if you want to keep the potato hot after it comes out of the oven. **Tip:** If you have a lot of potatoes to bake, place then on their ends vertically in a 12-cup muffin tin. **Tip:** Use leftover baked potatoes, diced, for tomorrow's breakfast hash browns. **Tip:** For a nice presentation, slit the baked potato in half and, with your hands, squeeze the skins causing the flesh to pop up out of the half.

Leftover baked potatoes: See recipes for leftover baked potatoes on page 302: Potato Skins, Baked Potato Cubes, and At-the-Ready Frozen Baked Potatoes.

Mash: You don't have to make mashed potatoes with boiled potatoes, use baked potatoes for more nutrition. Mash cooked potatoes with a fork or potato masher or an electric mixer. You can try using your blender, but it may cause the potatoes to take on a plastic consistency. Add a quarter cup of *warm* liquid (milk) and 1 or 2 teaspoons of *softened* butter for each medium potato, if you wish. Do not add flavorings (herbs, grated cheese, etc.) into mashed potatoes until immediately before serving. **Tip:** If mashed potatoes become too watery, add nonfat dried milk powder to make them fluffy. Too watery usually means that the potatoes have been overcooked. **Tip:** At the last minute, stir in ½-1 cup of shredded cheddar cheese into mashed potatoes and they will contain streaks of gold.

Leftover mashed potatoes: Coat leftover mashed potatoes with flour, wheat germ, or ground oatmeal and fry in a little butter or vegetable oil--see recipe for Potato Burgers, page 314. Or place them in a casserole dish, brush top with butter, cover, and bake 30 minutes at 250°F.

Freezing: Mashed potatoes will keep well-wrapped in the freezer for up to 10 months. Freeze whole baked potatoes for up to 3 months; thaw in the refrigerator overnight, wrap in foil and bake at 350°F for 30 minutes. Bake frozen, unthawed whole baked potatoes at 350°F for 45 minutes. Remove foil for last 10 minutes of baking.

Reheating: Dip whole cooked baked potatoes in hot water for a few minutes and re-bake for 20 minutes at 350°F.

Tip: Before boiling potatoes whole, peel a small band of skin around the "waistline" of the potato to prevent the skin from bursting.

Tip: If you have too many potatoes, store a few apples in with them to help prevent them from sprouting.

For Pumpkins, see Squash, Winter

For Prunes, see Plums

Rhubarb

Rhubarb, or "pieplant," is technically a vegetable, but frequently referred to as a fruit due to its flavor.

Baby must be at least: 9 months for cooked rhubarb. Never feed baby (or yourself) raw rhubarb.

Equivalents: 1 pound rhubarb = 3 cups slices = 2 cups cooked.

In season: Available January through August; peak May.

Choosing: Select bright, shiny, firm, crisp rhubarb that is a good red or pink color. Stalks should be neither too thick or too thin. Avoid wilted, flabby, stringy, or rough-textured rhubarb.

Storing: Store in plastic bag in refrigerator for up to one week.

Preparation for cooking: *Do not eat rhubarb leaves; they are toxic and can be fatal. Eat only the stalks.* Discard leaves, and wash and slice the stalks into 1½ inch slices.

Microwave: Microwave in covered container on high for 5 minutes. Let stand, covered, for 4 minutes.

Steam: Steam 20 minutes.

Bake: Bake in covered dish or wrapped in aluminum foil in a 350°F pre-heated oven for about 30 minutes.

Serve: Purée cooked rhubarb stalks and add about 3 tablespoons maple syrup for each pound. Add thickener (ground oatmeal, wheat germ, whole grain bread crumbs) if too watery. Store leftover cooked purée in refrigerator tightly covered for up to 5 days.

Freezing: Freeze using the Food Cube Method for up to 6 months.

Rutabagas and Turnips

These two root vegetables are very similar to each other, with rutabagas having the stronger flavor.
Baby must be at least: 9 months for cooked rutabagas or turnips. See warning about nitrates, page 38.
Equivalents: 2-3 medium sized rutabagas/turnips = 1 pound.
In season: Available all year; peak October through March.
Choosing: Choose those that are smooth, firm, solid, well-shaped, and heavy for their size. They should be no more than 3 or 4 inches in diameter. If turnips come with their green tops, make sure that they are fresh-looking and green. For turnip greens, see greens on page 442.
Storing: Store turnips in plastic bags in refrigerator for up to 1 week. As with other root vegetables, immediately remove the greens so that they do not pull moisture from the root. Store rutabagas for up to two weeks in plastic in the refrigerator and up to 1 week at room temperature.
Preparation for cooking: Wash, peel with a vegetable peeler, and cut into uniform, large pieces. Don't eat the peel because it tastes bitter. Do not overcook.
Microwave: Place in dish with 3 tablespoons water for each pound rutabagas or turnips. Microwave, covered, on high for 8 minutes, stirring halfway through cooking time. Let stand, covered, for 4 minutes.
Steam: Steam 10 minutes.
Bake: Place pieces in shallow baking dish. Dot with butter and/or sprinkle with a little water. Bake at 400°F for 30 to 45 minutes.
Freezing: Purée and freeze using the Food Cube Method for up to 10 months.
Growing: See how to grow a turnip plant, page 493.

For Snap Beans, see Green Beans

For Sorrel, see Greens

For Spinach, see Greens

Squash, Summer

The many summer squashes include: chayote or mirliton, English yellow, global, pattypan, scallopini, straight-neck, sunburst, yellow crookneck, and the zucchinis (also called courgettes, Italian marrows, or Italian squash). These squash grow quickly and are harvested while their seeds are still small and immature and their rinds are still thin and tender. Cook and purée squash for your baby. Or serve grated raw summer squash as a Healthy Addition to tofu, cottage cheese, yogurt, etc. Shredded zucchini is great in bread, see Zippity Zucchini bread, page 320.
Baby must be at least: 7 months for cooked summer squash, 10 months for raw grated summer squash.
Equivalents: 1 pound summer squash = 3½ cups sliced.
In season: Available year round; peak July through September.
Choosing: Select young, small or medium summer squash—they are soft and moist. Skin should be tender enough to be easily punctured with your fingernail. Skin also should be bright, smooth, glossy, and have good color. Zucchini skin should be bright green. Summer squash

should feel firm and heavy for their size. They should have an inch of stem still attached. The best size is about six inches long and one inch in diameter or smaller. Don't buy summer squash that is dull, flabby, soggy, dry, hard, tough, or with soft spots.

Storing: Refrigerate uncut in plastic bags for up to 5 days.

Preparation for cooking: Cut off ends and discard. Do not peel. Cook small, whole zucchini that are uniform in size, or cut larger zucchini into uniform slices.

Microwave: To microwave slices: Add 2 tablespoons of water for each pound and microwave on high, covered, for 7 minutes. Stir halfway through cooking time. Let stand, covered, for 3 minutes.

To microwave small, whole, uniformly sized zucchini: Pierce with fork. Place on at least two layers of paper towels and microwave on high for 8-10 minutes per pound, turning halfway through cooking time. Let stand for 5 minutes.

Steam: Steam small, whole squash for 12 minutes. Steam slices for 5 minutes.

Bake: Bake in covered baking dish or wrapped in aluminum foil in 350°F oven for 25 minutes. No need to add water for baking.

Freezing: Purée cooked squash and freeze using the Food Cube Method. Grate raw zucchini and freeze using the Nested Plastic Bag method. Pre-measure 1 cup per bag or the amount needed for zucchini bread or your favorite recipe.

Note: Chayote squash should be peeled. It will keep longer than other summer squash in the refrigerator—up to 2 weeks.

Squash, Winter

Winter squash have thick, hard shells and fully-grown seeds, unlike summer squash, with their thin rinds and immature seeds. Winter squash have those wonderful fall colors (indicating a high vitamin A content), such as deep-orange pumpkins and dark-green acorn squash. Other winter squash are banana, buttercup, butternut, and Hubbard. Less commonly-known are Chinese, delicata, golden acorn, and sweet dumpling.

Baby must be at least: 6 months for cooked winter squash.

Equivalents: 1 pound of raw winter squash = 1 cup cooked and puréed.

In season: September through March.

Choosing: Select those with bright, hard, tough, thick shells that feel heavy for their size. Variations in skin color are OK, but don't buy squash with tender or soft rinds or those with soft, decaying spots, mold, or cuts. If squash is cut, make sure that it has a bright orange or yellow color and that it is not stringy. Small pumpkins are best for eating; large pumpkins are best for jack-o-lanterns.

Storing: Whole winter squash will keep for up to 2 months if you keep them in a cool, dark, dry, and well ventilated spot. Store cut pieces in plastic in the refrigerator for up to 5 days.

Preparation for cooking one medium squash (1 pound): Cut squash in half lengthwise. Remove seeds and fibers, but leave skin intact. Or, peel squash and remove seeds and fiber. Cut into 1-inch cubes. If you're really having trouble cutting a very hard squash, try microwaving the whole squash very briefly (30 seconds or so), just enough to soften it up a little. Pierce several places with a fork first to prevent an explosion.

Microwave: Add 3 tablespoons water to each pound of squash halves or cubes. Microwave on high, covered, for 8 minutes. (For 2 pounds, 15 minutes.) Stir or rearrange halfway through cooking time. Let stand, covered, for 4 minutes.

Steam: Steam large squash pieces for 25 minutes.

Bake: Place prepared squash halves in a baking pan. Spread cut surfaces with butter or lemon juice (if your baby is old enough for citrus) if you wish. (Some suggest to place them cut side down, but I find baking them cut side up gives them a better flavor.) Bake in pre-heated 350°F oven for 30 to 45 minutes, depending on size. Peel or scoop out flesh and purée for baby. Or, place cubes into uncovered baking dish. Sprinkle with butter, lemon juice (if your baby is old enough for citrus) and/or water. Bake in pre-heated 350°F oven for 45 minutes.

Baking a whole squash: Place on a dry baking pan. Bake in a pre-heated 350°F oven for about one hour until done. After cool, slice off top and scoop out seeds and membranes.

Testing a whole squash for doneness: Test by wrapping your finger in a towel and pressing to see if it feels soft. Don't burn yourself! Or, test for doneness by piercing with fork—squash should be tender.

Tip: To remove the flesh from squash halves, especially acorn squash, try using a serrated scoop or grapefruit spoon. It will cut out the flesh easily and cleanly.

Purée: From squash halves, peel or scoop out flesh and purée. Do not feed peel from winter squash to baby. After baking, cooled squash peel very easily. Make sure to remove all strings from the purée— they are choking hazards (page 40). Use an electric mixer to purée and those pesky strings will adhere to the beaters. Then strain (page 152) to remove any remaining strings.

Freezing: Freeze purée using the Food Cube Method for up to 2 months.

Baking a large pumpkin: Cut the top off the pumpkin just under the stem. Scoop out seeds and membranes. (Save those wonderful, nutritious pumpkin seeds.) Replace the top and place on a dry baking pan. Bake in a pre-heated 350 °F oven for 1-1½ hours. Test for doneness by following directions for a whole squash above.

Baking pumpkin seeds: Remove pulp and string and rinse seeds. Place in a single layer on ungreased baking sheet. Bake in pre-heated 325°F oven for 15-20 minutes until dry and lightly brown, or for 30-40 minutes if you like them crispy. Use as a snack or garnish for adults.

Warning: Using fresh pumpkin for pies is a lot of work. I did it once and that was enough. If you are going to try it, make sure the pumpkin purée is not too watery. To make it thicker, cook the purée in a saucepan over low heat until enough water has evaporated to make it the proper consistency. What's the proper consistency? That of canned pumpkin, of course.

Pumpkin Leather Jack-O-Lanterns: See recipe, page 206.

Tips for Carving Jack-O-Lanterns: Cut stemmed top lid out of pumpkin with knife angled inward, not vertically, to prevent lid from falling inside. Make a mark or leave a notch on lid to indicate how to turn and place the lid so that it will fit perfectly every time. Cut a small hole in lid to act as a chimney for candle smoke. Use an ice cream scoop to make hollowing out pumpkin easier, and leave a thinner wall in front so that the face will be easier to cut. (Save seeds and bake as directed above.) Tape a paper pattern to front of pumpkin; use tip of knife to punch pinholes through paper into pumpkin rind, "tracing" the design into the rind with pinholes. (Use a copy of a picture from your child's favorite story book or a copy of a photograph of your child, carve your child's name, or have your child draw a picture.) Buy a saw-like knife made especially to cut jack-o-lanterns—they are cheap and it makes cutting so much easier. If your jack-o-lantern dries up, rehydrate by soaking in water until it's as good as new. To preserve your jack-o-lantern, spray inside and out with an antiseptic spray to kill bacteria. Place a candle on a small flat fire-proof dish or layers of aluminum foil. To stabilize, adhere candle to dish by "gluing" with melted wax. Light candle with fireplace match or dry stick of spaghetti or tape a few matches to a butter knife. Lighting the candle is easier if you cut the large initial hole in the bottom of the pumpkin instead of the top. To light the candle, lift the pumpkin by the stem, leaving the bottom hole and candle exposed for lighting. Or don't use a candle at all—line the jack-o-lantern with aluminum foil and place a small string of Christmas lights inside. The cord and plug can be pulled through a hole in the back of the pumpkin. Or use a small flashlight.

Toddlers: Toddlers can safely decorate their own jack-o-lantern by drawing on a pumpkin with washable, non-toxic, felt-tip markers.

For String Beans, see Beans

Beans with strings no longer exist. Green bean growers have worked hard to make beans stringless. You probably want green beans—see Beans.

Sweet Potatoes (Yams)

Puréed sweet potato is an excellent first food for baby. The sweet potato is one of the most complete foods. Like carrots, it is a super source of beta-carotene (vitamin A). Sweet potatoes are also a good source of magnesium, potassium, and other vitamins and minerals. The dry-fleshed variety (see next paragraph) can replace white potatoes in most recipes, and they take less time to cook and reheat better. Try them instead of white potatoes in potato salad and potato pancakes. (See recipes for these as well as Mr./Ms. Sweet Potato Heads, pages 301-303.) Sweet potatoes are also one of the easiest vegetables to prepare. Just pierce them with a fork, pop them in the microwave, cut them in half, scoop out the flesh, and fork-mash for baby.

There are two varieties of sweet potato sold in the United States: *moist-fleshed*, which has bright orange flesh that is sweet and moist when cooked, and *dry-fleshed*, which has ivory-colored flesh that is dry and mealy (like white potatoes) when cooked. The moister and sweeter variety is usually labeled "yam," even though it's really a sweet potato. Real yams are foreign-grown and cannot usually be found on our supermarket shelves. This is good because yams have virtually no vitamin A, but sweet potatoes are loaded with it. Be gentle with sweet potatoes, as they damage easily.

Baby must be at least: 4 months for cooked, puréed sweet potatoes.

Equivalents: 3 medium sweet potatoes = 1 pound = 3 cups sliced = 2½ cups puréed.

In season: Available year round; peak October through December.

Choosing: Buy them loose so you can get a good look at each one. Select small- to medium-sized, thick, chunky, well-shaped sweet potatoes that taper toward the ends. Skin should be dry, firm, bright, smooth, and uniformly colored. Try to get them unwaxed. Wax used on produce is supposedly safe, but it may contain pesticide residues. Avoid potatoes with cuts, worm holes, or other damage. Decay, found often in sweet potatoes, can be in the form of shriveled ends or wet, soft, discolored, or sunken areas in the skin. Cutting out a damaged area does no good. One bad spot ruins the whole potato and the rest of the potato that still looks good will probably be affected and taste bad. So, discard the entire potato if there is any serious injury.

Storing: Store in a dark, cool (50° F) place in a perforated (so moisture doesn't build) plastic bag for several weeks. Or, keep them at room temperature for up to one week. You may hear that you shouldn't store raw sweet potatoes in the refrigerator. Actually, you can store them in a plastic bag in the refrigerator for up to 10 days if you make sure they don't freeze. If even a little part of a potato freezes, the whole potato will taste bitter. After cooking, store them in the refrigerator for up to 5 days.

Preparation for cooking: Wash by scrubbing gently and do not peel.

Microwaving: Pierce several holes in the potatoes with a fork. Place on at least two layers of white paper towels. Microwave one ½-pound sweet potato on high for 5 minutes, turning halfway through cooking time. If you're microwaving more than one potato, add 2 to 3 minutes for each additional potato. If you're microwaving more than two potatoes, arrange like a star or wagon-wheel spokes. Let stand for 5 minutes.

Steaming: Steam whole sweet potatoes for 30 or more minutes.

Baking: Pierce several holes in the potatoes with a fork. If you wish, rub skin with butter. Bake, uncovered, in a 400°F oven for about 45 minutes, or in a 375°F oven for 55 minutes.
Boiling: Boil enough water to cover potatoes. Place washed, whole unpeeled, potatoes in boiling water, cover pot, and cook for 20-30 minutes until tender. Drain boiling water and drop potatoes into cold water and peels will slip right off.
Puréeing: Cut cooked potato in half. Scoop out flesh and mash with fork, potato masher, or mixer to purée. (If peeled, as in previous boiling paragraph, you can just put the whole potatoes in a bowl and mash.) For young babies who need a very smooth consistency, use your food processor or blender. For large sweet potatoes, which tend to be fibrous, a mixer is better to purée because the stringy fibers will collect on the beaters and leave the mash smooth. Make sure to remove all strings from the purée—they are choking hazards (page 40). Use an electric mixer to purée the strings will adhere to the beaters. Then strain (page 152) to remove any remaining strings.
Freezing: Freeze puréed sweet potatoes using the Food Cube Method for up to 2 months. Add a little lemon juice (if your baby is old enough for citrus) to prevent discoloration, if your baby is old enough for citrus. I never do, and my sweet potato cubes stay a nice orange color anyway.
Growing: See appendix for how to grow a sweet potato plant, page 493.

For Swiss Chard, see Greens

For Tangerines, see Citrus Fruits

Tomatoes

If you've ever tasted a fresh ripe red tomato right off the vine, you know that there's no comparison in taste to the supermarket variety. It would be too expensive to let mass-grown tomatoes ripen on the vine, so commercially grown tomatoes are picked before ripe and ripen in transit. Even "vine-ripened" tomatoes are picked when they are still pink and before they turn red. Some agribusiness tomatoes are even ripened in the truck while in transit. Ethylene gas is used in the truck to do the trick. If you can't get your hands on yours (or a friend's) home-grown tomatoes, the next best thing is your local Farmers' Market or a roadside stand. Vine-ripened tomatoes will have much more vitamin C and other nutrients than those gassed-to-ripeness or those ripened off the vine. Tomatoes are really a fruit, not a vegetable.

Small chunks of the soft inner part of raw tomatoes, without seeds or peels, are a nutritious finger food for toddlers.
Baby must be at least: 1 year for raw tomatoes or tomato juice.
Equivalents: 3 medium tomatoes = 1 pound = 1 ½ cups peeled, seeded, and chopped
In season: Available year round; peak June through August.
Choosing: Select firm, plump, smooth, well-formed tomatoes with good uniform color. They should feel heavy for their size. It's OK if there are a few small scars near the stem, but don't buy those with large cracks. Those that were vine-ripened have a fresh tomato-y smell, whereas those gas-ripened are odorless. Don't buy overripe tomatoes—soft or watery tomatoes and those with wet spots, depressions, mold, or bruises. Cherry tomatoes are usually flavorful.
Ripen: Ripen at room temperature away from sunlight for up to 5 days, but only if they have not been previously refrigerated. Ripe tomatoes will be a good red color and yield to gentle pressure. If you need a ripe tomato fast, put a tomato in a paper bag with an apple. The apple will release ethylene gas and speed the tomato's ripening. Sunlight will not speed tomatoes' ripening, it only softens them.

Storing: Once ripened, tomatoes will store for up to another week at room temperature. Keep them away from sunlight. Try to use tomatoes before you must refrigerate them, because cool temperatures take away their sweetness. If a tomato is becoming overripe, then go ahead and put it in the refrigerator. When it comes time to eat, place it at room temperature for an hour or so, until the chill goes. Tomatoes taste much better at room temperature than when chilled. Store cut tomatoes tightly wrapped in plastic in the refrigerator for up to 2 days. Remember to keep cut tomatoes out of air, warmth, and light to preserve the vitamin C.

Preparation: Cut tomato in half and remove seeds. Scoop out the flesh and purée.

Tip: For tomatoes in salads, slice vertically and the slices will stay firmer.

Freezing: Freeze purée using the Food Cube Method for up to 1 year. Whole tomatoes or pieces don't need blanching before you freeze them in freezer bags—core them first. Frozen tomatoes are very easy to peel. When thawed, tomato pieces will be mushy; use in sauces, soups, and stews.

Canned tomatoes: Sometimes canned tomatoes are better than the poor quality raw tomatoes discussed above. Read the label carefully and don't buy cans with salt, sugar, or preservatives added. Tomato paste or tomato purée in the can should not be fed to your baby—both are concentrated, but they are OK to use in baby's pasta sauce. Try to buy cans with an expiration date, as canned tomato products don't keep as long as other canned vegetables. Store opened canned tomato product leftovers in tightly covered glass jars for up to 1 week in the refrigerator. If you leave them in the can, they sometimes pick up a tinny or metallic flavor. See more about canned foods on page 37.

Sauce: Don't go through the trouble of peeling and seeding tomatoes for sauce. Throw the whole tomato in the processor and blend away.

For Turnips, see Rutabagas

Watermelon

Baby must be at least: 8 months.

In season: Available April through September; peak June through August.

Choosing: Select whole melons that feel smooth and look slightly dull, not shiny. They should be symmetrically shaped with full rounded, not flat, ends. The rind should be light green with dark green veins. The underside should have a cream or light yellowish color, not white or pale green. All of these indicators still do not insure a good watermelon. You just can't judge a watermelon by its cover. It's best to buy melon already cut. Look for red, crisp, firm, and juicy flesh, which is not dry, mushy, fibrous, or stringy and has no white streaks running lengthwise through it. Seeds should be dark and black or dark brown, not white, which is a sign of immaturity.

Storing: Keep whole melon in the refrigerator for up to one week. If you don't have the refrigerator room, whole melons can be kept at room temperature for a few days. If melon is cut, wrap pieces tightly in plastic and store in refrigerator for up to 4 days.

Freezing: Follow directions for freezing cantaloupe, page 433.

For Waxed Beans, see Beans
For Yellow Beans, see Beans
For Yams, see Sweet Potatoes
For Zucchini, see Squash, Summer

B. Homemade Baby Products

Baby's Personal Accessories

Commercial Baby Wipes. Stock up on commercial baby wipes when they go on sale. If they get too dry, simply add water. The cheapest wipes I've found are the big container of Wash-A-Bye®, but my favorite are Huggies® because they are so thick and cloth-like. Keep in mind that the bargain brands are not really a bargain if you have to use more than one or two wipes for one diaper change. Buy no more than one package of travel container baby wipes for the purpose of obtaining the container and keep re-filling it.

Homemade Baby Wipes. You can save money if you make your own homemade baby wipes. For the liquid, mix

two cups water
two tablespoons of baby oil
two tablespoons of *either* baby shampoo *or* baby wash
a tablespoon or two of aloe gel squeezed from a houseplant
(optional)
7-8 drops of lavender oil for a great fragrance that will also help kill
bacteria (optional) Lavender oil can be found at a natural foods
store or an arts and crafts store.

> **TIP:** If the wipes turn out too dry, add more water. If they are too wet, leave the top of the container off to allow some of the water to evaporate. Make a note on how much you had to adjust the water in the liquid recipe above so you will remember for next time.

For homemade **disposable** baby wipes, you can use a half a roll of paper towels. Use a brand that is re-usable or microwave-able because they tend to be the strongest and most like cloth. Kleenex Viva 55 sheets are good, and so are white Bounty quilted. Cut a roll in half by using an electric knife or a sharp non-serrated knife (serrated causes small bits of toweling). Remove the inside tube core—use a pair of plyers and it will be easy. Place the half roll in a cylindrical container (an old baby wipe container or a cylindrical Rubbermaid® container as shown in the picture above). Save the other half of the roll for the next batch or make up two containers at one time. Make two cups of liquid above. Pour the liquid into the container, cover, and turn the container upside down. Let it sit for 15 minutes to allow the liquid to be absorbed. Open the container and pull out the first towel from the *inside* of the roll and pull it through the hole in the top. If your container has no hole in the lid, take a sharp knife and cut an X in the lid. Cut off a little of the plastic from the four inside corners of the X to make a small hole. The hole will allow the paper towels to be pulled out without shredding.

Disposable wipes can be made more easily with individual paper towels in stacks. Use the kind that you pull out of dispensers in public restrooms, not the brown stuff that's as stiff as grocery bags. The softer white towels may be difficult to find. Try a restaurant supply or medical supply store.

Disposable cotton squares—the ones used for makeup removal—can also be used as baby wipes.

You may prefer to use plain **dry tissues** as baby wipes, because they are so easy and convenient and soooo soft. Use a good brand tissue, such as Puffs® Advanced Extra Strength—they are still much cheaper than paper towels. Keep the liquid recipe above in a spray bottle and shake well before use. Spritz baby's fanny with the liquid and wipe clean with tissue. Instead of the liquid recipe, a little baking soda in water can be used. The soda will neutralize the acidity of a diaper rash and soothe baby's skin. Or, use plain water or plain water with a little aloe mixed in. Some parents claim that their babies get reactions from wipe solutions.

For homemade **machine washable** baby wipes, use pieces of old cloth diapers cut to size. Or use pieces of terry cloth washcloths or an old towel. You can buy packs of cheap washcloths in department stores and cut them in halves or quarters. I found 50 all-cotton, *soft* washcloths at Sam's Club for about $10. These homemade cloth baby wipes can be washed with cloth diapers, if you use them. Huggies brand baby wipes can be machine washed and re-used.

Homemade Bibs. Cloth pullover bibs with —the ones that cost $4-5 in baby stores—can be homemade from an old sweatshirt, dickey style. Cut the neck and chest parts out of the sweatshirt. To prevent fraying, cut with pinking sheers or zig zag the edges. Fold up the bottom to form a food-catcher pocket.

A waterproof bib for baby or yourself can be made from an old sterile shower curtain (machine wash in hot water and bleach). Use duct tape, your sewing machine, and velcro tabs (available at craft and sewing stores) to finish. Don't use string to tie a bib around baby's neck; it's a strangulation hazard.

A large men's shirt worn backwards will also work as a bib for you; a smaller boy's/girl's shirt will work for baby.

Use the tops of old socks to protect your child's sleeves.

For Diaper Rash. Use plain white solid shortening (Crisco® or generic brand) as a preventative barrier to wetness and acidity as soon as you see your baby developing a diaper rash. If baby cries when you touch his bottom, smooth the shortening on the diaper instead of his skin and it will be applied painlessly when you put the diaper on.

> **TIP:** Use your pinky and ring finger to spread diaper cream and your other three fingers will remain clean and dry to tape the diaper.

Breast milk applied directly to baby's skin will soothe and help clear up a diaper rash. No kidding! Squeeze some liquid from your aloe house plant and smooth on baby's bottom to help soothe diaper rash. Put a few tablespoons of baking soda in baby's bath water to neutralize the acidity of a diaper rash and to soothe baby's skin. Or while changing a diaper and during potty training, rinse a wash cloth in a sink half filled with comfortably warm water and a few tablespoons of baking soda. Squeeze out excess water and wipe your little one clean to alleviate urine odor and soothe the rash. Or try the spray bottle with water and baking soda and dry tissue method on page 465.

Diaper Powder. The days of powder made from talc are gone, since it was discovered that talc can be inhaled into baby's lungs. Never let baby play with powder—some babies have actually died while playing with talc baby powder. If you do wish to use powder to keep baby dry, use a little cornstarch on an old powder puff or smooth it on baby directly with your hand. If using a commercial powder, save money and use less by taping most of the holes closed.

Diapers. Dundee sells irregular diapers direct from the factory via mail order. You may wish to call them before you purchase large amounts of cloth diapers: 800-522-3388.

I got tired of paying big bucks for the overnight diapers. Before my in-toilet-training son went to bed, I put on him my own cloth diaper contraption: I folded and placed two or three wipe-up towels, washcloths, or a cotton diaper between his legs inside his underpants, over which I put rubber training pants. Worked just fine for those nights when my son had an accident, and I figure I saved the better part of a dollar each time. By the way, I had to put this contraption on him after he had fallen fast asleep.

Diaper Mat. In an emergency, a large plastic storage bag or a sheet of wax paper can be used as a diaper changing mat. Keep one folded up in the diaper bag.

Hair Detanglers. The commercial spray detanglers and conditioners that you buy for your baby's hair are nothing more than very dilute solutions of hair conditioner. Make your own by adding one or two tablespoons of baby-safe hair conditioner into a pump or spray bottle and fill with water. Shake well before each use. I sometimes use this for my own hair after shampooing and towel drying. But most times, while I'm still in the shower and after shampooing, I take a tiny dollop (about ½ teaspoon) of regular hair conditioner, spread it on the palms of my hands, and massage it through my hair. I don't rinse and this "leave-in conditioner" makes my hair as soft and tangle free as when I use a lot of conditioner and rinse it out. This method makes a bottle of conditioner last for years. As a bonus, you also save time and water in the shower because you don't have to rinse.

Hairspray. Don't spray commercial hairspray around your baby and allow him to inhale it, or around yourself for that matter! Homemade hairspray can be made by mixing a little of any of the following sticky ingredients into water: lemon juice, honey, corn syrup, or even Elmer's glue! This may sound strange, but it's better than using the commercial hair sprays—who knows what goes into them. You will feel safer using homemade spray to hold down baby's stubborn hairs for those posed baby pictures (you know all about those "1000 pictures for $4.95 plus sitting fee" specials). Boil the water before adding the sticky stuff. Use an empty commercial hair spray pump bottle, cleaned well. For your first batch, try adding two tablespoons of corn syrup to ½ cup of boiling water, stir until dissolved, let cool, and pour into pump spray bottle. Or try this homemade citrus hair spray: Peel and chop one lemon (or for dry hair, one orange). Place in a pot and cover with two cups of water. Bring to a boil and keep boiling until liquid is reduced to one cup. Let cool, strain, and keep refrigerated in a spray bottle.

> **MONEY SAVER:** If you use non-aerosol commercial hairspray in a pump bottle, try diluting the liquid with an equal amount of water. You have just reduced your price by half and you will probably find that it works just as well. Use an empty pump bottle and mix half hair spray, half water. Try this with just a little hair spray first, not half of a bottle, in case you don't like it.

Hair Gel. Dissolve ½-1 teaspoon of unflavored gelatin in one cup of warm water. Keep refrigerated and use as you would a commercial hair gel—it works just as well. If you use commercial hair gel, try diluting it with water. You may find that it actually works better because it's less stiff and easier to smooth into your hair.

Mom's and Dad's Deodorant. If you are breastfeeding or even if you are not, it's probably a good idea to prevent your baby from inhaling deodorant when you are holding her close. I believe that deodorant isn't necessary at all, except maybe on hot sticky days. Plain baking soda will keep you dry and comfortable. Sprinkle about ½ teaspoon onto the palm of your hand and smooth it under your arm.

Baby Clothes

Don't discard baby clothes with minor damage which can be fixed. Use fabric markers to color in bleach spots. Or use paint, food coloring, or matching color crayon. Heat the spot with an iron, color with crayon, and set the color by placing a sheet of wax paper over the spot and ironing the spot again. Protect your iron from wax paper by placing a piece of brown paper from a grocery bag between the iron and the wax paper.

Spit-up stains are impossible to get out of used baby clothing. Try applying Dawn® dishwashing liquid directly to the stain, or try the Super Clothing Stain Remover, page 480. If nothing works, dye the entire item a darker color. Onsies® are cute when tie-dyed.

Camouflage tears or stains in clothing with a patch cut from a matching or contrasting fabric in a Simple Shape (pages 367-368). Sew it over the damage to make it look like it was a decoration originally designed into the clothes item. Add more patches for symmetry or a continuous pattern. Or use colored iron-on patches cut into Simple Shapes. Place aluminum foil on the ironing board under the hole, so that the glue doesn't melt onto the ironing board cover.

Baby clothes with stains can still be worn if they are under another clothes item. For example, who cares if a baby's t-shirt has a stain if it's under a new-looking shirt and cannot be seen.

Sew or iron patches to the inside or outside of a crawling baby's pants to strengthen the knees or to hide worn knees. For an expensive look, sew a corduroy, vinyl, or leather patch over the knees. (Cut the vinyl/leather patch from an old purse or boot.) Cut the patch into a Simple Shape (pages 367-368) for a cute touch. Knee pads can be made from sweatbands or the cuffs from an old pair of thick adult socks (cut the foot off). Fold to reduce to a few inches in length and to thicken, then zig zag stitch. These can be used on your crawling baby's bare knees or over his pants. Be sure they are not too tight around the knees. Make yourself a similar pair of knee pads with old socks and sponges or shoulder pads. Sure makes kneeling to clean floors easier!

Use the cuffs from white or colored socks as pony-tail holders or wrist sweat bands. Long cuffs from adult cotton socks can be used to protect children's sleeves from getting dirty while eating or painting.

Rings from milk jugs make good sock holders.

Buy many identical socks. All pairs will be a match and if you lose two socks, you've only lost one pair.

Make non-slip socks by putting non-toxic fabric puff paint on the bottom of baby's plain socks. (You can often find puff paint in undesirable colors on sale at fabric stores.) Follow washing instructions for puff paint. Check often to make sure pieces have not come off—they are choking hazards. Or sew on pieces of self-sticking bathtub appliques. Puff paint and appliques can also be used to prevent throw rugs from slipping. Be careful about ruining the floor underneath.

Sew non-slip patches to the bottom of a child's pajama feet to help prevent falls. Stick small bits of non-slip bath appliques to the bottom of new shoes to make them less slippery.

A missing zipper pull tab can be replaced with a paper clip. Sew matching fabric over the paper clip to camouflage it and to contain sharp wire ends. Zippers will slide more easily if you rub them with wax paper, a bar of soap, or a bit of petroleum jelly.

Pulled threads on sweaters or other clothing can be fixed by using a crochet needle to pull them through the fabric to the inside of the garment. Knot them to prevent the strings from catching and pulling, causing more damage.

Instead of using thread, use dental floss to sew buttons on your child's clothes, stuffed toys, or doll clothes. It is much stronger than thread and it can be touched up with marker to match the color of the garment.

Fix a shoe lace that is frayed on the end with a dab of nail polish, white glue, a piece of clear tape, or some melted crayon/candle wax to make it stiff again. (Use this same idea on a string that is difficult to thread. Dip it in a bottle of nail polish, let it dry, and thread away.)

Don't pay a fortune for fancy shoe laces. Decorate plain shoelaces with colorful permanent markers. Or use fancy or glittery ribbons as shoelaces. Strengthen the ribbon, if necessary, by folding and sewing around a plain shoelace. Or use colorful pipe cleaners as shoelaces.

Use a dab of petroleum jelly to polish baby's patent leather shoes and make them shine, and to protect them from snow and rain. Apply olive oil or a nut oil to leather with a chamois cloth.

Lace collars on baby's clothes (or doll clothes) can be freshened by ironing them between two sheets of wax paper. Protect your iron and ironing board by placing paper from a brown grocery bag between the wax paper and the iron and ironing board.

Use a damp sponge to remove hair and lint from clothing.

Bend the outer ends of wire hangers down to make baby clothes-sized hangers.

Styrofoam egg cartons will prevent the tops of boots from bending down.

If boots spring a leak, place plastic bags over your child's socks before putting on the boots. Your child's socks and feet will be kept dry and warm.

If over-the-shoe boots are too difficult to get on and off, try placing a plastic bag over the shoe before putting on the boot. Store the bag in the boot until it's time to go home.

When shoes and boots get wet inside, place a hand-held hair dryer into them part way and set the dryer on low heat. They will be dry in minutes. Watch very carefully for over-heating.

In my opinion, it was too expensive to buy snow boots for my twins when they were very young. They rarely used them, and when they did, it would be for only a few minutes outside and then they'd want to come back in the house. They grew out of them in one year, so I decided not to buy them boots until they were much older. Until then, for playing in the snow, first I put on their regular socks and shoes, second I put plastic freezer bags over their shoes, and third I put an old pair of adult thick socks over the bags to hold them in place. This worked just fine—it kept their feet and ankles dry and warm.

For gloves, I placed a cheap pair of baby gloves or a pair of cotton socks on their little hands. Then I placed over the gloves/socks a thick pair of adult wooly socks. The socks went up to their elbows and prevented snow from getting on their wrists and up their sleeves.

For snow pants, I sprayed a cheap pair of a size-too-big sweat pants with Scotchgard® protector for fabric that repels spills. The directions will tell you how to do this. (Spray outside so kids don't inhale it.) The twins wore these pants over a regular pair of sweat pants, winter pajama bottoms, or long winter underwear. The two pairs of pants kept them warm, and snow and water rolled off the outer Scotchgarded pair.

To prevent the loss of gloves, sew buttons on them. Your child can then button them into the front buttonholes of her coat. Two matching buttons on the knuckles will look like eyes if you add a nose and smile with yarn.

Safety

Metal seat belt buckles get burning hot when the sun shines on them or when the inside of your car gets hot. Cover the metal parts with terrycloth wrist bands or with the cuffs cut from old socks.

Tape old shoulder pads to the sharp corners of tables and other furniture to prevent baby from getting bruised. Or use stuffing from an old pillow, a rolled up sock, or half or a quarter of a tennis ball.

The corners and edges of cardboard boxes can be taped over the edges of table corners or on a brick fireplace raised hearth. Add some padding under the cardboard to prevent bruises. Or sew your baby's old crib bumpers together and use as a padding.

Instead of buying plastic covers for your electrical outlets, improvise a baby-proof cover with plain electrical tape. Unscrew and remove the cover of the outlet, place electrical tape over the slits, and then replace the cover. The cover should hold the tape securely in place. The disadvantage of this method, of course, is that you cannot plug an appliance into the outlet.

Keep kids riding bicycles out of the street by stretching an extension ladder across the end of the driveway.

For a clean play area, place a child who is not mobile on a large flat sheet. Toys can be picked up in a moment by gathering the corners, and the sheet is easily machine washed.

Drape a towel over the top of the bedroom/bathroom door to prevent children from locking themselves in.

Prevent your toddler from opening a door at Grandma's or a friend's house by using a strong rubber band to hold a sock over the doorknob.

Place large sponges under crib wheels to prevent it from the crib from "walking" when baby shakes it.

Keep unopened fast food packets of ketchup in your freezer for use as an ice pack for little boo-boos. Or small balloons filled with water and frozen. A package of frozen peas or other frozen vegetables wrapped in a thin cloth is good for bigger boo-boos.

Decorate a band-aid with stickers or non-toxic markers. If it hurts to remove a band-aid, try rubbing it with vegetable oil or heating the adhesive with a hair dryer.

Before removing a splinter, numb the area with an ice cube or some teething pain reliever.

In a public place, "label" your child with a suitcase address tag or a pet tag engraved with your child's name, address, and phone number. Use a safe diaper pin to attach it to your child's coat. A pet tag is small enough to fit on your child's shoe.

Be ready for anything while away from home. Keep emergency supplies in the trunk of your car along with the supplies listed on page 83.

When in public, your family should always have a pre-determined place to meet if you lose each other. Choose a unique, familiar, and easily-seen landmark: the center fountain in a mall, the ferris wheel at the amusement park, etc. A default rule to have in case you forgot to set a meeting place is this: young folks remain clearly visible in a safe place and wait for the adults to find them. Otherwise, if you both walk around looking for each other, you can pass each other like two ships in the night for hours. Teach your little one what to do if she gets lost. For example, go to the nearest cash register and tell the person in the dark blue coat that you are lost. Or put a sheet of paper with information in her pocket and tell her to give it to a "safe" adult. Go over the plan several times until she can repeat it back to you.

Baby Furniture

See tips for used high chairs on page 19.

Rub wax paper or petroleum jelly on your baby's high chair if the tray begins to stick. Or on your baby's crib runners to make them glide smoothly.

King size pillow cases will fit some baby changing table pads and infant beds.

Place an old sterile shower curtain (machine wash in hot water and bleach) between the mattress and bed covers to protect the mattress from a bed wetter.

Bath Accessories

Bathtub Toy Bag. Instead of buying the net bag for holding your child's toys in the tub, why not use a large nylon net from oranges or onions or a waterproof net laundry bag. Hang them with suction cups where the water will drain back into the tub. A plastic garbage bag with holes poked in the bottom for drainage works well, but remember that it is a suffocation hazard so hang it high out of baby's reach on the shower faucet. (The same can be used at the beach—fill it with toys and dunk to rinse off all of that sand.) I use a large laundry basket by the side of the tub. My little one can then take and return his toys by himself. When the basket needs a cleaning, I dip in into the tub when the baby is done and use the bath water to wash it..

Non-Slip Holders. Use a white cotton glove when bathing baby and you can keep a better grip on her. If you use bar soap, tie it inside part of an old pair of pantyhose. No more dropping slippery soap!

Bath Bottles. Buy the fancy bottles shaped like your child's favorite cartoon characters only once (when they are on sale and you have a coupon). Then keep refilling them with the cheaper bottles of baby shampoos, conditioners, baby washes, and soaps. If they get gooey, wash the bottles in the bathtub water with an old toothbrush.

Shampoo. It is less clumsy if you use a squeeze bottle for applying shampoo—you also use less and save money. Dilute baby shampoo with water (at least one part water to three parts shampoo) to use less and save more money. Make shampooing fun by forming your child's hair full of shampoo into spikes and other shapes and letting him look in a mirror. Kids usually hate to get their hair shampooed because water and soap get in their eyes and ears. Rub a slanted line of petroleum jelly on your child's forehead just over the eyebrows so shampoo will run off to the side instead of into his eyes. Give your child a small hand towel to hold over his eyes and ears while you shampoo. If your child will not lie down in the bathtub water, rinse the shampoo out by pouring water over his hair. Place your one hand over your child's eyes sun-visor style to help prevent water from running down his face. Use your second hand to pour rinse water down the back of his head while he holds his head way back. A lightweight pitcher filled one time for rinsing is easier and much faster than a small cup filled several times. Distract and relax him by asking him to "quack" at a rubber duck held over his head with your third hand.

Those of us with only two hands can hang the rubber duck from the shower curtain rod or shower head. Another possibility is some type of waterproof inclined plane that your child can lie back on while you wash his hair.

More bath tips. Let your child's towel double as a big bib for you to help keep you dry—use a large diaper pin to keep it around your neck. When bath time is over, you can hug your child dry! ✲Don't discard those leftover slivers of bar soap. Wet and stick them to a new bar of soap. They'll become one with the new bar. ✲At the end of your shower, place a little baby oil on a wet washcloth and rub it all over your skin. Unlike applying it with your hands, the washcloth prevents the shower floor from getting slippery and saves money because you use so little. ✲Unwrap bar soap and let it open to the air; it will freshen your cabinet and become harder and last longer. ✲Help your boy toddler-in-training improve his aim by floating a Cheerio or a square of toilet paper in the toilet as a target. ✲See page 400 for more bathtub fun!

Baby Linens

If you sew, even just a little, you can save money by buying baby sheets on sale and making a matching comforter, crib ruffle, and curtains for baby's windows. Buy a pattern that has bright primary colors, not pastels, for baby's room. A matching stretchy fabric can be folded into a triangle to make a stuffed toy hammock. Tie ends tightly around three large metal rings and place on three hooks on a wall in a corner of the room. Make an infant head support by stuffing a sleeve from an old sweatshirt and sewing it around a piece of semi-circular fabric. Use a friend's commercial head support as a pattern, to make sure that your design is safe.

Storage

For more organization and storage space, make shelves and cubby holes by hot-gluing cardboard boxes together. Or use large juice cans with no jagged edges. Decorate with wallpaper, decorative self-adhesive paper, fabric, or non-toxic paint. Hang smaller shelves on the wall above the changing table. Larger shelves on the floor can hold your toddler's toys.

Make your own modular toy holders with an old bookshelf unit (pick one up at a garage sale), or buy several plastic storage crates at the local hardware store. Place several kitchen dishpans on the shelves to hold toys. Note how much these modular units sell for in baby stores and toy catalogs!

Line baby's drawers with pretty baby gift wrapping paper. Iron the wrong side to remove wrinkles in used gift paper.

Use clean Styrofoam egg cartons as drawer organizers to hold baby's socks and other small items. Keep out of baby's reach—bitten pieces of Styrofoam are choking hazards.

A lower rod can be added to baby's closet with a shower curtain rod cut to size, swing chains, and metal self-closing shower curtain rings.

Make your child her own personal coat hanger from a piece of wood and golf tees. Paint it her favorite color and personalize it with her name.

An old dish drainer will hold children's books and records upright. Crayons and markers fit nicely in the silverware holder.

Use the playpen (that your child refuses to use) as a large toy chest.

C. Baby-Safe Household Cleaning Products

Children Are More Important than the Carpet

Brace yourself before reading this paragraph. This is a heartbreaking true story about someone I've known since childhood: Back a few generations ago, when most moms were stay-at-home and cabinet locks were not yet invented, a neighbor and dear friend of mine got under his mother's sink during his toddler years. The crystal drain opener, which looked like candy, was easy to reach. He tasted it. It burned his mouth instantly and so badly that he was deformed for life. He's embarrassed about his looks and his dribbling. Kids constantly made fun of him. He has had over a dozen painful plastic surgeries, but as an adult, his injuries are still obvious. He has suffered as much emotionally as physically. His mother never forgave herself.

I'm sorry. I know this is terribly upsetting. But I would rather have you be upset than to have anything like this happen to your child. Children are more important than a sparkling clean house. For your children's sake, choose to use only baby-safe products. Before your baby becomes mobile, go through your entire house, including the basement and garage, and get rid of any poisonous substances: insecticides, weed killers, drain cleaners, etc. You don't need them if you use the recipes in this chapter. Make sure that any other home or building your baby may visit—grandma's, the babysitter's, a friend's, etc.—is as safe for your baby as your home is.

WARNING: BLEACH + AMMONIA = DANGER!! Never mix bleach (or any product containing bleach) with ammonia (or any product containing ammonia). Mixing bleach and ammonia will cause a dangerous gas to form, which is a health hazard if inhaled and may even be lethal. The same is true for BLEACH+VINEGAR and BLEACH+TOILET BOWL CLEANER.

WARNING: A baby or toddler can drown in a pail or bucket of water within minutes. Watch both the pail and your baby every second until you've poured the water down the drain and put the pail away. Keep the lids locked down on your toilets, too. A little baby boy in my own home town tragically drown in a toilet. It can happen to anyone.

Please read the chapter *Important Safety Warnings* (page 35.)

Ingredients for Safe
Household Cleaning Solutions

Here are some staples to have on hand for the recipes in this section:

- **Baking soda** (sodium bicarbonate)—the same stuff you use in cakes and other baked goods. Buy it in bulk at the supermarket, department store, or your natural foods store.

- **Washing soda** is similar to baking soda in that it is mined from the same mineral (trona) and is refined to sodium bicarbonate. But not as refined as baking soda. It is therefore more caustic, non-edible, and less expensive. Look for it near the laundry detergents in the supermarket.

- Plain white **vinegar** is mentioned a lot in this section. It is much cheaper to buy the generic brand by the gallon than it is to buy the top named brands in the small glass bottles.

- **Vanilla** smells delicious and is used in some of the recipes here. Why buy vanilla scented cologne when you can dab real vanilla extract behind your ears to smell pretty? (Real vanilla extract is expensive, make your own—see recipe, page 355.)

- **Cornstarch**. The same white powder you use for thickening sauces.

- **Liquid soap**, not detergent, from the natural foods store. See the section *Laundry Soap and Detergent* on page 479 for how they differ.

- **Borax** is found near the laundry detergents at the supermarket. It is a mineral that occurs naturally and is safe for the environment, but it is not baby-safe so *keep it out of baby's reach*. It is also an eye and skin irritant and is harmful if swallowed. But sometimes you do need something strong to get parts of your home clean, and borax is one of the acceptable ingredients for these purposes. It is a disinfectant and a deodorant. Just be very careful when the baby is around.

- Next time you're at the local X-mart department store, pick up some empty transparent plastic trigger **spray bottles** for your homemade cleaning solutions. Do not use poisonous aerosol spray cans in your home; they only serve to deposit toxins in the air and into your family's lungs.

- Check out the cleaning products that are environmentally friendly and baby safe at your local natural foods store. *Soapworks* has soap that is "natural effective, human and earth-friendly." Call 888-883-SOAP (7627) or visit www.soapworks.com. Harmony (The Seventh Generation catalog) sells many "products in harmony with the earth," call 800-869-3446 or fax 800-456-1139 for a catalog.

- Products containing ammonia should not be used in a home with a baby (or any living beings). **Ammonia is dangerous** if swallowed and its fumes should not be inhaled. It is an eye and skin irritant and may cause burns. Never use any product containing ammonia in an aerosol can.

Economical, Homemade, Baby-Safe, and Environment-Friendly Cleaning Products

Window Cleaner

Mix water and white vinegar in a spray trigger bottle. Use anywhere from one tablespoon vinegar per cup of water to a solution of half vinegar and half water. Add a few drops of blue or green food coloring if you miss the tint. Try using newspaper as a lint-free "cloth" to wipe windows clean—it works! For a final touch that will make windows dazzling, rub dry windows with a clean blackboard eraser. To remove a scratch from window or glass, try rubbing a little toothpaste into it and polish.

> **NOTE:** If vinegar and water cause your windows to look streaky, there is probably a wax buildup on your windows from previous commercial window cleaners. Remove the wax with rubbing alcohol. Vinegar and water will then work just beautifully.

> **TIP:** Do your windows or drawers stick? Try "painting" their inside moldings or glides with petroleum jelly by using a small paint brush. Or rub them with soap.

In the winter on your car that is kept outside, coat the windows with a mixture of one part water and three parts vinegar to keep them frost- and ice-free.

All Purpose Cleaner

For general heavy-duty cleaning around the home, try this solution: Into a warm gallon of water, stir one tablespoon of borax and one tablespoon of liquid soap (not detergent). For grease cutting purposes, also include a tablespoon or more of vinegar. See warning about babies drowning, page 473. For all-purpose cleaning, mix ½ cup vinegar and ¼ cup baking soda into a gallon of warm water.

Furniture and Floor Polish

The main ingredient in most commercial furniture polishes is mineral oil, which gets absorbed into the wood. You can mix your own by adding a little lemon oil to mineral oil, but it is better with a baby around the house to use an edible oil. Mineral oil is not safe for a baby to drink. Any oil can be used to polish wood furniture: olive oil, corn oil, any vegetable oil, and even mayonnaise. Any smells will dissipate and the oil will not become rancid on your furniture. Be careful not to stain cloth, furniture, or rugs. Another recipe: Mix one part vinegar with two parts olive oil. (Use white vinegar for light furniture and cider vinegar for dark wood furniture.) Or, mix one part lemon juice to two parts olive or other vegetable oil in a spray bottle, shake well, and have fun dusting! Keep refrigerated. Clean the spray bottle as described in the Homemade Oil-Spray recipe on page 275. Clean mahogany with equal parts vinegar and water. Another more economical recipe for furniture polish: Add ½-1 tablespoon olive oil and ½-1 teaspoon vinegar to 1 cup *warm* tap water in a spray bottle. Mix it fresh each time because it should be warm while you are using it. Use a mixture of equal parts white vinegar and vegetable oil on wood floors. Apply a thin coat of this mixture and rub in well.

> **WARNING:** Use a disposable rag to polish with vegetable oil, which will become rancid on the cloth. See warning about vegetable oil and clothing, page 275.

Cleaner for Baby's Toys

Don't use poisonous disinfectants to wash your baby's things. Mix a little baking soda into a cup of warm water and wipe down baby's crib railing, car seats, playpens, etc. Also, plain white vinegar can be used as a mild disinfectant. Mix with water and clean baby's things, but first test on an inconspicuous spot for color fastness and to prevent other possible damage. Plain hot water will wash away and kill some of the germs.

Clean stuffed toys by sprinkling liberally with baking soda or cornstarch. (Put in a large plastic bag first for less mess.) Let remain for at least 15 minutes and then shake it off or vacuum or brush it off.

Sprinkle baking soda into plastic storage bags along with the summer toys before storing to keep mildew from forming: pool toys, beach toys, small blow-up children's pools (sprinkle inside before rolling up), canteens, picnic coolers, etc.

Place an old shower curtain under an inflatable children's pool to protect it from sharp rocks and keep it clean.

Dishwasher Detergent

Commercial dishwasher detergents are toxic and most release low levels of chlorine fumes into the air when mixed with water. The levels are considered "safe." A minute film of detergent remains on the dishes. An alternative homemade detergent for your dishwasher is equal parts borax and baking soda. Use about a quarter cup of this mixture (two tablespoons borax plus two tablespoons baking soda) per dishwasher load.   I put one tablespoon of each in both the open and closed detergent compartments. This mixture may not work quite as well as commercial detergents and some pre-rinsing may be necessary.

Bathroom Cleaner

Use plain white vinegar to clean your bathroom—it disinfects and gets rid of soap scum buildup. In a spray bottle, mix equal parts vinegar and water and use to clean bathroom fixtures, floor, bathtub, tile, and shower curtain. Rinse with water. To remove soap scum, mildew, and bathtub grime, wipe with undiluted white vinegar and then scrub with baking soda on a damp sponge. Rinse with water.

Clean the toilet bowl by pouring in one cup of white vinegar, let soak for five minutes, brush, and flush. A sprinkle of baking soda can be used in combination with the vinegar to remove a stubborn toilet bowl ring.

Never mix vinegar with bleach, see warning on page 473.

For a very stubborn toilet bowl ring, make a paste of borax and lemon juice. Flush to get sides of bowl wet, rub on the paste, let sit for two hours, and scrub.

Instead of using cleanser to scour a bathtub, try baking soda or salt or borax on a damp sponge as an abrasive cleanser. When kids leave a glop of toothpaste in the sink, take a washcloth and use the glop to scrub up the sink and fixtures. Bon Ami Cleaning Powder or Bon Ami Polishing Cleanser are also safe scouring cleansers. Check your natural foods store for others.

Prevent mold and mildew in your bathroom by keeping things as dry as possible. Heat will kill mold/mildew. If you can afford the utility bill, try leaving a portable electric heater running for several hours in your bathroom with windows and door closed, but do this while you remain at home and are awake, so you check it periodically for overheating and prevent a fire. For a small mold/mildew spot, hold a portable hair dryer on the spot to bake away those germies.

Remove hard lime deposits around faucets by covering with vinegar-soaked paper towels. Let sit for an hour before cleaning. Chrome will be clean and shiny. Soak a clogged shower head in vinegar and water to remove deposits.

Don't use soap to clean ceramic tile, it leaves a film. Use a mixture of ¼-½ cup vinegar in one gallon water.

Kitchen Cleaners

As with the bathroom, baking soda and vinegar can be used on kitchen sinks and faucets. To make your counter tops sparkle, pour club soda on them, clean with a wipe-up towel, rinse with water, and wipe dry.

Linoleum Floor Cleaners

You don't want your baby crawling on a poisonous floor cleaner, especially when she puts her wet fingers into her mouth while she's crawling. To clean, mop no-wax linoleum floors with plain water or water with a little mild detergent. Pour a cup of white vinegar into a gallon of warm water and go over the floor again to add luster. Instead of floor wax, mop your floor with water into which has been added one capful of baby oil. Or add some skim milk to the mop water for a shine. Keep water away from linoleum seams and edges to prevent loosening. See warning about babies drowning, page 473.

Drain Cleaners

Drain cleaners are lethal to your child, any living thing, and to the environment. Their main ingredient is lye, and one drop of it will cause severe skin damage and blindness. Do not have any drain cleaners in your home, Grandma's house, your babysitter's house, and any place where your child will be.

Prevent clogs before they happen by inserting a little nylon netting or a lint catcher under the drain cap to catch hair and soap gook. Use rubber gloves to replace often—yuck! Never pour grease or any other drain clogging materials down your drains. See warning about craft materials on page 386.

I used to have trouble with my kitchen and bathroom drains clogging often. Now I flush them at least once a month with just plain boiling water (being careful that my children are out of the way) and the problem is gone. Be very careful not to burn yourself: hold the water container as close to drain as possible and pour slowly and directly into drain. We eat whole grain pasta frequently and I save energy by draining the boiling water from the cooked pasta down the bathroom sinks alternately with the kitchen sink.

If you have a slow-running drain, and plain boiling water doesn't help, try this: Into the drain, pour ½ cup of baking soda/washing soda. Then pour in about one cup of white vinegar. If you wish, first heat the vinegar in the microwave until it's fairly hot. It should break down fat and soap scum. If possible, cover or close the drain tightly. Wait several minutes until the bubbling stops—this fizzing creates pressure to dislodge the clog. Then flush with lots of very hot or boiling water. Repeat if necessary. Do this regularly to keep your drains clear. Use baking soda and vinegar in your garbage disposal to keep it clean and sweet-smelling.

WARNING: Do not use baking or washing soda in drains which are blocked, because they may harden and cause the block to get worse. Use only in slow running drains or in clear drains to keep them clear.

For blocked drains or really tough clogs, use a small plumber's helper (a plunger). They are cheap and you can buy them in any hardware department. Cover the plunger's rubber cap with water before plunging and it will work better, but first drape an old bath towel around it before plunging to prevent splatters. It may take several plunges to clear the drain.

WARNING: Do not use a plunger after any commercial drain cleaner has been used in the drain or if commercial drain cleaner is present in the standing water.

If the above methods did not clear the drain, try pouring ¼ cup of 3% hydrogen peroxide into the drain, wait ten minutes, and plunge, being careful not to splatter the peroxide, especially into your eyes. Keep peroxide out of children's reach.

There are also garden hose pressure devices and mechanical snakes that you can buy to unclog drains. Or try carefully fishing down your drain pipes with an unbent wire hanger.

Oven Cleaner

If you do not have a self-cleaning oven, it's probably better to have a dirty oven than to use commercial oven cleaners. Like drain cleaners, they contain lye, ammonia, and other poisons. Avoid them as you would avoid plutonium, especially the aerosol sprays which disperse tiny droplets of the poison into the air and maybe into your lungs, on your skin, and into your eyes. Here's a safer method of cleaning that oven, which I found in Debra Lynn Dadd's wonderful book *Home Safe Home* (see bibliography). In a spray bottle, mix 2 tablespoons liquid soap (not detergent), 2 teaspoons borax, and fill to the top with warm water. Shake well until completely dissolved to prevent squirt device from clogging. With rubber gloves and safety glasses, spray very close to the inside surface of the oven so solution does not disperse into the air. Let sit for 20 minutes and scrub with plain steel wool and non-chlorine scouring powder. If necessary, use pumice (buy in hardware department) to scour off black spots.

Prevent oven stains on your oven by lining the oven floor with aluminum foil. Place foil under the burner, but don't let the foil touch the burner.

Laundry Soap and Detergent

Detergents, which were invented to clean synthetic fabrics, are very different from natural soaps, which have been used to clean natural fabrics (cotton, silk, wool, linen) for hundreds of years. Detergents are made from petrochemicals, synthetic whiteners, artificial fragrances, and other chemicals. Soaps are made from natural minerals and fats. As you know from your bathroom, soaps have the problem of leaving scum. Buy laundry soaps at your natural food store.

> **WARNING:** Do not use soap on clothing that is flame retardant, as are children's sleepwear. Follow the manufacturer's instructions on the label for cleaning flame retardant garments.

If you run out of laundry soap/detergent, here's a recipe you can use in a pinch: Mix one tablespoon of baking soda/washing soda plus ½ tablespoon of borax into one cup of water. Add to washing machine at the beginning of the wash, as you would laundry detergent.

> **WARNING:** Dryer lint is very flammable and should not be used to stuff homemade toys. Remember to clean out the lint trap of your dryer after every load and the lint trap on your washing machine according to recommendations in the instructions manual. Washing machines and clothes dryers should be taken apart to clean the lint out of their workings on a regular basis. Besides preventing a fire, this will cause them to work more efficiently and will save money on energy bills.

Take Advantage of Your Machines

Get away with any manual washing that you can! Run plastic toys through the dishwasher on the top shelf. I have done entire loads with only toys. Clean hair combs, toys, and other items by running them through the clothes washing machine, but be careful not to wash them with clothing that may be easily damaged. I wash them with a load of wipe-up towels (page 159).

Wash large items in the bathtub with the shower massage and an old vegetable brush. First line the bathtub with a towel to prevent scratches. Save water by re-using your baby's bath water, if the item doesn't need to be sterile. I often do this with my son's fully submersible plastic potty chair or the toy wagon he plays with outside.

Fabric Softener

Fabric softeners are just another chemical to keep away from your baby. They leave a film on clothing to prevent or reduce the static cling that develops on synthetic fabrics and often contain heavy perfumes and fragrances. Natural fibers (cotton, silk, wool, linen) do not need static reduction. Fabric softeners may irritate baby's sensitive skin and cause reactions in allergic persons. They may also make clothing more flammable. Instead, use ¼ cup of baking soda/washing soda in the rinse cycle of your clothes washing machine. Mix soda into water before adding to remove white clumps.

Plain white vinegar is another non-irritating fabric softener. Add ½-1 cup vinegar to the final rinse water, but do not pour it directly on clothing or it may damage the color. Clothes will not smell vinegar-y when they are dry. Vinegar will help eliminate soap residue—it is mild on fabrics but strong enough to dissolve the alkalies in soaps and detergents. Vinegar breaks down uric acid, so it's especially good for your baby's clothes. Be sure that the manufacturer's instructions say that vinegar is OK to use in your washing machine. Or call the manufacturer to be sure that vinegar will not damage the machine.

Do NOT use vinegar in your rinse water if you've used chlorine bleach during the wash cycle! See warning about dangerous vapors, page 473.

If you absolutely need a static reducer, the best commercial type to use is the unscented sheets, not the liquids. Bounce Free® is an example of such a fabric softener sheet, or use a brand from your natural foods store. Save money by cutting each sheet in half or in quarters. I've found that part of a sheet works just as well as a full sheet.

MONEY SAVER: If you do choose to use those scented fabric softener sheets, save money by using them for more than one dryer load. Save the used sheets, wet them with a little liquid fabric softener, let them air dry, and use them as you would the original new sheets. Or buy some cheap sponges and cut them up into small pieces. Soak the sponge pieces in liquid fabric softener. Remove a sponge piece, squeeze out excess softener, and toss into the dryer as you would use a fabric softener sheet. Keep reusing the sponges.

MONEY SAVER: No need to buy commercial spray starches, which are nothing more than cornstarch, chemicals, and water. Make your own by measuring one or two tablespoons of cornstarch into a spray bottle and filling with about one cup cold water. The more starch, the stiffer the result. Shake frequently during use and clean spritzer well after use to prevent clogging.

Bleach

Hydrogen peroxide can be used as a gentle bleach. It may also remove mildew from colored fabrics without bleaching them out. Always spot test first.

Super Clothing Stain Remover

This remover is not safe for you, the environment, or your clothes. It is to be used only in desperate stain situations when you are ready to throw the hopelessly-stained item out. Fill your washing machine to the low water level with hot water. Add one cup powdered Cascade® dishwasher detergent and one cup laundry bleach for whites (or Clorox II for colored fabrics) and let your washing machine begin agitating in order to stir the detergent until all powder has dissolved. Then stop the machine, add clothing, let agitate a few minutes, and stop the machine to let soak for a few hours or overnight. Then let the machine finish the entire wash and spin cycles. Hope it works for you!

Super Dirt Placer

Insert child into center of shallow puddle. Let soak five minutes. Move child over dirt pile and lower gently into sitting position. Spin.

Dry Cleaner's Secret

I heard from a friend that dry cleaning is not really necessary, except in very rare cases. Do your pocketbook and the environment a favor by hand washing almost any article of Dry Clean Only clothing in mild soap and water. Use a true soap (not Woolite® or Dawn® dishwashing detergent), such as Ivory® Soap Flakes, to prevent damage to fibers. Ironing the clothing is no fun, but you can take difficult items to the dry cleaner for a professional pressing. It's less expensive than a cleaning and pressing.

Use a baby gate over the bathtub to dry sweaters and other hand washables.

Irons and Babies Don't Mix

Ironing is too dangerous to do around a small child. Besides the possibility of serious burns, even a cold iron can cause serious injury if a baby pulls it off the ironing board by the cord. If you absolutely must iron when your child is in the house, keep your child in a playpen where he is in full view across the room from you. If your child won't stay in the playpen, get into it yourself with a small tabletop ironing board (here's my phobia of burns again!). Do this whenever you are working with any dangerous items, such as sharp scissors.

Making Clothing Flame Retardant

Some children's clothing, such as sleepwear, has a flame retardant film on it by law. This film can be washed off with soaps, so be careful to use the type of detergent recommended on the label of these flame-retardant clothes. I appreciated flame retardancy the time my son's shirt caught fire from a sparkler at a Fourth of July party. The flame fizzled out immediately. (I discovered that there are some situations where you immediately and willingly place your naked hand on an open flame. ☺) If you suspect that your children's old pajamas are no longer flame retardant, or when members of your family will be near an open flame, you may want to make their clothing flame retardant. They'll be much safer as they toast marshmallows and sing around that campfire.

I was all ready to print a recipe here with instructions on how to make clothing flame retardant, but I was strongly advised not to, due to the litigious society in which we now live. I suggest that you call your local department for the information. Or look on page 128 of Joey Green's book *Paint Your House with Powdered Milk*. See bibliography. Sorry for the inconvenience.

Human hair is extremely flammable. I saw this at a church service one day when one girl's hair caught fire from the unshielded candle she was holding. (Luckily, two adults put it out immediately and no injuries occurred, although she had to switch to a shorter hair style. After that we used only candles with large glass shields.) When children are around any type of fire, keep their long hair tied in a tight bun behind their necks.

Ice Melt and Traction

Sprinkle plain baking soda on your sidewalks to prevent slipping on ice and to melt the ice. If the baking soda comes in on people's shoes, your crawling baby will be safe with it. Soda will not damage your rugs, sidewalks, or shoes. For more traction, sprinkle some of your child's play sand.

Air Fresheners

On your stove top, simmer a small saucepan of water with natural aromatic food stuffs. Try a mixture of lemon/orange/tangerine peels, apple peels, cloves, cinnamon, allspice, and pine needles. What a delicious and homey smell! To rid the house of cabbage, cauliflower, and other cooking smells, mix a little vanilla flavoring into plain simmering water.

As an air freshener, place vanilla on a cotton ball and place in a saucer out of children's reach. (Vanilla contains alcohol.) Use in your home, the refrigerator, or even in your car.

For a homemade spray air freshener, place one teaspoon of baking soda into a trigger spray bottle and add about a cup of water. Spray a fine mist to remove odors from the air. Or spray plain white vinegar full strength.

Refrigerator Odors

Keep an opened box of baking soda in the back of your refrigerator to absorb odors and then pour it down a drain to freshen the drain too. Place a few drops of vanilla on a cotton ball in a custard cup and your refrigerator will soon smell great.

Carpets and Rugs

To deodorize, don't use the commercial powder. You don't want your baby crawling on chemicals. Instead, sprinkle baking soda or half baking soda/half cornstarch into your rugs. Let sit overnight and vacuum. No need for artificial fragrance if you add a pinch of cinnamon for a nice scent. First test on an inconspicuous spot if you have light-colored rugs. Instead of buying those vacuum scent inserts, put a cotton ball soaked with lemon juice or vanilla into your vacuum cleaner bag to freshen the air while you vacuum. Let the juice/vanilla dry before inserting.

To remove wet mud from your carpet, sprinkle liberally with cornstarch, wait 15 minutes, and vacuum. When carpeting has an absolutely unremovable stain, it's time to cut and paste. Use a utility knife or razor blade widget to cut out the rectangular or circular piece of carpet with the stain. Do not cut out the underpadding. Cut a matching piece of carpet from a closet floor or from under a piece of furniture that will never be moved. Use the cut piece of stained carpet to get the correct size and shape. (You may want to cut the unstained carpet piece a little bit bigger so you can trim it to fit exactly.) Then do the switch. Place the unstained carpet piece where the stained piece was. Use a glue gun to hot glue into place. Use plenty of glue so your vacuum cleaner won't pull up the carpet piece.

If the carpet has a stain that is lighter than the color of the carpet, try painting it back to its original color. Use a few shades of fabric paint close to the color of the carpet. Place paint globs on a paper plate, get down on the carpet, and mix the paints together until the color matches the carpet perfectly. Paint that stain away. More than one paint application may be necessary.

Prevent Newspaper from Yellowing

If you don't want to laminate a newspaper clipping, here's another way to prevent it from yellowing. Dissolve a milk of magnesia tablet in one quart of warm club soda. Let sit overnight. Pour some of this mixture into a shallow baking sheet and saturate newspaper clippings with it. Let newspaper dry thoroughly. Newspaper should not become yellow, as long as you keep it out of sunlight.

Hot Water Bottle

For cold toes, use a spill-proof plastic bottle as a hot water bottle.

First-Aid for Your Home

Resolve right now that you will not become upset or angry when (not if) your child writes with crayon on the good wallpaper, jumps on the couch with her shoes and breaks the springs, and spills boxed cereal all over the kitchen counter and floor while picking out just the raisins to eat. Here are a few fixes for some of the damage your little angel might cause to your unimportant home and material possessions.

Wood Scratches and Rings

Use your child's brown crayons to fix scratches in wood furniture. Walnut or pecan meat rubbed into scratches in wood furniture or wood floors helps erase them. Repeat several times for best results. Or, try mixing one teaspoon instant coffee or tea with two teaspoons water and applying with a cotton ball. Or, use equal parts of lemon juice and salad oil. For large holes, mix instant coffee with white toothpaste, Elmer's glue, or spackling paste to match the color of the wood, fill holes, and smooth with a damp paper towel. For white rings on wood furniture, try mixing cigarette/cigar ashes into corn oil and rub into the ring with the grain. Or try gently rubbing the ring with equal parts toothpaste and baking soda on a soft cloth, or with just plain toothpaste.

Loose Knobs

Kids love to unscrew dresser-drawer handles and knobs, making them too loose to stay securely in their holes. To create a snug fit again, coat screw with Elmer's glue or clear nail polish, screw into hole, and let dry thoroughly before touching.

Crayon Marks

From most flat surfaces (washable painted wall, washable wallpaper, table top, blackboard, etc.), remove crayons marks with one of these methods: rub with toothpaste on an old toothbrush and rinse well; spray on WD-40®, let sit 10 minutes, and blot with a paper towel; gently scrub with steel wool; apply rubber cement, let dry partially, and roll off; warm with hair dryer and wipe off; place paper towel over crayon mark and apply warm iron to absorb wax. Toothpaste will not work well on porous surfaces or wallpaper. Always test method on inconspicuous spot first in case damage results.

Melted Crayon Wax in the Carpet

Crayon wax melted into your carpet or car's cloth interior via the greenhouse effect can be removed. First ice the wax down until it is very cold. Pick off wax pieces with your fingernails, being careful not to pull the fibers. Spread a few layers of paper toweling or a brown grocery bag over the spot and apply a warm (not hot) iron. Some of the wax will be absorbed by the paper. Remove and replace with fresh paper and iron again. Repeat until all wax is gone. Be very careful with some car interiors and synthetic carpet which may melt—test on an inconspicuous spot first. (Newspaper can also be used but the ink may cause a spot problem.) A color stain may remain if the crayon was a dark color or one in contrast to the rug. Sorry.

Ink

To remove ink from hands or clothing, rub toothpaste into the spot, scrub, and rinse thoroughly. Or try squirting the ink stain with commercial hair spray.

Stickers, Adhesive-backed Paper, Chewing Gum, Silly Putty, Bathtub Decals, Price Tags, Stick-on Hooks

Remember to test on inconspicuous spot first before trying any of these methods: Rub full-strength hot white vinegar or saturate a cloth with the vinegar and place over the sticker. Squeeze the liquid so it gets on the glue behind the sticker. Give the vinegar time to soak in before rubbing off. Instead of vinegar, try vegetable oil (or spray WD-40®). Another method: Apply a warm iron directly to the sticker, or on a paper towel placed over the sticker, to melt the adhesive. Or hold a hair dryer over the spot until the adhesive melts. To remove chewing gum from hair, harden it by placing ice on it and pick it out of the hair, or try rubbing the gum with peanut butter.

Spit-up Stain and Odor Remover

When baby spits up, remove as much as possible, and then rub dry baking soda/washing soda into the spot to remove odor and prevent stain from setting. Let it dry and brush off. Keep a small container of baking soda in the diaper bag for this purpose. Or, fill a spray bottle with equal parts baking soda and water to spray on spit-up on furniture or clothes.

Urine Stain and Odor Remover

Get to that stain immediately. Rinse repeatedly with warm water, then apply a solution of 3 tablespoons white vinegar and 1 teaspoon liquid soap. (Test on inconspicious spot first.) Leave on for 15 minutes, rinse, and rub dry.

Blood Stains

One day I walked into my twins' room and there was blood all over—on the walls, the cribs, the carpet, everywhere! It looked like a murder scene! I almost lost it when I looked at their little hands and they were all blood! They had somehow knocked a picture with glass off the wall, and they had been playing with the pieces of broken glass! I spent a long time finding all the pieces and putting them back together like a puzzle to be sure I found every last sliver. To remove blood stains, you probably know to treat the stain immediately by soaking in COLD water (never hot water or it will set the stain) and scrubbing with a mild soap. Perhaps you didn't know that hydrogen peroxide is great for removing blood stains. I poured it directly on the blood stains on the carpet and they came right out! It was like magic! Club soda also works on some blood stains.

Those of you with twins (or more!) have a bit more to worry about in terms of your babies' safety. They can get into so much more trouble together! For example, one day my twins used the drawers as steps to climb up their high dresser and their combined weight made the dresser fall on them, pinning them to the floor. The adrenaline kicked in and I was able to lift the dresser, holding the drawers closed at the same time.

Twins are a blessing for a million reasons, and one is that they can watch out for each other. I was outside when one of my twins came running out of the house to tell me something. He was scared and I didn't wait to understand what he was trying to tell me—I knew something had happened. When I ran into the house, I found his brother pinned under our large game-room-sized video game, which had fallen on him! I don't know how, but I lifted that heavy machine as if it were light as a feather, just enough so that Freddy could crawl out from under it. I was expecting broken bones or worse, but fortunately he didn't have a scratch on him. I've tried to lift that machine many times since then, but couldn't budge it one inch. I believe the story about the grandmother who lifted a car to save her grandchild! Another incident happened when they were older and Freddy had gotten himself stuck in the snow at the playground. He was really stuck! His twin brother John, the only other person there, "saved" him by running to get me to shovel him out! Having twins is the greatest!! ☺

Stains

Read Don Aslett's *Stainbuster's Bible: The Complete Guide to Spot Removal.* See bibliography.

Baby-Safe Household Pesticides

Ants

Instant grits is a safe solution to your ant problems. Sprinkle where they enter and the workers will take the grits back to the queen ant. She'll eat them, expand, and blow up. Ants will not cross a line. Find where they are entering your home and draw a line with any of these: blackboard chalk, liquid dish soap, bath powder, white flour, paprika, red chili powder, dried peppermint, or cream of tartar. (Be careful with liquid dish soap. It may stain walls and is slippery and it's more trouble to wipe up.) Try dusting the area with ground cinnamon. Fill cracks with flour or white glue. Try washing countertops, floors, cabinets, etc. with equal parts white vinegar and water. Repel ants on vertical surfaces like windowsills, doors, and cracks in your home's foundation by spraying liberally with equal parts white vinegar and water. For places where children never go, mix two parts borax and one part sugar or white flour and sprinkle around the foundation of your home. Keep borax away from children.

Ants and Snails and Slugs

Place beer (yes, regular six-pack type beer) into a aluminum pie tin and place in the ground level with the soil. Keep snails from a young plant by pushing a soup can with both ends removed into the soil around the plant. The can encircles the plant and protects it from snails.

Cockroaches

Kill cockroaches by petrifying them. Mix equal parts cornstarch and Plaster of Paris and sprinkle in cracks and crevices. Keep Plaster of Paris away from children and follow warnings on the label. Or mix two parts flour, four parts borax, and one part cocoa and place in a saucer where they crawl. For cockroaches or silverfish, mix one part boric acid (keep away from children) with two parts sugar in a small amount of water. Leave bowl where insects crawl, but safely out of children's reach. Or try sprinkling equal parts baking soda and powdered sugar where they crawl.

Fleas

Remove vacuum cleaner bags immediately after vacuuming. Seal the bag and dispose of it *outside* your home. Add a bit of vinegar to your pet's drinking water—about one teaspoon to a quart of water and it will help repel fleas and ticks. Including brewer's yeast in your dog's diet may also help. Use Murphy's® Oil Soap to wash your dog. It kills fleas on contact (no 10 minute wait for flea soap to work), makes fur shine, and is natural so your dog can safely lick herself.

Flypaper

Make your own flypaper by mixing together and bringing to a boil corn syrup, sugar, and a little water. Coat strips cut from brown grocery bags and hang.

Mice

Mice hate peppermint. Repel them by placing fresh peppermint sprigs where they run. Or use a piece of cardboard saturated with oil of peppermint (available at some pharmacies). Nontoxic but cruel: Leave mashed potato buds or powder in their paths, along with a saucer of water nearby. They will eat it and die from bloating. Humane mouse traps are available at hardware stores.

Plant Pests

Place a raw white potato slice on the surface of soil in your potted plants. It will draw out plant-damaging worms.

Put hot sauce on a ball of cotton and place in your houseplant pot to repel plant pests.

In your blender, mix water and some garlic and pepper sauce or hot peppers or red pepper powder and optionally some raw onion. Strain and spray to coat plant leaves. Make sure to spray under leaves too. Or spray plants with one part Dawn® dishwashing detergent or other biodegradable dish soap to four parts water. Wait one hour before rinsing clean with water. Or soak raw onions and garlic in some water for a week. Place in spray bottle and use as a natural insecticide for plants.

Bugs don't like dead bugs, especially dead bugs that are in their family! Gather together some dead bugs and mix them in your blender with water. Strain until you can spray the mixture. Truly a bug spray! ☺

Ring a houseplant with your dog's flea collar. Cover plant and collar together in a plastic bag and let sit for two days. The tiny pests will be gone. Be sure to keep the collar and the plastic bag out of reach of children. Do not do this with houseplants that you plan to eat, such as herbs.

Kill grass growing in cracks by pouring boiling water on it. Or sprinkle with salt. Or wet with undiluted white vinegar.

See tip about grain bugs on page 208.

D. Your Kitchen Window is a Green Mine

Food plants grown in your own kitchen give you delicious fresh organic food. This chapter has directions on how to grow herbs. Herbs and sprouts (pages 245-249) are two green foods that are easy to grow in your kitchen for actual food. Directions are also given in this chapter for other food plants, which will not really supply very much food, but are fun and educational nonetheless. Watching them grow is a good lesson for your children, who will learn that food is alive and comes from the Earth, not from cans and boxes in the supermarket.

How to Grow Herbs on Your Windowsill

There's nothing like fresh herbs picked from a plant growing right in your own kitchen (or backyard). I've got pots of parsley and other herbs growing on my windowsill, from which I frequently pick leaves for healthy little snacks. Kids think it's really neat (and so do adults).

WARNING: Make sure your children know what is safe to eat and what is not. After seeing your kitchen herb garden, they may think it's OK to eat ANY green plant. Keep poisonous houseplants at a friend's house until your toddler gets older. Watch her carefully when she is outside, where green plants are everywhere.

Plants are dormant during the winter, so plan on planting indoor plants in the spring. If you plant herbs from seeds, you will be able to start eating leaves from the plants after several weeks, depending on the plant (read the seed package). Included here are the basics of growing herbs from seeds. If you find that you're really getting into indoor gardening, there are dozens of books at your local library that will give you all the details you need.

The Pots

Clay pots are best for growing herbs. Ready NEW clay pots by soaking them in plain water for at least one hour and allowing them to dry, so they won't absorb moisture from the soil. Wash old pots or those acquired from friends or yard sales thoroughly in soap and water. You can use plastic pots, but clay is porous and lets the soil "breath." All pots should have drainage holes in the bottom.

MONEY SAVER: Instead of buying pots, you can use milk cartons cut about 6 inches up from the bottom. Wash out the milk cartons thoroughly with hot water and soap. Poke a few small holes in the bottom for drainage.

The Soil

For the soil, mix together 1 part vermiculite, 1 part pearlite, and 2 parts sterilized potting soil. To know how much to buy, figure that a typical 4-inch (diagonal of the rim) pot takes about 2 cups. Or plug and fill your pots with water to figure the amount needed. If you're not sure how sterile your soil is, sterilize it yourself. Line shallow baking pans with aluminum foil. Spread soil very thinly on pans and bake in pre-heated 180°F oven for at least 30 minutes. Cool before using. DISCLAIMER: The author is not responsible for any strong odors emanating from the oven during or after the baking procedure.

Place screening, nylon net, flat rocks, nut shells, sponge pieces, pantyhose pieces, cheesecloth layers, coffee filter pieces, or pieces of broken clay pot in the bottom of the pots to prevent the soil from falling out the drainage holes. Then place a layer of small pebbles or gravel on the bottom of the pot. Fill each pot with the soil mixture to one inch from top. Place filled pots on the drip saucers that came with the pot to protect your windowsill from dirt and water. Or use an old tray, plastic tops or containers, an old baking pan, Styrofoam trays, or whatever. I have one of my plants on a Frisbee, which is borrowed occasionally by my kids.

TIP: Chlorine from tap water will evaporate in a day or two. After watering your plants, fill the watering can with tap water immediately and let sit until the next watering. Chlorine will be gone and the water will be at room temperature. Chlorine causes brown tips on plants. Brown tips are also caused by bottom roots remaining too wet.

Parsley, Sage, Rosemary, and Thyme

You can buy seeds from mail-order seed catalogs or your local garden or X-mart store. Common herbs that will grow well indoors are parsley (Extra Curly), basil (Green Ruffles Italian), and chives. You can also try anise, bay (bay leaves), chamomile (for tea), chervil, fennel, mint, mustard, oregano, rosemary, sage, and savory. Dill is my favorite. I usually wait to buy seeds at the end of the season when they are on sale for use the next summer. They germinate just fine even though they are a year old, if you store them in a cool dry place or in an airtight jar in the refrigerator.

Soak the soil in the pots until it is thoroughly wet before you plant the seeds. Plant a few seeds into each pot until they are ¼-½ inch deep in the soil. (A good rule of thumb to follow when planting any seeds is to plant them as deep as they are long.) You may wish to sprinkle a thin layer of sterile play sand on the top of the soil, which will help to keep it moist. The soil must be keep wet until the seeds germinate (sprout into little plants); however, don't water the seeds as you would houseplants or you'll flood and displace them. Keep the soil wet by misting it at least once a day, or use an old dropper from your baby's vitamins to gently drip water onto the soil.

Caring for Herb Plants

Herb plants should be kept warm (about 70°F) and in a sunny window. However, when the seeds are first sprouting, they are very delicate and must be protected from direct sunlight. Move them away from the window or cover them with cheesecloth so they don't burn up and die. In the winter, move them back from cold windows and make sure no leaves touch the cold window glass.

After a few weeks, sprouts will appear. When they are about 3 inches high, thin them. This means to remove the small, scrawny ones to leave room for the healthy, larger ones to grow. (Survival of the fittest.)

Keep the soil moist—you may have to water as often as once a day. Always have non-chlorinated water handy for your plants. See tip on previous page.

To help keep the air around your plants humid, place a layer of pebbles in a large shallow pan. Fill partway with water and place your plants in their pots on the pebbles and over the water.

Occasionally, spray your plants with the sink hose or soak them with a mister until they are dripping wet in order to rinse off any accumulated dirt and dust on the leaves.

Harvesting Herbs

When the plants grow to more than 4 inches high, you can pick off the largest leaves every few days. Take the outside leaves or the largest leaves from the top. Or, when taller, use sharp scissors to cut 2 or 3 inches off the top for eating or cooking. Always leave some leaves so you don't kill the plant, and leave the plants so that they are at least 4 inches high in the pot. If the plants grow into 3 sections, such as parsley, clip off the middle leaves.

Keep the picked leaves cool and eat them within 2-3 days, or freeze them (page 450) or dry them (page 450).

> **TIP:** Add fresh chopped parsley or dill to cream cheese or butter and use as a spread for crackers or baked potatoes. Or sprinkle fresh herbs into scrambled eggs or pasta sauces.

Aroma Therapy for You

Grow some English lavender in your bedroom. Anytime you need a quick pampering, take in the fragrance of this wonderful-smelling plant. Other fragrant herbs are scented geraniums, lemon verbena, patchouli, and tansy. Place mint leaves in your bath water for a wonderful scent.

Plant Tips

There's no need to buy special pots for plants—re-cycle containers you already have around the house: plastic containers of all sizes from small laundry detergent cups to large wastebaskets, old mugs, cups, bowls, etc. ▸Make a small greenhouse out of one of those plastic bottles with the dark saucer bottoms. Remove the dark saucer and put soil and plants in it. Cut off top of clear bottle, turn upside down over saucer, and punch air holes in the top. Keep out of direct sunlight. Water but don't drown your plants. If moisture builds up within the greenhouse, remove the top and let it dry out a bit. ⸙If you have an old aquarium that you no longer use for fish, use it for growing plants. ⸙Change a plain plant container into a fancy one by covering completely with small pebbles or by glueing on other textured art materials (page 392). ⸙Use an old bubble umbrella as a greenhouse. ⸙Germinate seeds indoors on top of the refrigerator, where they will be warm and cuddly. ⸙Wipe leaves with a mixture of half skim milk and half water to make them glossy. Or use mayonnaise or olive oil. Or use glycerin, which will not collect dust. ⸙Repot a plant into a large pot that is two inches larger. ⸙Mark each plant by placing a popsicle stick with its name and date written on it. Cover with transparent tape or clear nail polish to protect the writing. Or make plant markers by writing with permanent marker pen on white plastic spoons. ⸙A bent wire hanger will act as a trellis for a climbing houseplant. Bend into a heart or other shape and insert hook end in soil. ⸙Splint a bent houseplant with some clear tape and a toothpick or popsicle stick. ⸙Seal pruned stems and branches with Elmer's® Glue-All to prevent moisture loss and damage by insects. ⸙Fix cracks in a flowerpot with chewing gum. ⸙Keep egg shell halves and use as miniature planters. Paint a face on the front of the shells and the plants will look like hair growing out the top of the face. ⸙Make live potato heads: Cut raw potatoes in half and scoop out part of flesh. Plant grass seed in soil in the hollow. Growing grass looks like silly hair. Paint a face on the front of the potato. ⸙A layer of gravel on top of the soil in window boxes prevents dirt from splattering on windows during a rain. ⸙Free fertilizer! Feed your plants by watering them with nutrient-containing *gray water:* the soak water from your sprouts, the cooled water in which you boiled eggs or corn on the cob, water which contained cut flowers, weak tea (either orange pekoe and pekoe cut black tea, such as Lipton®), melted snow (minerals), flat club soda (minerals). To the soil, add a little wood ashes (controls pH), coffee grounds (adds acid), or egg shells that have been dried and pulverized in the blender (bone meal). Occasionally water them with skim milk. ⸙A good nutrition lesson for your child: Grow two plants side-by-side. Fertilize one and not the other and ask your child which one is healthier. ⸙Let your toddler water houseplants with squeeze bottles, for more control. ⸙Can plants spell!? Punch holes in the bottom of an aluminum baking sheet for drainage. Cover holes with nylon stocking or cheesecloth to prevent soil from falling out. Fill sheet with soil and trace your child's name into the soil with your finger. Plant small seeds along the soil lines. The small shoots will spell out your child's name. Write your child's name with small flowers in an outdoor garden. ⸙Cut black paper in the shape of your child's initial and glue it on the leaf of a tree outside or on a fruit before it ripens. Wait several weeks. Soak leaf in water to remove paper and let your child see her initial. ⸙Soak raw onions and garlic in some water for a week. Place in spray bottle and use as a natural insecticide for plants. ⸙My dog used to love to "dig" in the soil of my houseplants and eject soil all over the floor. I stopped her by covering the soil with plastic mesh, cut to fit around the plant like a big collar.

Fun Fruit Plants

Grow Citrus Plants

Take several plump-looking seeds from an orange (or grapefruit or lemon) and gently rinse them under cold water and dry them. Let them dry for 3-4 days. In a 4-inch pot, place several (in case some don't germinate) orange seeds one inch apart and ½-1 inch deep into the soil. Place the fat, rounded end of the seed down. Keep the soil moist (but not soaked) and in a sunny window, but not in direct sunlight. In 3-6 weeks (the seeds are slow to germinate), a plant will come up. Because it takes so long to germinate, you may wish to enclose the pot in a large plastic bag for a greenhouse effect and to keep moisture in. Or cut the top off a clear plastic two liter bottle and place over plants—punch some air holes in the top. Remove from plastic bag or bottle after germination. Keep in a sunny window and water when soil begins to dry.

Johnny Appleseed

Start an apple tree by following the directions above for citrus fruits.

Grow A Grape Vine

Take a few grape seeds and soak them in water overnight. Plant ¼ inch deep. Follow directions for citrus plants.

Grow a Pineapple Plant

Buy a whole pineapple with healthy, unbroken, symmetrical, green (no brown) leaves. Slice off the top green leafy part of a whole pineapple, leaving about an inch of flesh. Gently pull off the lower row of green leaves. Place it in a jar of water out of direct sunlight. In a week or two, roots will appear. Transplant to a 6-inch pot, covering brown skin and flesh with soil and keeping leaves above the soil. Keep in a sunny spot and water once a week, pouring water into the middle of the leaves. Take care of it and in a few years (good things take time), a little pineapple may appear.

Grow an Avocado Plant

Take the huge seed from the avocado, rinse off the green flesh, and remove the thin brown skin. Insert three toothpicks or nails equal distance around the middle of the seed. The toothpicks will support the seed in the top of a glass of water, larger flat side down, as shown in the professionally-drawn picture on the right. The glass's perimeter should be larger than the seed, to allow air to circulate around the seed. Keep the glass in a warm place out of direct sunlight. Each day or two, replace evaporated water so that the lower third of the seed remains under water. Change the water every week or so. In a few weeks, roots will grow underwater and the seed will split to allow a small green stalk to emerge. When the roots are several inches long and the stalk is 6 inches high, replant into a 6-inch clay pot, so that half the seed is exposed above the soil. To do this, make a hole in the soil large enough so that you can put in the seed, root side down, without damaging the delicate roots. Give it plenty of water and sun and watch it grow! When it is about a foot tall, cut 2 inches off the tip of the shoot, which will cause it to branch and get bushy. Periodically prune your avocado plant.

Grow a Sweet Potato Plant

Buy an unwaxed sweet potato (if you can find one). Grow using the same method as with an avocado seed above. Buds will appear on the top and roots will sprout under the water. In about a month, your windowsill will be crawling with potato vines.

Grow a Peanut Plant

Plant 5 raw shelled peanuts 1-inch deep into the soil of a clay pot, placing as far apart as possible from each other and the sides of the pot. Keep moist and in a sunny spot.

Grow a Carrot, Beet, Turnip, or Parsnip Plant

Unlike the boy in Ruth Krauss's book, *The Carrot Seed*, who started a carrot plant with a seed, have your child start with a whole, fully grown carrot with greens still attached. From carrot (or other veggie), slice the greens off the top so that ½-1 inch of orange flesh remains. Place orange part of carrot halfway into a saucer with water or into wet sterile sand or pearlite. Keep wet, and leaves will grow in a week or two.

Forest Plants

Take a nature walk and gather wild outdoor plants: moss from the side of a tree, small ferns, tiny plants. Make a forest terrarium with your gatherings.

Flowers

Collect seeds from yours or a friend's annual flowering plants for next year. Place a plastic bag over a dried up blossom and wait several days for seeds to fall into bag. Shake occasionally to help the process. Place seeds in an envelope labeled with the name of the flower. Store the envelope in a cool dry place.

Collect several different types of seeds and give as gifts along with gardening accessories: a trowel, gardening gloves, a planter, etc. Include instructions.

When you spouse brings you flowers and they slump in the vase, stretch lengths of clear tape from one edge of the vase to another and perpendicular to each other. Place flowers between crisscrossed tape to "straighten them up." For flower stems that are damaged or too short, lengthen by inserting into plastic straws cut to the length you need. Cut stems at an angle with sharp scissors. Remove leaves below water line—they'll decay and poison the water. To keep cut flowers fresher longer, refrigerate them overnight and as much as possible. Preserve cut flowers by placing them in water mixed with a little white vinegar (antibacterial) and cane sugar (food). Use about one tablespoon each of vinegar and sugar per pint of water.

Learning About Seeds

Viewing Seeds Through Glass

Let your child see a seed sprout by placing paper towels around the edges the inside of a glass jar. Stuff more paper towels inside to keep the outside towels flat against the sides of the jar. Wet the towels and insert seeds (use large seeds like garbanzos, kidney beans, etc.) between the paper toweling and the glass as shown in the picture. Plant at least three seeds, in case some do not germinate. Keep the towels wet and watch the seeds sprout. Keep seeds out of sunlight so they don't cook and die. When the sprouts grow to two inches long and have two leaves on them, transplant to soil.

Soak a seed overnight in water. Remove its protective seed coat and split lengthwise. Show your child the tiny plant inside and explain that the rest of the inside of the bean is food for the plant.

Sponge Sprouting

Place seeds on a sterile sponge to germinate. Keep sponge wet and seeds out of direct sunlight. For more fun, first cut sponge into a Simple Shape (pages 367-368).

Plants Drink Water Too

To show your toddler that plants drink water, place a white carnation or other light-colored flower into a jar of water colored red with food coloring. In a few hours, the carnation blossom will turn red. The analogy can be made that plants drink water from the soil as we drink liquids through a straw, although I'm not sure how botanically correct it is.

This experiment also can be done with a celery or carrot. Cut the bottom off first before placing in colored water. After a few hours, split open the carrot/celery and see the results.

Split a white carnation stem in half and place one of the halves in a glass with red-colored water and the other half in a glass with blue-colored water. It will look like the carnation has two legs—one leg in each glass. In a few hours the carnation will turn half red and half blue!

E. Nutrition 101: A Crash Course in Nutrition

Proper nutrition is about eating the proper foods in the correct amounts and combinations so that our bodies can carry on their biological processes and use energy. The more you study the minute details of nutrition, the more complicated it gets, and the more you realize that you should just leave it to nature. In other words, eating a variety of whole, natural foods—whole grains, legumes, nuts, seeds, vegetables, fruits, and yogurt—is the best diet we can eat to insure optimum health.

This chapter gives the basics of nutrition, an understanding of which will help you to give your baby and yourself a good diet. Also included in this chapter are many warnings about the food industry and their advertising practices, which, I believe, are meant to mislead the uninformed consumer and increase their profits.

Nutrients

The food we eat provides our body with the substances necessary for energy and with the structural components necessary for bodily growth and repair. These substances are called **nutrients**. The amount of nutrients we need depend on body weight, age, activity level, and many other factors.

In general, the younger a person is, the more nutrients he needs per pound of body weight. For example, a 150-pound, 30-year old woman requires more or less 13 calories per pound of body weight per day or about 2000 (13x150) calories. But a 25-pound, 18-month old toddler requires about 50 calories per pound of body weight per day or 1250 calories. A toddler needs more than 3 times more calories per pound than an adult! This disparity exists with almost all other nutrients. Nutrients are needed in much greater proportions by your baby because of her fast growth rate and her activity level—as we parents know so well. It is therefore very important that you feed your baby the healthiest foods possible, to insure that she grows up to be big and strong!

The Major Nutrient Classes

The nutrients needed by the human body are classified into 6 types:

1. Carbohydrates
2. Fats
3. Proteins
4. Vitamins
5. Minerals
6. Water

Carbohydrates, fats, and proteins are called **macronutrients** because you body needs lots of them. Vitamins and minerals are called **micronutrients** because your body needs very little of them, relative to the macros. However, the fact that we only need a little bit of the micros doesn't mean that they aren't just as important as the macros.

No nutrient works alone. Nutrients are needed in proper proportions, as they are found in whole, natural food.

Macronutrients

Carbohydrates and fats from foods are the main sources of energy for the body. Each gram of carbohydrate supplies 4.1 calories, and each gram of fat supplies 9.3 calories. Fat is a more concentrated source of fuel for the body, and is more "fattening" than carbohydrate. Although proteins are mainly for maintenance and repair, they can also be used for energy when carbohydrates and fats are not available. Proteins, like carbohydrates, supply 4.1 calories per gram. The breakfast cereal commercial that reminds you to lose the fat, not the muscle, is referring to the loss of protein when muscle tissue is broken down and used for energy because of a lack of carbohydrates and fat in the diet, due to crash dieting. (Incidentally, that cereal is not whole grain.)

Carbohydrates Supply Energy

Carbohydrates are the most important source of energy for the body. There are three classifications of carbohydrates: sugars (simple carbohydrates), starches (complex carbohydrates), and fibers (also complex carbohydrates). Carbohydrates are found almost exclusively in plant foods, with the exception of milk, which contains lactose or milk sugar, a simple carbohydrate.

Simple Carbohydrates or Sugars

Sugars are called simple carbohydrates because their simple molecular makeup allows them to be digested very easily and quickly—in fact, too easily and too quickly. These sugars include common white sugar or table sugar, brown sugar, powdered sugar, honey, molasses, and the crystallized white fructose that looks like white sugar.

NOTE: Please be sure to read about too much sugar in your baby's fruit juice on page 64.

Empty Calories and Nutrient Debt

We know that too much of these sugars are not good for us, but why? After all, they are natural: sucrose (table sugar) is found in sugar beets and sugar cane, fructose (fruit sugar) is found in fruits, which are very good for us, and honey is very healthy for bees. Well, first of all and probably least important is the fact that these concentrated sugars are a major cause of tooth decay. A bigger problem with these sugars is that they supply _empty calories_—calories with only energy and without any significant amounts of other vitamins and minerals. Eating large amounts of them makes you feel full for a short while, but you burn them up very quickly and soon find yourself hungry again. It's like building a campfire out of leaves instead of logs: You get a big, big fire for a few minutes, but then it quickly fizzles out. Complex carbohydrates (covered next) are like logs—they burn slowly and steadily for a long time.

And here's a surprising fact about sugars: Not only do simple carbohydrates supply no other nutrients, but they actually rob vitamins and minerals already existing in your body to digest them! _Eating refined sugars is like going into nutrient debt._ This occurs with all simple carbohydrates, even honey, which is not much better than table sugar, with only a minute amount of nutrients.

Refined Sugars Wreak Havoc with Blood Sugar Levels

The main problem with simple carbohydrates exists in their _concentration_. In nature, sugars are found diluted in large amounts of water in fruit and sugar beets, coexisting with fiber and many other nutrients. When removed from their original plant sources, table sugar and other simple carbos are refined, processed, and concentrated. They cause a reaction in the human body more akin to that of a drug or chemical than that which would occur from the natural, whole foods from which they were derived. When eaten in large amounts, these concentrated sugars cause a rapid and dramatic rise in blood sugar levels, which causes the pancreas (a digestive organ that produces insulin to counteract blood sugar) and other digestive organs to go wild trying to handle this instantaneous influx of excessive sugar. This over-reaction eats up too much sugar, causing a precipitous drop in your blood sugar level. This plummet affects your brain before any other organ: You feel tired, irritable, nervous, and light-headed, and may have other low blood sugar (or hypoglycemic) symptoms. In order to alleviate these symptoms, you grab a jelly doughnut and a cup of sugared coffee, and the roller coaster ride starts all over again.

Macronutrient Food Sources

Macronutrient	Super Baby Food Sources	Other Sources
Carbohydrates	whole grains beans and legumes nuts and seeds starchy and other vegetables and their juices fruits and their juices dairy products blackstrap molasses	wheat flour (not whole), same as white flour white sugar white rice cakes, pies ice cream colas and other soft drinks
Fats	nuts and seeds flaxseed (linseed) oil avocado eggs dairy products whole grains	meat butter margarine processed vegetable oils lard shortening
Proteins	eggs dairy products combinations of grains, beans, legumes, nuts, seeds, and brewer's yeast	red meat pork poultry fish

BUYER BEWARE: Avoid the OSEs on the Label

The food industry takes full advantage of the fact that these sugars can technically be labeled "natural." To increase sales, they make their food products taste good by loading them with lots of sweet-tasting sugary additives, and mislead the uninformed public that their product is healthy because it's "all natural." Think about it, a five-pound bag of white sugar (sucrose) is, in fact, all natural. Don't fall for the advertising. Ignore all healthy and natural claims written in big, brightly-colored letters on the front of the package and go for the jugular—the ingredients list. In general, look for ingredients that end in -ose; they're the sugars.

Names That Mean Sugar in Lists of Ingredients

sucrose	molasses	syrup
dextrose	corn sweetener	sorghum syrup
maltose	mannitol	high fructose corn syrup
fructose	sorbitol	fruit juice concentrate
glucose	honey	and, of course, sugar
lactose		

BUYER BEWARE: The Hidden Sugar Amount Trick

Here's a trick that food manufacturers use to make you think you're getting less sugar than is actually in their products. Let's say that a jar of peaches actually has more sugar than peaches, but the manufacturer doesn't want you to realize this. The list of ingredients on the side of the jar may read: peaches, dextrose, sucrose, and fructose. (This is a simplified version of the trick. A real package intersperses several other ingredients between the ose's, so they're not as obvious.) Because peaches is first on the ingredient list, the unwary consumer may think that they are actually getting more peaches than anything else. Well, there may be more peaches than dextrose, and more dextrose than sucrose, and more sucrose than fructose, but when you add up the quantities of dextrose, sucrose, and fructose, the total sugar content is greater than the amount of peaches.

5 grams=1 teaspoon

The new mandatory nutrition labels make it difficult for a food manufacturer to hide the actual total sugar amount in their products. Look at the second line from the bottom in the label; it has the word *Sugars* followed by a number of grams. Consider every 5 grams of sugar one teaspoon. (Actually, 1 teaspoon of sugar is equivalent to 4.76 grams or about 4¾ grams.) For instance, if a cereal has 15 grams of sugar per serving, that's the equivalent of more than 3 teaspoons of sugar. Some children's breakfast cereals are more than 50% sugar! Soft drinks are other high-sugar offenders, with colas containing about 9 teaspoons of sugar per 12 ounces, and orange soda with almost 12 teaspoons per 12 ounces. Picture taking a 12-ounce glass of water and stirring 12 teaspoons of sugar into it and feeding it to your children! This is what you are giving your children when you feed them soft drinks, except soft drinks have more junk added: chemicals, food colorings, etc.

Our Taste Buds Previously Insured a Balanced Diet

It's a shame that the stuff that tastes so good to us is so bad for us. Every wonder why? I once heard a good explanation. In the environments of our ancestors, complex carbohydrates were plentiful and easily acquired from the abundance of plant life. Foods containing fats and sugars were more scarce, so nature (knowing that a variety of foods helps to insure a balanced diet) supposedly built into our taste buds a love for the rare fats and sweets. Hence, our ancestors had a great desire for them, and would go through more difficult maneuvers to obtain them.

A friend of mine has a cute cartoon on his office door. Under a picture of a little boy saying a prayer at his bedside reads this caption: Dear Lord, Please put my vitamins in candy instead of broccoli.

Sugar Substitutes

Sugar substitutes have no place in a baby's diet. Nutrasweet® and saccharin® are not natural, in my opinion, no matter what the ads say. Artificial additives and chemicals should not be put into your baby's body. At the time this book was printed, some scientists believe that the risk of brain cancer may be increased by the use of some artificial sweeteners, which have been sold for years as being "safe." How true this is, we don't know, but why take the chance!

Sugar in Baby Foods

Baby food manufacturers have stopped adding sugars to most baby foods, thanks to pressure from the public, but they still add it to the dessert-type baby foods. Read the label and don't buy them.

Complex Carbohydrates or Starches

Whereas simple carbohydrates (sugars) have simple molecular structures that are digested too quickly and easily by the body, complex carbohydrates have complex molecular structures that take hours to be digested. A complex carbohydrate molecule is actually a very long chain of thousands of simple sugar molecules, which gets broken down and released into the bloodstream slowly and steadily. Blood sugar levels stay at an even keel, along with organ activity and your emotions. After eating complex carbos, you don't feel hungry again for several hours and your desire for food again comes back slowly. It is much healthier to eat whole foods with complex carbohydrates that your body breaks down into sugars, than to let food manufacturers refine whole foods into simple sugars before they even reach your plate.

Complex carbohydrates, also called starches, are found in grains, beans, legumes, nuts, seeds, and the products made from them, such as breads and pastas, and in starchy foods such as potatoes and other vegetables.

BUYER BEWARE:
   "Complex carbohydrates" does not necessarily mean "whole grain."
At the time this book was printed, a breakfast cereal manufacturer was advertising that their product contained "complex carbohydrates." Beware that this could mean that the product is made out of white flour. Read the chapter on Whole Grains beginning on page 218 to find out why white flour is so nutritionally inferior to whole grain flour.

Fiber

Although some refer to fiber as a nutrient class by itself, it is actually a type of complex carbohydrate. Fibers, like starches, are long chains of sugar units, but the bonds between them cannot be broken by our systems, and they pass through the body undigested. Fiber, sometimes imprecisely referred to as "roughage," comes only from plant foods. There is no fiber in meat, milk, eggs, and cheese. It is found in whole grains, legumes, nuts, seeds, and in parts of fruits and vegetables, such as in the peels of fruits, the membranes between orange segments, and in the strings of celery. Fiber is listed in the ingredients on commercial food products as pectin, cellulose, and guar gum. Fibrous additives change the texture of the food. Another fiber ingredient is lignin, which is actually a woody material from the stems and bark of plants.

There are two types of fiber found in food: insoluble and soluble. Insoluble fiber (lignin, cellulose, hemicellulose) does not dissolve in water and adds bulk to the diet. It speeds up passage of food through the intestine, which helps prevent constipation and speeds carcinogens out of the body before they can do much harm, thereby reducing cancer risk. Soluble fiber (pectin, gums, psyllium), which does dissolve in water, also increases bulk in the diet. It slows down the absorption of carbohydrates and sugars, which helps manage diabetes. Soluble fiber has also been found to lower blood cholesterol levels.

Babies Eating Super Baby Food Do Not Need Bran

We all know that bran is a good source of fiber, but I don't recommend adding it to your baby's foods. If he is eating the Super Baby Food Diet, he is getting plenty of fiber and he doesn't need bran. In fact, too much bran is not good because it binds with certain nutrients and carries them out of the body before they can be assimilated.

Food Sources of Water Soluble Fiber	Food Sources of Water Insoluble Fiber
whole grains (in cereal, bread, pasta, crackers, muffins, rolls, etc.) vegetables and fruits with peels nuts and seeds	legumes (dried beans, peas, and lentils) oats and oat bran, barley apples, pears, plums oranges and other citrus fruits

There is NO Fiber in Meat

People are beginning to become aware of the importance of a high-fiber, low-fat diet for good health. The Department of Agriculture's two food pyramids *for adults* are shown on this page and the next. The older pyramid below depicts a diet containing meat and the pyramid on the opposite page shows the pyramid for a vegetarian diet. The major difference between the two pyramids is the replacement of meat in the top right box with the meat alternative group. Meat has fat and no fiber, whereas fiber is plentiful in the meat alternatives: legumes, nuts, and seeds. There are a few other differences, such as the healthier-for-adults low-fat dairy products and the healthier whole grain bread products shown in the vegetarian pyramid.

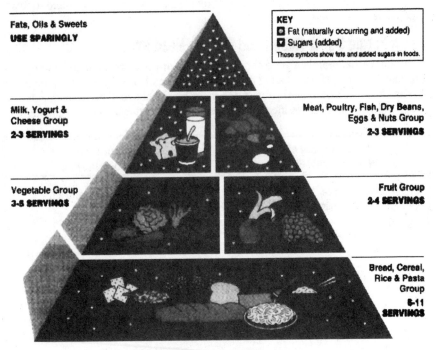

Food Pyramid **for Adults**
Source: Department of Agriculture

Vegetable Fats and Oils,
Sweets, and Salt

EAT SPARINGLY

Low-Fat or Non-Fat,
Milk, Yogurt, Fresh Cheese,
and fortified
Alternative Group
2 - 3 Servings
EAT MODERATELY

Legume, Nut, Seed, and
Meat Alternative Group
2 - 3 Servings
EAT MODERATELY

Vegetable Group
3 - 5 Servings
EAT
GENEROUSLY

Fruit Group
2 - 4 Servings

EAT
GENEROUSLY

Whole Grain
Bread, Cereal,
Pasta, and Rice
Group
6 - 11 Servings
EAT LIBERALLY

Vegetarian Food Pyramid **for Adults**
Source: Department of Agriculture

Fats: The Good, the Bad, and the Ugly

The family of lipids (the scientific name for what we commonly call fats) includes fats, oils, cholesterol, triglycerides, and other lipids. Fats, along with carbohydrates, are the two major sources of energy for the body. Fats are also needed to provide insulation to keep the body warm. In general, women have a higher percentage of fat stored in their bodies than men, which is why they can supposedly stand colder temperatures than men. Fats are also needed in the body to hold essential fatty acids and the fat-soluble vitamins (A, D, E, and K).

Fatty acids (so named because their molecular structure contains an acid group) are classified as either saturated or unsaturated, depending on whether their structures are holding a maximum amount of hydrogen. If they contain a maximum amount of hydrogen, they are referred to as saturated fatty acids, because they are "saturated" with hydrogen. If it is possible for a fat to hold more hydrogen, and hence not saturated with hydrogen, they are called unsaturated fatty acids. Knowing this is important later in understanding hydrogenation (page 507).

The Bad—Saturated Fats

Saturated fats are found mostly in animal products, such as meats, poultry, lard, shortening, butter, and eggs. They are also found in a few vegetable products: cocoa butter, coconut oil, palm oil, and palm kernel oil. Saturated fats are solid at room temperature.

BUYER BEWARE: Saturated Fat in Plant Oils

Some vegetable products (cocoa butter, coconut oil, palm oil, and palm kernel oil) do contain large proportions of saturated fats. If a product is labeled "Non-dairy" or "No animal products," that doesn't necessarily mean that it contains no saturated fats.

Our bodies are able to internally manufacture all the saturated fat it needs from other fat sources in our diets, and therefore we can be perfectly healthy if we never ate a gram of saturated fat. Studies have shown that saturated fats from animal products clog arteries and increase the chance of heart disease. They also interfere with the body's production of the good fats, such as EFAs (discussed next). But there is good news for us chocoholics: Recent studies have brought into question the heart-damaging effects of saturated fats from plant products, such as cocoa butter. They might not be so bad after all.

BUYER BEWARE: Pork—The Other White Meat.

White meat generally contains less fat than red meat. The slogan "Pork. The other white meat," in my opinion, misleads the uninformed public into thinking that pork has a low fat content similar to poultry. Not true. Most pork is much more fatty than white meat, and some pork is actually more fatty than some red meat. Compare:

Grams of Fat in 3½ ounces:					
Pork:		**Beef:**		**Roasted Chicken:**	
ground pork	31	hamburger	20	with skin	15
pork chop	32	rib roast	40	without skin	3
bacon	52			fried drumstick:	10

The Good—Unsaturated Fats

Unsaturated fats are usually supplied by plants, and include oils from vegetables, such as corn oil. Unsaturated fats are liquid at room temperature. The two types of unsaturated fats are **monounsaturated fats**, found primarily in vegetable oils such as avocado, olive, and canola or rapeseed, and **polyunsaturated fats** (PUFAs), found mostly in seed and nut oils, such as sunflower, safflower, walnut, corn, and soy. PUFAs are also found in fish oils, because of the sea plants eaten by the fish. It is important to note that although we need some unsaturated fats in our diet, an overabundance may lead to serious health problems. PUFAs, when consumed in excess, may lower HDL (the "good" cholesterol, page 508) levels in the bloodstream. Monounsaturated fats are the only fats that have managed to keep a clean bill of health through all the scientific studies.

The Refrigerator Test

Most oils are part saturated fat and part unsaturated fat. The more saturated the fat, the more it tends to solidify at room temperature or at temperatures slightly cooler. To determine the amount of saturated fat contained in a bottle of oil, place it in the refrigerator and wait for it to get cold. The parts that become solid are the saturated fat, and the parts that become thick or cloudy, but remain liquid, are the polyunsaturated fat, and the liquid parts are the monounsaturated fat.

Essential Fatty Acids or EFAs

The word "essential" in the world of nutrition refers to a nutrient that cannot be made by the body, and therefore must be supplied by the diet. In other words, it is essential that an "essential nutrient" be part of your diet.

Essential fatty acids (EFAs) are the fats we must get from our diet, because our bodies cannot manufacture them. Of all the fatty acids, only two are essential: **linoleic acid** (LA) and **linolenic acid** (LNA or ALENA). The two EFAs are both polyunsaturated fats. They are part of every single solitary cell in our bodies, and make up a large percent of brain tissues. EFAs also have a lot to do with the way cholesterol works in our systems. (See page 554.)

Omega-3 (ω3) and Omega-6 (ω6)

Lately, the EFAs omega-3, a linolenic acid, and omega-6, a linoleic acid, have been mentioned frequently in the popular press. Omega-6 is found in corn oils and other oils from warm weather plants, such as sunflower and safflower oils. Omega-3 is found in cold-water fatty fish (tuna, cod, mackerel, salmon), green leafy vegetables, some nuts, and cold weather plants like flaxseed. You may have heard that Eskimos, who eat lots of cold-water fish, have a low incidence of heart disease.

The typical American diet contains more than enough omega-6, but is sorely lacking in omega-3. Researchers believe that there should be a one-to-one ratio of omega-3's to omega-6's in the human diet. It is estimated that the current ratio is about ten-to-one (10 omega-6's to one omega-3)! Omega-3 deficiencies are believed to cause heart disease, arthritis, skin problems, problems in the immune system, and mental illness.

Forget Fish Oils and Go for the Flax

The popular press has been giving much attention to the fact that eating more fish can decrease the incidence of heart disease because of its omega-3 content. This is true, but fish may have high amounts of heavy metals from water pollution, such as lead (page 556) and mercury (page 558). I don't understand why the press, along with some authors of "good fat" and omega-3 books, seem to concentrate only on fish. They completely ignore the absolute best source of omega-3: the small brown flaxseed.

We "health faddists" have known for years about the fabulous flaxseed. Flaxseed is THE food highest in the omega-3 fatty acid linolenic acid, and one of the best food sources of the other essential fatty acid, linoleic acid. Flax doesn't have the problem of heavy metals, and no fish have to be slaughtered in order to get flax. To get the amount of omega-3 found in flaxseed, you would have to eat quite a few fish meals, probably more than most people would want to eat. For example, four grams of flax seeds (about ½ tablespoon) have 2372 mg of omega-3 fatty acids, whereas a half a can of white tuna fish has only 700 mg and 3½ ounces of rainbow trout has less than 600 mg.

Somehow I feel I must be fair to the fish, though, and say that the best fish source, sardines, does have quite a bit of omega-3—5000 mg per 3½ ounce serving. And two other fish—sockeye salmon and Atlantic mackerel, have 2500-3000 per 3½ ounce serving. All other fish are under the 2000 mg mark. Other non-fish sources of omega-3 are: walnuts and walnut butter, canola oil, olive oil, alfalfa sprouts, soybeans, and spinach.

Flax for Your Baby

I suggest that you feed your baby about a ½ teaspoon of whole raw flax seeds every day. First, you must grind them well in your blender or they may pass through your baby's system undigested. Feed them to your baby immediately after grinding, because they become rancid in just a few hours after grinding. Mix them into his Super Porridge, yogurt, or other food.

You can buy flaxseed oil at the natural foods store. (Flaxseed or linseed oil from the hardware store is not for human consumption. Do not eat!) Dr. Leo Galland, on pages 67-68 of *SuperImmunity for Kids*, recommends a teaspoon of flaxseed oil per day added to baby's formula bottle. Or you can rub a teaspoon on his skin and let it get absorbed. If it smells "fishy," don't worry, that's normal.

You must keep flaxseed oil refrigerated or frozen. Keep only until the date on the label, or ask the natural foods store cashier how long it will keep. The oil usually keeps for up to 2 months in the refrigerator, or up to 4 months in the freezer. Be careful that the oil has not become rancid. Taste it every time and if it is even slightly bitter, throw the whole bottle out.

WARNING: Flaxseed oil should never be used for frying, as the high temperatures destroy all of the beneficial EFAs and may create TFAs (discussed later).

I prefer flaxseed over flaxseed oil because it is a whole food and contains the fiber, whereas the oil does not. Also, whole flaxseed (before it is ground in the blender) does not become rancid quickly as the oil does.

WARNING: Omega-3 greatly increases the effectiveness of B vitamins. If you eat flaxseed regularly, do not take megadoses of the B vitamins.

Essential Fatty Acids and Rancidity

Essential fatty acids and other unsaturated fatty acids are unstable and become rancid quickly if not stored carefully. When the oils containing EFAs are exposed to air, they attract oxygen. This ability to easily attract oxygen is one property that is very beneficial to the body, because EFAs help carry oxygen through the body. Unfortunately, it is also the property that causes a problem with rancidity.

This problem with air exposure causing rancidity is the reason why it is so important to eat seeds immediately after grinding. Ground seeds are broken open and their oils are exposed to oxygen, causing oxidation to occur and the seeds' oils to become rancid.

One way to prevent rancidity in vegetable oils is to keep them under refrigeration, a storage method that is expensive for the food industry. A much cheaper method of preventing rancidity is hydrogenation.

The Ugly and Very Bad—Partially Hydrogenated Oils and TFAs

Hydrogenation is a chemical process that adds hydrogen to unsaturated fatty acids. Remember that unsaturated fatty acids are not holding the maximum amount of hydrogen—they are not saturated with hydrogen (page 504). Hydrogenation makes oils more saturated: monounsaturated oils become more polyunsaturated, and polyunsaturated oils become more saturated. Hydrogenation adds to the saturation, and therefore also to the solidity, of previously liquid vegetable oils, making their texture more palatable to some people.

Adding hydrogen is a cheap way to make fats less prone to rancidity. It greatly extends the shelf life of fats. Unfortunately, it may also greatly reduce the life of people that eat them. If an oil is completely hydrogenated, it is similar to a saturated fat and as stable. Partially hydrogenated oils are worse than fully hydrogenated or totally saturated oils. If an oil is only partially hydrogenated, the part that has not taken on hydrogen—the unsaturated part—is open to the formation of trans fatty acids. **Trans fatty acids (TFAs)** are carcinogens (cancer-causing agents), and also have been found to raise LDL (the bad cholesterol) levels in the bloodstream and decrease HDL (the good cholesterol) levels. They are not found naturally in foods, and are brought about by heating oils to high temperatures or by chemical processes such as hydrogenation.

BUYER BEWARE: Partially Hydrogenated Oils
Avoid any food products containing partially hydrogenated oils as you would avoid plutonium.

BUYER BEWARE: Margarine and TFAs
Margarine is more solid than liquid because their healthy liquid oils have been partially hydrogenated to make them solid. Even though margarine may not contain TFAs (and the manufacturers advertise that they do not contain trans fatty acids, trans fats, or TFAs), their partially hydrogenated oils most likely will turn to TFAs.

Cholesterol

Cholesterol is a not really a fat—it's actually a sterol, another member of the lipid family. Cholesterol, unlike fats, is not an energy source of the body. It is an essential structural component in every cell in our bodies, and is also needed to build hormones like testosterone and estrogen. The cholesterol contained in human skin is converted into vitamin D by exposure to sunlight. The brain contains a higher concentration of cholesterol than any other organ in the body. Cholesterol is not essential in the diet because the liver can manufacture it. Dietary cholesterol (the cholesterol in the foods we eat) is present only in animal products like meat, poultry, eggs, and dairy products. Serum cholesterol (or blood cholesterol) is the cholesterol in the bloodstream resulting from cholesterol in the diet or from being manufactured by the liver. High levels of dietary or serum cholesterol have been associated with greater risk of heart attack. But authorities believe that it's not just the cholesterol in our diets that promotes heart disease, it's more the total amount of fat and lipids that we consume. We Americans just eat too much fat! Although we adults should restrict all dietary fats, including cholesterol and saturated fats, we should not restrict fats in our babies' diets.

HDL and LDL

Because fats and cholesterol cannot dissolve in blood, they must hitch a ride on a certain kind of protein in order to get around the body through the bloodstream. These proteins, called transport proteins or **lipoproteins** (lipo for fats, proteins for proteins), act as little taxis to move fats and cholesterol around in the body. There are two types of lipoproteins: high-density lipoproteins or **HDLs** (the "good" cholesterol) and low-density lipoproteins or **LDLs** (the "bad" cholesterol). HDLs carry cholesterol out of the arteries back to the liver for reprocessing or out of the body. Therefore we consider them good lipoproteins because their act of removing fats helps prevent heart disease. A way to remember that HDL's are the good cholesterol is to remember that we want a *high* level of *high*-density lipoproteins in our bloodstream. LDLs carry cholesterol out of the liver and into the bloodstream. An excess of LDLs causes cholesterol to get deposited in the artery walls, a process known as "hardening of the arteries." We want a *low* level of LDLs in our blood. So, you see, all cholesterol is the same. When people say that cholesterol is "good" or "bad," they are actually referring to the type of lipoprotein that is carrying it in the blood.

BUYER BEWARE: "No Cholesterol!" May Raise Your Cholesterol

An excess of saturated fat in the diet has been proven to contribute to elevated blood cholesterol levels. On some food products with high saturated fat, I believe that the food manufacturer purposely puts the words *No Cholesterol!* on the labels to mislead the consumer that their product is heart-healthy. Although it may be true that their product contains no cholesterol, the high level of saturated fat contributes to high blood cholesterol and makes it very heart-UNhealthy.

Triglycerides

Triglycerides are "bundles" of individual saturated and unsaturated fats and are a major form of storage for fatty acids in the body. Triglycerides are also found in the bloodstream, and a common question heard in the doctor's office is, "How are my triglycerides?" High triglycerides levels are correlated with heart disease.

Free Radicals

Fats in the body sometimes change into reactive compounds called "free radicals," which do serious damage to body cells. Free radicals are believed to cause cancer and heart disease. The more fats you eat, the higher the chance that free radicals will occur in your body. Antioxidants (vitamins A, C, E, and selenium) have been found to help rid the body of free radicals. And, as nature would design it, the low-fat foods—fruits, vegetables, and whole grains—are the foods that contain lots of antioxidants. Fill up on them and you won't have room for fatty foods.

Fake Fat—Olestra®

Proctor and Gamble finally did it—came up with a fat that feels like a fat in your mouth, but has no calories. If it sounds to good to be true, it is. Do not feed this to your baby. Olestra, like any other unnatural, synthetically-manufactured food product, is not, in my opinion, safe to eat. Besides robbing your body of the fat-soluble vitamins and carotenoids, it can cause digestive problems. It also stimulates your taste for high-fat foods, an eating habit we can do without.

Fats and Your Baby

Babies need fats. One of the main problems with a STRICT vegetarian diet for babies is a lack of fat *and* calories, because fat is a concentrated source of calories. The Super Baby Food Diet includes these foods that contain fats: eggs, dairy products, nuts, and seeds. Breast milk and formula contain fat. Some fats also exist in whole grains and beans, especially soybeans and tofu. For the number of fat grams contained in the Super Baby Foods, see the table on pages 523-524.

Food Sources of Fats and Oils

The table below summarizes the main food sources of saturated and unsaturated fatty acids.

Food Sources of Saturated Fatty Acids	Food Sources of Unsaturated Fatty Acids	
	Monounsaturated*	Polyunsaturated*
hydrogenated oil	avocado	pumpkin seeds
margarine with partially	avocado oil	flaxseeds
hydrogenated oil	canola (rapeseed) oil	sesame seeds
meat	safflower oil	sesame oil
bacon	sunflower oil	sunflower seeds
beef tallow	olives	sunflower oil
chicken fat	olive oil	safflower oil
lamb tallow	peanuts	Brazil nuts
salt pork	peanut oil	walnuts
poultry	almonds	pine nuts
shortening	almond oil	butternuts
lard	filberts or hazelnuts	soybeans
dairy products, such as	cashews	soybean oil
butter, milk (not skim),	macadamia nuts	mayonnaise made from non-hydrogenated oils
cheese, yogurt	pecans	
coconut oil	pistachios	
palm oil	acorns	
palm kernel oil	beechnuts	
	hickory nuts	

*Nuts contain both monounsaturated and polyunsaturated fatty acids. Nuts are classified here in the category of the predominant fatty acid.

BUYER BEWARE: Misleading Advertising: "90% Fat Free" Can Mean 75% Fat
Products often claim to contain some percentage of fat that is very misleading, because the percentage is calculated by weight instead of by calories. Here is a simple example to see how this trick is done. Let's say that you have in one glass 10 grams of oil, which is all fat and contains 90 calories because each fat gram is 9 calories. In another glass you have 90 grams of sugared water that has no fat and 30 calories. Mix the two glasses and you have 100 grams altogether, 10 grams of which are fat and 90 grams of which are nonfat. By weight, the fat content is 10 grams out of 100, which is 10% fat by weight, or 90% nonfat. The mixture can be legally advertised as 90% fat free! But by calories, the more appropriate way to measure fat content, the fat percentage is much higher. The mixture is 90 calories from the all-fat oil and 30 calories from the no-

fat sugar water, for a total of 120 calories. Since 90 calories out of the 120 calories come from fat, 75% (90÷120) of the calories come from fat. By calories, the mixture is 75% fat, even though by weight it was only 10% fat. So go by the nutrition label and not the advertising on the front of the package. To get the percentage of fat by calories, take the number of fat grams from the nutrition label, multiply by 9, and divide by the total number of calories.

How Many Calories Does My Baby Need?

You may know that to approximate your daily caloric requirements, you multiply your body weight in pounds by about 13 calories. A 150-pound woman needs about 13x150 or about 2000 calories per day to maintain her weight. You can do the same to get the approximate number of calories needed daily by your baby. But instead of using 13, use the number 50, because your baby needs about 50 calories per pound of body weight. Wouldn't it be nice if we could use that number? That same 150-pound woman would be able to eat 7500 calories a day without gaining weight!

A baby needs a lot more energy per pound than we do, because of his fast growth rate and activity level. More details about figuring your baby's daily caloric requirements are on pages 522-525.

Vitamins and Minerals—The Micronutrients

Vitamins act as catalysts in the biochemical reactions of the human body. Our bodies need very small amounts of vitamins and minerals, which is why they are called "micronutrients," but if we don't get the proper amounts, severe illness or even death may result. Whereas the macronutrients are measured in grams, vitamins and minerals are measured in milligrams (mg) or micrograms (mcg). There are 28 grams in one ounce. A milligram (mg) is one thousandth of a gram; a microgram (mcg) is one millionth of a gram, and that's pretty small!

Fat-soluble vs Water-soluble Vitamins

Vitamins come in two varieties: those that are fat-soluble (vitamins A, D, E, and K) and those that are water-soluble (all other vitamins). The water-soluble vitamins are found in the watery parts of foods and do their work in the water-filled parts of the body. Excesses of water-soluble vitamins get flushed out of the body in the urine and therefore are rarely toxic. In contrast, excesses of the fat-soluble vitamins are stored in the body, making toxicity possible. Because excesses of the water-soluble vitamins are excreted and not stored by the body, it is important that they be part of your diet every day. You can be a little more lax about getting fat-soluble vitamins daily, because of the body's ability to store them.

Nutrient Supplements

Many experts now agree that vitamin and mineral supplements are helpful, but only in small doses and in the same proportions in which they are found in nature, as in a good multivitamin/multimineral supplement. Our food supply does not always supply us with the vital nutrients we need because of nutrient-depleted chemicalized soils, too-early harvesting, long transportation times, and less-than-optimal storage conditions. Nutrient supplements can help assure that we are getting the vitamins and minerals missing in our foods. Some people eat too much processed, denatured, sugared, salted, canned and boxed pretend foods. They think they can make up for it by pumping vitamin pills into their systems. But supplements are meant to be just that—supplements. They should supplement a good diet, not make up for a bad one.

Today, there's much talk about taking megavitamins and megaminerals. Taking large amounts of pills may not only be unhelpful, it may actually be harmful. No nutrient works alone, it must be in proper proportion with other nutrients as they are found in nature. Taking megadoses of one nutrient can leave us deficient in another, or worse yet, can cause toxicity. This is especially true of the fat-soluble nutrients. Fat-soluble nutrients are stored in body fat, unlike the water-soluble nutrients, which are not stored by the body. Too much of the fat-soluble vitamins can build to toxic amounts in the body. In contrast, too much of the water-soluble vitamins will most likely be excreted in the urine. It is said that Americans have the healthiest urine in the world.

> **REMEMBER:** Take fat-soluble vitamin supplements with foods that contain fat (as little as 3-4 grams of fat is all you need) so that they will be better assimilated. See more about vitamin supplements on page 68.

The next appendix, *Appendix F. Nutrient Tables with Baby-Sized Portions*, contains tables showing the nutritional food composition of the Super Baby Foods.

Proteins—The Body-Building Nutrient

The human body is constantly in need of protein to continuously replace its parts. Perhaps you've heard that your body completely replaces its skin every seven years. All of our fat cells get replaced within a year's time, and no blood cell in our bodies is more than 4 months old. Your baby needs even more protein than an adult proportionate to his size, because along with all of this replacing of body cells, he also is growing at a rapid rate and adding new body cells each day. While the adult body needs about one-third gram of protein for each pound of body weight, your baby needs approximately a full gram of protein for each pound of body weight, or proportionately 3 times the adult amount. The information on pages 526-527 discusses the number of protein grams your baby needs each day, and the table shows the number of grams of complete protein in the Super Baby Foods.

The Super Baby Food Diet Supplies Lots of Protein

It is the norm for Americans to overconsume protein. In our meat-centered culture, many people believe that meat is required in the diet to supply protein requirements and other nutrients. They may be concerned that the Super Baby Food Diet, a lacto-ovo vegetarian diet (defined on page 278), will cause stunted growth or other health problems in their baby. If you have this concern, perhaps the table on page 527 will reassure you that your baby will get more than enough of her protein requirements from the Super Baby Food Diet. Pediatricians agree that a lacto-ovo vegetarian diet is a healthy and safe diet for a growing baby. It is a strict vegan diet that causes concern for most health professionals.

Amino Acids are the Building Blocks of Proteins

Our bodies are constantly building proteins to be used for maintenance, growth, and repair. The substances it uses for all this protein synthesis are called "amino acids." Surely you remember eighth-grade health science class—"amino acids are the building blocks of proteins." You rotely answered the test question on this memorized fact correctly, but had no idea why you had to know it. Well, here's why: It will help you to understand protein complementarity so that you can give your baby a super healthy diet.

Essential Amino Acids (EAAs)

There are 22 amino acids. Of the 22, only 8 amino acids cannot be manufactured by the body and must be provided by foods in the diet. These 8 amino acids are called *essential amino acids* or *EAAs*. (Remember what *essential* means in nutrition, page 505.) Here's the kicker: Not only do you need all 8 of these EAAs in your diet, you also have to eat them together in the same meal. For example, if you eat a meal with only 6 of these EAAs, complete proteins cannot be manufactured. (Recent studies show that this may not be true, but I'm going to assume that it is to be on the safe side.)

Protein Complementarity

With few exceptions, only foods from animals, such as meat, milk, and eggs, contain all 8 EAAs in the proper proportions to make significant amounts of complete proteins. Grains, beans, vegetables, and other plant foods, when eaten alone, do not supply enough complete proteins for the body because they are lacking in one or more EAAs. However, if we combine a plant food lacking in one EAA with another plant food strong in that EAA, complete protein is formed. The protein is equal to or better than the protein from meat and other animal products, and you don't have to kill any animals or eat all of the fat and toxins that go along with meat. This process of combining non-meat foods to make complete protein, so that one food's weakness in EAAs is compensated by another food's strength in those EAAs, is referred to as *protein complementarity*.

The next table shows some plant food combinations that form complete protein. You can learn more about protein complementarity by reading the single best book on the subject: Frances Moore Lappé's classic book *Diet for a Small Planet*. *Recipes for a Small Planet*, by Ellen Buchman Ewald, has many great vegetarian recipes using the principles of protein complementarity. See bibliography.

The measures in the table below are for dry, uncooked grains and legumes. For example, when you see 2 C rice, that means 2 cups of dry brown rice before cooking in water. 1 C beans means 1 cup of dry beans or legumes before soaking and cooking in water. Rice can be replaced with oats, barley, millet, and other grains with a similar effect in protein complementarity. Peanuts are technically legumes (because of the pod), but they should be treated like nuts when combining foods for complete proteins.

If you're not interested in more details about protein complementarity, skip over the next section and go to page 520.

High Protein Plant Food Combinations

Super Baby Food Combinations That Form Complete Protein	Example Food Combinations (C=cups, T=tablespoon, t=teaspoon)
2 GRAINS+1 LEGUMES Combine approximately 2 parts grains with 1 part beans, peas, or other legumes.	2 C rice + 1 C beans ½ C rice + ¼ C lentils ½ C millet + ¼ C soy grits 1 C whole wheat flour + ¼ C soy flour or powder 1 C bulgur + ⅓ C split peas ½ C rice + 3 oz tofu 1 slice whole wheat bread + 1 oz tofu 1 slice whole wheat bread + 1 T peanut butter ½ cup pasta + 8 oz tofu
PEANUTS + MILK	½ C milk + 5 T peanut butter ¼ C yogurt + 2½ T peanut butter
SEEDS + MILK	½ C yogurt + 5 T tahini 1 T yogurt + ½ C sunflower seed sprouts
GRAINS + MILK	¼ C rice + ⅓ C milk or yogurt 1 C whole wheat flour + ⅔ C milk or yogurt 1 slice whole wheat bread + 1 t cheese 1 cup macaroni + ½ oz cheese
MISCELLANEOUS	¼ C rice + 1 T brewer's yeast 1 slice whole wheat bread + 1 T peanut butter ½ pound white potatoes + ¼ C grated cheese 1 C milk or yogurt + ½ C beans ½ pound white potatoes + ¾ C yogurt ½ C cornmeal + ⅛ C dry beans scalloped potatoes broccoli with cheese sauce eggplant Parmesan

An Example to Help in the Understanding of Protein Complementarity

This example is to help you understand the concept of protein complementarity. It is optional reading and can be skipped without losing any continuity in this book.

This example, where chairs are being assembled instead of complete proteins, may help you to understand protein complementarity. Let's say that we are making only one type of chair, made from only one type of seat, one type of armrest, and one type of leg. To get these parts for the chairs, we go to a supply house and buy any of the 4 different boxes containing the chair parts shown below. For example, one box (Box A) contains these chair parts: 22 legs, 4 seats, and 5 armrests.

Each chair is made of: 1 seat + 2 arms + 4 legs

Box **A**	Box **B**	Box **C**	Box **D**
22 legs 4 seats 5 arms	4 legs 2 seats 8 arms	6 legs 2 seats 4 arms	4 legs 2 seats 2 arms

If we buy one of Box A, we can make only 2 chairs. Even though we have enough legs to make 5 chairs and enough seats to make 4 chairs, we are limited by the fact that we have only 5 arms, which will make only 2 chairs. With only 5 arms, no matter how many surplus legs and seats, only 2 chairs can be assembled. *In Box A, arms are the limiting chair parts.*

How many chairs can we make with Box B? Only 1, because even though we have enough seats for 2 chairs and enough arms for 4 chairs, we can make only one 4-legged chair. Legs is the limiting chair part. Below is the number of chairs and the limiting chair parts for each of the four boxes.

Box **A**	Box **B**	Box **C**	Box **D**
2 chairs limited by arms	1 chair limited by legs	1 chair limited by legs	1 chair limited by legs and arms

If we bought 1 Box A and 1 Box B, we can make 2 chairs + 1 chair or 3 chairs, right? No, we can actually make 6 chairs! Why? Because they complement each other—Box A's weakness in arms is compensated by Box B's strength in arms, and Box B's leg limitation is counterbalanced by Box A's abundance in legs. By buying two boxes which complement each other, we have doubled the number of complete chairs we can assemble—6 chairs instead of 3.

Box **A**		Box **B**		A + B
22 legs 4 seats 5 arms	+	4 legs 2 seats 8 arms	=	26 legs 6 seats 13 arms
2 chairs	+	1 chair	=	6 chairs

A+B make 6 chairs, with 2 legs and 1 arm leftover. If, instead of combining these 2 different boxes, we used 2 Box A's, we'd only have 4 chairs instead of 6. With 2 Box B's, we'd have only 2 chairs.

❶ **In combining different boxes, we are able to manufacture more complete chairs than we would if we used chair parts from two of the same box.**

What if we assemble chairs using Box B and Box C?

Each chair is made of: 1 seat + 2 arms + 4 legs

Box **B**		Box **C**		B + C
4 legs 2 seats 8 arms	+	6 legs 2 seats 4 arms	=	10 legs 4 seats 12 arms
1 chair	+	1 chair	=	2 chairs

Instead of being able to make *more* than 1 + 1, we still get only 2 chairs. Why? Because B and C are both limited by the same chair parts, legs. In order to get a total greater than the sum of its parts, we must complement one box's strengths with another box's weakness, as was done in the previous example.

❷ **Note that we still are able to manufacture some chairs, but not as many as when we use complementarity.**

Look at boxes C and D. Do they complement each other? Yes, they do to a certain extent.

Box **C**		Box **D**		C + D
6 legs 2 seats 4 arms	+	4 legs 2 seats 2 arms	=	10 legs 4 seats 6 arms
1 chair	+	1 chair	=	2 chairs

We still get only 1+1=2 chairs, so there doesn't seem to be any point in combining C and D. But, in fact, there is, if you could buy a partial box. Let's say we can buy ½ of a Box D.

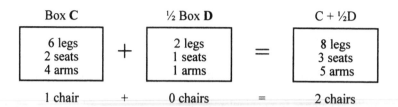

Box **C**

| 6 legs |
| 2 seats |
| 4 arms |

+

½ Box **D**

| 2 legs |
| 1 seats |
| 1 arms |

=

C + ½D

| 8 legs |
| 3 seats |
| 5 arms |

| 1 chair | + | 0 chairs | = | 2 chairs |

We have been able to make as many chairs with only half of a Box D, and hence saved half the cost of D with no ill results.

Allow me to give you just one more example: Look back at the first example, where boxes A and B were combined to make 6 chairs, with 2 legs and 1 arm leftover. To make one additional chair for a total of 7 chairs, we need 2 more legs, 1 more seat, and 1 more arm. Sound familiar? It's the contents of half of box D as shown in the previous example. Therefore A+B+½D will make 7 chairs instead of 6.

❸ **The last two examples show that if you combine different partial boxes *in the right proportions*, you can manufacture chairs even more economically than if you combine entire boxes together.**

If we wanted to have a quick graphical reference for an inventory of which chair parts are supplied by which types of boxes, we might set up a table like the one on the next page.

Looking at the table, it is easy to see that limiting chair part for Box A is arms, and that Boxes B and C have limited legs. Box D is well proportioned, when it comes to chairs. Also apparent is the fact that Box A and Box B complement each other when combined, because A's strength in legs makes up for B's leg weakness, and B's arm strength complements A's arm weakness. The table makes it evident that Boxes B and C do not make a good combination, because they both have the same weakness—legs. The table doesn't give us much information about how well Box C and D would complement each other. We can tell that they are not as poor a combination as B+C and not as good a combination of A+B or A+C. But this table does give us some very helpful information nonetheless.

Chair Part Complementarity Table	Legs	Seats	Arms
Box A	☺	●	☹
Box B	☹	●	☺
Box C	☹	●	●
Box D	●	●	●

In all of the boxes, there are always enough seats; seats are never a limiting chair part. And because of this, the seat column could be left out of the table. Only legs and arms need to be considered when combining boxes for the manufacturing of chairs.

This chair example actually was meant to give you the basics of manufacturing complete proteins by using protein complementarity. In chair part complementarity, arms, legs, and seats combine to form complete chairs. In protein complementarity, amino acids combine to form complete proteins.

The same concepts in bold print in the chair manufacturing examples above can be applied to amino acid combining to make complete proteins:

❶ When we combined different boxes, we were able to manufacture more complete chairs than if we used chair parts from two of the same box. In combining the different complementing foods, we are able to obtain more complete proteins than we would if we used two portions of the same food.

❷ We still were able to manufacture some chairs, but not as many as when we use box complementarity. In eating only one plant food, we are getting some complete protein, but not as much as when we use protein complementarity.

❸ The last two examples show that if you combine partial boxes in the right proportions, you can manufacture chairs even more economically than if you combine entire boxes together. By mixing the proper foods together in predefined proportions, we obtain complete proteins even more efficiently. For example, 2 parts grains and 1 part beans is an efficient protein combination, as shown in the first row in the table on page 514.

Like the chair complementarity table on the bottom of page 517, we can set up a similar table to depict efficient combinations of foods for protein complementarity. The table on the next page shows the EAA strengths and weaknesses of selected foods. Even though there are 8 EAAs, only 4 of them (tryptophane, isoleucine, lysine, and the sulfur-containing amino acids) are shown in the table. Just as the seats in the chair example were not limiting chair parts, the 4 EAAs not shown in the table are not often limiting amino acids, so we can ignore them and leave them out of the next table for simplicity.

PROTEIN COMPLEMENTARITY	Tryp	Isol	Lys	S-C
Millet	☺☺	●	☹	☺
Wheat Germ	☹	●	☺☺	●
Grains[*]	●	☹	☹	●
Pasta	●	●	☹	☹
Whole cornmeal	●	●	●	☹
Rye and rye flour	☹	☹	☹	●
Brewer's Yeast	●	☺	☺☺	☹
Soybeans/Tofu/Grits	☺	●	☺	☹
Garbanzos & Lima Beans	☹	●	☺☺	☹
Legumes[**]	☹	●	☺☺	☹☹
Mung Beans	☹	☹	☺☺	☹☹
Broad Beans	☹	●	☺	☹☹
Black-Eyed Peas (Cowpeas)	●	☹	☺☺	☹
Black Beans	●	☺☺	☺	☹
Peanuts/peanut butter	●	☹	☹	☹
Tahini (Sesame seed butter)	☺	☹	☹	☺
Pumpkin/Squash Seeds	☺	●	●	Unknown
Sunflower Seeds/Meal	☺	●	☹	●
Brazil nuts	☺☺	☹	☹	☺☺
Walnuts	●	☹	☹	●
Milk/Yogurt	☺	☺	☺☺	●
Nonfat Dry Milk	☺	☺	☺☺	●
Cheese[***]	●	☺	☺☺	●
Eggs	☺	☺	☺☺	☺

The symbols signify the amounts of essential amino acid (EAA) supplied by the food:

☺☺=very high ☺=high ●=adequate ☹=low
☹☹= very low Unknown=no data available.

[*] Grains include: brown rice, whole wheat, bulgur, whole wheat flour
[**] Legumes include: peas, pea beans, lentils, white beans, kidney beans
[***] Cheese includes: cottage, ricotta, Parmesan, Swiss, cheddar, bleu, Camembert

F. Nutrient Tables with Baby-Sized Portions

This appendix contains detailed nutritional information on the Super Baby Foods. The nutrient amounts supplied by each food are listed in the tables, which allow you to determine how well a food meets your baby's daily requirement for that nutrient. The foods are listed in decreasing order, with the best Super Baby Food source at the top of the list.

In these tables, the National Research Council's Recommended Daily Dietary Allowances (RDA's) for 1989 include a margin of safety. In other words, if your baby gets a little less than the recommended amount, it's probably OK. (The old minimum daily requirements were just that—minimums, which means that you were expected to get more than the amounts recommended.) The sources used in these tables for the nutrient amounts in foods were the books in the bibliography by these authors: National Research Council, the United States Department of Agriculture, Audrey H. Ensminger, and Jean A. T. Pennington.

The numbers in the tables are meant to give you a rough idea of the Super Baby Foods that supply significant amounts of the nutrients. None of these numbers should be considered extremely accurate, because nutrient content depends on several factors including the age of the food, cooking method used, the soil in which it was grown, the method and length of storage, maturity and ripeness at harvest, and other factors. Adding to the variability is the fact that every baby's nutrient requirements are different, depending on age, weight, activity level, climate, genetics, and other variables. However, I hope you find these tables helpful in planning a healthy diet for your baby.

In the tables, peanut butter means natural creamy peanut butter with no oils or salt added. Unless otherwise specified, milk means cow's milk and is either whole milk or 2%. Foods not part of the Super Baby Food Diet, such as meat, fish, commercial baby foods, processed supermarket foods, chocolate, etc. are not usually included in the tables, even though they may be good food sources of the nutrients.

Baby-Sized Portions

Note that the food portions are baby-sized for your convenience. Keep this in mind if you compare these numbers to numbers in other books, which will usually be much larger because of adult-sized portions. Most of the vegetable servings are one ounce (1 oz) servings. **One ounce is approximately equal to 30 grams, 2 tablespoons, ⅛ cup, or approximately 1 food cube.** Of course, your food cubes may be slightly larger or smaller and they contain varying amounts of water from puréeing, so allow for inaccuracies. If your baby is eating two food cubes instead of one, remember to double the number in the table. Many fruit portions for babies are given in fractions: ⅛ cantaloupe, ¼ orange, ½ kiwi fruit, etc. When trying to figure the size of these portions, picture in your mind a medium-sized fruit. The fruit portions are quite small. If your baby loves fruit and eats more than these small portions (like mine does), adjust the numbers accordingly. The portions for grains, legumes, nuts, and seeds are also 1 ounce. The nutrient numbers are for *dry, uncooked grains and legumes* as you buy them from the store before grinding in the blender.

> **REMEMBER:** The 1 ounce portions in the table are approximately ⅛ cup or 2 tablespoons. To get a feel for a 1 oz portion, picture the amount of veggies, grains, beans, nuts, or seeds that would fit in a small scoop or a ⅛-cup measuring cup.

Example: Here's a word problem (similar to those you enjoyed in high school math class). Let's say your 7-month old baby just started eating homemade brown rice cereal, and you are making Super Porridge this way: You measure ¼ cup of brown rice into the blender before grinding. Then you stir the ground brown rice into 1 cup of boiling water and cook for 10 minutes. Your baby eats ½ of the cooked cereal for lunch. How much vitamin B6 did your baby get in his lunch?

Answer: Concentrate on the amount of dry, uncooked rice your baby ate, or the amount of rice before you ground it in the blender and cooked it. The porridge was made from ¼ cup of dry, uncooked rice, and your baby ate half of the porridge you cooked. Half of ¼ cup is ⅛ cup, which just so happens to be the portion-size used in the tables. Look up ⅛ cup of brown rice in the B6 table on pages 535-536 and you can see that your baby has received .12 of his daily requirements of .60 units or one fifth of his daily needs.

Your Baby's Caloric Needs

Your baby knows how many calories she needs and will eat accordingly. If you are concerned that she is eating too little or too much, the next table may help in determining if your concerns are legitimate. Of course, calorie requirements vary with each baby, but the averages in the table will give you a rough idea of the number of calories your baby should be eating. If your baby is eating significantly less or more than the amount recommended for her age, consult your pediatrician.

Use the table on page 523 to total up the calories for each food your baby eats during the day and compare the total calories with the average daily recommended calories for your baby's age group at the top of the table. These numbers are average caloric recommendations for babies at the age and weight.

A More Accurate Daily Caloric Requirement for Your Baby

A more accurate number for your individual baby's recommended daily calories can be computed by multiplying her weight in pounds by the number associated with her age below. Depending on the individual baby and the particular day, calorie requirements will still vary from this number by up to 10% above or below.

0-3 months	55 calories per pound of body weight
3-6 months	52 calories per pound of body weight
6-9 months	50 calories per pound of body weight
9-12 months	47 calories per pound of body weight
1-3 years	45 calories per pound of body weight

Example: If your baby is 10 months old and weighs 19 pounds, multiply 19 by 47 to get 893. Caloric needs can vary by 10% above or below. 10% of 893 is about 89, so the lower limit is 893-89=804, and the upper limit is 893+89=982. Therefore, your baby should be getting between 804 and 982 calories per day.

Your Baby's Fat Needs

It is important for proper growth and development that your baby get enough fat. The table below lists the amounts of fat in the Super Baby Foods. The second numeric column gives the fat grams in the food, and the third column gives the number of calories in the food that come from fat. The fourth column gives the percentage of fat in the foods. Nuts, seeds, and avocado are mostly fat—the good fat that your baby needs for growth and proper brain development. Eggs, milk, yogurt, and cheese also supply good amounts of fats, but these fats are saturated and less healthy than the unsaturated fats in nuts and seeds, as discussed in the section *Fats: The Good, the Bad, and the Ugly* beginning on page 504.

To use the table to determine if your baby is getting enough (or too much) fat in his diet, total up the number of fat grams from the food that your baby has eaten in one day and confirm that the number fits in the recommended range at the top of the table for your baby's age group.

Your Baby's Average Daily Recommended Calories and Fat:

0 to 6 months (13 lbs):	650 calories and 25-40 fat grams
6 to 12 months (20 lbs):	850 calories and 33-52 fat grams
1 to 3 years (29 lbs):	1300 calories and 50-79 fat grams

Calories and Fat in the Super Baby Foods:	Calories	Fat Grams	Calories from Fat	Percent Fat
1 oz Brazil nuts	186	19	170	91%
1 oz walnuts	182	18	158	87%
1 oz filberts	179	18	160	89%
1 oz almonds	167	15	133	80%
1 oz cashews	163	13	118	73%
1 oz sunflower seeds	162	14	127	78%
1 oz peanuts	159	14	124	78%
1 oz pumpkin seeds	154	13	117	76%
1 oz flaxseed	139	9	81	58%
2 T chia seeds	130	7	67	52%
1 T toasted wheat germ	108	8	75	69%
1 oz cheddar cheese	108	9	77	72%
½ C creamed cottage cheese	117	5	45	39%
1 T raw wheat germ	104	3	25	24%
1 oz natural Swiss cheese	104	8	69	67%
½ C cottage cheese, 2%	102	2	20	20%
1 T almond butter	101	9	85	84%
¾ cup Super Porridge[6]	**100**	**2**	**18**	**18%**
⅛ C soybeans	97	5	42	43%
⅛ C millet	95	1	9	10%
⅛ C amaranth	92	2	14	16%
1 oz teff	92	1	6	6%
⅛ C chick peas	91	2	14	15%
⅛ C mung beans	90	0	3	3%
⅛ C pearled barley	88	0	3	3%
⅛ C navy beans	87	0	3	3%
⅛ C couscous	87	0	1	2%
1 T tahini	87	8	72	83%
½ C breast milk	85	4	46	42%
⅛ C brown rice	86	1	6	7%
⅛ C split peas	84	0	3	3%

---

[6] The amount of calories and fat in Super Porridge depends, of course, on the grain and legume ingredients. As an average, use these numbers for a ¾ cup serving of cooked Super Porridge: 100 calories and 2 fat grams.

	Calories	Fat Grams	Calories from Fat	Percent Fat
⅛ C pinto beans	82	0	2	3%
⅛ C lentils	81	0	2	3%
⅛ C adzuki beans	81	0	1	1%
⅛ C triticale	81	1	5	6%
½ C milk, 3.7%	80	5	41	50%
⅛ C quinoa	80	1	11	14%
½ C formula	78	4	36	46%
⅛ C black turtle beans	78	0	2	2%
1 oz mozzarella, part skim	78	5	43	55%
⅛ C Great Northern beans	77	0	2	3%
⅛ C kidney beans	77	0	2	2%
½ C milk, 3.3%	75	4	37	49%
⅛ C lima beans	75	0	1	2%
⅛ C buckwheat groats	71	1	5	7%
⅛ C rye berries	71	1	5	7%
½ C whole milk yogurt	70	4	33	47%
½ C milk, 2%	61	2	21	35%
1 large egg yolk	59	5	46	78%
½ C orange juice	56	0	0	0%
⅛ C cornmeal, whole grain	55	1	5	9%
⅛ C whole wheat flour	51	0	3	5%
1 oz Calif. avocado	48	4	36	75%
1 T blackstrap molasses	47	0	0	0%
⅛ C rolled oats/oatmeal	39	1	6	15%
1 oz ricotta, part skim	39	2	20	51%
⅛ C bulgur	38	0	1	3%
1 T butter	36	4	36	100%
1 oz mashed banana	26	0	1	5%
1 T grated Parmesan	23	2	14	59%
2 T sweet potatoes	22	0	0	1%
1 oz tofu	21	1	12	57%
2 T canned pumpkin	10	0	1	7%
2 T Brussels sprouts	8	0	1	8%
2 T beets	7	0	0	1%
2 T carrots	6	0	0	5%
2 T broccoli	6	0	0	4%
2 T asparagus	6	0	1	11%
2 T beet greens	5	0	0	6%
2 T cauliflower	4	0	0	10%

How to Calculate Percentage of Calories from Fat

You may skip this section if you wish and there will be no loss of continuity in this book.

Perhaps you are aware that most medical authorities advise that adults restrict their fat calories to 30% (or less) of total calories. This is not true for babies, who need a much higher percentage of fat calories than we do. Experts have quoted figures ranging from 35% to 55%. When baby becomes a toddler, however, the percentage should be decreased to about 30% (some say 20%, but some think 20% is much too low). To calculate the percentage of calories your baby is receiving from fat, use one of the two methods below.

Method 1. Use the first column of numbers from the table on page 523 to find the total calories your baby has eaten for the day. Use the third column to find total calories from fat. Divide the total calories from fat by total calories from the first column.

Method 2. Use the first column of numbers from the table to find the total calories your baby has eaten for the day. Use the second column to find total number of fat grams. Multiply the number of fat grams by 9 and divide the product by the total calories from the first column.

The number after dividing should be greater than .35 (35%) and less than .55 (55%) for a baby. For a toddler, the number should be approximately .30 (30%).

Example: Let's say that you totaled up the number of calories and fat grams or calories from fat that your baby has eaten today.

Method 1. Your totals show that your baby ate 800 calories and 344 calories from fat. Divide 344 by 800 to get 0.43. The percentage of calories from fat is therefore 43%, which fits nicely in the recommended range of 35% to 55%.

Method 2. Your totals show that your baby ate 800 calories and 38 fat grams. Multiply 38x9=342. Divide 342 by 800 to get 0.4275 or approximately 0.43. The percentage of calories from fat is therefore 43%, which fits nicely in the recommended range of 35% to 55%.

For another example, see the bottom of page 528.

Your Baby's Protein Needs

The Super Baby Food Diet supplies your baby with more than enough protein. Please look at the next table. It shows the number of protein grams in the foods if they are eaten separately, in other words, if you discount any protein complementarity that may be taking place. Many of the foods in the Super Baby Food Diet naturally complement each other for additional protein. (T=tablespoons) For example:

★ ½ cup cooked Super Porridge made with brown rice and lentils (approximately 1½ T dry uncooked rice + ½ T uncooked lentils) contains 3 grams of complete protein

★ ¼ cup yogurt mixed with 2⅔ tablespoons tahini contains 8 grams of complete protein

★ ½ cup cooked brown rice cereal (2 T dry rice) mixed with 1½ teaspoons brewer's yeast contains 3 grams of complete protein

★ ½ cup cooked brown rice cereal (2 T dry rice) mixed with 1⅛ teaspoon tahini contains 2 grams of complete protein

★ ½ cup cooked cornmeal (¼ cup dry) + ⅛ cup cooked beans (1 tablespoon dry beans)contains 4 grams of complete protein

★ 2 tablespoons tahini + ⅓ cup cooked beans (1/6 cup dry beans) contains 10 grams of complete protein

★ ½ slice whole wheat bread spread with 1 tablespoon yogurt cheese (or 5 teaspoons yogurt or milk) contains 3 grams of complete protein

★ ½ cup cooked bulgur or wheat cereal (2 T dry bulgur/wheat) mixed with ½ ounce tofu contains 3 grams of complete protein

A More Accurate Daily Protein Requirement for Your Baby

The daily required grams of protein in the table are averages for children in the age groups. You can determine a more exact number of daily protein grams for your baby by multiplying the number associated with his age group below by his body weight:

For babies 0-6 months old, multiply your baby's weight in pounds by 1.
For babies 6-12 months old, multiply your baby's weight by .9.
For toddlers 1-3 years old, multiply your baby's weight by .81.

For example, if your baby is 9 months old and weights 18 pounds, the number of daily protein grams your baby needs is .9x18=16.2 grams.

Your Baby's Average Daily Protein Requirements:

0 to 6 months (13 lbs): 13 grams
6 to 12 months (20 lbs): 18 grams
1 to 3 years (29 lbs): 23 grams

Protein Grams from Super Baby Foods Eaten Separately:

⅛ C soybeans	8.5	1 oz filberts	3.7
1 oz natural Swiss cheese	8.2	⅛ C amaranth	3.5
1 oz mozzarella, part skim	7.7	1 oz ricotta, part skim	3.1
1 oz peanuts	7.2	⅛ C triticale	3.1
¼ C cottage cheese	7.0	⅛ C rye berries	3.1
1 oz cheese	7.0	⅛ C couscous	2.9
1 oz pumpkin/squash seeds	7.0	1 large egg yolk	2.8
⅛ C lentils	6.7	⅛ C quinoa	2.8
1 oz cheddar cheese	6.5	⅛ C millet	2.8
1 oz sunflower seeds	6.5	1 T tahini	2.6
⅛ C mung beans	6.2	⅛ C teff	2.5
½ oz soy flour	6.0	⅛ C pearled barley	2.5
1 egg yolk	6.0	1 T almond butter	2.4
½ C yogurt	6.0	⅛ C buckwheat groats	2.4
⅛ C split peas	6.0	1 oz tofu	2.2
⅛ C navy beans	5.8	1 T toasted wheat germ	2.1
1 oz almonds	5.7	1 T grated Parmesan	2.1
1 T dry TVP	5.5	⅛ C whole wheat flour	2.1
⅛ C kidney beans	5.4	⅛ C brown rice	1.8
1 oz flaxseed	5.0	1 T raw wheat germ	1.7
⅛ C Great Northern beans	5.0	⅛ C rolled oats/oatmeal	1.6
⅛ C pinto beans	5.0	⅛ C bulgur	1.4
⅛ C adzuki beans	4.9	⅛ C cornmeal, whole grain	1.2
⅛ C black turtle beans	4.9	½ C fresh orange juice	0.9
⅛ C lima beans	4.8	2 T broccoli	0.7
⅛ C chick peas	4.8	2 T Brussels sprouts	0.7
2 T chia seeds	4.7	2 T asparagus	0.6
1 oz cashews	4.4	2 T beet greens	0.5
1 oz Eng walnuts	4.1	1 oz Calif. avocado	0.5
1 oz Brazil nuts	4.1	2 T sweet potatoes	0.4
1 T peanut butter	4.0	2 T cauliflower	0.4
1 T brewer's yeast	4.0	2 T canned pumpkin	0.3
½ C milk	4.0	1 oz mashed banana	0.3
½ C most formula	4.0	2 T beets	0.2
½ C breast milk	4.0	2 T carrots	0.2
½ C whole milk yogurt	3.9		

Nutritional Analysis

You can use this part of this book to do a nutritional analysis of your baby's diet. For the sample menu on page 136, the calories and fat table (page 523) and the protein table (page 527) were used to do the analysis below. The tables on the next several pages can be used to determine if your baby's diet is meeting her daily needs for all other major nutrients.

**Nutritional Analysis of the Sample Menu on Page 136
for Calories, Fat Grams, Protein Grams, and % of Calories from Fat**

	Calories	Fat	Protein
morning 8 oz bottle	160	8	8
Breakfast:			
3/4 cup Super Porridge	100	2	4
egg yolk	60	5	2
broccoli	12	0	0.7
brewer's yeast	10	0	1.3
orange juice	55	0	0.9
Morning Snack:			
Oatios	60	0	2
carrot	10	0	0.2
½ cup (4 oz) formula/breast	80	4	4
Lunch:			
yogurt	70	4	6
tahini	87	8	2.6
flax seeds	20	2	1
2 cubes avocado	100	8	1
Afternoon Snack:			
kiwi fruit	45	0	0
½ slice whole wheat	40	1	2
½ cup formula/breast	80	4	4
Supper:			
3/4 cup Super Porridge	100	2	4
banana	100	0	0.3
½ cup formula/breast	80	4	4
Bedtime:			
8 oz formula/breast	160	8	8
TOTAL	1429	60	56

To calculate percent of calories from fat, use method 2 on page 525: 60 fat grams times 9 calories per fat gram is 540 calories from fat. 540÷1429= 38% calories from fat.

Vitamin A— Beta Carotene
(Retinol, Retinal, Carotene)

RDA in IUs:

Birth to 6 months:	1500
6 to 12 months:	2000
1 to 3 years:	2000

Best Super Baby Food Sources:

2 T canned pumpkin	6727
2 T sweet potatoes	3610
2 T carrots	3405
⅛ cantaloupe	2300
2 T spinach	1800
2 T collard greens	1620
⅛ mango	1200
2 T kale	1140
2 T butternut squash	1100
2 T mustard greens	1010
2 T beet greens	918
½ C watermelon	590
1 oz papaya juice	560
½ medium apricot	500
⅓ peach	450
2 T broccoli	435
2 T dandelion greens	340
1 large egg yolk	323
⅓ medium nectarine	275
1 oz most cheeses	250
1 medium egg yolk	250
½ C 1%, 2% milk	250
¼ small raw tomato	225
½ C whole milk	150
½ C yogurt, whole milk	139
2 T asparagus	121
2 T Brussels sprouts	115

There are two forms of Vitamin A in foods: Preformed or active Vitamin A (retinol) and Provitamin A (carotene or beta carotene). Our bodies must convert beta carotene, which is found in vegetables and fruits, to Vitamin A. Carotene is a yellow-orange pigment, and gives carrots and sweet potatoes their color. (The name carotene was derived from the word carrots.) The pigment is also found in green vegetables, but can't be seen because of chlorophyll, which gives leaves their green color. In general, the deeper the green or yellow-orange color, the higher the carotene content. Retinol is found in animal products, such as liver and fish oils; the animal has done the work for us and changed the carotene to Vitamin A. Some animal products, like butter, have both forms of Vitamin A.

Stability: Vitamin A is not destroyed by heat, but is lost when exposed to light or oxygen.

Functions in the human body: Vitamin A is an antioxidant (page 509). Reduces susceptibility to infection by aiding secretion of mucus by mucous membranes to keep them moist and healthy. Promotes growth and repair of body tissues, bones, and teeth. Maintains healthy skin. Aids digestion. Maintains good eyesight and helps prevent night blindness, when eyes are unable to adjust to bright light and darkness.

Deficiency symptoms: Night blindness. Dry eyes. Dry, scaly, itchy, rough skin. Loss of taste or smell. Increased number of respiratory infections. Poor bone growth. Numerous dental cavities. Slow healing of wounds.

Toxicity symptoms: Toxicity occurs only with retinol, not with carotene; therefore, vegetarians don't have to worry much about Vitamin A toxicity. However, an extreme excess of carotene may cause the skin to turn yellow. Some vitamin pill manufacturers emphasize that the Vitamin A in their products come from carotene. I guess they mean to quell any fears their customers may have about Vitamin A toxicity. Possible toxicity symptoms of retinol are dizziness, headaches, nausea, vomiting, fatigue, deep bone pain, hair loss, and loss of appetite. Toxicity occurs at daily levels of 50,000 units or more in adults. In children, 20,000 units can cause toxicity symptoms. In the opinion of the National Research Council, these doses are so large that, unless you live on liver or fish oils like cod liver oil, it is very difficult to get Vitamin A overdose from food. Toxicity almost always occurs from vitamin pill supplements and rarely from foods. Symptoms quickly disappear when high doses are discontinued.

Vitamin D
(Sunshine Vitamin, Calciferol,
Cholecalciferol, Ergocalciferol)

RDA in mcg:

Birth to 6 months:	300
6 to 12 months:	400
1 to 3 years:	400

Best Super Baby Food Sources:

1 teaspoon cod liver oil	400
½ C milk	50
½ cup some soy milk	50
1 medium egg yolk	22

The body produces Vitamin D when ultraviolet rays from the sun shine on the skin. Only a few minutes a day of sunshine may be enough to meet Vitamin D requirements. The amount of Vitamin D produced by sunlight on the skin depends on the climate, the area of skin exposed and the length of time it is exposed, and the wavelength of the ultraviolet light. Darker skinned peoples' bodies take longer to manufacture Vitamin D than lighter skinned people under the same circumstances because a higher melanin content acts as a natural sun screen. It has been estimated that light-skinned children need only 15 minutes of sunlight per week to meet their vitamin D requirements. It is probably best to make sure you are drinking enough vitamin D-fortified milk or taking a regular vitamin D supplement. Ask your doctor. *Fortified* soy milks are a good source of vitamin D. Compare the "Nutrition Facts" label on a box of soy milk to the label on a carton of cow's milk to see how the vitamin D contents compare.

Stability: Vitamin D is not destroyed by heat, but is sensitive to light.

Functions in the human body: Helps the body absorb calcium and phosphorus; therefore, it is needed for strong bones and teeth.

Deficiency symptoms: A major deficiency causes the disease rickets, which causes soft bones that bend easily. A child's legs will be bowed by his/her body weight and the ribs will protrude. In adults, calcium loss from the bones will cause deep bone pain and pressure in the back and pelvis. A baby's teeth will not come in on time and will get cavities easily.

Fractures will heal slowly. Milk and infant formula are fortified with Vitamin D, so deficiencies are rare in developed countries. Vitamin D deficiency can occur in some infants who ingest only breastmilk and are rarely exposed to sunlight.

Toxicity symptoms: May occur in adults if more than 2000 IU daily are taken. Toxicity symptoms include kidney stones, loss of appetite and weight loss, diarrhea, excessive thirst, poor rate of growth, weakness, headache, vomiting, irritability, high blood pressure, tissue calcification, and elevated blood cholesterol.

Vitamin E
(Tocopherol)

RDA in mg alpha TE:

Birth to 6 months:	3.0
6 to 12 months:	4.0
1 to 3 years:	6.0

Best Super Baby Food Sources:

1 T wheat germ oil	5.3
⅛ C filberts	3.5
⅛ C almonds	2.8
½ C raw blackberries	2.5
⅛ C sunflower seeds	2.4
⅛ C peanuts	1.7
⅛ C rolled oats/oatmeal	1.7
1 T peanut butter	1.5
1 T raw wheat germ	1.2
⅛ C Brazil nuts	1.1
¼ California avocado	1.0

Vitamin E is actually a group of compounds called tocopherols. There are seven forms of tocopherol: alpha, beta, delta, epsilon, eta, gamma, and zeta. Alpha tocopherol has the most Vitamin E. Vitamin E slows down the rancidity process in fats and oils. Adelle Davis recommends 30 IU's daily for infants and children, about 10 times the RDA. Ask for your pediatrician's advice on this.

Stability: Cooking does not affect Vitamin E content. Vitamin E is destroyed by light, oxygen, and food rancidity.

Functions in the human body: Antioxidant (page 509). Vitamin E acts as a preservative of Vitamin A, Vitamin B, Vitamin C and other compounds in the body by protecting them against oxidation. Protects red blood cell membranes. May protect against ozone pollution. Helps linoleic acid function in the body and may help metabolize calcium. Increases stamina and endurance. Helps in circulation and helps lower blood pressure by acting as a natural diuretic. Helps in reproductive problems like impotence, lack of sex drive, and spontaneous abortions.

Deficiency symptoms: In premature and under-nourished infants, anemia, hemorrhaging, and edema. In all people, shrinking of collagen in skin, and of connective tissue, and easy rupturing of red blood cell membranes. Sterility. Kidney and liver damage.

Toxicity symptoms: Few symptoms have been discovered and it is generally considered nontoxic in healthy persons. Vitamin E, because it is fat-soluble, can be toxic if large vitamin pill supplements are taken. Very large doses might cause extensive bleeding due to an interference with Vitamin K, which has a coagulant function in the human body.

Vitamin K
(Anti-hemorrhagic Vitamin, Menadione)

RDA in mcg:

Birth to 6 months:	5
6 to 12 months:	10
1 to 3 years:	15

Best Super Baby Food Sources:

2 T Brussels sprouts	228
2 T green beans	83
2 T turnip greens	41
2 T broccoli	31
2 T cabbage	20
2 T asparagus	16

Vitamin K is not a single vitamin, but a group of "quinones" that occur naturally in foods. The synthetic Vitamin K is called "menadione."

Stability: Destroyed by radiation and x-rays, aspirin, and air pollution. Antibiotics ant other drugs destroy intestinal flora which manufacture natural Vitamin K. See information about yogurt and antibiotics, page 252.

Functions in the human body: Essential for protein formation and blood clotting. Possibly relieves menstrual cramps and reduces unusually long menstrual bleeding. Typically, newborn babies are routinely given an injection of vitamin K to prevent hemorrhage.

Deficiency symptoms: Prolonged bleeding due to problems with blood clotting. Nosebleeds, miscarriages, brain hemorrhages, and hemorrhages in other parts of the body.

Toxicity symptoms: Abnormal blood clotting, sweating, chest constrictions, and red blood cell breakdown can occur when large doses are taken in supplements. Giving large doses of supplements to infants causes damage to their red blood cells.

B-Complex Vitamins

The B Vitamins are a family of related water-soluble vitamins that work together. It is important that they be ingested in the proper proportions. Taking a single B vitamin by itself may cause deficiencies of other B vitamins, and if a there is a deficiency in one of the B vitamins, others in the group will not function properly. You see, the B vitamins are all "team players." The B complex vitamins found naturally in food are, of course, in the correct balance and they tend to be found in the same food groups. Whole grains, legumes, beans, and seeds are all good sources of the B-complex. If the most important B's—niacin, thiamine, and riboflavin—are present in adequate amounts, there usually is not a problem with serious deficiencies. This reason, along with the fact that B-vitamins get destroyed during processing, is why processed grain foods are enriched with these three B vitamins. Folic acid will be be added beginning in the year 1998.

The B-complex vitamins help the body produce antibodies, provide energy by converting carbohydrates into glucose, metabolize fats and proteins, and help regenerate red blood cells. The brain is very sensitive to glucose levels, therefore proper functioning of the brain depends upon adequate amount of B vitamins.

Vitamin pill manufacturers market B-complex vitamins as stress-reducers. Stress does increase the body's need for nutrients.

Information on the individual B vitamins follows.

Thiamine
(Vitamin B1)

RDA in mg:

Birth to 6 months:	.30
6 to 12 months:	.40
1 to 3 years:	.70

Best Super Baby Food Sources:

1 oz sunflower seeds	.65
1 T raw wheat germ	.55
1 T toasted wheat germ	.47
1 T brewer's yeast	.30
1 oz Brazil nuts	.28
1/8 C raw peanuts	.28
1/8 C sesame seeds	.28
2 T chia seeds	.25
1/8 C pecans	.24
1 T tahini	.23
1/8 C black turtle	.21
1/8 C soybeans	.20
1/8 C pistachio nuts	.19
1/8 C split peas	.18
1/8 C navy beans	.17
1/8 C mung beans	.16
1/8 C Great Northern beans	.15
1 oz filberts	.14
1/8 C pinto beans	.13
1/8 C kidney beans	.12
1/8 C chick peas	.12
1 oz English walnuts	.11
1 oz teff, white	.11
1/8 C millet	.11
1/8 C adzuki beans	.11
1/8 C lima beans	.11
1/8 C lentils	.11
1/8 C brown rice	.10
1/8 C triticale	.10
1/8 C macadamia	.10
1/8 C bulgur	.09
1/8 C whole wheat flour	.07
1 oz pumpkin/squash seeds	.06
1/8 C cornmeal, whole grain	.06
1 oz cashews	.06
1 oz almonds	.06

1 medium egg yolk	.06
2 T fresh peas, cooked	.06
1/8 C buckwheat groats	.05
1 oz flaxseed	.05
1/8 C pearled barley	.05
1 T peanut butter	.05
1 oz teff, red	.04
1/8 C couscous	.04
1/8 C quinoa	.04
1 T dry TVP	.03
1/2 C yogurt, whole milk	.03

Because thiamine is believed to affect mental attitude, it is also known as the "morale" vitamin.

Stability: Destroyed by heat and exposure to air. Extremely unstable in water, therefore use as little water as possible in cooking. Thiamine is leached out into the water, so save the water and use it in soups or beverages. Baking soda destroys thiamine. Sulfur dioxide, commonly used in the drying of fruits, destroys thiamine.

Functions in the human body: See page 531 for information on the B vitamins. Needed to prevent the disease beriberi. Necessary for a healthy nervous system. Improves learning capacity and mental alertness. Necessary for children's healthy, consistent growth and development. A must for cardiovascular health.

Deficiency symptoms: The disease beriberi occurs when thiamine is seriously deficient. In the United States, beriberi is rare because of the enrichment of foods, but is seen in chronic alcoholics. Excessive tea-drinking, due to tannins, inhibits thiamine absorption. Symptoms of thiamine deficiency include mental illness, neuroses, fatigue, depression and the symptoms of depression, headaches, loss of appetite and weight loss, nausea, constipation and abdominal pains, and tingling or numbness of the feet.

Toxicity symptoms: None.

Riboflavin
(Vitamin B2, Vitamin G)

RDA in mg:

Birth to 6 months:	.40
6 to 12 months:	.50
1 to 3 years:	.80

Best Super Baby Food Sources:

1 T brewer's yeast	.34
1 T toasted wheat germ	.23
1 T blackstrap molasses	.22
1 oz almonds	.22
⅛ C soybeans	.20
½ C yogurt, whole milk	.16
1 T raw wheat germ	.15
⅛ C filberts	.15
1 large egg yolk	.11
⅛ C brown rice	.10
1 oz pumpkin or squash seeds	.09
⅛ C quinoa	.08
⅛ C rolled oats/oatmeal	.08
⅛ C sesame seeds	.07
1 T almond butter	.07
1 oz sunflower seeds	.07
⅛ C millet	.07
2 T turnip greens	.07
2 T broccoli	.06
⅛ C whole rye berries	.06
⅛ C pinto beans	.06
⅛ C mung beans	.06
1 oz cashews	.06
⅛ C navy beans	.06
⅛ C buckwheat groats	.06
⅛ C lentils	.06
⅛ C amaranth	.05
⅛ C kidney beans	.05
2 T beet greens	.05
⅛ C split peas	.05
⅛ C adzuki beans	.05
⅛ C chick peas	.05
⅛ C Great Northern beans	.05
2 T chia seeds	.05
1 oz flaxseed	.05
2 T dandelion greens	.05
⅛ C lima beans	.05
2 T asparagus	.05
1 oz Brazil nuts	.04
1 oz peanuts	.04
1 oz teff, white	.04
⅛ C black turtle	.04
1 oz English walnuts	.04
1 T peanut butter	.04
2 T spinach	.04
1 oz teff, red	.03

Excesses of riboflavin are excreted by the body and cause a fluorescent yellow color of urine.

Stability: A small amount of riboflavin is lost during cooking. Baking soda destroys riboflavin. Light, especially sunlight, destroys riboflavin very quickly. Direct sunlight can destroy up to 40% of riboflavin in one hour and up to 70% in two hours. Buy milk in opaque, cardboard cartons instead of transparent glass or plastic. Store grains in dark, cool cupboards.

Functions in the human body: See page 531 for information on the B vitamins. Helps prevent eye problems in pregnant women. Sometimes alleviates eczema in children.

Deficiency symptoms: Problems with the mouth and tongue, including cracked lips and cracks in the corners of the mouth and dry, scaly, purple tongue. Irritated, watery eyes that are sensitive to light, or a feeling that there is sand or grit in the eyes, cataracts. Vaginal itching, an inability to urinate. Trembling, fatigue, dizziness. Stunted growth in children.

Toxicity symptoms: None.

Niacin
(Vitamin B3, Niacinamide,
Nicotinic Acid, Nicotinamide)

RDA in mg NE:

Birth to 6 months:	5.0
6 to 12 months:	6.0
1 to 3 years:	9.0

Best Super Baby Food Sources:

1 T peanut butter	4.9
1 oz peanuts	3.4
1 T brewer's yeast	2.0
1 T raw wheat germ	2.0
2 T chia seeds	1.7
1 T toasted wheat germ	1.6
⅛ C sesame seeds	1.5
1 oz sunflower seeds	1.3

⅛ C millet	1.2
⅛ C pearled barley	1.2
⅛ C buckwheat groats	1.1
⅛ C brown rice	1.0
1 oz almonds	1.0
⅛ C whole wheat flour	1.0
1 T tahini	.8
⅛ C couscous	.8
⅛ C split peas	.7
⅛ C adzuki beans	.6
⅛ C mung beans	.6
⅛ C quinoa	.6
⅛ C lentils	.6
1 oz pumpkin or squash seeds	.5
1 oz teff, white	.5
⅛ C navy beans	.5
⅛ C bulgur	.5
1 T almond butter	.5
1 oz Brazil nuts	.5
⅛ C kidney beans	.5
2 T potatoes	.5
⅛ C cashews	.5
⅛ C cornmeal, whole grain	.5
1 oz teff, red	.4

The human body can manufacture niacin using tryptophan and vitamin B6. Foods with high tryptophan content, such as milk and eggs, are beneficial in meeting the body's niacin needs. Nicotinamide should not be confused with the nicotine found in cigarettes.

Stability: Fairly stable. Some niacin is leached into water during cooking.

Functions in the human body: See page 531 for information on the B vitamins. Niacin is involved in more than fifty body processes. Helps keep you calm. Stabilizes blood sugar levels. Necessary for production of sex hormones. Helps in the treatment of alcoholism. Niacin, but not niacinamide, may lower cholesterol and triglycerides and reverse atherosclerosis.

Deficiency symptoms: Extreme niacin deficiency causes the disease pellagra. Moderate deficiency symptoms include temper tantrums, aggressive behavior, restlessness, hyperactivity. (Actually these four are the result of tryptophan deficiency, whose absorption is

impaired because of inadequate niacin.) Other symptoms include diarrhea, red rash on skin, headache, irritability, depression, dizziness and delusions, loss of appetite and weight, insomnia, sore mouth or tongue, and fatigue.

Toxicity symptoms: None for nicotinamide, but large doses of nicotinic acid may cause upset stomach, nervousness, dizziness or head throbbing, and skin flushing. Adult doses greater than 2000 grams daily of niacinamide can cause liver damage.

Pantothenic Acid
(Calcium Pantothenate, Vitamin B5, once called Vitamin B3)

RDA in mg:
Birth to 6 months:	2
6 to 12 months:	3
1 to 3 years:	3

Best Super Baby Food Sources:
1 T raw wheat germ	.66
1 large egg yolk	.63
¼ California avocado	.60
⅛ C mung beans	.50
1 oz peanuts	.50
⅛ C lentils	.44
½ C yogurt, whole milk	.44
⅛ C split peas	.43
⅛ C chick peas	.40
1 T toasted wheat germ	.39
1 oz cashews	.35
⅛ C brown rice	.35
1 oz filberts	.33
⅛ C triticale	.32
⅛ C lima beans	.30
½ C watermelon	.30
⅛ C couscous	.29
⅛ C amaranth	.26
⅛ C buckwheat groats	.25
¼ C canned pumpkin	.25
⅛ C Great Northern beans	.25
½ C tomato juice	.25
½ C orange juice	.24
⅛ honeydew melon	.23
⅛ C millet	.21
⅛ C black turtle	.21
1 oz English walnuts	.18
⅛ C kidney beans	.18

⅛ C soybeans	.18
⅛ C pinto beans	.18
⅛ C navy beans	.18
1 T brewer's yeast	.13
¼ C sweet cherries	.13
½ C raw pineapple	.11
1 slice canned pineapple	.10
½ medium apple	.08
⅛ papaya	.08
½ raw pear	.07
1 T blackstrap molasses	.07
1 T dry TVP	.07
½ C strawberries	.06
½ C blueberries	.06
½ plum (not Caissa)	.05
½ medium apricot	.05
⅛ mango	.04

Pantothenic acid is present in all living cells. It comes from food and also is manufactured by intestinal bacteria. Antibiotics decrease intestinal flora and may cause a deficiency. See information about yogurt and antibiotics, page 252. It works as an antioxidant by disabling free radicals before they do damage to body cells. This vitamin is lost in the processing of grains and is not replaced by enrichment (see table on page 219).

Stability: Some pantothenic acid is lost during cooking. Also, vinegar and baking soda destroy it.

Functions in the human body: See page 531 for information on the B vitamins. Stimulates healing of wounds. Manufacturers antibodies. Helps in Vitamin D production.

Deficiency symptoms: Decreased resistance to respiratory infections, decreased production of antibodies, poor wound healing, ulcers, abdominal pain and vomiting, muscle cramps, depression, insomnia, headache, fatigue, irritability, fainting, rapid pulse, appetite loss, tingling and numbness in the hands and feet, "burning feet" syndrome. Inability to handle stressful situations.

Toxicity symptoms: Very large doses may cause diarrhea.

Vitamin B6
(Pyridoxine, Pyridoxamine, Pyridoxal)

RDA in Mgs:

Birth to 6 months:	.30
6 to 12 months:	.60
1 to 3 years:	1.0

Best Super Baby Food Sources:

1 T raw wheat germ	.38
1 T toasted wheat germ	.28
1 T brewer's yeast	.20
1 oz filberts	.17
1 oz mashed banana	.16
1 oz English walnuts	.16
⅛ C chick peas	.13
⅛ C lentils	.13
½ C tomato juice	.13
⅛ C brown rice	.12
½ C pineapple juice	.12
⅛ C pinto beans	.11
⅛ C lima beans	.11
⅛ C navy beans	.11
⅛ C mung beans	.10
⅛ C Great Northern beans	.10
½ C grape juice	.10
1 oz peanuts	.10
⅛ C millet	.10
⅛ C kidney beans	.09
⅛ C soybeans	.09
½ C cottage cheese	.08
1 large egg yolk	.07
⅛ C black turtle	.07
⅛ C pearled barley	.07
½ C watermelon	.07
⅛ C buckwheat groats	.07
1 oz cashews	.07
1 oz Brazil nuts	.07
1 T blackstrap molasses	.07
2 T Brussels sprouts	.06
⅛ C rye berries	.06
½ C raw pineapple	.06
⅛ cantaloupe	.05
½ orange	.05
½ C blueberries	.05
⅛ C amaranth	.05
½ C orange juice	.05
½ C milk	.05
⅛ C whole wheat flour	.05
⅛ C cornmeal, whole grain	.05

½ C buttermilk	.05
½ C yogurt, whole milk	.04
⅛ C bulgur	.04
⅛ C split peas	.04
2 T sweet potatoes	.04
½ C apple juice	.04
½ C raspberries	.04
½ C strawberries	.04
½ C blackberries	.04
2 T asparagus	.03
⅛ C couscous	.03
2 T broccoli	.03
⅛ C triticale	.03
2 T carrots	.03
1 T dry TVP	.03

During the processing of grains, up to 90% of Vitamin B6 is lost and not replaced during enrichment (see table on page 219). Many Americans have low levels of this vitamin, probably due to grain processing. Smoking depletes this vitamin. Vitamin B6 is excreted in urine 8 hours after ingested, so you must frequently eat foods that contain it. Large supplemental doses of Vitamin B6 causes an imbalance in the other B vitamins.

Stability: Some Vitamin B6 is destroyed by light, air, and the cooking process. Significant amounts are lost when foods are frozen and in cooking water.

Functions in the human body: See page 531 for information on the B vitamins. The body uses Vitamin B6 with tryptophan to produce niacin. B6 is needed for healthy sex organs and may reduce premenstrual fluid retention. May cure carpal tunnel syndrome, anemia, sleep disorders, PMS, kidney problems, and heart disease.

Deficiency symptoms: Anemia, shortness of breath, decreased immunity function, nausea, sore mouth and red tongue, cracks in the corners of the mouth, dermatitis, kidney problems, hair loss, stunted growth, abdominal pain or vomiting, depression, lethargy, and sensitivity to insulin. In infants, convulsions and malformation of bones. In pregnant women, water retention.

Toxicity symptoms: Extremely large doses—more than 500 mg daily for adults—from supplements cause nerve impairment including tingling sensations in lips and tongue, tingling in hands and numbness in feet and skin, pain in the limbs, clumsiness, loss of balance and difficulty walking, and headache, bloating, and irritability. Pregnant mothers taking excessive B6 doses have had children with birth defects similar to those of thalidomide; pregnant mothers should keep their doses under 200 mg daily. Discuss this with your obstetrician.

Vitamin B12
(Cobalamins)

RDA in mcg:

Birth to 6 months:	.30
6 to 12 months:	.50
1 to 3 years:	.70

Best Super Baby Food Sources:

½ C cottage cheese	.75
1 medium egg yolk	.60
½ C milk	.45
½ C yogurt	.42
1 T brewer's yeast with B12	.40
½ C buttermilk	.27

Vitamin B12 is the one nutrient that may be lacking in a **strict** vegetarian diet, because it is found almost exclusively in animal products. Only trace amounts occur in plant foods. The Super Baby Food Diet includes foods containing vitamin B12 because it includes dairy products and milk—animal products that contain vitamin B12. If your baby is on a strict vegetarian diet, make sure that her prescription vitamins or daily brewer's yeast is supplemented with vitamin B12. Some soy products are also enriched with B12. Read the labels.

B12 is sometimes referred to as the "red vitamin" because it is bright red in color. It is the only vitamin that also contains a mineral—cobalt. The amount of B12 stored in the human liver is so great that it can prevent deficiency in a person ingesting no B12 for several years. The amount of B12 stored in the liver increases with age; children may show deficiencies in as little as two years. Laxatives taken regularly may eliminate too much B12, causing a deficiency. Vitamin B12 and folate work closely together and have similar deficiency symptoms (see page 538).

Stability: Cooking destroys some Vitamin B12.

Functions in the human body: See page 531 for information on the B vitamins. Increases energy and promotes growth. Scientific studies have proven that Vitamin B12 improves children's growth rates. B12 shots are given for pernicious anemia (insufficient red blood cells in bone marrow).

Deficiency symptoms: Pernicious anemia, sore mouth and tongue, weakness, mental disorders, memory loss, depression, nervous disorders, nervousness, insomnia, loss of appetite and weight, difficulty walking, shooting pains, needles-and-pins and hot-and-cold sensations, which are warnings of central nerve system damage, unpleasant body odor, menstrual disturbances, and neuritis. If deficiency is not caught in its early stages, spinal cord degeneration, permanent mental problems, and paralysis may result. Enough calcium must be present in the body for proper functioning of Vitamin B12. A tapeworm infestation can cause B12 deficiency.

Toxicity symptoms: None.

Biotin
(once called Vitamin H)

RDA in mcg:

Birth to 6 months:	10
6 to 12 months:	15
1 to 3 years:	20

Best Super Baby Food Sources:

1 oz American cheese, pasteurized process	23.1
1/8 C Pers/Eng walnuts	5.0
1 small banana	4.4
1/2 C whole milk	3.7
1/2 C watermelon	3.6

1 T brewer's yeast	3.2
1/8 C almonds	3.0
1/8 cantaloupe	3.0
1/4 avocado	3.0
1 T wheat germ	2.0
1 T blackstrap molasses	1.8
strawberries	1.1
1/4 small raw tomato	1.0

Biotin is a member of the B complex. It appears in very small amounts in all living tissue, animal and plant. The protein avidin in raw egg whites binds with biotin, which prevents its absorption into the body. Biotin comes from foods and also is made by bacteria in the intestine. Antibiotics decrease intestinal flora and may cause a deficiency of biotin. See information about yogurt and antibiotics, page 252.

Stability: Cooking destroys some biotin.

Functions in the human body: See page 531 for information on the B vitamins. Necessary for healthy skin. Helps prevent depression.

Deficiency symptoms: Deficiencies are rare and were reported in humans only when large numbers of antibiotics were taken and when the diet consisted of too many raw egg whites. Symptoms include anemia, skin eruptions and dry skin, pain in the muscles, fatigue, lethargy, insomnia, muscle pain, anorexia, nausea, vomiting, rise in cholesterol levels, and hair loss.

Toxicity symptoms: None.

Folate
(Folacin, Folic Acid)

RDA in mcg:

Birth to 6 months:	25
6 to 12 months:	35
1 to 3 years:	50

Best Super Baby Food Sources:

1/8 C mung beans	162
1/8 C chick peas	139
1/8 C pinto beans	122
1/8 C Great Northern beans	110
1/8 C lentils	104

⅛ C black turtle	102
1 T toasted wheat germ	100
⅛ C navy beans	96
⅛ C lima beans	88
⅛ C soybeans	87
1 T raw wheat germ	82
⅛ C kidney beans	79
½ C fresh orange juice	69
⅛ C split peas	67
1 oz peanuts	67
2 T asparagus	33
¼ avocado	32
⅛ cantaloupe	29
2 T spinach	27
½ C tomato juice	26
1 large egg yolk	24
1 oz cashews	20
2 T Brussels sprouts	20
1 oz filberts	20
1 oz English walnuts	19
⅛ C triticale	18
1 T peanut butter	17
1 oz almonds	17
½ C cottage cheese	14
½ pear	13
2 T broccoli	13
2 T collard greens	12
½ C strawberries	12
⅛ C amaranth	12
2 T beets	11
1 T brewer's yeast	11
¼ small raw tomato	10
2 T turnip greens	10
1 T almond butter	10
½ C blackberries	10
2 T corn	9
⅛ C buckwheat groats	9
⅛ C bulgur	9
2 T cauliflower	9
½ C cherries	8
½ C yogurt, whole milk	8
½ C raw pineapple	8
⅛ C whole wheat flour	7
⅛ C pearled barley	6
½ medium apple	6
½ C milk	6
⅛ C brown rice	5
1 oz mashed banana	5
⅛ C couscous	5

2 T sweet potatoes	5
2 T canned pumpkin	4
1 oz tofu	4
2 T eggplant	4
2 T yellow squash	4
1 slice canned pineapple	4
2 T turnips	4
½ medium peach	4
½ C blueberries	4
⅛ C rolled oats/oatmeal	3
2 T carrots	2
1 oz Brazil nuts	1

The word *folate* comes from the same Latin root of foliage, folium meaning leaf. Folate should bring to mind green, leafy plants or vegetables, which are some of the good sources of the vitamin. Folate and Vitamin B12 work closely together and have similar deficiency symptoms. An excessive folate intake from supplements can hide a vitamin B12 deficiency (page 537).

Folic acid will begin being added to white flour in the year 1998 in order to prevent some birth defects (see table on page 219). Folic acid is the B vitamin that a fetus needs in the first few weeks of pregnancy—usually before the woman knows that she is pregnant.

Stability: Cooking, improper storing (leaving at room temperature for long time periods), heat, and light destroys folate. Folate leaches into cooking water.

Functions in the human body: See page 531 for information on the B vitamins. Maintains the genetic code for the cells of the body.

Deficiency symptoms: Folate deficiency is one of the most common; some experts estimate that half of all women have folate deficiency. Stress, sickness, pregnancy, breast feeding, using oral contraceptives (the pill), and drinking alcohol increase the need for folate. Any illness that prevents absorption of food, such as illnesses accompanied by diarrhea or vomiting, may cause a folate deficiency. Symptoms include pernicious anemia, diarrhea, constipation, gastrointestinal disturbances, gray hair, weakness, fatigue, forgetfulness, headaches, heart palpitation, irritability, behavioral disorders, infertility, possible cervical cancer. Sore tongue and mouth, smooth red tongue, bleeding gums. Stunted growth and repair of body cells. Folate deficiency in the fetus may cause deformities, such as cleft palate, slow development, learning disabilities, and brain damage.

Toxicity symptoms: None.

Vitamin C
(Ascorbic Acid)

RDA in mg:

Birth to 6 months:	30
6 to 12 months:	35
1 to 3 years:	40

Best Super Baby Food Sources:

½ C fresh orange juice	63
½ C canned papaya juice	51
½ medium kiwi fruit	38
⅛ cantaloupe	32
¼ C fresh lemon juice	28
2 T green peppers	25
½ C canned tomato juice	24
½ C green raw cabbage	24
¼ C strawberries	22
⅛ papaya	21
¼ C fresh lime juice	20
2 T raw parsley	17
½ C blackberries	15
2 T Brussels sprouts	14
2 T broccoli	14
¼ Florida avocado	13
2 T turnip greens	13
½ C pineapple juice	12
½ raw tomato	12
½ C raspberries	11
¼ orange	11
½ C raw pineapple	11
½ C blueberries	10
1 small banana	10
½ C cherries	10
½ C mashed potatoes	10
⅛ mango	9
2 T collard greens	9
2 T kale	9
1 slice canned pineapple	7
½ C watermelon	7
⅛ mango	7
2 T cauliflower	7
2 T spinach	7
¼ California avocado	6
½ medium apple	6
2 T lima beans	5
2 T mustard greens	5
¼ C canned pumpkin	5
2 T beet greens	4
½ nectarine	4

Perhaps you've heard the story of the British sailors in the eighteenth century who came down with scurvy approximately three months into a long ocean trip. Their diet consisted of meat and cereals and no fresh vegetables and fruits. This complete lack of vitamin C caused scurvy, which is a disease characterized by bleeding under the skin, bleeding and swollen gums, swollen legs and arms, bleeding in eyes, very dry skin, shortness of breath, and hair loss. By the late eighteenth century, all British ships were regularly supplied with lime juice, and British sailors came to be known as "limey"s. The sailors were subsequently "without scurvy." And to increase your language origins trivia knowledge, know that the Latin word for "without scurvy" is *ascorbic*. The body cannot manufacture Vitamin C. It must be obtained from foods. It is easily absorbed in the intestine and excesses are excreted in the urine. Vitamin C foods should be eaten with foods containing iron, because it increases absorption in the intestines. It also helps the body use folic acid and manganese. Of course, breastmilk has enough vitamin C for your baby. If you are formula feeding, give your baby a vitamin C fruit juice or puréed fresh fruit with vitamin C. The body can absorb only so much vitamin C at one time, therefore it is better to eat small amounts of vitamin C foods several times a day than to eat all of your vitamin C foods in one meal. The body excretes vitamin C in the urine, even if body tissues are not saturated.

Stability: Vitamin C is very unstable, in fact, it is the most unstable of all vitamins. Exposure to heat, light, and air quickly destroys Vitamin C. For example, approximately half of the vitamin C of an orange slice is gone after being exposed to air for only 30 minutes. Keep this in mind when looking at the Best Sources table for vitamin C. Squeeze fresh orange juice and have your baby drink it immediately. Keep foods cold, fresh, and in a dark environment to preserve vitamin C. Don't let foods sit on the counter at room temperature, return them to the refrigerator right away. Freezing preserves some vitamin C in foods. Cooking by boiling destroys twice as much vitamin C than steaming, and microwave cooking is slightly better than steaming. Using copper utensils in cooking also destroys vitamin C.

Functions in the human body: Antioxidant (page 509). Vitamin C is necessary for healthy skin and red blood cells, wound and bone healing, and infection prevention. It helps form collagen, which forms connective tissue that binds cells together. Collagen is found in bones, teeth, and tendons, and in the skin, eyes, and blood vessels. Vitamin C promotes stress hormone production and requirements for this vitamin increase when the body is under stress. Vitamin C may increase resistance to colds and infection. Eating lots of fresh fruits and vegetables with vitamin C has been associated with a decreased incidence of some cancers, but there is no definite correlation yet (so what?).

Deficiency symptoms: Scurvy is rare in the United States, but marginal Vitamin C deficiency is common due to alcohol, smoking (smoking one pack eats up the vitamin C in eight oranges), stress, lack of fresh fruits and vegetables in the diet, and some medications. Symptoms include bleeding and spongy gums, nosebleeds, pinpoint hemorrhages under the skin, dry skin, slow healing wounds and fractures, swollen and painful joints, loose or weakened teeth, muscle cramps, poor lactation, fatigue, irritability, weakness, restlessness, and loss of appetite. In infants and children, stunted growth.

Toxicity symptoms: None. Some adverse effects have been reported with excessive supplementation (1000+ mg daily in adults) for long periods of time, such as kidney stone development, diarrhea or flatulence, skin rash, anemia, burning sensation during urination, and low blood sugar. Too much vitamin C might also destroy copper and selenium in the body.

My personal vitamin C story: I have taken between 500 to 1000 mg per day for the last 20 years. There was a time when I stopped taking vitamin C for a few months. Ironically, it was during a very stressful period in my life when I needed more than my usual amount of vitamin C. My gums began to bleed every time I brushed my teeth. It took four dental visits to have my gums scraped. (This is definitely something you want to avoid.) I believe my gum problems were caused by the vitamin C supplementation stoppage. What's the moral of my story? If you consume large doses of vitamin C for a long time and then stop, you may develop deficiency symptoms, even if your diet is high in vitamin C compared to the RDA. If you want to reduce your intake, do so slowly over a period of time so your body can adjust. If you took supplements while pregnant, your infant may be used to a high vitamin C intake. Ask your doctor if you should give her supplements.

Calcium

RDA in mg:

Birth to 6 months:	400
6 to 12 months:	600
1 to 3 years:	800

Best Super Baby Food Sources:

1 T blackstrap molasses	172
2 T chia seeds	150
½ C milk, skim or with fat	150
½ cup of some soy milk	150
½ C buttermilk	150
2 oz. evaporated milk	150
½ C yogurt, whole milk	137
½ C fortified soy milks	100
½ oz most natural cheeses	100

1 oz flaxseed	76
1 oz almonds	75
½C cottage cheese	70
⅛ C soybeans	64
1 T tahini	63
1 oz filberts	53
1 oz Brazil nuts	50
2 T collard greens	45
2 T kale	44
2 T mustard greens	43
1 T almond butter	43
⅛ C Great Northern beans	40
⅛ C navy beans	40
⅛ C amaranth	38
1 oz tofu (calcium coagulated)	37
2 T broccoli	21

Of the minerals in the human body, calcium is the most abundant. Your body contains between two and three pounds of calcium. For proper calcium absorption, vitamin D, fluoride, and silicon are needed. Your doctor has probably told you to get enough calcium during your pregnancy, especially in the last three months, to insure proper bone and teeth formation in your unborn baby. During lactation, if the mother is not getting enough calcium, calcium will be taken from the mother's body to provide for the child. This may result in future bone disease for the mother. Calcium must be properly balanced with phosphorus—too much phosphorus can cause a calcium deficiency. Some soft drinks have a very high phosphorus content from sodium phosphate, an additive that gives it the fizz. Please don't replace high-calcium milk with carbonated beverages (soda) in your child's diet or you'll get a double whammy—the lack of calcium from the milk and too much phosphorus from the soda. Milk also has lots of phosphorus, but that's OK because it has the calcium to balance it. *Fortified* soy milks are a good source of calcium. Compare the "Nutrition Facts" label on a box of soy milk to the label on a carton of cow's milk to see how the calcium contents compare. In the Best Sources for calcium table above, I did not list beet greens, spinach, and Swiss chard, even though they do contain calcium. These green vegetables contain significant amounts of oxalic acid, which combines with calcium during digestion, causing it to be passed out of the body without being absorbed. The green vegetables without this oxalic acid problem that can be used as sources of calcium are kale, broccoli, and turnip, mustard, dandelion and collard greens. The same problem with oxalic acid holds true for phytic acid in beans' and grains' outer husks. Sprouting or soaking beans and grains before cooking decreases the phytic acid content. Hard drinking water contains more calcium than soft water. Don't use a water softener for the water you drink, as discussed on page 63.

Read about the dangers of lead in some calcium supplements on page 557.

Functions in the human body: Almost all (99%) of the calcium in your body is found in bones and teeth, where it works with phosphorus and silicon to keep them strong. But calcium is needed for more than healthy bones and teeth. In your baby, calcium helps her body use iron, and enough iron is essential in infants and children. See iron, page 547. Calcium is necessary for muscle contraction, especially the heart; a lack of calcium can lead to irregular heart rhythms. It's also needed for proper blood clotting, maintenance of the connective tissue collagen, parathyroid hormone function, and proper functioning of the nerves. Calcium helps control blood pressure, which helps to prevent heart disease and stroke. It also helps prevent colorectal cancer. Proper calcium intake and absorption can help prevent osteoporosis, the bone disease associated with aging. Calcium, along with iron, is critical in preventing low-level lead poisoning. See lead, page 556.

Deficiency symptoms: Muscle cramps, tingling or numbness in the arms and legs, cramps, pain in joints, slow pulse, heart palpitations, dental cavities, insomnia, irritability, and stunted growth. In children, extreme calcium deficiency causes rickets, a disease characterized by deformed bones.

Smoking and excessive intake of alcohol, caffeine, and soft drinks can cause calcium deficiency. Too much magnesium or phosphorus in the diet may also lead to deficiency.

Toxicity symptoms: If more than several thousand mg of calcium are ingested daily in adults, these toxicity symptoms may occur: constipation, nausea, bloating, excessive bone calcification, kidney stones, decreased absorption of zinc and iron, and calcium deposits in arteries and veins.

Phosphorus

RDA in mg:

Birth to 6 months:	300
6 to 12 months:	500
1 to 3 years:	800

Best Super Baby Food Sources:

1 oz pumpkin or squash seeds	333
1 T toasted wheat germ	325
1 T raw wheat germ	244
1 oz pasteurized Amer cheese	200
1 oz sunflower seeds	200
½ C whole milk, 3.7%	185
1 T brewer's yeast	175
2 T chia seeds	172
1 oz Brazil nuts	170
½ C cottage cheese	170
⅛ C soybeans	164
1 oz almonds	148
1 oz cashews	139
1 oz flaxseed	129
⅛ C navy beans	115
⅛ C amaranth	112
1 T tahini	112
½ C whole milk, 3.3%	110
½ C milk, 2%, 1%, skim	110
1 oz most natural cheeses	110
⅛ C lentils	109
½ C buttermilk	109
½ C yogurt, whole milk	108
1 T peanut butter	106
1 oz peanuts	105
⅛ C Great Northern beans	102
⅛ C black turtle	101
⅛ C pinto beans	100
⅛ C mung beans	95
⅛ C kidney beans	94
⅛ C adzuki beans	93
⅛ C chick peas	92
⅛ C split peas	90
1 oz English walnuts	90
1 oz filberts	89
⅛ C quinoa	87
⅛ C triticale	86
⅛ C lima beans	86
1 T almond butter	84
1 large egg yolk	81
⅛ C rye berries	79
⅛ C millet	71
⅛ C buckwheat groats	65
½ C soybean milk	65
⅛ C brown rice	63
⅛ C pearled barley	55
⅛ C whole wheat flour	52
⅛ C rolled oats/oatmeal	48
⅛ C couscous	39
⅛ C cornmeal, whole grain	36
1 T dry TVP	35
1 oz tofu	27
¼ C dried cooked prunes	25

Phosphorus is the second most abundant mineral in the human body, after calcium. You probably don't hear nearly as much about phosphorus as you do about calcium. It is found so abundantly in plant and animal foods that deficiency is rare; toxicity is more likely. Recommended allowances usually depend on calcium and are set at approximately the same as calcium, although it can be as much as twice that of calcium and still be well-utilized.

Functions in the human body: Phosphorus is involved in almost all body processes and is part of all body cells' genetic codes. Along with calcium, it forms bones and teeth. It is also part of the structure of all soft tissues, and in all organs from the brain to the kidneys.

Deficiency symptoms: Deficiency is rare. Large amounts of aluminum hydroxide, found in some antacids and anticonvulsant medications, might cause a phosphorus deficiency.

Toxicity symptoms: Toxicity results if there is an imbalance of phosphorus and calcium in the diet. The ratio should be approximately one to one. People at risk are those who eat too many phosphorus-rich foods (meat, fast foods, soft drinks) and too little calcium-rich foods (see calcium table, page 540). Bone problems, such as osteoporosis, can occur if too much phosphorus is in the diet.

Magnesium

RDA in mg:

Birth to 6 months:	40
6 to 12 months:	60
1 to 3 years:	80

Best Super Baby Food Sources:

1 oz pumpkin or squash seeds	152
1 oz sunflower seeds	100
1 T toasted wheat germ	91
1 oz almonds	84
1 oz filberts	81
1 oz cashews	74
1 T raw wheat germ	69
⅛ C soybeans	65
⅛ C amaranth	65
1 oz Brazil nuts	64
1 T tahini	50
⅛ C lima beans	50
⅛ C mung beans	49
1 T almond butter	48
1 oz English walnuts	48
1 oz peanuts	47
⅛ C buckwheat groats	45
⅛ C quinoa	45
⅛ C navy beans	45
1 T blackstrap molasses	43
⅛ C Great Northern beans	43
⅛ C pinto beans	38
⅛ C black turtle	37
⅛ C brown rice	34
⅛ C kidney beans	32
⅛ C adzuki beans	31
⅛ C triticale	31
⅛ C chick peas	29
⅛ C millet	29
⅛ C split peas	28
1 oz tofu	28
1 T peanut butter	28
¼ avocado	28
⅛ C lentils	26
⅛ C rye berries	26

1 oz pistachio nuts	25
½ C fresh orange juice	24
1 T brewer's yeast	23
⅛ C whole wheat flour	21
⅛ C pearled barley	20
⅛ C cornmeal, whole grain	19
½ C black raspberries	18
½ C sweet cherries	16
½ C pineapple juice	15
1 oz pecans	15
½ C blackberries	15
⅛ C rolled oats/oatmeal	15
⅛ C bulgur	15
¼ C dried cooked prunes	14
½ C buttermilk	13
½ C yogurt, whole milk	13
2 T spinach	13
½ C red raspberries	13
2 T beet greens	12
½ C sour red cherries	12
⅛ C couscous	10
½ C tomato juice	10
½ C watermelon	10
½ C strawberries	9
1 oz Amer cheese, pasteurized	9
1 oz mashed banana	8
2 T beets	8
⅛ honeydew melon	8
⅛ raw cantaloupe	8
2 T canned pumpkin	7
¼ C raw pumpkin	6
2 T broccoli	5
2 T Brussels sprouts	5
2 T sweet potatoes	5
½ medium pear	4
¼ small raw tomato	4
½ C blueberries	4

A magnesium deficiency is not uncommon in this country. Processing and refining of foods removes most of the magnesium, which is not replaced during the enrichment process. Also, cooking, freezing, and canning destroys magnesium, so eat the foods listed in the Best Sources table raw. Chemical fertilization, our most common farming method, depletes the soil of magnesium, whereas organic gardening does not. Soft-water, which is typical of drinking supplies in many areas of this country, lacks the magnesium content of hard water. Feel lucky if your soap doesn't lather well, that's a sign of hard water and high magnesium content. Don't use a water softener for the water you drink, as discussed on page 63. More than half of the human body's magnesium is found in bone, the rest is in cells, soft tissues, muscle, and blood. If magnesium is lacking in the diet, it is taken from bone to insure an adequate amount exists in blood. Calcium and magnesium are closely related in their body functions and must be in proper proportion. One part magnesium should be accompanied by approximately two parts calcium. (Note that the RDA's are not in that proportion. They are way off—1 to 10 instead of 1 to 2.) There is a reciprocal relationship between calcium and magnesium in muscle functioning, calcium stimulates muscles and magnesium relaxes muscles. Remember that the heart is a muscle and needs calcium to stay healthy. Excess calcium may cause a magnesium deficiency.

Functions in the human body: Necessary in formation of bones and teeth. Activates enzymes which help the body use energy from food. Controls blood pressure. Regulates body temperature. Regulates acid-alkaline balance in the body. Helps in the manufacture of protein, RNA, and DNA. Used in muscle contraction and relaxation and in nerve functioning. Helps with constipation by acting as a laxative and flushing out intestines. Neutralizes stomach acid. Helps stiff joints.

Deficiency symptoms: Magnesium deficiency is sometimes hard to recognize because the symptoms may be linked to other problems or deficiencies. Severe deficiency symptoms include weak muscles, muscle spasms, poor coordination, tremors or convulsions, hypertension, loss of appetite, depression, apprehensiveness, change in personality, a desire to commit suicide, confusion, nausea, gastrointestinal problems, hair loss, swollen gums, irregular heartbeat, calcium deposits in the kidneys, heart, and blood vessels. Long-term magnesium deficiency can cause heart and cardiovascular problems. All of these can cause magnesium deficiency: stress, alcohol,

diuretics, highly refined, processed foods, lack of protein in the diet, a high carbohydrate diet, too much calcium in the diet, vomiting, diarrhea, and taking too many diuretics. Magnesium deficiency can cause painful uterine contractions in women in the later stages of pregnancy. The children's disease, kwashiorkor, which means "the disease of the deposed baby when the next one is born" is caused by magnesium deficiency. It is very common in some developing countries. When a second child is born, the first is weaned from the breast and placed on a diet lacking in magnesium and other nutrients. Malnutrition develops and death may result.

Toxicity symptoms: Toxicity is unlikely, being that the kidneys excrete excess magnesium. If kidneys are not functioning properly, as in the aged and in those with kidney problems, magnesium toxicity may result. People with kidney problems should not take magnesium supplements unless their doctors approve. Symptoms include weakness, lethargy, drowsiness, and difficulty breathing.

Potassium

RDA in mg:

Birth to 6 months:	500
6 to 12 months:	700
1 to 3 years:	1000

Best Super Baby Food Sources:

1 T blackstrap molasses	498
¼ Calif or Florida avocado	425
⅛ C soybeans	418
⅛ C lima beans	384
⅛ C black turtle	345
⅛ C mung beans	324
⅛ C kidney beans	324
⅛ C pinto beans	319
⅛ C Great Northern beans	316
⅛ C adzuki beans	307
⅛ C navy beans	297
⅛ honeydew melon	282
1 T toasted wheat germ	269
1 T raw wheat germ	259
½ C orange juice	250
⅛ cantaloupe	242

⅛ C split peas	240
1 oz pumpkin or squash seeds	229
½ C tomato juice	227
⅛ C chick peas	219
⅛ C lentils	217
1 oz almonds	208
½ C cherries	200
1 T peanut butter	200
1 oz peanuts	197
1 oz sunflower seeds	196
2 T lima beans	195
1 T brewer's yeast	189
½ C buttermilk	185
½ C yogurt, whole milk	175
½ C pineapple juice	170
½ C milk	170
1 oz Brazil nuts	170
2 T beet greens	164
1 oz cashews	160
⅛ C quinoa	157
½ C blackberries	152
½ C grape juice	145
1 oz English walnuts	142
½ medium kiwi fruit	126
1 oz filberts	126
½ C apple juice	125
½ C strawberries	123
1 T almond butter	121
1 T dry TVP	110
1 oz mashed banana	110
½ C raspberries	110
½ peach	101
½ C cottage cheese	100
½ orange	100
½ C watermelon	100
1 slice canned pineapple	99
½ C raw pineapple	96
½ pear	93
⅛ C amaranth	90
⅛ papaya	88
½ apple	88
2 T butternut & acorn squash	88
2 T beet greens	83
2 T sweet potatoes	83
1 oz macadamia nuts	82
2 T spinach	81
⅛ C triticale	80
½ nectarine	74
⅛ C pearled barley	70

2 T beets	67
2 T Swiss chard	67
⅛ C buckwheat groats	66
1 T tahini	65
⅛ C brown rice	64
2 T Brussels sprouts	64
2 T canned pumpkin	63
¼ raw tomato	61
⅛ C whole wheat flour	61
½ apricot	60
2 T collard greens	60
2 T raw parsley	60
1 oz fresh orange juice	56
⅛ C rye berries	56
½ C blueberries	56
2 T dandelion greens	55
⅛ C millet	49
⅛ mango	47

Potassium and sodium are partners in the body to maintain the water balance in the body and to keep the heart muscle beating properly. Potassium works inside the cells while sodium works outside the cells to regulate the amount of water inside and outside of the cell walls. A high-sodium, low-potassium diet, typical in developed cultures, is detrimental to cardiovascular health. Your body is designed to flush out mass amounts of potassium and hoard sodium, because natural foods like fresh vegetables have a lot potassium and very little sodium. Unfortunately, refinement of foods produces food that is just the opposite. For instance, **canned vegetables have horrendously high levels of sodium and depleted potassium levels.** The ill health effects of too much sodium are discussed on page 546. There are rare instances where processing helps, such as when potassium chloride is added to butter/margarine blends to balance with the high sodium chloride (salt) content.

Potassium is a major nutrient of plants and therefore eating plants, that is, eating fruits, vegetables, and other plant products, is a good way for people to get potassium in their diet. Plants receive potassium through the soil. Perhaps you have fertilized your vegetable garden with wood ashes, which contain a lot of potash, a form of potassium chloride that is easily absorbed by plants.

Functions in the human body: Necessary for healthy skin, proper muscle and nerve functioning, and for the manufacture of protein. Maintains the acid-base balance in body fluids. Helps body cells release energy. Maintains a normal heart beat and blood pressure. Along with sodium and chloride, maintains the normal balance of water and dissolved substances in body cells. Stimulates the kidneys to empty toxins from the body.

Deficiency symptoms: Potassium deficiency is common, due to high salt intake. Symptoms include muscle weakness, muscle damage, poor reflexes, heart muscle irregularities, respiratory failure, kidney problems, constipation, nervous disorders, insomnia, and acne or dry skin. In infants, diarrhea decreases potassium absorption and may cause potassium deficiency. Diuretics, some blood pressure medications, some hormone products, digestive tract disease, vomiting, excessive sugar intake, stress, and saline solution administered intravenously may also lead to deficiency.

Toxicity symptoms: Excessive potassium intake (greater than 18,000 mg for adults) may cause any of these symptoms: kidney problems, improper fluid balance in the body, hemorrhages in the digestive system, infections, breakdown of muscle tissue, and heart problems including cardiac arrest.

Sodium

RDA in mg:

Birth to 6 months:	120
6 to 12 months:	200
1 to 3 years:	225

Best Super Baby Food Sources:

½ C cottage cheese	460
½ C canned tomato juice	200
½ C buttermilk	128
½ C milk	60
½ C yogurt, whole milk	53
2 T beet greens	43

1 T blackstrap molasses	19
beet greens	19
⅛ honeydew melon	13
spinach	12
1 T brewer's yeast	12
dandelion greens	11
⅛ cantaloupe	11
2 T beets	11
2 T carrots	10

Sodium exists in the body in fluids outside of the cells and in bones. The body needs sodium, but the typical American is more likely to have too much in the diet rather than too little. Cured meats, canned vegetables, processed cheese, soups, breads, snack foods, fast foods, condiments, and fermented foods like pickles, all typically contain horrendous amounts of salt. Read the labels and avoid these high-salt junk foods. Even our tap water is poisoned with too much salt. The water softening process, used to make soap lather more easily and to decrease mineral buildup in pipes, adds sodium to water, as discussed on page 63. If you must soften your water, soften only that which is used for cleaning and not that which your family drinks. Sodium is also added to our drinking water when the tons of de-icing highway salt leach into the water table.

Sodium has a very bad reputation for causing hypertension and with just cause. In some people, an increase of sodium in the diet causes a rise in blood pressure. One of the highest sources of sodium is, of course, table salt. For your health and that of the rest of your family, chuck that salt shaker. Most importantly, you should not add table salt to any of your baby's food or cooking water, either as a source of dietary sodium or as a flavor enhancer. Some parents mistakenly think they are doing the baby a favor by adding salt to make the food taste better. Not so. The delicious natural flavors of fresh, whole foods are so much better than processed, tasteless food perked up by added salt. You don't want your baby to acquire a taste for salt, which is way too abundant in the typical American diet. Fortunately, the practice of adding salt to commercial baby food has become less common, although some is still added to the dessert-type baby foods. Don't buy them and read labels on all the food you buy.

Functions in the human body: Sodium is the chief regulator of the body's water balance. It works together with potassium to maintain the balance of water in and around body cells. It is also necessary for muscle and nerve functioning, and maintaining proper acid-base balance in the body.

Deficiency symptoms: Sodium is more likely to be found in excess in the American diet. Excessive sweating, fever, diarrhea, starvation dieting, fasting, and very low salt diets are the rare circumstances when sodium deficiency exists. Symptoms include muscle twitching, weak muscles, dehydration, loss of memory or poor concentration, and loss of appetite.

Toxicity symptoms: Sodium excesses in modern diets are common, due to the addition of salt to processed foods, the popularity of high-salt snack foods, and the common practice of keeping a salt shaker at the dining room table. Symptoms include edema (water retention) and hypertension.

Iron

RDA in mg:

Birth to 6 months:	6
6 to 12 months:	10
1 to 3 years:	10

IRON FROM PLANT FOODS IS POORLY ABSORBED. IRON FORTIFIED FORMULA, IRON-FORTIFIED CEREALS, OR IRON SUPPLEMENT DROPS MAY BE RECOMMENDED. CONSULT YOUR PEDIATRICIAN.

Best Super Baby Food Sources:

1 oz teff, red	21.14
1 oz flaxseed	12.26
1 oz teff, white	5.85
1 oz pumpkin or squash seeds	4.25
⅛ C soybeans	3.65
1 T blackstrap molasses	3.50
2 T chia seeds	2.84

1 T toasted wheat germ	2.58
⅛ C lentils	2.17
⅛ C black turtle	2.00
1 T brewer's yeast	2.00
⅛ C quinoa	1.97
1 oz sunflower seeds	1.92
⅛ C kidney beans	1.89
⅛ C amaranth	1.86
1 T raw wheat germ	1.82
⅛ C mung beans	1.75
1 oz cashews	1.70
⅛ C navy beans	1.68
⅛ C lima beans	1.67
⅛ C chick peas	1.56
1 oz tofu	1.49
⅛ C pinto beans	1.41
1 oz peanuts	1.28
⅛ C Great Northern beans	1.25
⅛ C adzuki beans	1.22
¼ C dried cooked prunes	1.21
1 T medium molasses	1.20
1 T fortified infant cereal	1.10
⅛ C split peas	1.09
½ C soybean milk	1.05
1 oz almonds	1.04
¼ California avocado	1.02
1 oz Brazil nuts	.97
1 oz filberts	.93
1 T tahini	.90
1 small red banana	.80
½ C strawberries	.75
⅛ C millet	.75
½ C blueberries	.70
1 oz English walnuts	.69
⅛ C pearled barley	.63
1 average dwarf banana	.63
⅛ C triticale	.62
½ C tomato juice	.60
1 large egg yolk	.59
1 T almond butter	.59
⅛ C whole wheat flour	.58
⅛ C rye berries	.56
½ C raspberries	.56
⅛ C cornmeal, whole grain	.52
⅛ C buckwheat groats	.51

Note: Although spinach, beet greens, and chard contain iron, they also contain oxalic acid, which interferes with iron absorption (and absorption of other minerals). Greens that are sources of iron, which don't have the oxalic acid problem are: kale, broccoli, collard, dandelion, mustard, and turnip greens, cabbage, and romaine lettuce.

Iron is a very important nutrient for your baby. This is evident in the supermarket, where every baby cereal box package and infant formula can states in bold letters that the product is iron-fortified. Iron is found in whole grain cereals and some is destroyed during grain refinement, which is another reason to eat only whole grains. Infants are born with only 4-6 months' supply of iron in their bodies. Low birth weight babies and premature babies may have as little as 2 months' supply. After this time, infants must get iron from their diet, supplements, or iron-fortified food. Some nutritionists believe that infants (and pregnant and lactating women) cannot possibly get the iron they need from diet and must supplement to prevent anemia. Talk to your pediatrician about an iron supplement for your baby.

Although breast milk contains small amounts of iron, it is very efficiently used by the baby. Pediatricians usually recommend an iron supplement for a baby that is exclusively breast-fed. The typical dose is 0.5 mg of iron per day per pound of baby's body weight.

And for yourself, look on the label of over-the-counter vitamins and buy those that get iron from ferrous, not ferric, compounds. Ferrous compounds are more readily absorbed by the body than ferric. Unfortunately, it's ferric compounds that are used for fortification and enrichment in processed flours and cereals. Why do food manufacturers use the type that isn't readily absorbed? Because it causes the breads to turn gray, so they are no longer pretty white, it shortens shelf life, and it doesn't bake as well. We must start letting manufacturers know by the products we choose to buy that we care more about our health than about aesthetics!

Vitamin C greatly improves iron absorption, so make sure your baby eats a vitamin C food with an iron food. Fresh orange juice with whole

grain millet or brown rice cereal is a good combination. Your doctor probably has prescribed liquid vitamins containing vitamin C, which you give to your baby daily. If you don't have fresh orange juice or a vitamin C food in the meal containing iron, give your baby his prescription vitamins. Fruit juices and purées fortified with vitamin C are also good sources.

If you are not a vegetarian, you may want to include small amounts of meat, poultry, or fish with meals containing iron-rich foods, as these animal foods also increase iron absorption. Desiccated liver is a good source of iron.

Again, stay away from processed foods such as white flour, ice cream, and soft drinks, which contain additives (phosphates) that decrease iron absorption.

Iron leaches into cooking water, so use as little water as possible. Cooking acidic foods, such as spaghetti sauce, in cast iron cookware greatly increases the iron content of the food. So simmer your spaghetti sauce for a long time in that cast iron pot, and it will be high in iron.

Adequate copper is also necessary for proper iron absorption. See copper, page 549.

Functions in the human body: Iron's main function is to carry oxygen to every corner of the body. When the blood goes through the lungs' blood vessels, inhaled oxygen binds to the iron contained in the blood and off it goes to the rest of the body. Iron helps the body resist colds and infections and promotes a strong immune system. Iron also helps to prevent lead poisoning by reducing lead absorption in the intestine.

Deficiency symptoms: Feeling of being tired or "washed-out." (Sorry, I know it's ridiculous to tell the parent of a 10-month old that she shouldn't feel tired.) Also, iron-deficiency anemia (decrease in red blood cells or the size of red blood cells), lethargy, poor concentration, shortness of breath, and heart problems. Another symptom might be the craving to eat things that are not food, such as ice, clay, or starch (pica). Although it is suspected that pica is caused by lack of iron, it has not been proven. Infants with iron deficiency are more inactive, fussier, and less responsive than infants with adequate iron. Children with iron deficiency score lower on intelligence tests, do poorer in school, have shorter attention spans, and may be hyperactive. Iron, along with calcium, is critical in preventing low-level lead poisoning in children. (See lead, page 556.) Women are more at risk for anemia than men, due to menstruation, the late stages of pregnancy, birth, and lactation. We can't win—if we're not losing iron from our periods, then we are losing it through birthing or nursing babies! ☺

Toxicity symptoms: Iron toxicity is possible from supplements and iron-fortified foods, but it is rare from diet alone. Infants should not get more than 15 mg of iron per day. Each year, approximately 2,000 children get iron toxicity, usually because they ingest adult iron supplements.

Some people are born with a tendency to absorb and store too much iron (hemochromatosis) and they are at very high risk for iron poisoning. Symptoms of iron toxicity include damage to organs, especially the liver and the spleen, tissue damage, and organ failure. Too much iron may also cause zinc deficiency.

Copper

RDA in mg:
Birth to 6 months:.40 to .60
6 to 12 months: .60 to .70
1 to 3 years: .70 to 1.0

Best Super Baby Food Sources:

1 oz cashews	.63
1 oz sunflower seeds	.50
1 oz Brazil nuts	.50
2 T chia seeds	.47
1 oz filberts	.43
1 T blackstrap molasses	.41
1 oz pumpkin or squash seeds	.39
⅛ C soybeans	.39
1 oz English walnuts	.38
1 oz peanuts	.32
⅛ C adzuki beans	.27
1 oz almonds	.27
⅛ C mung beans	.24
⅛ C navy beans	.23
⅛ C black turtle	.23
1 T raw wheat germ	.23
1 T peanut butter	.22
⅛ C kidney beans	.22
⅛ C chick peas	.21
r⅛ C split peas	.21
⅛ C lentils	.20
⅛ C amaranth	.19
⅛ C millet	.19
⅛ C pinto beans	.19
⅛ C Great Northern beans	.19
1 T toasted wheat germ	.18
⅛ C quinoa	.17
⅛ C lima beans	.16
1 slice canned pineapple	.15
½ C sweet cherries	.14
1 T almond butter	.14
⅛ C buckwheat groats	.13
⅛ C pearled barley	.11
⅛ C triticale	.11
½ medium pear	.10
½ C raw pineapple	.10
½ C sour red cherries	.09
⅛ C rye berries	.09
½ C blackberries	.08
½ C black raspberries	.08
1 small banana	.08
½ C blueberries	.08
⅛ C brown rice	.07
1 T dry TVP	.07
⅛ C couscous	.06
⅛ C whole wheat flour	.06
⅛ honeydew melon	.05
2 T beet greens	.05
1 oz tofu	.05
2 T sweet potatoes	.04
2 T fresh peas, cooked	.04
⅛ mango	.04
2 T asparagus	.04
½ peach	.04
½ C red raspberries	.04
⅛ C bulgur	.03
⅛ C rolled oats/oatmeal	.03

Copper is found in the bones, the muscles, and in the brain, heart, kidneys, and liver.

Processing of foods, especially refining whole wheat flour into white flour, removes the majority of the copper content (see table, page 219). American diet staples—bread, rolls, cereals, pasta—are deficient in copper because they are made from white flour.

Functions in the human body: Copper is an important part of the cardiovascular, nervous, and skeletal systems. It helps in the formation of red blood cells by converting iron into hemoglobin. Copper may help prevent heart problems, lower cancer risk, and prevent cell damage, anemia, and premature aging. In pregnant women, copper may prevent miscarriage.

Deficiency symptoms: Severe copper deficiency is rare, marginal deficiencies are more common. Hospital food may be marginally deficient. Too much zinc may cause copper deficiency. In children with chronic diarrhea or lack of protein in their diet, deficiency is possible. Symptoms include anemia, loss of color from skin and hair, defects in the skeletal system, scoliosis, heart disease, raised cholesterol levels, low elasticity of arteries, decreased resistance to infections, nervous system disorders, poor concentration, lack of coordination, and tingling and numbness.

Toxicity symptoms: Taking too many supplements (more than 15 mg daily) may cause diarrhea, intestinal cramps, nausea, and vomiting. Too much copper may cause a zinc deficiency and also may block absorption of selenium; low selenium is linked to high cancer risk. The inherited disease called Wilson's disease is characterized by too much copper in the body. There is a remote chance that copper pipes may introduce too much copper into your tap water. See tap water, page 62.

Zinc

RDA in mg:

Birth to 6 months:	5
6 to 12 months:	5
1 to 3 years:	10

Best Super Baby Food Sources:

1 T toasted wheat germ	4.7
1 T raw wheat germ	3.6
1 oz pumpkin or squash seeds	2.1
1 oz cashews	1.6
1 T tahini	1.5
2 T chia seeds	1.5
1 oz sunflower seeds	1.4
1 oz Brazil nuts	1.3
⅛ C adzuki beans	1.2
⅛ C soybeans	1.1
1 oz peanuts	.9
⅛ C chick peas	.9
1 T peanut butter	.9
⅛ C lentils	.9
⅛ C amaranth	.8
⅛ C rye berries	.8
⅛ C triticale	.8
1 oz almonds	.8
1 oz English walnuts	.8
1 oz filberts	.7
⅛ C navy beans	.7
½ C yogurt, whole milk	.7
⅛ C mung beans	.7
⅛ C quinoa	.7
⅛ C split peas	.7
⅛ C lima beans	.6
⅛ C kidney beans	.6
⅛ C pinto beans	.6
⅛ C pecans	.6
⅛ C brown rice	.5
1 T almond butter	.5
⅛ C Great Northern beans	.5
⅛ C black turtle	.5
1 large egg yolk	.5
⅛ C buckwheat groats	.5
1 T wheat germ oil	.5
½ C cottage cheese	.5
⅛ C pearled barley	.5
½ C milk	.5
1 T blackstrap molasses	.4
⅛ C whole wheat flour	.4
⅛ C millet	.4

Functions in the human body: Needed for formation of approximately 100 enzymes, including insulin, and proteins, nucleic acids, and hormones. Necessary for growth and repair of tissue, and for energy conversion. Needed for a strong immune system. Regulates blood sugar, blood pressure, heart rate, and blood cholesterol levels. Detoxifies alcohol in the liver. May help prevent cancer or any disease characterized by abnormal cell growth. May help prevent cadmium poisoning (page 556).

Deficiency symptoms: Anemia, slow wound healing, dwarfism or stunted growth, birth defects and miscarriages, sterility, mental problems, skin problems, hair loss, bowel problems, poor ability to taste food. Too much iron or copper in the diet may cause a zinc deficiency. Vegetarians should be careful to get enough zinc in their diet. Children with zinc deficiency may have slow growth and be shorter than if zinc was adequate in the diet. They also may suffer slow intellectual development.

Toxicity symptoms: More than 25 mg daily can cause copper deficiency. A dose of more than 150 mg of zinc can decrease the body's resistance to infection. If daily intake exceeds 2000 mg per day, nausea and vomiting may result.

Manganese

RDA in mgs:

Birth to 6 months:	0.3 to 0.6
6 to 12 months:	0.6 to 1.0
1 to 3 years:	1.0 to 1.5

Best Super Baby Food Sources:

1 T toasted wheat germ	5.67
1 T raw wheat germ	3.86
⅛ C brown rice	0.89
1 oz Eng walnuts	0.82
⅛ C triticale	0.77
1 oz almonds	0.65
⅛ C soybeans	0.59
1 oz sunflower seeds	0.57
1 oz filberts	0.57
⅛ C whole wheat	0.57
⅛ C rye berries	0.56
⅛ C amaranth	0.55
⅛ C chick peas	0.55
1 oz peanuts	0.54
1 T blackstrap	0.52
⅛ C adzuki beans	0.42
⅛ C millet	0.41
1 T almond butter	0.38
⅛ C lima beans	0.37
⅛ C rolled	0.37
⅛ C lentils	0.34
⅛ C split peas	0.34
⅛ C navy beans	0.34
⅛ C buckwheat groats	0.33
⅛ C pearled barley	0.33
⅛ C Great Northern	0.32
⅛ C bulgur	0.28
⅛ C pinto beans	0.27
⅛ C mung beans	0.27
⅛ C kidney beans	0.23
⅛ C black turtle	0.23
1 oz Brazil nuts	0.22
⅛ C couscous	0.18
1 oz tofu	0.17
2 T sweet potatoes	0.15
1 T dry TVP	0.13
2 T broccoli	0.07
⅛ C cornmeal	0.07
2 T carrots	0.06
2 T Brussels sprouts	0.06
2 T beets	0.05
1 oz mashed banana	0.04
2 T asparagus	0.03
2 T cauliflower	0.03

Our bodies contain about 10 mg of manganese, most of which is in the bones, and the liver, kidneys, and pancreas.

Functions in the human body: Necessary for bone development and muscle coordination, and a healthy nervous system and reproductive system. Used by the body to produce some enzymes having to do with muscles, tendons, skin, cartilage, and bone. It is also used in the metabolism of carbohydrates and fats and along with vitamin K in the blood clotting process.

Deficiency symptoms: Seizures and epilepsy, poor muscle coordination and abnormal muscular movements, face twitching, impaired growth, birth defects, bone deformities, general weakness.

Toxicity symptoms: Too much manganese causes problems with iron absorption and can cause iron-deficiency anemia (see iron).

Selenium

RDA in mcgs:

Birth to 6 months:	10-40
6 to 12 months:	15-60
1 to 3 years:	20-80

Best Super Baby Food Sources:
Brazil nuts, whole grains, dairy, vegetables, Cheerios.

Selenium is an antioxidant (page 509). The amount of selenium found in food depends on the soil in which it is grown and it varies widely. Processing of whole grain and other foods removes selenium. Artificial fertilizers used in non-organic farming cause selenium depletion of soil. Brazil nuts are very high in selenium: 1 oz contains 18 mcg, so you and your baby should not eat too many of them.

Functions in the human body: Necessary for healthy skin, muscles, and proper heart function. Promotes formation of antibodies and therefore helps prevent infection. Helps to build red blood cells. May prevent cancer, cataracts, and arthritis, high blood pressure, stroke, heart attack. Helps to prevent the absorption of metals such as cadmium, mercury, silver, and thallium. It may protect against radiation.

Deficiency symptoms: Deficiency symptoms are premature aging, muscular aches and pains, nerve cell damage, mental retardation, nervous disorders, and infertility. Deficiency in infants may cause crib death.

Toxicity symptoms: Selenium can be very toxic at levels above 2400 mcg for adults, proportionately much less for a small infant. The recommended maximum intake for each age group is shown above. Symptoms include nausea, diarrhea, vomiting, abdominal pain, irritability, fatigue, sour-milk breath odor, hair loss, and hair and nail changes.

Bioflavinoids
(Vitamin P, Flavinoids)

Bioflavinoids may help the body absorb vitamin C. They are actually a group of over 200 substances, some of which are: citrin, flavonals, flavones, hesperidin, quercetin, and rutin. Bioflavinoids are found mostly in the non-juice part of citrus fruits, that is, the skin, peel, and white rinds, although there is a minute amount in the strained juice. Bioflavinoids may prevent damaged blood vessels, high blood pressure, arthritis, and cancer. Some, but not all, scientists claim they act as antioxidants.

Best Sources: apricots, blackberries, cherries, citrus fruits, grapes, plums, red onions, (tea, coffee, and wine).

Boron

This trace mineral is important in regulating the levels of calcium in the body, which may help to prevent osteoporosis.

Best Sources: legumes, nuts, vegetables, and fruits.

Chloride
(Chlorine)

Chlorine is a mineral found in the body along with sodium or potassium. As does sodium and potassium, chloride helps to keep the fluid balance in and out of cells. It is necessary for proper functioning of the liver and for healthy joints and tendons. Deficiency symptoms include digestive problems, problems with the muscles, hair loss, and tooth loss. A good diet of natural, whole foods contains adequate chloride.

Best sources: table salt, seaweed, olives, some water.

Choline

Choline is present in all living cells and is considered by some, but not all, as a B-complex vitamin. It helps the body use fat and cholesterol (it dissolves them) and helps rid the liver of fat. It is necessary for healthy kidneys, blood vessels, nerves, and liver. The body can manufacture choline, and therefore, it is not necessary in the diet, although some disagree that the body is capable of producing an adequate amount. Choline and inositol are the basic constituents of lecithin. Choline and inositol should be ingested in equal amounts. Choline deficiency may cause bleeding stomach ulcers, liver and kidney problems, high blood pressure, and atherosclerosis. Toxicity may cause a vitamin B6 deficiency—remember that the B vitamins must be in proper balance.

Best sources: lecithin, egg yolk, liver, brewer's yeast, soybeans, peanuts, peas, and wheat germ.

Chromium

Chromium is a mineral involved in metabolism, enzyme functions, and the manufacture of proteins. It is contained in glucose tolerance factor (GTF), which works with insulin to regulate blood sugar levels. Chromium is sometimes effective in managing hypoglycemia, because it helps to keep blood sugar on an even keel. Deficiency is common in Americans (some estimate 90% of Americans are deficient) because of the processing of grains (page 219) and white sugar and because of lack of chromium in the soil and ground water. Pregnant women are often deficient because the fetus needs lots of chromium. When the baby is born, he has a higher concentration of chromium in his body than he will the rest of his life. Deficiency symptoms include numbness and tingling in fingers and toes, high blood sugar, glucose intolerance, clumsiness, and nerve disorders in the extremities. Even moderate chromium deficiency causes problems in the human body, such as sugar intolerance, stunted growth, and atherosclerosis.

Best sources: brewer's yeast, whole grains, liver, broccoli and other vegetables, orange juice, some hard water.

Cobalt

Cobalt is a necessary partner for vitamin B12 in the functioning of enzymes and body cells, especially red blood cells. Like vitamin B12, it is found mostly in animal products and deficiency can be a problem for strict vegetarians. Deficiency symptoms include anemia and nervous disorders. Some toxicity symptoms are fatigue, heart palpitations, diarrhea, and numbness in fingers and toes.

Best sources: liver, milk, some seaweed.

Fluoride
(Fluorine)

About half of the United States population has fluoride added to their tap water. Studies have proven that fluoride significantly decreases the incidence of tooth decay in children, especially when fluoride is ingested *before* teeth have erupted.

We all know that most toothpastes now contain fluoride and, yes, fluoride in the body is found mainly in the teeth. Fluoride helps prevent tooth decay because it helps prevent acid formation in the mouth caused from food, especially sugars. A fluoride deficiency can result in tooth development problems and cavities. Relatively large amounts also are found in the body in bone and there are minute amounts in just about every body tissue. Fluorine is necessary for strong bones because it helps calcium to deposit in them and it is used to prevent osteoporosis. Tap water sometimes contains fluoride, and if your water is not fluoridated, your pediatrician may prescribe vitamins containing fluoride. Too much fluoride can be toxic, which is probably why it is not found in over-the-counter vitamins. Excess intake of fluoride by your child from supplements, fluoridated water, concentrated baby formula mixed with fluoridated water, and the swallowing of fluoridated toothpaste and mouthwashes, can also cause dental problems.

See more about fluoride on page 70 and in the section *Preventing Dental Problems*, page 48.

Toxicity: may cause stunted growth, calcification of tendons and ligaments, mongolism, and organ damage. Also, toxicity may cause brown stains to form on the teeth and enamel may acquire a high degree of porosity. Fluorosis, a condition where the permanent teeth become mottled, can also be caused by too much fluoride. Excess fluoride may also cause gas, irritability, and fussiness.

Best sources: baby prescription vitamins with fluoride, fluoridated water, some cheese.

Inositol

Inositol is considered by some scientists to be one of the B vitamins. It is found in bones, muscles, and nerves. The body can manufacture inositol, but whether or not the body can make enough is unknown. It is added to infant formula not based on cow's milk. Inositol and choline are the basic constituents of lecithin. Like choline, it helps the body use fat and cholesterol and aids in the movement of fat out of the liver. And like choline, it is necessary for healthy kidneys, blood vessels, nerves, and liver. Inositol and choline should be ingested in equal amounts. Too much caffeine may cause inositol deficiency. Deficiency symptoms are eczema, constipation, eye problems, hair loss, and high blood cholesterol. Inositol is believed to act as a sedative and may help insomnia. There is no known inositol toxicity.

Best sources: lecithin, whole grains, brewer's yeast, blackstrap molasses, liver, and citrus fruits.

Iodide
(Iodine)

Iodine is a trace mineral commonly known to be necessary for proper thyroid gland function and development. It is also necessary for all over growth and development, helps with metabolism, and has various other functions in the human body. Deficiency symptoms include goiter (thyroid gland enlargement), dry hair, irritability, nervousness, slow metabolism, and obesity. If pregnant women have iodine deficiency, it can cause cretinism, a disease characterized by physical and mental retardation, in the baby. Cretinism symptoms may be reversed if iodine treatment is begun soon after birth. Iodine toxicity is known to be caused only from supplements, and not from food.

Best sources: kelp and other seaweeds, mushrooms grown in iodine-rich soil, iodized table salt.

Linoleic Acid and Linolenic Acid

These two unsaturated fatty acids cannot be manufactured by the body, and therefore must be supplied in the diet. The body needs unsaturated fatty acids for cell lubrication, healthy mucous membranes, nerves, skin, and reproductive organs. They also help transport oxygen to all body cells, break down cholesterol from the walls of arteries, help convert carotene into vitamin A, and help in the assimilation of phosphorus and calcium. Take vitamin E in combination to increase absorption. Deficiency symptoms include hair and nail problems, dry skin, eczema, dandruff, acne, problems with tooth development, allergies, underweight, varicose veins, diarrhea, and gallstones. For more information, see EFAs on page 505.

Molybdenum

Molybdenum is an essential trace mineral found in almost all plant and animal tissues. In the human body, it is found in the liver, kidneys, bones and teeth. It may prevent anemia, tooth decay, impotency, and esophagus cancer. Toxicity symptoms include stunted growth, diarrhea, anemia, and copper deficiency.

Best sources: whole grains, legumes, some green leafy vegetables. All must have been grown in soil with good molybdenum content.

Nickel

Nickel is an essential trace mineral necessary in metabolism and other body functions. Deficiency symptoms can be caused from excessive sweating, intestinal malabsorption, stress, kidney failure, and cirrhosis of the liver. Nickel becomes very toxic when combined with carbon dioxide, as in cigarette smoke, and may be a cause of lung cancer. Toxicity may occur in people who experience stroke, myocardial infarction, uterine cancer, burns, and toxemia during pregnancy. Toxicity symptoms include headache, nausea, vomiting, chest pain, and cough.

Best sources: whole grains, seeds, beans, and veggies. Depends on soil content.

Silicon

Silicon is an essential mineral for strong bones and connective tissues in the body and healthy blood vessels. It is very important in iron formation.

Best sources: hard drinking water, plant fiber, and whole grains.

Sulfur

Sulfur is an element that is present in every animal and plant cell. It is needed for metabolism, in the building of body cells, and a healthy nervous system. It is used by the body to manufacture collagen and is therefore needed for healthy skin. Sulfur is found in large amounts in keratin, which is needed for healthy skin, nails, and hair. Sulfur is used in ointments for treating skin problems, such as eczema, psoriasis, and dermatitis. Sulfur is a component of insulin, which helps to regulate blood sugar levels. Sulfur deficiency goes hand-in-hand with protein deficiency, and can be corrected by increasing protein in the diet. Strict vegetarians may be deficient in sulfur. Toxicity from diet is non-existent; excess sulfur is excreted in the urine.

Best sources: eggs, cheese, milk, yogurt, dried beans and peas.

TOXIC SUBSTANCES FOUND IN THE HUMAN BODY

Aluminum

Aluminum is a trace mineral found in plant and animal foods, but its function in the human body is not known. Too much aluminum is dangerous. Toxicity symptoms include loss of energy or appetite, nausea, constipation, leg muscle twitching, skin problems, and excessive perspiration. It can cause colic in your baby.

Sources to be avoided: Aluminum is added to table salt, baking powder, some antacids, some processed cheeses, and in white flour during the bleaching process. Tap water usually contains aluminum. Try not to use aluminum cookware, as some aluminum will wind up in the food.

Asbestos

Asbestos causes lung cancer. It is in mineral fibers found in rocks that was used in patching compounds and other building products before its dangers became known. The CPSC (page 16) banned its use in 1977. The fibers are so small that they are invisible to the human eye and can pass through vacuum cleaner filters. Dangers of asbestos occur when airborne fibers are released during building demolitions and renovation projects. Only professionals should be involved in asbestos removal or in any projects involving building structures containing asbestos. For information, call the CPSC (page 16) or the EPA (page 39).

Cadmium

Cadmium is a trace mineral that is poison in the human body. It may cause hypertension, atherosclerosis, emphysema (if inhaled), and kidney damage. Cadmium toxicity may be prevented if enough zinc is present in the body, because zinc combats cadmium. If zinc intake is low, cadmium is stored in the body in zinc's place. Whole wheat has 120 times more zinc than cadmium, but when processed into white flour, zinc is significantly depleted. Cadmium is present in soft water, which leaches cadmium from pipes. It is also present in white sugar and cigarette smoke.

Sources to be avoided: Processed grains and flours, processed white sugar, soft tap water, cigarette smoke, and second-hand cigarette smoke.

Lead

Lead is infamous as a poison to the human body. Television commercials warn parents about possible lead poisoning from babies eating paint chips or wall plaster. Warn children about paint on the outside of the house, too. Pica is a condition in children characterized by the eating of lead-containing paint, paper, and dirt. If you have any old toys, cribs, or furniture from the 1960's or before, don't let your baby put them in her mouth or chew on them—the paint may contain lead. Warn your children not to chew pencils; the paint on them may contain lead. Don't allow your children to put newspaper, especially sections with colored ink (cartoons, advertising flyers, magazine inserts) in their mouths, as the ink may contain lead.

Lead may be found in some calcium supplements, especially those from made from "natural" sources such as oyster shells and bone meal. Other causes of lead poisoning include: eating food or drinking liquids from lead-glazed earthenware pottery or lead crystal; drinking soft, acidic tap water that erodes lead from pipes; cigarette smoke; inhaling fumes from coal burning; inhaling automobile exhaust fumes; and eating plant foods grown in urban areas and from fields bordering on highways where the atmosphere contains a lot of automobile exhaust fumes. You cannot see, smell, or taste lead. Pregnant women should be careful not to ingest lead from drinking water or other sources, as the lead passes into the brain of the fetus causing mental retardation. Lead toxicity in children causes mental retardation, hyperactivity, autism, blindness, learning disorders, anemia, and epilepsy. Other symptoms include headaches, nausea, indigestion, restlessness, irritability, depression, memory impairment, hallucination, and muscular aches.

Lead poisoning is more common than you think. Approximately 10% of America's children have dangerous levels of lead in the bloodstream! Children are at higher risk than adults because they absorb a much higher percentage of lead in their environment. Unfortunately, lead causes brain damage in children before any deficiency symptoms begin. They can appear perfectly healthy even though they have high blood levels of lead. Children at risk are those who live or frequently visit buildings built before 1978 (when lead-based paint was banned from housing) and especially those buildings built before 1960. Children who live near an industry that releases lead into the atmosphere and soil are also at risk. Wipe soil from shoes before entering your house to keep lead outside. If you find reason to be concerned, please read Richard M. Stapleton's book listed in the bibliography. Or call the National Lead Information Center 800-LEAD-FYI or call your state agency.

To help prevent lead poisoning, include a little Pacific kelp (seaweed) in the diet everyday. This kelp contains a substance that binds with lead and carries it safely out of the body. Also, make sure your child's diet is high in calcium and iron, especially iron. Vitamin C also helps decrease lead absorption. Fatty foods help the body retain lead. Children with good diets (like the Super Baby Food Diet) absorb less lead!

Lead in Cans. Before 1992, it was possible to buy food in cans that contained lead. Actually, it was the solder in the seams of the cans that contained lead; therefore, cans with rolled seams never had a lead problem because, of course, they contained no solder. Although the FDA (page 38) no longer allows lead-containing solder to be used to seam cans in the United States, there may still be trouble with imported cans. In fact, around 1994, lead was found in imported canned foods in a specialty store. To be sure that you are safe from lead, stick with non-imported canned food products only. Supposedly, any old cans manufactured in the United States that contained lead are long gone from stores' food inventories.

Lead in Canned Foods. See page 37.

Lead in Window Blinds. One household source of lead is the very common vinyl mini-blinds. (The more expensive metal blinds do not have any currently-known lead problems.) It is recommended that you should not have them in rooms where children are, but I say get rid of all of them. The CPSC (page 16) can answer questions on the vinyl blinds and on other products hazardous to children.

Lead in Tap Water. See page 62.

Lead Paint on Public Playground Equipment. Contact your local or city government to make sure that your child's neighborhood playground has not been painted with a lead-based paint. Or call the CPSC Hotline (page 16).

Lead Dust from Remodeling. For guidelines on how to protect your family during home remodeling/renovating your home, call the National Lead Information Clearinghouse at 800-424-LEAD.

Lead in Paint on Plastic Bags. See page 170.

Mercury

Mercury is toxic to the human body. Most people know that they should avoid the mercury from broken thermometers. Industrial waste containing mercury is dumped into bodies of water, where it ends up in fish used as food for people. If you are a fish-eater, be aware that, in general, the larger the fish, the more mercury it contains, because the higher up on the food chain, the more concentrated the mercury. Other sources of mercury: mercury-containing industrial products and fumes, tooth fillings, some over-the-counter laxatives, some cosmetics, and meat from some wild game. Toxicity symptoms include excessive salivation; digestive problems; loss of coordination, intellectual ability, hearing, and sight; skin problems; chills, fever, cough, and chest pain; tremors; depression; and tooth loss.

Radon

Radon is a gas that may be present in rocks, soil, natural gas, and other sources. The EPA (page 39) estimates that inhaling radon is second only to cigarette smoking as the most common cause of lung cancer. To get a free brochure about how to find and reduce radon in your home and a listing with your local contact, call the National Radon Hotline operated by the National Safety Council 800-SOS-RADON. If you have a specific question concerning radon, call 800-55-RADON.

G. Measures and Metric Equivalents

COMMON COOKBOOK ABBREVIATIONS	
t = tsp = teaspoon T = tbsp = tablespoon c = cups pt = pint qt = quart gal = gallon	oz = ounce lb = pound L = liters ml = milliliters g = grams kg = kilograms

COMMON EQUIVALENT MEASURES

3 teaspoons = 1 tablespoon= ½ fluid ounce
2 tablespoons = 1 fluid ounce
3 tablespoons = 1½ fluid ounces = 1 jigger
4 tablespoons = ¼ cup = 2 fluid ounces
8 tablespoons = ½ cup = 4 fluid ounces
12 tablespoons = ¾ cup = 6 fluid ounces
16 tablespoons = 1 cup = 8 fluid ounces
⅓ cup = 5 tablespoons + 1 teaspoon
⅔ cup = 10 tablespoons + 2 teaspoons
2 cups = 16 fluid ounces = 1 pint
4 cups = 32 fluid ounces = 2 pints = 1 quart
4 quarts = 1 gallon
pinch = less than ⅛ teaspoon
1 food cube = 2-3 tablespoons
1 stick butter = ½ cup = ¼ pound =
8 tablespoons
1 liter = 1000 milliliters
1 milliliter = 0.001 liter
1 kilogram = 1000 grams
1 gram = .001 kilograms

METRIC EQUIVALENTS
Common *Approximate* Measures

1 teaspoon ≅ 5 milliliters
1 tablespoon ≅ 15 milliliters
¼ cup ≅ 60 milliliters
⅓ cup ≅ 80 milliliters
½ cup ≅ 120 milliliters
⅔ cup ≅ 140 milliliters
¾ cup ≅ 180 milliliters
1 cup ≅ 240 milliliters
1 ounce ≅ 30 milliliters
1 teaspoon ≅ 5 grams
1 tablespoon ≅ 15 grams
1 ounce ≅ 30 grams
1 pound ≅ 454 grams
1 quart ≅ 0.95 liter
1 gallon ≅ 3.8 liters
1 gram = 0.035 ounces
1 kilogram = 2.21 pounds
1 liter = 1.06 quarts

METRIC EQUIVALENTS

Temperature

0°F =	-18°C
32°F =	0°C
40°F =	4°C
60°F =	16°C
120°F =	49°C
140°F =	60°C
165°F =	74°C
200°F =	93°C
212°F =	100°C
225°F =	107°C
250°F =	121°C
275°F =	135°C
300°F =	149°C
325°F =	163°C
350°F =	177°C
375°F =	191°C
400°F =	204°C
425°F =	218°C
450°F =	232°C

To convert to Centigrade, subtract 32° from Fahrenheit temperature and multiply the difference by 5/9 (or .5556).

Growth Charts For the height and weight growth charts on pages 54-55:

Multiply pounds by 0.454 to get kilograms. Multiply pounds by 454 to get grams.

Multiply inches by 2.54 to get centimeters.

Liquid Measure

⅛ teaspoon = 0.61 milliliters
¼ teaspoon = 1.23 milliliters
½ teaspoon = 2.47 milliliters
¾ teaspoon = 3.70 milliliters
1 teaspoon = 4.94 milliliters
Multiply teaspoons by 4.94 to get milliliters.
⅛ tablespoon = 1.84 milliliters
¼ tablespoon = 3.69 milliliters
½ tablespoon = 7.39 milliliters
¾ tablespoon = 11.08 milliliters
1 tablespoon = 14.78 milliliters
Multiply tablespoons by 14.79 to get milliliters.
1 ounce = 29.57 milliliters
Multiply fluid ounces by 29.57 to get milliliters.
⅛ cup = 29.57 milliliters
¼ cup = 59.14 milliliters
½ cup = 118.28 milliliters
¾ cup = 177.42 milliliters
1 cup = 236.56 milliliters
Multiply cups by 236.56 to get milliliters. Multiply cups by 2.37 to get liters.
1 pint = 473.18 milliliters
Multiply pints by 473.18 to get milliliters. Multiply pints by .473 to get liters.
1 quart = 946.00 milliliters
½ gallon = 1.89 liters
¾ gallon = 2.83 liters
1 gallon = 3.78 liters

Dry Measure

⅛ teaspoon = 0.54 grams
¼ teaspoon = 1.09 grams
½ teaspoon= 2.19 grams
¾ teaspoon = 3.28 grams
1 teaspoon = 4.38 grams
Multiply teaspoons by 4.38 to get grams.
⅛ tablespoon = 1.77 grams
¼ tablespoon = 3.54 grams
½ tablespoon = 7.09 grams
¾ tablespoon = 10.63 grams
1 tablespoon = 14.18 grams
Multiply tablespoons by 14.18 to get grams.
⅛ ounce = 3.59 grams
¼ ounce = 7.39 grams
½ ounce = 14.18 grams
¾ ounce = 21.34 grams
1 ounce = 28.35 grams
Multiply ounces by 28.35 to get grams.
2 ounce ≅ 60 grams
4 ounces = ¼ pound ≅ 115 grams
8 ounces = ½ pound ≅ 225 grams
16 ounces = 1 pound = 453.59 grams
Multiply pounds by 454 to get grams.

≅ means "is approximately equal to"

Bibliography

You will find many of these books on the shelves in your local library. If your library does not have a book that you want, ask your librarian for assistance with an interlibrary loan. These loans are usually free.

Adams, Ruth and Frank Murray. With foreword by S. Marshall Fram. *Health Foods.* New York: Larchmont Books, 1975.

American Academy of Pediatrics. *Caring for Your Baby and Young Child.* New York: Bantam Books, 1991.

Ames, Louise Bates and Frances L. Ilg. *Your 2 Year Old: Terrible or Tender.* Delacorte Press, 1993.

Ames, Louise Bates, Frances L. Ilg, and Carol Chase Haber. *Your One-Year-Old: The Fun-Loving, Fussy 12-to 24-Month Old.* New York: Doubleday and Company, Inc., 1995.

Allergy Information Association. *The Food Allergy Cookbook.* New York: St. Martin's Press, 1983.

Aslett, Don. *Stainbuster's Bible The Complete Guide to Spot Removal.* New York: Penguin Books, 1990.

Bailey, Emma and the Prevention editors. *Prevention's Better Living Cookbook.* Emmaus, Pennsylvania: Rodale Press, Inc., 1976.

Bailey, Janet. *Keeping Food Fresh.* New York: The Dial Press, 1985.

Bingham, Rita. *Country Beans.* With an introduction by Lendon Smith. Edmond, OK: Natural Meals in Minutes, 1994.

Birnes, Nancy. *Cheaper & Better: Homemade Alternatives to Storebought Goods.* New York : Harper & Row, c1987.

_____. *Zapcrafts : Microwaves Are for Much More than Cooking.* Berkeley, California: Ten Speed Press, 1990.

Blonz, Edward R. *The Really Simple, No Nonsense Nutrition Guide.* Emeryville, California: Conari Press, 1993.

Blue Goose, Inc. *The Buying Guide for Fresh Fruits, Vegetables, Herbs, and Nuts.* Hagerstown, Maryland: Blue Goose, Inc., 1980.

Bosque, Elena, and Sheila Watson. *Safe and Sound: How to Prevent and Treat the Most Common Childhood Emergencies.* New York: St. Martin's Press, 1988.

Boston Children's Hospital with Susan Baker and Roberta R. Henry. *Parents' Guide to Nutrition.* Reading, Massachusetts: Addison-Wesley Publishing Company, Inc., 1986.

Bradley, Hassell, and Carole Sundberg. *Keeping Food Safe.* Garden City, New York: Doubleday and Company, Inc., 1975.

Brazelton, T. Berry, M.D. *Touchpoints.* Reading, Massachusetts: A Merloyd Lawrence Book, 1992.

Brody, Jane E. *Jane Brody's Good Food Gourmet.* New York: W. W. Norton & Company, 1990.

_____. *Jane Brody's Nutrition Book.* New York: W. W. Norton & Company, 1981.

Burck, Frances Wells. *Babysense.* New York: St. Martin's Press, 1991.

Caplan, Theresa. *The First Twelve Months of Life.* New York: Putnam Publishing, 1993.

Case-Smith, Jane. *Development of Hand Skills in the Child.* Rockville, Maryland: The American Occupational Therapy Association, Inc., 1992.

Castle, Sue. *The Complete New Guide to Preparing Baby Foods.* With a foreword by Jeffrey L. Brown. New York: Bantam Books, 1992.

Cohen, Stanley A. *Healthy Babies, Happy Kids.* New York: Delilah, 1982.

Cooking with Bon Appétit Vegetables. Los Angeles: The Knapp Press, 1983.

Consumer Guide editors. *The Ultimate House-Holder's Book.* New York: A & W Publishers, 1982.

Costenbader, Carol W. *The Big Book of Preserving the Harvest.* Pownal, Vermont: Storey Communications, 1997.

Coyle, Rena, and Patricia Messing. *Baby Let's Eat!* with foreword by Michael A. Levi. New York: Workman Publishing Company, Inc, 1987.

Dadd, Debra Lynn. *Home Safe Home.* New York: Penguin Putnam, Inc., 1997.

Delahoyde, Michael, and Susan C. Despenich. "Creating Meat-Eaters: The Child as Advertising Target," *Journal of Popular Culture* 28, Summer 1994, 135-49.

DeLong, Deanna. *How to Dry Foods.* Tucson, Arizona: H. P. Books, 1979.

Dodson, Fitzhugh, M.D., and Ann Alexander, M.D. *Your Child Birth to Age 6.* New York: Simon and Schuster, 1986.

Dominguez, Joseph R., and Vicki Robin. *Your Money or Your Life : Transforming Your Relationship with Money and Achieving Financial Independence.* New York: Viking, 1992.

Doyle, Rodger P., and James L. Redding. *The Complete Food Handbook.* New York: Grove Press, Inc., 1976.

Dribin, Lois, and Denise Marina. *Cooking with Sun-Dried Tomatoes.* Tucson, Arizona: Fisher Books, 1990.

Duncan, Alice Likowski, D.C. *Your Healthy Child* with forward by Lendon Smith, M.D. Los Angeles: Jeremy P. Tarcher, Inc., 1991.

Dworkin, Floss Romm, and Stan Dworkin. *Bake Your Own Bread.* New York: NAL Penguin, Inc., 1987.

Easterday, Kate Cusick. *The Peaceable Kitchen Cookbook.* New York: Paulist Press, 1980.

Eden, Alvin, M.D. *Dr. Eden's Healthy Kids.* New York: Plume, 1987.

Eiger, Marvin S., M.D. and Sally Wendkos Olds. *The Complete Book of Breastfeeding.* New York: Bantam Books, 1987.

Eisenberg, Arlene, Heidi E. Murkoff, and Sandee E. Hathaway. *What to Expect the First Year.* New York: Workman Publishing Company, Inc., 1989.

Elliot, Rose. *Vegetarian Mother and Baby Book: A Complete Guide to Nutrition, Health, and Diet During Pregnancy and After.* New York: Pantheon, 1987.

Ensminger, Audrey H, et al. *Foods & Nutrition Encyclopedia.* Boca Raton, Florida: CRC Press, 1994.

Ewald, Ellen Buchman. With introduction by Frances Moore Lappé. *Recipes for a Small Planet.* New York: Ballantine Books, 1973.

Finkaly, Susan Tate. *Into the Mouths of Babes.* Cincinnati, Ohio: Betterway Books, 1995.

Galland, Leo, M.D. *SuperImmunity for Kids.* New York: E. P. Dutton, 1988.

Garland, Anne Witte. *For Our Kids' Sake How to Protect Your Child Against Pesticides in Food* with forward by T. Berry Brazelton. San Francisco: Sierra Club Books, 1989.

General Mills, Inc. *Betty Crocker's Vegetarian Cooking.* New York: Prentice Hall, 1994.

German, Don and Joan German. *Make Your Own Convenience Foods: How to Make Chemical-free Foods That Are Fast, Simple and Economical.* New York: Macmillan Publishing Co, Inc, 1978.

Goldbeck, Nikki, and David Goldbeck. *The Supermarket Handbook.* New York: The New American Library, Inc., 1976.

Gooch, Sandy. *If You Love Me, Don't Feed Me Junk!* with forwards by Earl Mindell, Lendon Smith, and Dick Gregory. Reston, Virginia: Reston Publishing Company, Inc., 1983.

Green, Joey. *Paint Your House with Powdered Milk.* New York: Hyperion, 1996.

Green, Martin I. *A Sigh of Relief: First-Aid Handbook for Childhood Emergencies.* New York: Bantam, 1984.

Hamilton, Eva May Nunnelley, Eleanor Noss Whitney, and Frances Sienkiewicz Sizer. *Nutrition: Concepts and Controversies.* St. Paul, Minnesota: West Publishing Company, 1988.

Haxelton, Nika. *The Unabridged Vegetable Cookbook.* New York: M. Evans and Company, Inc., 1976.

Haynes, Linda. *The Vegetarian Lunchbasket.* Willow Springs, MO: Nucleus Publications, 1994.

Herbst, Sharon Tyler. *The Food Lover's Tiptionary.* New York: Hearst Books, 1994.

Hertzberg, Ruth, Beatrice Vaughan, and Janet Greene. *Putting Food By.* Brattleboro, Vermont: The Stephen Greene Press, 1975.

Heslin, Jo-Ann, Annette B. Natow, and Barbara C. Raven. *No-Nonsense Nutrition for Your Baby's First Year.* Boston: CBI Publishing Company, Inc., 1978.

Hillman, Howard. *Kitchen Science.* Boston: Houghton Mifflin Co., 1981.

Hobson, Phyllis. *Making and Using Dried Foods.* Pownal, Vermont: Storey Communications, Inc., 1994.

Holt, Tamara, M.S. and Maureen Callahan, R.D. *The Miracle Nutrient Cookbook 100 Delicious Antioxidant-Enriched Recipes and Menu Suggestions for Optimum Health.* New York: Simon and Schuster, 1995.

Hood, Joan, compiler for Home and Freezer Digest. *Will It Freeze?* New York: Charles Scribner's Sons, 1982.

Hoshijo, Kathy. *Kathy Cooks...Naturally.* Hawaii: The Self-Sufficiency Association, 1981.

Hostage, Jacqueline. *Living...Without Milk.* White Hall, Virginia: Betterway Publications, 1981.

Hunter, Beatrice Trum. *Wheat, Millet and Other Grains.* New Canaan, Connecticut: Keats Publishing, Inc., 1982.

Illingsworth, Ronald S. *The Development of the Infant and Young Child. Eighth edition.* New York: Churchill Livingstone, 1983.

Jensen, Bernard. *Foods that Heal.* New York: Avery Publishing Group, Inc., 1993.

Johnston, Ingeborg M., and James R. Johnston. *Flaxseed (Linseed) Oil and the Power of Omega-3.* Connecticut: Keats Publishing, Inc., 1990.

Jones, Dorothea Van Gundy. *The Soybean Cookbook.* With forward by Ruth Stout. New York: Arco Publishing, Inc., 1982.

Jones, Helen Taylor. *Grain Power.* With introduction by Beth Allen. New York: Dell Publishing, 1993.

Karmel, Annabel. *The Healthy Baby Meal Planner.* New York: Simon & Schuster, Inc., 1992.

Keane, Maureen B., and Daniella Chace. *Grains for Better Health.* Rocklin, California: Prima Publishing, 1994.

_____. *The Natural Baby Food Cookbook.* New York: Avon Books, 1982.

Kimmel, Martha, David Kimmel, and Suzanne Goldenson. *Mommy Made Home Cooking for a Healthy Baby & Toddler.* New York: Bantam Books, 1990.

Klaper, Michael, M.D. *Pregnancy, Children, and the Vegan Diet.* Umatilla, Florida: Gentle World, Inc., 1987.

Kloss, Jethro. *Back to Eden second edition.* California: Back to Eden Publishing Co., 1992.

Knight, Karin, and Jeannie Lumley. *The Baby Cookbook.* New York: William Morrow and Company, Inc., 1992.

Kowalski, Robert E. With forward by Dennis M. Davidson, M.D. *Cholesterol & Children A Parent's Guide to Giving Children a Future Free of Heart Disease.* New York: Harper and Row, 1988.

Krauss, Michael with Sue Castle and Joan Lunden. *Your Newborn Baby.* New York: Warner Books, Inc., 1988.

Kreschollek, Margie. *The Guaranteed Goof-Proof Microwave Cookbook.* New York: Bantam Books, 1988.

Kuntzleman, Charles. *Healthy Kids for Life.* New York: Simon and Schuster, 1988.

La Leche League International. *The Womanly Art of Breastfeeding.* New York: NAL Penguin, Inc., 1987.

Lambert-Lagacé, Louise. *Feeding Your Baby from Conception to Age Two.* Chicago: Surrey Books, 1991.

Lansky, Vicki. *Fat-Proofing Your Children.* New York: Bantam Books, 1988.

_____. *Feed Me! I'm Yours.* New York: Meadowbrook Press, 1994.

_____. *Baby Proofing Basics.* Book Peddlers, 1991.

_____. and Consumer Guide editors. *Complete Pregnancy and Baby Book.* Skokie, Illinois: Publications International, Ltd, 1987.

Lappé, Frances Moore. *Diet for a Small Planet.* New York: Ballantine Books, 1975.

Larson, Gena. *Better Food for Better Babies and Their Families.* New Canaan, Connecticut: Keats Publishing, Inc., 1972.

Levy, Faye. *Faye Levy's International Vegetable Cookbook: Over 300 Sensational Recipes from Argentina to Zaire and Artichokes to Zucchini.* New York: Warner Books, Inc., 1993.

Margen, Sheldon, and the University of California at Berkeley Wellness Letter editors. *The Wellness Encyclopedia of Food and Nutrition.* New York: Rebus, 1992.

Meyerowitz, Steve. *Sprout It!* Massachusetts: The Sprout House, Inc., 1994.

McClure, Joy, and Kendall Layne. *Cooking for Consciousness.* Willow Springs, MO: Nucleus Publications, 1993.

McCoy, Jonni. *Miserly Moms.* Elkton, MD: Full Quart Press, 1996.

National Research Council. *Recommended Dietary Allowances 10th edition.* Washington, D.C.: National Academy Press, 1989.

Newhouse, Sonia. *Complete Natural Food Facts.* London: Thorsons, 1991.

Norman, Cecilia. *Vegetarian Microwave Cookbook.* San Francisco: HarperCollins Publishers, 1993.

Nugent, Nancy, and the editors of Prevention Magazine. *Food and Nutrition.* Emmaus, Pennsylvania: Rodale Press, 1983.

Null, Gary. *Vegetarian Cooking for Good Health.* New York: Macmillan Publishing Company, 1991.

Nutrition Search, Inc. with John D. Kirschmann and Lavon J. Dunne. *Nutrition Almanac Cookbook.* New York: McGraw-Hill Book Company, 1983.

Ojakangas, Beatrice. *Great Whole Grain Breads.* New York: E. P. Dutton, Inc., 1984.

Olds, Sally B., Marcia L. London, and Patricia A. Ladewig. *Maternal Newborn Nursing.* Menlo Park, California: Addison-Wesley Publishing Company, Inc., 1988.

Ornish, Dean. *Eat More, Weigh Less.* New York: HarperCollins Publishers, Inc., 1993.

Packard, Vernal S. *Human Milk and Infant Formula.* New York: Academic Press, 1982.

Parham, Barbara. *What's Wrong with Eating Meat?* Denver, Colorado: Ananda Marga Publications, 1979.

Parker, Dorothy. *The Wonderful World of Yogurt.* New York: Hawthorn Books, Inc., 1972.

Pennington, Jean A. T., and Helen Nichols Church. *Food Values of Portions Commonly Used 14th edition.* New York: Harper and Row Publishers, Inc., 1985.

Phipps, Marlynn, Jan Woolley, Venecia Phipps, and Jenny Phipps. *A Bite of Independence Through Self-sufficiency Learn How to Feed a Family of Four for as Low as $10 per Week.* Higley, Arizona: SSL, Inc.,1991.

Pickard, Mary Ann. With foreword by Lendon H. Smith. *Feasting...Naturally.* Olathe, Kansas: Cookbook Publishers, Inc., 1979.

Pickarski, Brother Ron. *Friendly Foods.* California: Ten Speed Press, 1991.

Prevention Magazine editors. *All About Vitamins and Minerals.* Stamford, Connecticut: Longmeadow Press, 1989.

_____. *The Healing Foods Cookbook.* Emmaus, Pennsylvania: Rodale Press, Inc., 1991.

_____. *Understanding Vitamins and Minerals.* Emmaus, Pennsylvania: Rodale Press, Inc., 1984.

Frince, Francine and Harold Prince. *Feed Your Kids Bright.* New York: Simon and Schuster, 1987.

Rapp, Doris J., M.D. *Allergies and Your Child.* New York: Holt, Rinehart, and Winston, 1972.

_____. *Is This Your Child? : Discovering and Treating Unrecognized Allergies.* New York: William Morrow & Co, 1991.

Reader's Digest editors. *Live Longer Cookbook.* Pleasantville, New York: The Reader's Digest Association, Inc., 1992.

Reader's Digest editors. *Great Recipes for Good Health.* Pleasantville, New York: The Reader's Digest Association, Inc., 1988.

Riccio, Dolores. *Superfoods 300 Recipes for Foods that Heal Body and Mind.* New York: Warner Books, Inc., 1992.

Richert, Barbara. With forward by William Shevin, M.D. *Getting Your Kids to Eat Right.* New York: Simon and Schuster, 1981.

Robertson, Laurel, Carol Flinders, and Bronwen Godfrey. *The Laurel's Kitchen Bread Book A Guide to Whole-Grain Breadmaking.* New York: Random House, 1984.

Robertson, Laurel, Carol Flinders, and Brian Ruppenthal. *The New Laurel's Kitchen: A Handbook for Vegetarian Cookery and Nutrition.* Berkeley, California: Ten Speed Press, 1986.

Rodale Books editors. *The Good Grains.* Emmaus, Pennsylvania: Rodale Press, Inc., 1982.

_____. *Nuts and Seeds The Natural Snacks.* Emmaus, Pennsylvania: Rodale Press, Inc., 1973.

Rombauer, Irma S., and Marion Rombauer Becker. *Joy of Cooking.* Indiana: The Bobbs-Merrill Company, Inc., 1973.

Satter, Ellyn, R.D. *Child of Mine: Feeding with Love and Good Sense.* Palo Alto, California: Bull Publishing Co., 1986.

Scharffenberg, John A., M.D. *Problems with Meat.* Santa Barbara, California: Woodbridge Press publishing Company, 1982.

Scott, Cyril, and John Lust. *Crude Black Molasses.* New York: Benedict Lust Publications, 1992.

Smith, Lois. *Baby Eats!* New York: The Berkley Publishing Group, 1994.

Somer, Elizabeth and Health Media of America. *The Essential Guide to Vitamins and Minerals.* New York: HarperCollins Publishers, Inc., 1992.

Spock, Benjamin, M.D., and Michael B. Rothenberg, M.D. *Dr. Spock's Baby and Child Care.* New York: Dutton, 1992.

Stanfield, Peggy. *Nutrition and Diet Therapy.* Boston: Jones and Bartlett Publishers, Inc., 1986.

Stapleton, Richard M. *Lead is a Silent Hazard.* New York: Walker Publishing Company, Inc., 1994.

Stoppard, Miriam, M.D. *Complete Baby and Child Care.* New York: Dorling Kindersley Limited, 1995.

_____. *Day-By-Day Baby Care.* New York: Villard Books, 1983.

Stoner, Carol and Organic Gardening and Farming editors. *Stocking Up How to Preserve the Foods You Grow, Naturally.* Emmaus, Pennsylvania: Rodale Press, Inc., 1974.

Sunset Books and Sunset Magazine editors. *Fresh Produce.* Menlo Park, California: Lane Publishing Co., 1987.

_____. *Good Cook's Handbook.* Menlo Park, California: Lane Publishing Co., 1986.

_____. *Vegetarian Favorites.* Menlo Park, California: Lane Publishing Co., 1987.

Sweet, O. Robin, and Thomas Bloom. *The Well-Fed Baby.* New York: Macmillan, 1994.

Tudor, Mary. *Child Development.* New York: McGraw-Hill, 1981.

United States Department of Agriculture. *Agriculture Handbook No. 8 Composition of Foods Series: 8-1 Dairy and Egg Products*, 1976; *8-4 Fats and Oils*, 1979; *8-5 Poultry Products*, 1979; *8-9 Fruits and Fruit Juices*, 1982; *8-10 Pork Products*, 1983; *8-11 Vegetables and Vegetable Products*, 1984; *8-12 Nut and Seed Products*, 1984; *8-13 Beef Products*, 1986; *8-16 Legume and Legume Products*, 1986; *8-20 Cereal Grains and Pasta*, 1989.

Watson, Susan. *Sugar-Free Toddlers.* Charlotte, Vermont: Williamson Publishing, 1991.

Webb, Densi. *Feeding Infants and Children.* New York: Bantam Books, 1995.

Whaley, Lucille F., and Donna L. Wong. *Nursing Care of Infants and Children.* St. Louis, Missouri: The C. V. Mosby Company, 1987.

White, Burton L. *The First Three Years of Life.* New York: Fireside Books, 1995.

Whitney, Eleanor Noss, and Eva May Nunnelley Hamilton. *Understanding Nutrition.* St. Paul, Minnesota: West Publishing Company, 1984.

Winick, Myron, M.D. *Growing Up Healthy A Parent's Guide to Good Nutrition.* New York: William Morrow and Company, Inc., 1982.

Yntema, Sharon. *Vegetarian Baby.* Ithaca, New York: McBooks Press, 1991.

_____. *Vegetarian Children.* Ithaca, New York: McBooks Press, 1987.

Yoder, Eileen Rhude. *Allergy-Free Cooking.* Reading, Massachusetts: Addison-Wesley, 1987.

Recipe Index

Index

Quick Reference Pages:

Foods to introduce each month and consistency 86-87
Amount of food your baby might eat per day 58
Worksheet 134-135
Overview of the Super Baby Food Diet 120
Super Snacks and Finger Foods List 291
Baby Food Safety Precautions 165
Choking Hazards 40-41
Simple Shapes 367-368
Height and Weight Growth Charts 54-55
Grain Cooking Quick Reference 222
Bean Cooking Quick Reference 235

Other Often-Used Pages: